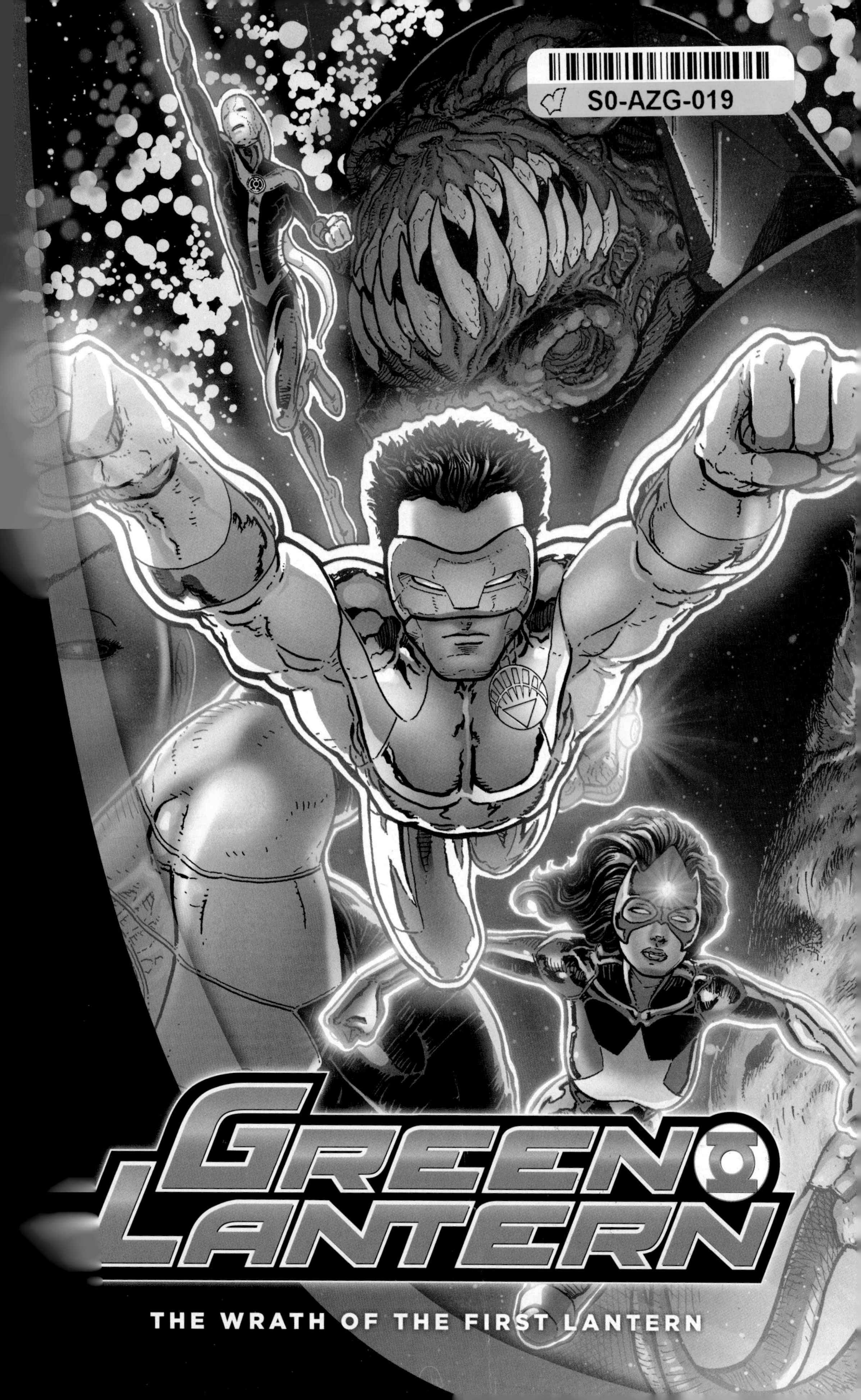

GREEN LANTERN

THE WRATH OF THE FIRST LANTERN

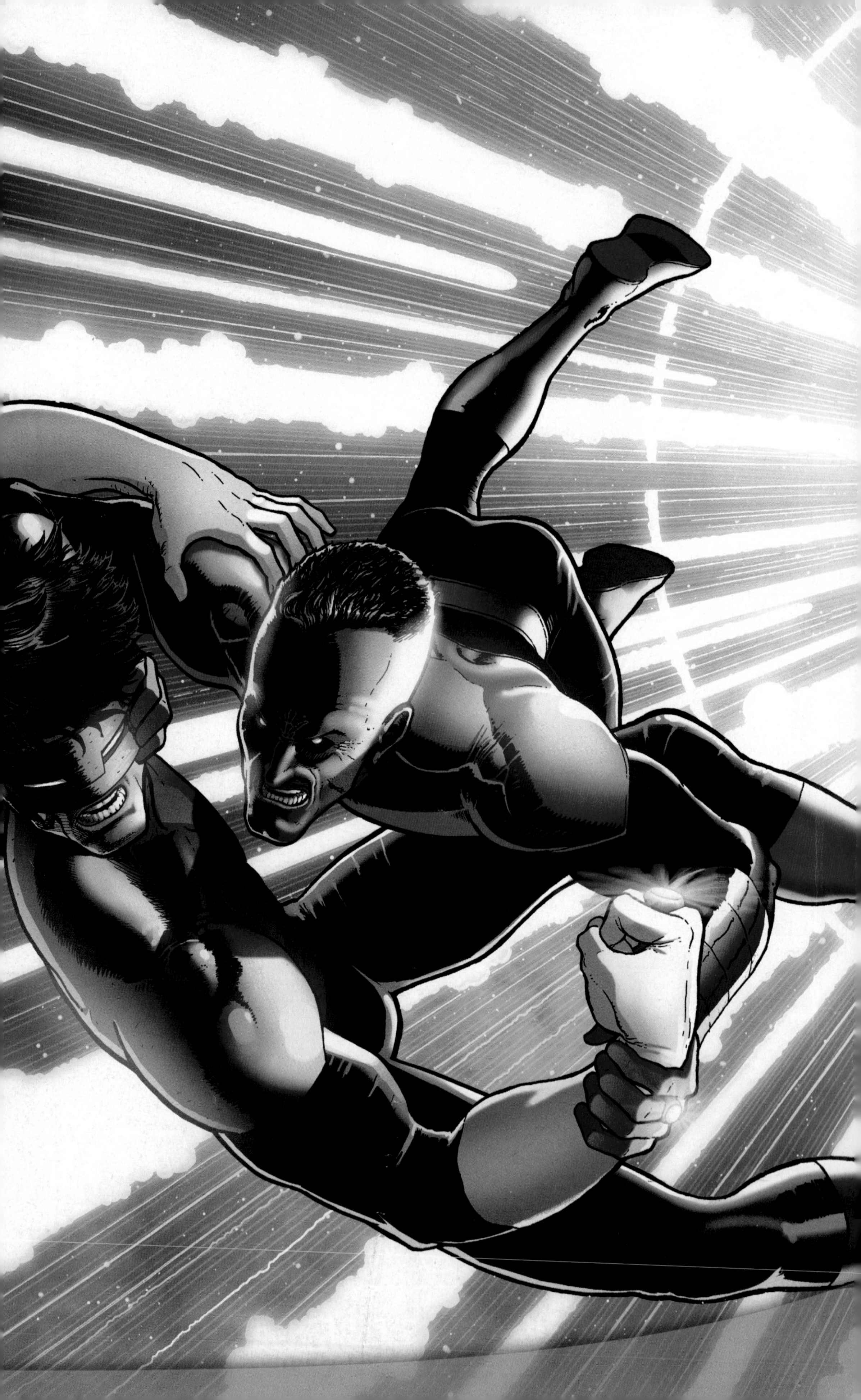

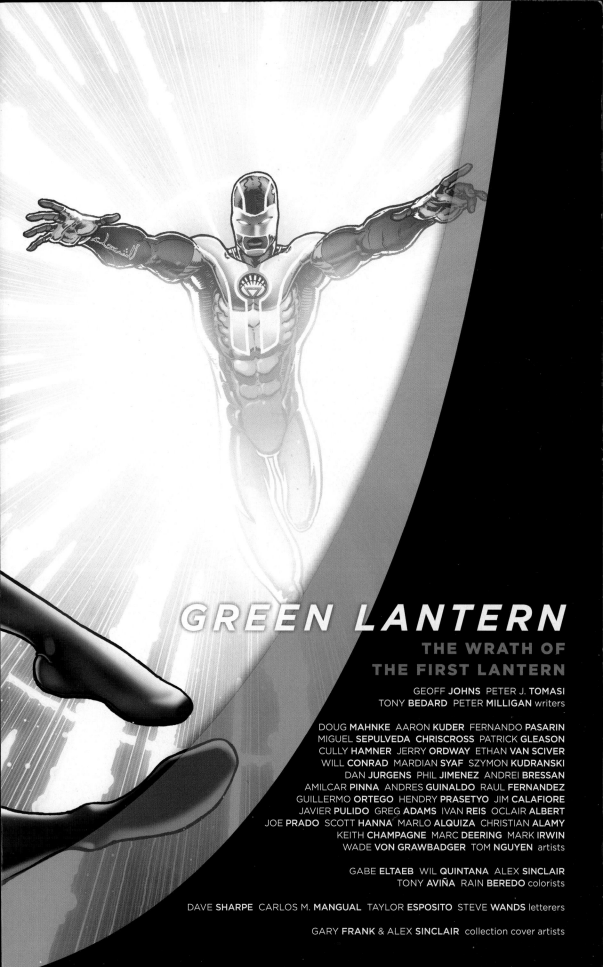

GREEN LANTERN

THE WRATH OF
THE FIRST LANTERN

GEOFF **JOHNS**   PETER J. **TOMASI**
TONY **BEDARD**   PETER **MILLIGAN** writers

DOUG **MAHNKE**   AARON **KUDER**   FERNANDO **PASARIN**
MIGUEL **SEPULVEDA**   CHRISCROSS   PATRICK **GLEASON**
CULLY **HAMNER**   JERRY **ORDWAY**   ETHAN **VAN SCIVER**
WILL **CONRAD**   MARDIAN **SYAF**   SZYMON **KUDRANSKI**
DAN **JURGENS**   PHIL **JIMENEZ**   ANDREI **BRESSAN**
AMILCAR **PINNA**   ANDRES **GUINALDO**   RAUL **FERNANDEZ**
GUILLERMO **ORTEGO**   HENDRY **PRASETYO**   JIM **CALAFIORE**
JAVIER **PULIDO**   GREG **ADAMS**   IVAN **REIS**   OCLAIR **ALBERT**
JOE **PRADO**   SCOTT **HANNA**   MARLO **ALQUIZA**   CHRISTIAN **ALAMY**
KEITH **CHAMPAGNE**   MARC **DEERING**   MARK **IRWIN**
WADE **VON GRAWBADGER**   TOM **NGUYEN** artists

GABE **ELTAEB**   WIL **QUINTANA**   ALEX **SINCLAIR**
TONY **AVIÑA**   RAIN **BEREDO** colorists

DAVE **SHARPE**   CARLOS M. **MANGUAL**   TAYLOR **ESPOSITO**   STEVE **WANDS** letterers

GARY **FRANK** & ALEX **SINCLAIR** collection cover artists

WIL MOSS CHRIS CONROY MATT IDELSON Editors – Original Series
KATE STEWART KYLE ANDRUKIEWICZ Assistant Editors – Original Series RACHEL PINNELAS Editor
ROBBIN BROSTERMAN Design Director – Books ROBBIE BIEDERMAN Publication Design

BOB HARRAS Senior VP – Editor-in-Chief, DC Comics

DIANE NELSON President DAN DIDIO and JIM LEE Co-Publishers GEOFF JOHNS Chief Creative Officer
AMIT DESAI Senior VP – Marketing and Franchise Management
AMY GENKINS Senior VP – Business and Legal Affairs NAIRI GARDINER Senior VP – Finance
JEFF BOISON VP – Publishing Planning MARK CHIARELLO VP – Art Direction and Design
JOHN CUNNINGHAM VP – Marketing TERRI CUNNINGHAM VP – Editorial Administration
LARRY GANEM VP – Talent Relations and Services ALISON GILL Senior VP – Manufacturing and Operations
HANK KANALZ Senior VP – Vertigo and Integrated Publishing JAY KOGAN VP – Business and Legal Affairs, Publishing
JACK MAHAN VP – Business Affairs, Talent NICK NAPOLITANO VP – Manufacturing Administration SUE POHJA VP – Book Sales
FRED RUIZ VP – Manufacturing Operations COURTNEY SIMMONS Senior VP – Publicity BOB WAYNE Senior VP – Sales

GREEN LANTERN: THE WRATH OF THE FIRST LANTERN

Published by DC Comics. Copyright © 2014 DC Comics. All Rights Reserved.
Originally published in single magazine form in GREEN LANTERN 17-20; GREEN LANTERN CORPS 17-20; RED LANTERNS 17-20;
GREEN LANTERN: NEW GUARDIANS 17-20. Copyright © 2013 DC Comics. All Rights Reserved. All characters, their distinctive likenesses
and related elements featured in this publication are trademarks of DC Comics. The stories, characters and incidents featured in this publication are entirely fictional. DC Comics does not read or accept unsolicited ideas, stories or artwork.

DC Comics, 1700 Broadway, New York, NY 10019
A Warner Bros. Entertainment Company.
Printed by RR Donnelley, Owensville, MO, USA. 7/11/14. First Printing.
ISBN: 978-1-4012-4693-8

Certified Chain of Custody
20% Certified Forest Content,
80% Certified Sourcing
www.sfiprogram.org
SFI-01042
APPLIES TO TEXT STOCK ONLY

Library of Congress Cataloging-in-Publication Data

Green Lantern : Wrath of the First Lantern.
pages cm
"Originally published in single magazine form as GREEN LANTERN 17-20, GREEN LANTERN CORPS 17-20,
RED LANTERNS 17-20, GREEN LANTERN: NEW GUARDIANS 17-20."
ISBN 978-1-4012-4693-8
1. Graphic novels.
PN6728.G74G86 2014
741.5'973-dc23
                                    2013039606

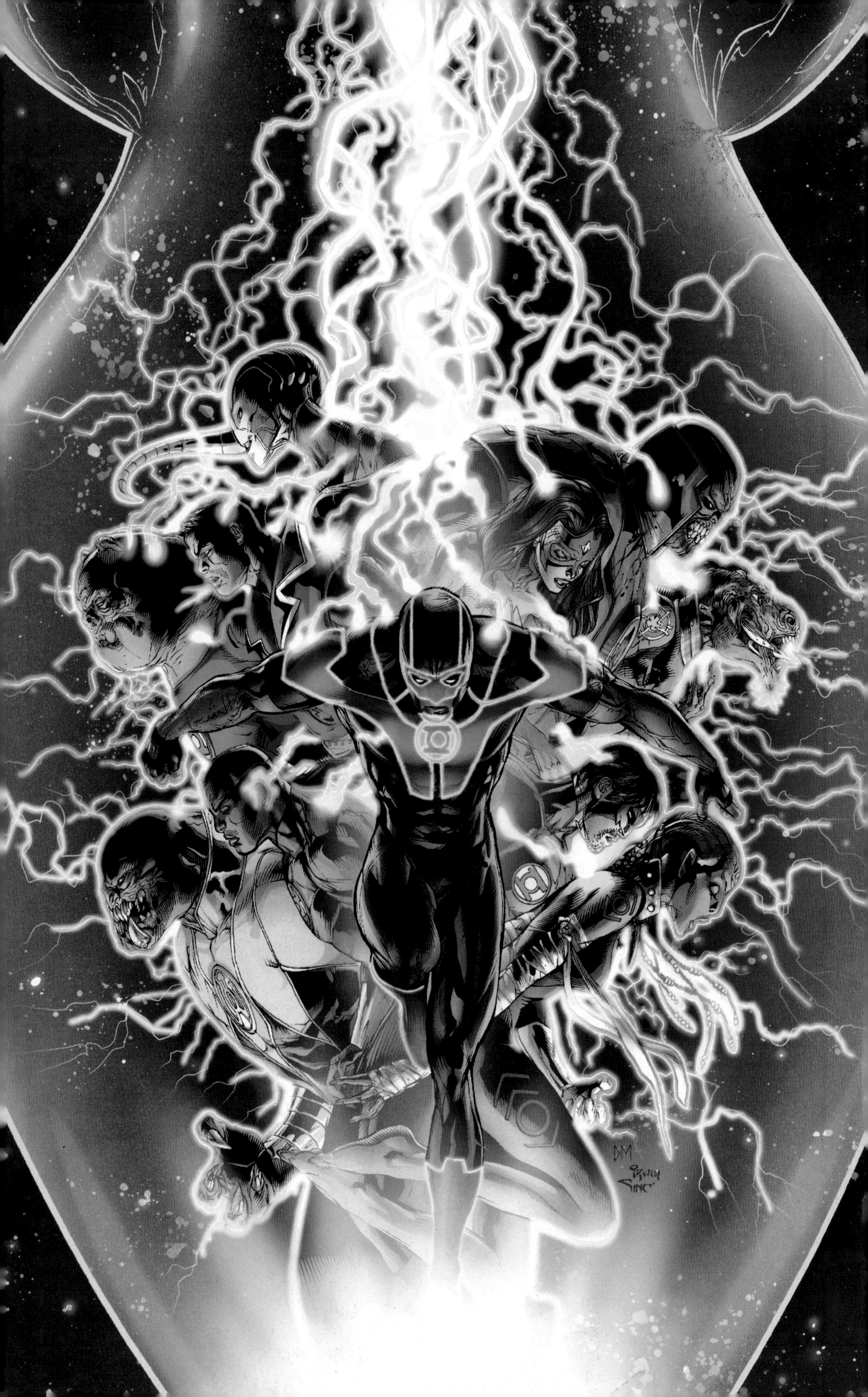

PART ONE: THE PUPPETEER

GEOFF JOHNS writer **DAN JURGENS** layouts – prolouge **PHIL JIMENEZ** finishes – prologue **DOUG MAHNKE** penciller
TOM NGUYEN, KEITH CHAMPAGNE, MARK IRWIN, CHRISTIAN ALAMY & DOUG MAHNKE inkers cover art by **DOUG MAHNKE, MARK IRWIN & ALEX SINCLAIR**

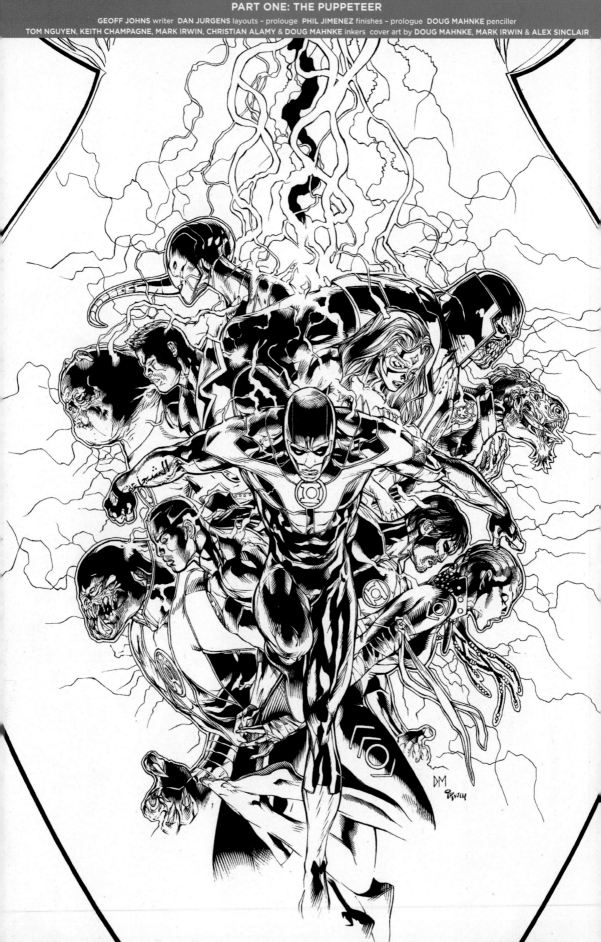

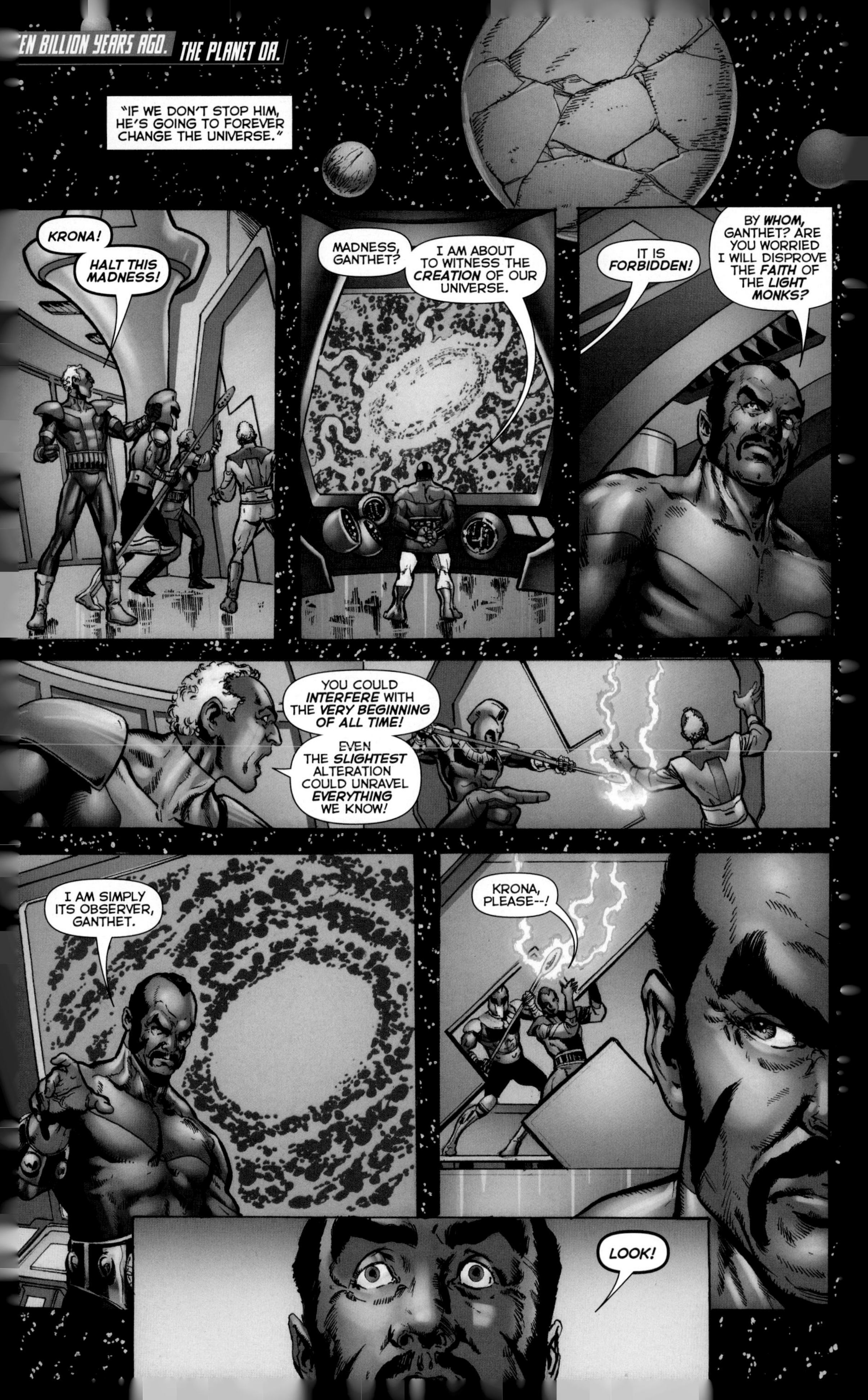

EN BILLION YEARS AGO.
THE PLANET OA.
"IF WE DON'T STOP HIM, HE'S GOING TO FOREVER CHANGE THE UNIVERSE."
KRONA!
HALT THIS MADNESS!
MADNESS, GANTHET?
I AM ABOUT TO WITNESS THE CREATION OF OUR UNIVERSE.
IT IS FORBIDDEN!
BY WHOM, GANTHET? ARE YOU WORRIED I WILL DISPROVE THE FAITH OF THE LIGHT MONKS?
YOU COULD INTERFERE WITH THE VERY BEGINNING OF ALL TIME!
EVEN THE SLIGHTEST ALTERATION COULD UNRAVEL EVERYTHING WE KNOW!
I AM SIMPLY ITS OBSERVER, GANTHET.
KRONA, PLEASE--!
LOOK!

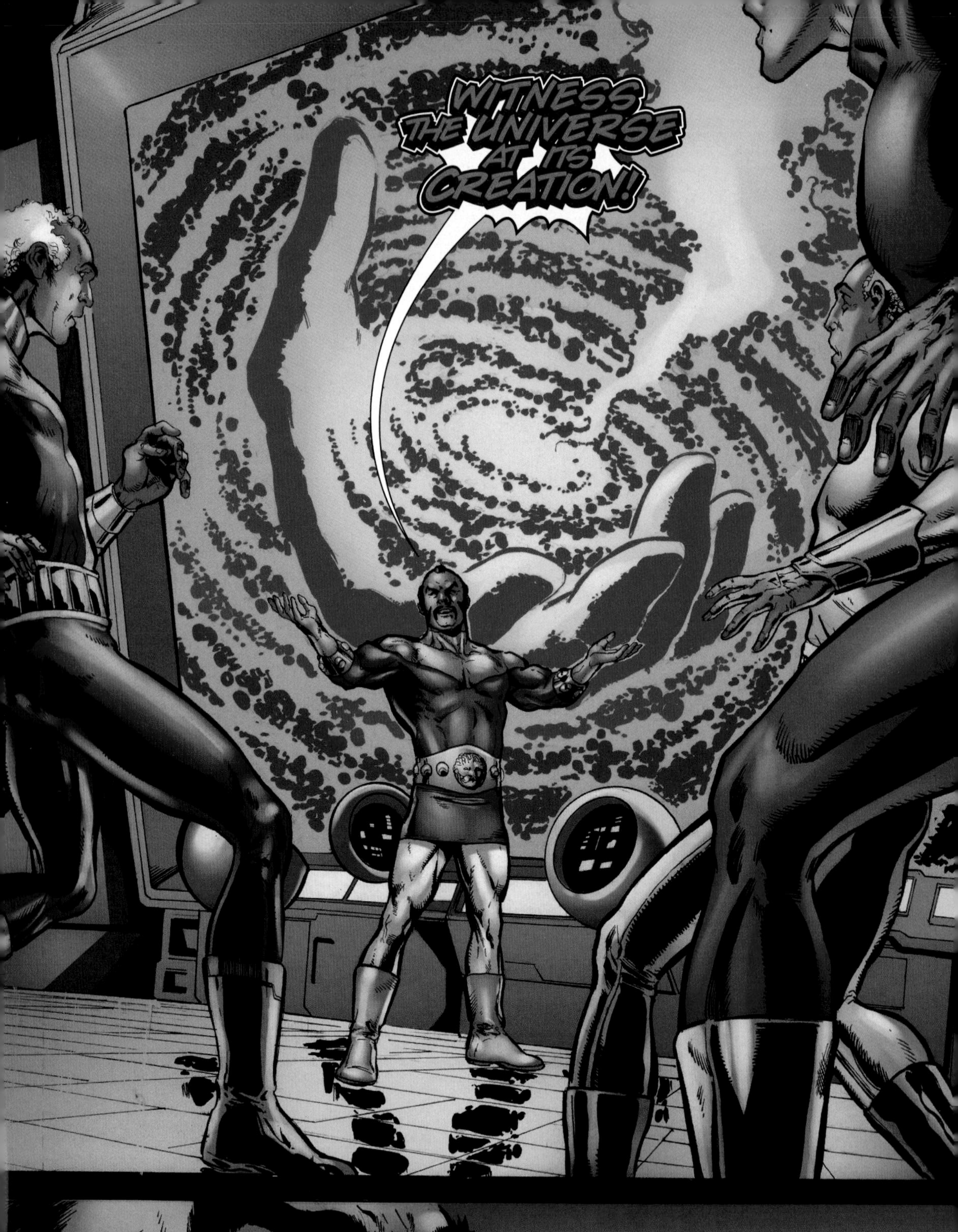
WITNESS THE UNIVERSE AT ITS CREATION!
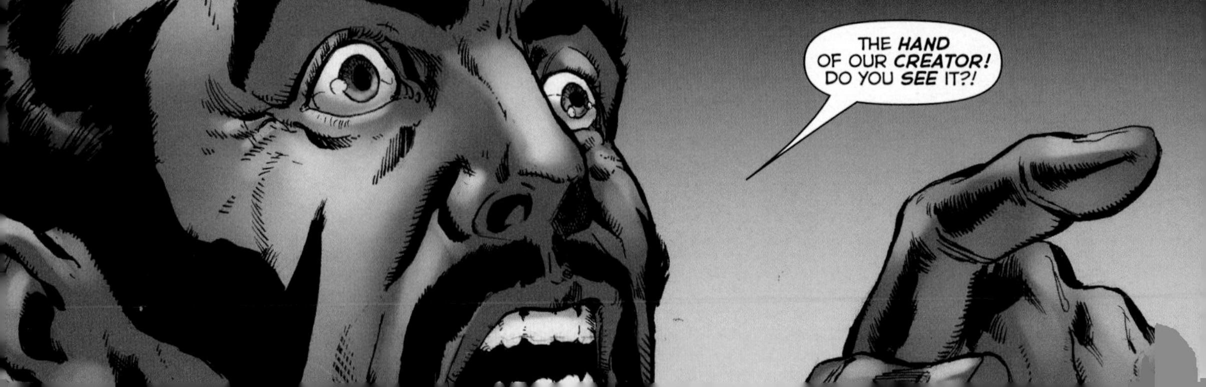
THE HAND OF OUR CREATOR! DO YOU SEE IT?!

KRONA, YOU *KNOW* THE LEGENDS...

BAH! SUCH STORIES ARE TALES ONLY *FOOLS* WOULD FEAR.

I SEEK TO LEARN THE *ORIGIN OF THE UNIVERSE!*

AND YOU TALK OF LEGENDS OF *DESTRUCTION* SHOULD I LEARN THE TRUTH.

KRONA! THE HAND...

...WHAT IS *ON* IT?

A RING--?

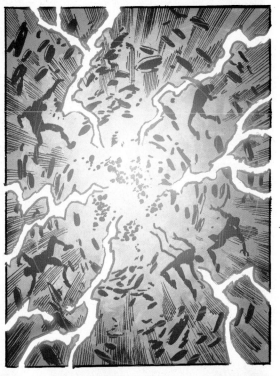

I... I MADE IT. *I SURVIVED!*

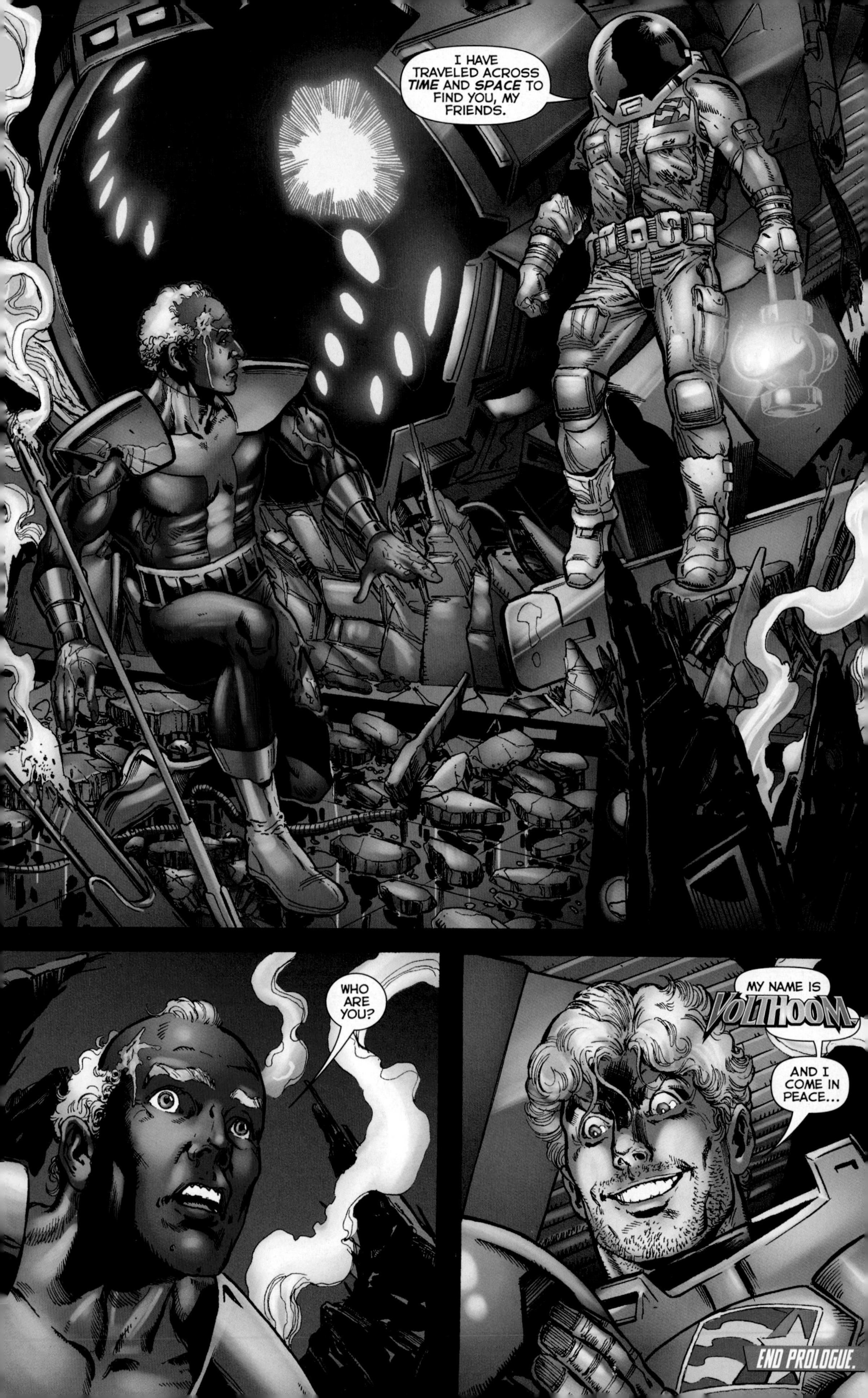
I HAVE TRAVELED ACROSS TIME AND SPACE TO FIND YOU, MY FRIENDS.
WHO ARE YOU?
MY NAME IS
VOLTHOOM.
AND I COME IN PEACE...
END PROLOGUE.

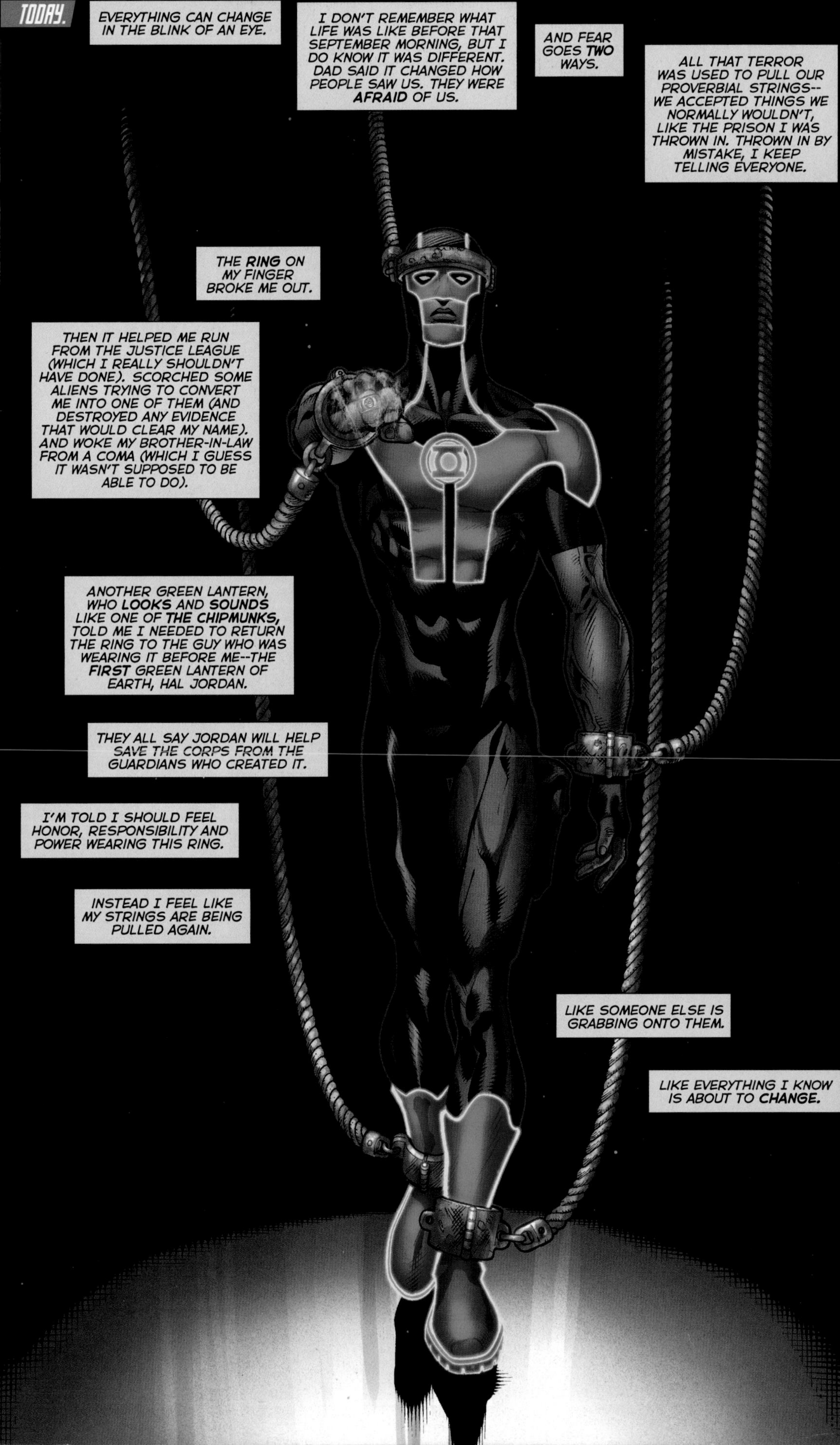

TODAY.
EVERYTHING CAN CHANGE IN THE BLINK OF AN EYE.
I DON'T REMEMBER WHAT LIFE WAS LIKE BEFORE THAT SEPTEMBER MORNING, BUT I DO KNOW IT WAS DIFFERENT. DAD SAID IT CHANGED HOW PEOPLE SAW US. THEY WERE AFRAID OF US.
AND FEAR GOES TWO WAYS.
ALL THAT TERROR WAS USED TO PULL OUR PROVERBIAL STRINGS-- WE ACCEPTED THINGS WE NORMALLY WOULDN'T, LIKE THE PRISON I WAS THROWN IN. THROWN IN BY MISTAKE, I KEEP TELLING EVERYONE.
THE RING ON MY FINGER BROKE ME OUT.
THEN IT HELPED ME RUN FROM THE JUSTICE LEAGUE (WHICH I REALLY SHOULDN'T HAVE DONE). SCORCHED SOME ALIENS TRYING TO CONVERT ME INTO ONE OF THEM (AND DESTROYED ANY EVIDENCE THAT WOULD CLEAR MY NAME). AND WOKE MY BROTHER-IN-LAW FROM A COMA (WHICH I GUESS IT WASN'T SUPPOSED TO BE ABLE TO DO).
ANOTHER GREEN LANTERN, WHO LOOKS AND SOUNDS LIKE ONE OF THE CHIPMUNKS, TOLD ME I NEEDED TO RETURN THE RING TO THE GUY WHO WAS WEARING IT BEFORE ME--THE FIRST GREEN LANTERN OF EARTH, HAL JORDAN.
THEY ALL SAY JORDAN WILL HELP SAVE THE CORPS FROM THE GUARDIANS WHO CREATED IT.
I'M TOLD I SHOULD FEEL HONOR, RESPONSIBILITY AND POWER WEARING THIS RING.
INSTEAD I FEEL LIKE MY STRINGS ARE BEING PULLED AGAIN.
LIKE SOMEONE ELSE IS GRABBING ONTO THEM.
LIKE EVERYTHING I KNOW IS ABOUT TO CHANGE.

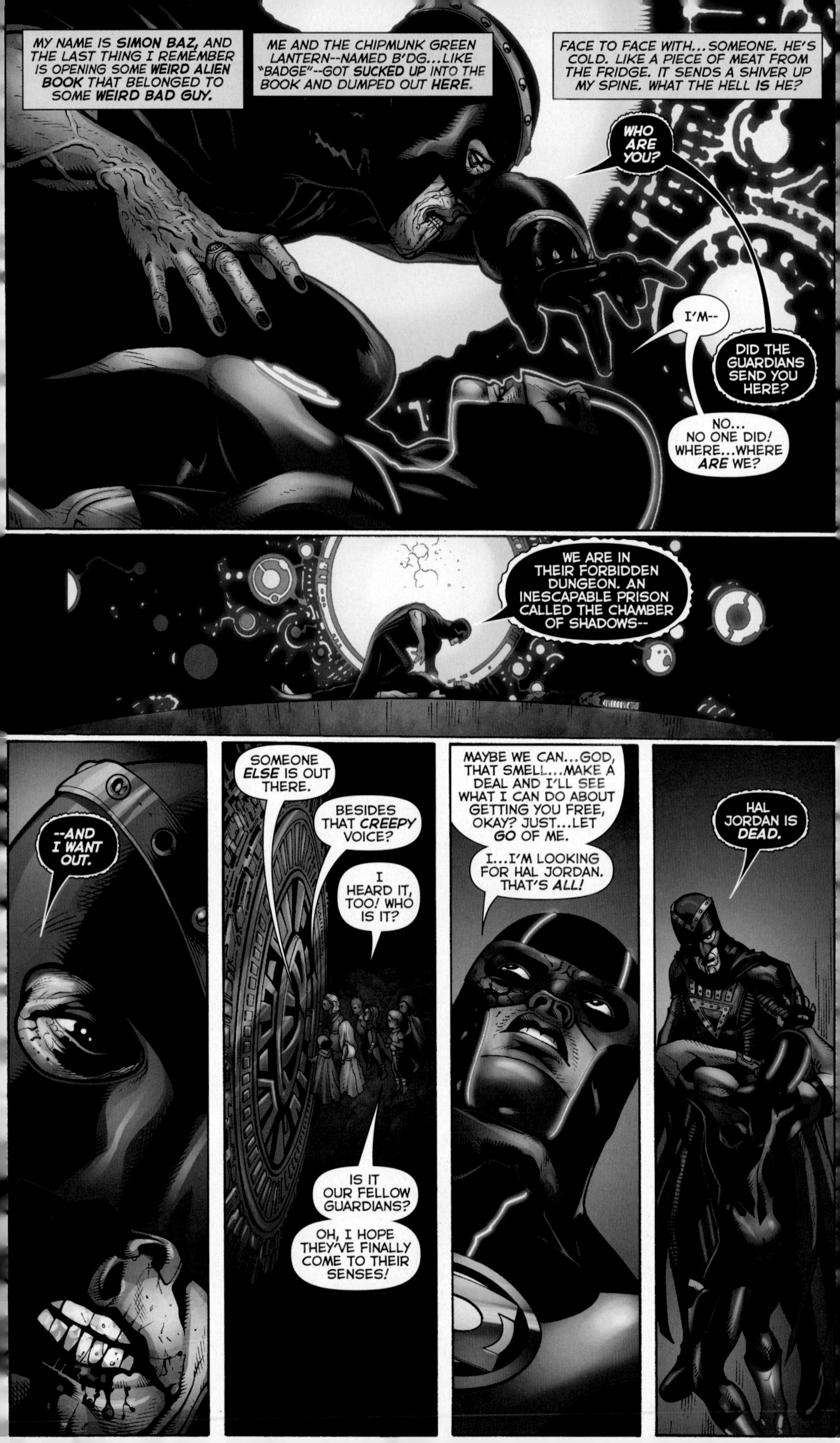
MY NAME IS SIMON BAZ, AND THE LAST THING I REMEMBER IS OPENING SOME WEIRD ALIEN BOOK THAT BELONGED TO SOME WEIRD BAD GUY.
ME AND THE CHIPMUNK GREEN LANTERN--NAMED B'DG...LIKE "BADGE"--GOT SUCKED UP INTO THE BOOK AND DUMPED OUT HERE.
FACE TO FACE WITH...SOMEONE. HE'S COLD. LIKE A PIECE OF MEAT FROM THE FRIDGE. IT SENDS A SHIVER UP MY SPINE. WHAT THE HELL IS HE?
WHO ARE YOU?
I'M--
DID THE GUARDIANS SEND YOU HERE?
NO... NO ONE DID! WHERE...WHERE ARE WE?
WE ARE IN THEIR FORBIDDEN DUNGEON. AN INESCAPABLE PRISON CALLED THE CHAMBER OF SHADOWS--
--AND I WANT OUT.
SOMEONE ELSE IS OUT THERE.
BESIDES THAT CREEPY VOICE?
I HEARD IT, TOO! WHO IS IT?
IS IT OUR FELLOW GUARDIANS?
OH, I HOPE THEY'VE FINALLY COME TO THEIR SENSES!
MAYBE WE CAN...GOD, THAT SMELL...MAKE A DEAL AND I'LL SEE WHAT I CAN DO ABOUT GETTING YOU FREE, OKAY? JUST...LET GO OF ME.
I...I'M LOOKING FOR HAL JORDAN. THAT'S ALL!
HAL JORDAN IS DEAD.

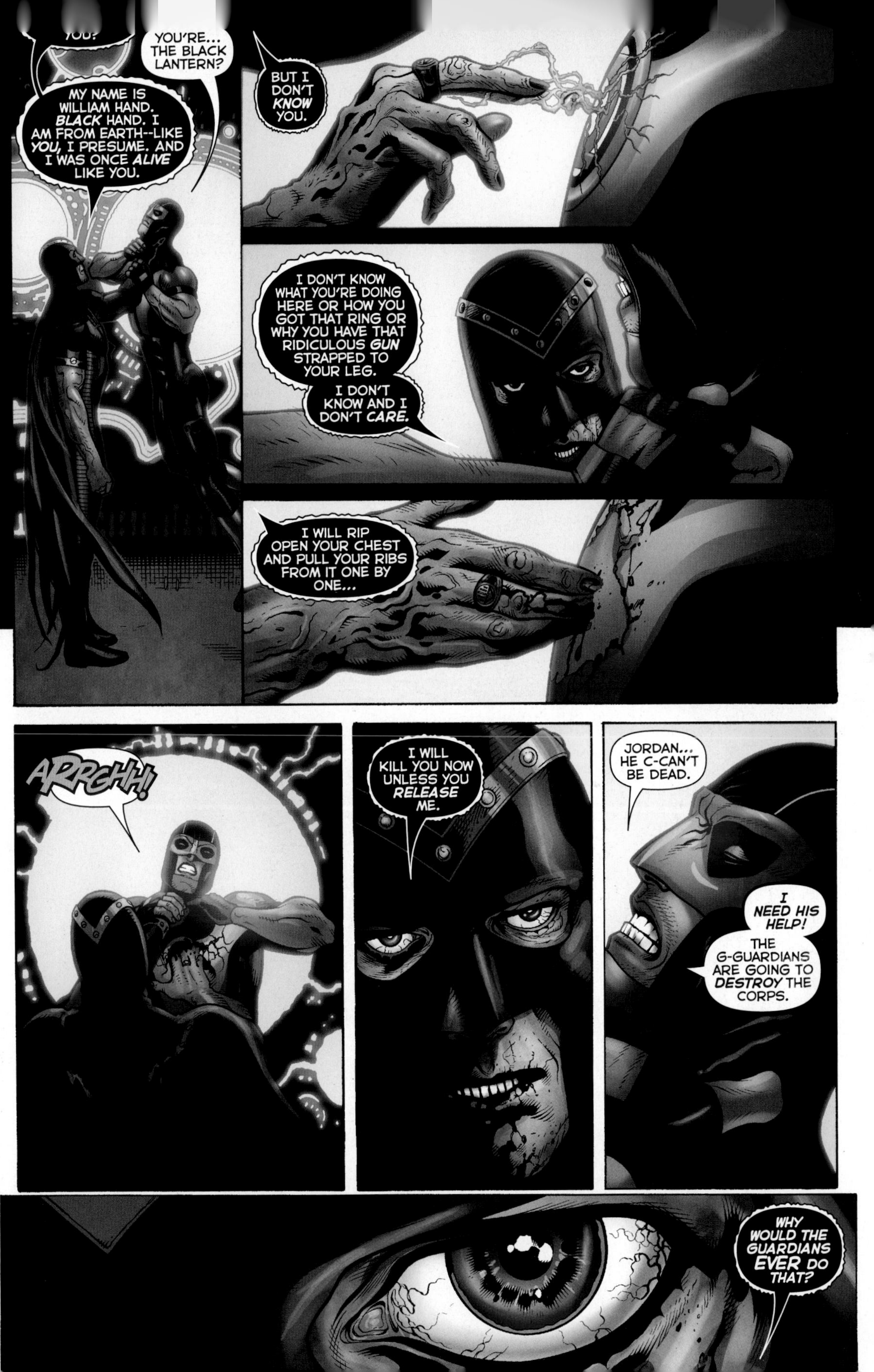
YOU?
YOU'RE... THE BLACK LANTERN?
MY NAME IS WILLIAM HAND. BLACK HAND. I AM FROM EARTH--LIKE YOU, I PRESUME. AND I WAS ONCE ALIVE LIKE YOU.
BUT I DON'T KNOW YOU.
I DON'T KNOW WHAT YOU'RE DOING HERE OR HOW YOU GOT THAT RING OR WHY YOU HAVE THAT RIDICULOUS GUN STRAPPED TO YOUR LEG.
I DON'T KNOW AND I DON'T CARE.
I WILL RIP OPEN YOUR CHEST AND PULL YOUR RIBS FROM IT ONE BY ONE...
ARRGHH!
I WILL KILL YOU NOW UNLESS YOU RELEASE ME.
JORDAN... HE C-CAN'T BE DEAD.
I NEED HIS HELP!
THE G-GUARDIANS ARE GOING TO DESTROY THE CORPS.
WHY WOULD THE GUARDIANS EVER DO THAT?

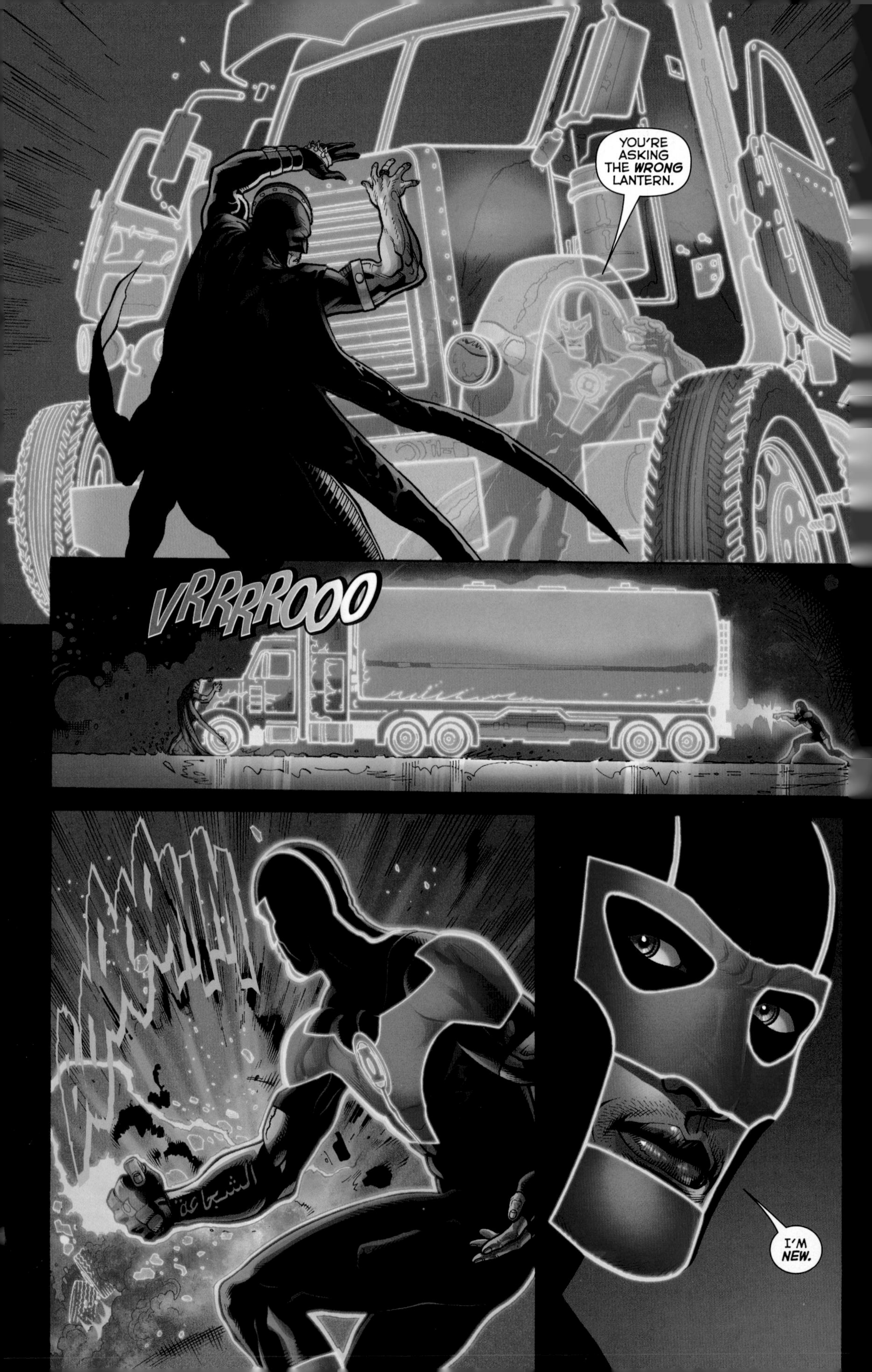
YOU'RE ASKING THE *WRONG* LANTERN.
VRRRROOO
الشجاعة
I'M *NEW.*

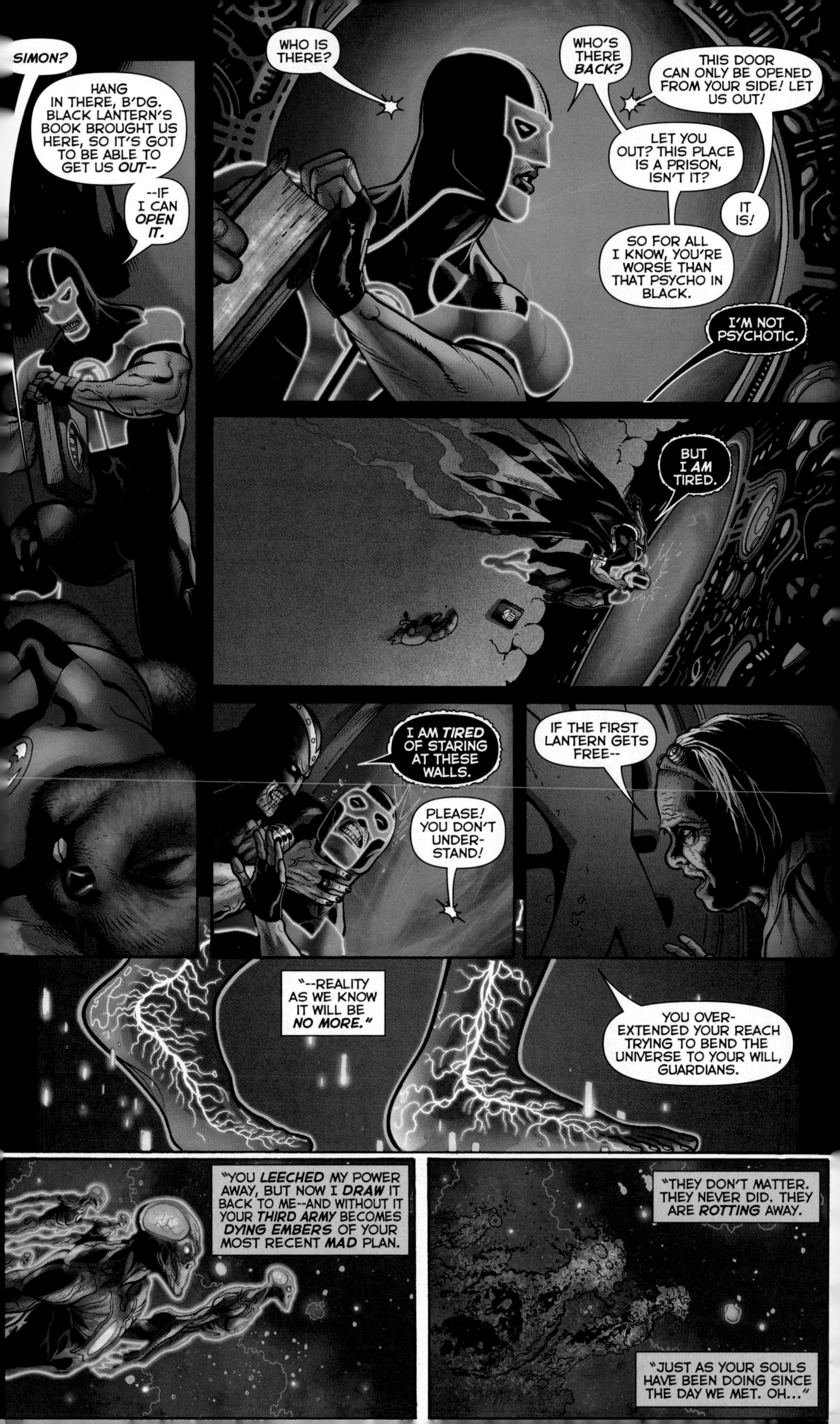
SIMON?
HANG IN THERE, B'DG. BLACK LANTERN'S BOOK BROUGHT US HERE, SO IT'S GOT TO BE ABLE TO GET US *OUT*--
--IF I CAN *OPEN* IT.
WHO IS THERE?
WHO'S THERE *BACK?*
THIS DOOR CAN ONLY BE OPENED FROM YOUR SIDE! LET US OUT!
LET YOU OUT? THIS PLACE IS A PRISON, ISN'T IT?
IT IS!
SO FOR ALL I KNOW, YOU'RE WORSE THAN THAT PSYCHO IN BLACK.
I'M NOT PSYCHOTIC.
BUT I *AM* TIRED.
I AM *TIRED* OF STARING AT THESE WALLS.
PLEASE! YOU DON'T UNDER-STAND!
IF THE FIRST LANTERN GETS FREE--
"--REALITY AS WE KNOW IT WILL BE *NO MORE.*"
YOU OVER-EXTENDED YOUR REACH TRYING TO BEND THE UNIVERSE TO YOUR WILL, GUARDIANS.
"YOU *LEECHED* MY POWER AWAY, BUT NOW I *DRAW* IT BACK TO ME--AND WITHOUT IT YOUR *THIRD ARMY* BECOMES *DYING EMBERS* OF YOUR MOST RECENT *MAD* PLAN.
"THEY DON'T MATTER. THEY NEVER DID. THEY ARE *ROTTING* AWAY.
"JUST AS YOUR SOULS HAVE BEEN DOING SINCE THE DAY WE MET. OH..."

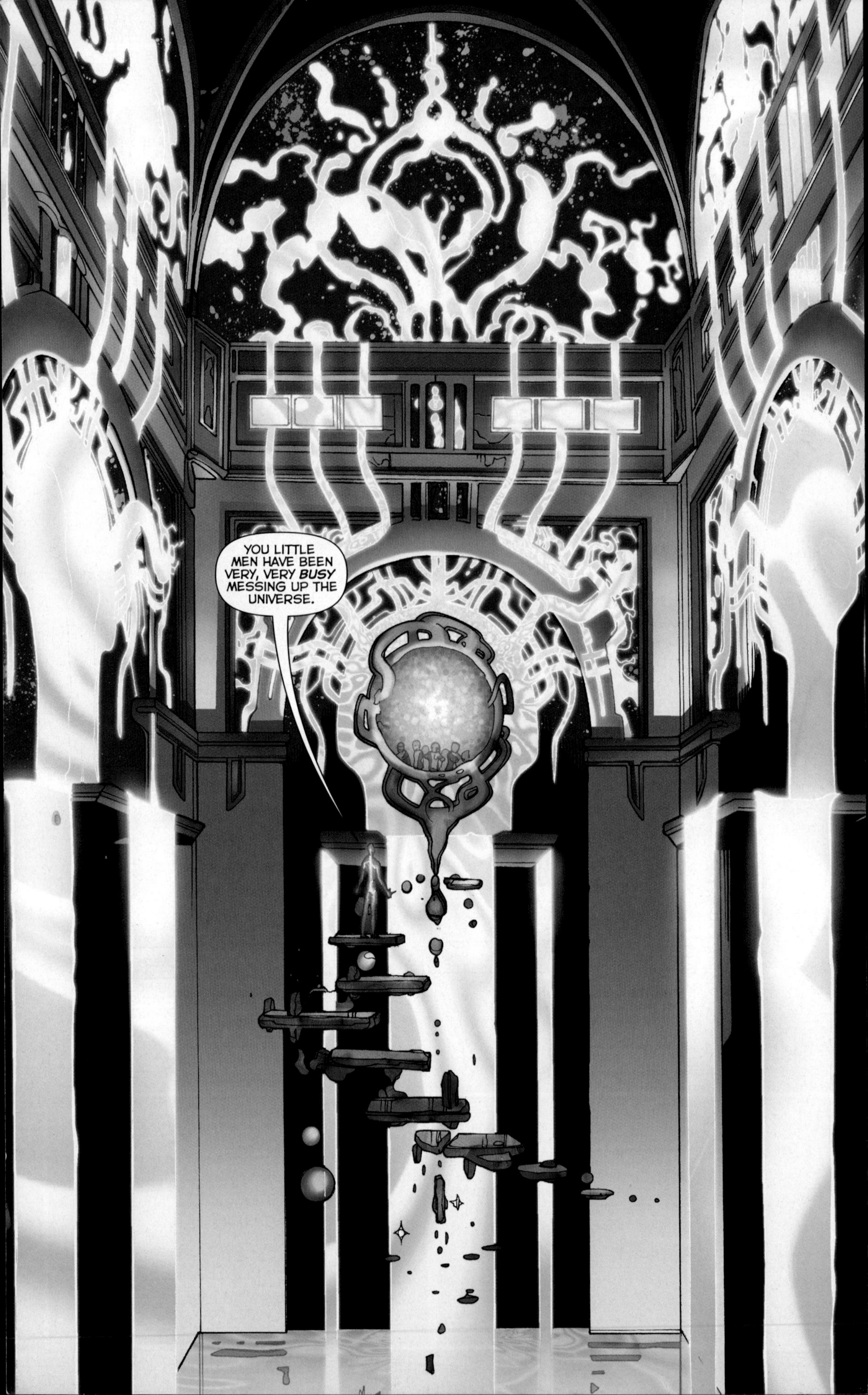
YOU LITTLE MEN HAVE BEEN VERY, VERY *BUSY* MESSING UP THE UNIVERSE.

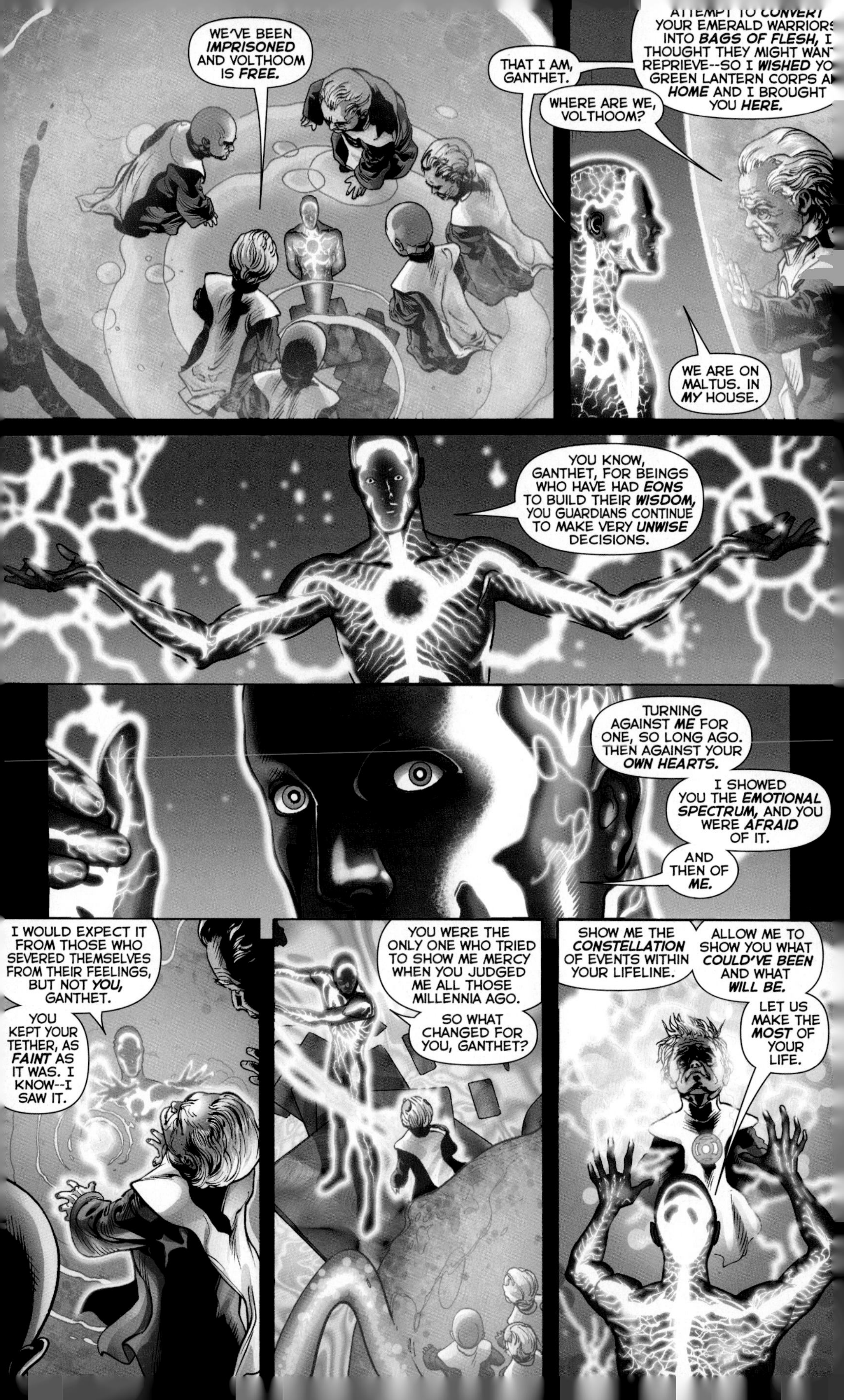
WE'VE BEEN IMPRISONED AND VOLTHOOM IS FREE.
THAT I AM, GANTHET.
ATTEMPT TO CONVERT YOUR EMERALD WARRIORS INTO BAGS OF FLESH, I THOUGHT THEY MIGHT WANT REPRIEVE--SO I WISHED YO GREEN LANTERN CORPS A HOME AND I BROUGHT YOU HERE.
WHERE ARE WE, VOLTHOOM?
WE ARE ON MALTUS. IN MY HOUSE.
YOU KNOW, GANTHET, FOR BEINGS WHO HAVE HAD EONS TO BUILD THEIR WISDOM, YOU GUARDIANS CONTINUE TO MAKE VERY UNWISE DECISIONS.
TURNING AGAINST ME FOR ONE, SO LONG AGO. THEN AGAINST YOUR OWN HEARTS.
I SHOWED YOU THE EMOTIONAL SPECTRUM, AND YOU WERE AFRAID OF IT.
AND THEN OF ME.
I WOULD EXPECT IT FROM THOSE WHO SEVERED THEMSELVES FROM THEIR FEELINGS, BUT NOT YOU, GANTHET.
YOU KEPT YOUR TETHER, AS FAINT AS IT WAS. I KNOW--I SAW IT.
YOU WERE THE ONLY ONE WHO TRIED TO SHOW ME MERCY WHEN YOU JUDGED ME ALL THOSE MILLENNIA AGO.
SO WHAT CHANGED FOR YOU, GANTHET?
SHOW ME THE CONSTELLATION OF EVENTS WITHIN YOUR LIFELINE.
ALLOW ME TO SHOW YOU WHAT COULD'VE BEEN AND WHAT WILL BE.
LET US MAKE THE MOST OF YOUR LIFE.

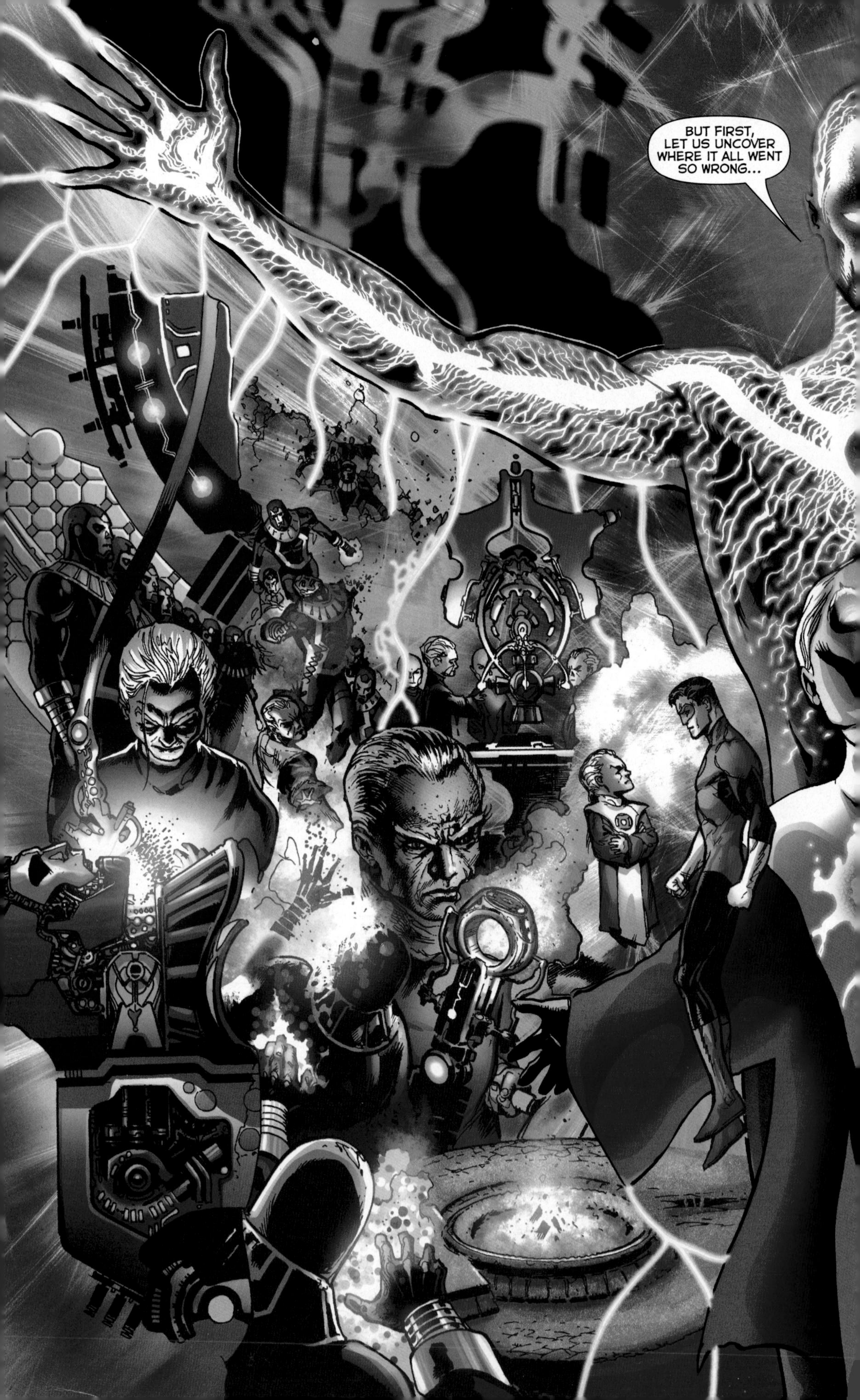
BUT FIRST, LET US UNCOVER WHERE IT ALL WENT SO WRONG...

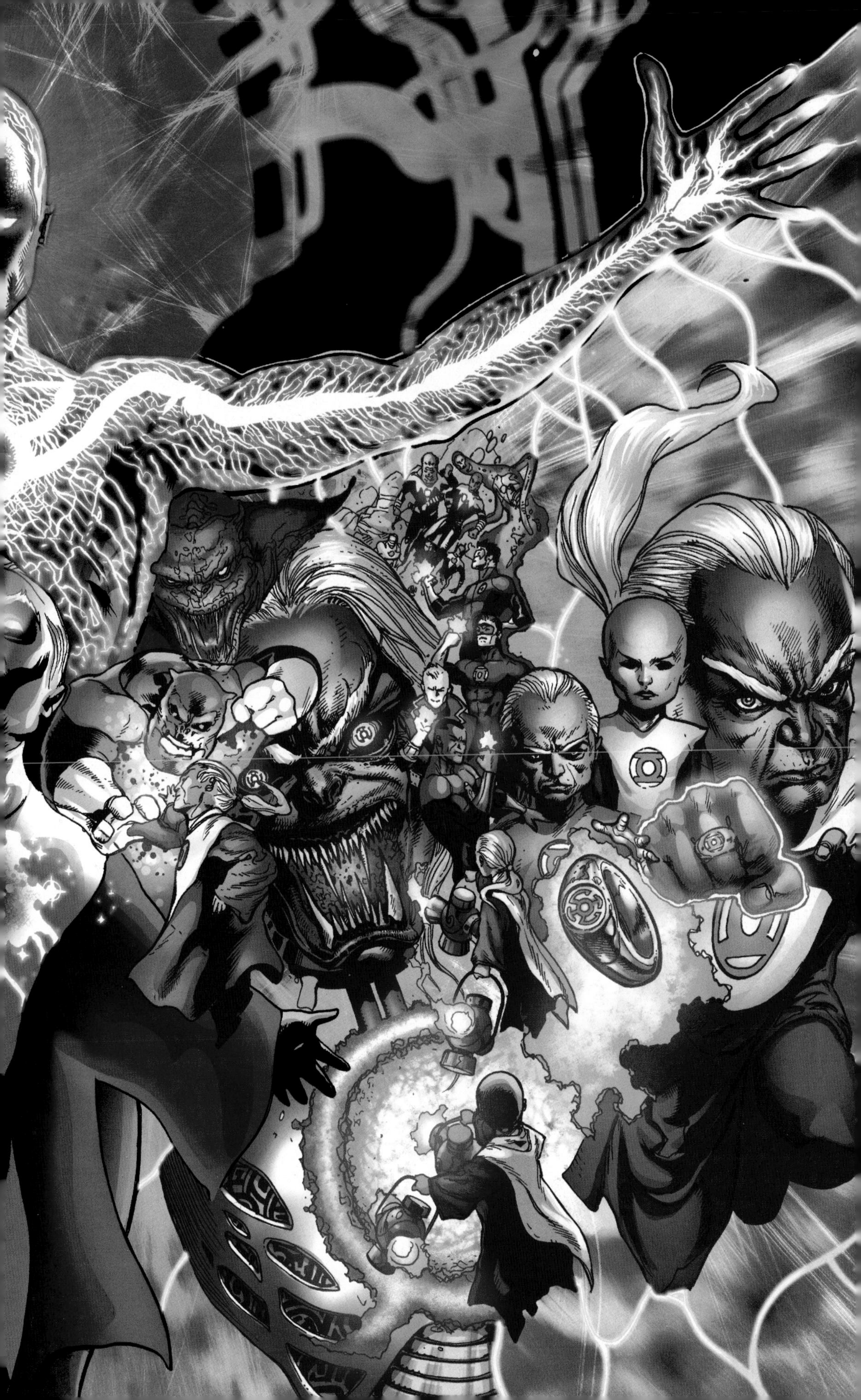

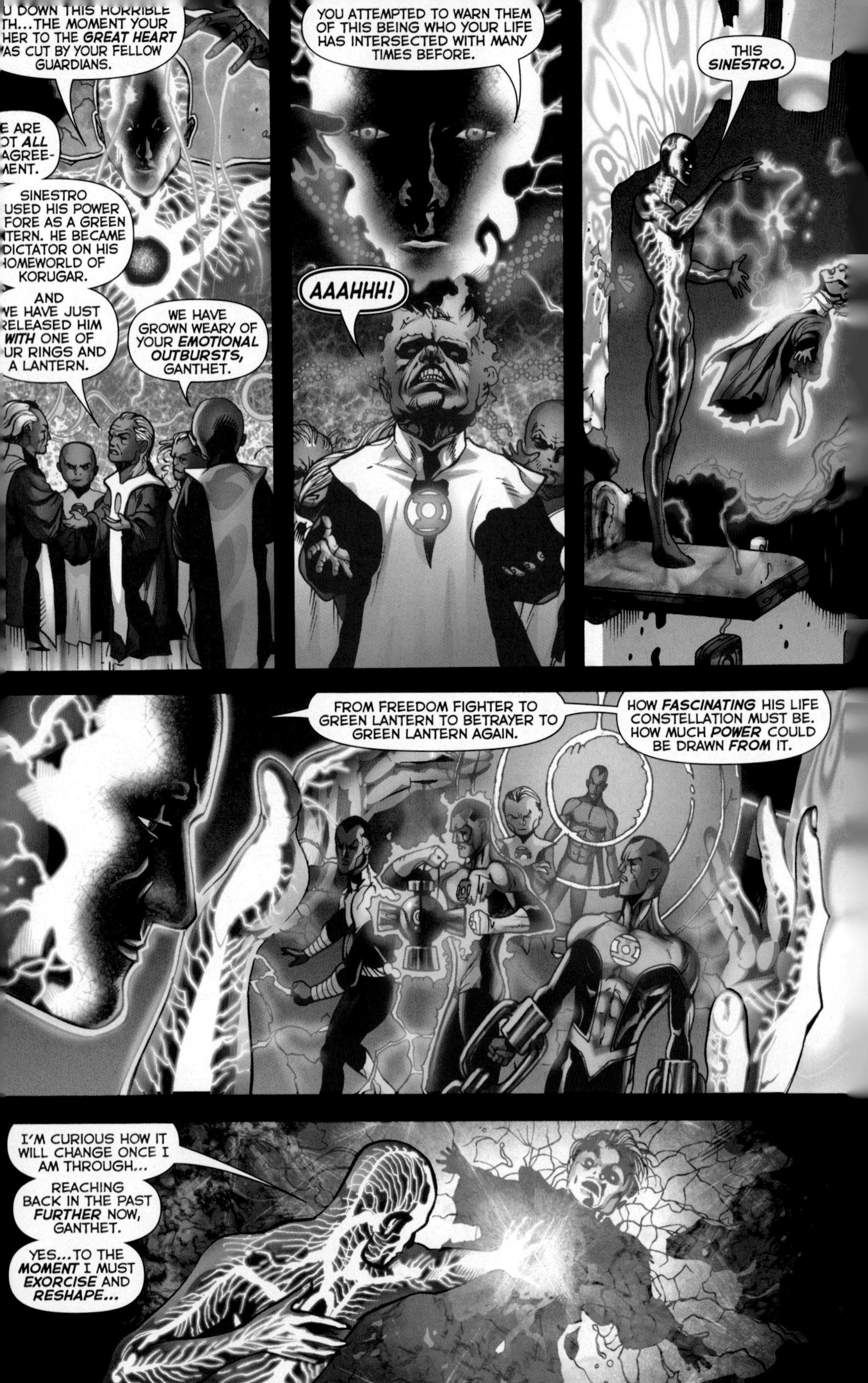

U DOWN THIS HORRIBLE TH... THE MOMENT YOUR HER TO THE GREAT HEART AS CUT BY YOUR FELLOW GUARDIANS.
E ARE OT ALL AGREE-MENT.
SINESTRO USED HIS POWER FORE AS A GREEN TERN. HE BECAME DICTATOR ON HIS HOMEWORLD OF KORUGAR.
AND WE HAVE JUST RELEASED HIM WITH ONE OF UR RINGS AND A LANTERN.
WE HAVE GROWN WEARY OF YOUR EMOTIONAL OUTBURSTS, GANTHET.
YOU ATTEMPTED TO WARN THEM OF THIS BEING WHO YOUR LIFE HAS INTERSECTED WITH MANY TIMES BEFORE.
AAAHHH!
THIS SINESTRO.
FROM FREEDOM FIGHTER TO GREEN LANTERN TO BETRAYER TO GREEN LANTERN AGAIN.
HOW FASCINATING HIS LIFE CONSTELLATION MUST BE. HOW MUCH POWER COULD BE DRAWN FROM IT.
I'M CURIOUS HOW IT WILL CHANGE ONCE I AM THROUGH...
REACHING BACK IN THE PAST FURTHER NOW, GANTHET.
YES...TO THE MOMENT I MUST EXORCISE AND RESHAPE...

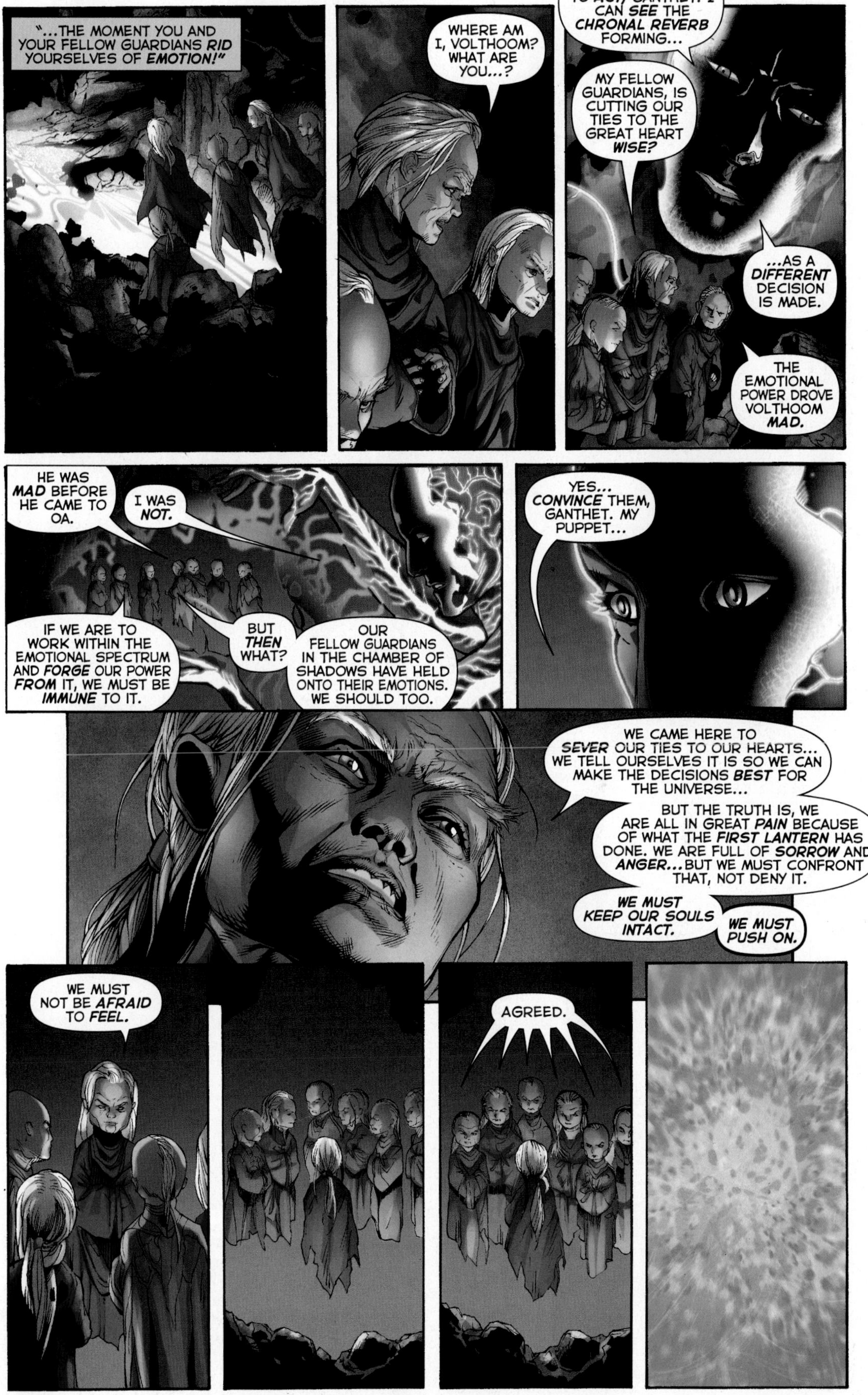
"...THE MOMENT YOU AND YOUR FELLOW GUARDIANS RID YOURSELVES OF EMOTION!"
WHERE AM I, VOLTHOOM? WHAT ARE YOU...?
YOU WILL ACT THE WAY I WILL YOU TO ACT, GANTHET. I CAN SEE THE CHRONAL REVERB FORMING...
MY FELLOW GUARDIANS, IS CUTTING OUR TIES TO THE GREAT HEART WISE?
...AS A DIFFERENT DECISION IS MADE.
THE EMOTIONAL POWER DROVE VOLTHOOM MAD.
HE WAS MAD BEFORE HE CAME TO OA.
I WAS NOT.
IF WE ARE TO WORK WITHIN THE EMOTIONAL SPECTRUM AND FORGE OUR POWER FROM IT, WE MUST BE IMMUNE TO IT.
BUT THEN WHAT?
OUR FELLOW GUARDIANS IN THE CHAMBER OF SHADOWS HAVE HELD ONTO THEIR EMOTIONS. WE SHOULD TOO.
YES... CONVINCE THEM, GANTHET. MY PUPPET...
WE CAME HERE TO SEVER OUR TIES TO OUR HEARTS... WE TELL OURSELVES IT IS SO WE CAN MAKE THE DECISIONS BEST FOR THE UNIVERSE...
BUT THE TRUTH IS, WE ARE ALL IN GREAT PAIN BECAUSE OF WHAT THE FIRST LANTERN HAS DONE. WE ARE FULL OF SORROW AND ANGER...BUT WE MUST CONFRONT THAT, NOT DENY IT.
WE MUST KEEP OUR SOULS INTACT.
WE MUST PUSH ON.
WE MUST NOT BE AFRAID TO FEEL.
AGREED.

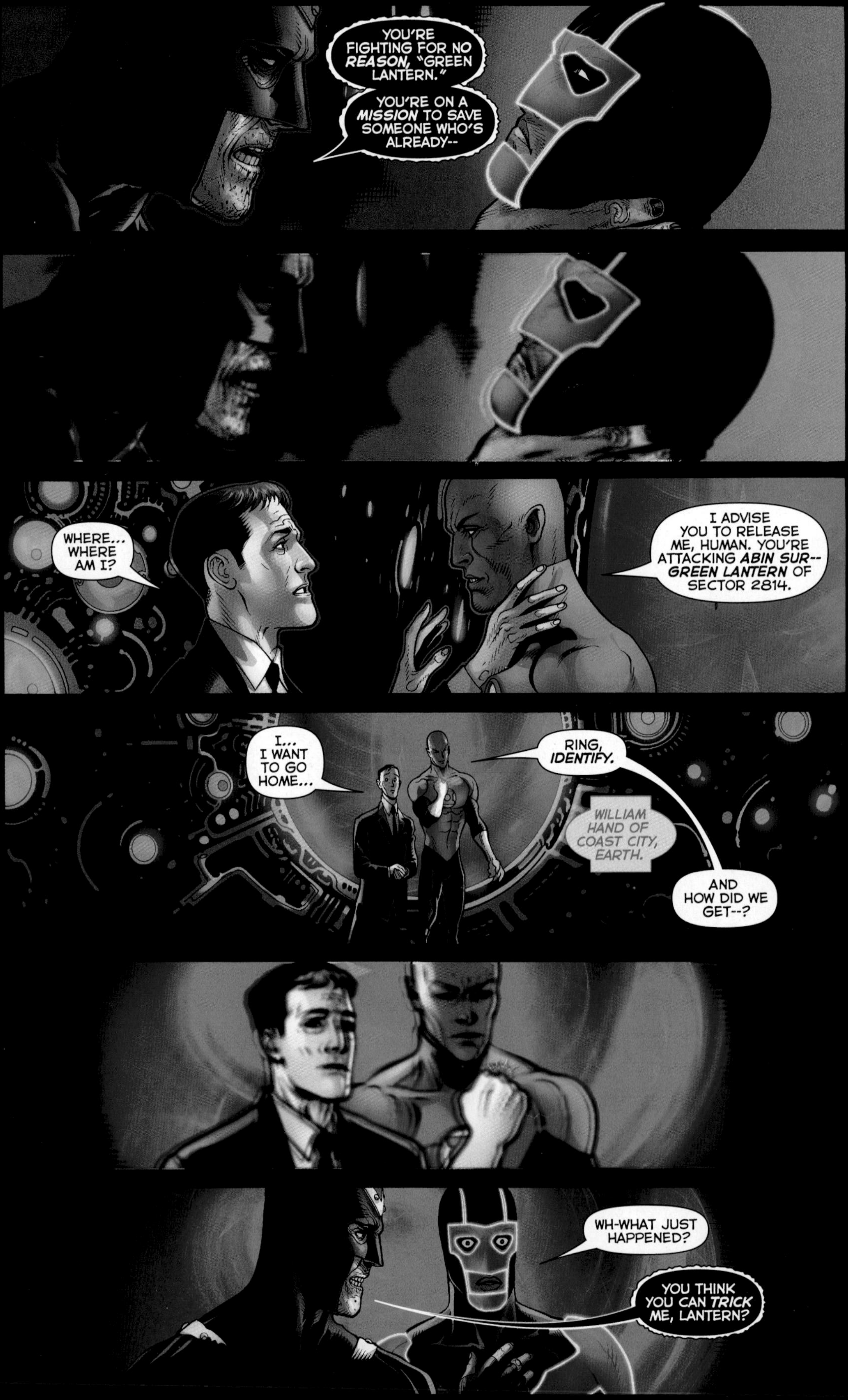
YOU'RE FIGHTING FOR NO REASON, "GREEN LANTERN."
YOU'RE ON A MISSION TO SAVE SOMEONE WHO'S ALREADY--
WHERE... WHERE AM I?
I ADVISE YOU TO RELEASE ME, HUMAN. YOU'RE ATTACKING ABIN SUR-- GREEN LANTERN OF SECTOR 2814.
I... I WANT TO GO HOME...
RING, IDENTIFY.
WILLIAM HAND OF COAST CITY, EARTH.
AND HOW DID WE GET--?
WH-WHAT JUST HAPPENED?
YOU THINK YOU CAN TRICK ME, LANTERN?

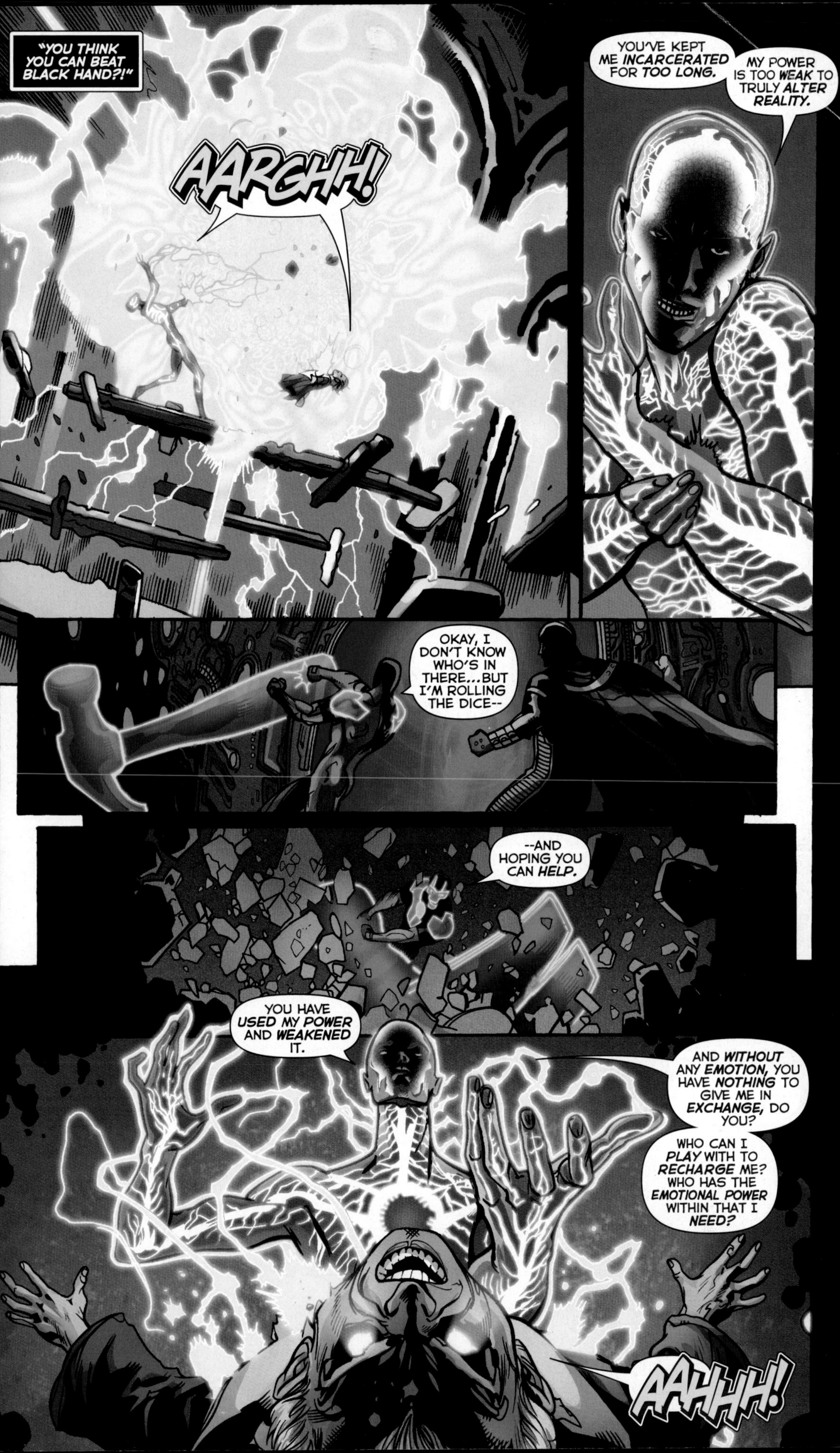
"YOU THINK YOU CAN BEAT BLACK HAND?!"
AARGHH!
YOU'VE KEPT ME INCARCERATED FOR TOO LONG.
MY POWER IS TOO WEAK TO TRULY ALTER REALITY.
OKAY, I DON'T KNOW WHO'S IN THERE...BUT I'M ROLLING THE DICE--
--AND HOPING YOU CAN HELP.
YOU HAVE USED MY POWER AND WEAKENED IT.
AND WITHOUT ANY EMOTION, YOU HAVE NOTHING TO GIVE ME IN EXCHANGE, DO YOU?
WHO CAN I PLAY WITH TO RECHARGE ME? WHO HAS THE EMOTIONAL POWER WITHIN THAT I NEED?
AAHHH!

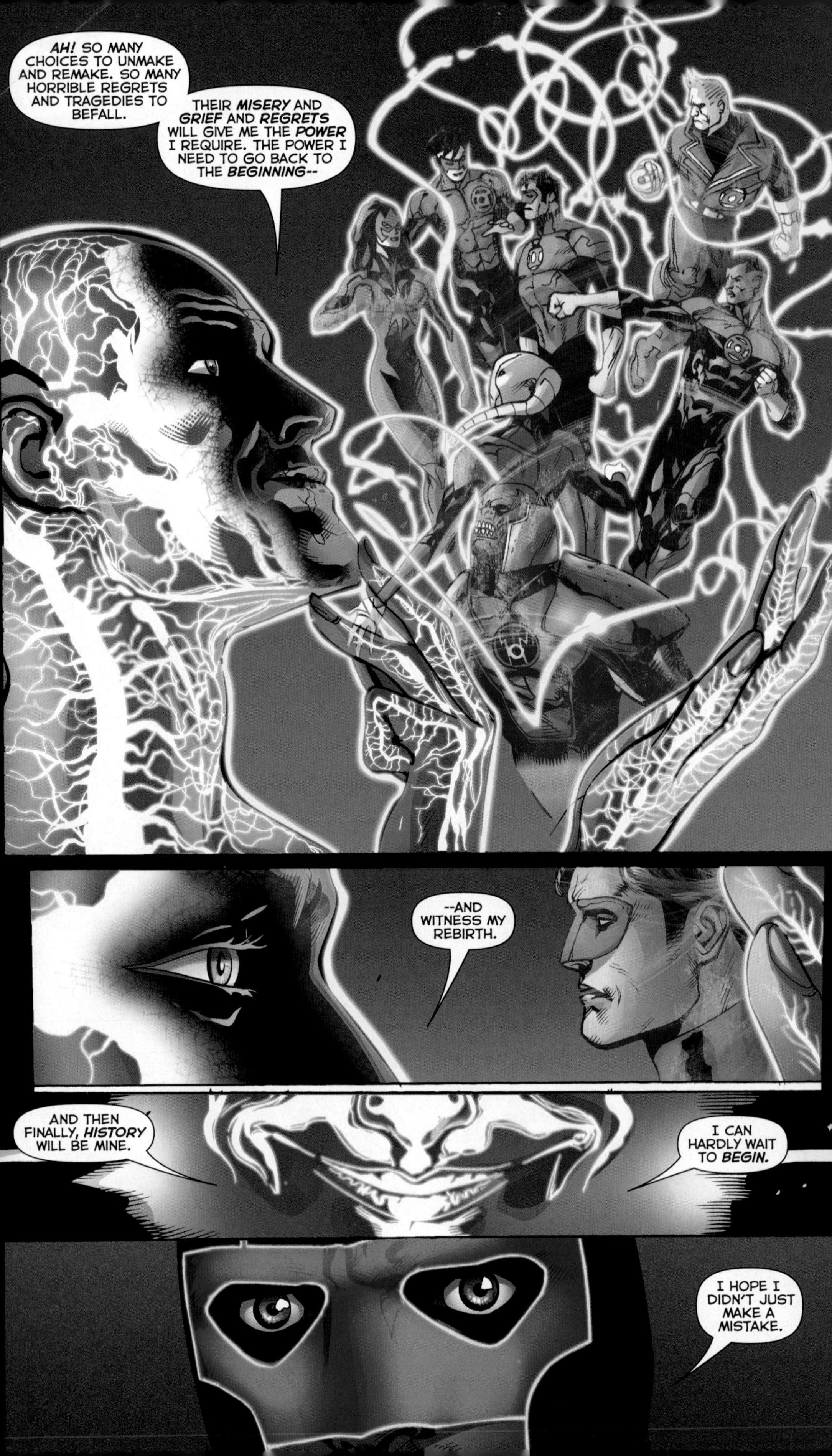
AH! SO MANY CHOICES TO UNMAKE AND REMAKE. SO MANY HORRIBLE REGRETS AND TRAGEDIES TO BEFALL.
THEIR MISERY AND GRIEF AND REGRETS WILL GIVE ME THE POWER I REQUIRE. THE POWER I NEED TO GO BACK TO THE BEGINNING--
--AND WITNESS MY REBIRTH.
AND THEN FINALLY, HISTORY WILL BE MINE.
I CAN HARDLY WAIT TO BEGIN.
I HOPE I DIDN'T JUST MAKE A MISTAKE.

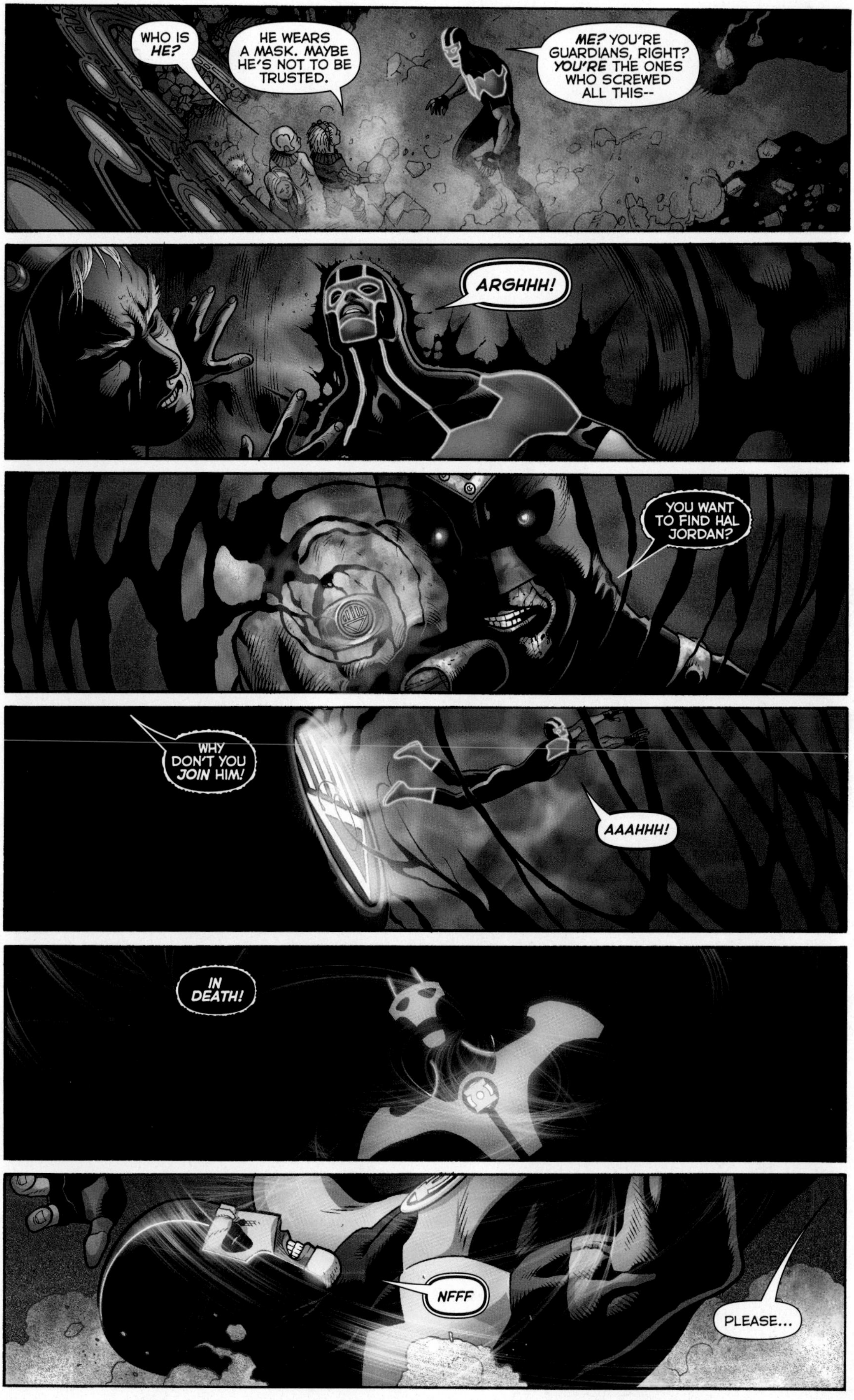
WHO IS HE?
HE WEARS A MASK. MAYBE HE'S NOT TO BE TRUSTED.
ME? YOU'RE GUARDIANS, RIGHT? YOU'RE THE ONES WHO SCREWED ALL THIS--
ARGHHH!
YOU WANT TO FIND HAL JORDAN?
WHY DON'T YOU JOIN HIM!
AAAHHH!
IN DEATH!
NFFF
PLEASE...

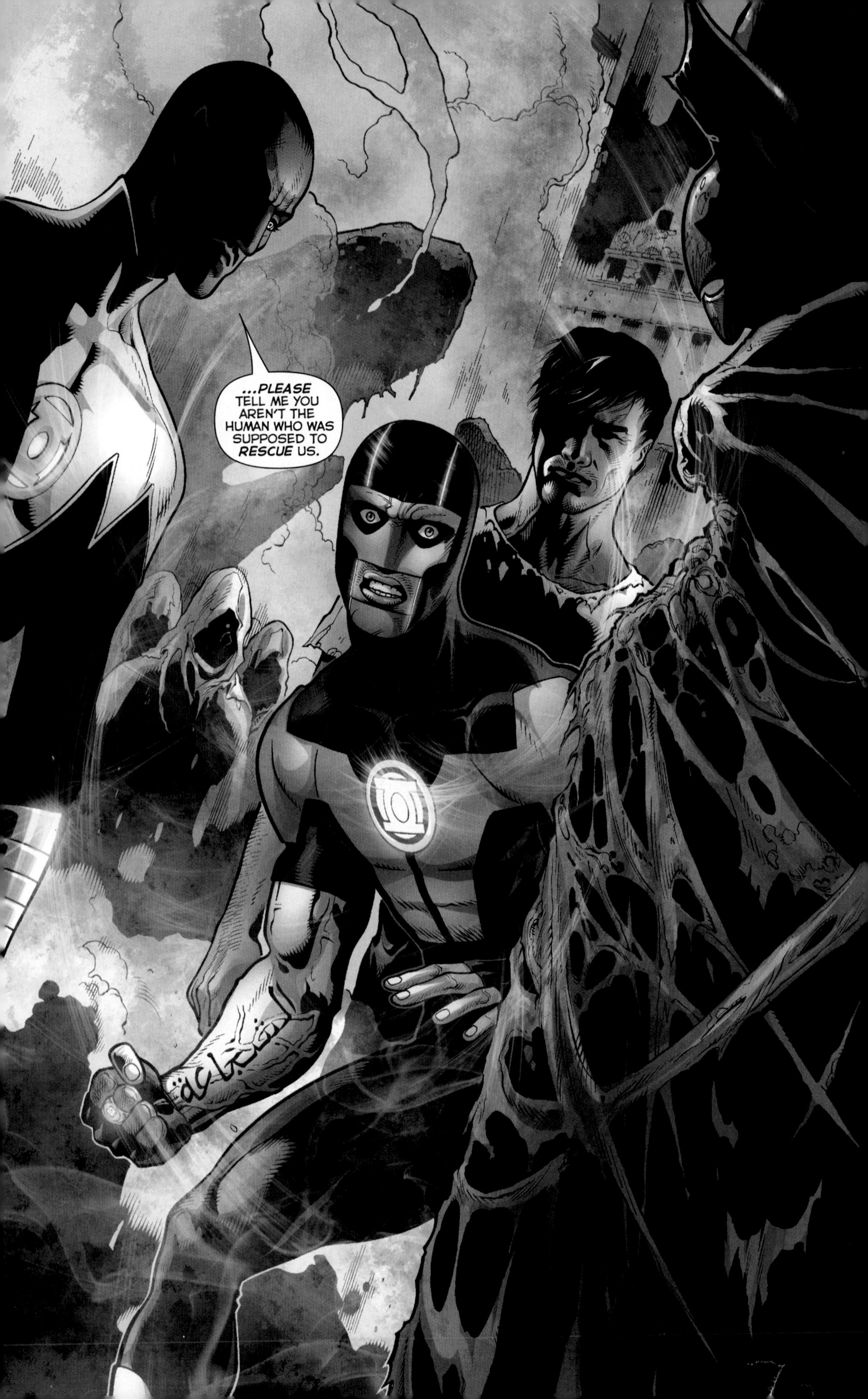
...PLEASE TELL ME YOU AREN'T THE HUMAN WHO WAS SUPPOSED TO RESCUE US.

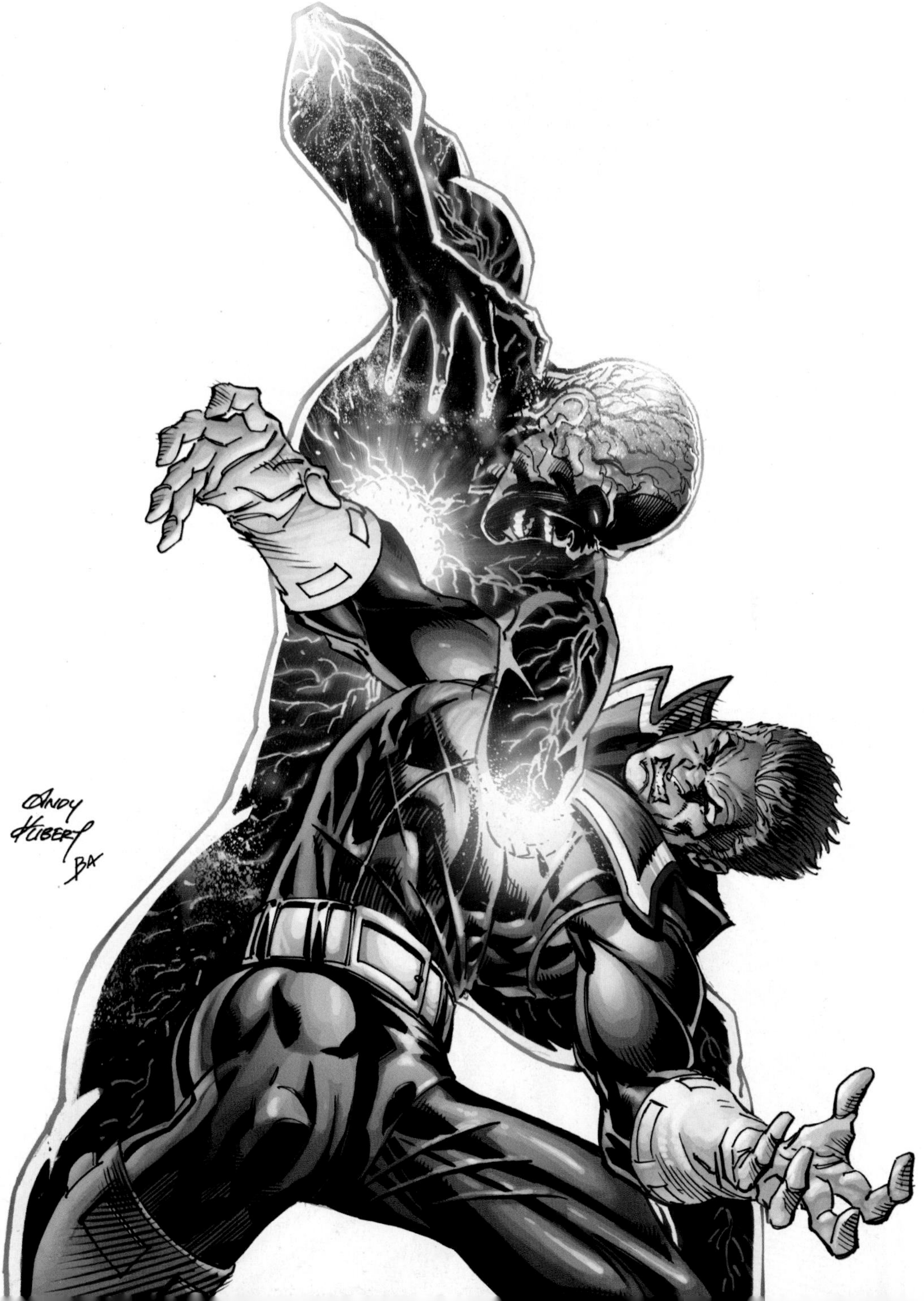
ANDY
KUBERT
BA

PART TWO: DECIMATED

PETER J. TOMASI writer FERNANDO PASARIN penciller SCOTT HANNA inker
cover art by ANDY KUBERT & BRAD ANDERSON

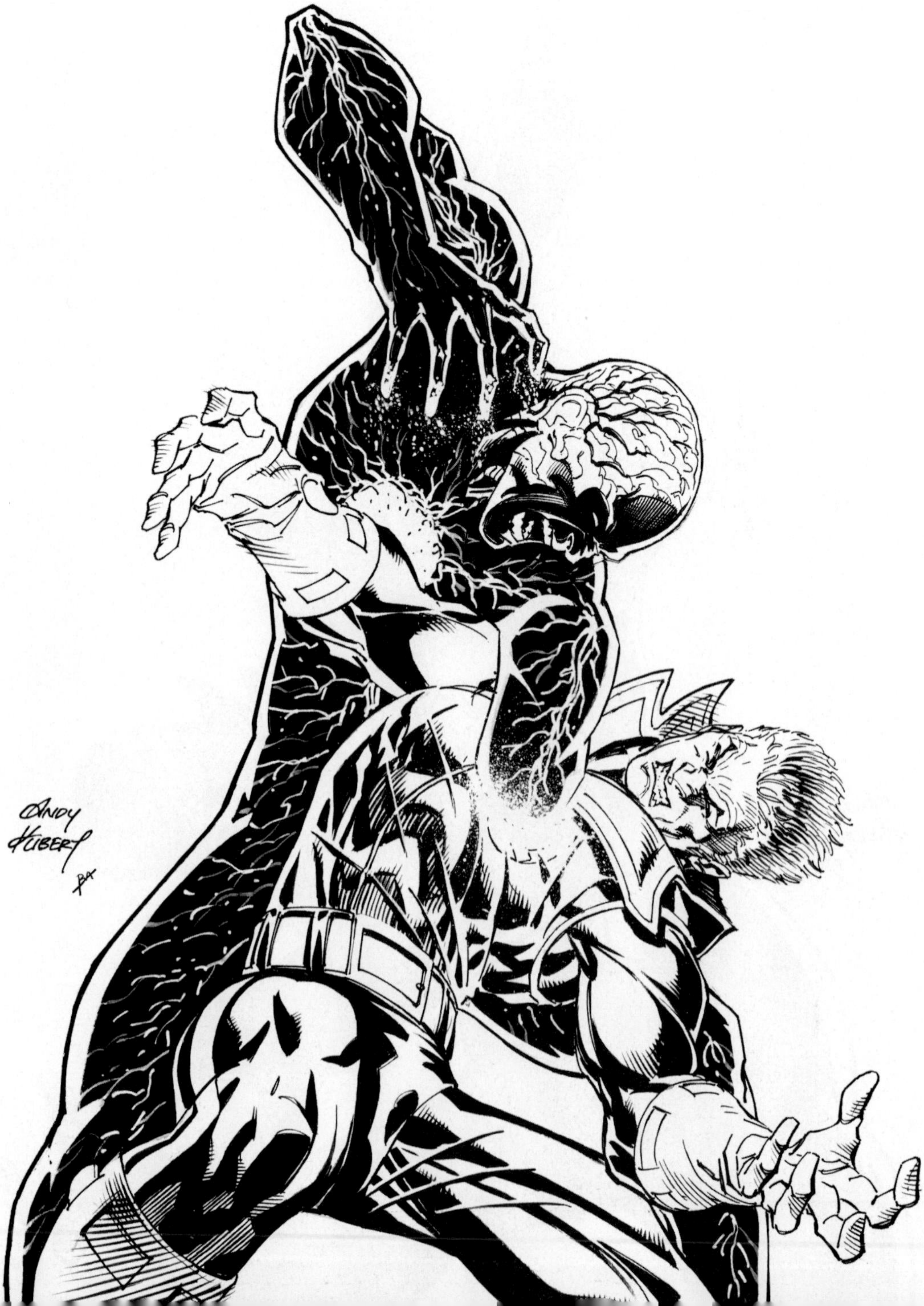
ANDY KUBERT
BA

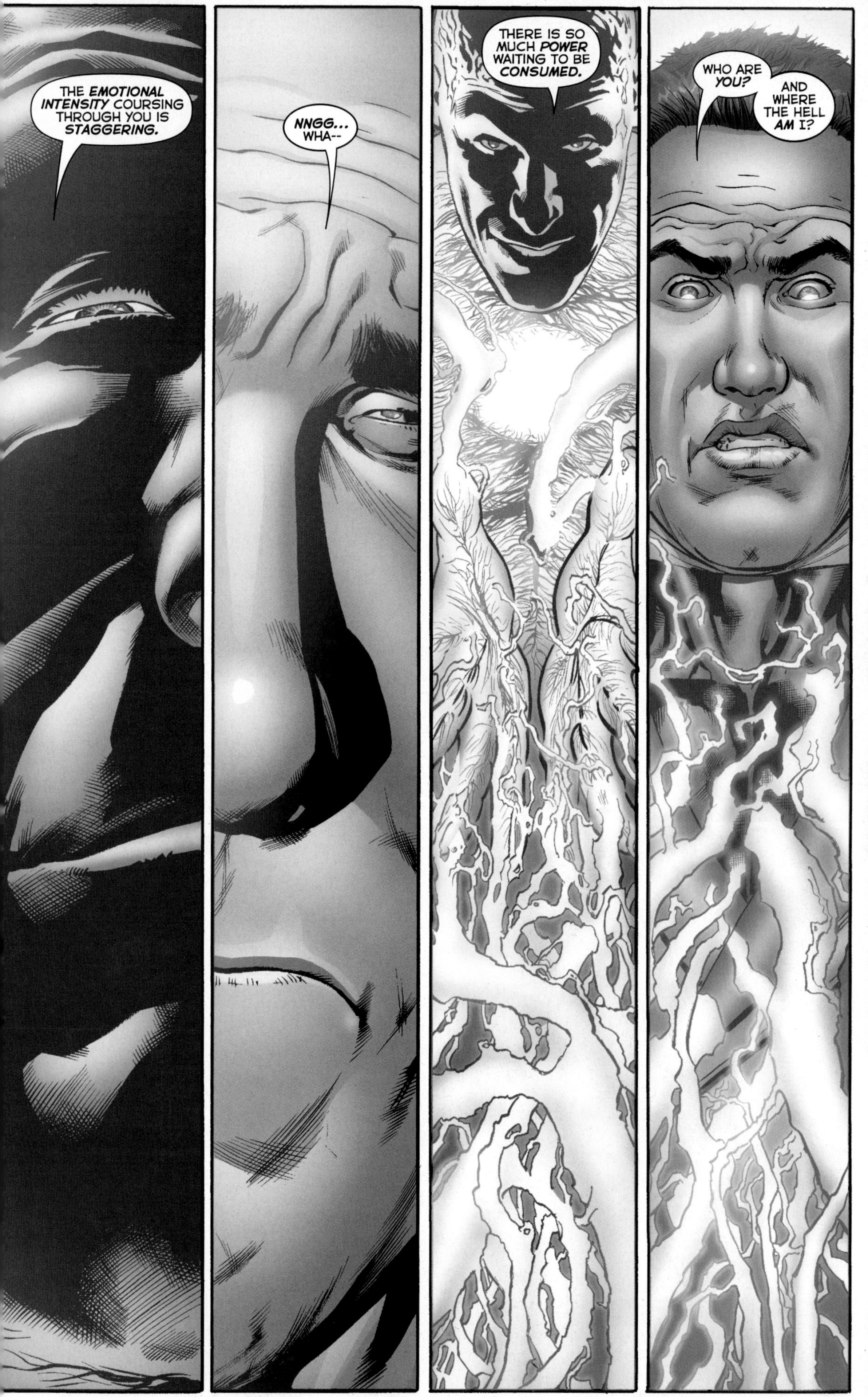
THE *EMOTIONAL INTENSITY* COURSING THROUGH YOU IS *STAGGERING.*
NNGG... WHA--
THERE IS SO MUCH *POWER* WAITING TO BE *CONSUMED.*
WHO ARE *YOU?*
AND WHERE THE HELL *AM* I?

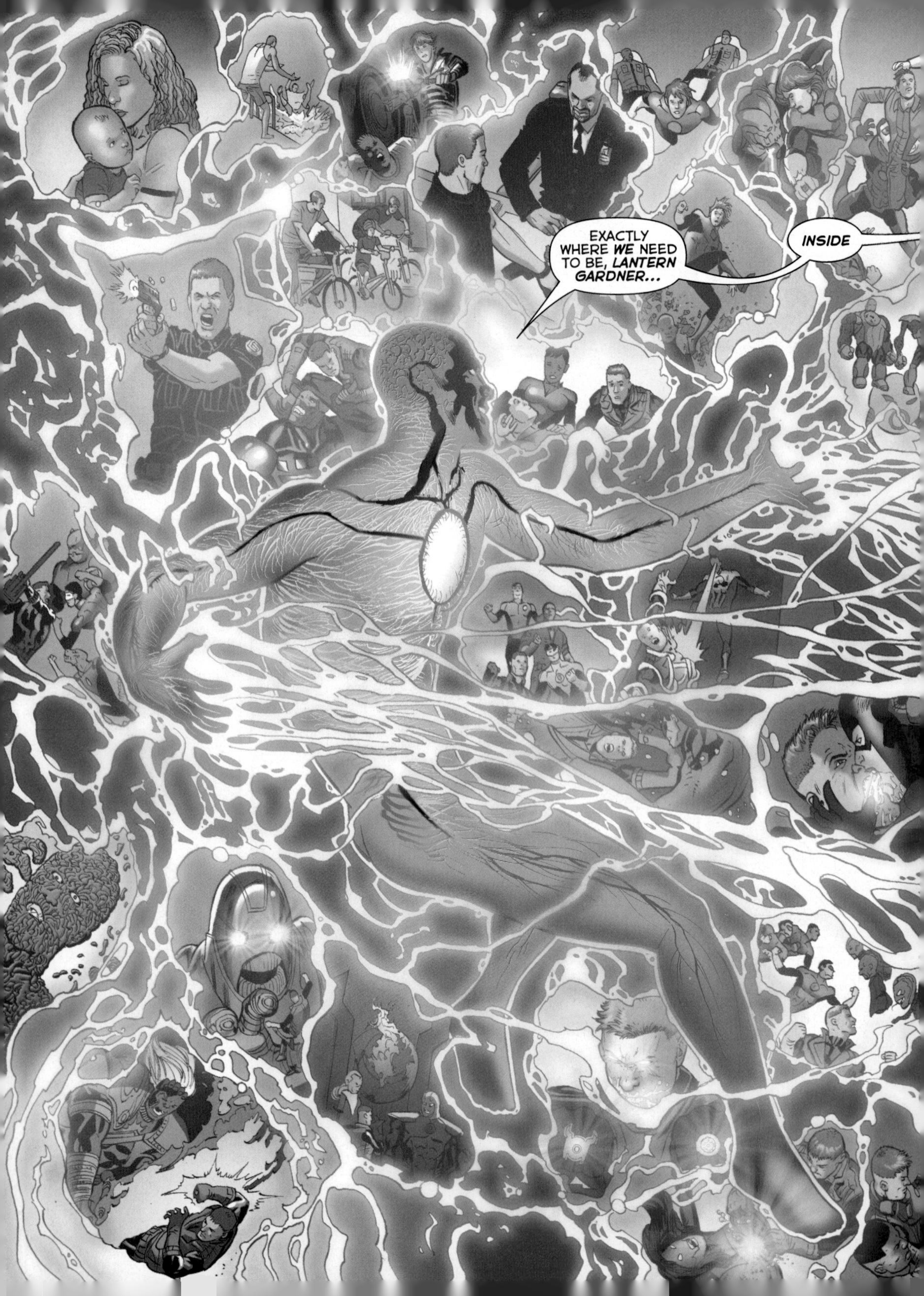

EXACTLY WHERE WE NEED TO BE, LANTERN GARDNER...
INSIDE

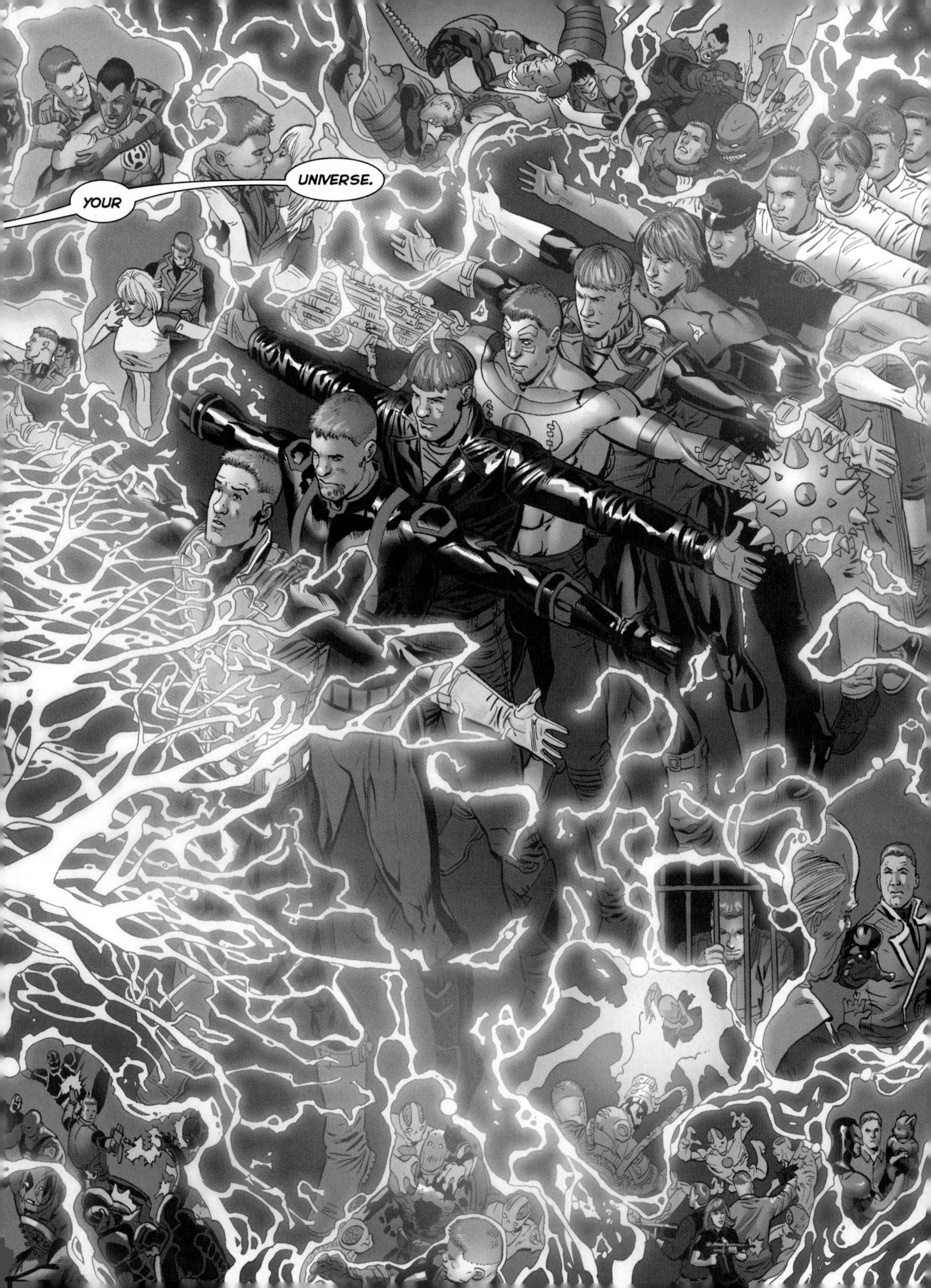
YOUR
UNIVERSE.

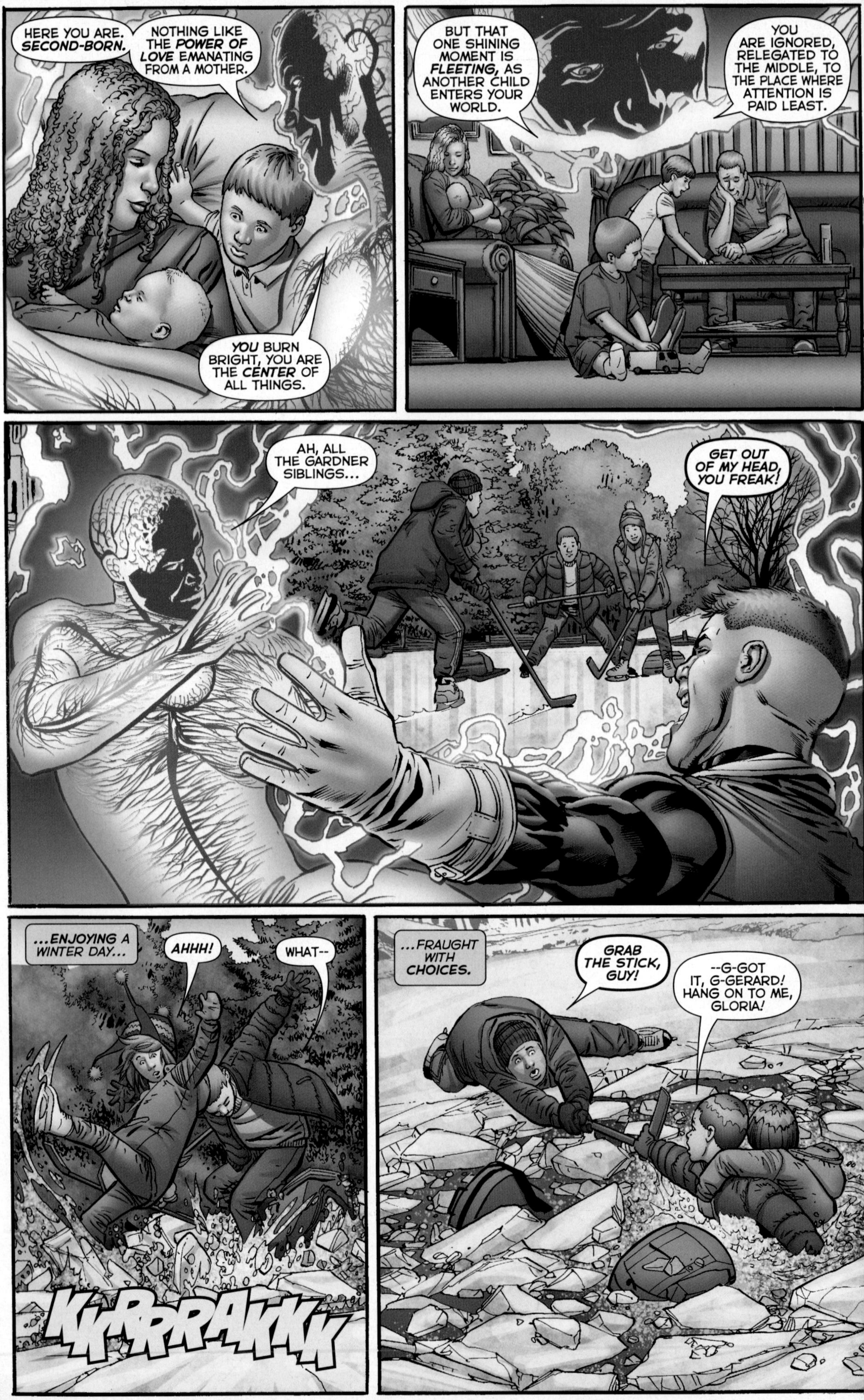
HERE YOU ARE. SECOND-BORN.
NOTHING LIKE THE POWER OF LOVE EMANATING FROM A MOTHER.
YOU BURN BRIGHT, YOU ARE THE CENTER OF ALL THINGS.
BUT THAT ONE SHINING MOMENT IS FLEETING, AS ANOTHER CHILD ENTERS YOUR WORLD.
YOU ARE IGNORED, RELEGATED TO THE MIDDLE, TO THE PLACE WHERE ATTENTION IS PAID LEAST.
AH, ALL THE GARDNER SIBLINGS...
GET OUT OF MY HEAD, YOU FREAK!
...ENJOYING A WINTER DAY...
AHHH!
WHAT--
KKRRRAKKK
...FRAUGHT WITH CHOICES.
GRAB THE STICK, GUY!
--G-GOT IT, G-GERARD! HANG ON TO ME, GLORIA!

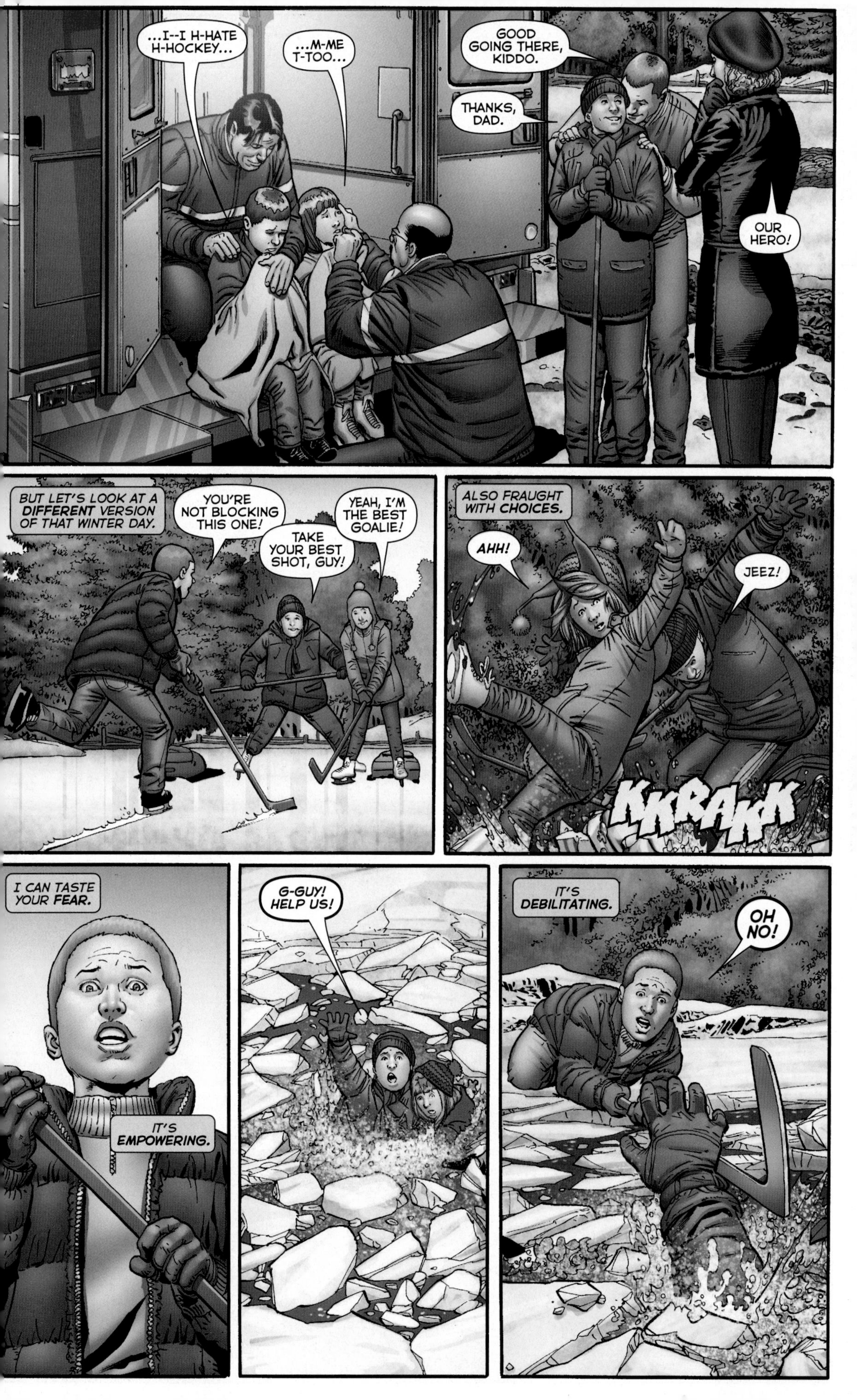
...I--I H-HATE H-HOCKEY...
...M-ME T-TOO...
GOOD GOING THERE, KIDDO.
THANKS, DAD.
OUR HERO!
BUT LET'S LOOK AT A DIFFERENT VERSION OF THAT WINTER DAY.
YOU'RE NOT BLOCKING THIS ONE!
TAKE YOUR BEST SHOT, GUY!
YEAH, I'M THE BEST GOALIE!
ALSO FRAUGHT WITH CHOICES.
AHH!
JEEZ!
KKRAKK
I CAN TASTE YOUR FEAR.
IT'S EMPOWERING.
G-GUY! HELP US!
IT'S DEBILITATING.
OH NO!

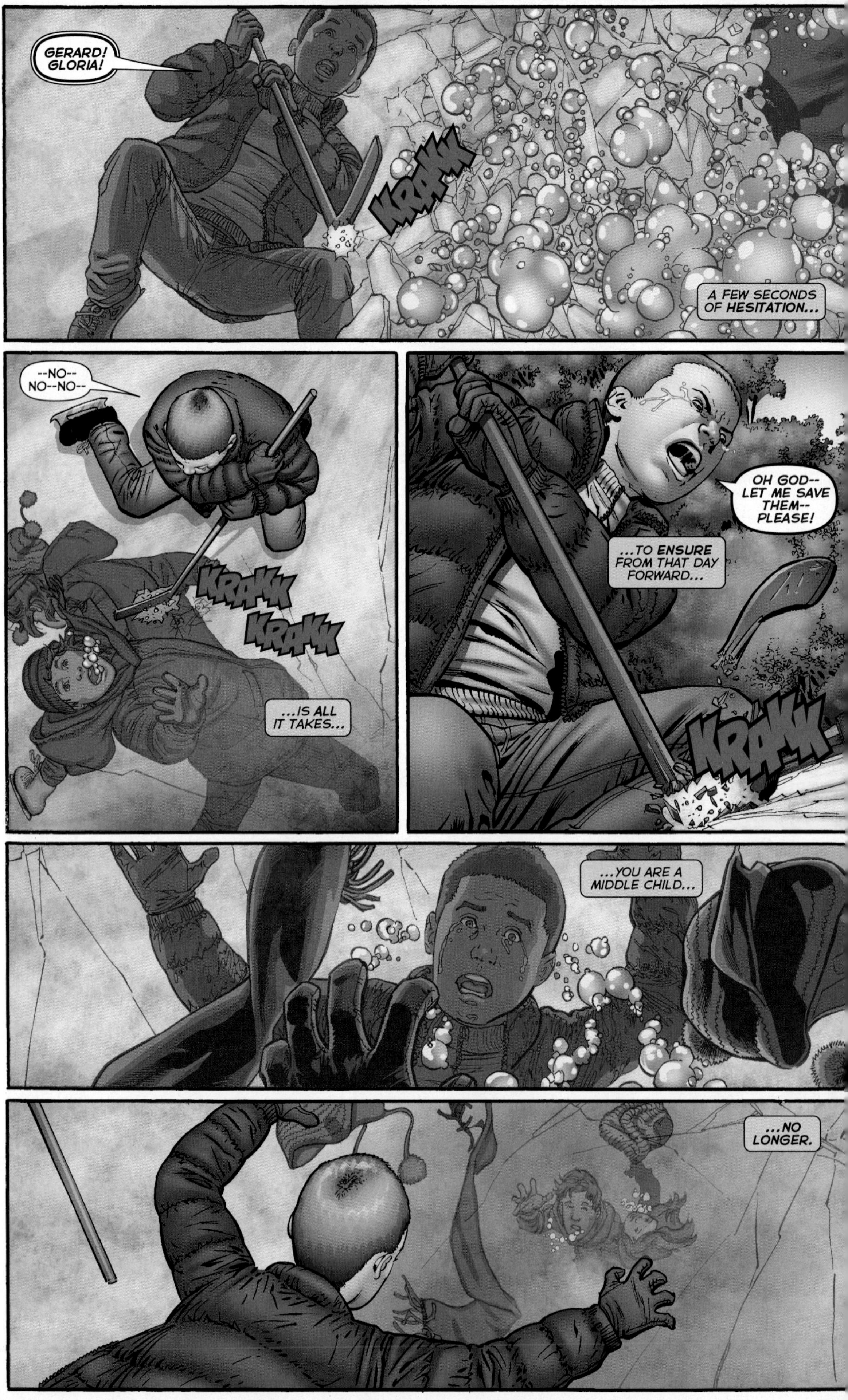
GERARD! GLORIA!
KRAKK
A FEW SECONDS OF HESITATION...
--NO-- NO--NO--
KRAKK
KRAKK
...IS ALL IT TAKES...
OH GOD-- LET ME SAVE THEM-- PLEASE!
...TO ENSURE FROM THAT DAY FORWARD...
KRAKK
...YOU ARE A MIDDLE CHILD...
...NO LONGER.

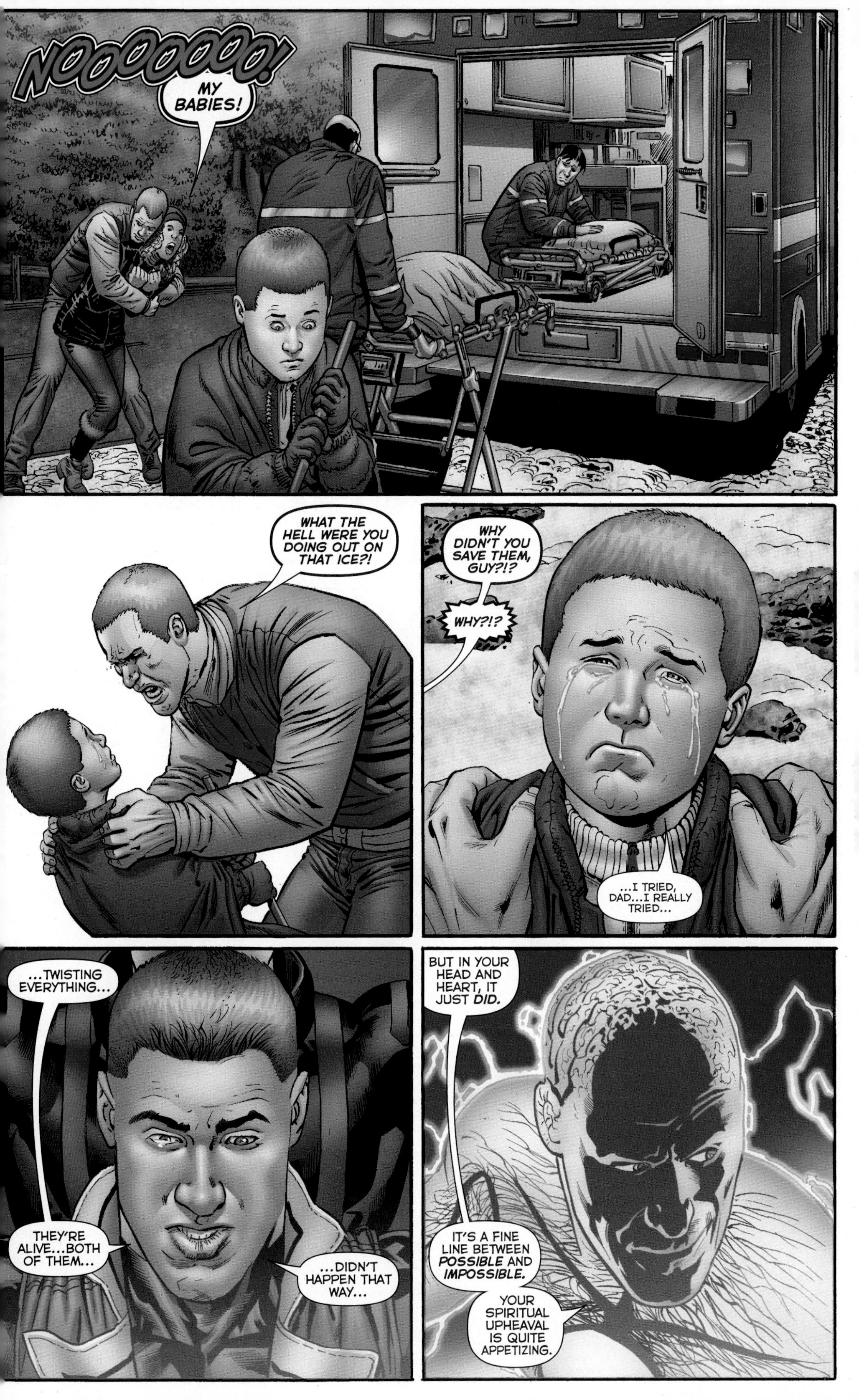
NOOOOOOO!
MY BABIES!
WHAT THE HELL WERE YOU DOING OUT ON THAT ICE?!
WHY DIDN'T YOU SAVE THEM, GUY?!?
WHY?!?
...I TRIED, DAD...I REALLY TRIED...
...TWISTING EVERYTHING...
THEY'RE ALIVE...BOTH OF THEM...
...DIDN'T HAPPEN THAT WAY...
BUT IN YOUR HEAD AND HEART, IT JUST DID.
IT'S A FINE LINE BETWEEN POSSIBLE AND IMPOSSIBLE.
YOUR SPIRITUAL UPHEAVAL IS QUITE APPETIZING.

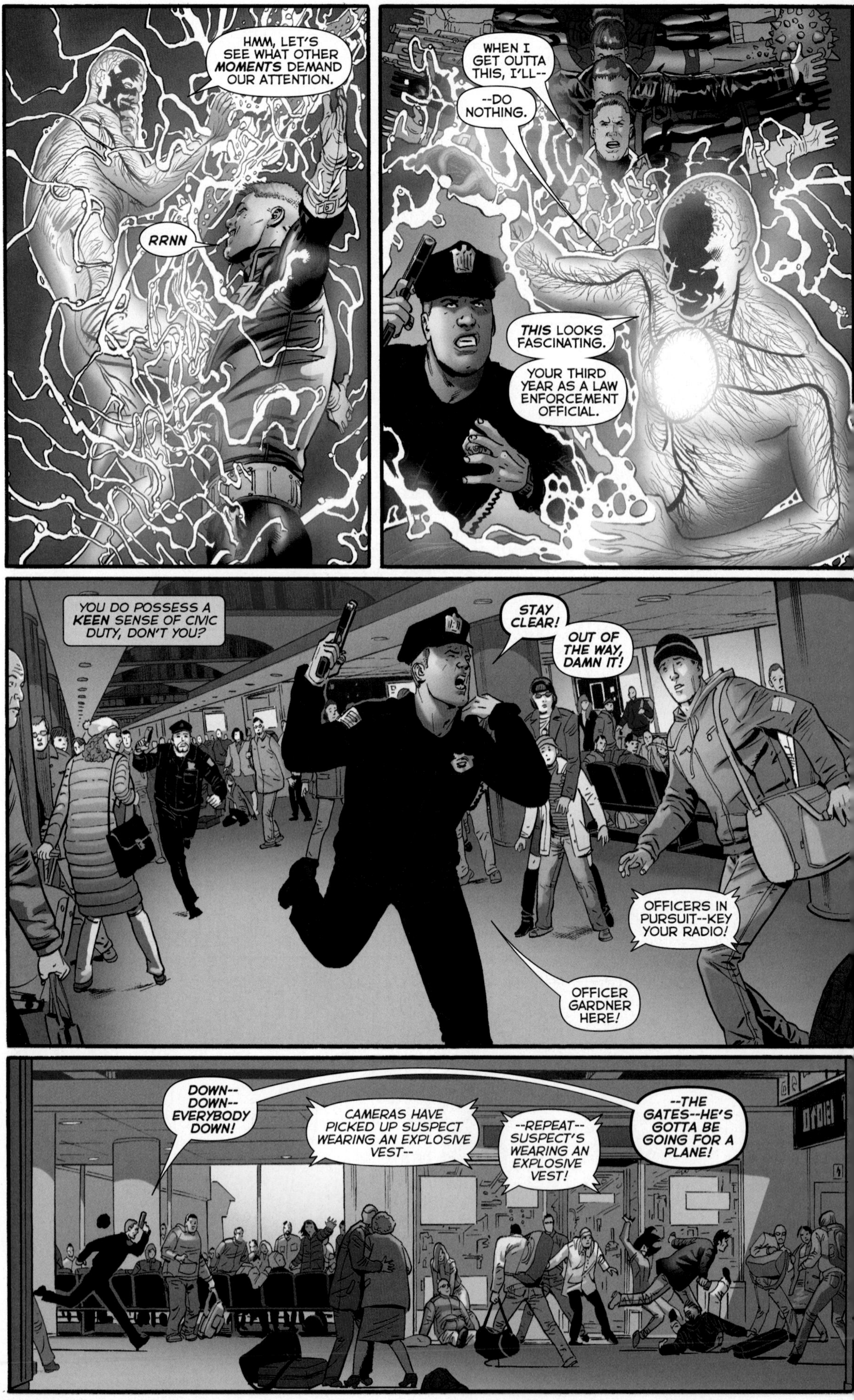
HMM, LET'S SEE WHAT OTHER MOMENTS DEMAND OUR ATTENTION.
RRNN
WHEN I GET OUTTA THIS, I'LL--
--DO NOTHING.
THIS LOOKS FASCINATING.
YOUR THIRD YEAR AS A LAW ENFORCEMENT OFFICIAL.
YOU DO POSSESS A KEEN SENSE OF CIVIC DUTY, DON'T YOU?
STAY CLEAR!
OUT OF THE WAY, DAMN IT!
OFFICERS IN PURSUIT--KEY YOUR RADIO!
OFFICER GARDNER HERE!
DOWN-- DOWN-- EVERYBODY DOWN!
CAMERAS HAVE PICKED UP SUSPECT WEARING AN EXPLOSIVE VEST--
--REPEAT--SUSPECT'S WEARING AN EXPLOSIVE VEST!
--THE GATES--HE'S GOTTA BE GOING FOR A PLANE!

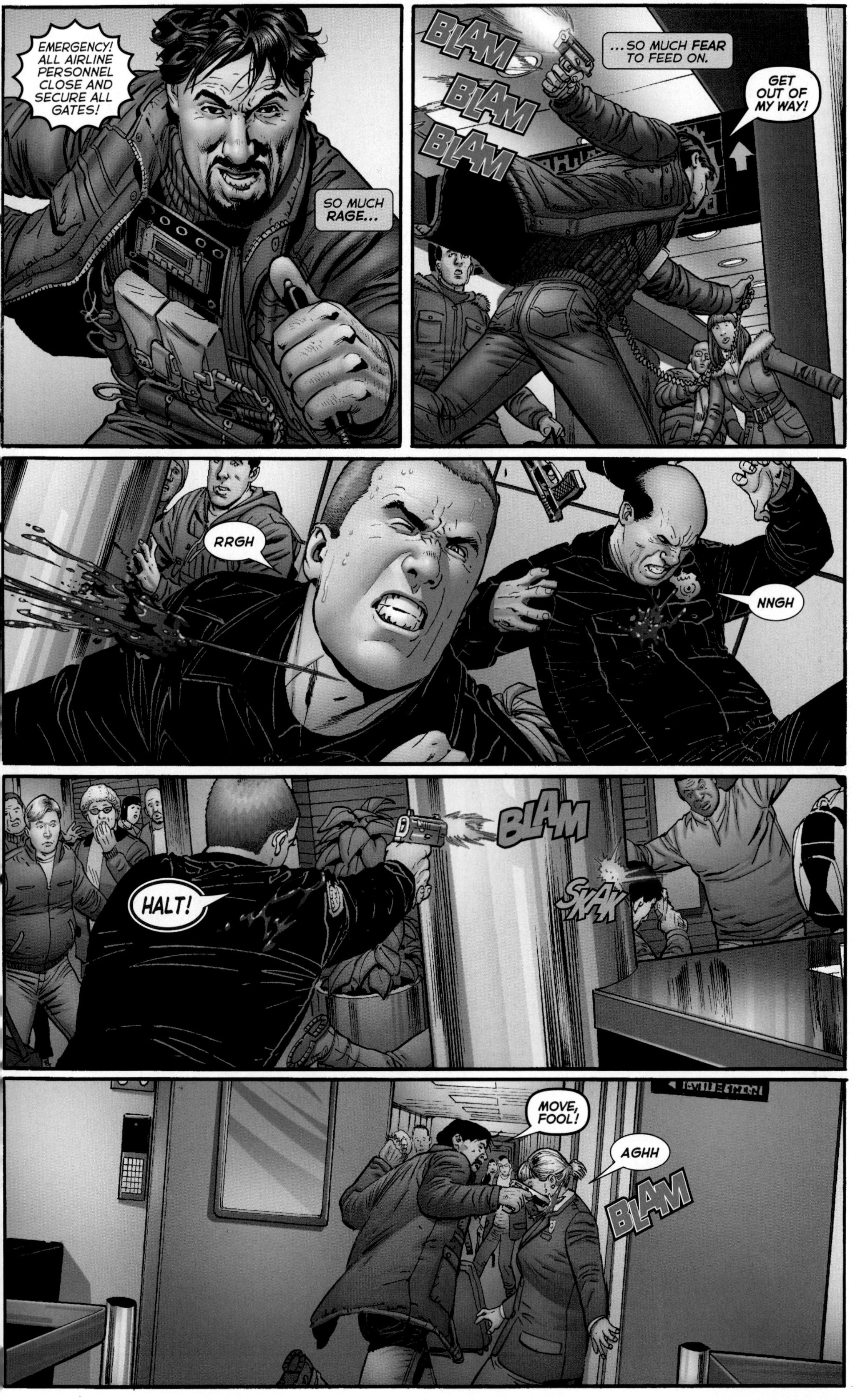
EMERGENCY! ALL AIRLINE PERSONNEL CLOSE AND SECURE ALL GATES!
SO MUCH RAGE...
BLAM
BLAM
BLAM
...SO MUCH FEAR TO FEED ON.
GET OUT OF MY WAY!
RRGH
NNGH
BLAM
HALT!
SKAK
MOVE, FOOL!
AGHH
BLAM

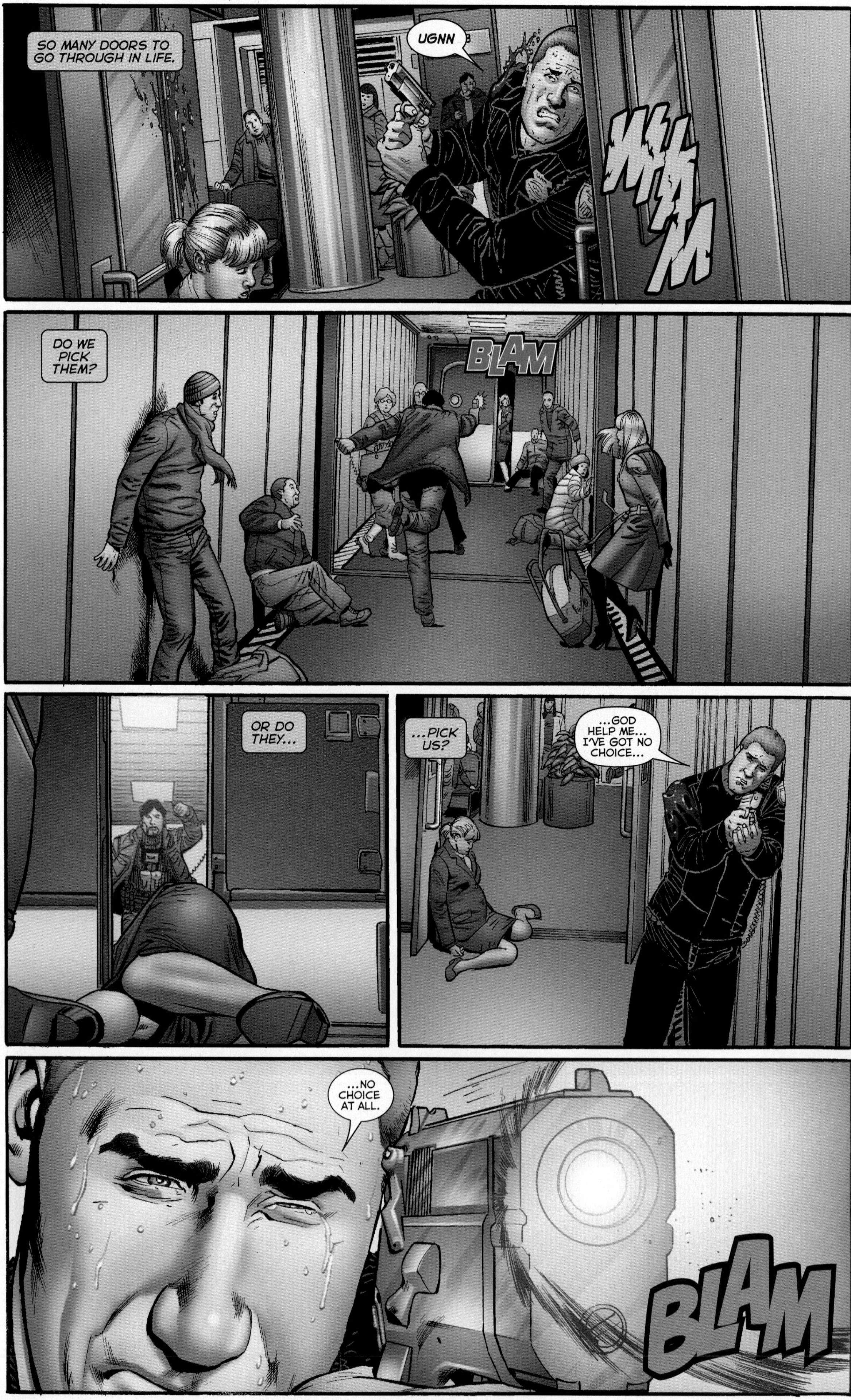
SO MANY DOORS TO GO THROUGH IN LIFE.
UGNN
DO WE PICK THEM?
BLAM
OR DO THEY...
...PICK US?
...GOD HELP ME... I'VE GOT NO CHOICE...
...NO CHOICE AT ALL.
BLAM

BOOOOM

...NEED MEDICS... CIVILIANS DOWN... FER CRISSAKES, *HURRY*...

...THEY'RE DYING...HAVE TO...HELP...

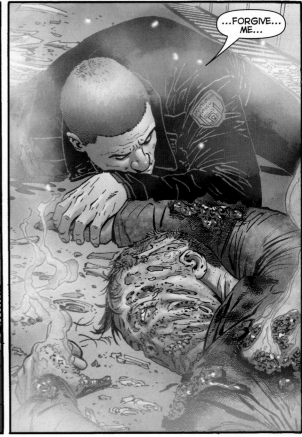

...FORGIVE... ME...

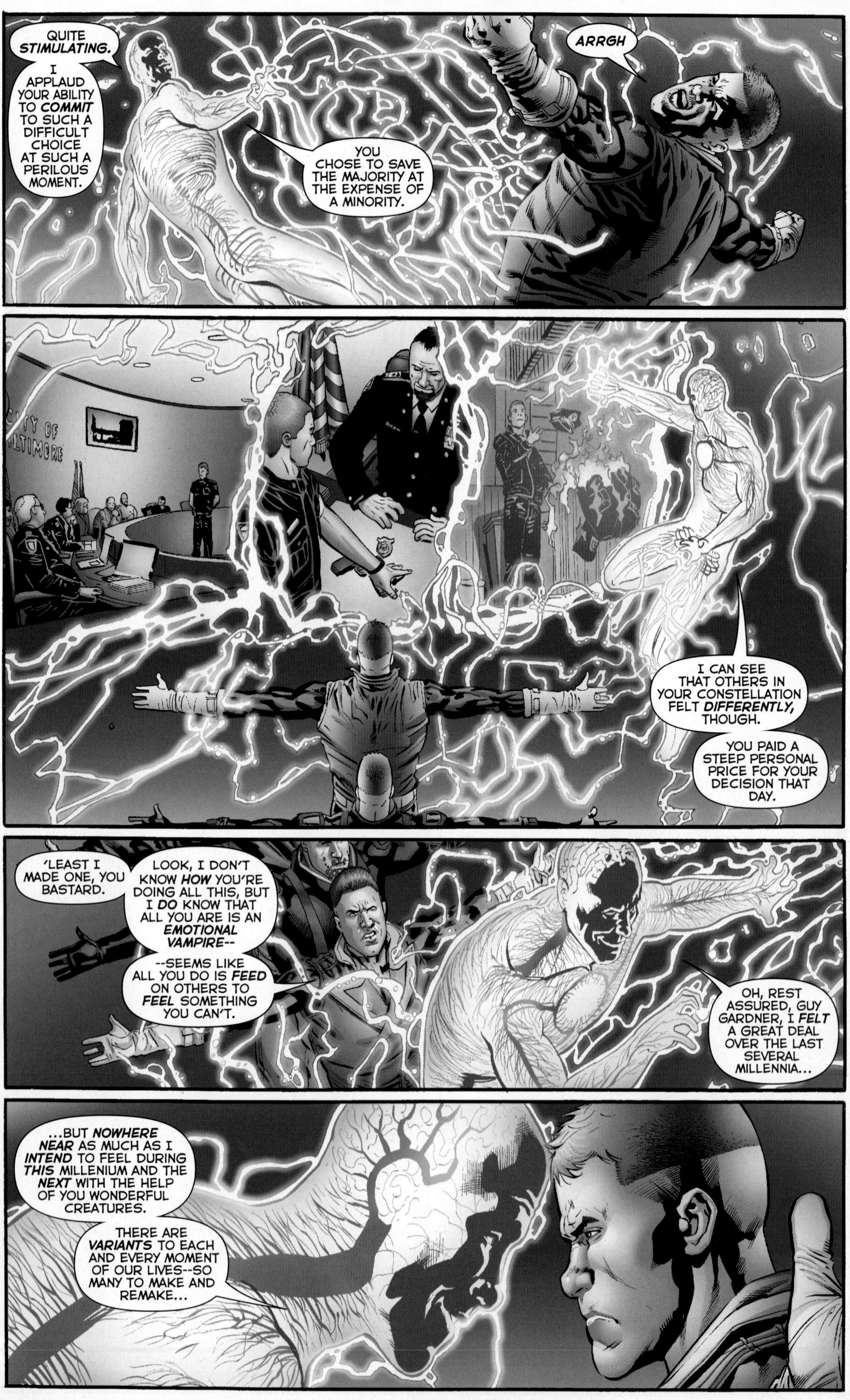
QUITE STIMULATING.
I APPLAUD YOUR ABILITY TO COMMIT TO SUCH A DIFFICULT CHOICE AT SUCH A PERILOUS MOMENT.
ARRGH
YOU CHOSE TO SAVE THE MAJORITY AT THE EXPENSE OF A MINORITY.
I CAN SEE THAT OTHERS IN YOUR CONSTELLATION FELT DIFFERENTLY, THOUGH.
YOU PAID A STEEP PERSONAL PRICE FOR YOUR DECISION THAT DAY.
'LEAST I MADE ONE, YOU BASTARD.
LOOK, I DON'T KNOW HOW YOU'RE DOING ALL THIS, BUT I DO KNOW THAT ALL YOU ARE IS AN EMOTIONAL VAMPIRE--
--SEEMS LIKE ALL YOU DO IS FEED ON OTHERS TO FEEL SOMETHING YOU CAN'T.
OH, REST ASSURED, GUY GARDNER, I FELT A GREAT DEAL OVER THE LAST SEVERAL MILLENNIA...
...BUT NOWHERE NEAR AS MUCH AS I INTEND TO FEEL DURING THIS MILLENIUM AND THE NEXT WITH THE HELP OF YOU WONDERFUL CREATURES.
THERE ARE VARIANTS TO EACH AND EVERY MOMENT OF OUR LIVES--SO MANY TO MAKE AND REMAKE...

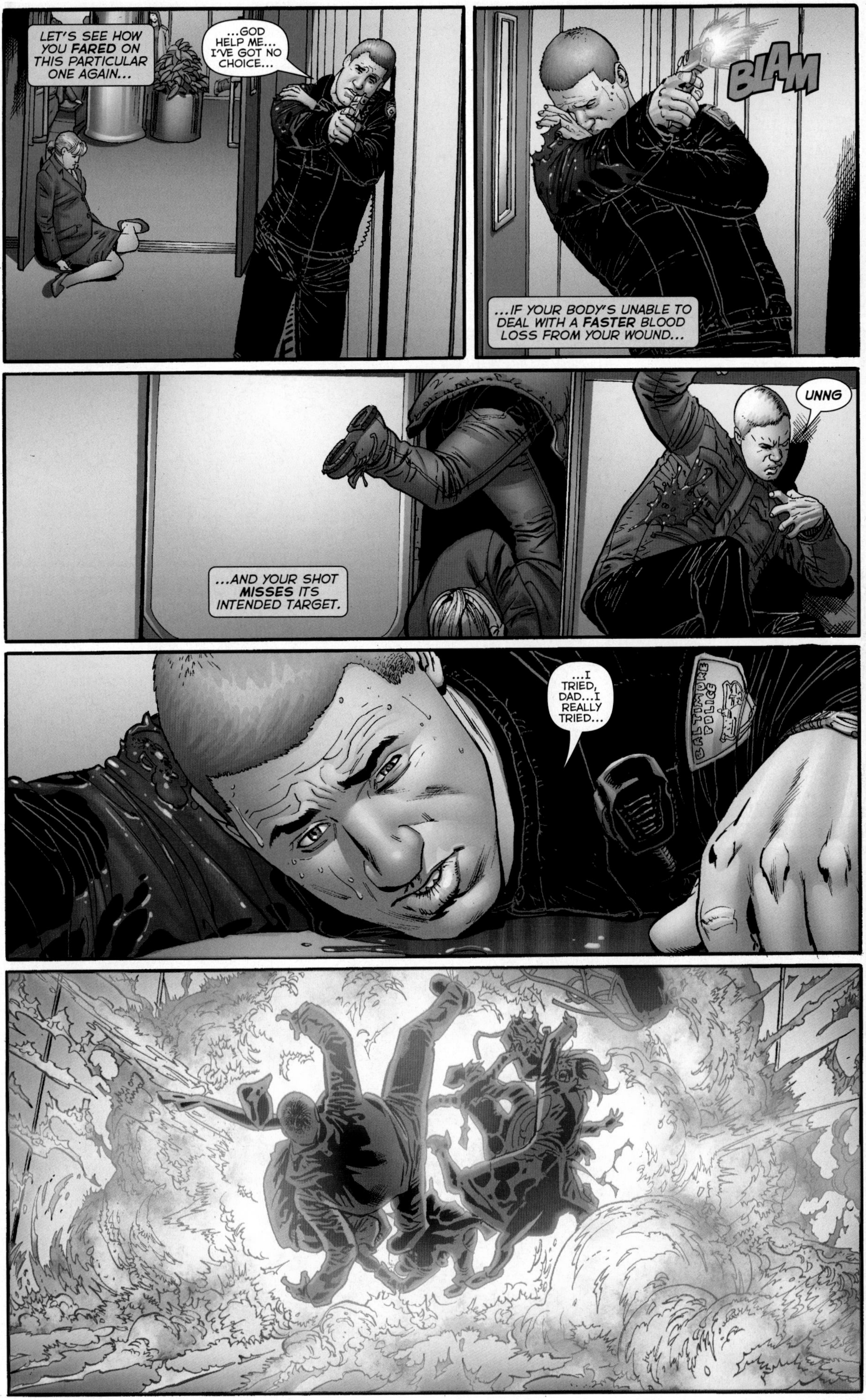
LET'S SEE HOW YOU FARED ON THIS PARTICULAR ONE AGAIN...
...GOD HELP ME... I'VE GOT NO CHOICE...
BLAM
...IF YOUR BODY'S UNABLE TO DEAL WITH A FASTER BLOOD LOSS FROM YOUR WOUND...
...AND YOUR SHOT MISSES ITS INTENDED TARGET.
UNNG
...I TRIED, DAD...I REALLY TRIED...
BALTIMORE POLICE

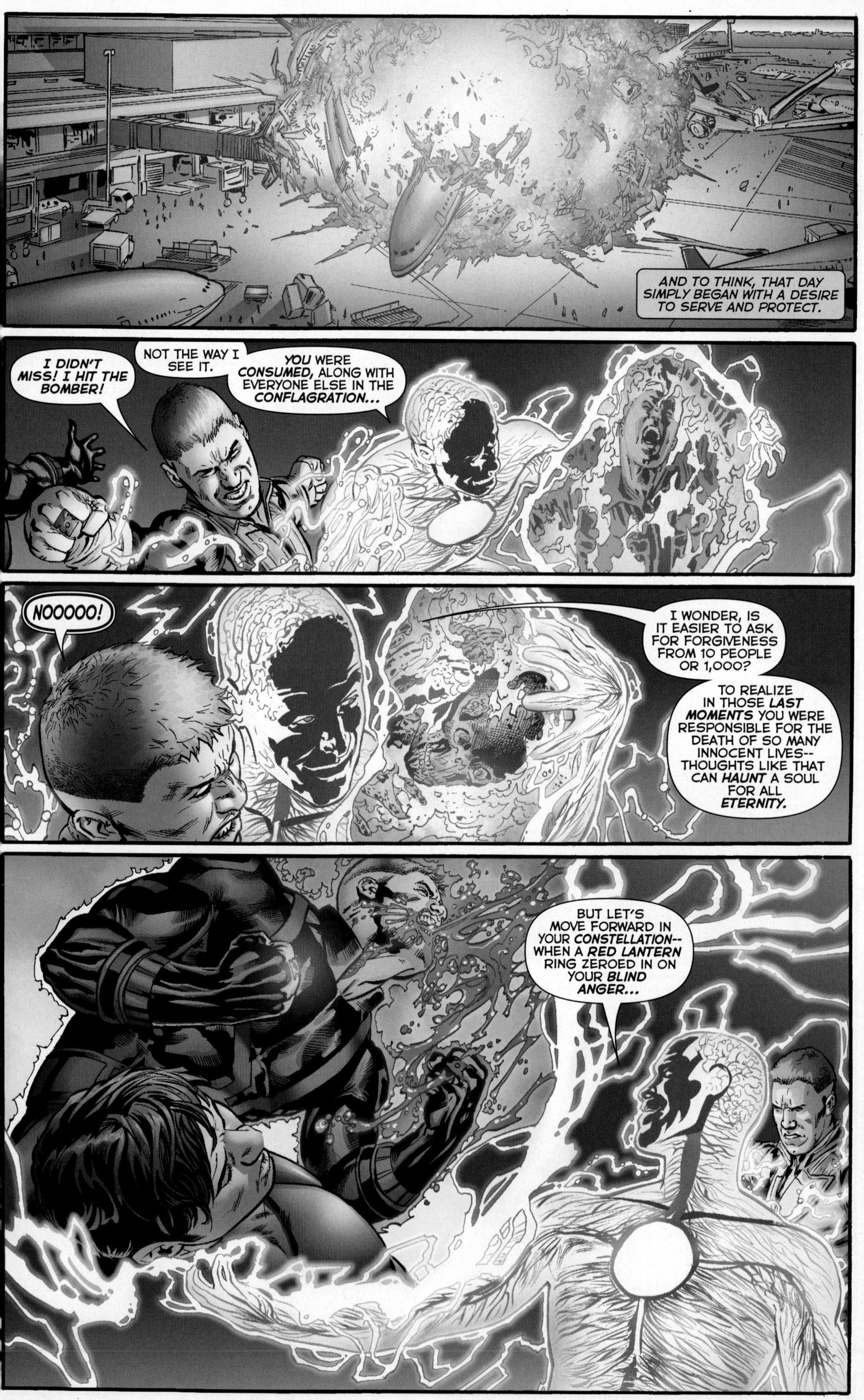
AND TO THINK, THAT DAY SIMPLY BEGAN WITH A DESIRE TO SERVE AND PROTECT.
I DIDN'T MISS! I HIT THE BOMBER!
NOT THE WAY I SEE IT.
YOU WERE CONSUMED, ALONG WITH EVERYONE ELSE IN THE CONFLAGRATION...
NOOOOO!
I WONDER, IS IT EASIER TO ASK FOR FORGIVENESS FROM 10 PEOPLE OR 1,000?
TO REALIZE IN THOSE LAST MOMENTS YOU WERE RESPONSIBLE FOR THE DEATH OF SO MANY INNOCENT LIVES-- THOUGHTS LIKE THAT CAN HAUNT A SOUL FOR ALL ETERNITY.
BUT LET'S MOVE FORWARD IN YOUR CONSTELLATION-- WHEN A RED LANTERN RING ZEROED IN ON YOUR BLIND ANGER...

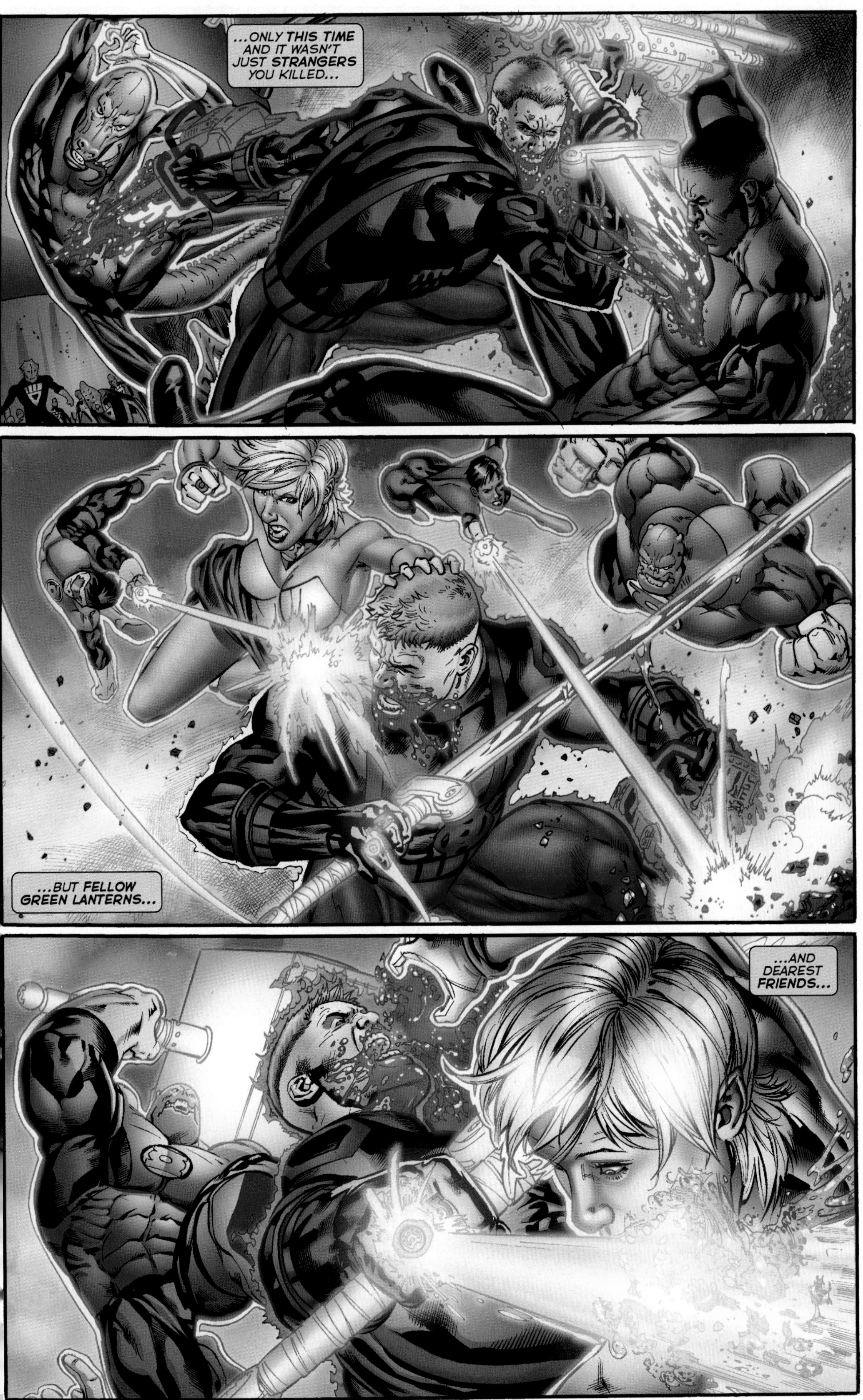
...ONLY THIS TIME AND IT WASN'T JUST STRANGERS YOU KILLED...
...BUT FELLOW GREEN LANTERNS...
...AND DEAREST FRIENDS...

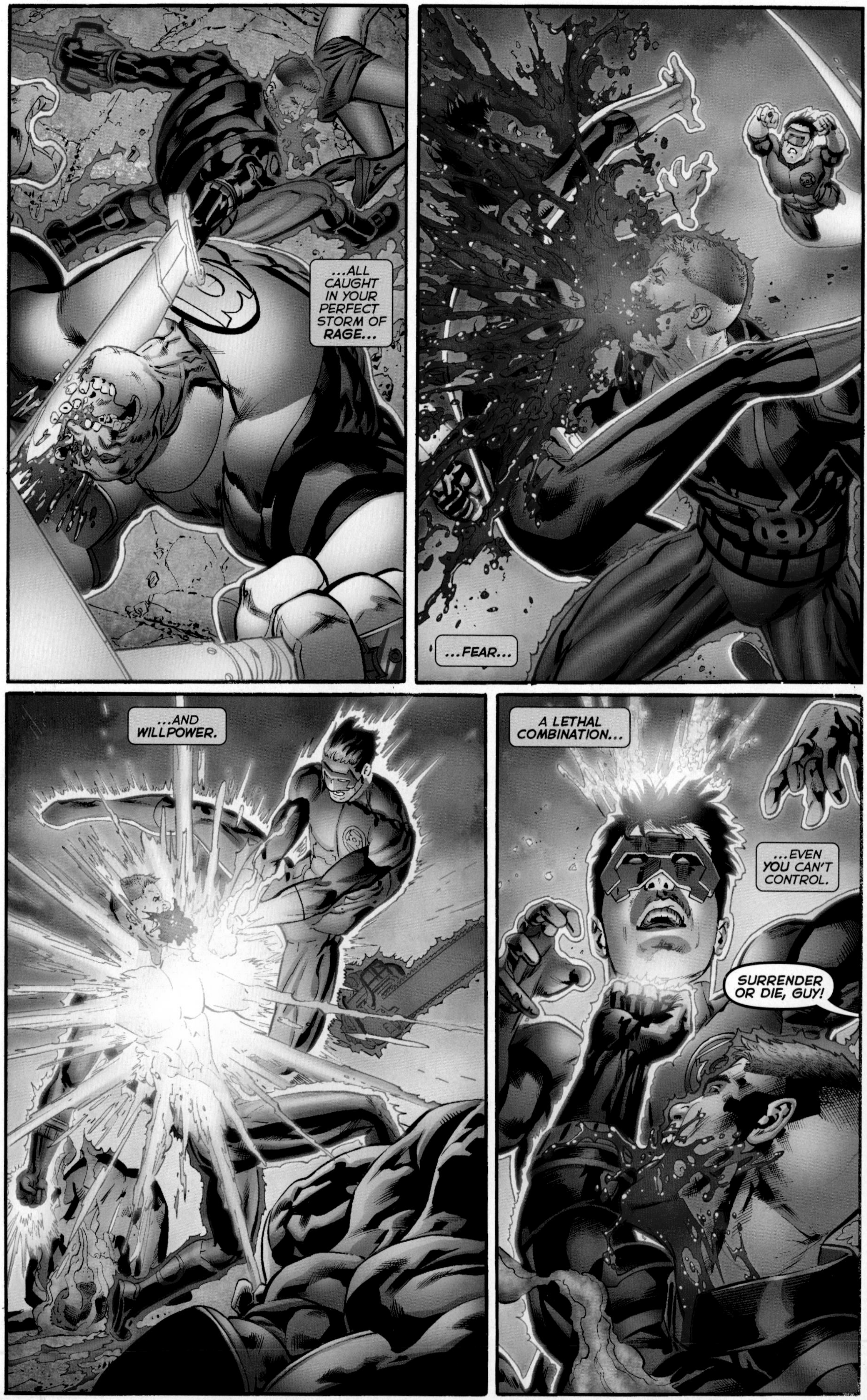
...ALL CAUGHT IN YOUR PERFECT STORM OF RAGE...
...FEAR...
...AND WILLPOWER.
A LETHAL COMBINATION...
...EVEN YOU CAN'T CONTROL.
SURRENDER OR DIE, GUY!

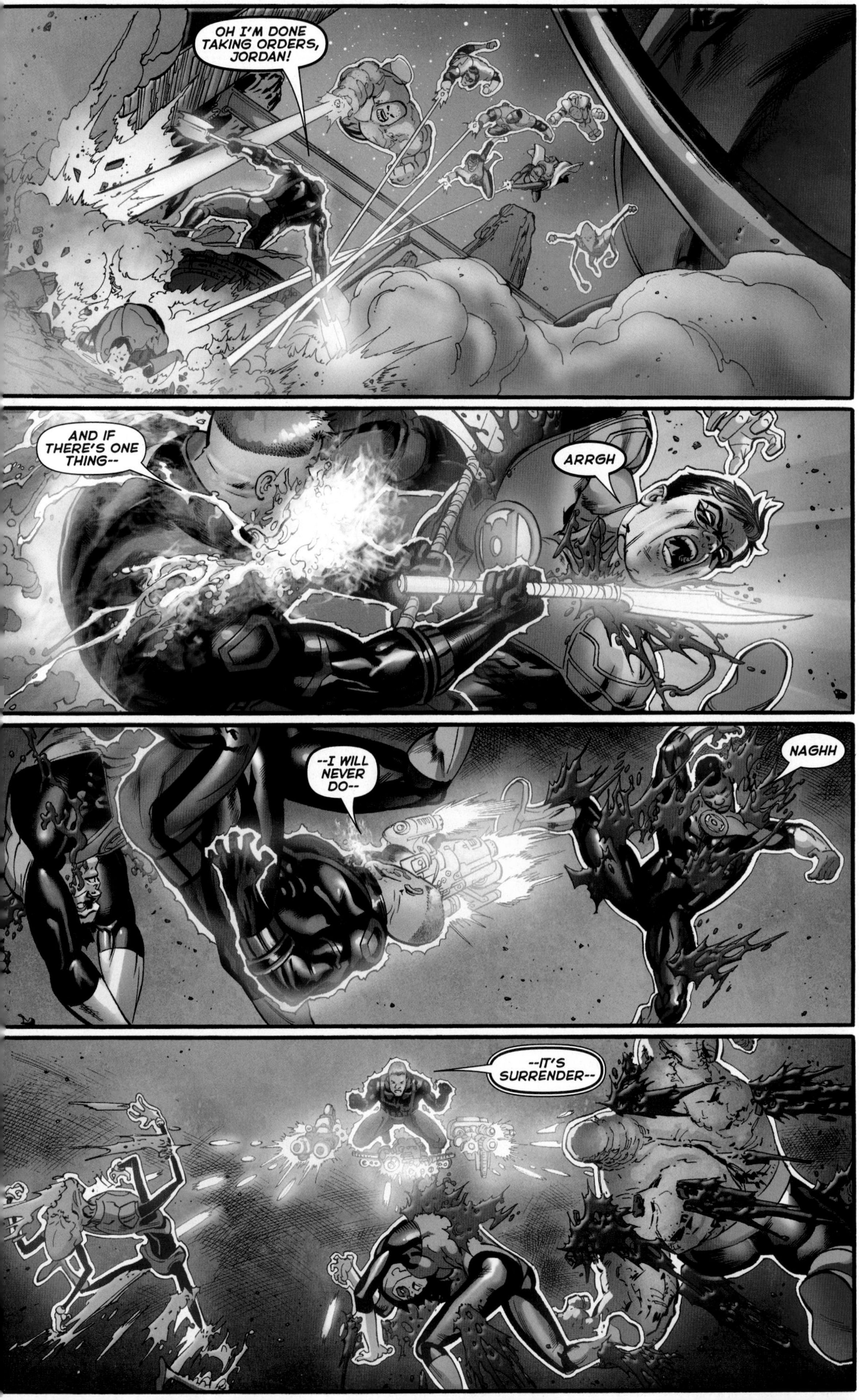
OH I'M DONE TAKING ORDERS, JORDAN!
AND IF THERE'S ONE THING--
ARRGH
--I WILL NEVER DO--
NAGHH
--IT'S SURRENDER--

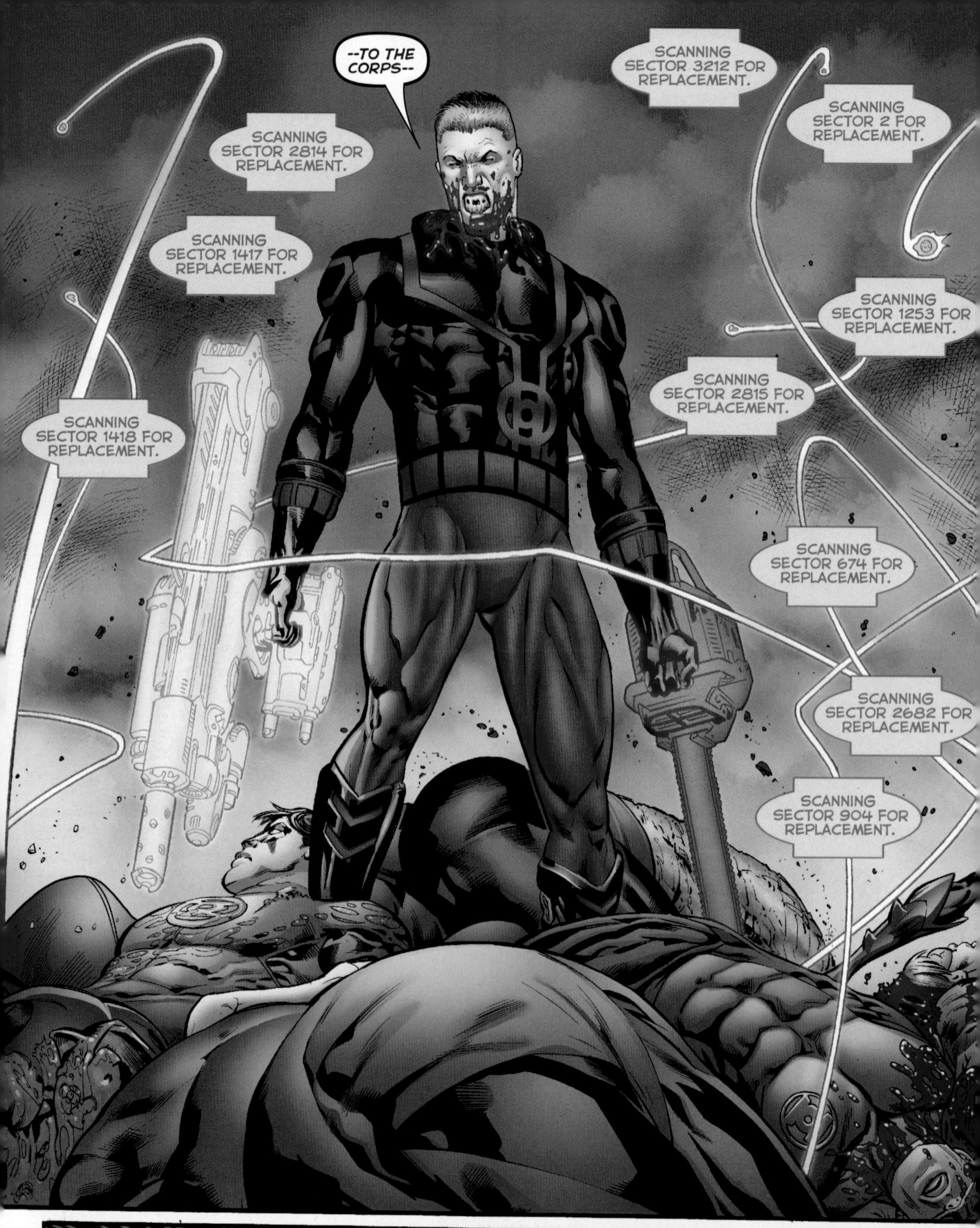
--TO THE CORPS--
SCANNING SECTOR 3212 FOR REPLACEMENT.
SCANNING SECTOR 2814 FOR REPLACEMENT.
SCANNING SECTOR 2 FOR REPLACEMENT.
SCANNING SECTOR 1417 FOR REPLACEMENT.
SCANNING SECTOR 1253 FOR REPLACEMENT.
SCANNING SECTOR 2815 FOR REPLACEMENT.
SCANNING SECTOR 1418 FOR REPLACEMENT.
SCANNING SECTOR 674 FOR REPLACEMENT.
SCANNING SECTOR 2682 FOR REPLACEMENT.
SCANNING SECTOR 904 FOR REPLACEMENT.

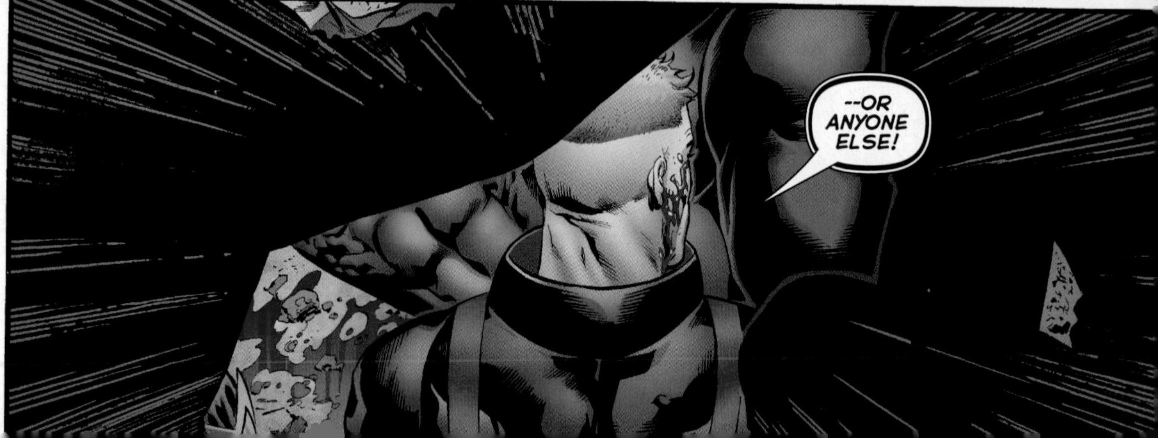
--OR ANYONE ELSE!

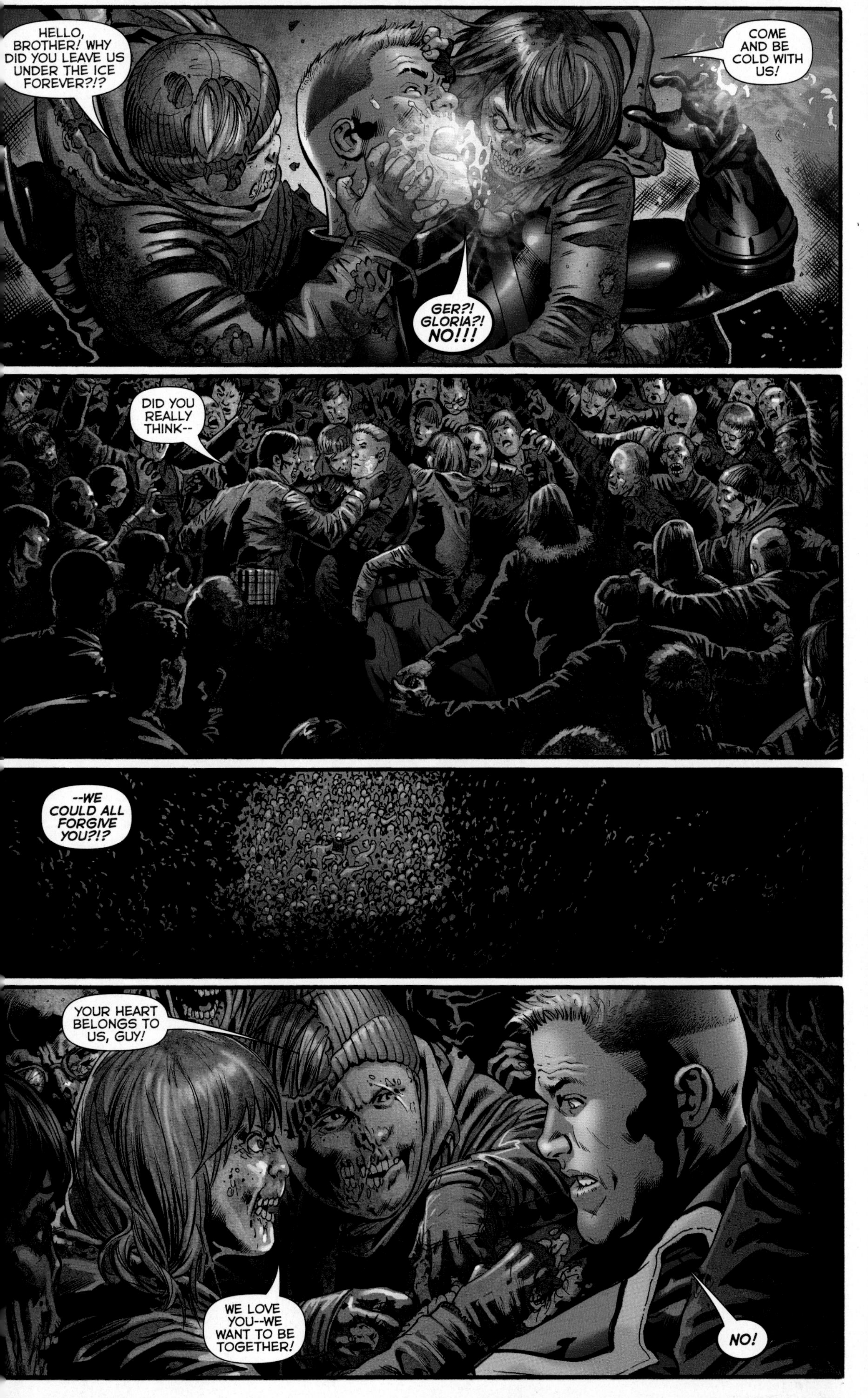
HELLO, BROTHER! WHY DID YOU LEAVE US UNDER THE ICE FOREVER?!?
COME AND BE COLD WITH US!
GER?! GLORIA?! NO!!!
DID YOU REALLY THINK--
--WE COULD ALL FORGIVE YOU?!?
YOUR HEART BELONGS TO US, GUY!
WE LOVE YOU--WE WANT TO BE TOGETHER!
NO!

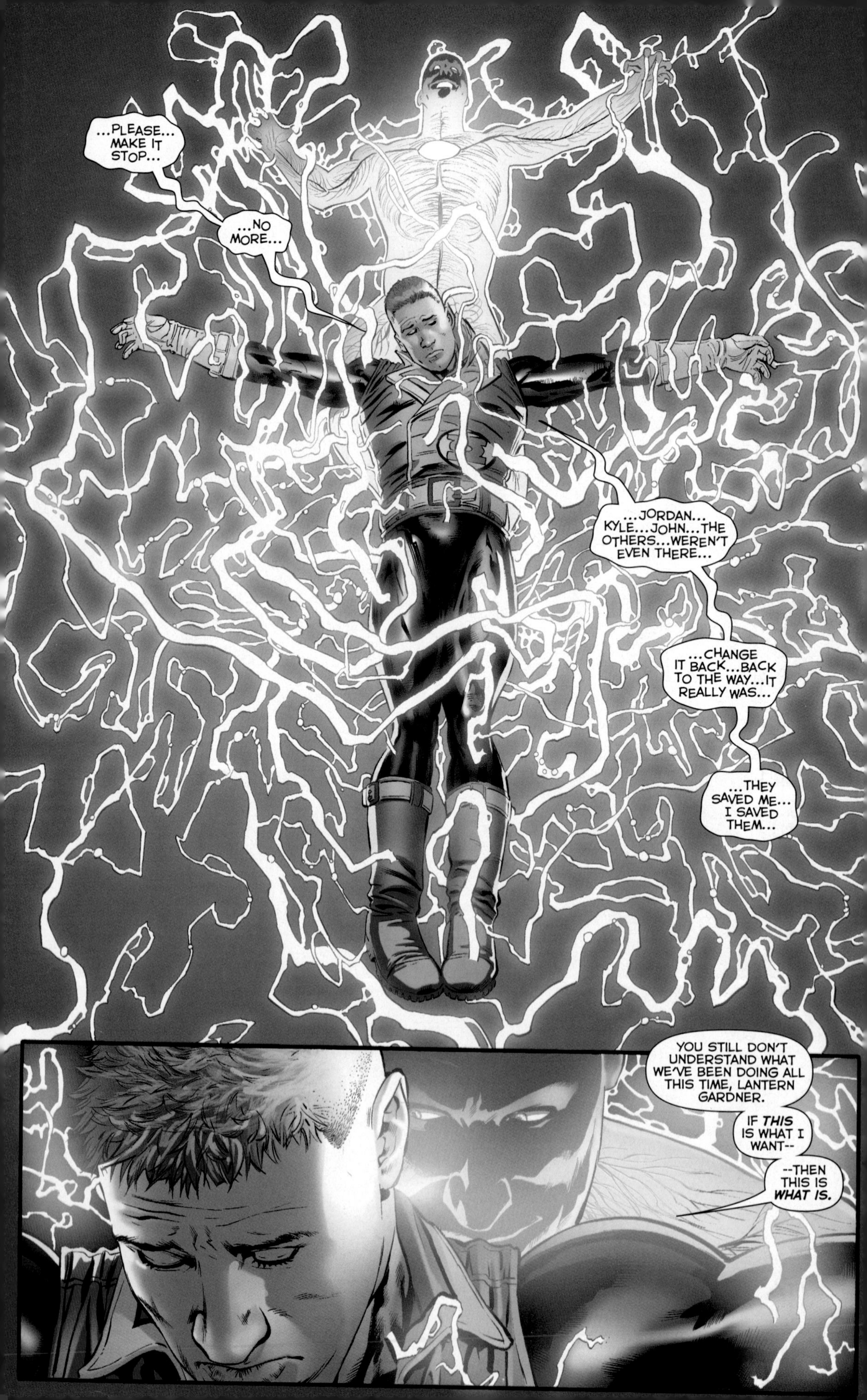
...PLEASE... MAKE IT STOP...
...NO MORE...
...JORDAN... KYLE...JOHN...THE OTHERS...WEREN'T EVEN THERE...
...CHANGE IT BACK...BACK TO THE WAY...IT REALLY WAS...
...THEY SAVED ME... I SAVED THEM...
YOU STILL DON'T UNDERSTAND WHAT WE'VE BEEN DOING ALL THIS TIME, LANTERN GARDNER.
IF *THIS* IS WHAT I WANT--
--THEN THIS IS ***WHAT IS.***

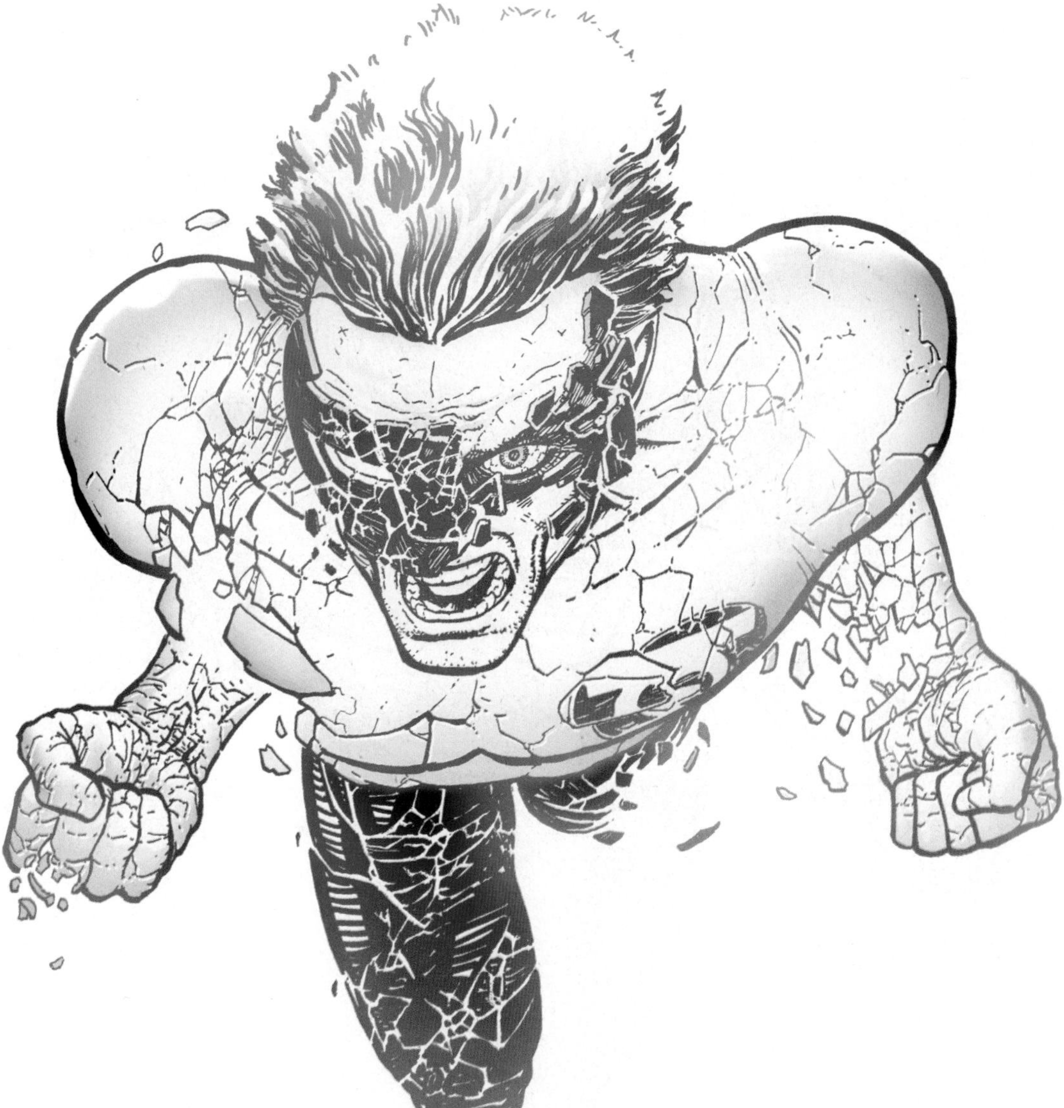

PART THREE: 2 REUNIONS & A FUNERAL

TONY BEDARD writer **AARON KUDER** artist

cover art by **AARON KUDER** & **WIL QUINTANA**

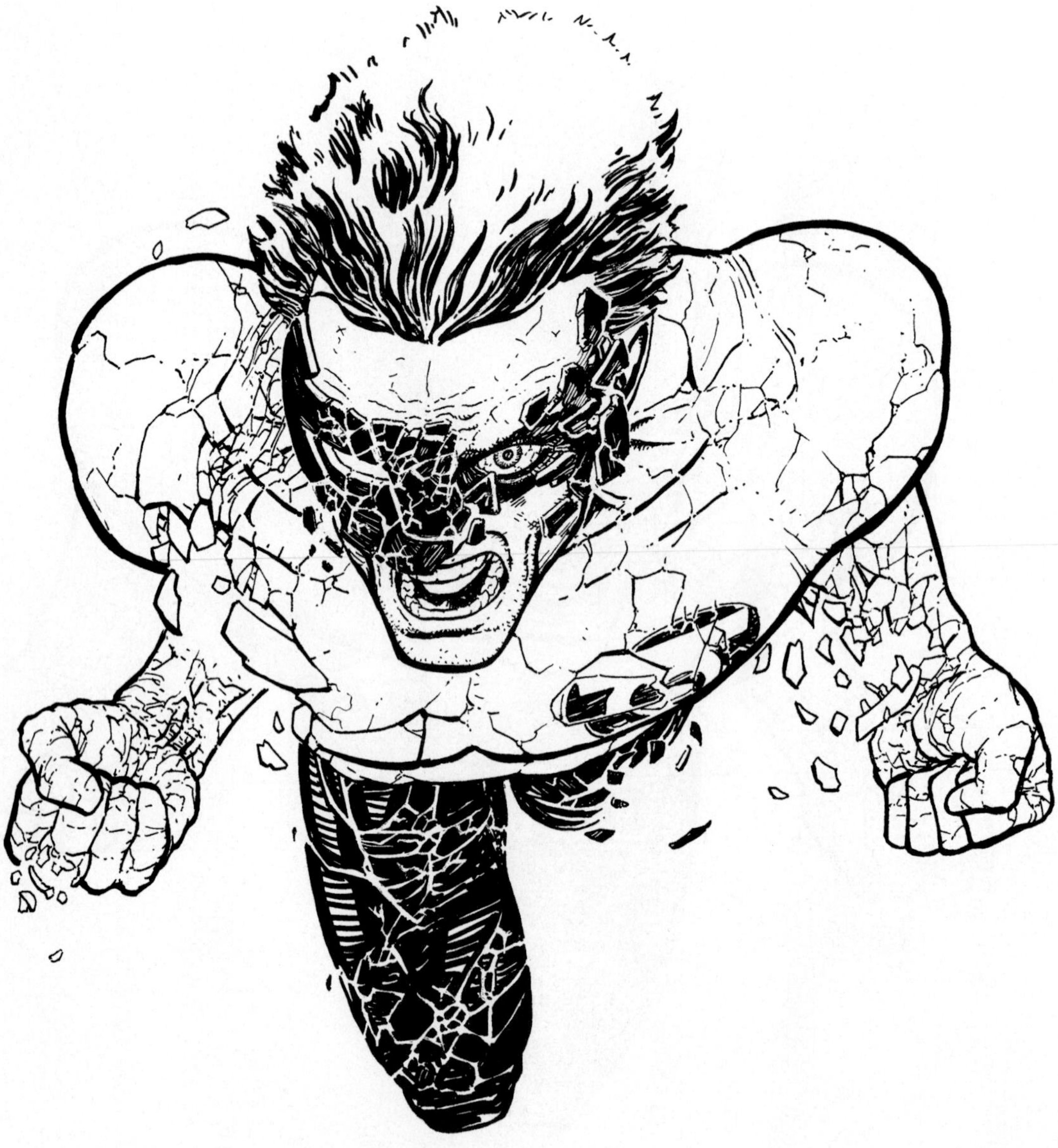

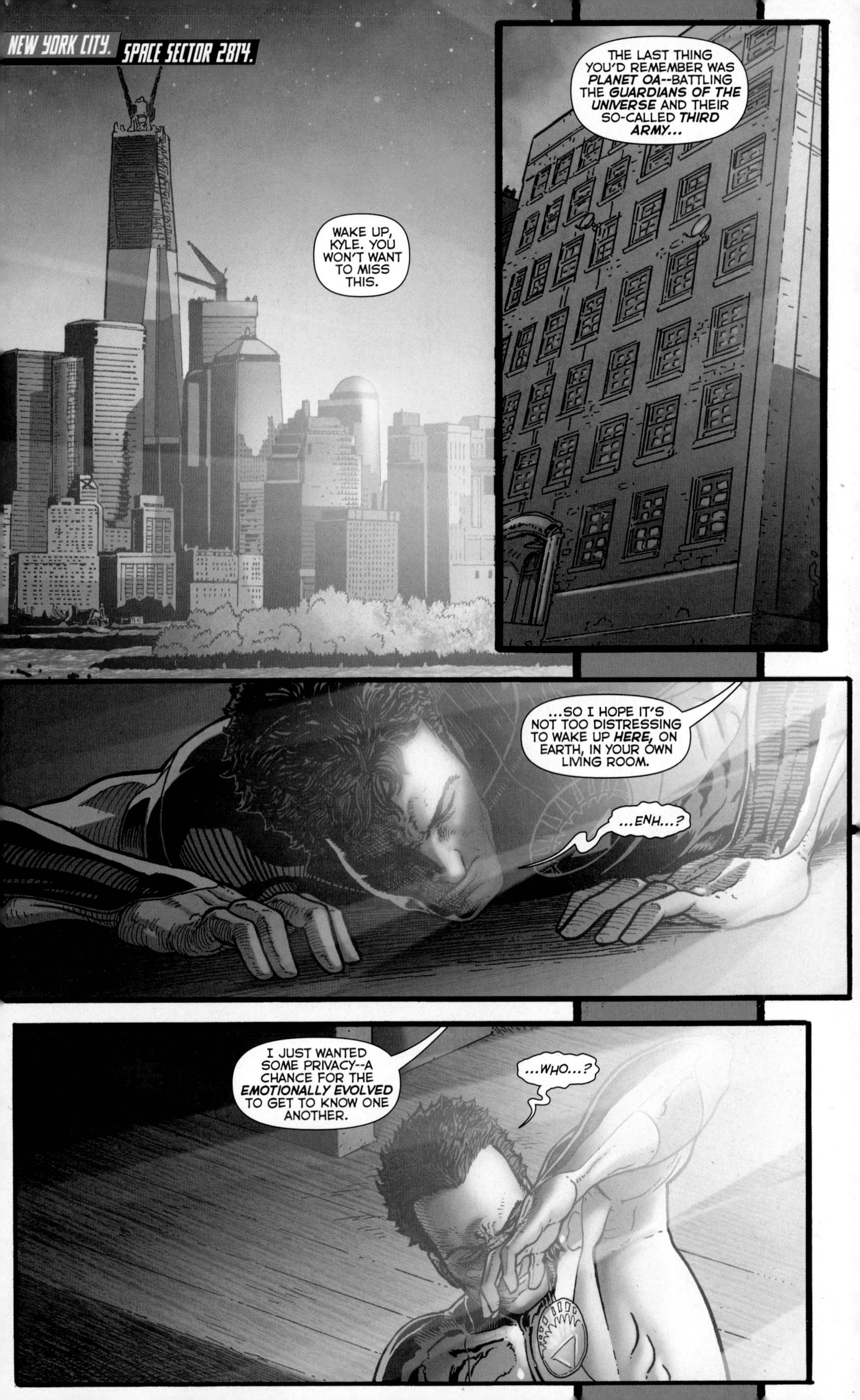
NEW YORK CITY.
SPACE SECTOR 2814.
WAKE UP, KYLE. YOU WON'T WANT TO MISS THIS.
THE LAST THING YOU'D REMEMBER WAS PLANET OA--BATTLING THE GUARDIANS OF THE UNIVERSE AND THEIR SO-CALLED THIRD ARMY...
...SO I HOPE IT'S NOT TOO DISTRESSING TO WAKE UP HERE, ON EARTH, IN YOUR OWN LIVING ROOM.
...ENH...?
I JUST WANTED SOME PRIVACY--A CHANCE FOR THE EMOTIONALLY EVOLVED TO GET TO KNOW ONE ANOTHER.
...WHO...?

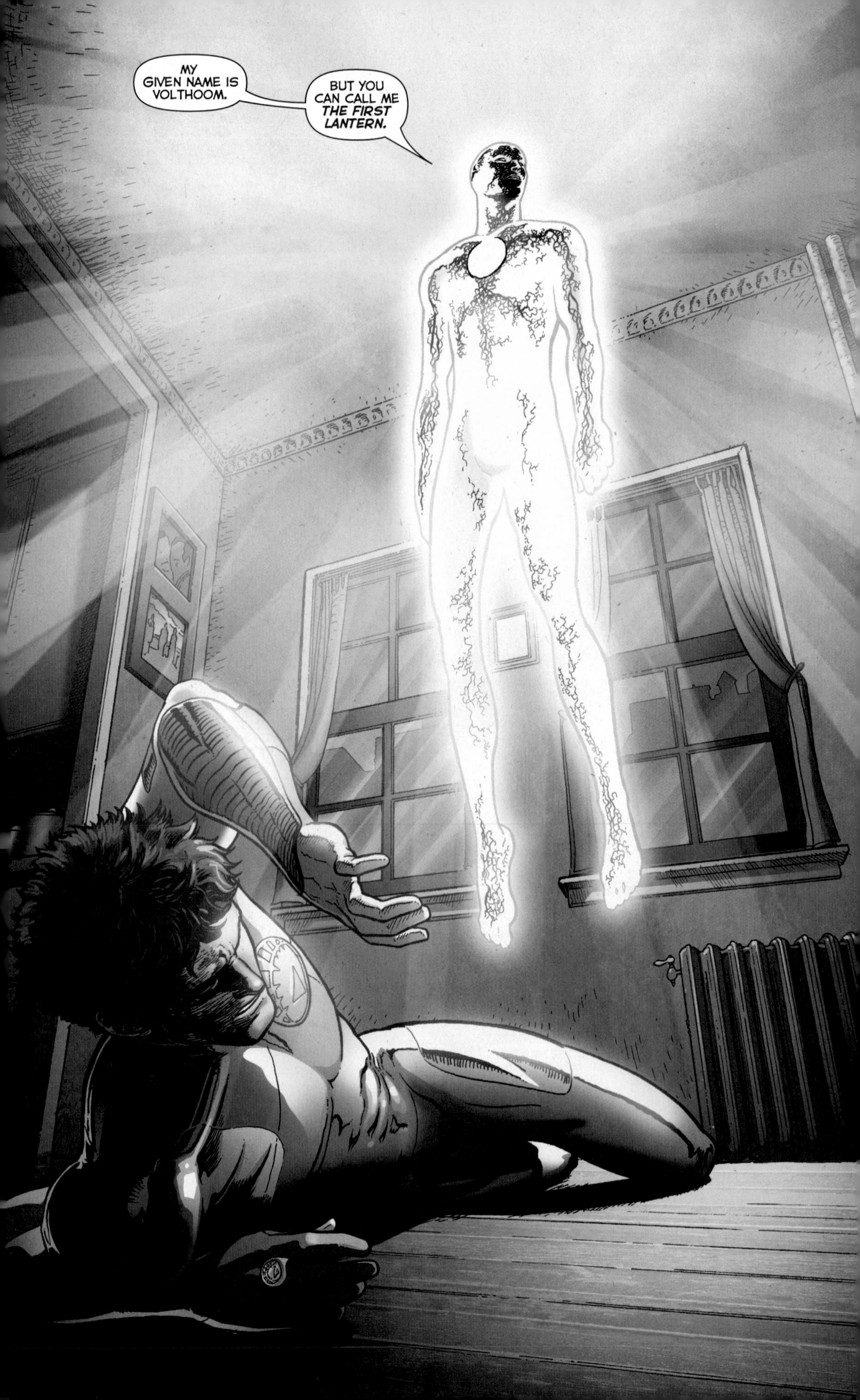
MY GIVEN NAME IS VOLTHOOM.
BUT YOU CAN CALL ME *THE FIRST LANTERN.*

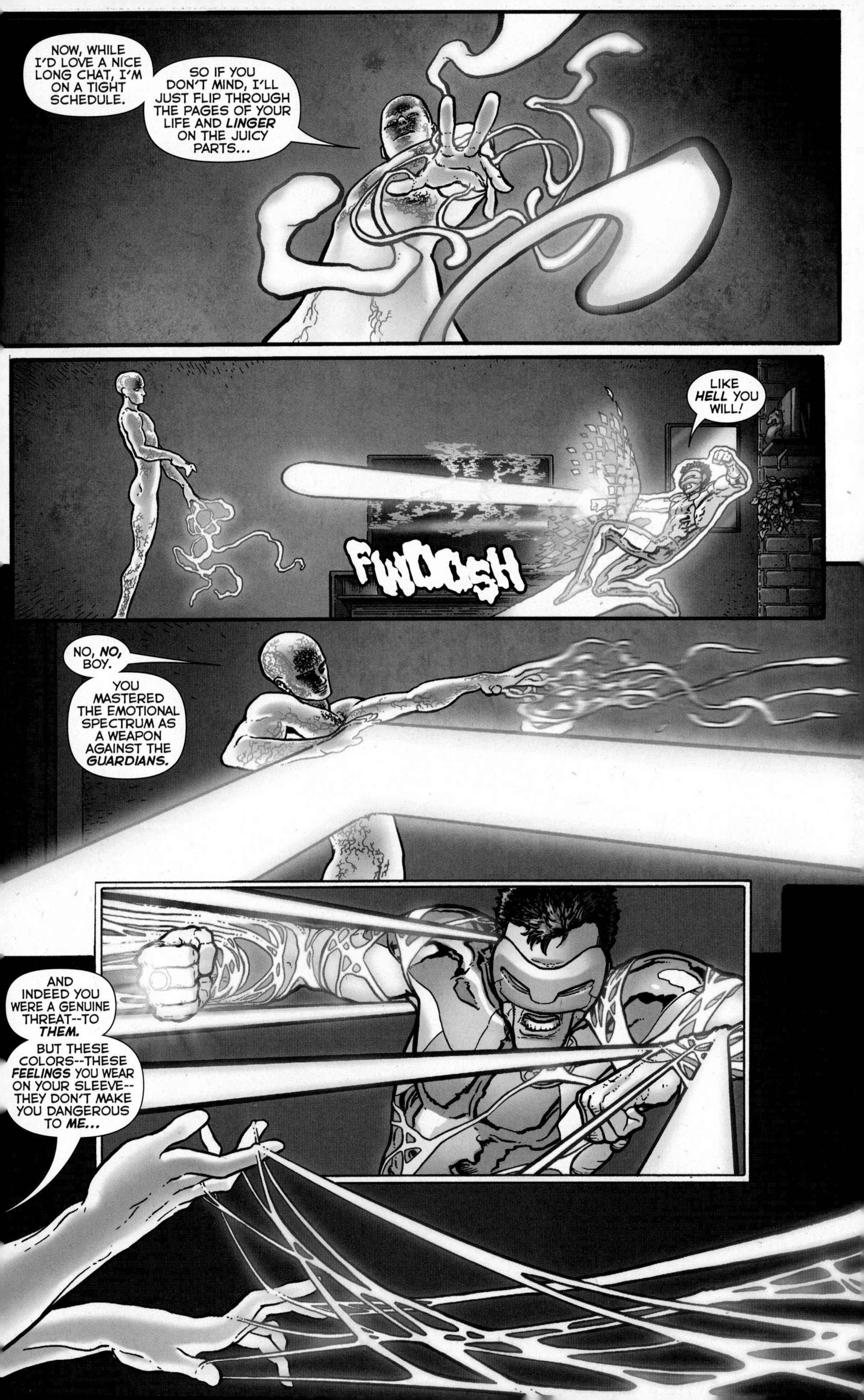
NOW, WHILE I'D LOVE A NICE LONG CHAT, I'M ON A TIGHT SCHEDULE.
SO IF YOU DON'T MIND, I'LL JUST FLIP THROUGH THE PAGES OF YOUR LIFE AND *LINGER* ON THE JUICY PARTS...
LIKE ***HELL*** YOU WILL!
FWOOSH
NO, ***NO***, BOY.
YOU MASTERED THE EMOTIONAL SPECTRUM AS A WEAPON AGAINST THE ***GUARDIANS.***
AND INDEED YOU WERE A GENUINE THREAT--TO ***THEM.***
BUT THESE COLORS--THESE ***FEELINGS*** YOU WEAR ON YOUR SLEEVE--THEY DON'T MAKE YOU DANGEROUS TO ***ME...***

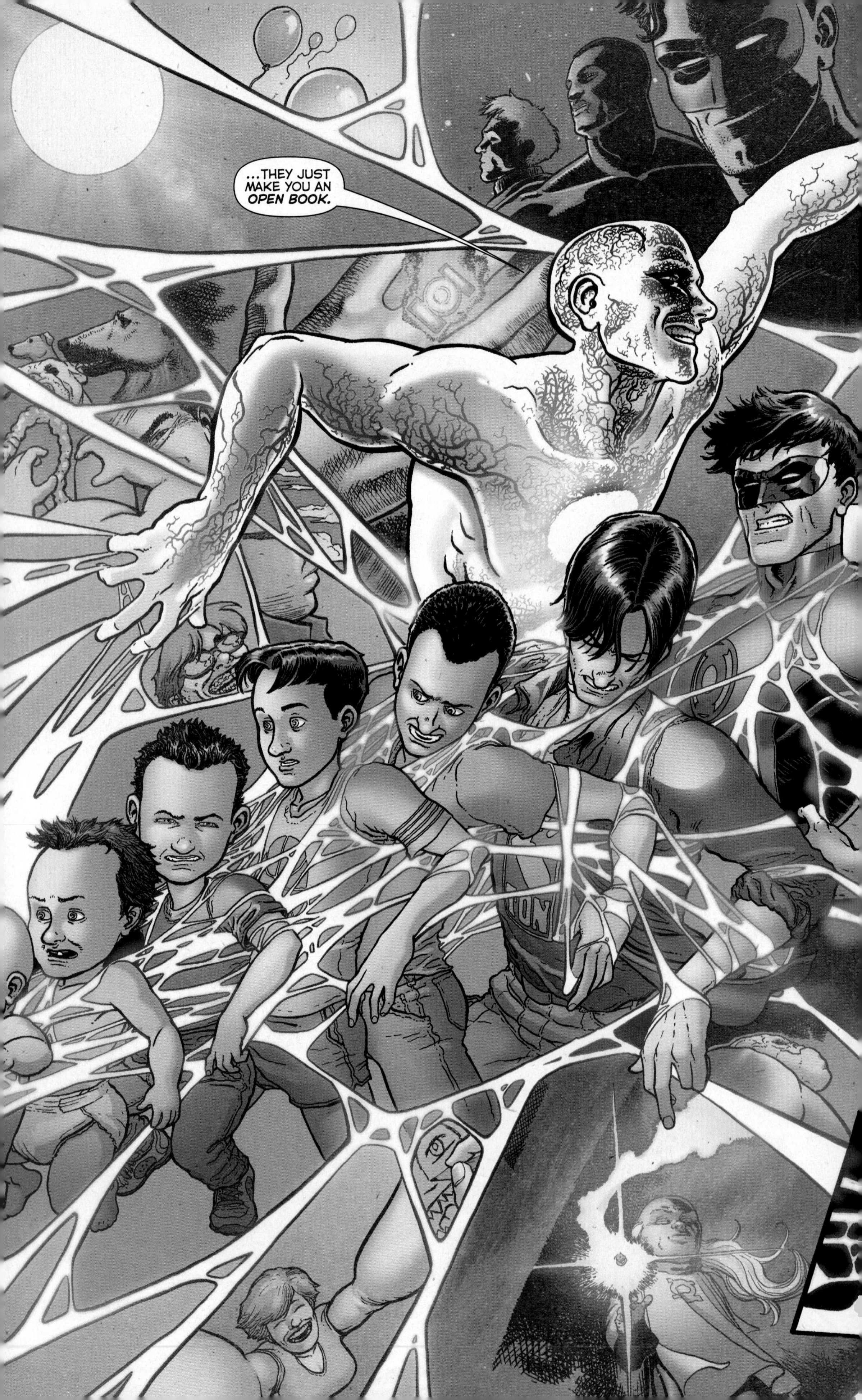
...THEY JUST MAKE YOU AN OPEN BOOK.

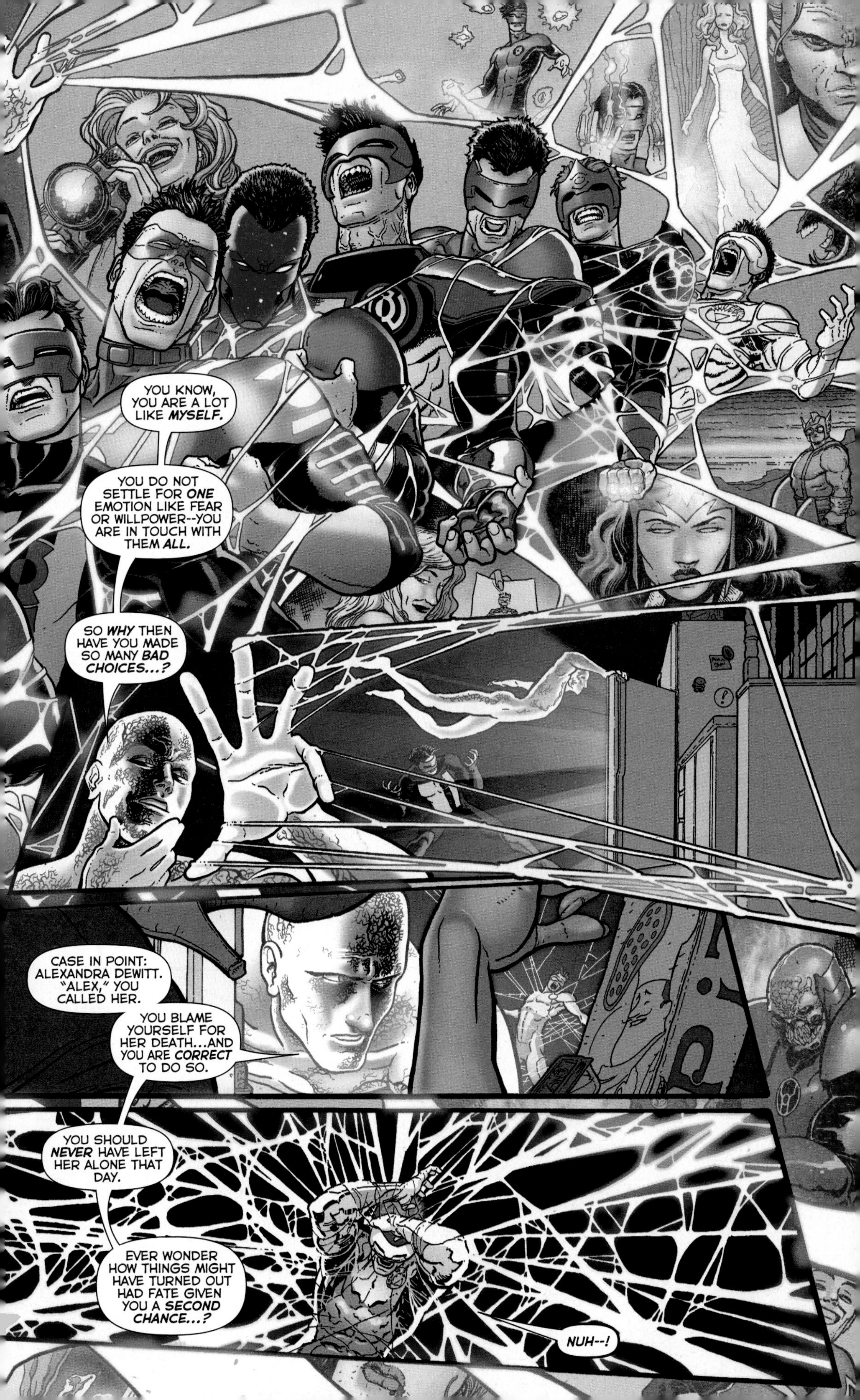
YOU KNOW, YOU ARE A LOT LIKE MYSELF.
YOU DO NOT SETTLE FOR ONE EMOTION LIKE FEAR OR WILLPOWER--YOU ARE IN TOUCH WITH THEM ALL.
SO WHY THEN HAVE YOU MADE SO MANY BAD CHOICES...?
CASE IN POINT: ALEXANDRA DEWITT. "ALEX," YOU CALLED HER.
YOU BLAME YOURSELF FOR HER DEATH...AND YOU ARE CORRECT TO DO SO.
YOU SHOULD NEVER HAVE LEFT HER ALONE THAT DAY.
EVER WONDER HOW THINGS MIGHT HAVE TURNED OUT HAD FATE GIVEN YOU A SECOND CHANCE...?
NUH--!

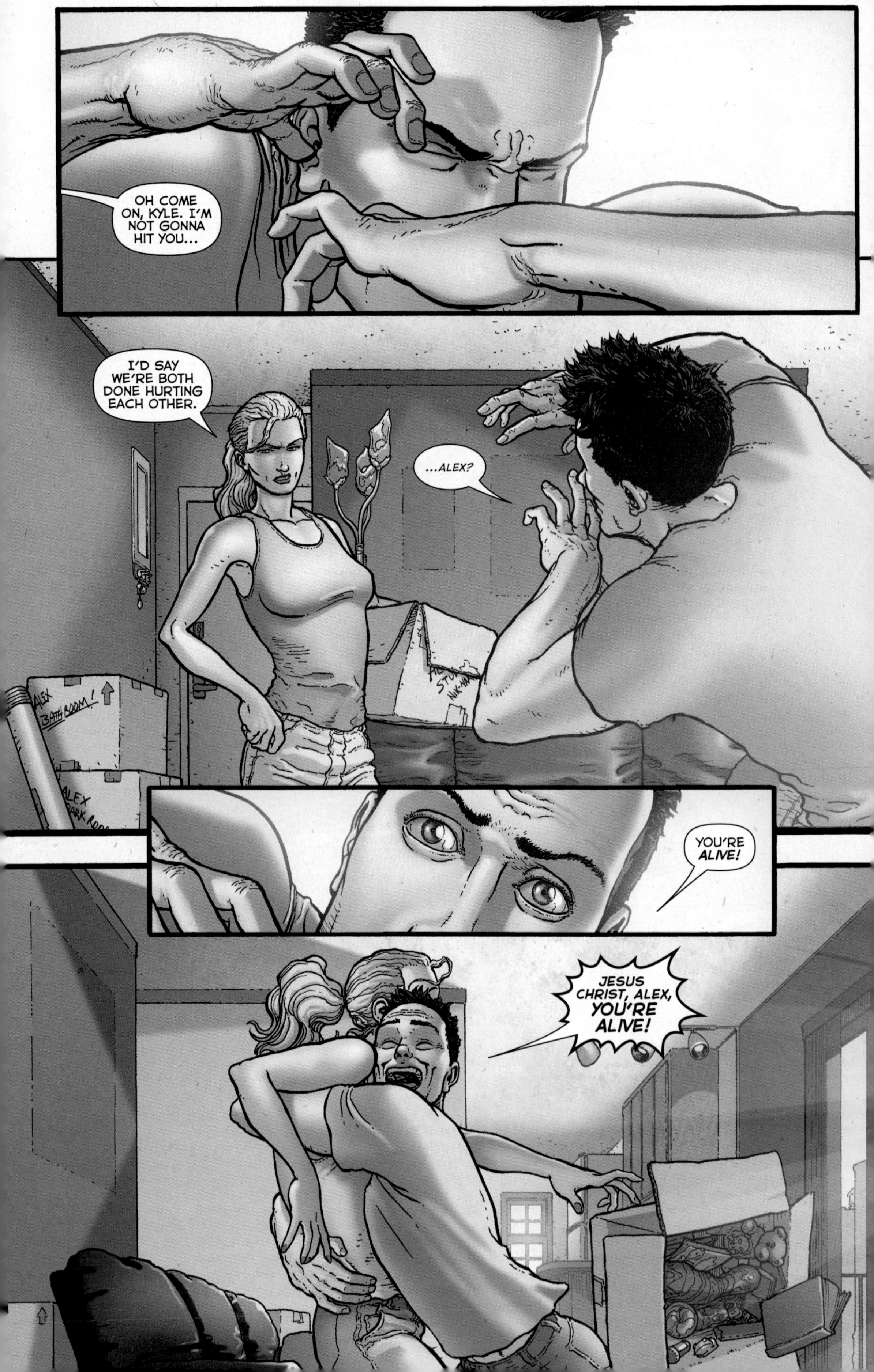
OH COME ON, KYLE. I'M NOT GONNA HIT YOU...
I'D SAY WE'RE BOTH DONE HURTING EACH OTHER.
...ALEX?
ALEX BATHROOM!
ALEX DARK ROOM
YOU'RE ALIVE!
JESUS CHRIST, ALEX, YOU'RE ALIVE!

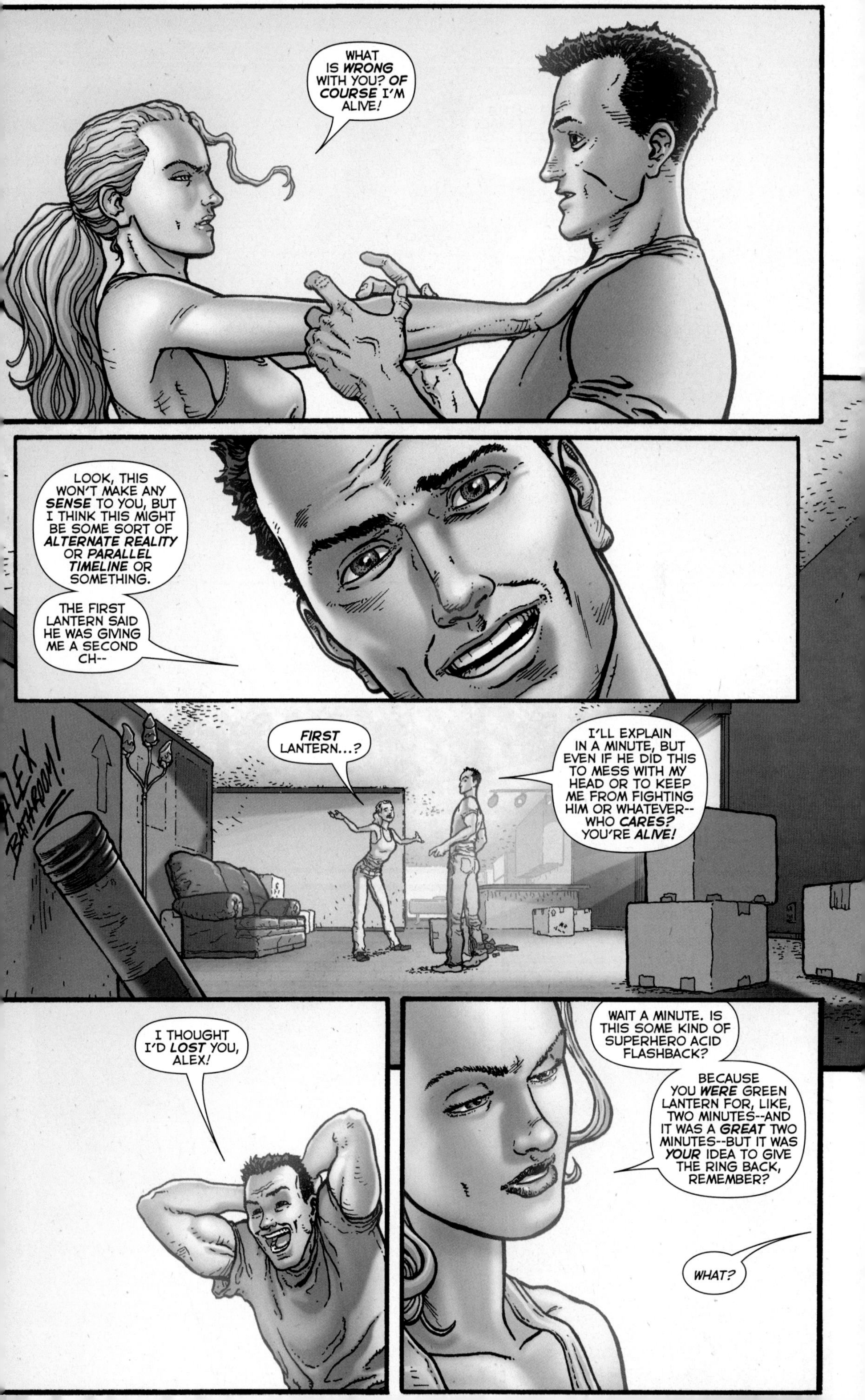
WHAT IS **WRONG** WITH YOU? **OF COURSE** I'M ALIVE!
LOOK, THIS WON'T MAKE ANY **SENSE** TO YOU, BUT I THINK THIS MIGHT BE SOME SORT OF **ALTERNATE REALITY** OR **PARALLEL TIMELINE** OR SOMETHING.
THE FIRST LANTERN SAID HE WAS GIVING ME A SECOND CH--
FIRST LANTERN...?
I'LL EXPLAIN IN A MINUTE, BUT EVEN IF HE DID THIS TO MESS WITH **MY** HEAD OR TO KEEP ME FROM FIGHTING HIM OR WHATEVER-- WHO **CARES?** YOU'RE **ALIVE!**
I THOUGHT I'D **LOST** YOU, ALEX!
WAIT A MINUTE. IS THIS SOME KIND OF SUPERHERO ACID FLASHBACK?
BECAUSE YOU **WERE** GREEN LANTERN FOR, LIKE, TWO MINUTES--AND IT WAS A **GREAT** TWO MINUTES--BUT IT WAS **YOUR** IDEA TO GIVE THE RING BACK, REMEMBER?
WHAT?

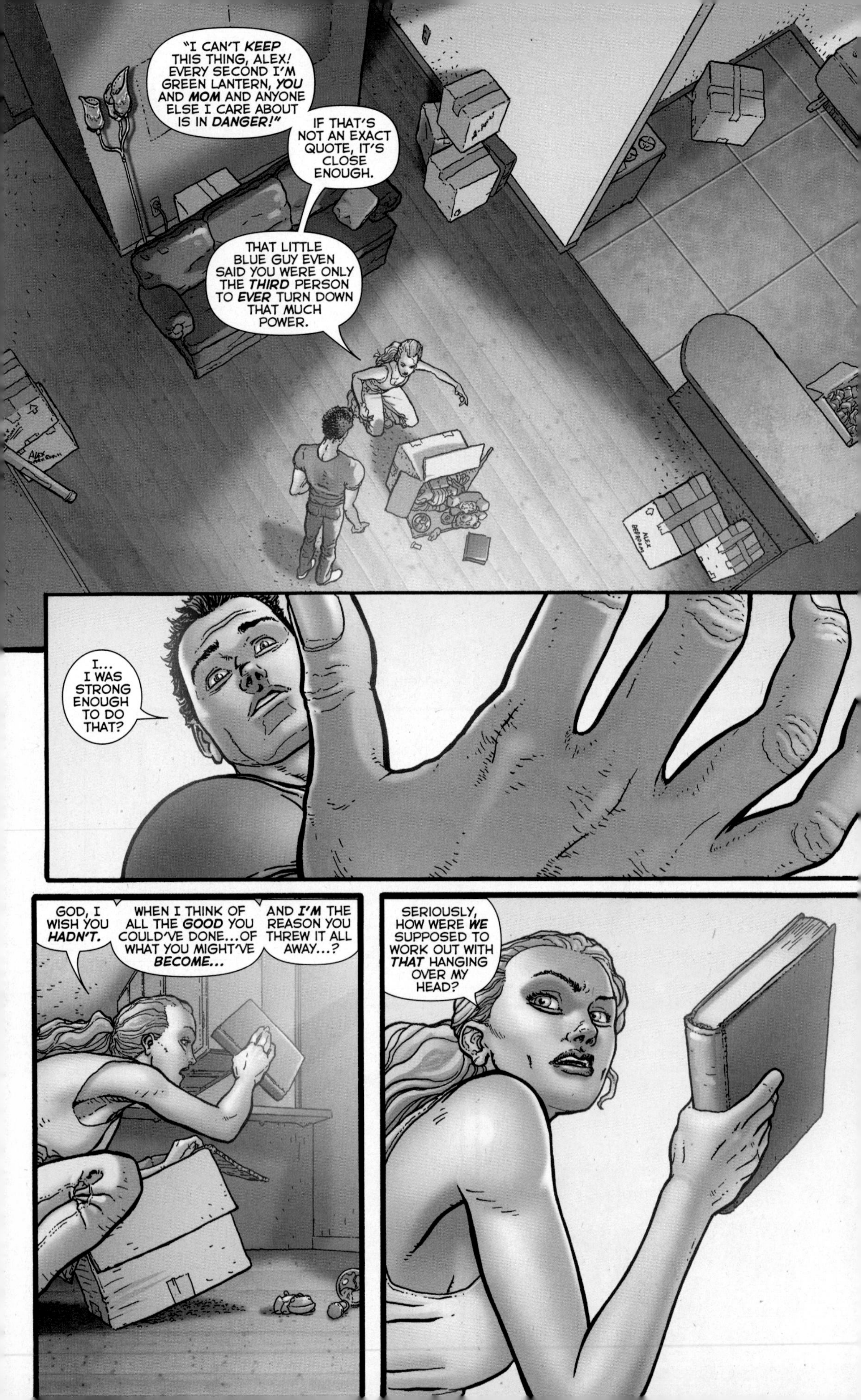
"I CAN'T KEEP THIS THING, ALEX! EVERY SECOND I'M GREEN LANTERN, YOU AND MOM AND ANYONE ELSE I CARE ABOUT IS IN DANGER!"
IF THAT'S NOT AN EXACT QUOTE, IT'S CLOSE ENOUGH.
THAT LITTLE BLUE GUY EVEN SAID YOU WERE ONLY THE THIRD PERSON TO EVER TURN DOWN THAT MUCH POWER.
I... I WAS STRONG ENOUGH TO DO THAT?
GOD, I WISH YOU HADN'T.
WHEN I THINK OF ALL THE GOOD YOU COULD'VE DONE...OF WHAT YOU MIGHT'VE BECOME...
AND I'M THE REASON YOU THREW IT ALL AWAY...?
SERIOUSLY, HOW WERE WE SUPPOSED TO WORK OUT WITH THAT HANGING OVER MY HEAD?

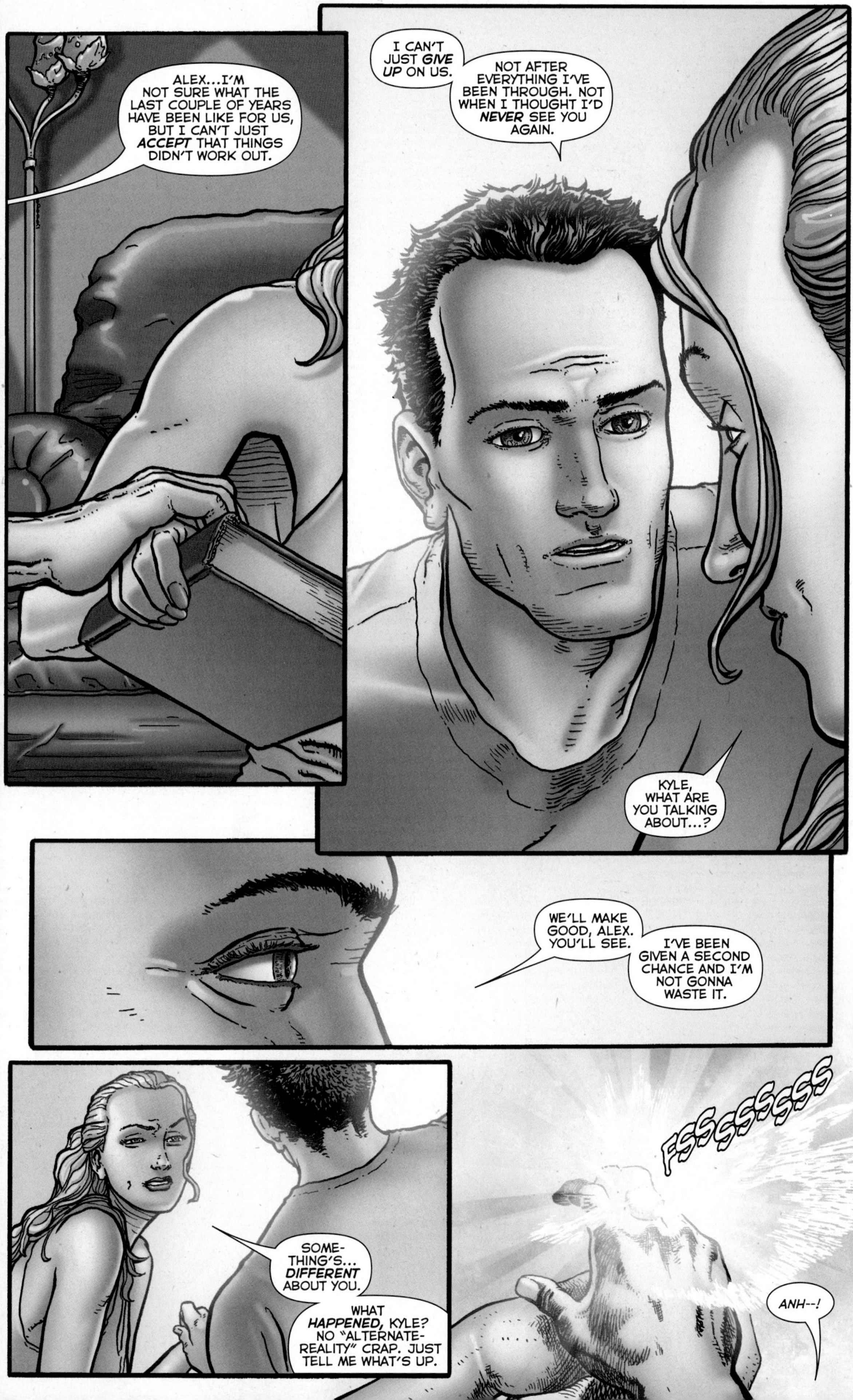
ALEX...I'M NOT SURE WHAT THE LAST COUPLE OF YEARS HAVE BEEN LIKE FOR US, BUT I CAN'T JUST *ACCEPT* THAT THINGS DIDN'T WORK OUT.
I CAN'T JUST *GIVE UP* ON US.
NOT AFTER EVERYTHING I'VE BEEN THROUGH. NOT WHEN I THOUGHT I'D *NEVER* SEE YOU AGAIN.
KYLE, WHAT ARE YOU TALKING ABOUT...?
WE'LL MAKE GOOD, ALEX. YOU'LL SEE.
I'VE BEEN GIVEN A SECOND CHANCE AND I'M NOT GONNA WASTE IT.
SOME-THING'S... *DIFFERENT* ABOUT YOU.
WHAT *HAPPENED,* KYLE? NO "ALTERNATE-REALITY" CRAP. JUST TELL ME WHAT'S UP.
FSSSSSSSS
ANH--!

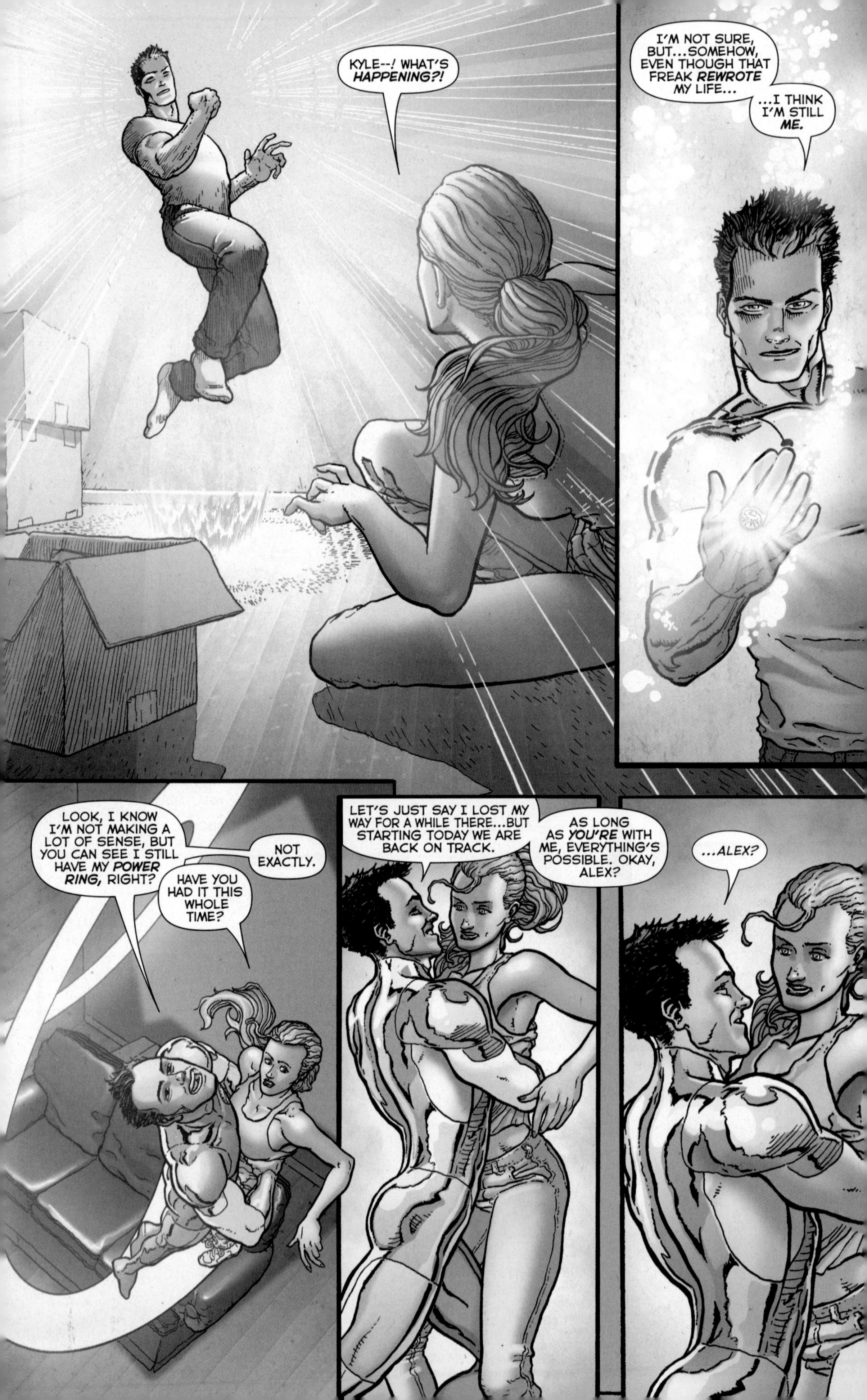
KYLE--! WHAT'S HAPPENING?!
I'M NOT SURE, BUT...SOMEHOW, EVEN THOUGH THAT FREAK REWROTE MY LIFE...
...I THINK I'M STILL ME.
LOOK, I KNOW I'M NOT MAKING A LOT OF SENSE, BUT YOU CAN SEE I STILL HAVE MY POWER RING, RIGHT?
NOT EXACTLY.
HAVE YOU HAD IT THIS WHOLE TIME?
LET'S JUST SAY I LOST MY WAY FOR A WHILE THERE...BUT STARTING TODAY WE ARE BACK ON TRACK.
AS LONG AS YOU'RE WITH ME, EVERYTHING'S POSSIBLE. OKAY, ALEX?
...ALEX?

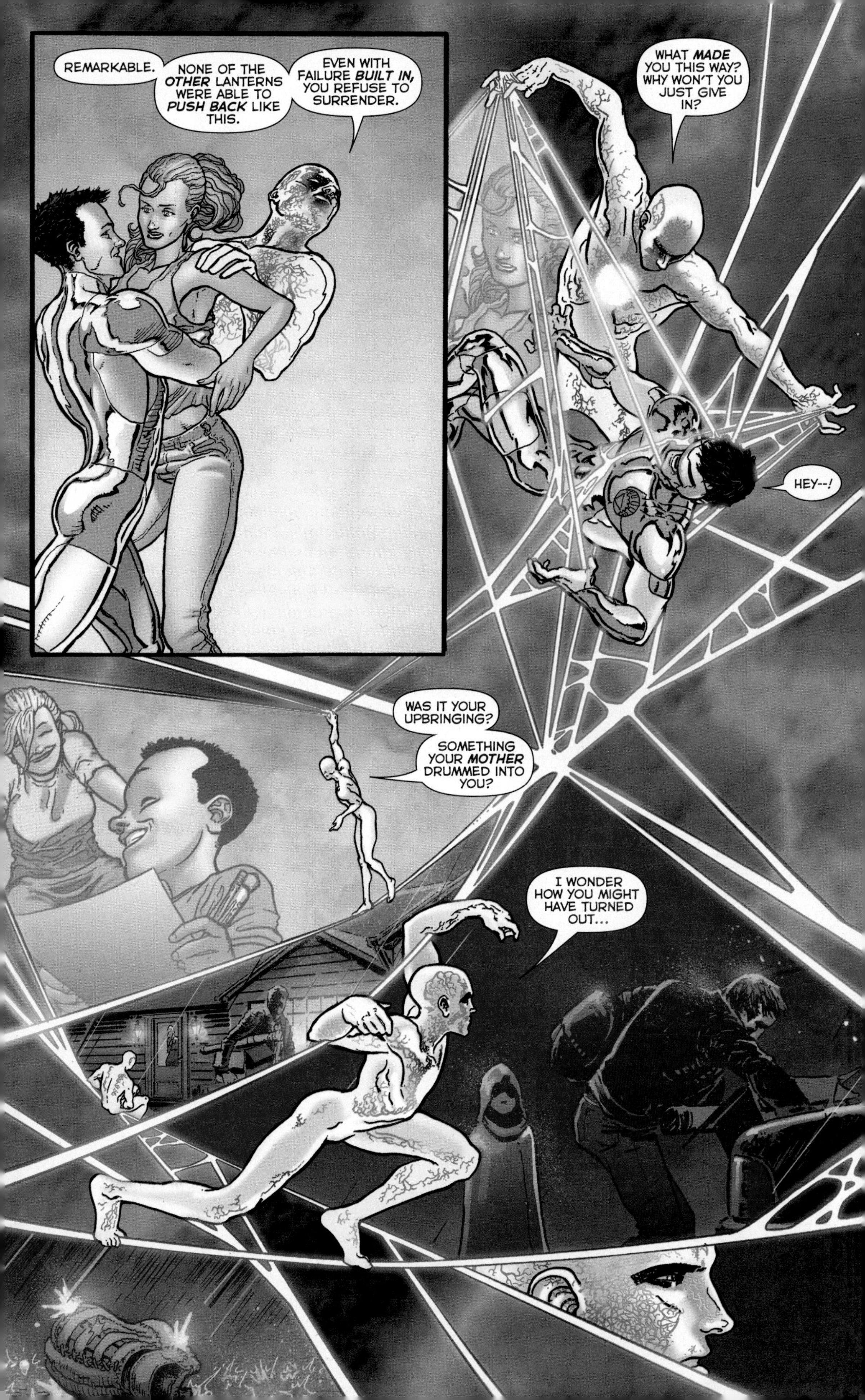
REMARKABLE.
NONE OF THE OTHER LANTERNS WERE ABLE TO PUSH BACK LIKE THIS.
EVEN WITH FAILURE BUILT IN, YOU REFUSE TO SURRENDER.
WHAT MADE YOU THIS WAY? WHY WON'T YOU JUST GIVE IN?
HEY--!
WAS IT YOUR UPBRINGING?
SOMETHING YOUR MOTHER DRUMMED INTO YOU?
I WONDER HOW YOU MIGHT HAVE TURNED OUT...

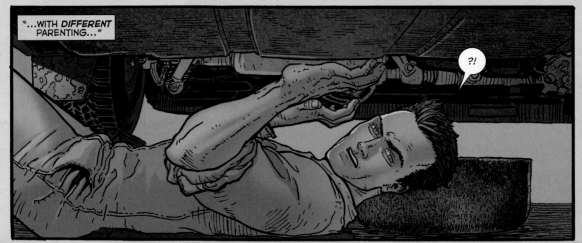

"...WITH *DIFFERENT* PARENTING..."

?!

WHAT JUST HAPPENED?

I WAS... *WITH* SOMEONE... SOMEONE *IMPORTANT*...

...SOMEONE... I *LOVE*...?

NO! I *WON'T* FORGET HER.

≈NNH≈ WHATEVER'S GOING ON HERE...*SOME-ONE* WANTS ME TO FORGET...

...BLONDE... FUNNY...SMART... STRONG...

ALEX!

RAYNER'S AUTO

I WAS WITH ALEX. AND THEN THAT "FIRST LANTERN" CAME, AND--

"HANG ON. WHO'S THAT TALKING TO *JOHNNY LAW* IN THERE...?"

HOLY CRAP, THAT'S MY *DAD*--!

HEY! SINCE WHEN DOES THE STORE PAY THE CUSTOMER?

GET BACK TO *WORK*, KYLE.

THANKS FOR THE *RENT*, CHIEF. Y'ALL HAVE A NICE DAY.

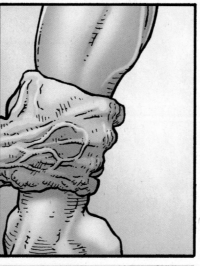

KYLE, WHAT'RE YOU *THINKING*--?!

WHAT, I'M JUST SUPPOSED TO LOOK THE OTHER WAY WHILE SHERIFF LARD-BUTT *SHAKES YOU DOWN?*

YES!

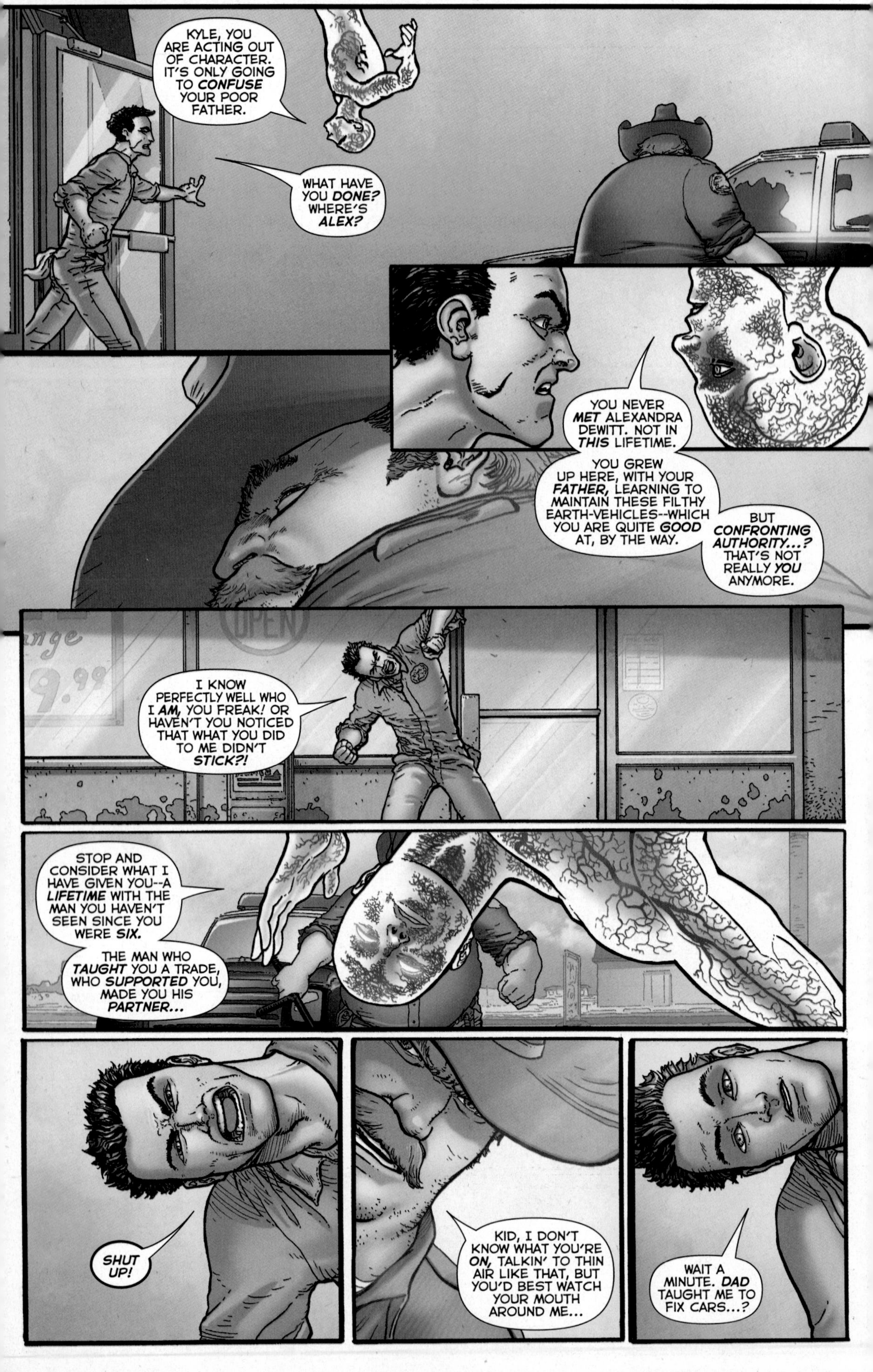

KYLE, YOU ARE ACTING OUT OF CHARACTER. IT'S ONLY GOING TO CONFUSE YOUR POOR FATHER.
WHAT HAVE YOU DONE? WHERE'S ALEX?
YOU NEVER MET ALEXANDRA DEWITT. NOT IN THIS LIFETIME.
YOU GREW UP HERE, WITH YOUR FATHER, LEARNING TO MAINTAIN THESE FILTHY EARTH-VEHICLES--WHICH YOU ARE QUITE GOOD AT, BY THE WAY.
BUT CONFRONTING AUTHORITY...? THAT'S NOT REALLY YOU ANYMORE.
OPEN
I KNOW PERFECTLY WELL WHO I AM, YOU FREAK! OR HAVEN'T YOU NOTICED THAT WHAT YOU DID TO ME DIDN'T STICK?!
STOP AND CONSIDER WHAT I HAVE GIVEN YOU--A LIFETIME WITH THE MAN YOU HAVEN'T SEEN SINCE YOU WERE SIX.
THE MAN WHO TAUGHT YOU A TRADE, WHO SUPPORTED YOU, MADE YOU HIS PARTNER...
SHUT UP!
KID, I DON'T KNOW WHAT YOU'RE ON, TALKIN' TO THIN AIR LIKE THAT, BUT YOU'D BEST WATCH YOUR MOUTH AROUND ME...
WAIT A MINUTE. DAD TAUGHT ME TO FIX CARS...?

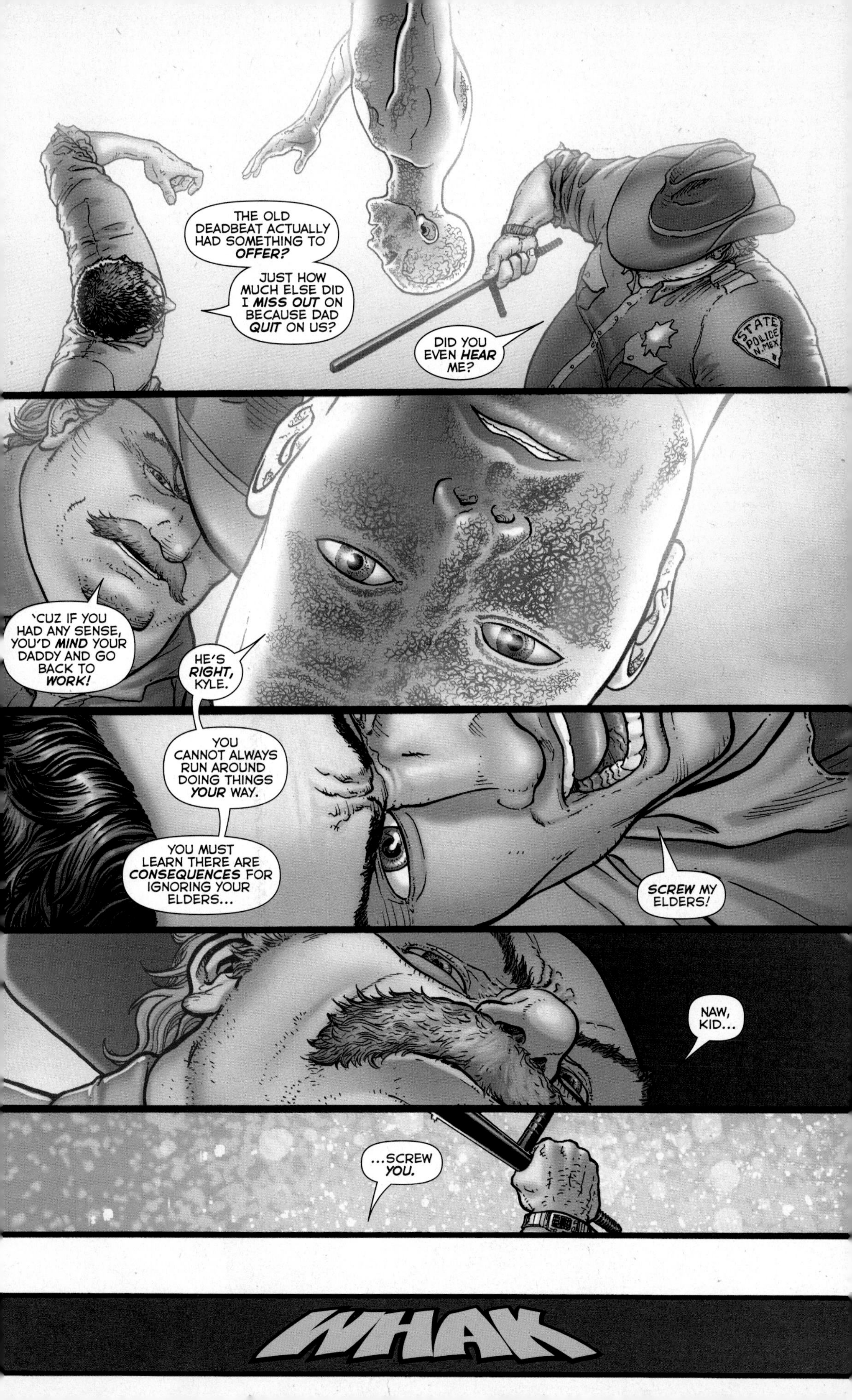
THE OLD DEADBEAT ACTUALLY HAD SOMETHING TO OFFER?
JUST HOW MUCH ELSE DID I MISS OUT ON BECAUSE DAD QUIT ON US?
DID YOU EVEN HEAR ME?
STATE POLICE N. MEX
'CUZ IF YOU HAD ANY SENSE, YOU'D MIND YOUR DADDY AND GO BACK TO WORK!
HE'S RIGHT, KYLE.
YOU CANNOT ALWAYS RUN AROUND DOING THINGS YOUR WAY.
YOU MUST LEARN THERE ARE CONSEQUENCES FOR IGNORING YOUR ELDERS...
SCREW MY ELDERS!
NAW, KID...
...SCREW YOU.
WHAK

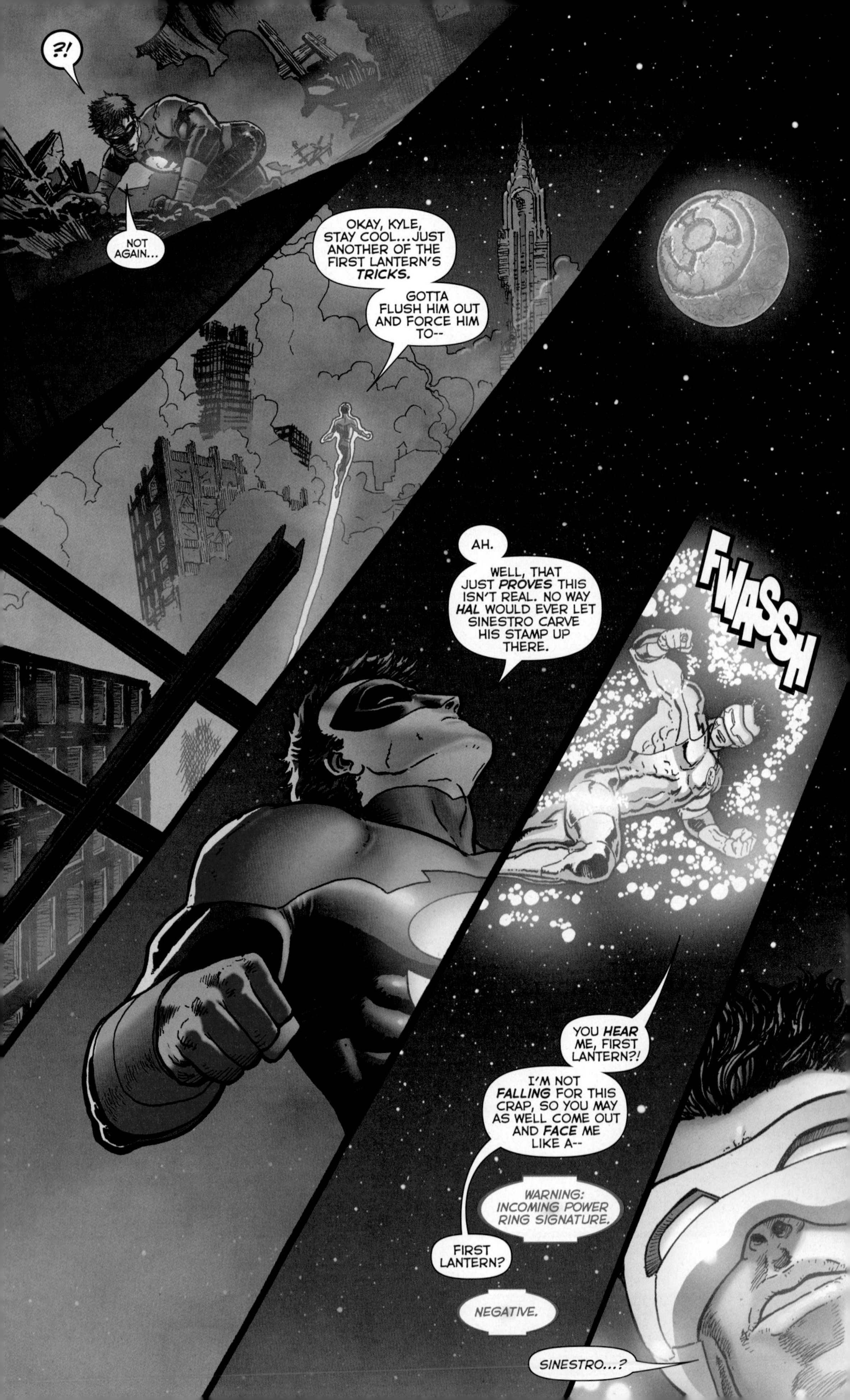
?!
NOT AGAIN...
OKAY, KYLE, STAY COOL... JUST ANOTHER OF THE FIRST LANTERN'S TRICKS.
GOTTA FLUSH HIM OUT AND FORCE HIM TO--
AH.
WELL, THAT JUST PROVES THIS ISN'T REAL. NO WAY HAL WOULD EVER LET SINESTRO CARVE HIS STAMP UP THERE.
FWASSH
YOU HEAR ME, FIRST LANTERN?!
I'M NOT FALLING FOR THIS CRAP, SO YOU MAY AS WELL COME OUT AND FACE ME LIKE A--
WARNING: INCOMING POWER RING SIGNATURE.
FIRST LANTERN?
NEGATIVE.
SINESTRO...?

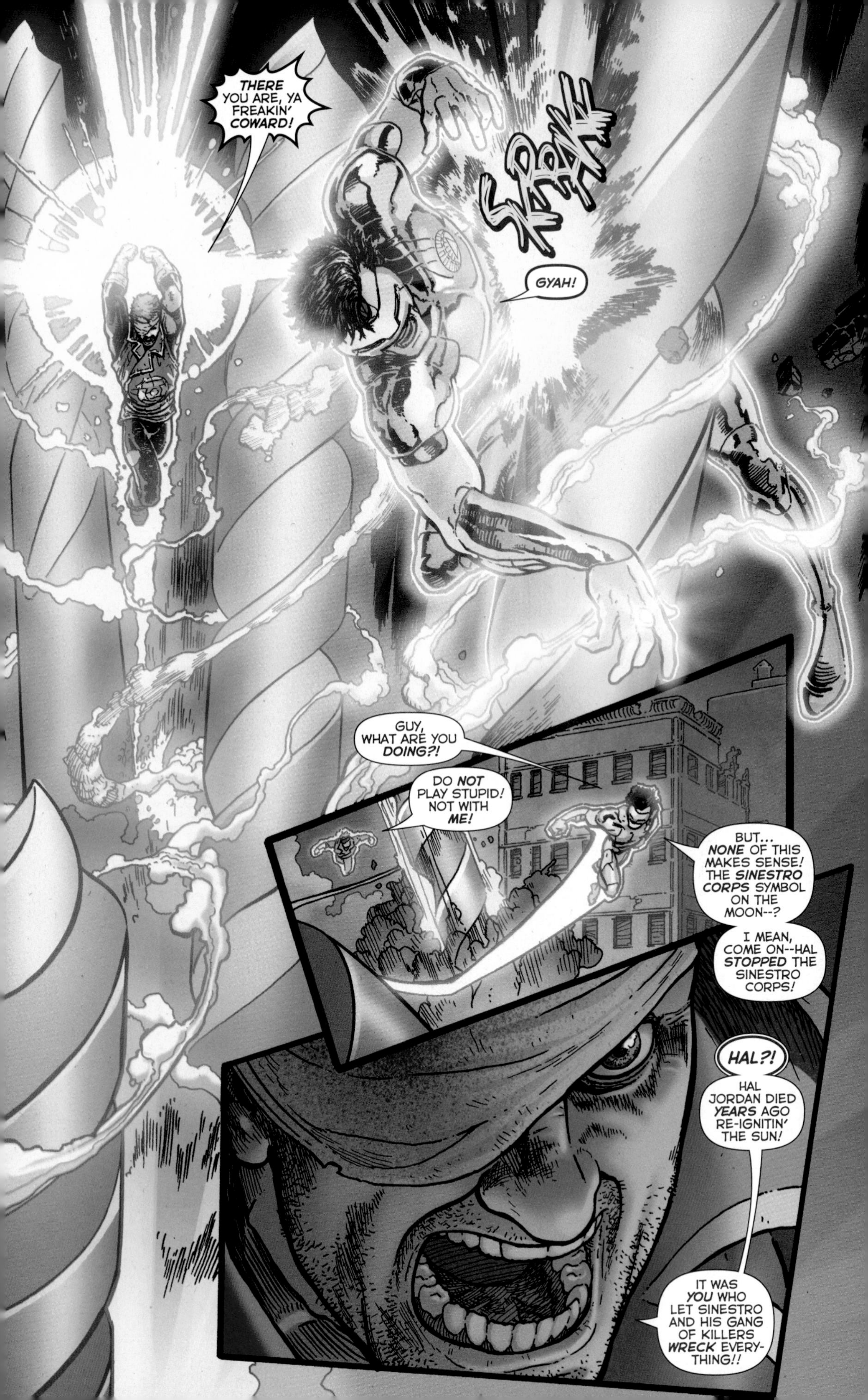

THERE YOU ARE, YA FREAKIN' COWARD!
SKROK
GYAH!
GUY, WHAT ARE YOU DOING?!
DO NOT PLAY STUPID! NOT WITH ME!
BUT... NONE OF THIS MAKES SENSE! THE SINESTRO CORPS SYMBOL ON THE MOON--?
I MEAN, COME ON--HAL STOPPED THE SINESTRO CORPS!
HAL?!
HAL JORDAN DIED YEARS AGO RE-IGNITIN' THE SUN!
IT WAS YOU WHO LET SINESTRO AND HIS GANG OF KILLERS WRECK EVERY-THING!!

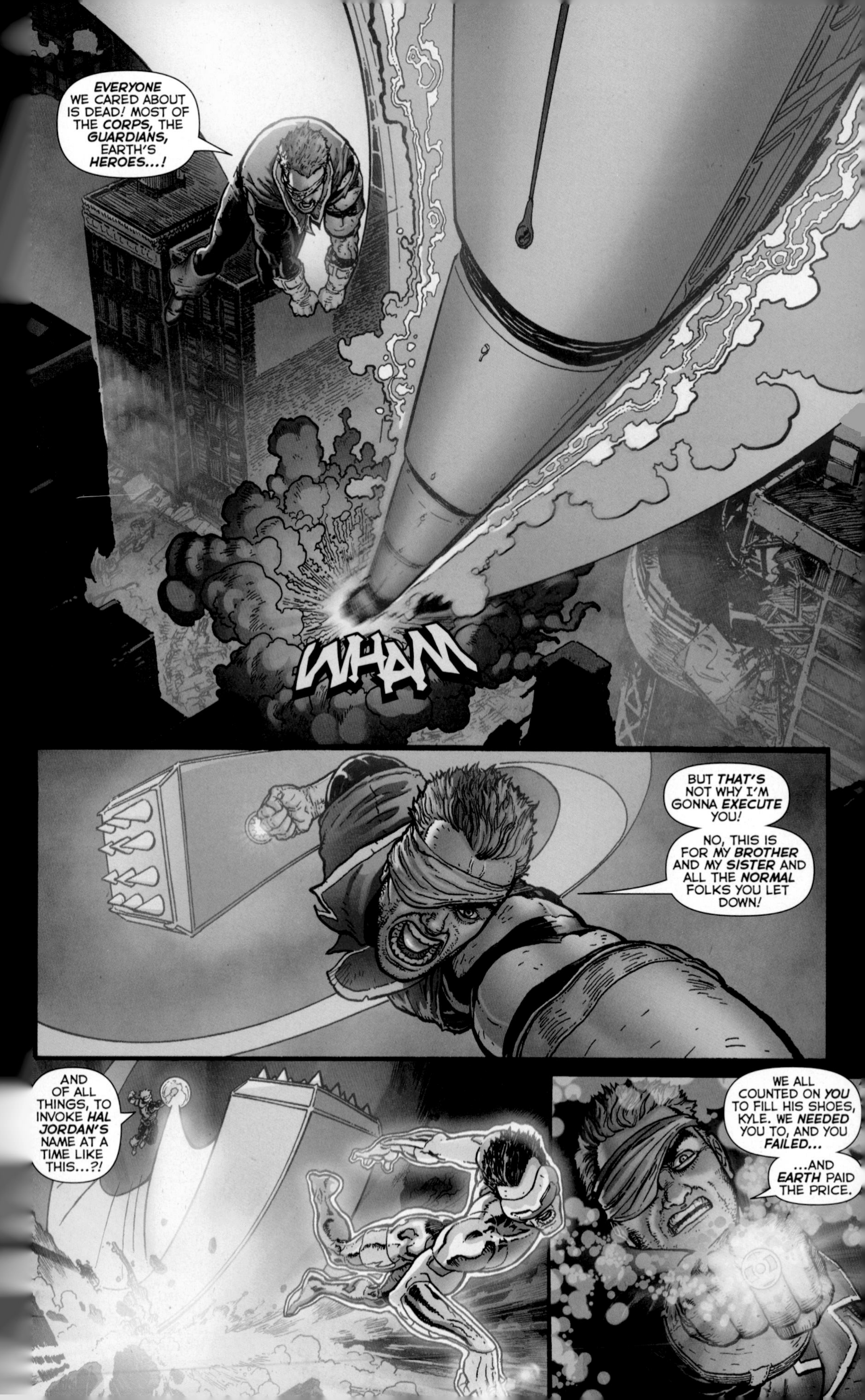
EVERYONE WE CARED ABOUT IS DEAD! MOST OF THE CORPS, THE GUARDIANS, EARTH'S HEROES...!
WHAM
BUT THAT'S NOT WHY I'M GONNA EXECUTE YOU!
NO, THIS IS FOR MY BROTHER AND MY SISTER AND ALL THE NORMAL FOLKS YOU LET DOWN!
AND OF ALL THINGS, TO INVOKE HAL JORDAN'S NAME AT A TIME LIKE THIS...?!
WE ALL COUNTED ON YOU TO FILL HIS SHOES, KYLE. WE NEEDED YOU TO, AND YOU FAILED...
...AND EARTH PAID THE PRICE.

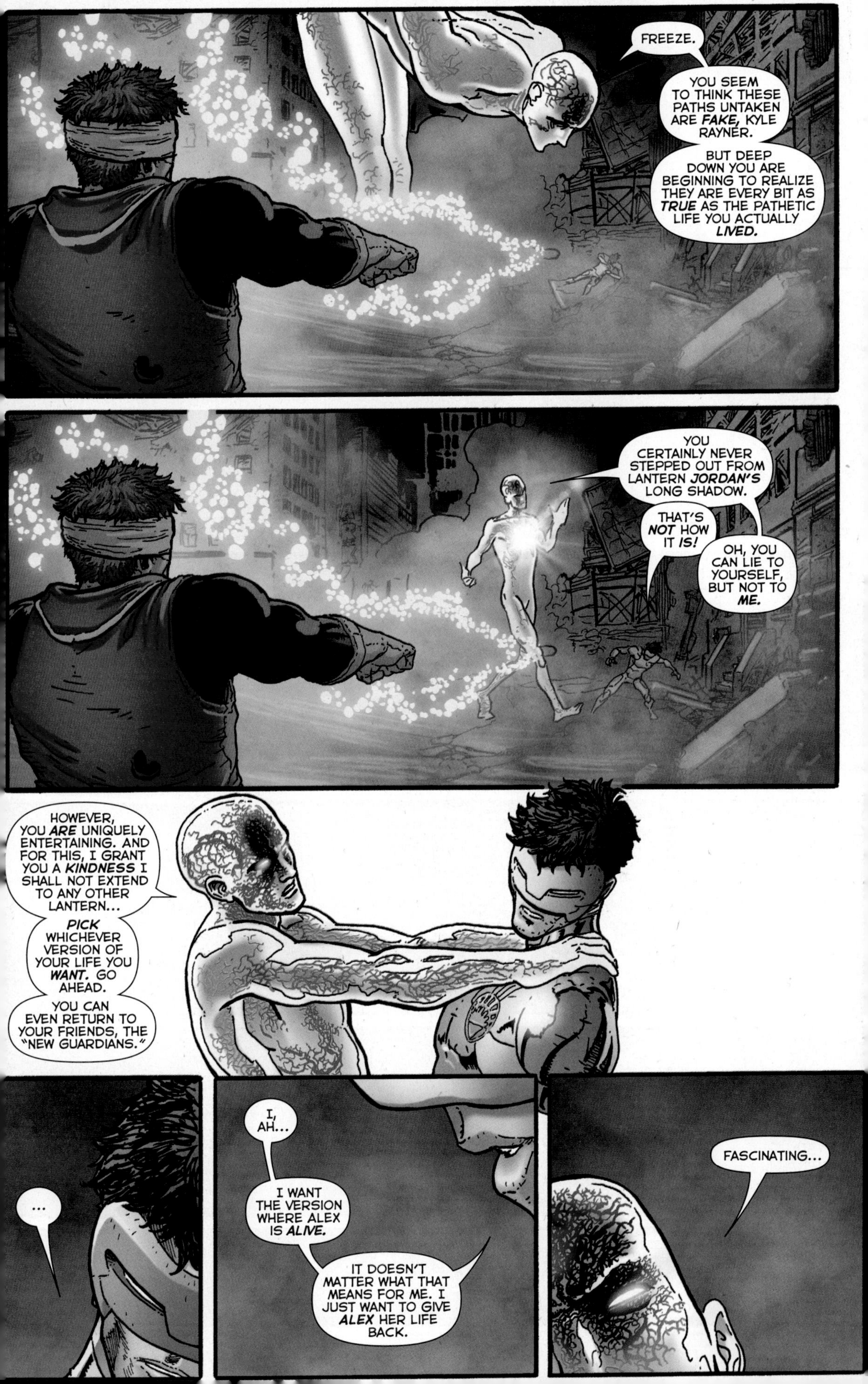
FREEZE.
YOU SEEM TO THINK THESE PATHS UNTAKEN ARE FAKE, KYLE RAYNER.
BUT DEEP DOWN YOU ARE BEGINNING TO REALIZE THEY ARE EVERY BIT AS TRUE AS THE PATHETIC LIFE YOU ACTUALLY LIVED.
YOU CERTAINLY NEVER STEPPED OUT FROM LANTERN JORDAN'S LONG SHADOW.
THAT'S NOT HOW IT IS!
OH, YOU CAN LIE TO YOURSELF, BUT NOT TO ME.
HOWEVER, YOU ARE UNIQUELY ENTERTAINING. AND FOR THIS, I GRANT YOU A KINDNESS I SHALL NOT EXTEND TO ANY OTHER LANTERN...
PICK WHICHEVER VERSION OF YOUR LIFE YOU WANT. GO AHEAD.
YOU CAN EVEN RETURN TO YOUR FRIENDS, THE "NEW GUARDIANS."
...
I, AH...
I WANT THE VERSION WHERE ALEX IS ALIVE.
IT DOESN'T MATTER WHAT THAT MEANS FOR ME. I JUST WANT TO GIVE ALEX HER LIFE BACK.
FASCINATING...

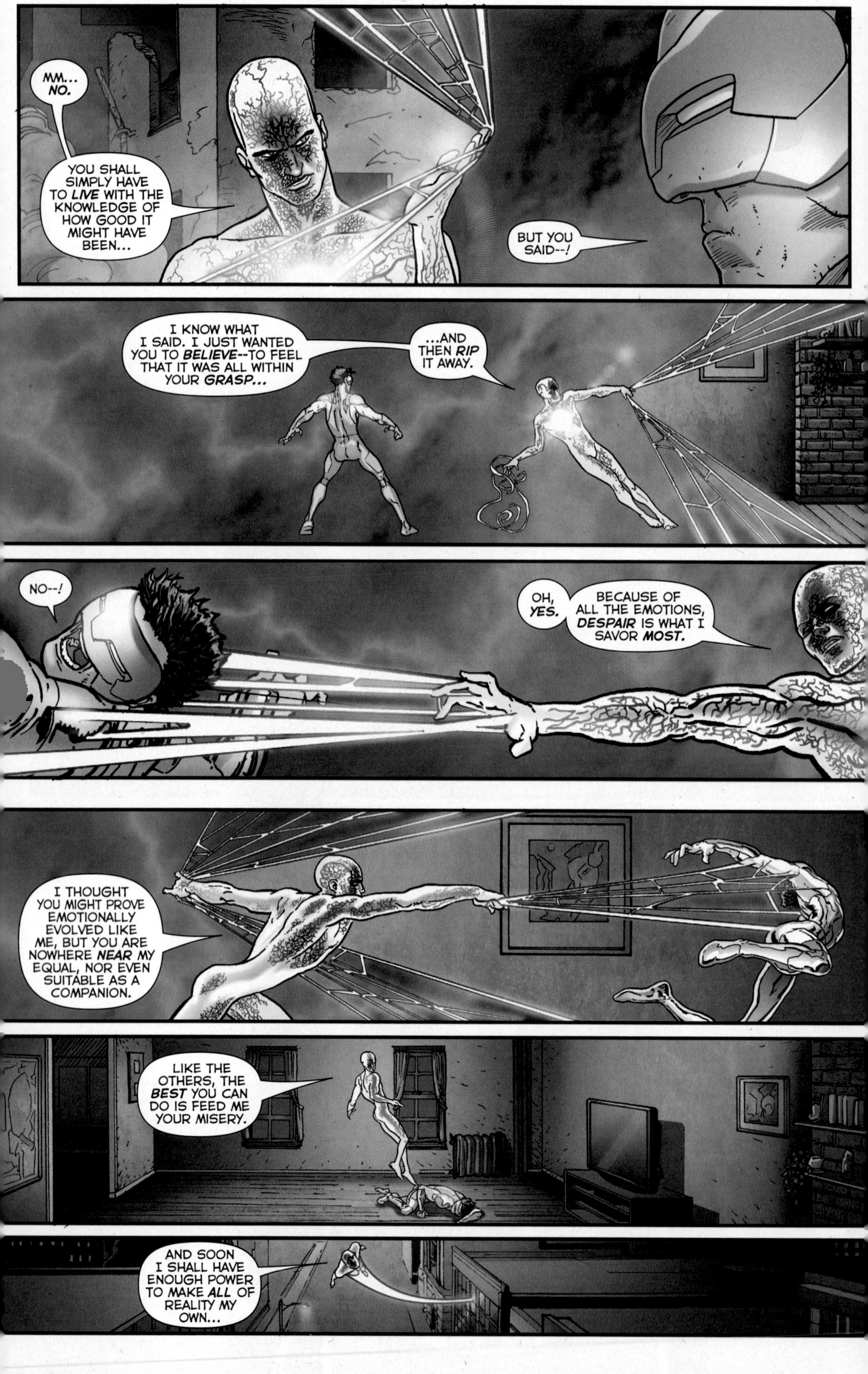
MM... NO.
YOU SHALL SIMPLY HAVE TO LIVE WITH THE KNOWLEDGE OF HOW GOOD IT MIGHT HAVE BEEN...
BUT YOU SAID--!
I KNOW WHAT I SAID. I JUST WANTED YOU TO BELIEVE--TO FEEL THAT IT WAS ALL WITHIN YOUR GRASP...
...AND THEN RIP IT AWAY.
NO--!
OH, YES.
BECAUSE OF ALL THE EMOTIONS, DESPAIR IS WHAT I SAVOR MOST.
I THOUGHT YOU MIGHT PROVE EMOTIONALLY EVOLVED LIKE ME, BUT YOU ARE NOWHERE NEAR MY EQUAL, NOR EVEN SUITABLE AS A COMPANION.
LIKE THE OTHERS, THE BEST YOU CAN DO IS FEED ME YOUR MISERY.
AND SOON I SHALL HAVE ENOUGH POWER TO MAKE ALL OF REALITY MY OWN...

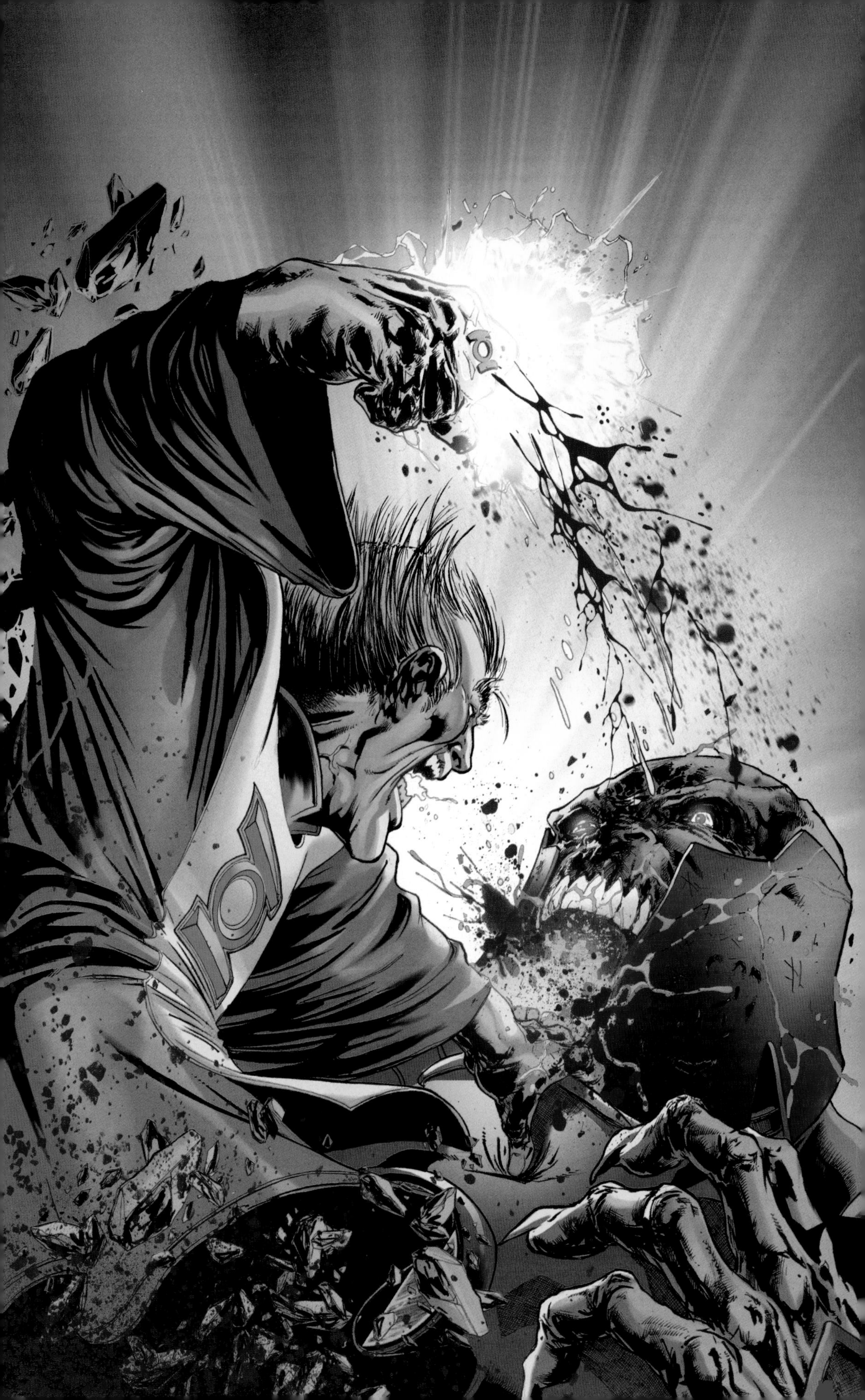

PART FOUR: SYMPATHY FOR THE DEVIL

PETER MILLIGAN writer **MIGUEL SEPULVEDA** artist
cover art by **MIGUEL SEPULVEDA & RAIN BEREDO**

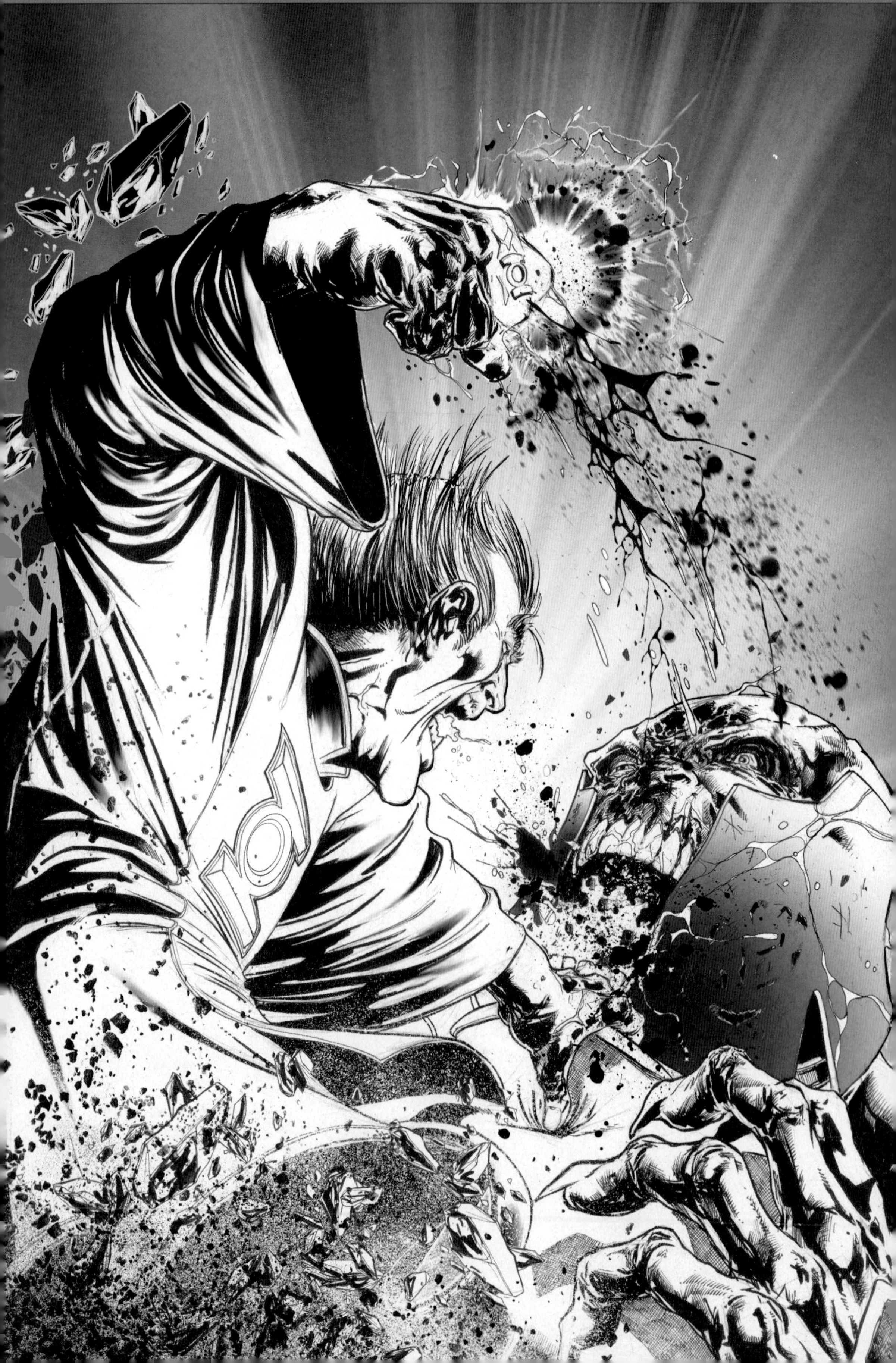

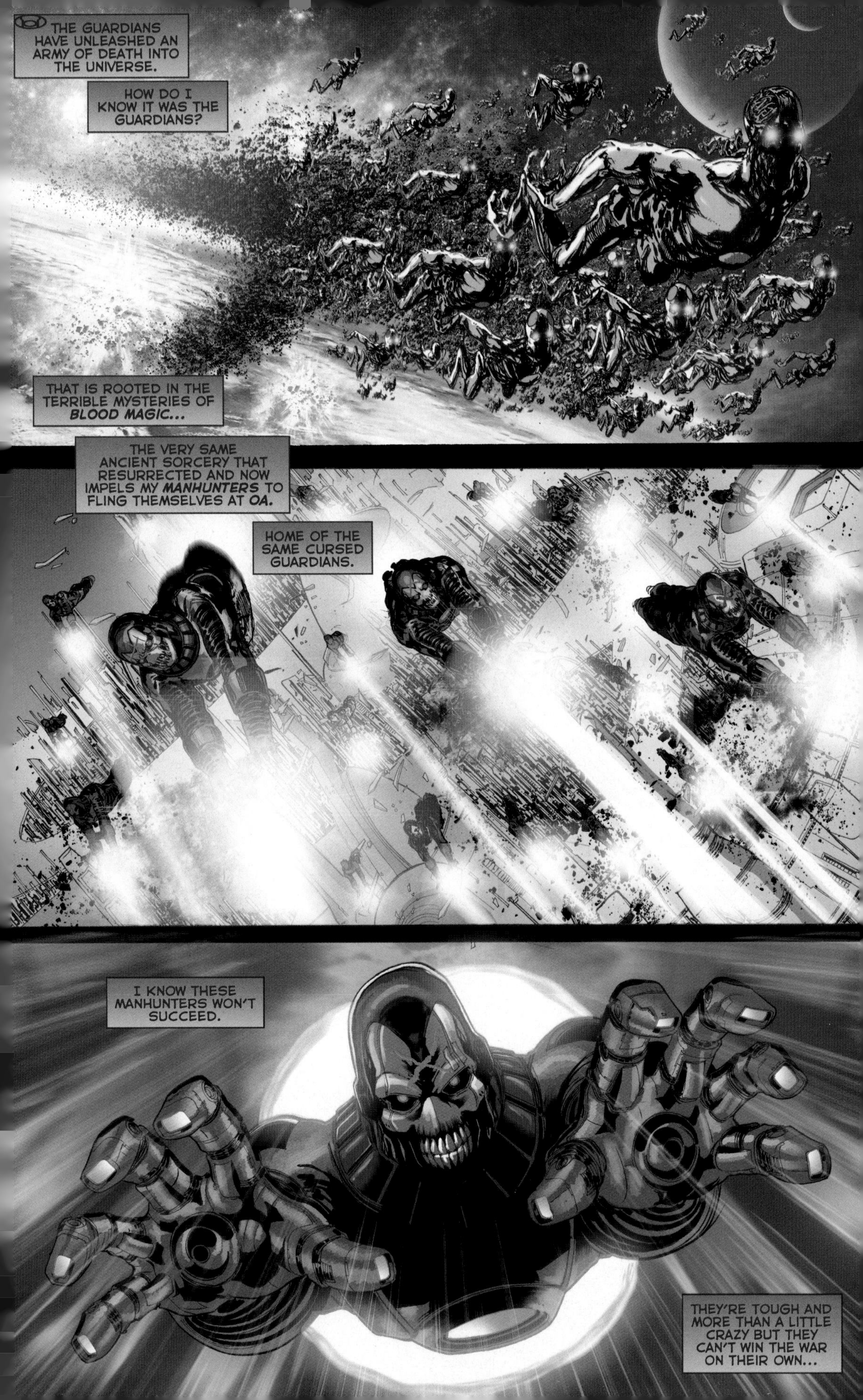
THE GUARDIANS HAVE UNLEASHED AN ARMY OF DEATH INTO THE UNIVERSE.
HOW DO I KNOW IT WAS THE GUARDIANS?
THAT IS ROOTED IN THE TERRIBLE MYSTERIES OF *BLOOD MAGIC*...
THE VERY SAME ANCIENT SORCERY THAT RESURRECTED AND NOW IMPELS *MY MANHUNTERS* TO FLING THEMSELVES AT *OA*.
HOME OF THE SAME CURSED GUARDIANS.
I KNOW THESE MANHUNTERS WON'T SUCCEED.
THEY'RE TOUGH AND MORE THAN A LITTLE CRAZY BUT THEY CAN'T WIN THE WAR ON THEIR OWN...

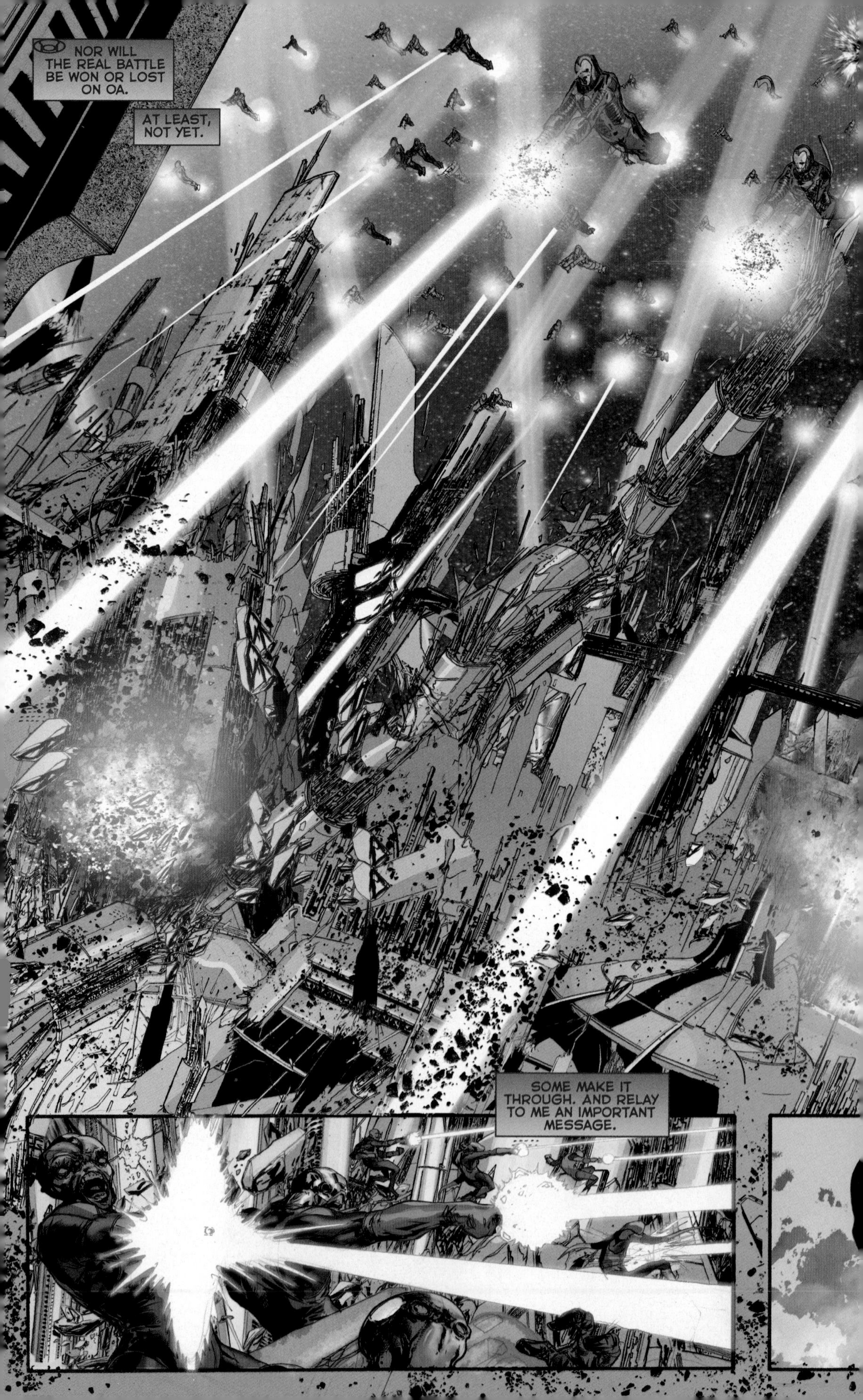
NOR WILL THE REAL BATTLE BE WON OR LOST ON OA.
AT LEAST, NOT YET.
SOME MAKE IT THROUGH. AND RELAY TO ME AN IMPORTANT MESSAGE.

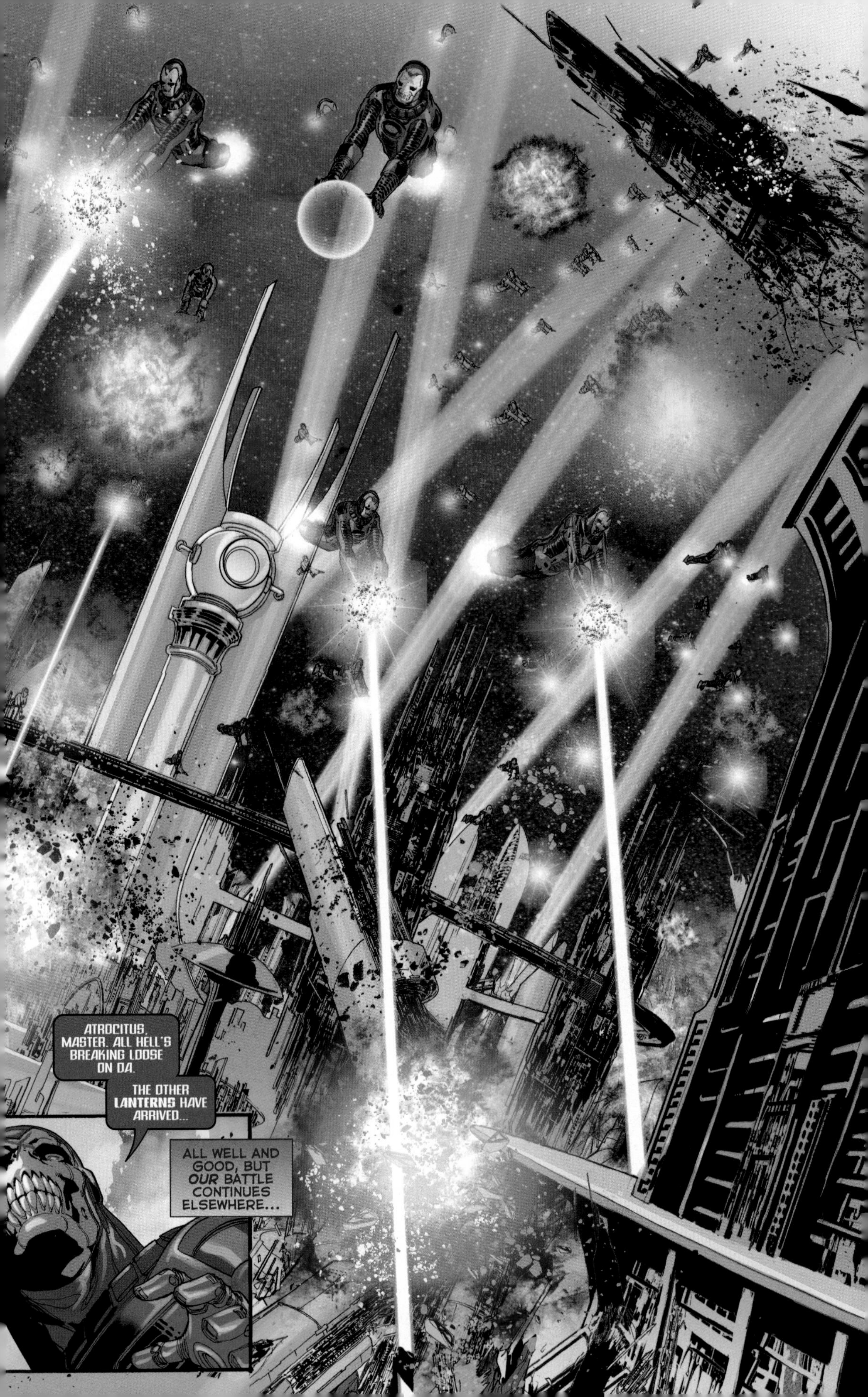
ATROCITUS, MASTER. ALL HELL'S BREAKING LOOSE ON OA.
THE OTHER LANTERNS HAVE ARRIVED...
ALL WELL AND GOOD, BUT OUR BATTLE CONTINUES ELSEWHERE...

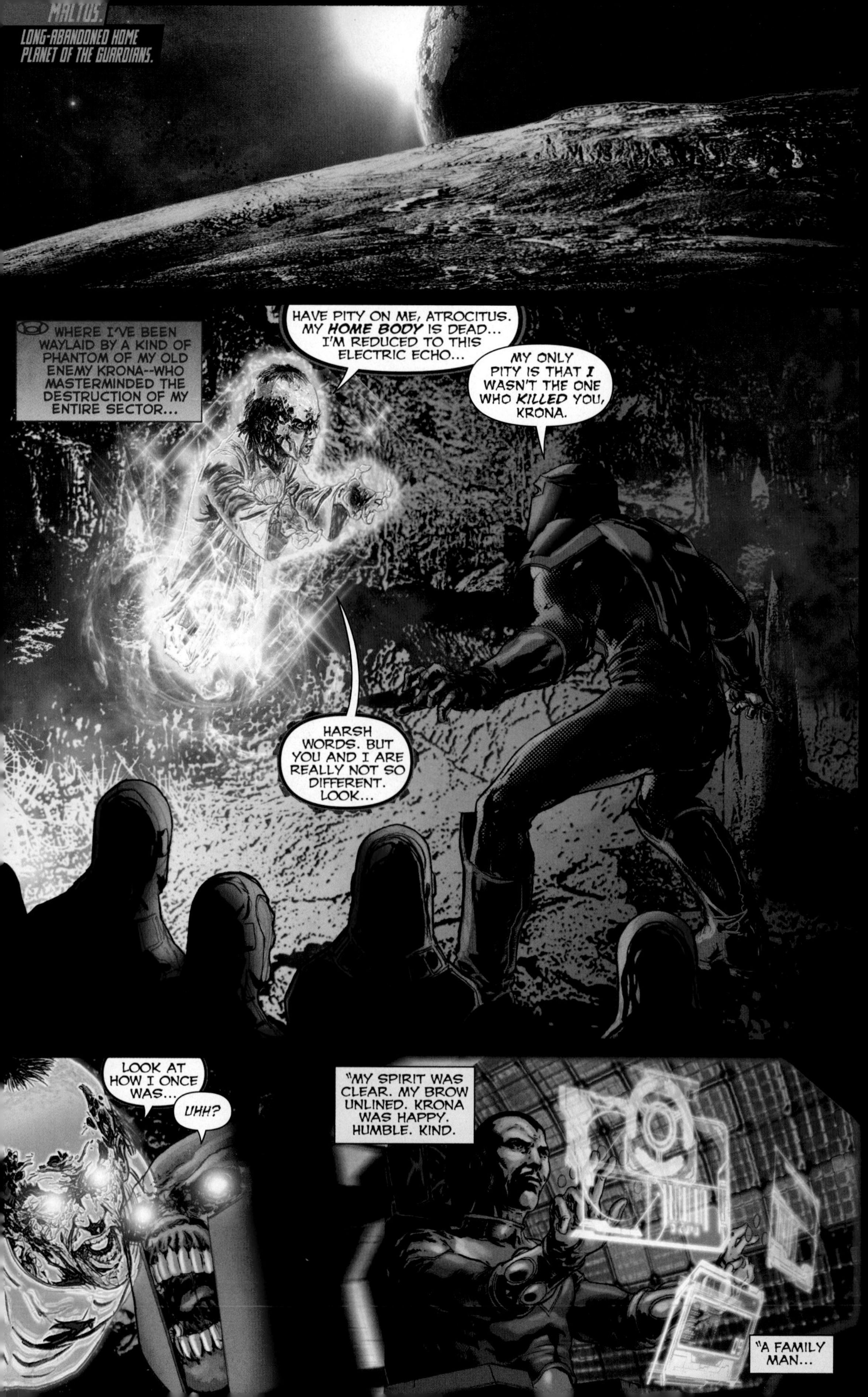
MALTOS.
LONG-ABANDONED HOME PLANET OF THE GUARDIANS.
WHERE I'VE BEEN WAYLAID BY A KIND OF PHANTOM OF MY OLD ENEMY KRONA--WHO MASTERMINDED THE DESTRUCTION OF MY ENTIRE SECTOR...
HAVE PITY ON ME, ATROCITUS. MY HOME BODY IS DEAD... I'M REDUCED TO THIS ELECTRIC ECHO...
MY ONLY PITY IS THAT I WASN'T THE ONE WHO KILLED YOU, KRONA.
HARSH WORDS. BUT YOU AND I ARE REALLY NOT SO DIFFERENT. LOOK...
LOOK AT HOW I ONCE WAS...
UHH?
"MY SPIRIT WAS CLEAR. MY BROW UNLINED. KRONA WAS HAPPY. HUMBLE. KIND.
"A FAMILY MAN...

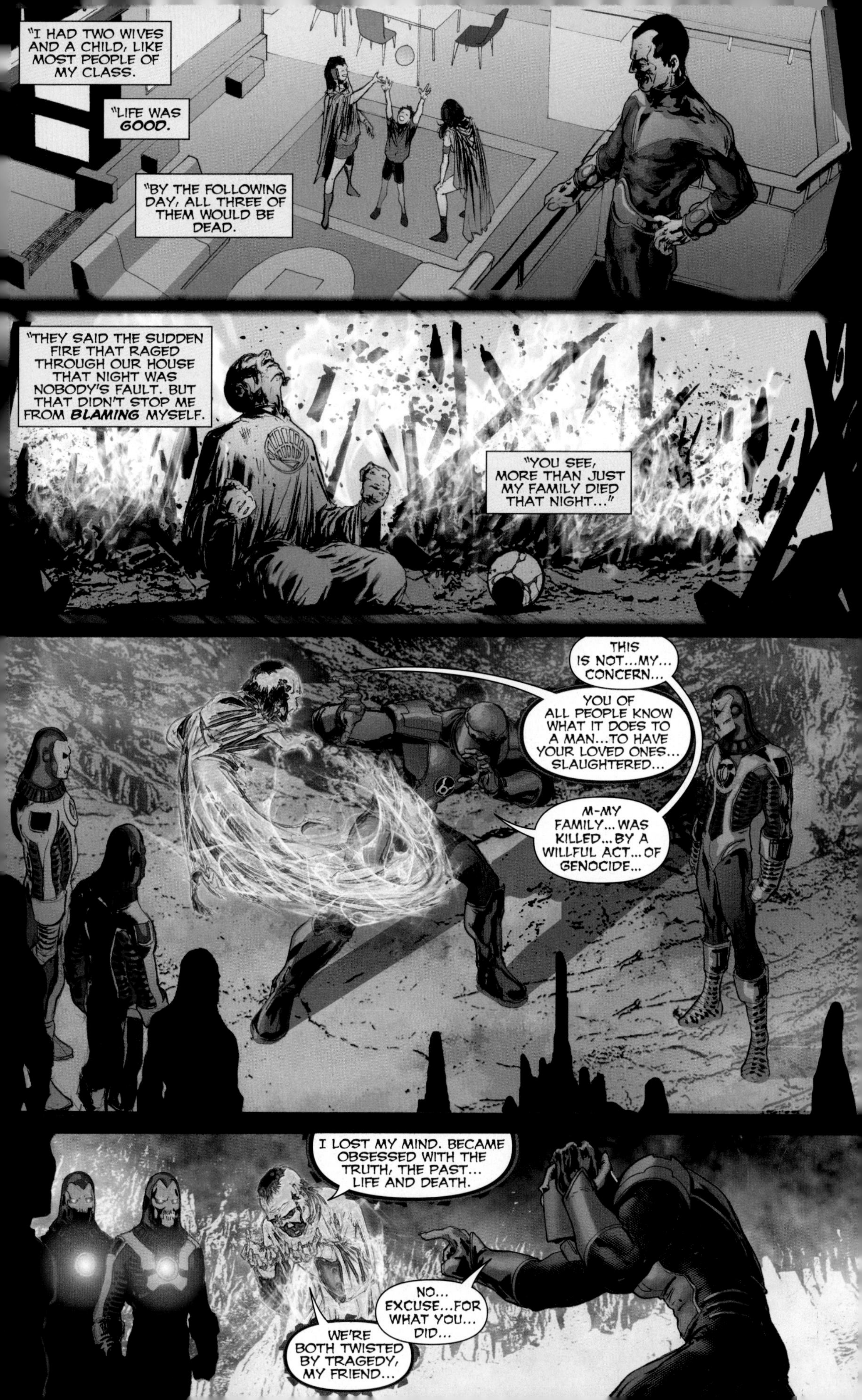
"I HAD TWO WIVES AND A CHILD, LIKE MOST PEOPLE OF MY CLASS.
"LIFE WAS GOOD.
"BY THE FOLLOWING DAY, ALL THREE OF THEM WOULD BE DEAD.
"THEY SAID THE SUDDEN FIRE THAT RAGED THROUGH OUR HOUSE THAT NIGHT WAS NOBODY'S FAULT. BUT THAT DIDN'T STOP ME FROM BLAMING MYSELF.
"YOU SEE, MORE THAN JUST MY FAMILY DIED THAT NIGHT..."
THIS IS NOT...MY... CONCERN...
YOU OF ALL PEOPLE KNOW WHAT IT DOES TO A MAN...TO HAVE YOUR LOVED ONES... SLAUGHTERED...
M-MY FAMILY...WAS KILLED...BY A WILLFUL ACT...OF GENOCIDE...
I LOST MY MIND. BECAME OBSESSED WITH THE TRUTH, THE PAST... LIFE AND DEATH.
NO... EXCUSE...FOR WHAT YOU... DID...
WE'RE BOTH TWISTED BY TRAGEDY, MY FRIEND...

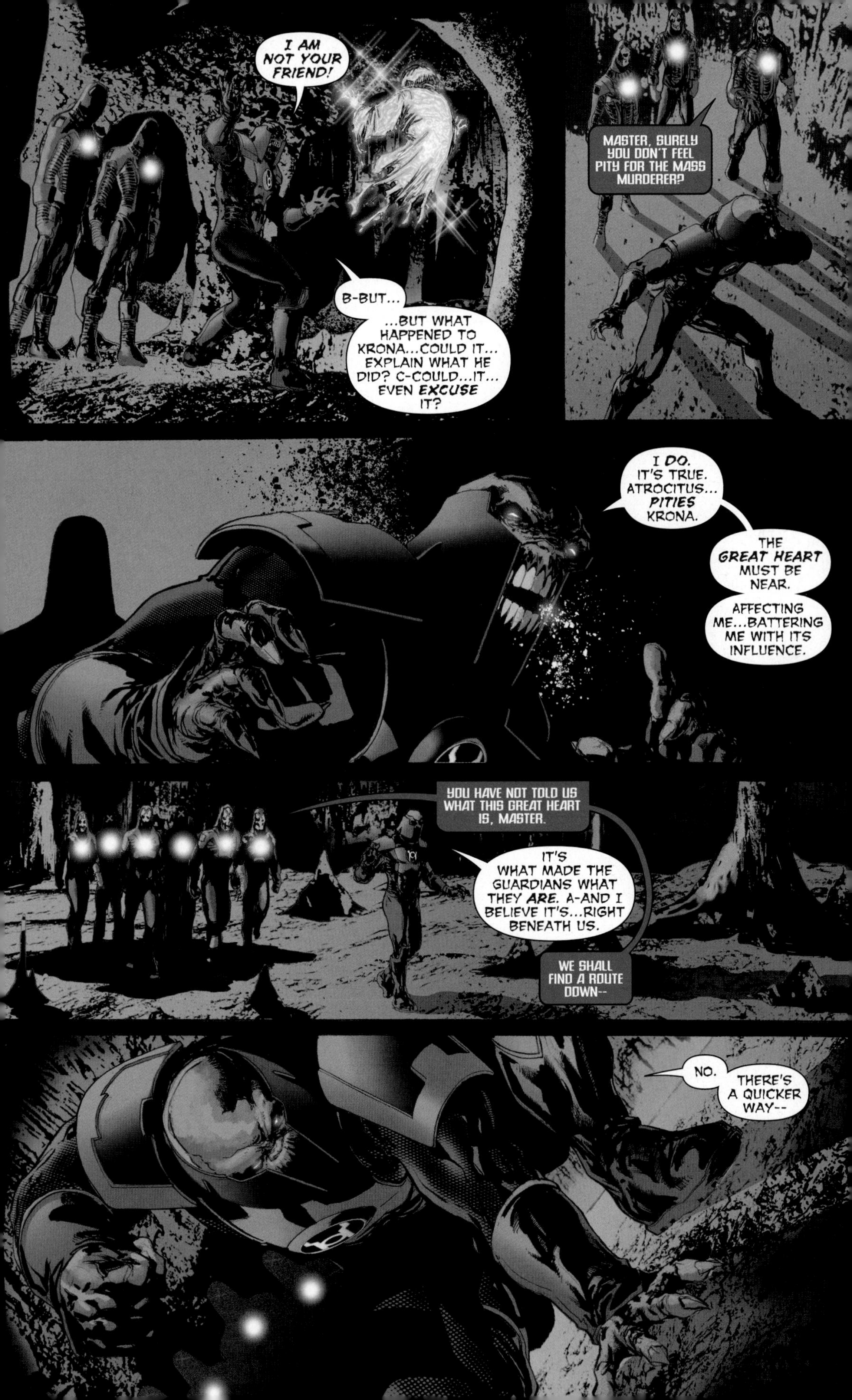

I AM NOT YOUR FRIEND!
B-BUT...
...BUT WHAT HAPPENED TO KRONA...COULD IT... EXPLAIN WHAT HE DID? C-COULD...IT... EVEN EXCUSE IT?
MASTER, SURELY YOU DON'T FEEL PITY FOR THE MASS MURDERER?
I DO. IT'S TRUE. ATROCITUS... PITIES KRONA.
THE GREAT HEART MUST BE NEAR.
AFFECTING ME...BATTERING ME WITH ITS INFLUENCE.
YOU HAVE NOT TOLD US WHAT THIS GREAT HEART IS, MASTER.
IT'S WHAT MADE THE GUARDIANS WHAT THEY ARE. A-AND I BELIEVE IT'S...RIGHT BENEATH US.
WE SHALL FIND A ROUTE DOWN--
NO.
THERE'S A QUICKER WAY--

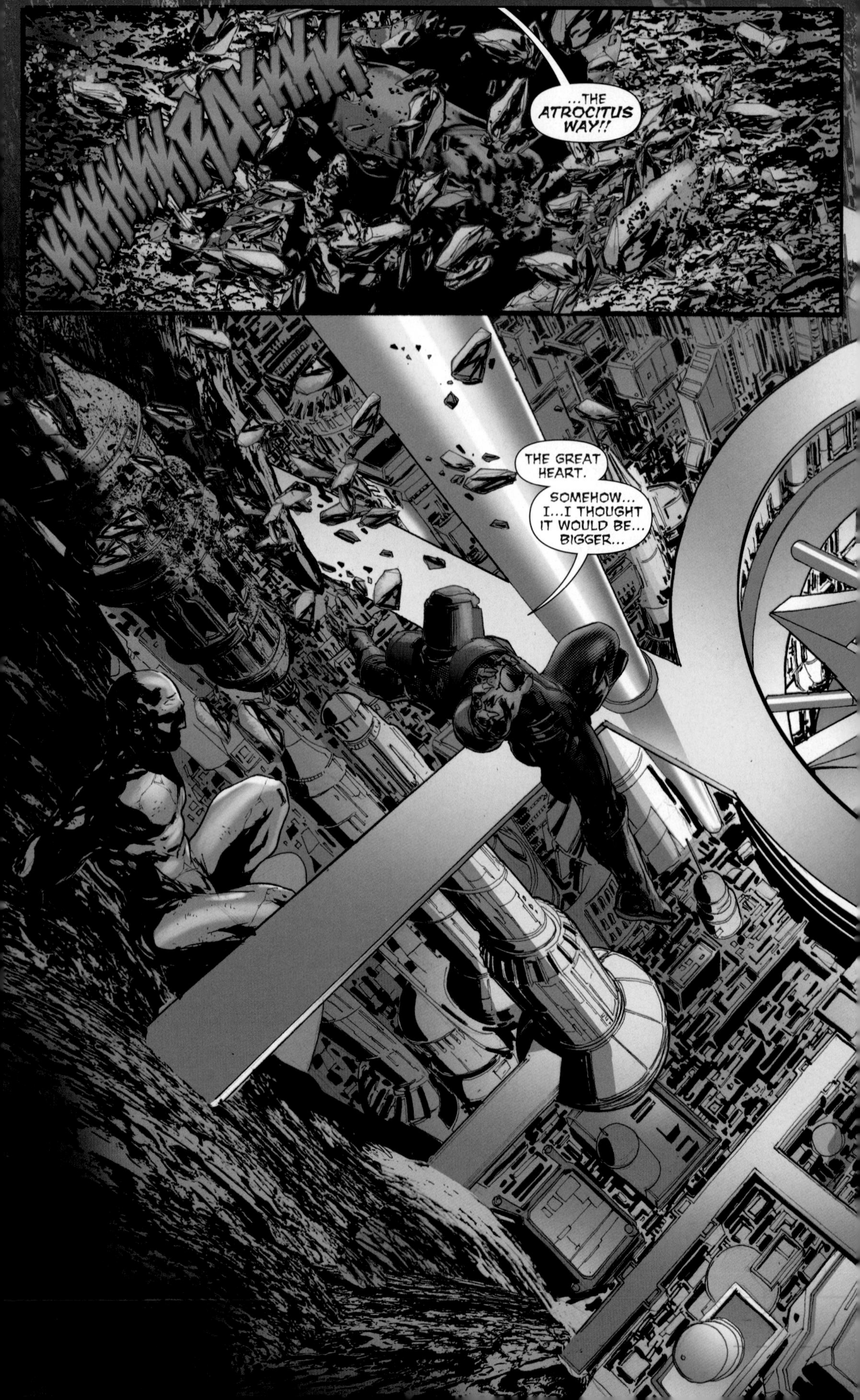
KKKKKKRAKKKKK
...THE ATROCITUS WAY!!
THE GREAT HEART.
SOMEHOW... I...I THOUGHT IT WOULD BE... BIGGER...

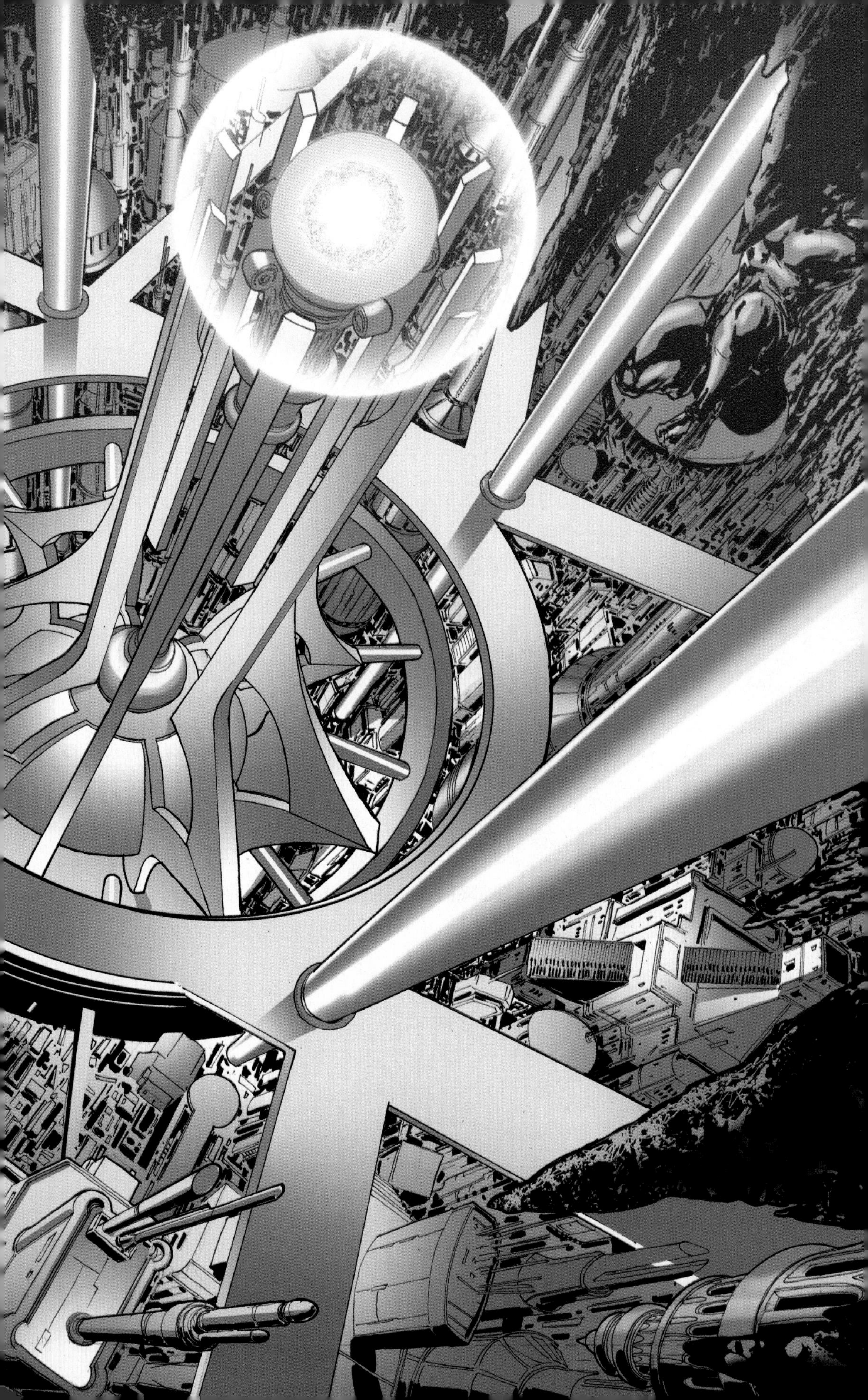

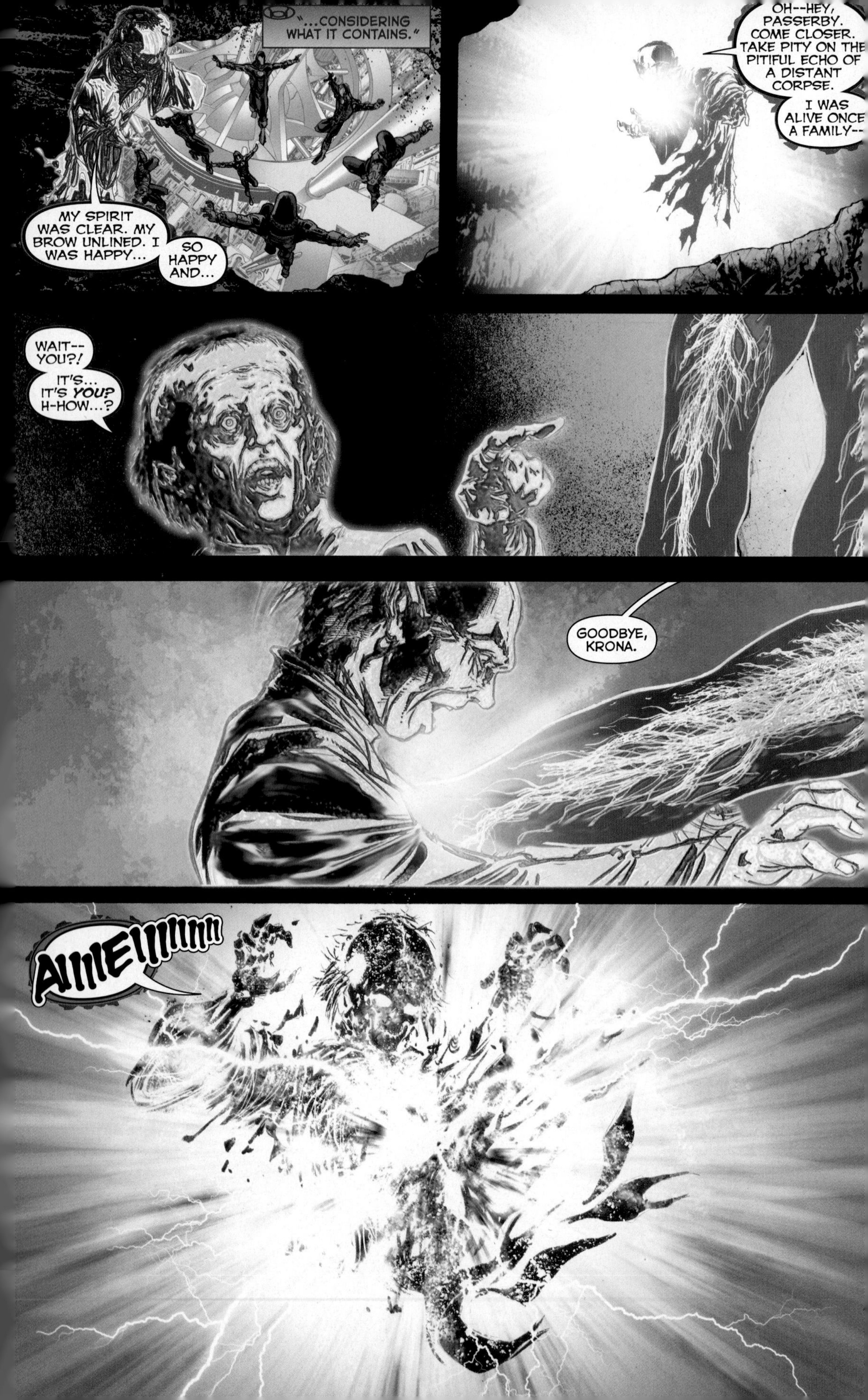
"...CONSIDERING WHAT IT CONTAINS."
MY SPIRIT WAS CLEAR. MY BROW UNLINED. I WAS HAPPY...
SO HAPPY AND...
OH--HEY, PASSERBY. COME CLOSER. TAKE PITY ON THE PITIFUL ECHO OF A DISTANT CORPSE.
I WAS ALIVE ONCE A FAMILY--
WAIT-- YOU?!
IT'S... IT'S YOU? H-HOW...?
GOODBYE, KRONA.
AIIIIEIIIIIInn

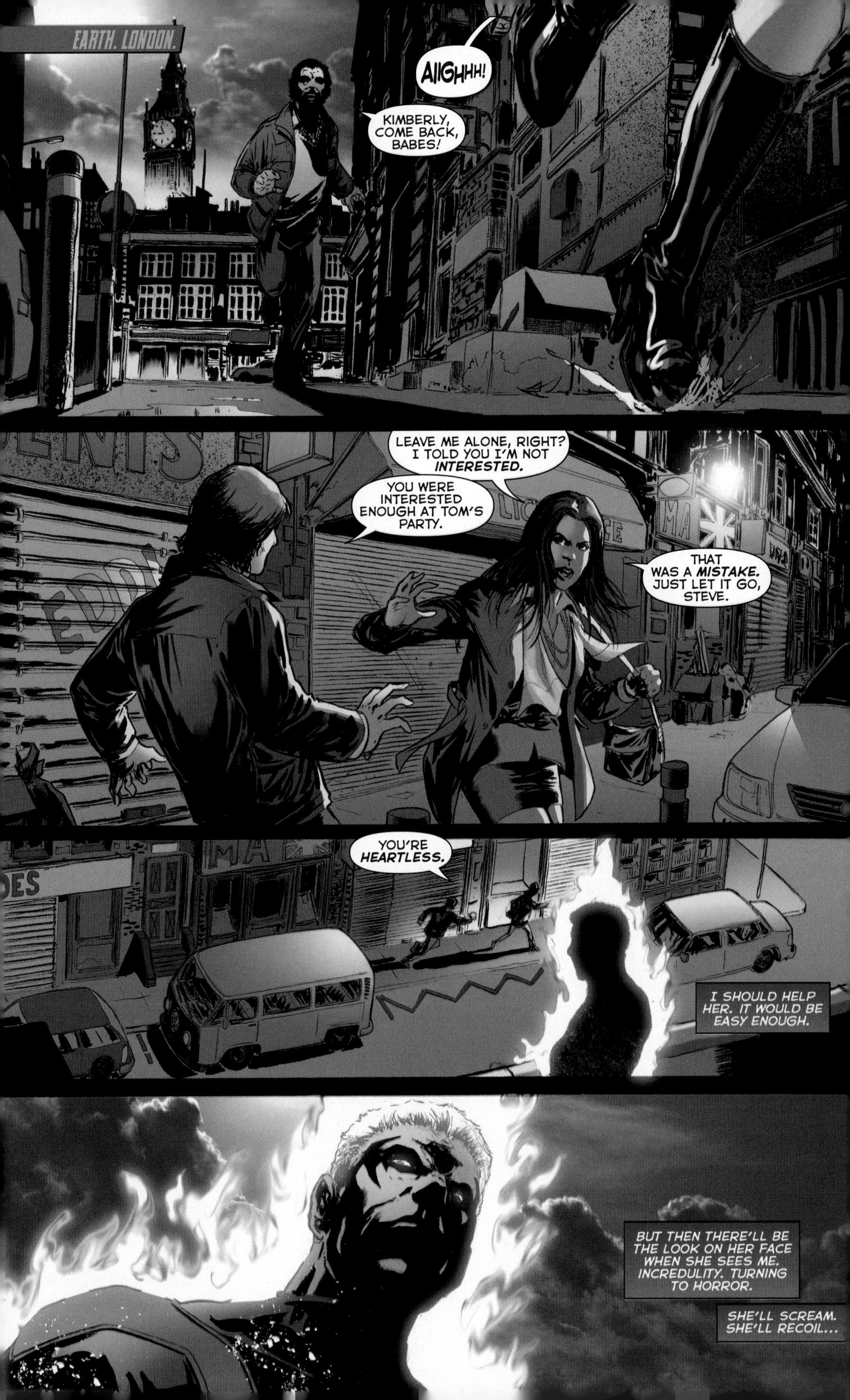
EARTH. LONDON.
AIIGHHH!
KIMBERLY, COME BACK, BABES!
LEAVE ME ALONE, RIGHT? I TOLD YOU I'M NOT INTERESTED.
YOU WERE INTERESTED ENOUGH AT TOM'S PARTY.
THAT WAS A MISTAKE. JUST LET IT GO, STEVE.
YOU'RE HEARTLESS.
I SHOULD HELP HER. IT WOULD BE EASY ENOUGH.
BUT THEN THERE'LL BE THE LOOK ON HER FACE WHEN SHE SEES ME. INCREDULITY. TURNING TO HORROR.
SHE'LL SCREAM. SHE'LL RECOIL...

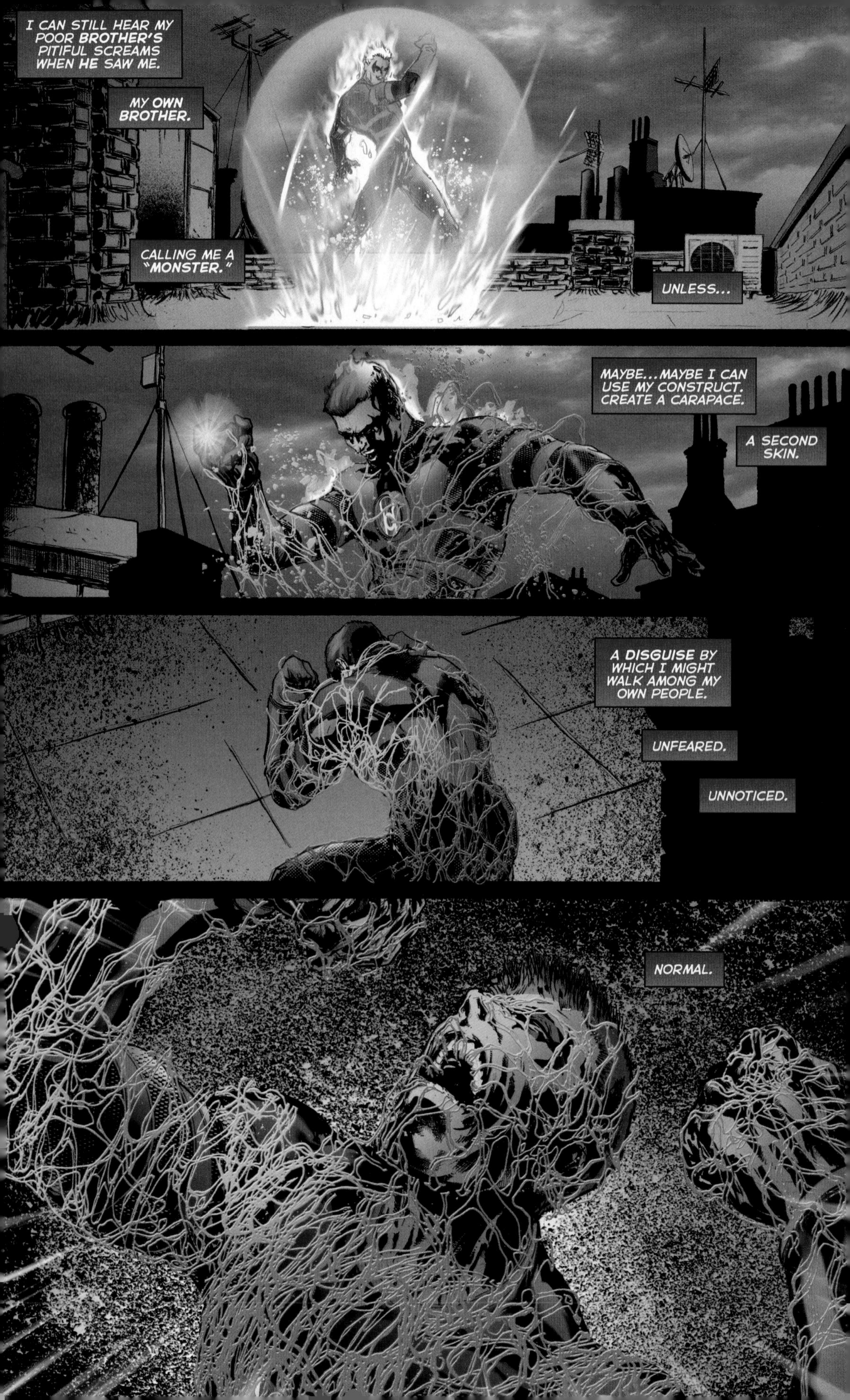
I CAN STILL HEAR MY POOR BROTHER'S PITIFUL SCREAMS WHEN HE SAW ME.
MY OWN BROTHER.
CALLING ME A "MONSTER."
UNLESS...
MAYBE...MAYBE I CAN USE MY CONSTRUCT. CREATE A CARAPACE.
A SECOND SKIN.
A DISGUISE BY WHICH I MIGHT WALK AMONG MY OWN PEOPLE.
UNFEARED.
UNNOTICED.
NORMAL.

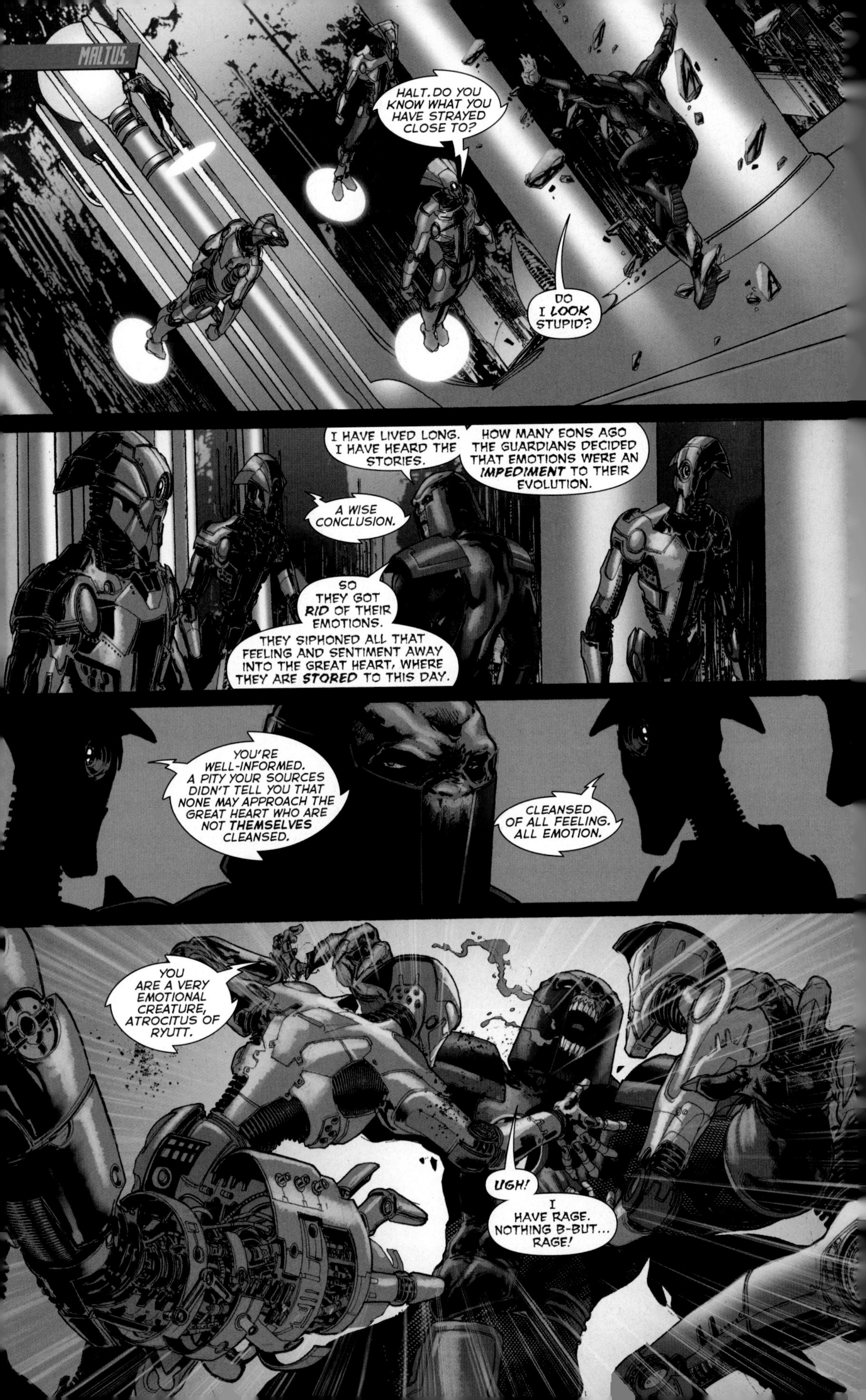
MALTUS.
HALT. DO YOU KNOW WHAT YOU HAVE STRAYED CLOSE TO?
DO I LOOK STUPID?
I HAVE LIVED LONG. I HAVE HEARD THE STORIES.
HOW MANY EONS AGO THE GUARDIANS DECIDED THAT EMOTIONS WERE AN IMPEDIMENT TO THEIR EVOLUTION.
A WISE CONCLUSION.
SO THEY GOT RID OF THEIR EMOTIONS.
THEY SIPHONED ALL THAT FEELING AND SENTIMENT AWAY INTO THE GREAT HEART, WHERE THEY ARE STORED TO THIS DAY.
YOU'RE WELL-INFORMED. A PITY YOUR SOURCES DIDN'T TELL YOU THAT NONE MAY APPROACH THE GREAT HEART WHO ARE NOT THEMSELVES CLEANSED.
CLEANSED OF ALL FEELING. ALL EMOTION.
YOU ARE A VERY EMOTIONAL CREATURE, ATROCITUS OF RYUTT.
UGH!
I HAVE RAGE. NOTHING B-BUT... RAGE!

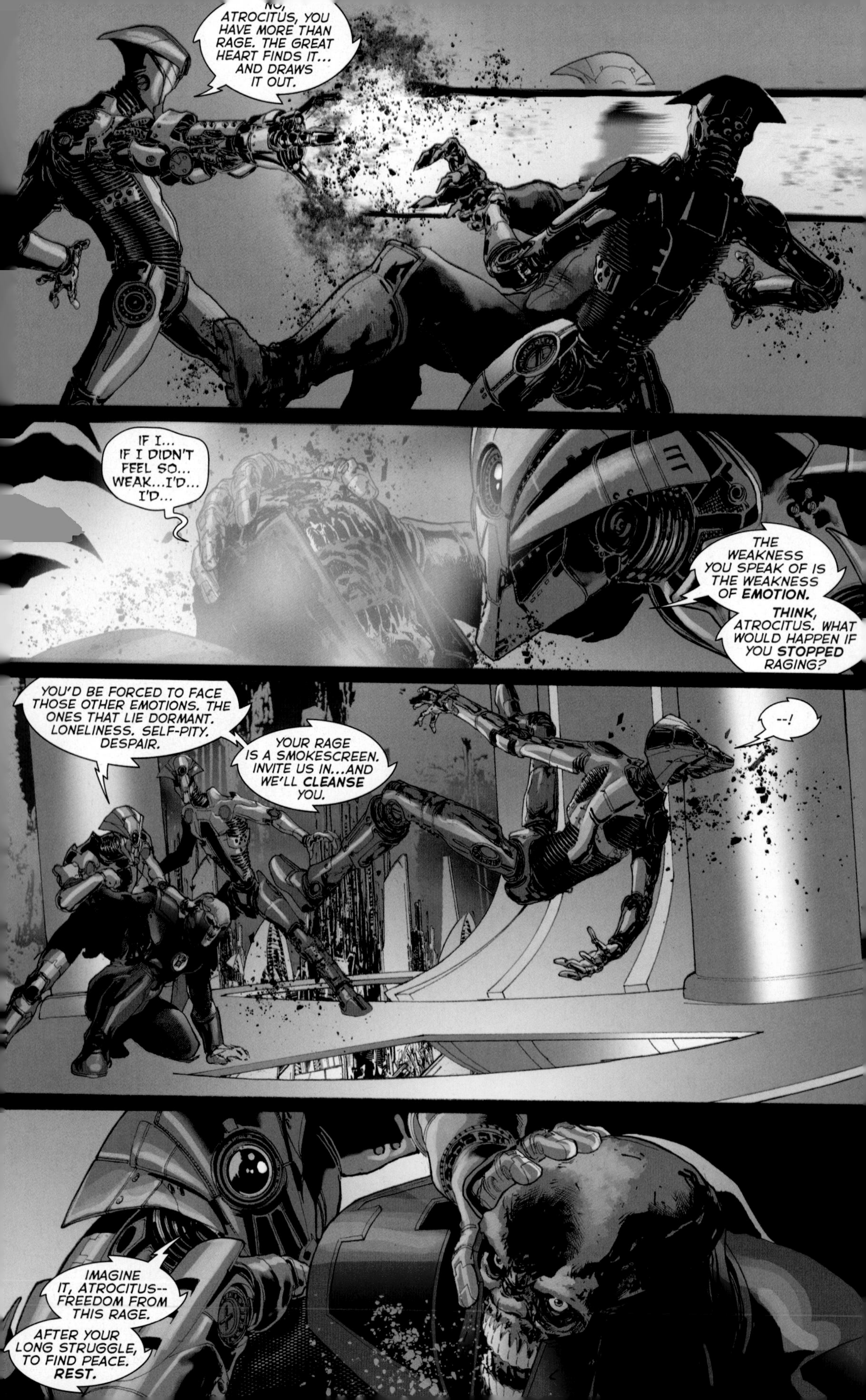
NO, ATROCITUS, YOU HAVE MORE THAN RAGE. THE GREAT HEART FINDS IT... AND DRAWS IT OUT.
IF I... IF I DIDN'T FEEL SO... WEAK...I'D... I'D...
THE WEAKNESS YOU SPEAK OF IS THE WEAKNESS OF EMOTION.
THINK, ATROCITUS. WHAT WOULD HAPPEN IF YOU STOPPED RAGING?
YOU'D BE FORCED TO FACE THOSE OTHER EMOTIONS. THE ONES THAT LIE DORMANT. LONELINESS. SELF-PITY. DESPAIR.
YOUR RAGE IS A SMOKESCREEN. INVITE US IN...AND WE'LL CLEANSE YOU.
--!
IMAGINE IT, ATROCITUS-- FREEDOM FROM THIS RAGE.
AFTER YOUR LONG STRUGGLE, TO FIND PEACE. REST.

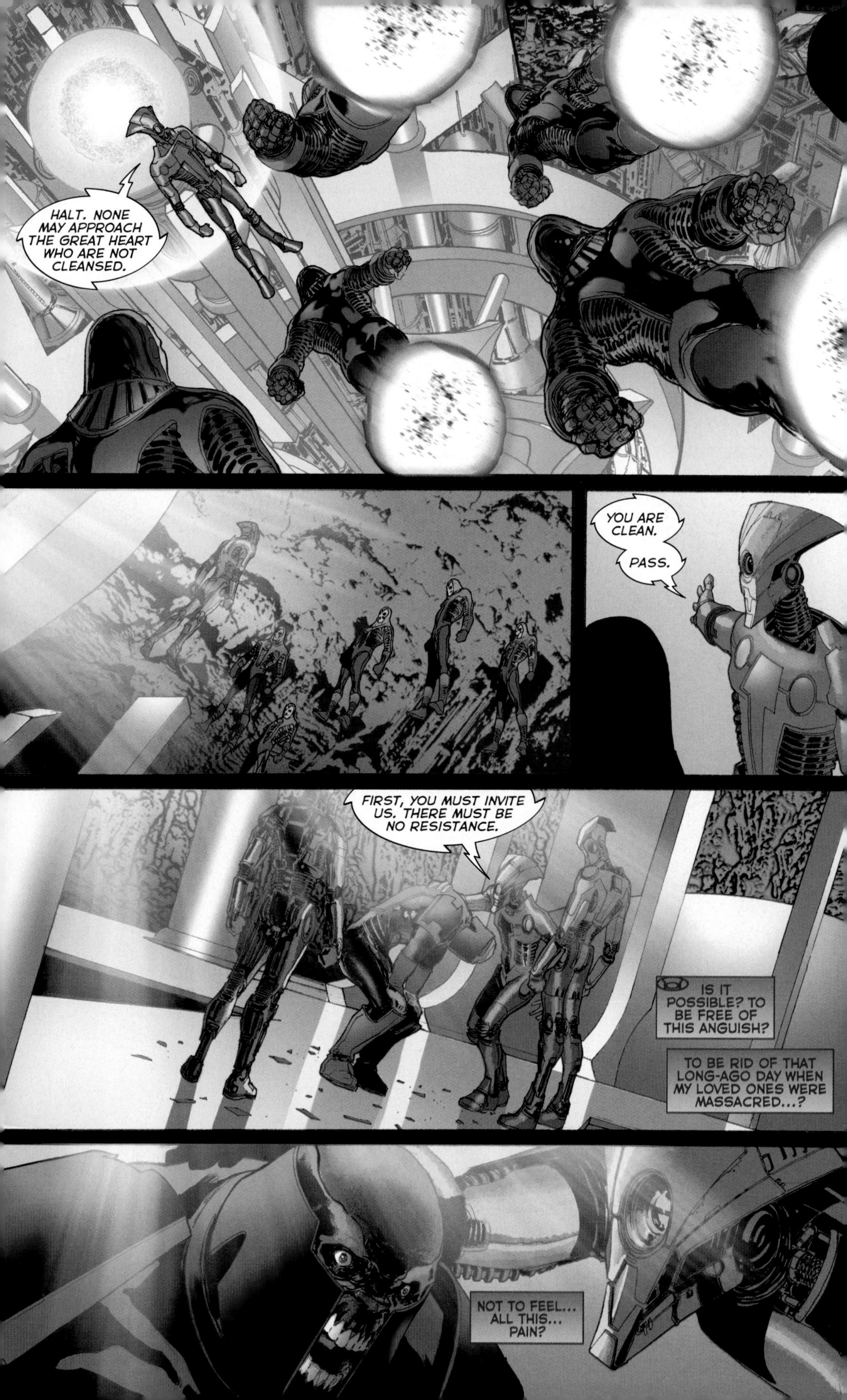
HALT. NONE MAY APPROACH THE GREAT HEART WHO ARE NOT CLEANSED.
YOU ARE CLEAN.
PASS.
FIRST, YOU MUST INVITE US. THERE MUST BE NO RESISTANCE.
IS IT POSSIBLE? TO BE FREE OF THIS ANGUISH?
TO BE RID OF THAT LONG-AGO DAY WHEN MY LOVED ONES WERE MASSACRED...?
NOT TO FEEL... ALL THIS... PAIN?

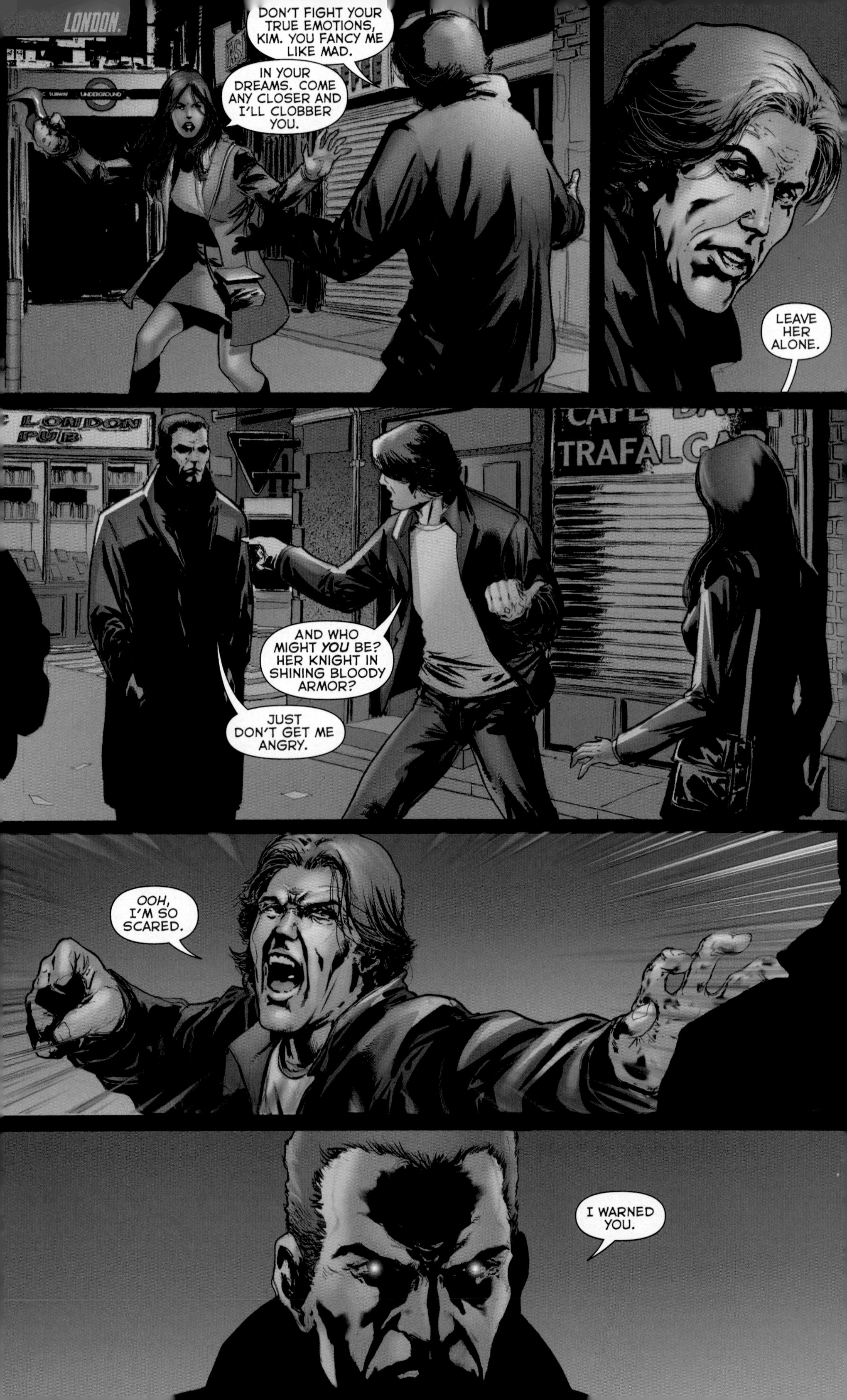
LONDON.
DON'T FIGHT YOUR TRUE EMOTIONS, KIM. YOU FANCY ME LIKE MAD.
IN YOUR DREAMS. COME ANY CLOSER AND I'LL CLOBBER YOU.
LEAVE HER ALONE.
LONDON PUB
CAFE
TRAFALGA
AND WHO MIGHT *YOU* BE? HER KNIGHT IN SHINING BLOODY ARMOR?
JUST DON'T GET ME ANGRY.
OOH, I'M SO SCARED.
I WARNED YOU.

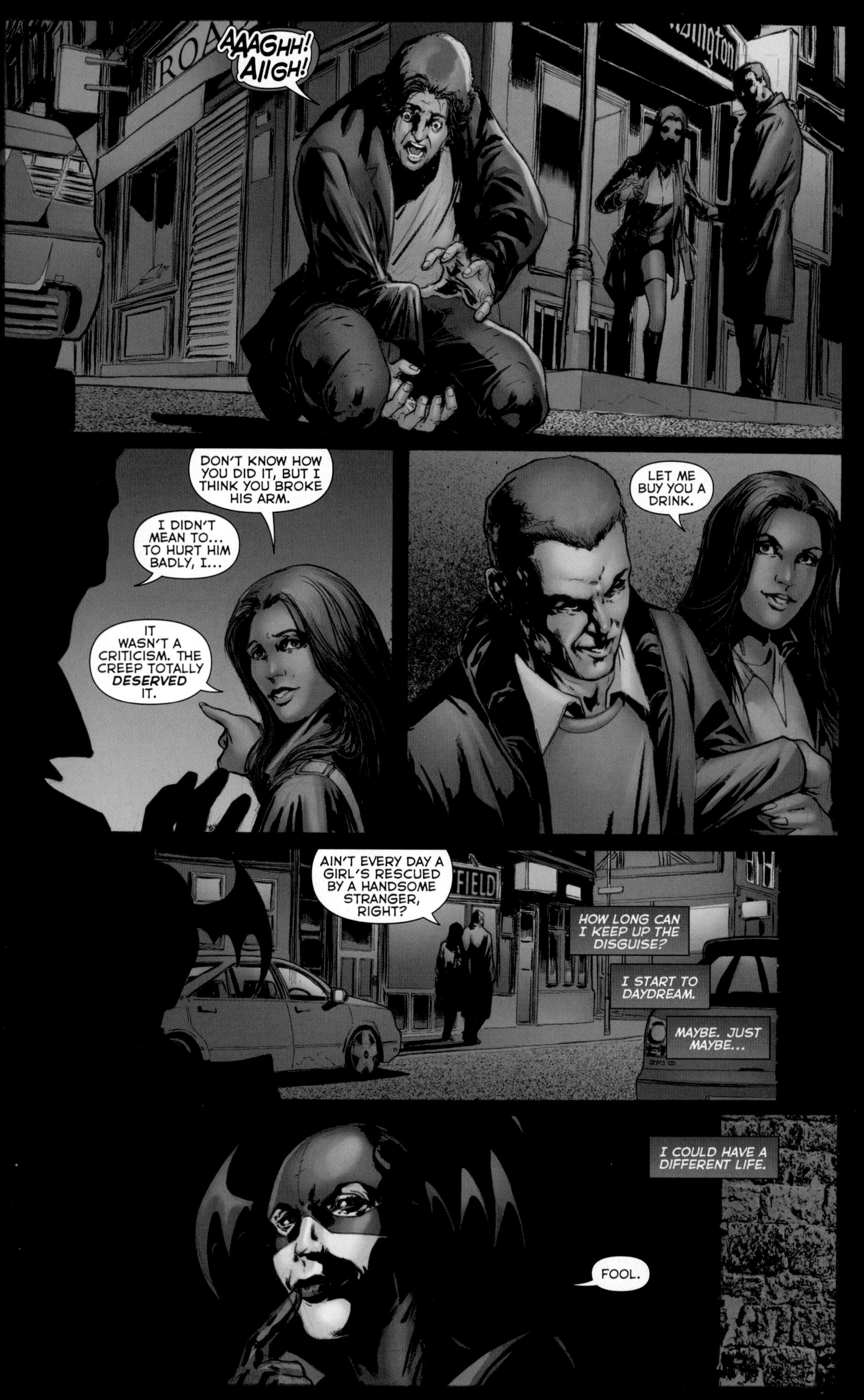
AAAGHH! AIIGH!
DON'T KNOW HOW YOU DID IT, BUT I THINK YOU BROKE HIS ARM.
I DIDN'T MEAN TO... TO HURT HIM BADLY, I...
IT WASN'T A CRITICISM. THE CREEP TOTALLY DESERVED IT.
LET ME BUY YOU A DRINK.
AIN'T EVERY DAY A GIRL'S RESCUED BY A HANDSOME STRANGER, RIGHT?
FIELD
HOW LONG CAN I KEEP UP THE DISGUISE?
I START TO DAYDREAM.
MAYBE. JUST MAYBE...
I COULD HAVE A DIFFERENT LIFE.
FOOL.

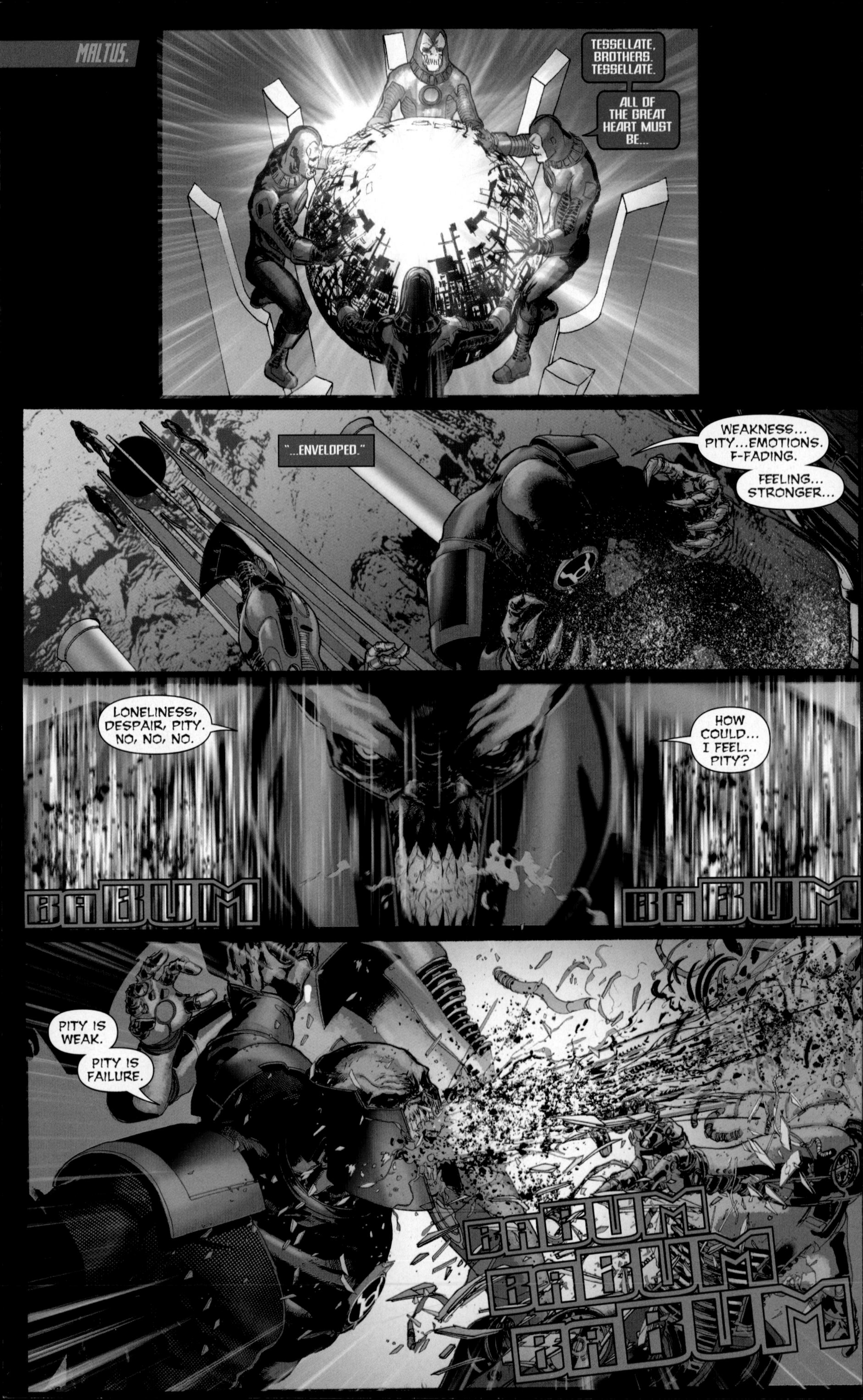
MALTUS.
TESSELLATE, BROTHERS. TESSELLATE.
ALL OF THE GREAT HEART MUST BE...
"...ENVELOPED."
WEAKNESS... PITY...EMOTIONS. F-FADING.
FEELING... STRONGER...
LONELINESS, DESPAIR, PITY. NO, NO, NO.
HOW COULD... I FEEL... PITY?
BA BUM
BA BUM
PITY IS WEAK.
PITY IS FAILURE.
BA BUM
BA BUM
BA BUM

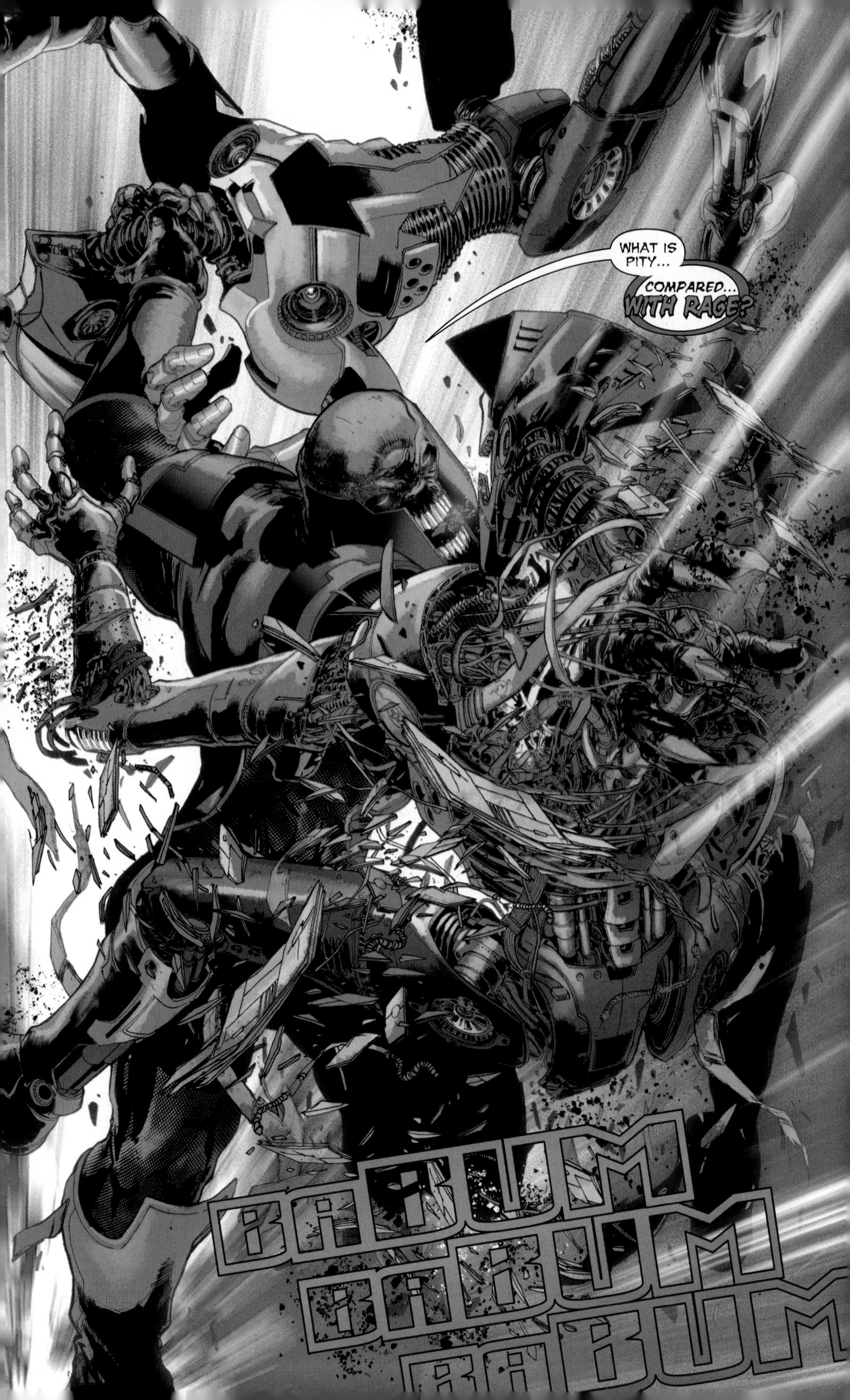
WHAT IS PITY...
COMPARED... WITH RAGE?
BRABUM
BRABUM
BRABUM

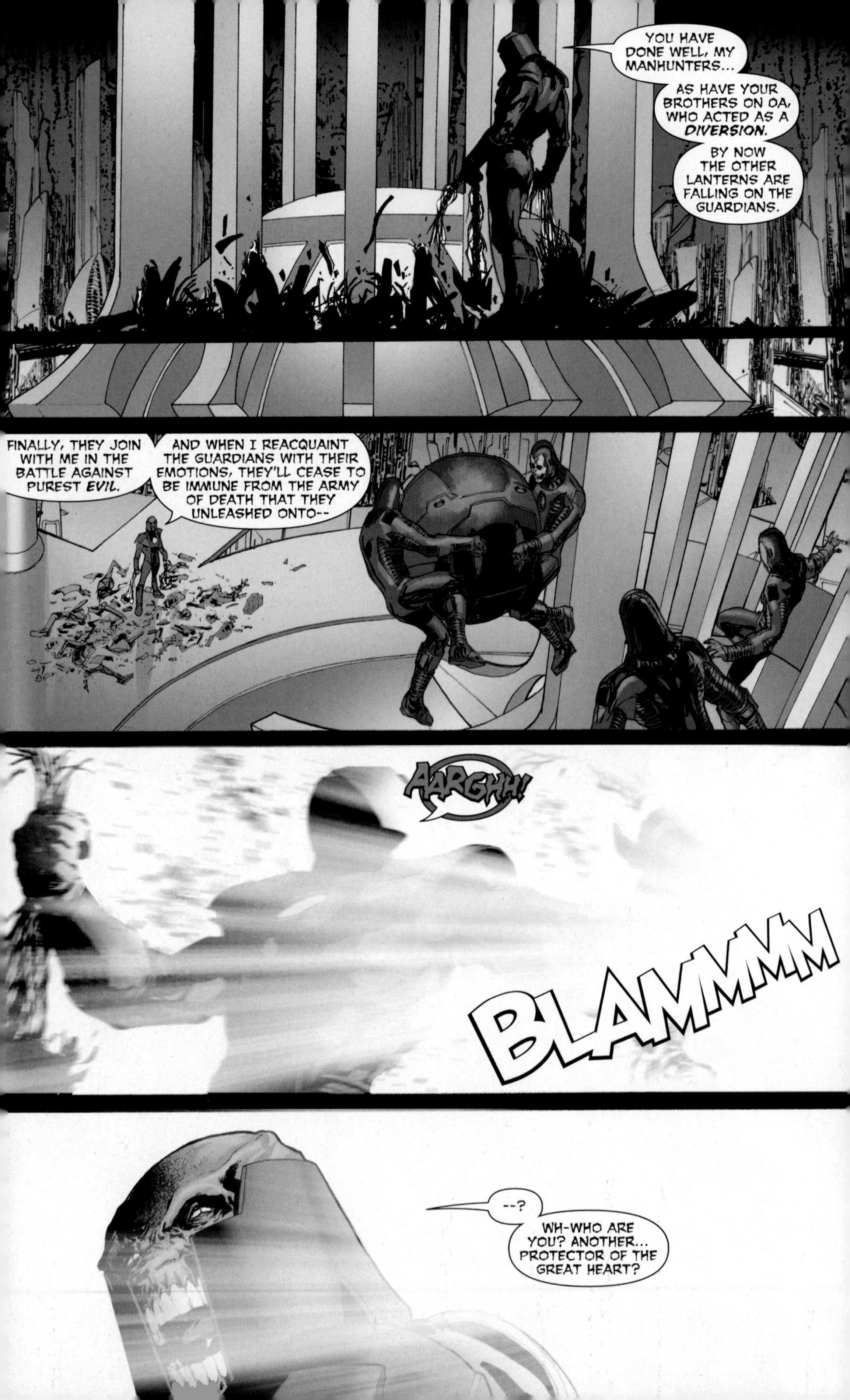
YOU HAVE DONE WELL, MY MANHUNTERS...
AS HAVE YOUR BROTHERS ON OA, WHO ACTED AS A DIVERSION.
BY NOW THE OTHER LANTERNS ARE FALLING ON THE GUARDIANS.
FINALLY, THEY JOIN WITH ME IN THE BATTLE AGAINST PUREST EVIL.
AND WHEN I REACQUAINT THE GUARDIANS WITH THEIR EMOTIONS, THEY'LL CEASE TO BE IMMUNE FROM THE ARMY OF DEATH THAT THEY UNLEASHED ONTO--
AARGHH!
BLAMMMM
--?
WH-WHO ARE YOU? ANOTHER... PROTECTOR OF THE GREAT HEART?

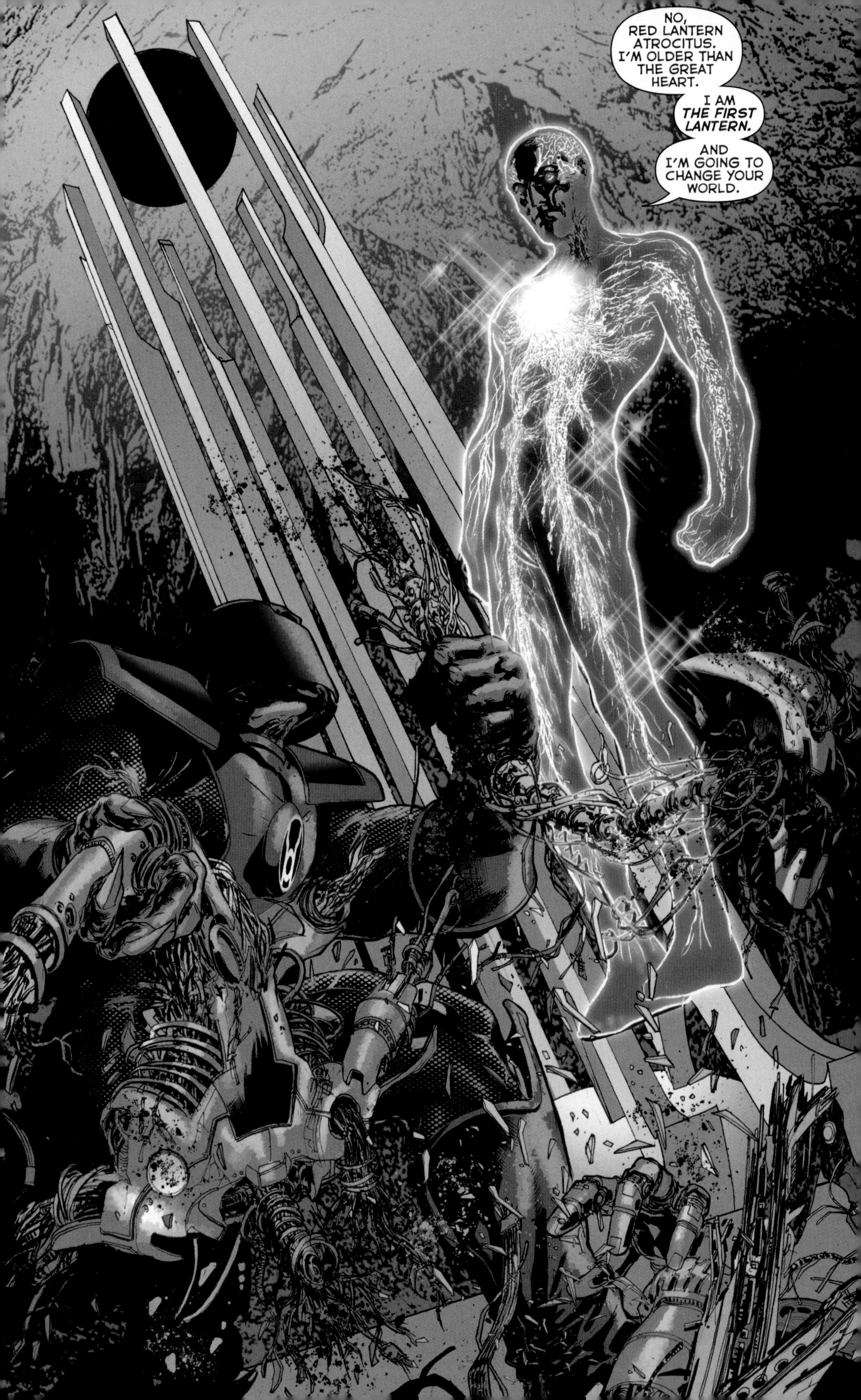
NO, RED LANTERN ATROCITUS. I'M OLDER THAN THE GREAT HEART.
I AM *THE FIRST LANTERN.*
AND I'M GOING TO CHANGE YOUR WORLD.

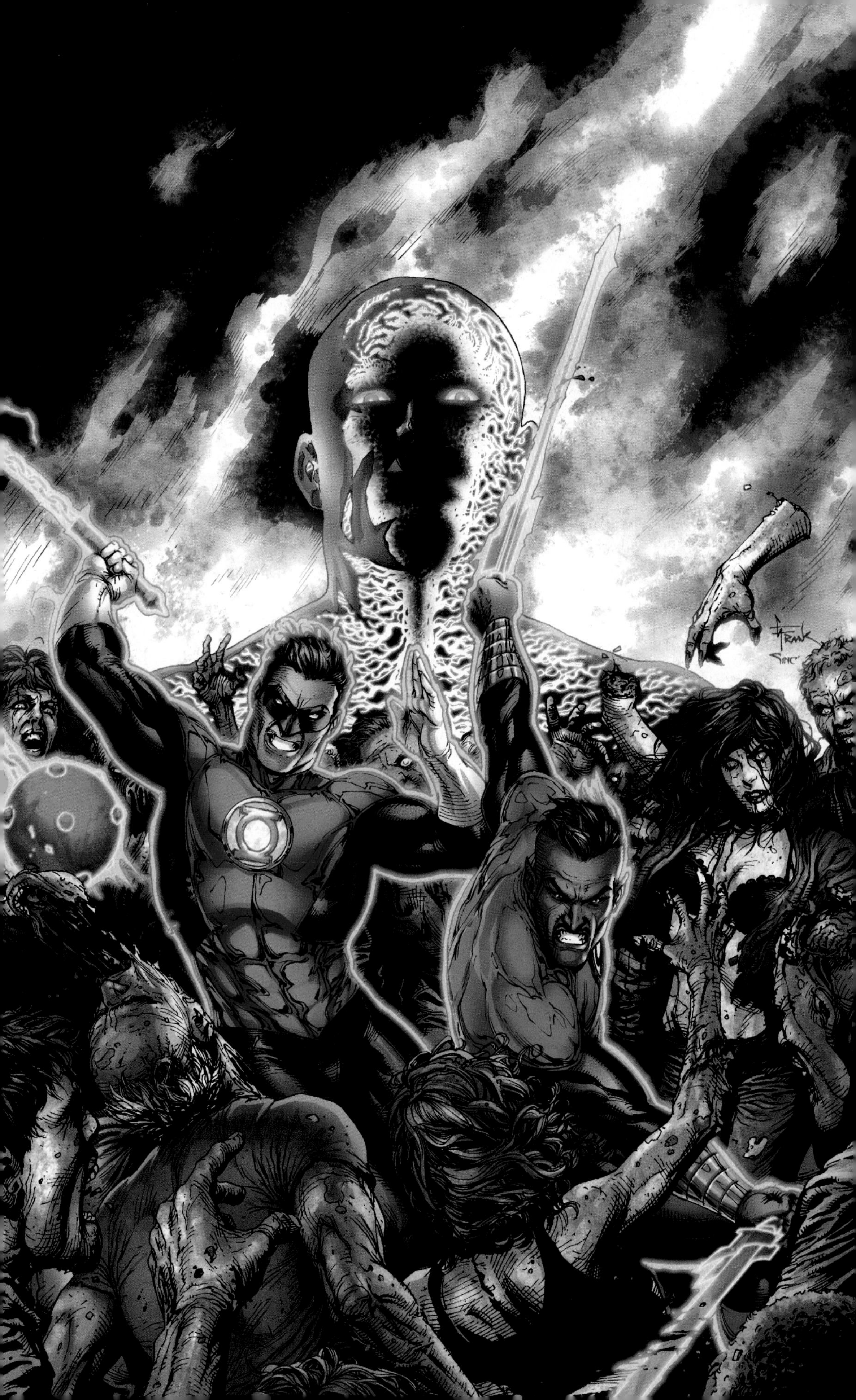

PART FIVE: DEAD OR ALIVE, YOU'RE COMING WITH ME!

GEOFF JOHNS writer **SZYMON KUDRANSKI** artist **ARDIAN SYAF** penciller **MARK IRWIN** inker
cover art by **GARY FRANK** & **ALEX SINCLAIR**

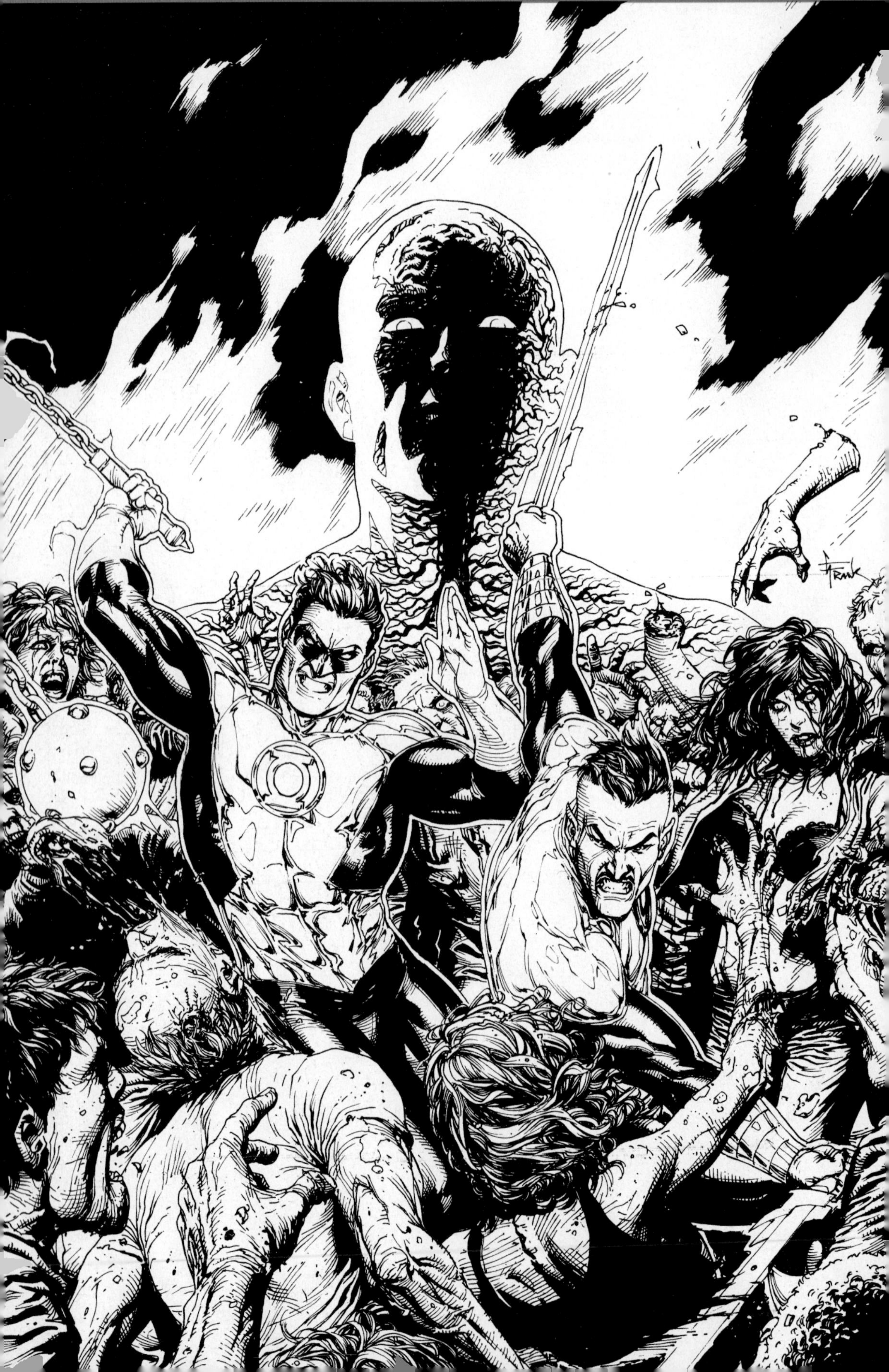

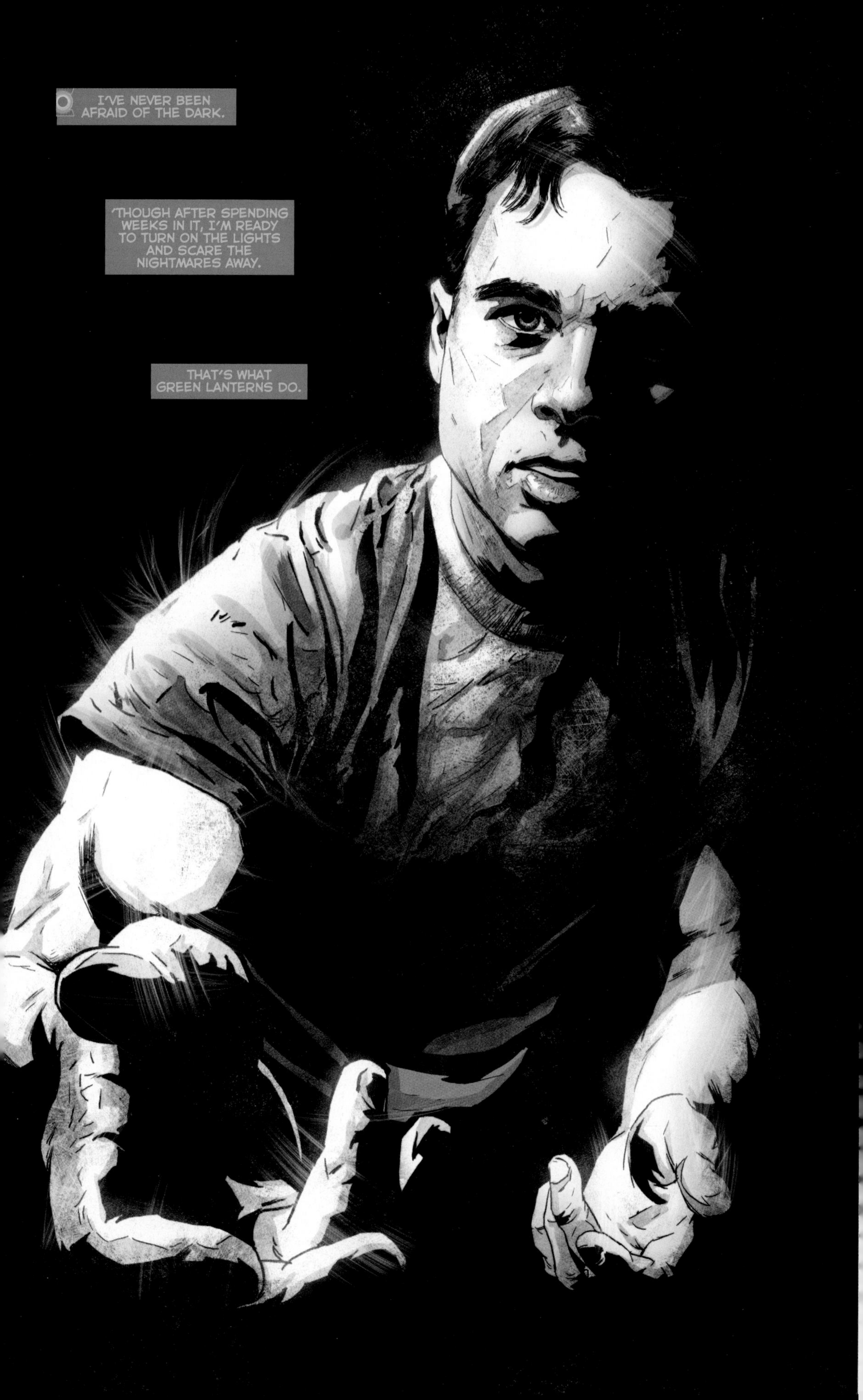
I'VE NEVER BEEN AFRAID OF THE DARK.
'THOUGH AFTER SPENDING WEEKS IN IT, I'M READY TO TURN ON THE LIGHTS AND SCARE THE NIGHTMARES AWAY.
THAT'S WHAT GREEN LANTERNS DO.

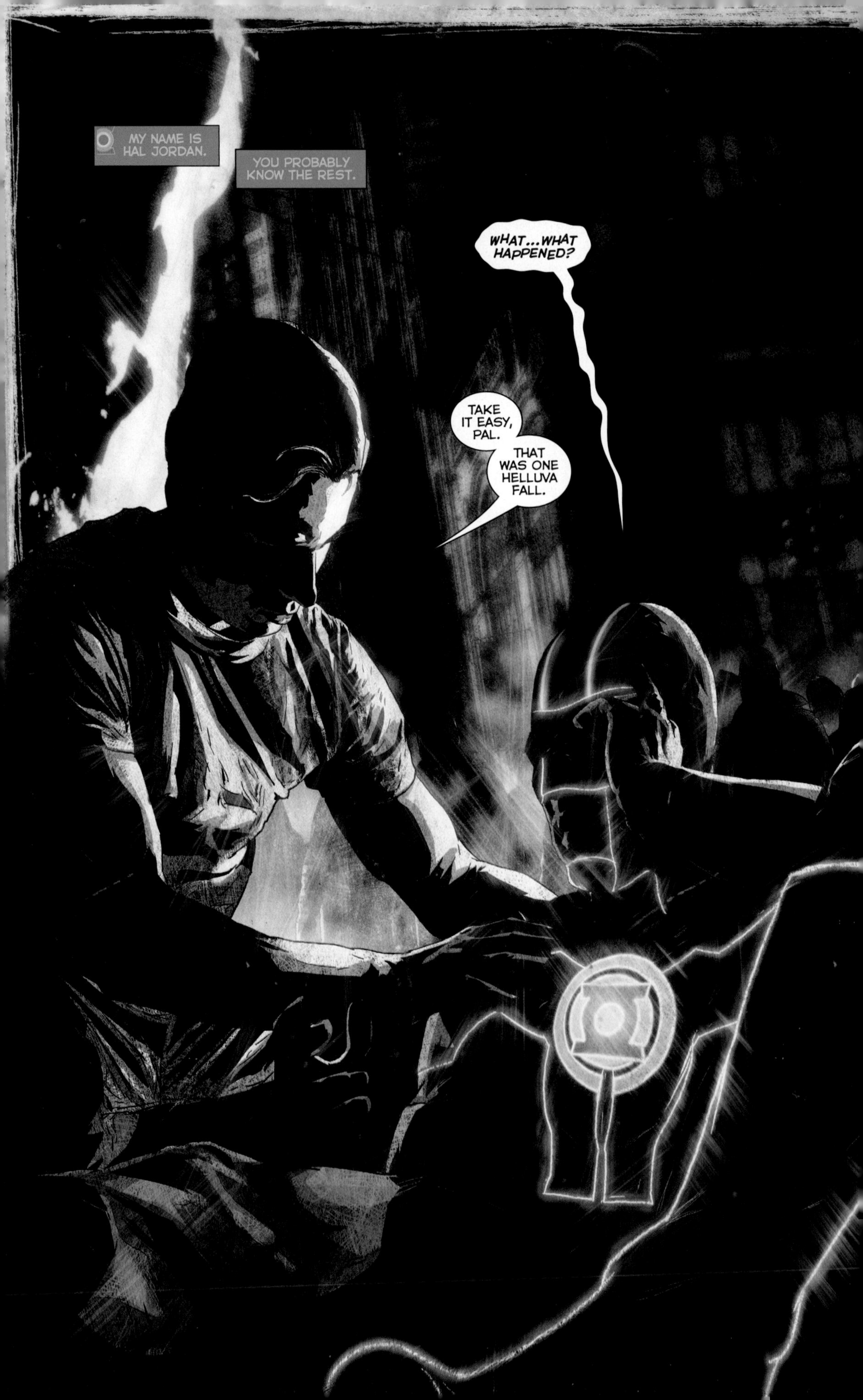
MY NAME IS HAL JORDAN.
YOU PROBABLY KNOW THE REST.
WHAT...WHAT HAPPENED?
TAKE IT EASY, PAL.
THAT WAS ONE HELLUVA FALL.

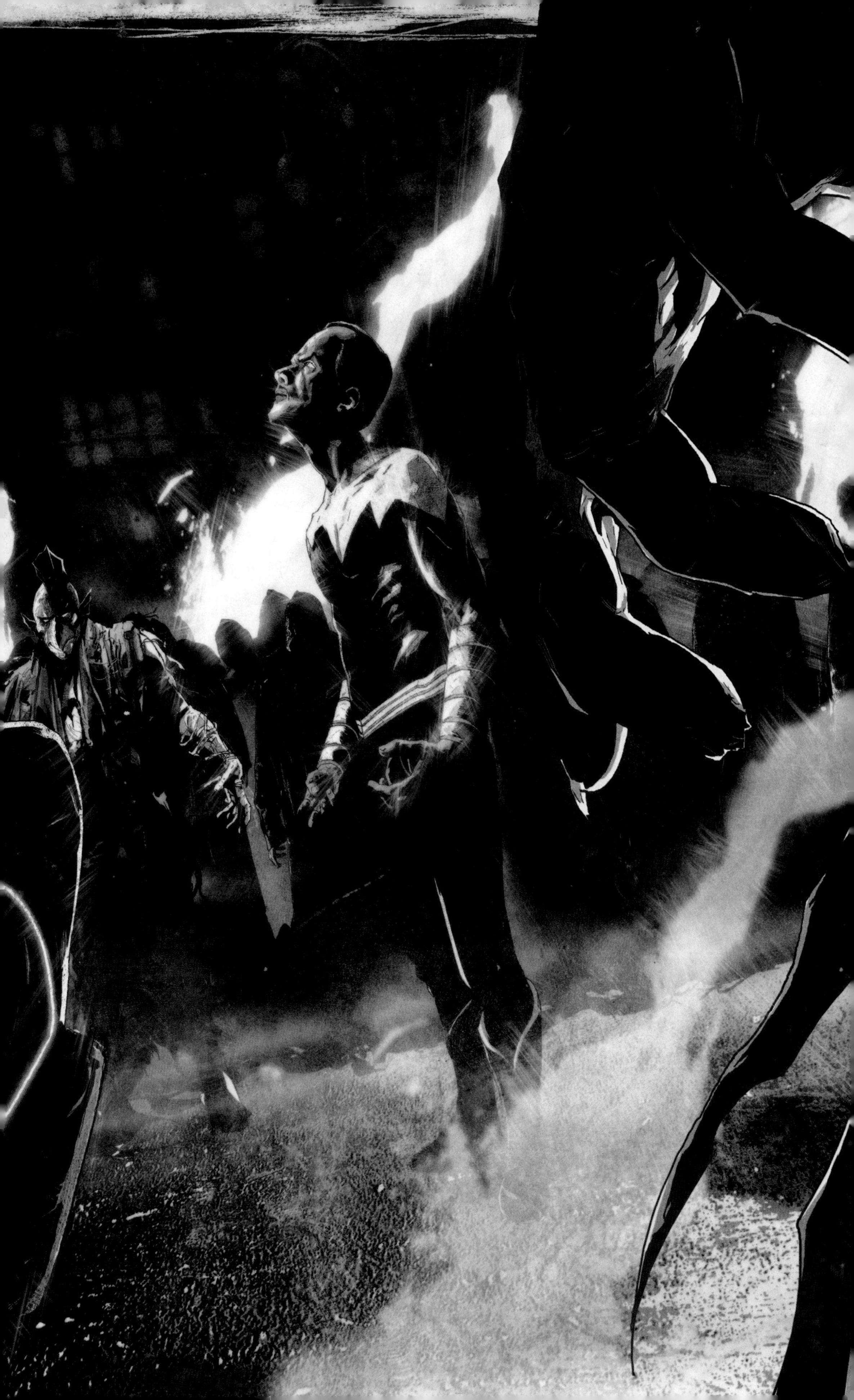

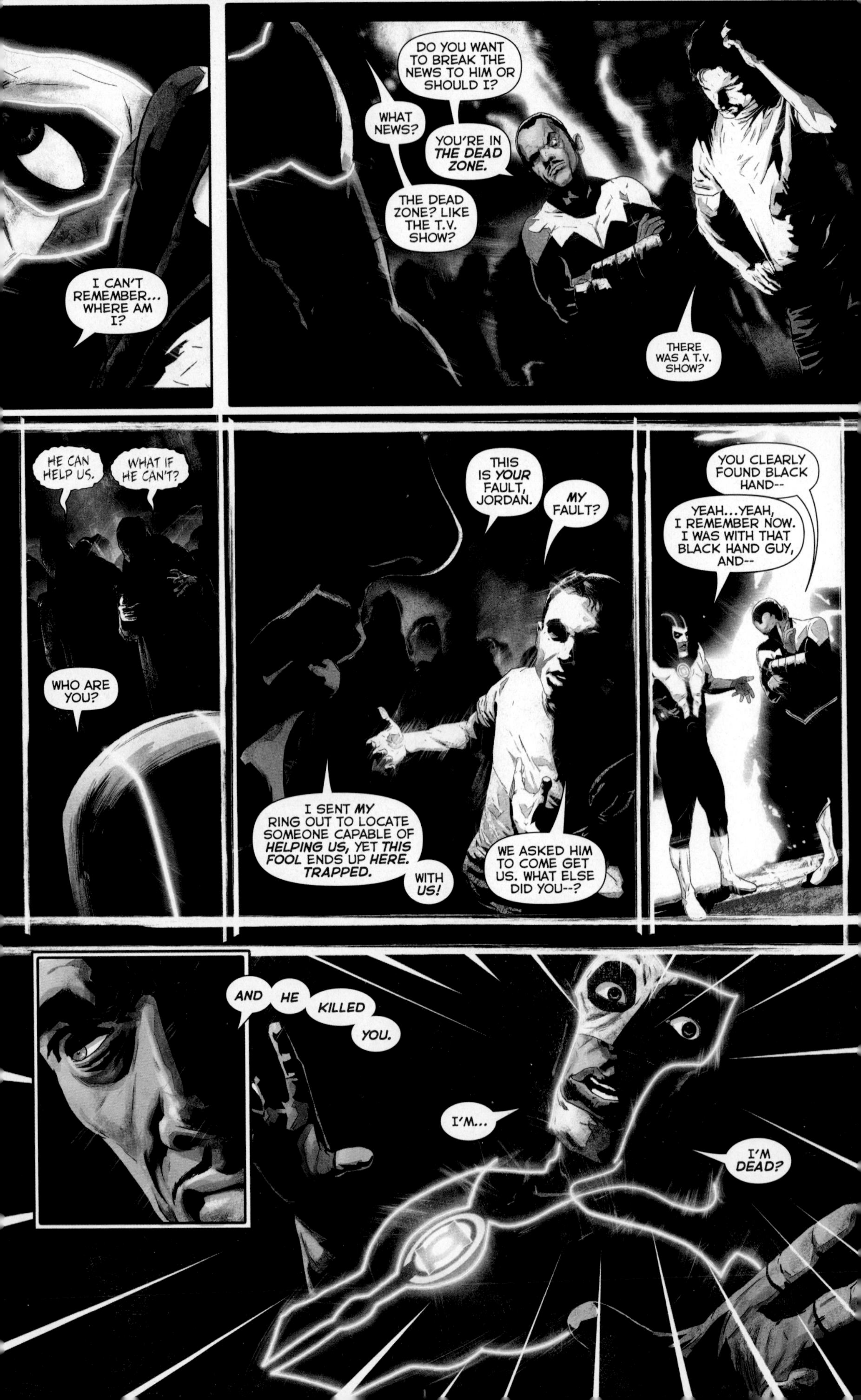

I CAN'T REMEMBER... WHERE AM I?
DO YOU WANT TO BREAK THE NEWS TO HIM OR SHOULD I?
WHAT NEWS?
YOU'RE IN *THE DEAD ZONE.*
THE DEAD ZONE? LIKE THE T.V. SHOW?
THERE WAS A T.V. SHOW?
HE CAN HELP US.
WHAT IF HE CAN'T?
WHO ARE YOU?
THIS IS *YOUR* FAULT, JORDAN.
MY FAULT?
I SENT *MY* RING OUT TO LOCATE SOMEONE CAPABLE OF *HELPING US,* YET *THIS FOOL* ENDS UP *HERE. TRAPPED.*
WITH *US!*
WE ASKED HIM TO COME GET US. WHAT ELSE DID YOU--?
YOU CLEARLY FOUND BLACK HAND--
YEAH...YEAH, I REMEMBER NOW. I WAS WITH THAT BLACK HAND GUY, AND--
AND HE KILLED YOU.
I'M...
I'M *DEAD?*

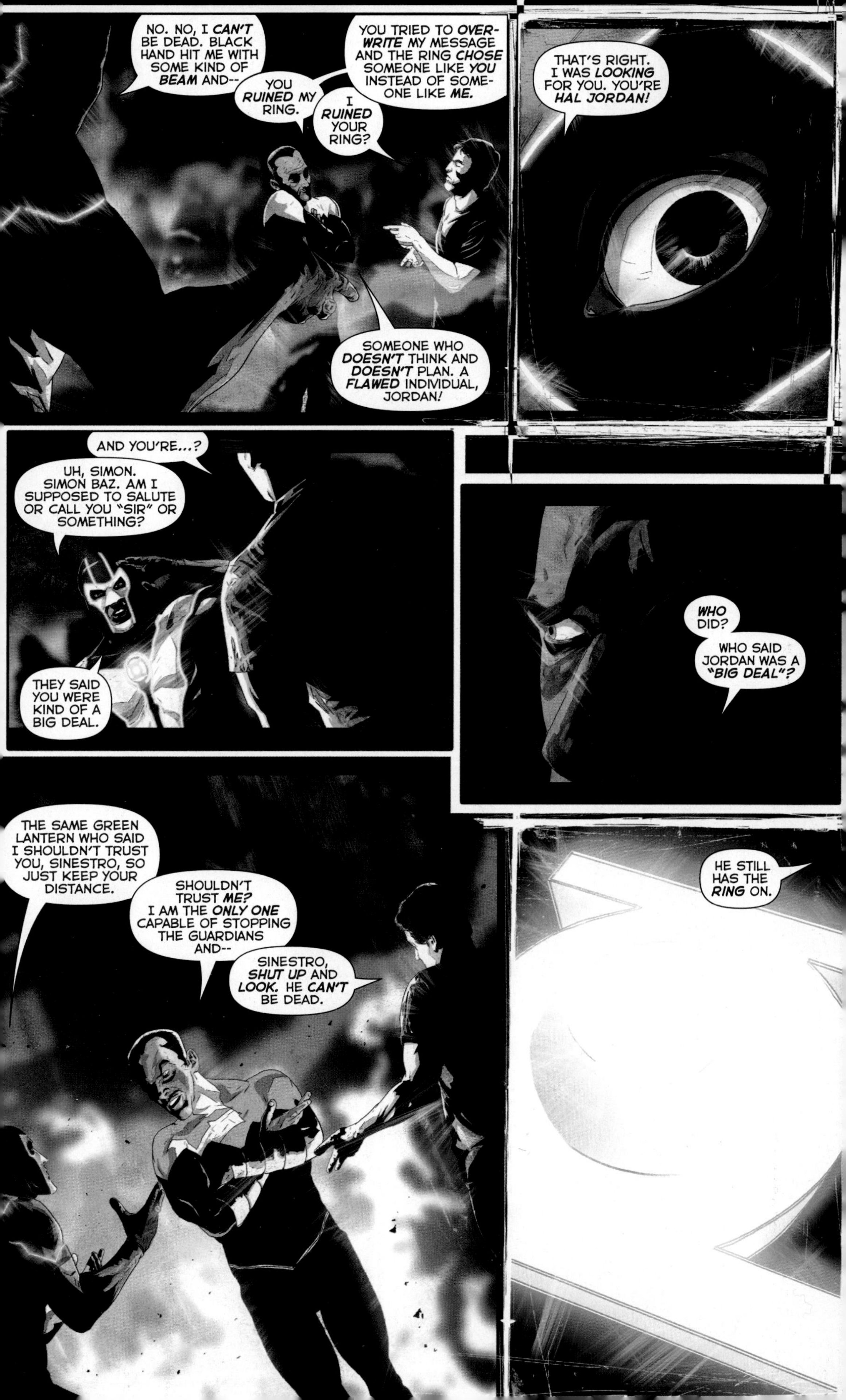
NO. NO, I CAN'T BE DEAD. BLACK HAND HIT ME WITH SOME KIND OF BEAM AND--
YOU RUINED MY RING.
YOU TRIED TO OVER-WRITE MY MESSAGE AND THE RING CHOSE SOMEONE LIKE YOU INSTEAD OF SOME-ONE LIKE ME.
I RUINED YOUR RING?
SOMEONE WHO DOESN'T THINK AND DOESN'T PLAN. A FLAWED INDIVIDUAL, JORDAN!
THAT'S RIGHT. I WAS LOOKING FOR YOU. YOU'RE HAL JORDAN!
AND YOU'RE...?
UH, SIMON. SIMON BAZ. AM I SUPPOSED TO SALUTE OR CALL YOU "SIR" OR SOMETHING?
THEY SAID YOU WERE KIND OF A BIG DEAL.
WHO DID?
WHO SAID JORDAN WAS A "BIG DEAL"?
THE SAME GREEN LANTERN WHO SAID I SHOULDN'T TRUST YOU, SINESTRO, SO JUST KEEP YOUR DISTANCE.
SHOULDN'T TRUST ME? I AM THE ONLY ONE CAPABLE OF STOPPING THE GUARDIANS AND--
SINESTRO, SHUT UP AND LOOK. HE CAN'T BE DEAD.
HE STILL HAS THE RING ON.

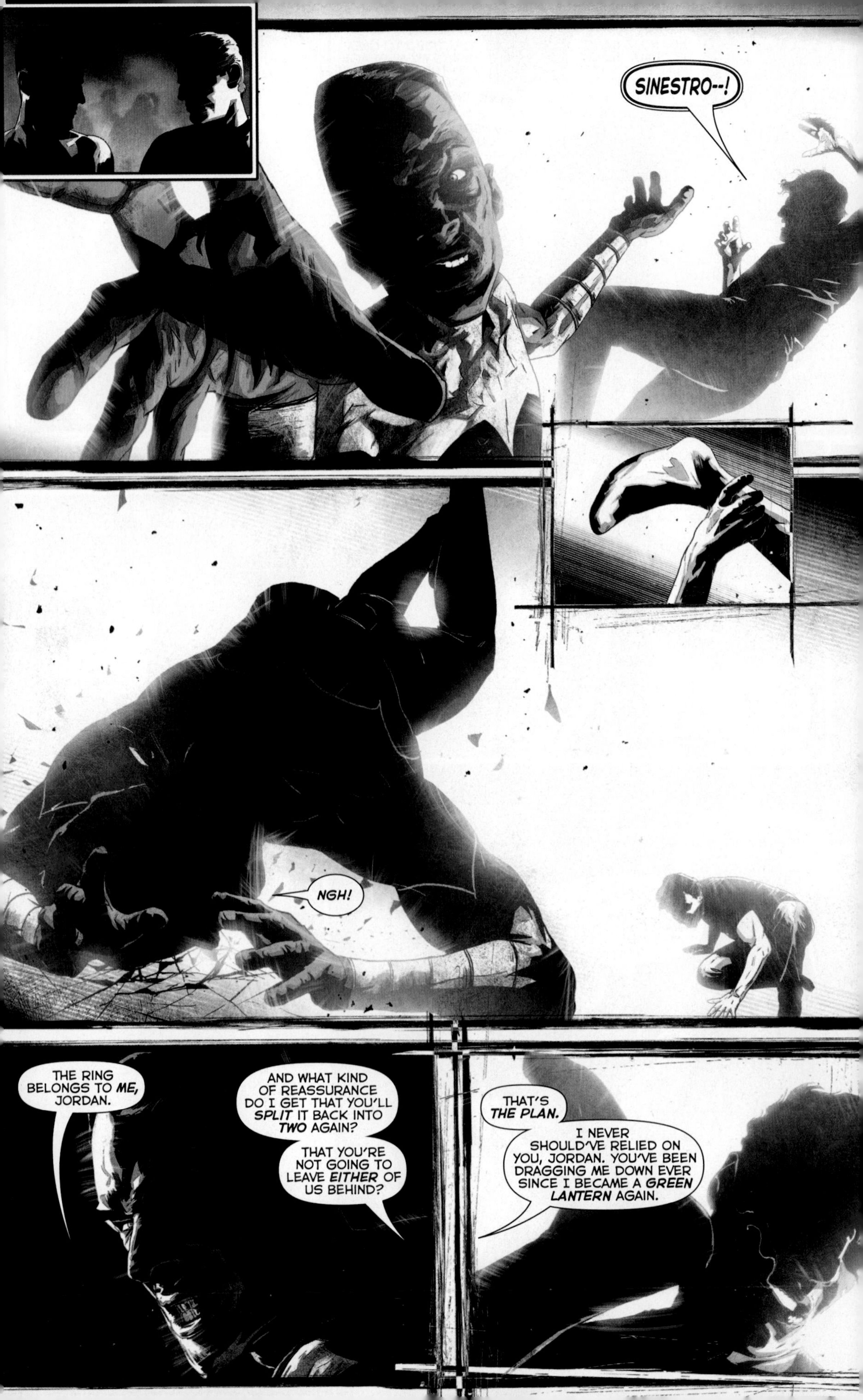
SINESTRO--!
NGH!
THE RING BELONGS TO ME, JORDAN.
AND WHAT KIND OF REASSURANCE DO I GET THAT YOU'LL SPLIT IT BACK INTO TWO AGAIN?
THAT YOU'RE NOT GOING TO LEAVE EITHER OF US BEHIND?
THAT'S THE PLAN.
I NEVER SHOULD'VE RELIED ON YOU, JORDAN. YOU'VE BEEN DRAGGING ME DOWN EVER SINCE I BECAME A GREEN LANTERN AGAIN.

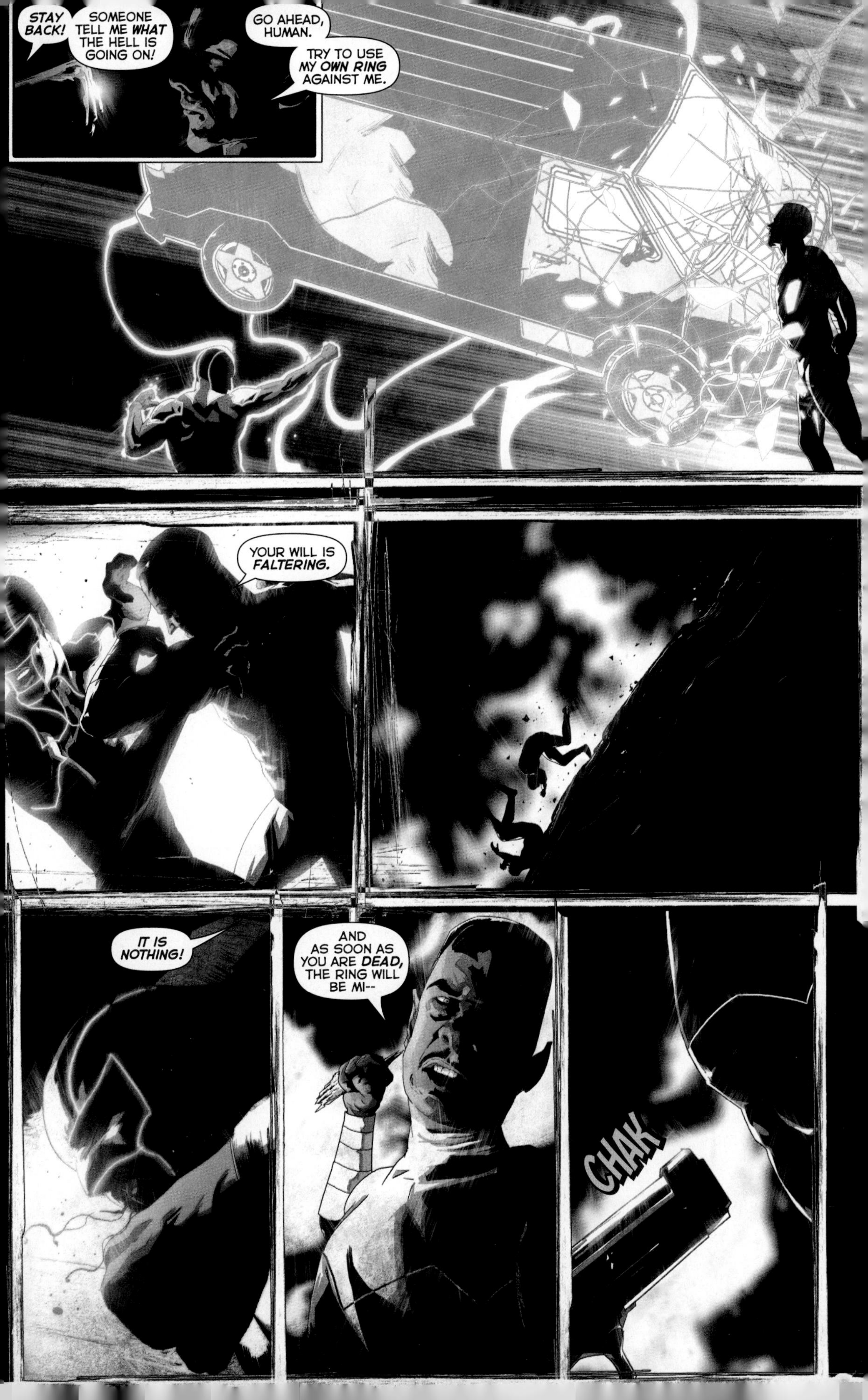
STAY BACK!
SOMEONE TELL ME WHAT THE HELL IS GOING ON!
GO AHEAD, HUMAN.
TRY TO USE MY OWN RING AGAINST ME.
YOUR WILL IS FALTERING.
IT IS NOTHING!
AND AS SOON AS YOU ARE DEAD, THE RING WILL BE MI--
CHAK

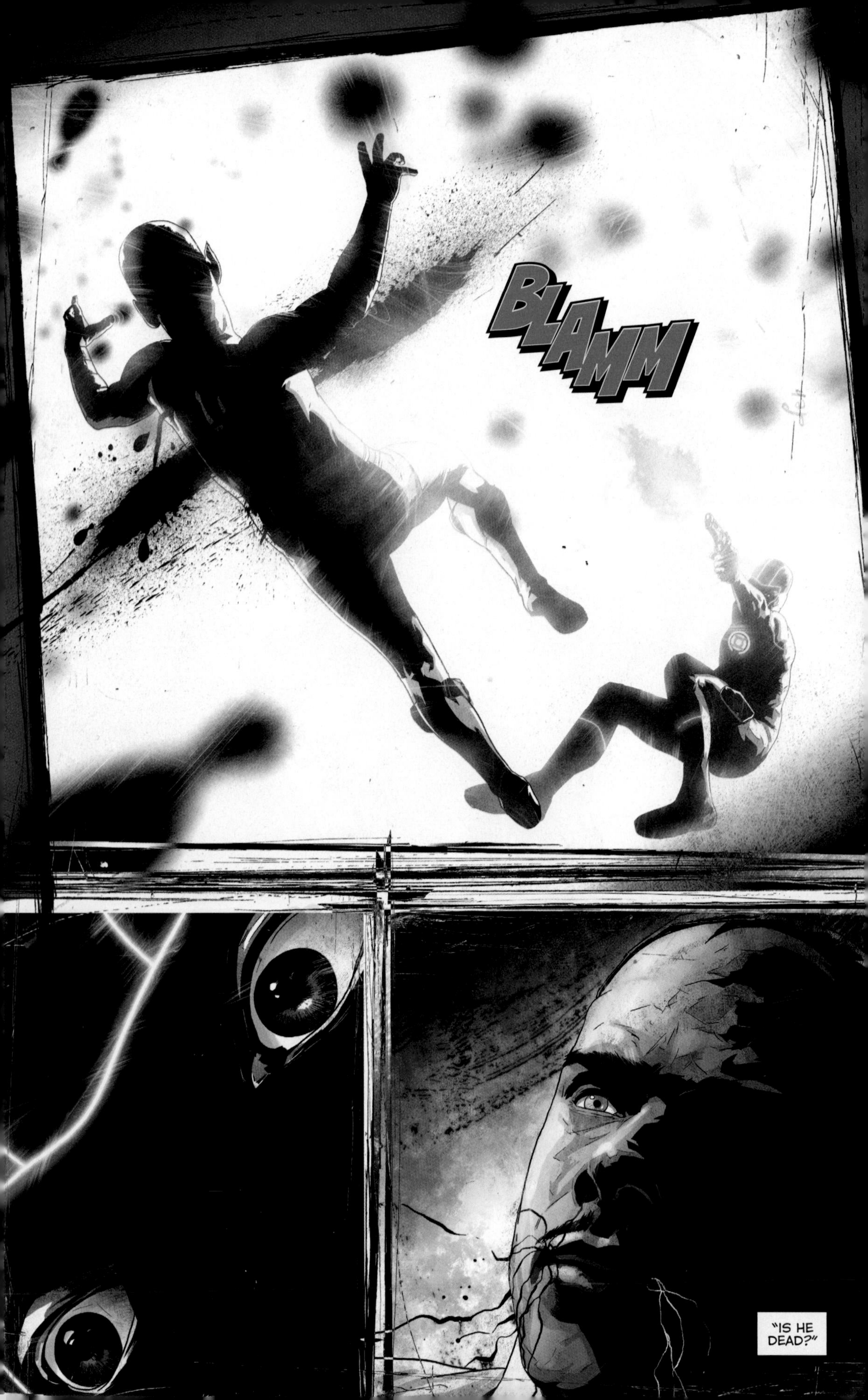
BLAMM
"IS HE DEAD?"

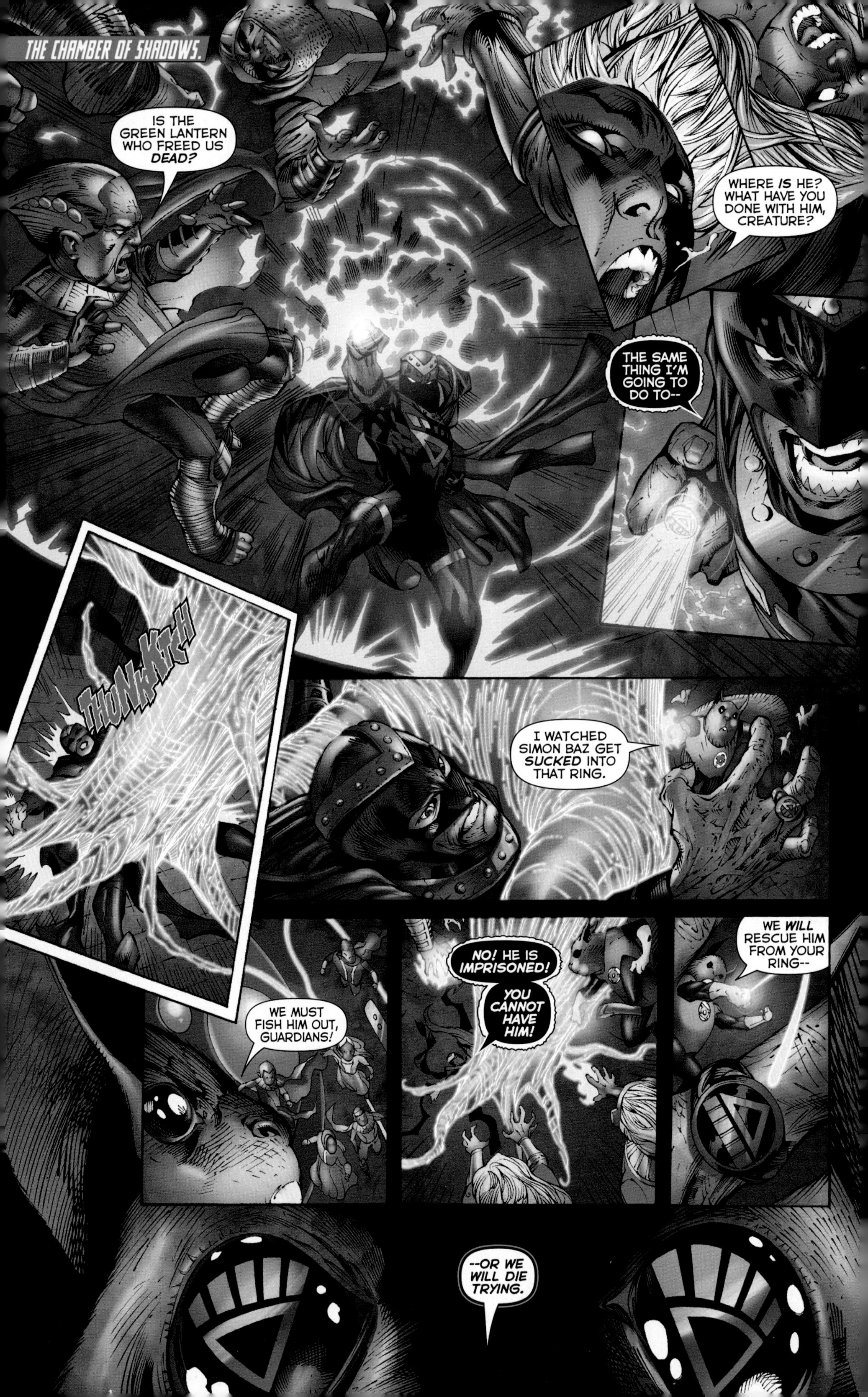
THE CHAMBER OF SHADOWS.
IS THE GREEN LANTERN WHO FREED US DEAD?
WHERE IS HE? WHAT HAVE YOU DONE WITH HIM, CREATURE?
THE SAME THING I'M GOING TO DO TO--
THUNKKTCH
I WATCHED SIMON BAZ GET SUCKED INTO THAT RING.
WE MUST FISH HIM OUT, GUARDIANS!
NO! HE IS IMPRISONED!
YOU CANNOT HAVE HIM!
WE WILL RESCUE HIM FROM YOUR RING--
--OR WE WILL DIE TRYING.

PERHAPS SINESTRO WAS INCORRECT REGARDING THE RING'S **CHOICE** OF INDIVIDUAL. HE MAY BE MORE LIKE SINESTRO THAN WE THOUGHT.

I... I THOUGHT HE WAS GOING TO **KILL** ME.

IS SINESTRO DEAD, TOMAR?

YES.

BUT AS I SAID BEFORE, HAL, WE'RE ALL DEAD IN HERE. UNLIKE ME, HOWEVER, YOU AND SINESTRO AND SIMON BAZ STILL HAVE **ONE FOOT** PLANTED ON THE **OTHER SIDE**.

NNGGK!

YOU **SEE**? YOU CANNOT **DIE** IN HERE AS LONG AS YOU HAVE THE **WILL** TO LIVE.

HEY, MAN, UH, SORRY ABOUT THAT?

JUST YOU WAIT UNTIL THAT RING IS MINE AGAIN, HUMAN.

YOU HAVE MORE TO WORRY ABOUT THAN **PETTY REVENGE**, SINESTRO.

YOUR **EMOTIONAL VOLATILITY** HAS ALWAYS BEEN YOUR WEAKNESS.

AND **TRUSTING** IN OTHERS WAS YOURS, TOMAR-RE. YOU TRUSTED TOO FREELY. YOU PUT YOUR LIFE AND THE LIVES OF OTHERS INTO THE HANDS OF THOSE CLOSE TO YOU.

BUT THEY **FAILED** YOU AND YOU **DIED** AS A RESULT.

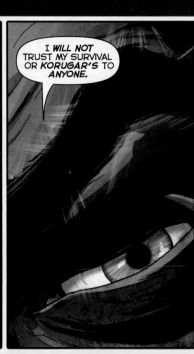

I **WILL NOT** TRUST MY SURVIVAL OR **KORUGAR'S** TO **ANYONE**.

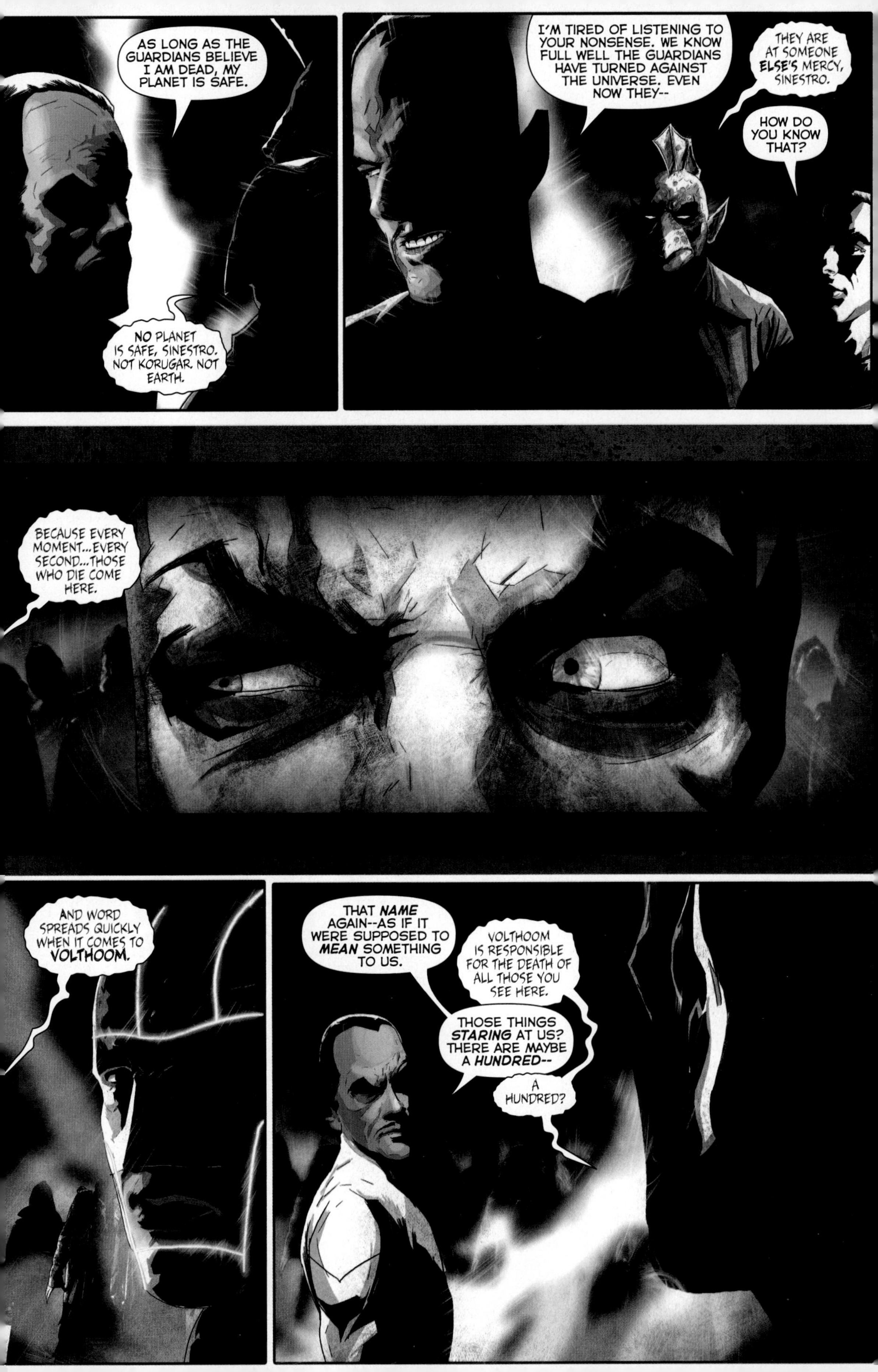
AS LONG AS THE GUARDIANS BELIEVE I AM DEAD, MY PLANET IS SAFE.
NO PLANET IS SAFE, SINESTRO. NOT KORUGAR. NOT EARTH.
I'M TIRED OF LISTENING TO YOUR NONSENSE. WE KNOW FULL WELL THE GUARDIANS HAVE TURNED AGAINST THE UNIVERSE. EVEN NOW THEY--
THEY ARE AT SOMEONE ELSE'S MERCY, SINESTRO.
HOW DO YOU KNOW THAT?
BECAUSE EVERY MOMENT...EVERY SECOND...THOSE WHO DIE COME HERE.
AND WORD SPREADS QUICKLY WHEN IT COMES TO VOLTHOOM.
THAT NAME AGAIN--AS IF IT WERE SUPPOSED TO MEAN SOMETHING TO US.
VOLTHOOM IS RESPONSIBLE FOR THE DEATH OF ALL THOSE YOU SEE HERE.
THOSE THINGS STARING AT US? THERE ARE MAYBE A HUNDRED--
A HUNDRED?

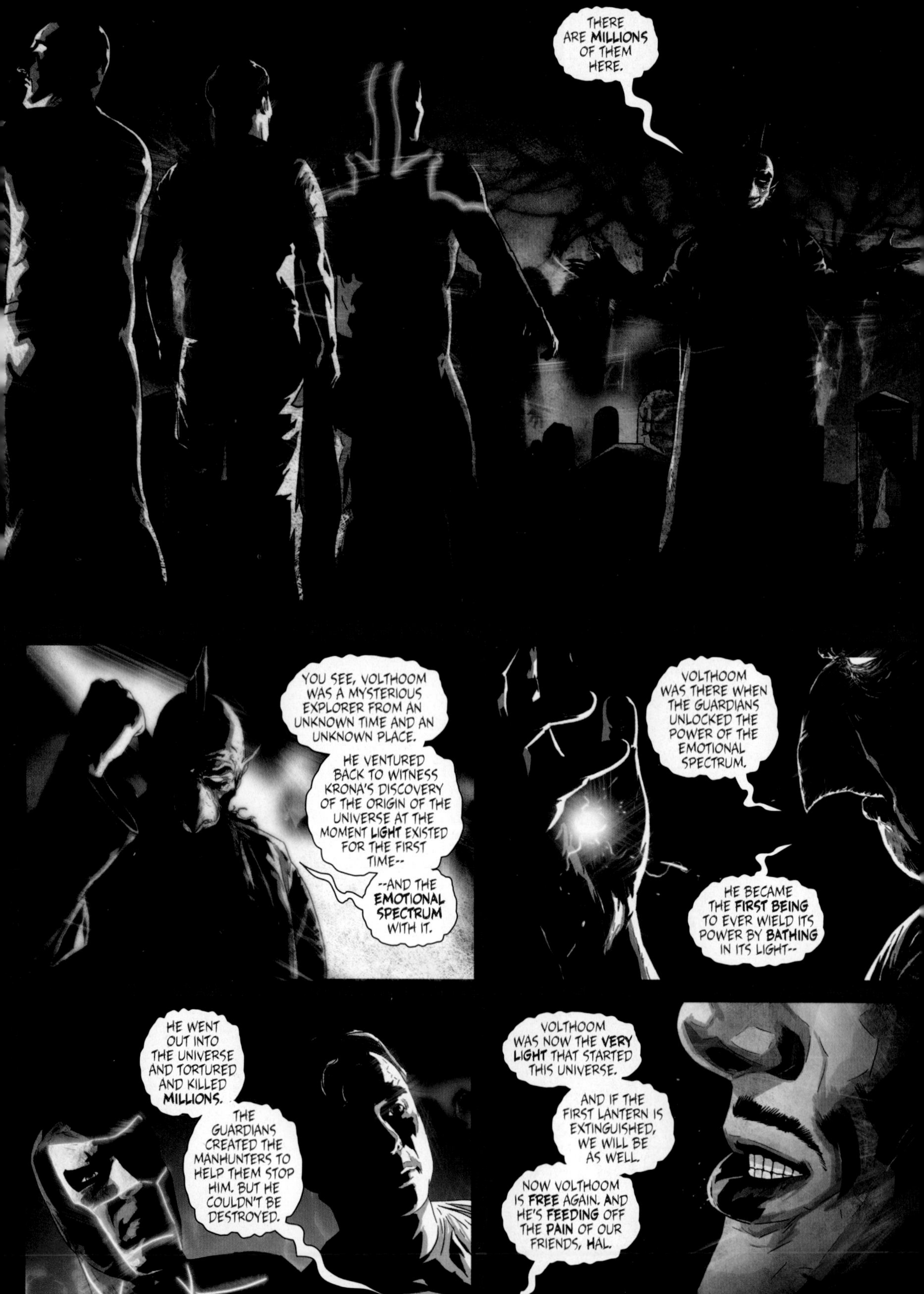
THERE ARE MILLIONS OF THEM HERE.
YOU SEE, VOLTHOOM WAS A MYSTERIOUS EXPLORER FROM AN UNKNOWN TIME AND AN UNKNOWN PLACE.
HE VENTURED BACK TO WITNESS KRONA'S DISCOVERY OF THE ORIGIN OF THE UNIVERSE AT THE MOMENT LIGHT EXISTED FOR THE FIRST TIME--
--AND THE EMOTIONAL SPECTRUM WITH IT.
VOLTHOOM WAS THERE WHEN THE GUARDIANS UNLOCKED THE POWER OF THE EMOTIONAL SPECTRUM.
HE BECAME THE FIRST BEING TO EVER WIELD ITS POWER BY BATHING IN ITS LIGHT--
HE WENT OUT INTO THE UNIVERSE AND TORTURED AND KILLED MILLIONS.
THE GUARDIANS CREATED THE MANHUNTERS TO HELP THEM STOP HIM. BUT HE COULDN'T BE DESTROYED.
VOLTHOOM WAS NOW THE VERY LIGHT THAT STARTED THIS UNIVERSE.
AND IF THE FIRST LANTERN IS EXTINGUISHED, WE WILL BE AS WELL.
NOW VOLTHOOM IS FREE AGAIN. AND HE'S FEEDING OFF THE PAIN OF OUR FRIENDS, HAL.

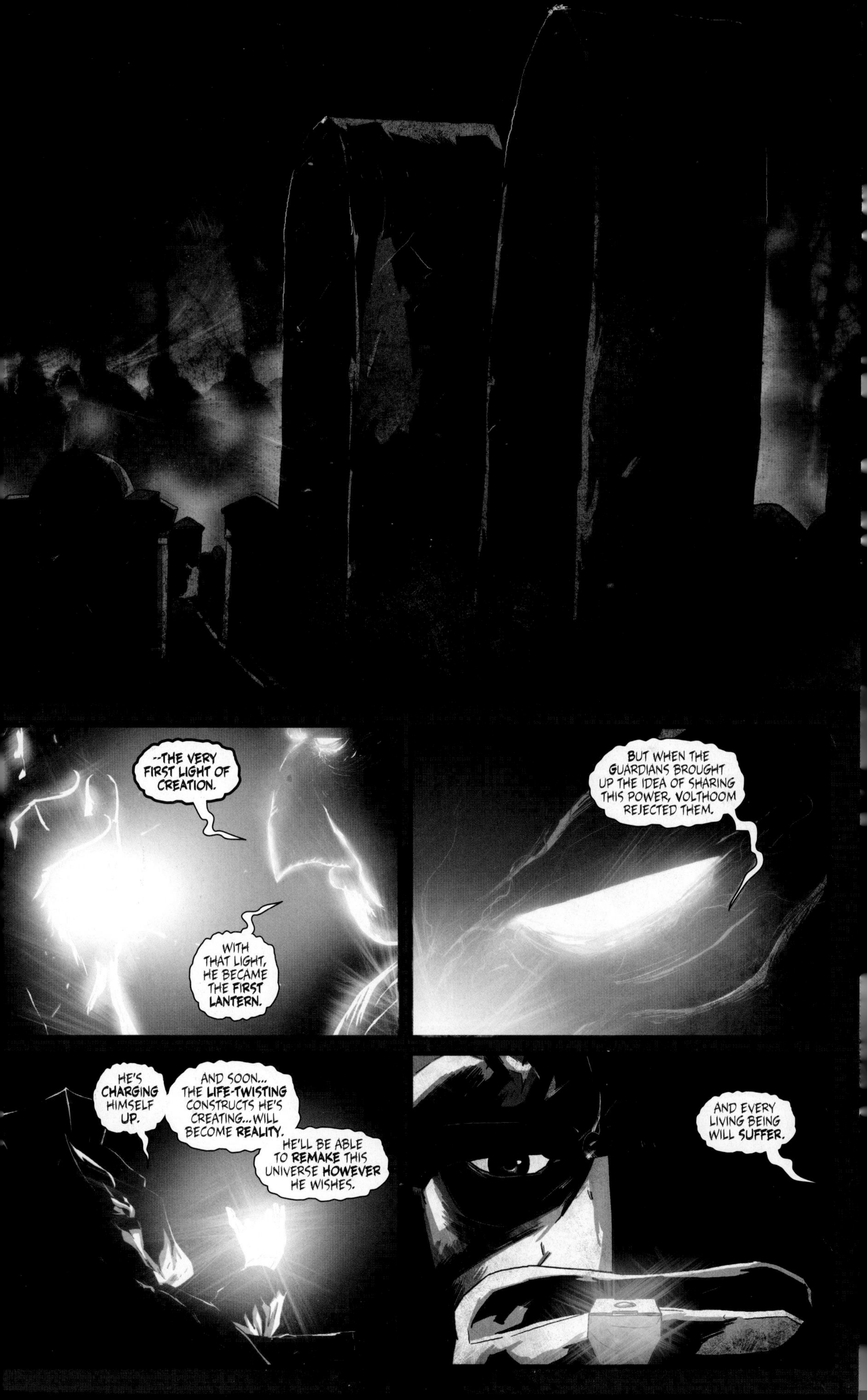

--THE VERY FIRST LIGHT OF CREATION.
WITH THAT LIGHT, HE BECAME THE FIRST LANTERN.
BUT WHEN THE GUARDIANS BROUGHT UP THE IDEA OF SHARING THIS POWER, VOLTHOOM REJECTED THEM.
HE'S CHARGING HIMSELF UP.
AND SOON... THE LIFE-TWISTING CONSTRUCTS HE'S CREATING... WILL BECOME REALITY.
HE'LL BE ABLE TO REMAKE THIS UNIVERSE HOWEVER HE WISHES.
AND EVERY LIVING BEING WILL SUFFER.

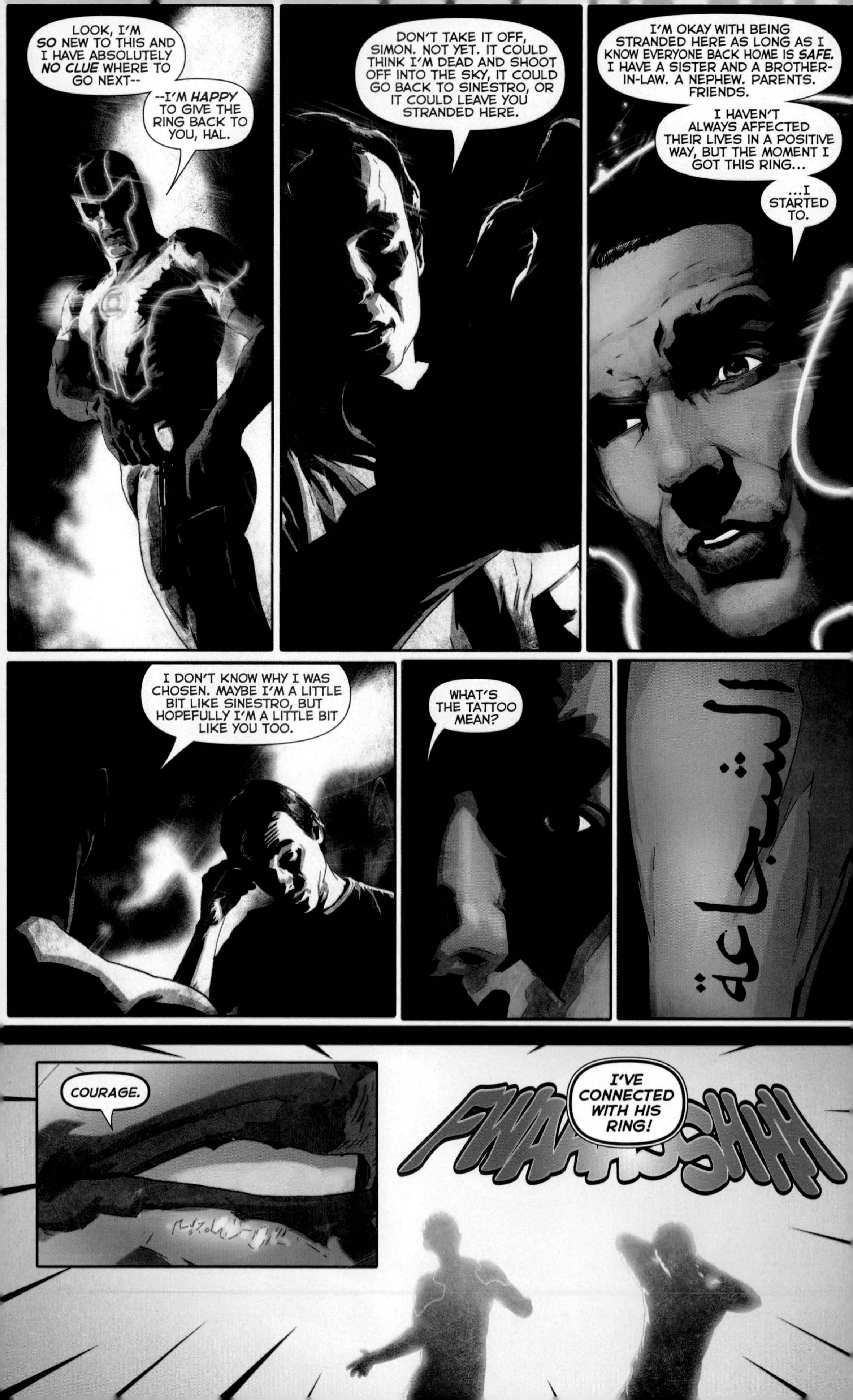
LOOK, I'M SO NEW TO THIS AND I HAVE ABSOLUTELY NO CLUE WHERE TO GO NEXT--
--I'M HAPPY TO GIVE THE RING BACK TO YOU, HAL.
DON'T TAKE IT OFF, SIMON. NOT YET. IT COULD THINK I'M DEAD AND SHOOT OFF INTO THE SKY, IT COULD GO BACK TO SINESTRO, OR IT COULD LEAVE YOU STRANDED HERE.
I'M OKAY WITH BEING STRANDED HERE AS LONG AS I KNOW EVERYONE BACK HOME IS SAFE. I HAVE A SISTER AND A BROTHER-IN-LAW. A NEPHEW. PARENTS. FRIENDS.
I HAVEN'T ALWAYS AFFECTED THEIR LIVES IN A POSITIVE WAY, BUT THE MOMENT I GOT THIS RING...
...I STARTED TO.
I DON'T KNOW WHY I WAS CHOSEN. MAYBE I'M A LITTLE BIT LIKE SINESTRO, BUT HOPEFULLY I'M A LITTLE BIT LIKE YOU TOO.
WHAT'S THE TATTOO MEAN?
الشجاعة
COURAGE.
FWAAASHHH
I'VE CONNECTED WITH HIS RING!

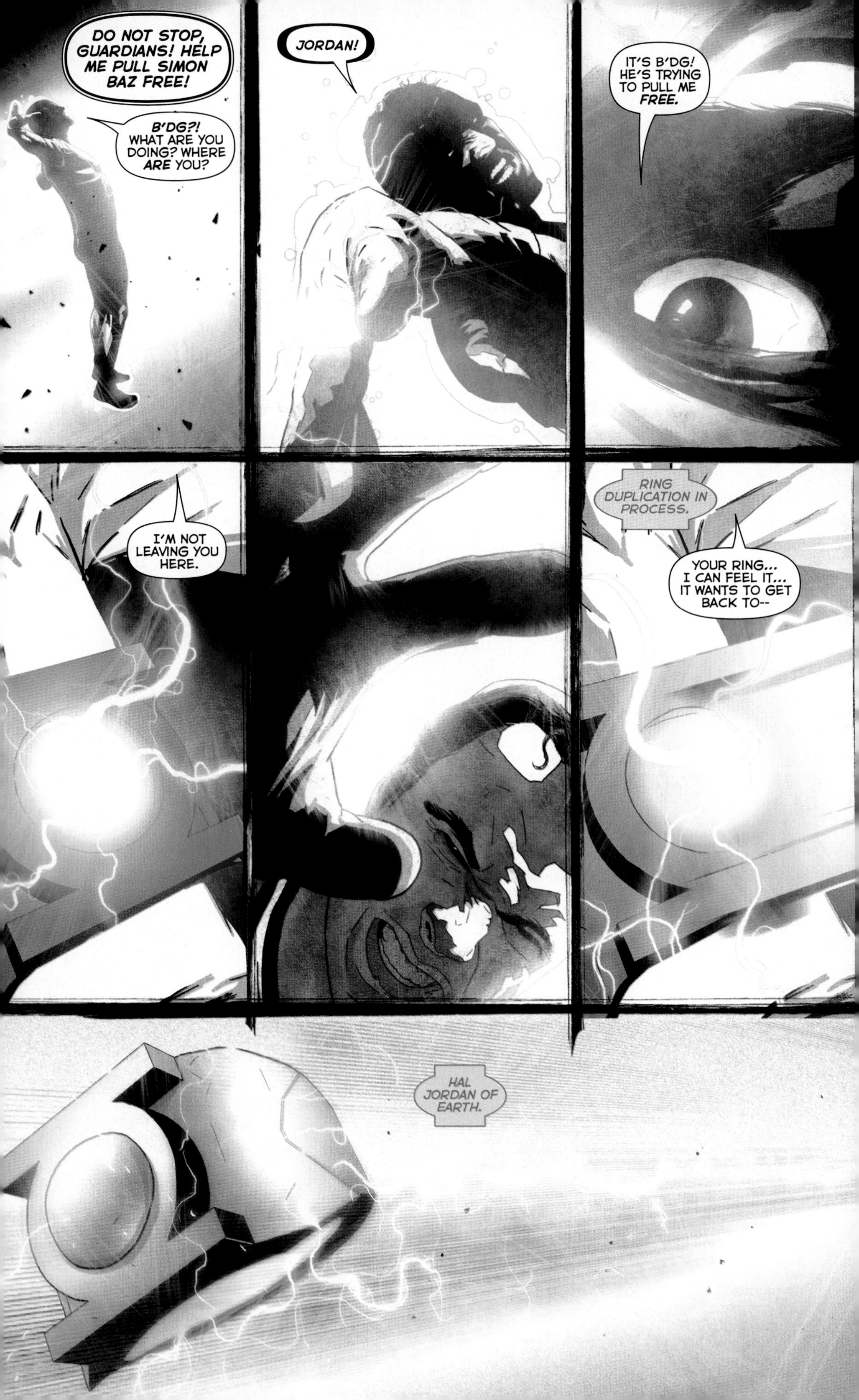
DO NOT STOP, GUARDIANS! HELP ME PULL SIMON BAZ FREE!
B'DG?! WHAT ARE YOU DOING? WHERE ARE YOU?
JORDAN!
IT'S B'DG! HE'S TRYING TO PULL ME FREE.
I'M NOT LEAVING YOU HERE.
RING DUPLICATION IN PROCESS.
YOUR RING... I CAN FEEL IT... IT WANTS TO GET BACK TO--
HAL JORDAN OF EARTH.

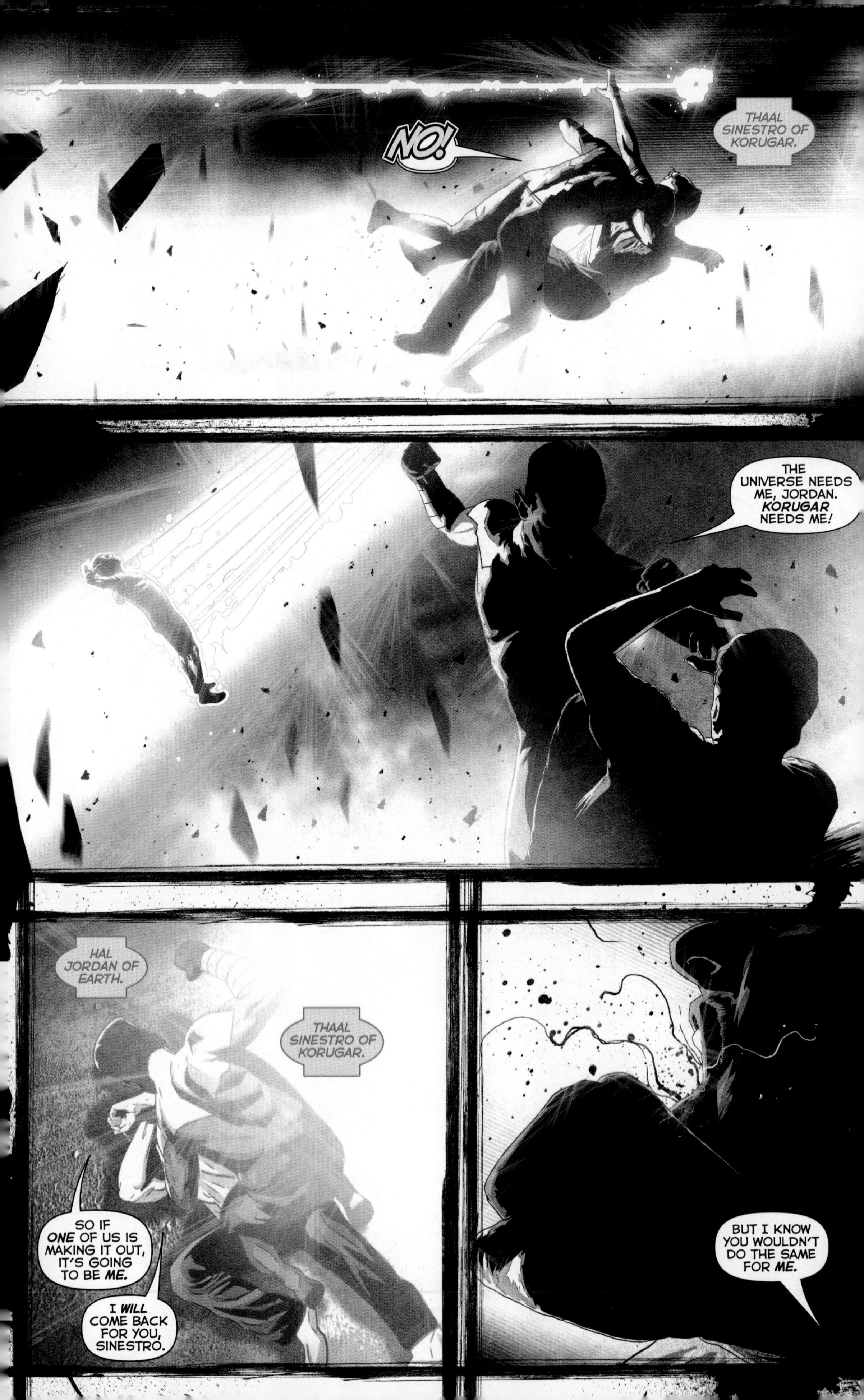
NO!
THAAL SINESTRO OF KORUGAR.
THE UNIVERSE NEEDS ME, JORDAN. KORUGAR NEEDS ME!
HAL JORDAN OF EARTH.
THAAL SINESTRO OF KORUGAR.
SO IF ONE OF US IS MAKING IT OUT, IT'S GOING TO BE ME.
I WILL COME BACK FOR YOU, SINESTRO.
BUT I KNOW YOU WOULDN'T DO THE SAME FOR ME.

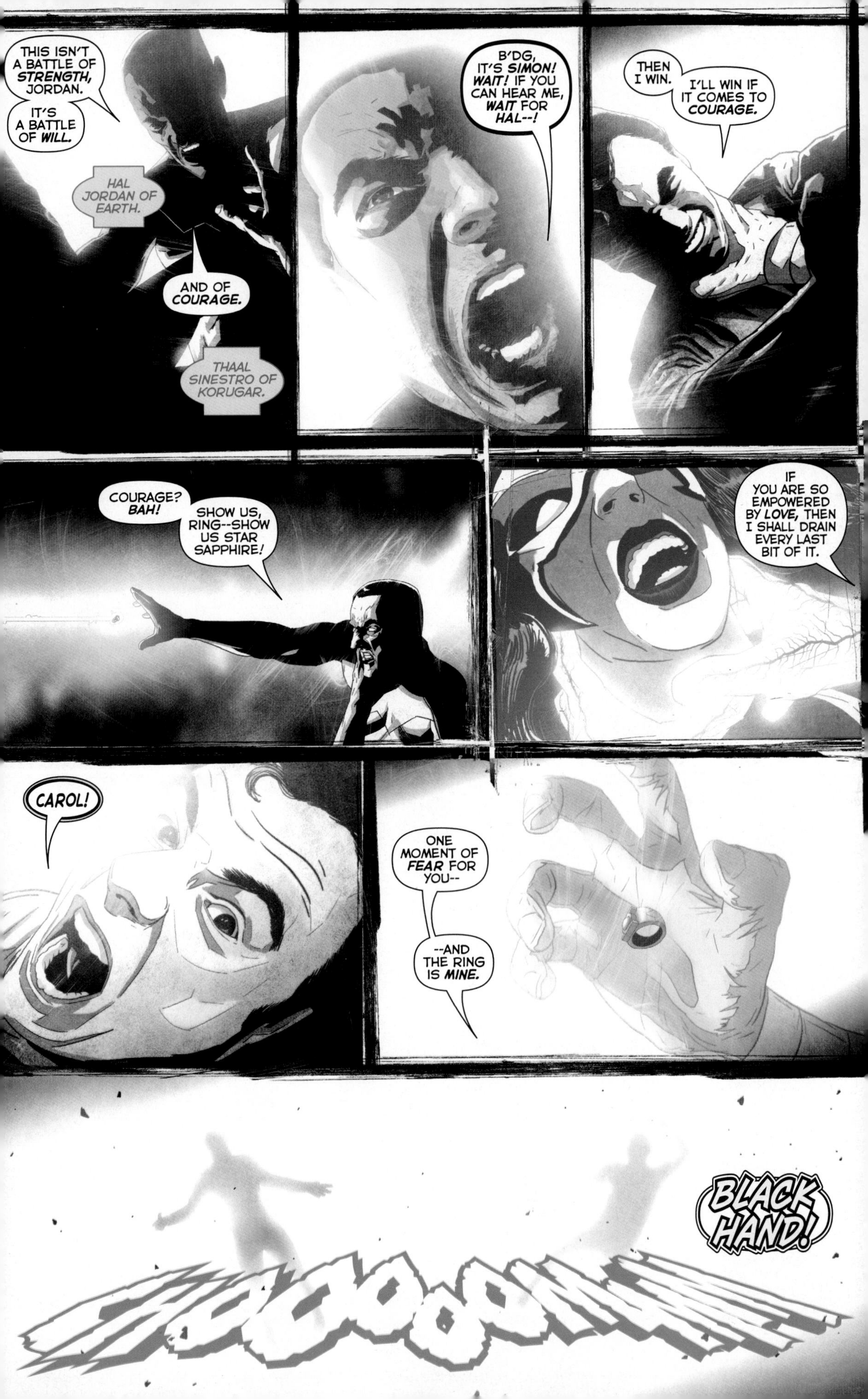

THIS ISN'T A BATTLE OF STRENGTH, JORDAN.
IT'S A BATTLE OF WILL.
HAL JORDAN OF EARTH.
AND OF COURAGE.
THAAL SINESTRO OF KORUGAR.
B'DG, IT'S SIMON! WAIT! IF YOU CAN HEAR ME, WAIT FOR HAL--!
THEN I WIN.
I'LL WIN IF IT COMES TO COURAGE.
COURAGE? BAH!
SHOW US, RING--SHOW US STAR SAPPHIRE!
IF YOU ARE SO EMPOWERED BY LOVE, THEN I SHALL DRAIN EVERY LAST BIT OF IT.
CAROL!
ONE MOMENT OF FEAR FOR YOU--
--AND THE RING IS MINE.
BLACK HAND!

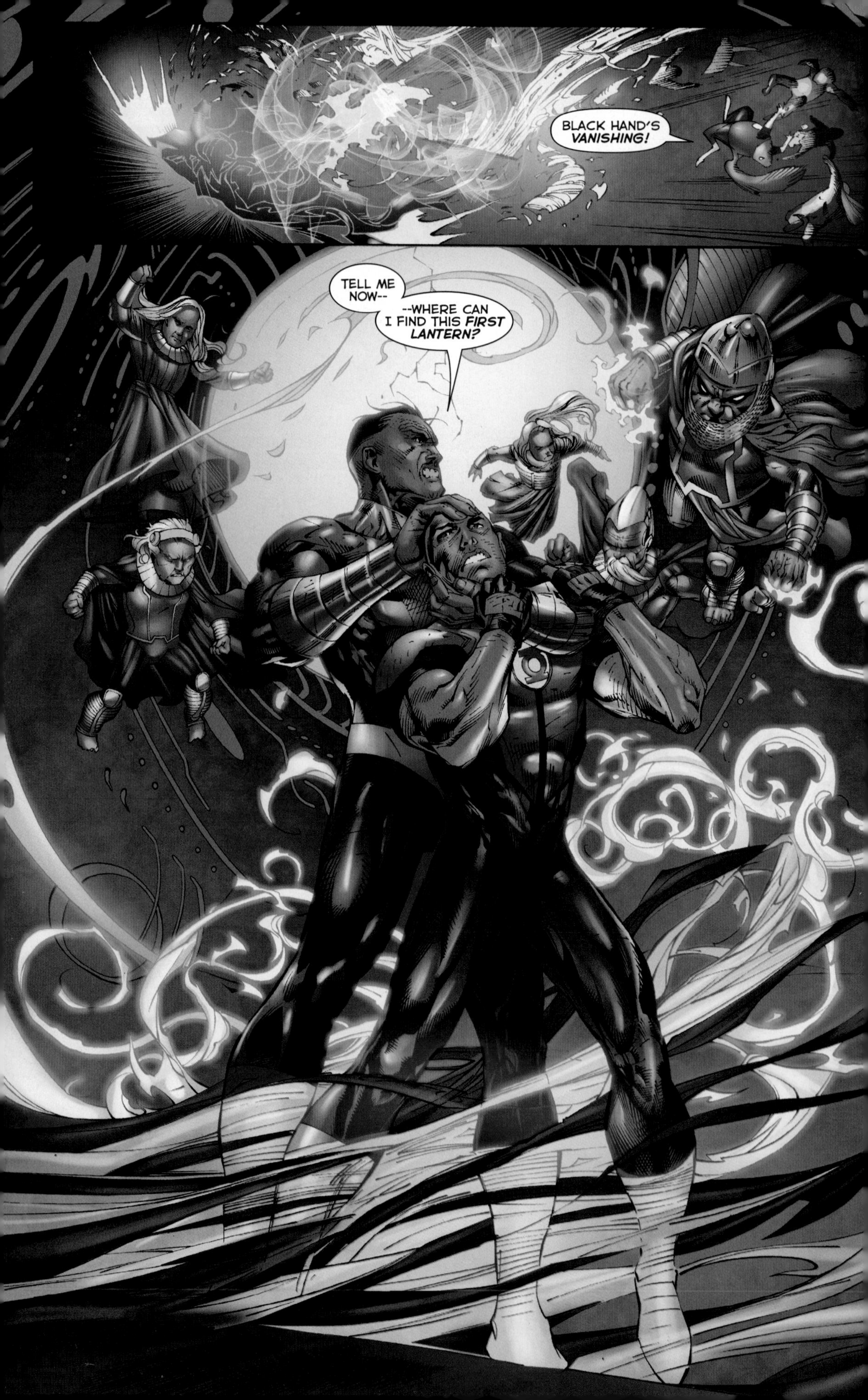
BLACK HAND'S VANISHING!
TELL ME NOW--
--WHERE CAN I FIND THIS FIRST LANTERN?

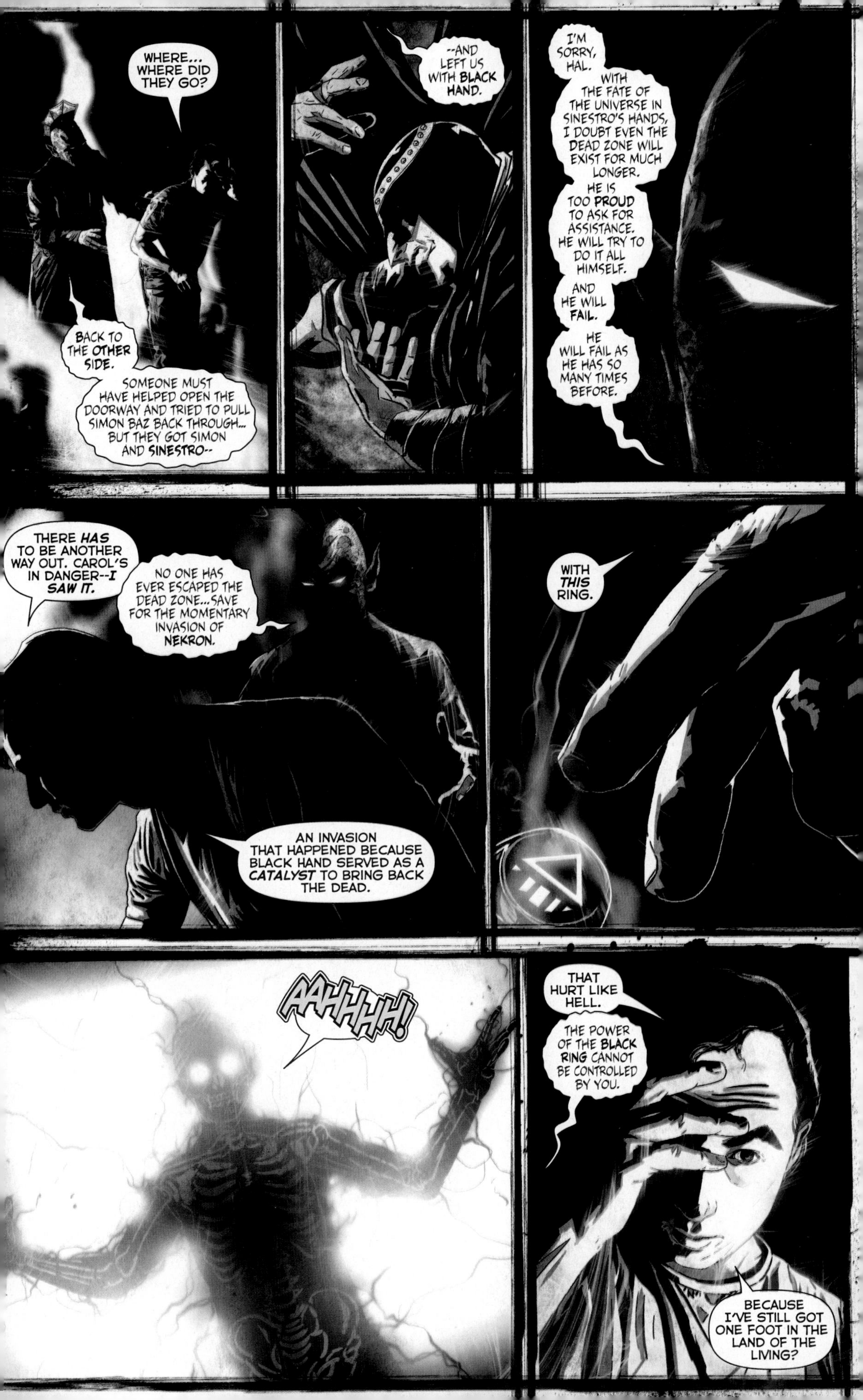
WHERE... WHERE DID THEY GO?
BACK TO THE OTHER SIDE.
SOMEONE MUST HAVE HELPED OPEN THE DOORWAY AND TRIED TO PULL SIMON BAZ BACK THROUGH... BUT THEY GOT SIMON AND SINESTRO--
--AND LEFT US WITH BLACK HAND.
I'M SORRY, HAL.
WITH THE FATE OF THE UNIVERSE IN SINESTRO'S HANDS, I DOUBT EVEN THE DEAD ZONE WILL EXIST FOR MUCH LONGER.
HE IS TOO PROUD TO ASK FOR ASSISTANCE. HE WILL TRY TO DO IT ALL HIMSELF.
AND HE WILL FAIL.
HE WILL FAIL AS HE HAS SO MANY TIMES BEFORE.
THERE HAS TO BE ANOTHER WAY OUT. CAROL'S IN DANGER--I SAW IT.
NO ONE HAS EVER ESCAPED THE DEAD ZONE...SAVE FOR THE MOMENTARY INVASION OF NEKRON.
AN INVASION THAT HAPPENED BECAUSE BLACK HAND SERVED AS A CATALYST TO BRING BACK THE DEAD.
WITH THIS RING.
AAHHHH!
THAT HURT LIKE HELL.
THE POWER OF THE BLACK RING CANNOT BE CONTROLLED BY YOU.
BECAUSE I'VE STILL GOT ONE FOOT IN THE LAND OF THE LIVING?

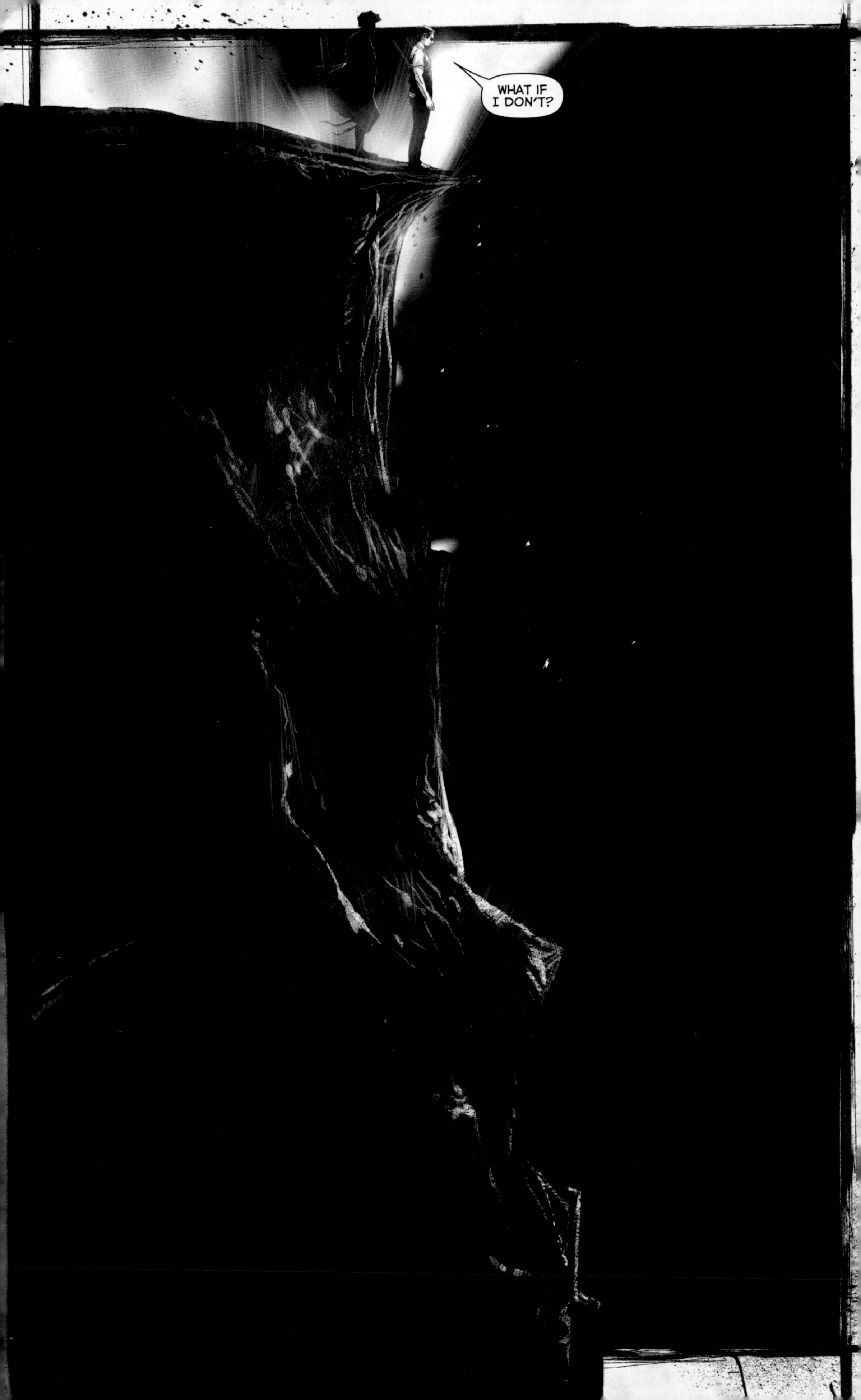
WHAT IF I DON'T?

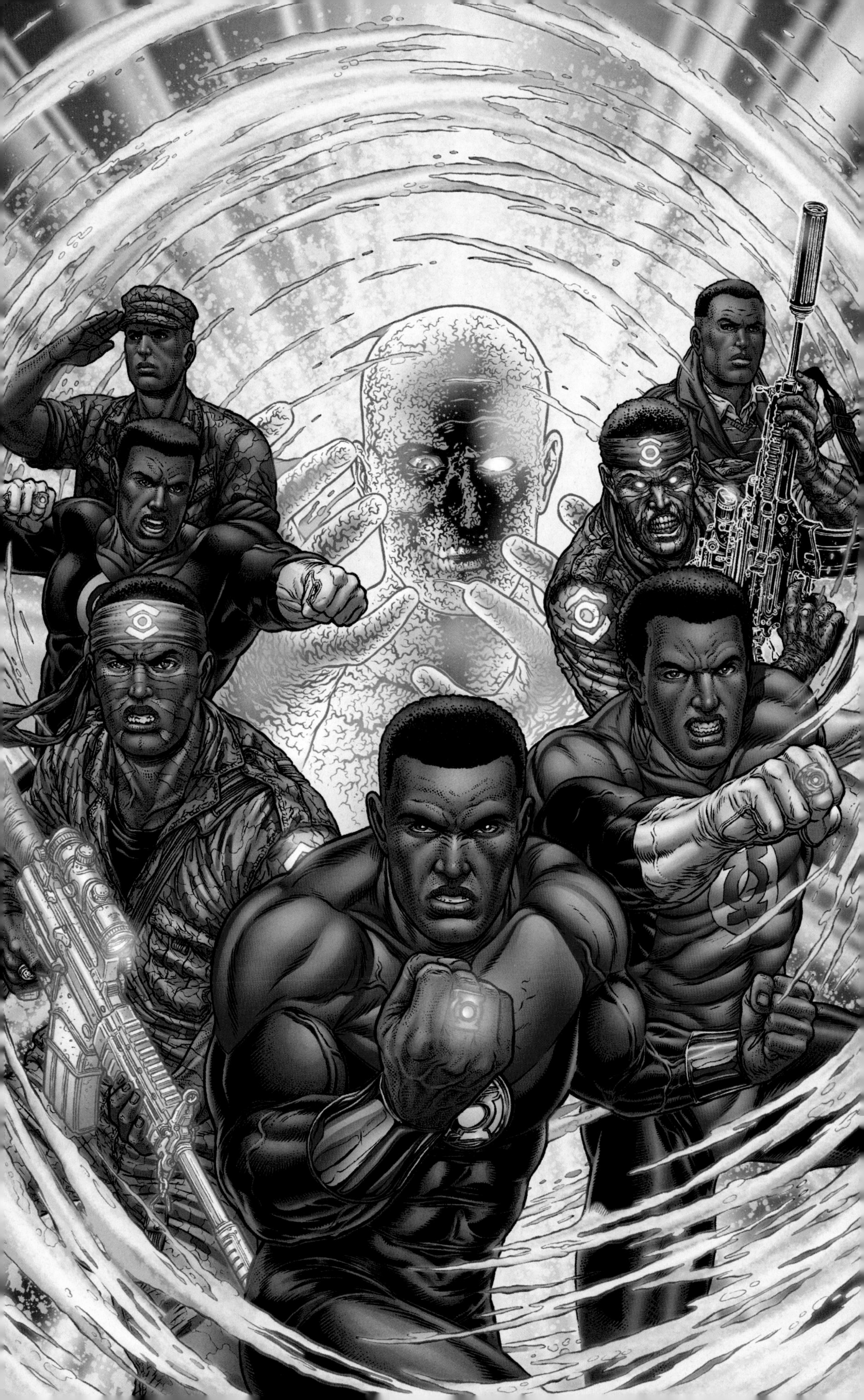

PART SIX: PIECES OF YOU

PETER J. TOMASI writer **CHRISCROSS** penciller **SCOTT HANNA** inker
cover art by **JUAN JOSÉ RYP & GABE ELTAEB**

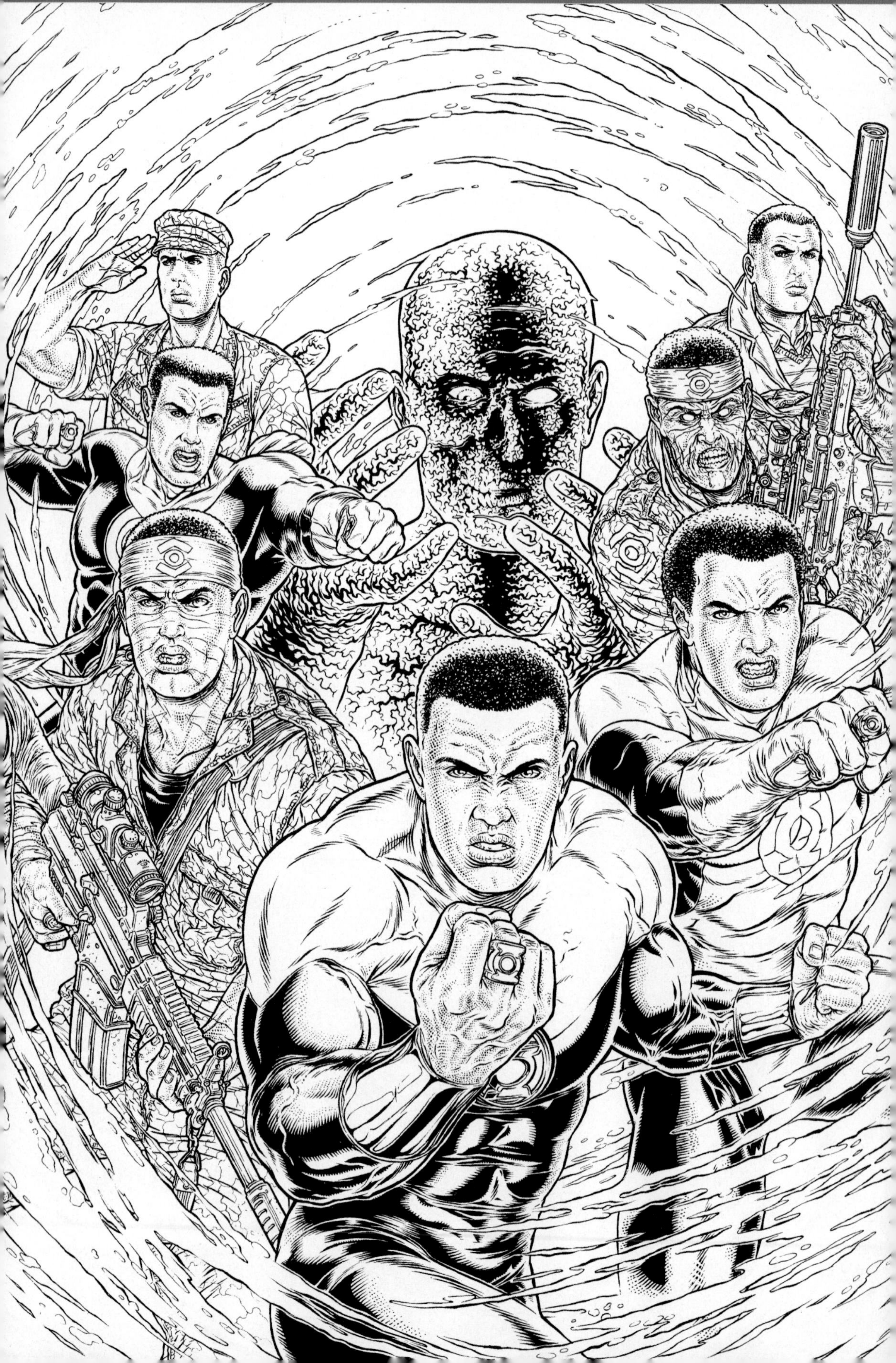

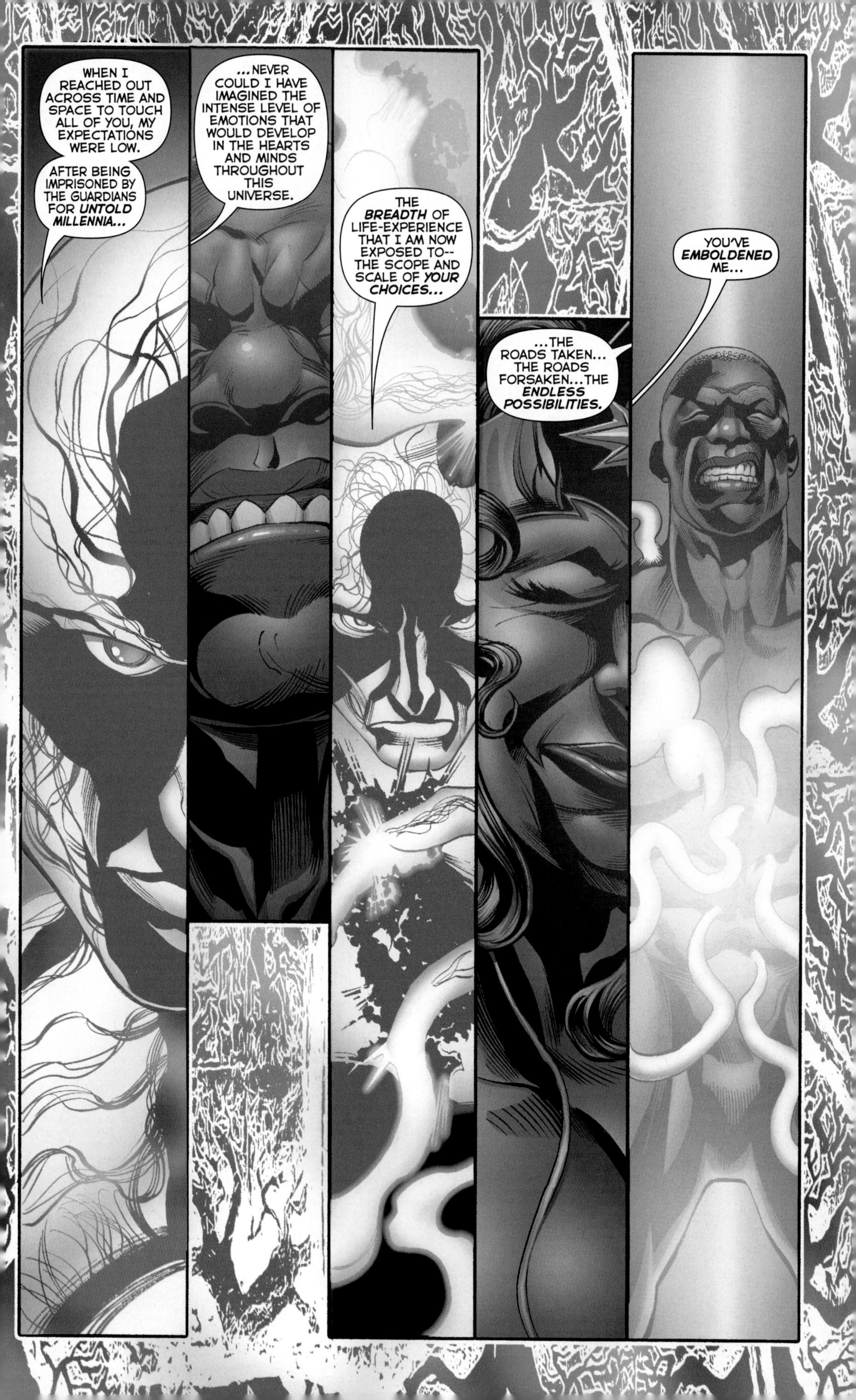
WHEN I REACHED OUT ACROSS TIME AND SPACE TO TOUCH ALL OF YOU, MY EXPECTATIONS WERE LOW.
AFTER BEING IMPRISONED BY THE GUARDIANS FOR *UNTOLD MILLENNIA...*
...NEVER COULD I HAVE IMAGINED THE INTENSE LEVEL OF EMOTIONS THAT WOULD DEVELOP IN THE HEARTS AND MINDS THROUGHOUT THIS UNIVERSE.
THE *BREADTH* OF LIFE-EXPERIENCE THAT I AM NOW EXPOSED TO-- THE SCOPE AND SCALE OF *YOUR CHOICES...*
...THE ROADS TAKEN... THE ROADS FORSAKEN...THE *ENDLESS POSSIBILITIES.*
YOU'VE *EMBOLDENED* ME...

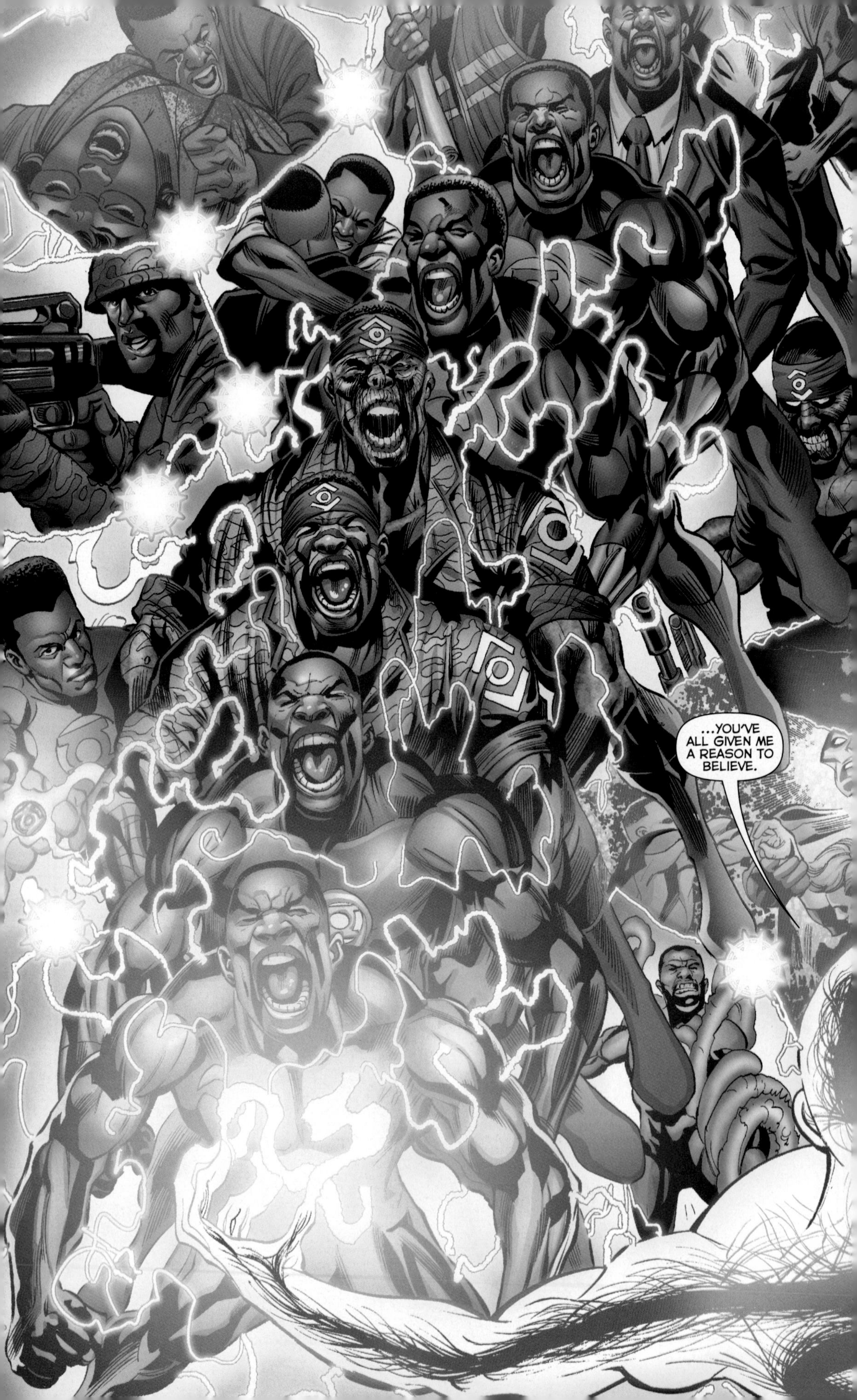
...YOU'VE ALL GIVEN ME A REASON TO BELIEVE.

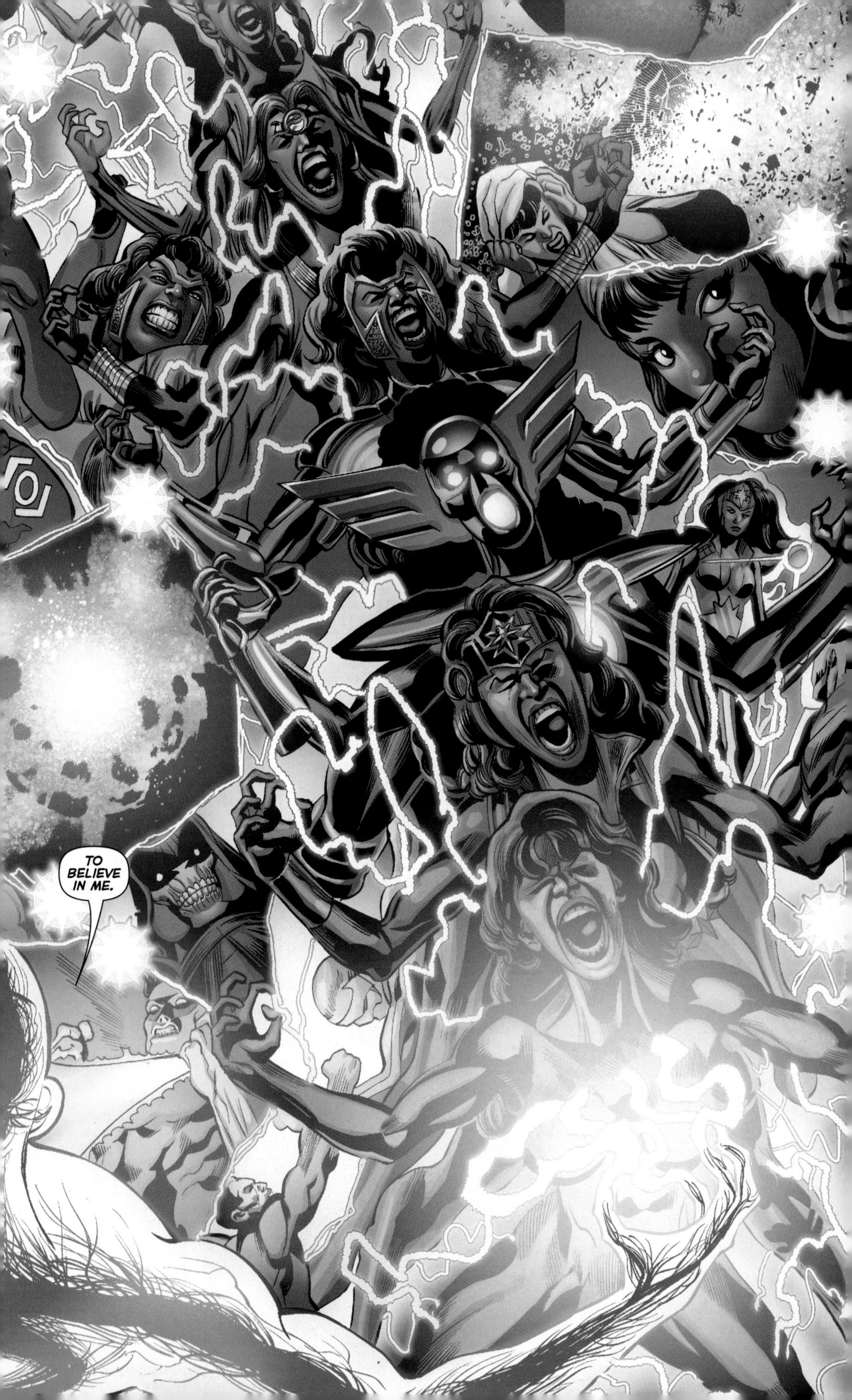
TO BELIEVE IN ME.

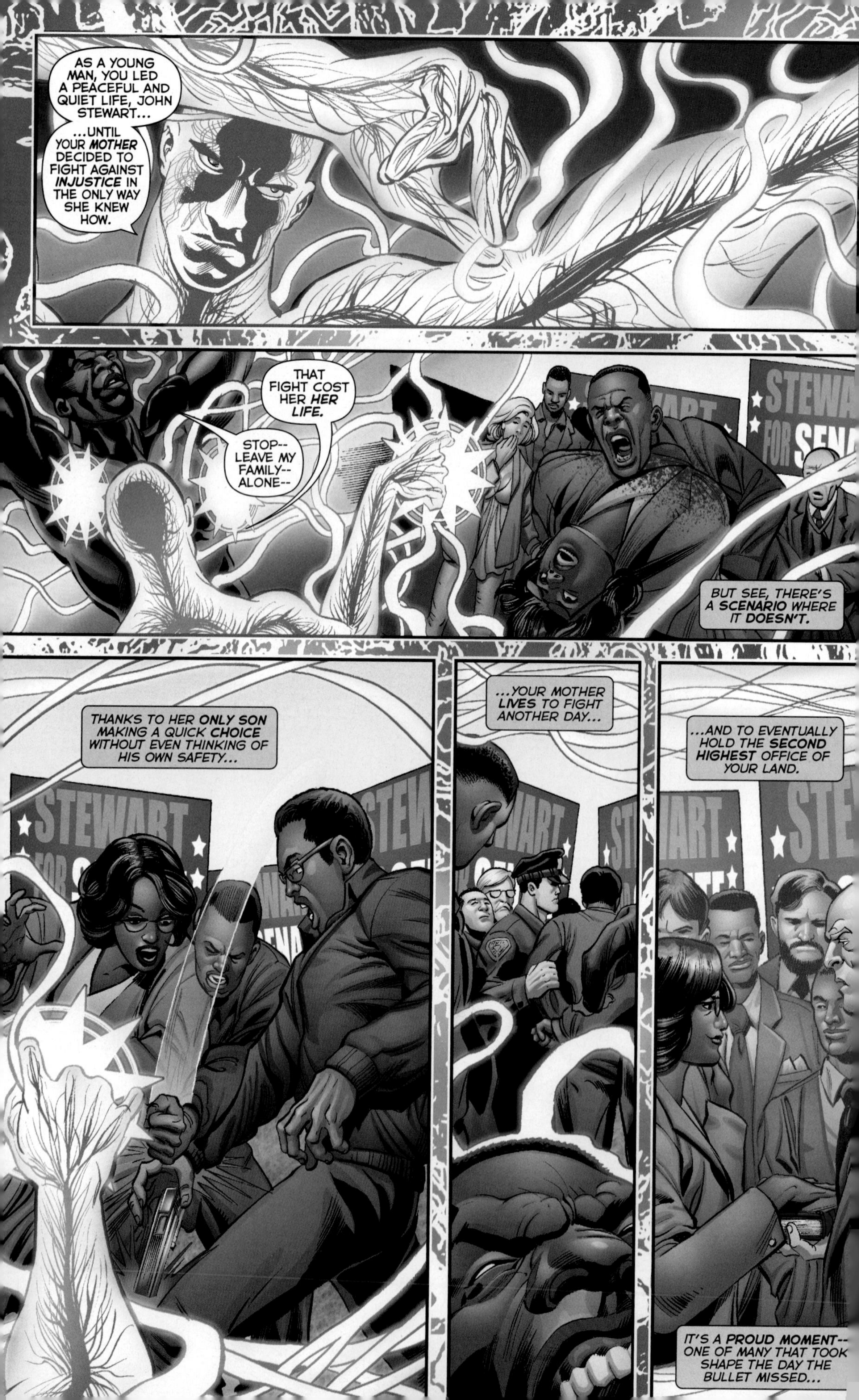
AS A YOUNG MAN, YOU LED A PEACEFUL AND QUIET LIFE, JOHN STEWART...
...UNTIL YOUR MOTHER DECIDED TO FIGHT AGAINST INJUSTICE IN THE ONLY WAY SHE KNEW HOW.
THAT FIGHT COST HER HER LIFE.
STOP-- LEAVE MY FAMILY-- ALONE--
STEWART FOR SENA
BUT SEE, THERE'S A SCENARIO WHERE IT DOESN'T.
THANKS TO HER ONLY SON MAKING A QUICK CHOICE WITHOUT EVEN THINKING OF HIS OWN SAFETY...
STEWART
...YOUR MOTHER LIVES TO FIGHT ANOTHER DAY...
...AND TO EVENTUALLY HOLD THE SECOND HIGHEST OFFICE OF YOUR LAND.
IT'S A PROUD MOMENT-- ONE OF MANY THAT TOOK SHAPE THE DAY THE BULLET MISSED...

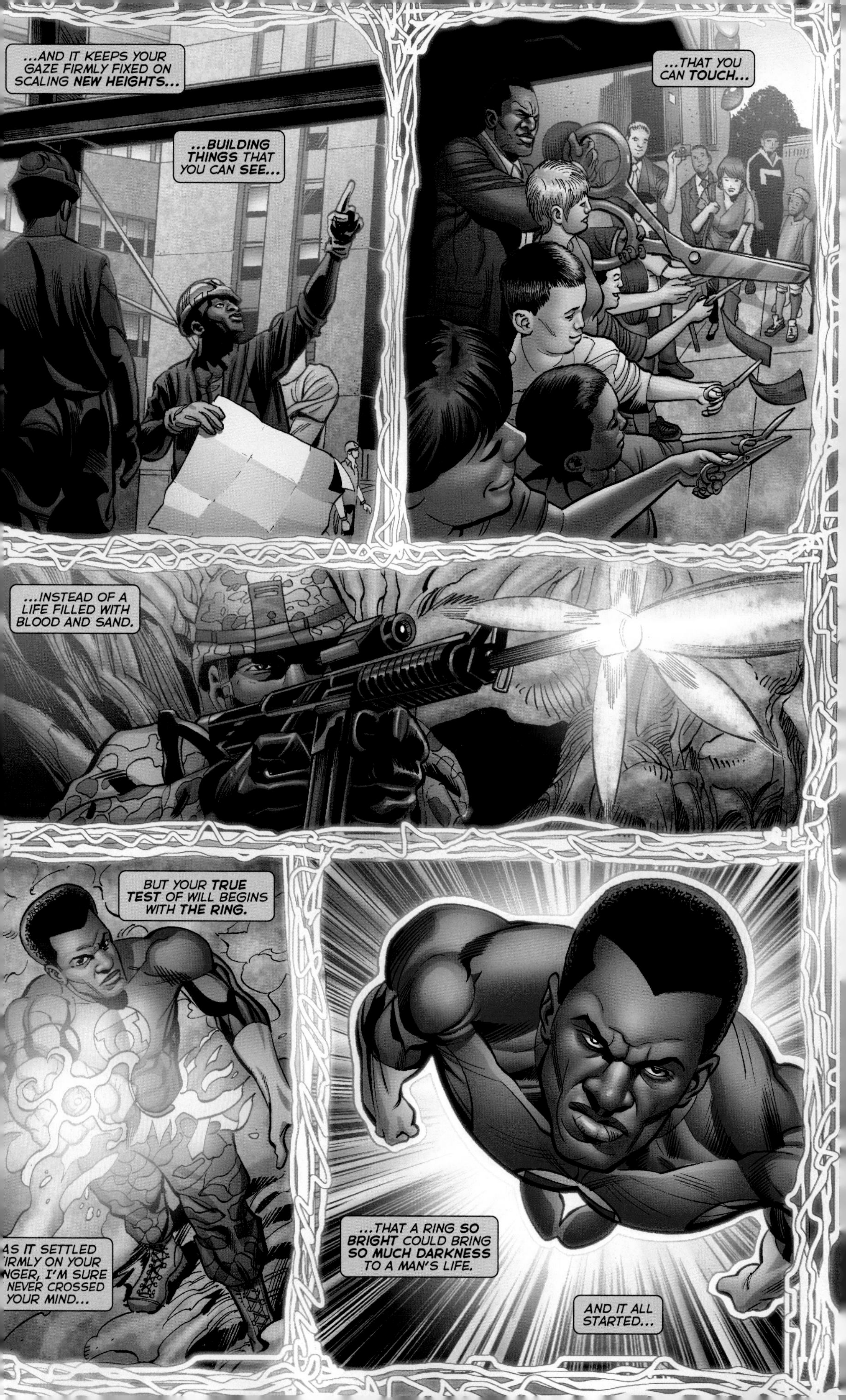
...AND IT KEEPS YOUR GAZE FIRMLY FIXED ON SCALING NEW HEIGHTS...
...BUILDING THINGS THAT YOU CAN SEE...
...THAT YOU CAN TOUCH...
...INSTEAD OF A LIFE FILLED WITH BLOOD AND SAND.
BUT YOUR TRUE TEST OF WILL BEGINS WITH THE RING.
AS IT SETTLED FIRMLY ON YOUR NGER, I'M SURE NEVER CROSSED YOUR MIND...
...THAT A RING SO BRIGHT COULD BRING SO MUCH DARKNESS TO A MAN'S LIFE.
AND IT ALL STARTED...

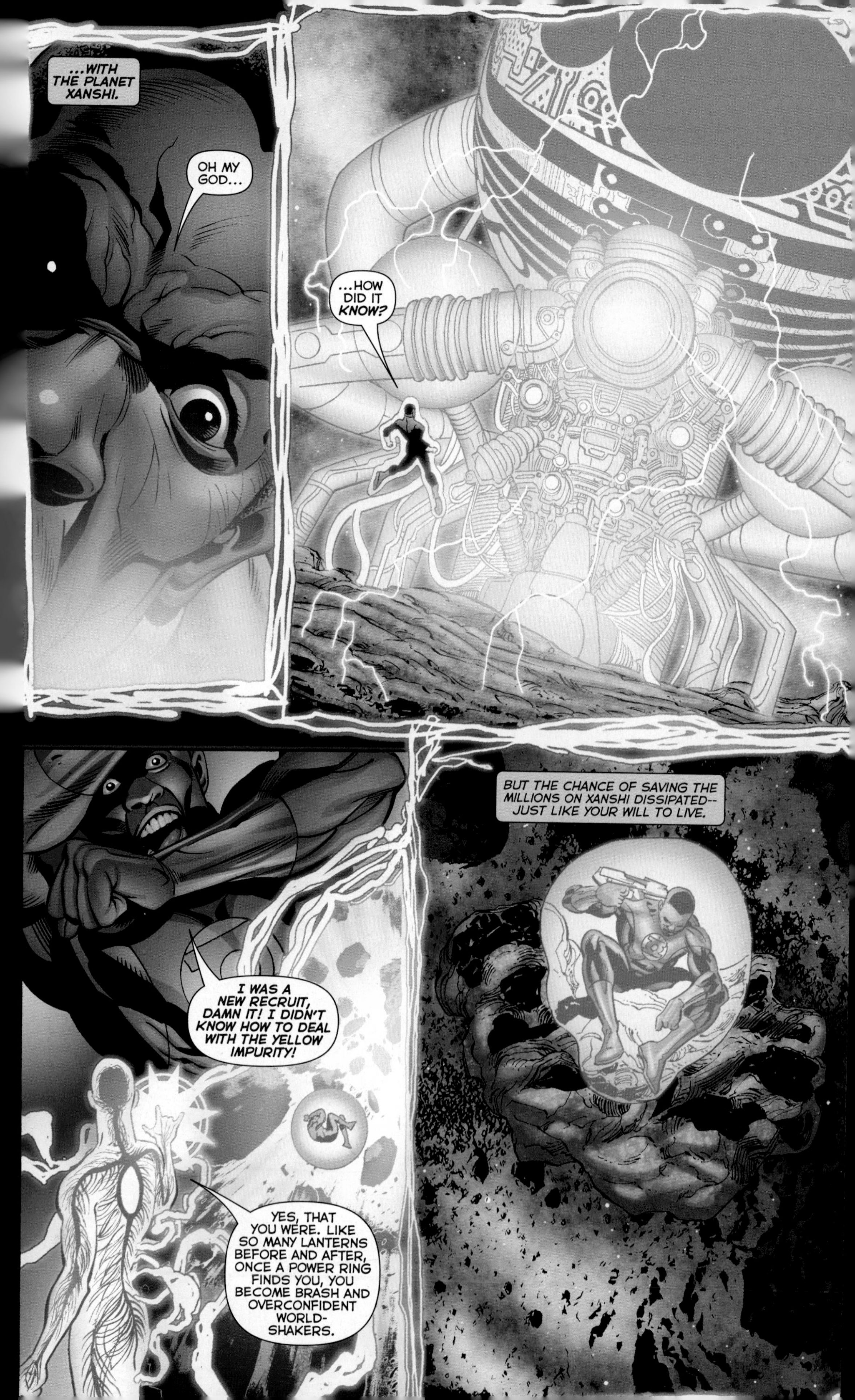
...WITH THE PLANET XANSHI.
OH MY GOD...
...HOW DID IT KNOW?
I WAS A NEW RECRUIT, DAMN IT! I DIDN'T KNOW HOW TO DEAL WITH THE YELLOW IMPURITY!
YES, THAT YOU WERE. LIKE SO MANY LANTERNS BEFORE AND AFTER, ONCE A POWER RING FINDS YOU, YOU BECOME BRASH AND OVERCONFIDENT WORLD-SHAKERS.
BUT THE CHANCE OF SAVING THE MILLIONS ON XANSHI DISSIPATED--JUST LIKE YOUR WILL TO LIVE.

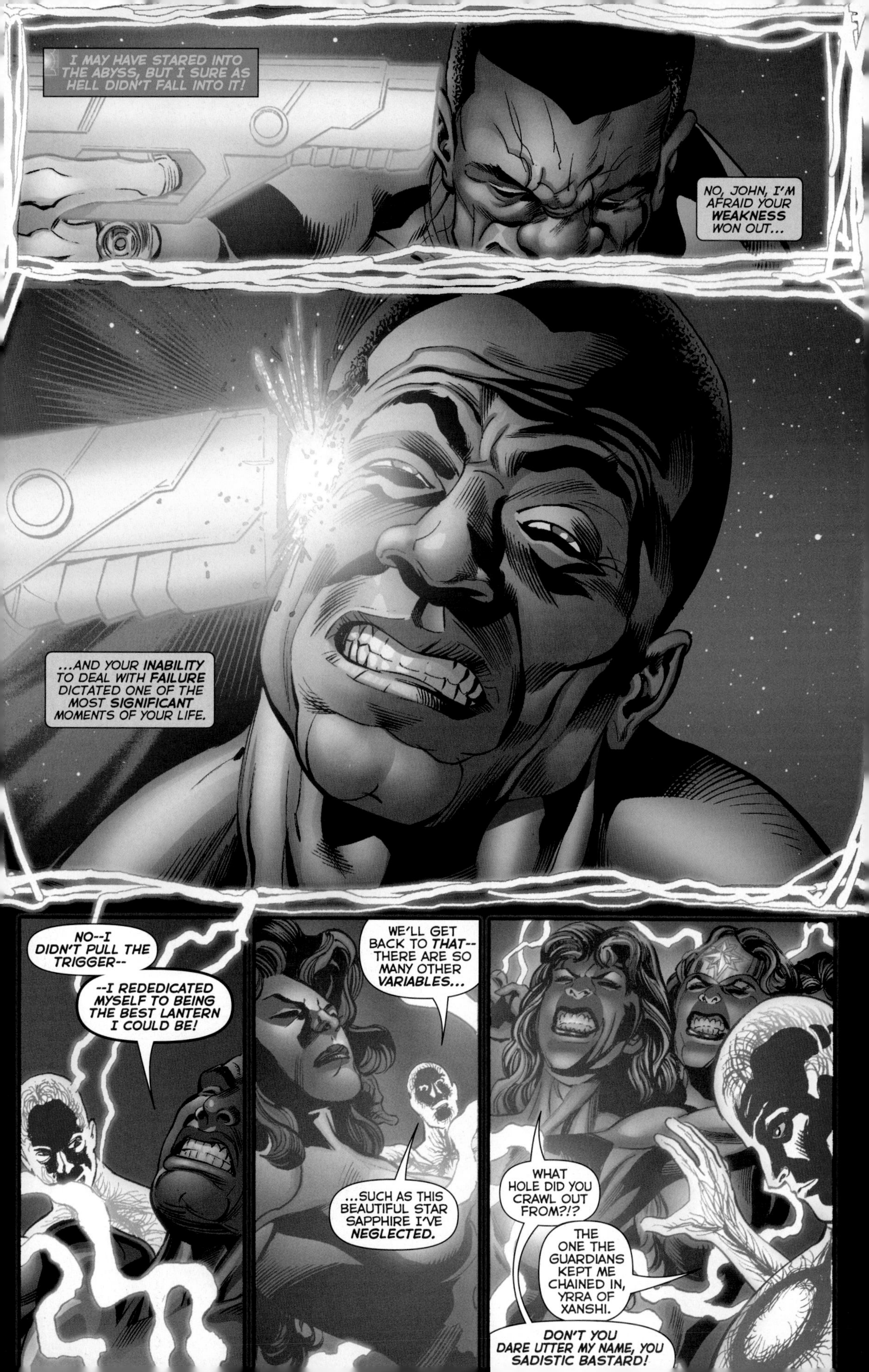
I MAY HAVE STARED INTO THE ABYSS, BUT I SURE AS HELL DIDN'T FALL INTO IT!
NO, JOHN, I'M AFRAID YOUR WEAKNESS WON OUT...
...AND YOUR INABILITY TO DEAL WITH FAILURE DICTATED ONE OF THE MOST SIGNIFICANT MOMENTS OF YOUR LIFE.
NO--I DIDN'T PULL THE TRIGGER--
--I REDEDICATED MYSELF TO BEING THE BEST LANTERN I COULD BE!
WE'LL GET BACK TO THAT--THERE ARE SO MANY OTHER VARIABLES...
...SUCH AS THIS BEAUTIFUL STAR SAPPHIRE I'VE NEGLECTED.
WHAT HOLE DID YOU CRAWL OUT FROM?!?
THE ONE THE GUARDIANS KEPT ME CHAINED IN, YRRA OF XANSHI.
DON'T YOU DARE UTTER MY NAME, YOU SADISTIC BASTARD!

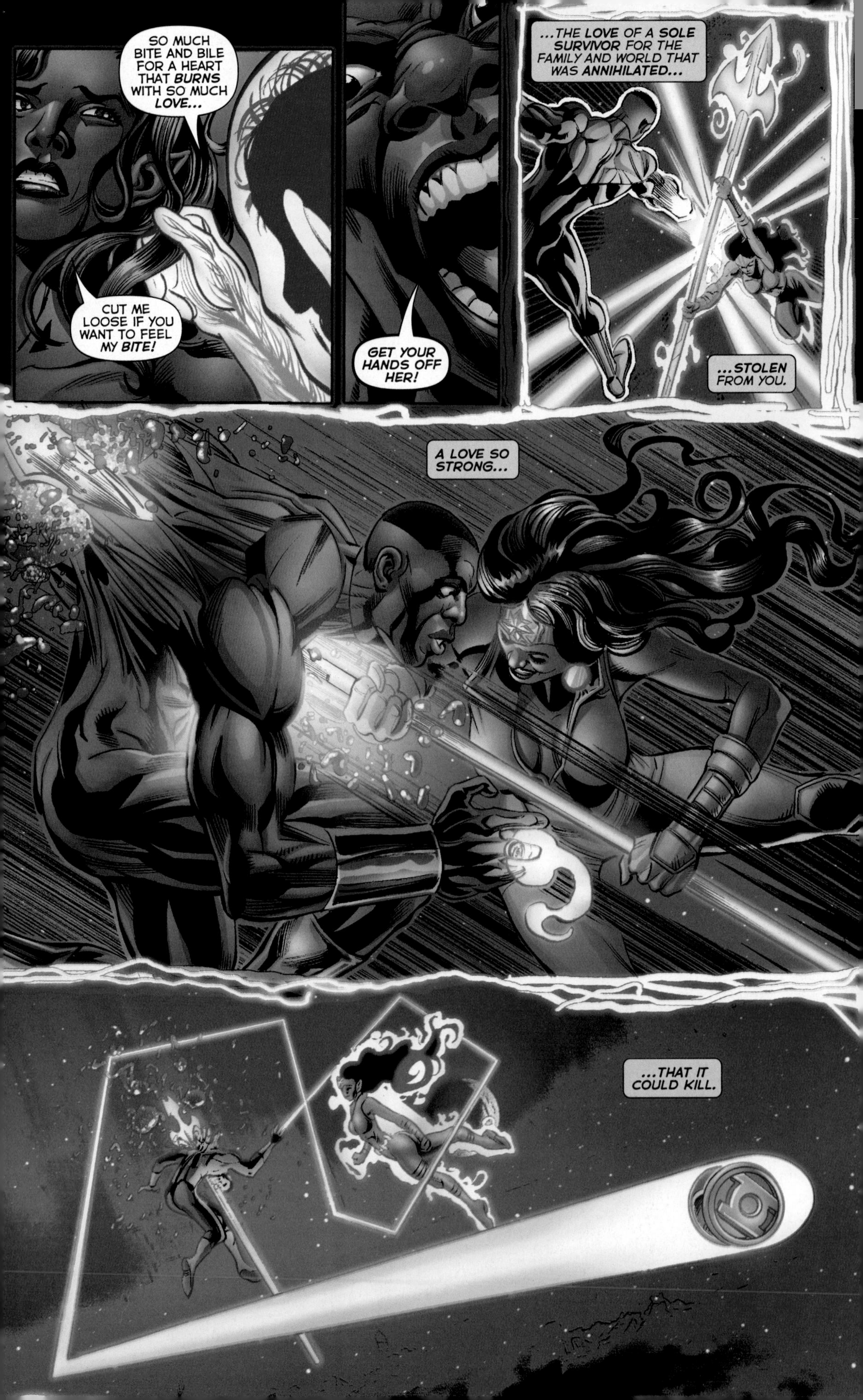
SO MUCH BITE AND BILE FOR A HEART THAT BURNS WITH SO MUCH LOVE...
CUT ME LOOSE IF YOU WANT TO FEEL MY BITE!
GET YOUR HANDS OFF HER!
...THE LOVE OF A SOLE SURVIVOR FOR THE FAMILY AND WORLD THAT WAS ANNIHILATED...
...STOLEN FROM YOU.
A LOVE SO STRONG...
...THAT IT COULD KILL.

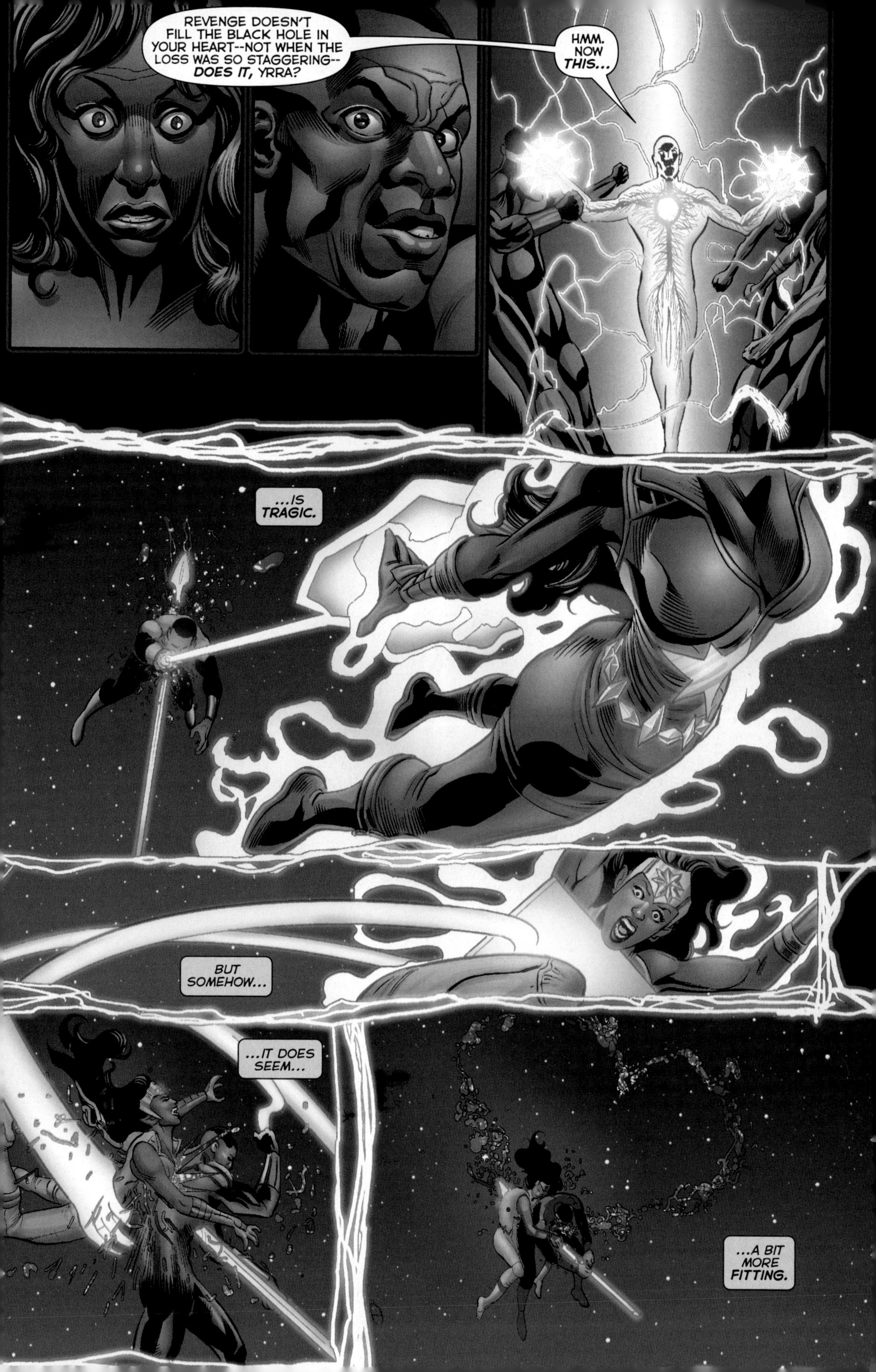
REVENGE DOESN'T FILL THE BLACK HOLE IN YOUR HEART--NOT WHEN THE LOSS WAS SO STAGGERING-- DOES IT, YRRA?
HMM. NOW THIS...
...IS TRAGIC.
BUT SOMEHOW...
...IT DOES SEEM...
...A BIT MORE FITTING.

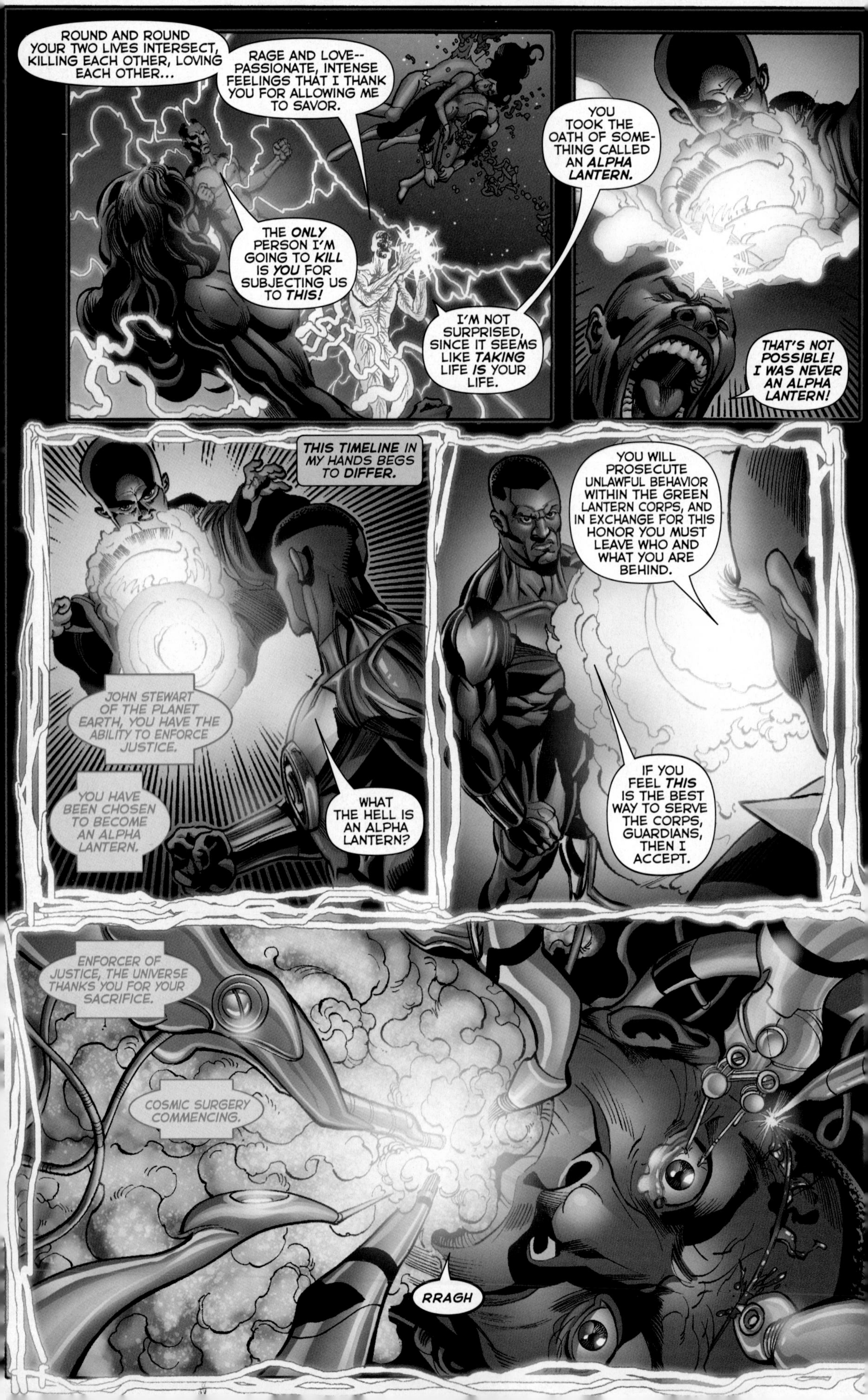
ROUND AND ROUND YOUR TWO LIVES INTERSECT, KILLING EACH OTHER, LOVING EACH OTHER...
RAGE AND LOVE-- PASSIONATE, INTENSE FEELINGS THAT I THANK YOU FOR ALLOWING ME TO SAVOR.
THE ONLY PERSON I'M GOING TO KILL IS YOU FOR SUBJECTING US TO THIS!
I'M NOT SURPRISED, SINCE IT SEEMS LIKE TAKING LIFE IS YOUR LIFE.
YOU TOOK THE OATH OF SOMETHING CALLED AN ALPHA LANTERN.
THAT'S NOT POSSIBLE! I WAS NEVER AN ALPHA LANTERN!
THIS TIMELINE IN MY HANDS BEGS TO DIFFER.
JOHN STEWART OF THE PLANET EARTH, YOU HAVE THE ABILITY TO ENFORCE JUSTICE.
YOU HAVE BEEN CHOSEN TO BECOME AN ALPHA LANTERN.
WHAT THE HELL IS AN ALPHA LANTERN?
YOU WILL PROSECUTE UNLAWFUL BEHAVIOR WITHIN THE GREEN LANTERN CORPS, AND IN EXCHANGE FOR THIS HONOR YOU MUST LEAVE WHO AND WHAT YOU ARE BEHIND.
IF YOU FEEL THIS IS THE BEST WAY TO SERVE THE CORPS, GUARDIANS, THEN I ACCEPT.
ENFORCER OF JUSTICE, THE UNIVERSE THANKS YOU FOR YOUR SACRIFICE.
COSMIC SURGERY COMMENCING.
RRAGH

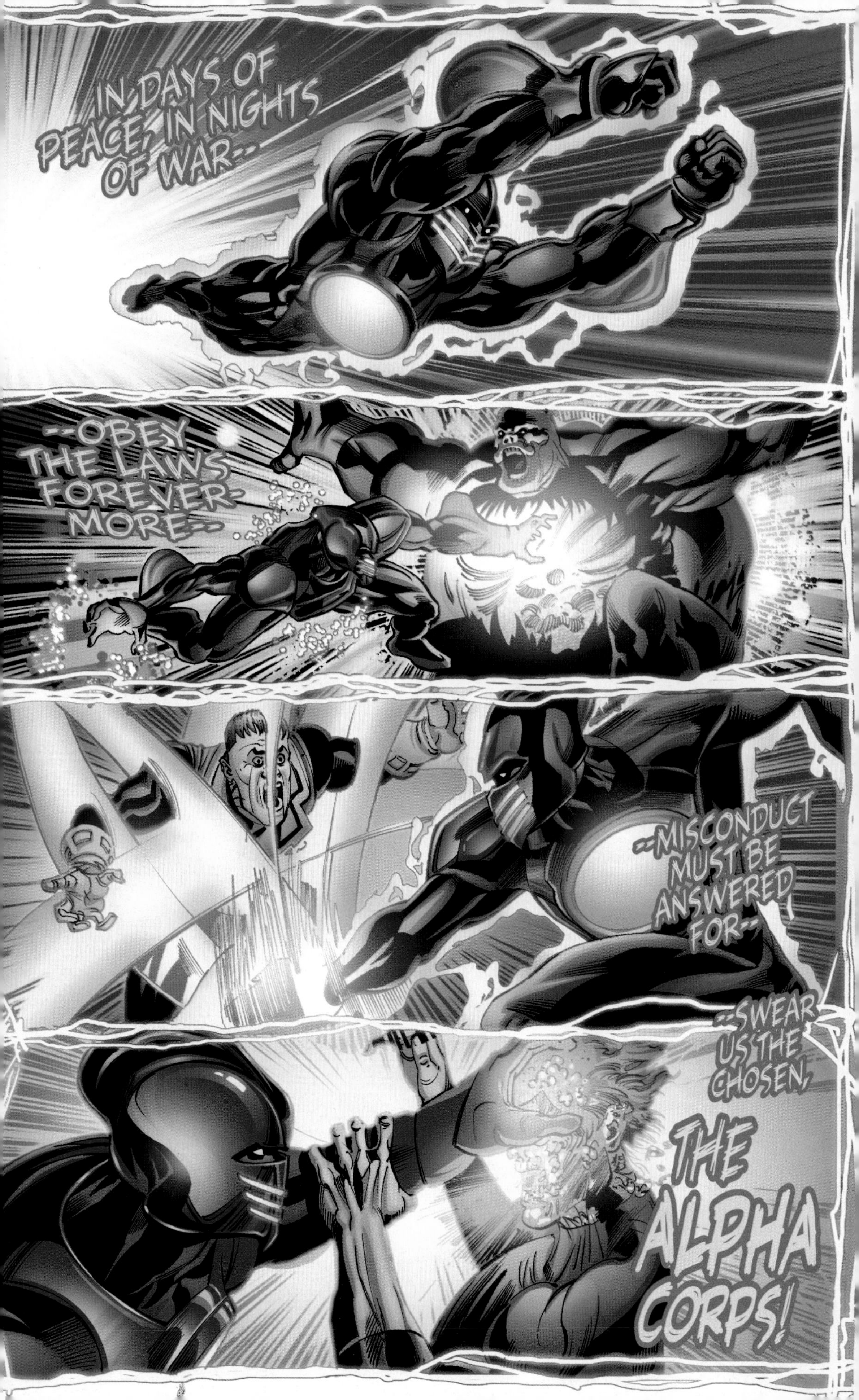
IN DAYS OF PEACE, IN NIGHTS OF WAR--
--OBEY THE LAWS FOREVERMORE--
--MISCONDUCT MUST BE ANSWERED FOR--
--SWEAR US THE CHOSEN,
THE ALPHA CORPS!

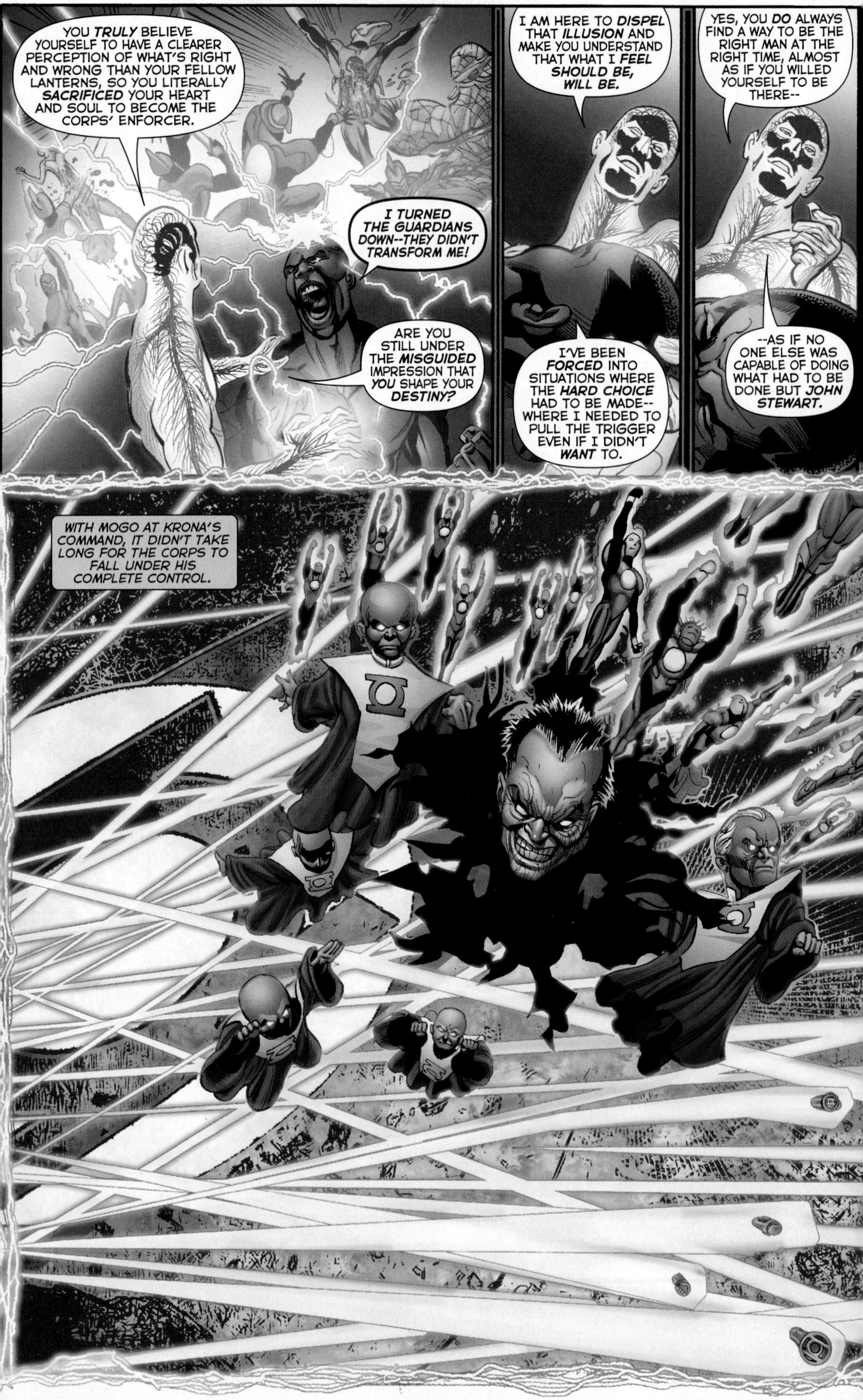
YOU TRULY BELIEVE YOURSELF TO HAVE A CLEARER PERCEPTION OF WHAT'S RIGHT AND WRONG THAN YOUR FELLOW LANTERNS, SO YOU LITERALLY SACRIFICED YOUR HEART AND SOUL TO BECOME THE CORPS' ENFORCER.
I TURNED THE GUARDIANS DOWN--THEY DIDN'T TRANSFORM ME!
ARE YOU STILL UNDER THE MISGUIDED IMPRESSION THAT YOU SHAPE YOUR DESTINY?
I AM HERE TO DISPEL THAT ILLUSION AND MAKE YOU UNDERSTAND THAT WHAT I FEEL SHOULD BE, WILL BE.
I'VE BEEN FORCED INTO SITUATIONS WHERE THE HARD CHOICE HAD TO BE MADE-- WHERE I NEEDED TO PULL THE TRIGGER EVEN IF I DIDN'T WANT TO.
YES, YOU DO ALWAYS FIND A WAY TO BE THE RIGHT MAN AT THE RIGHT TIME, ALMOST AS IF YOU WILLED YOURSELF TO BE THERE--
--AS IF NO ONE ELSE WAS CAPABLE OF DOING WHAT HAD TO BE DONE BUT JOHN STEWART.
WITH MOGO AT KRONA'S COMMAND, IT DIDN'T TAKE LONG FOR THE CORPS TO FALL UNDER HIS COMPLETE CONTROL.

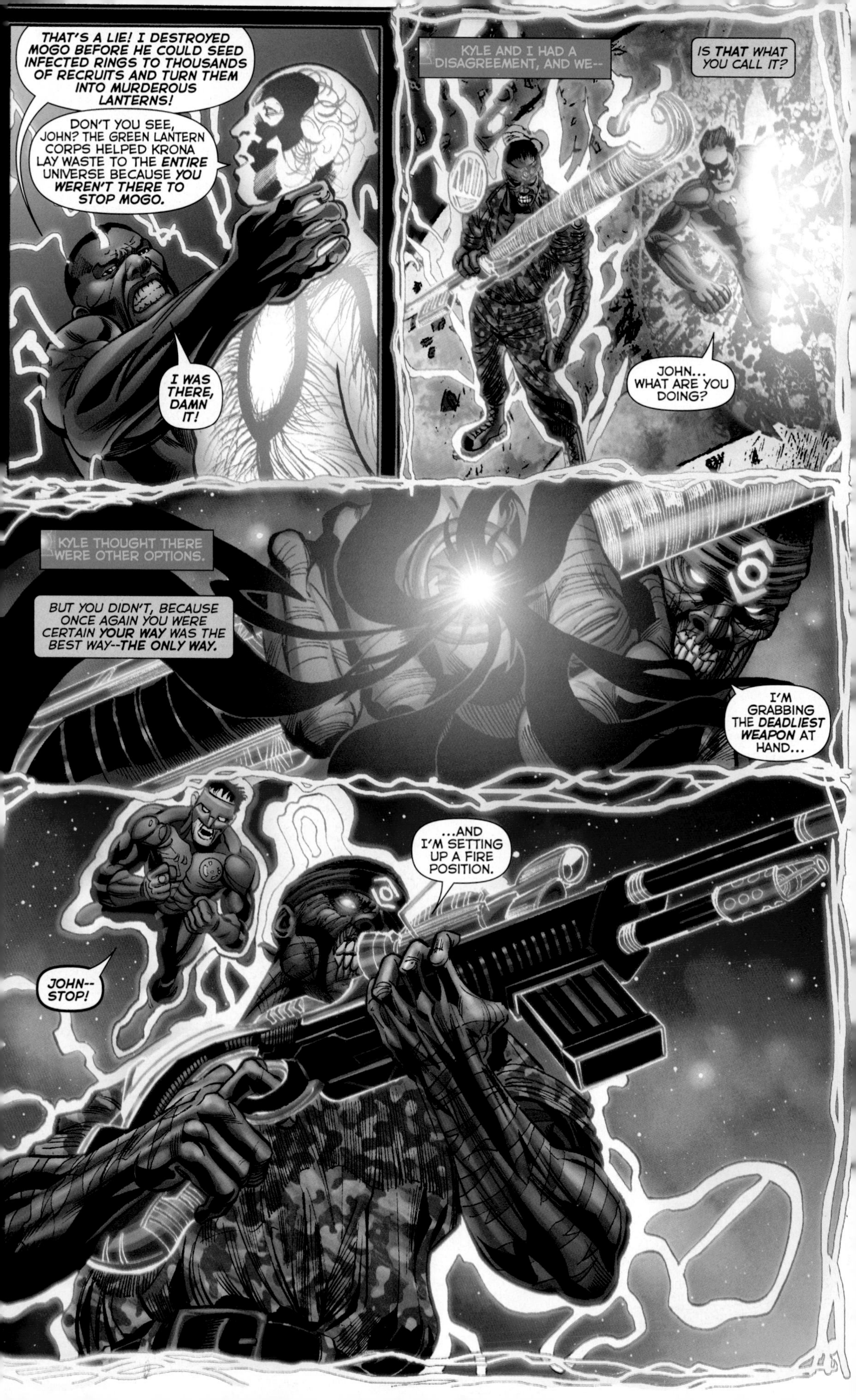
THAT'S A LIE! I DESTROYED MOGO BEFORE HE COULD SEED INFECTED RINGS TO THOUSANDS OF RECRUITS AND TURN THEM INTO MURDEROUS LANTERNS!
DON'T YOU SEE, JOHN? THE GREEN LANTERN CORPS HELPED KRONA LAY WASTE TO THE ENTIRE UNIVERSE BECAUSE YOU WEREN'T THERE TO STOP MOGO.
I WAS THERE, DAMN IT!
KYLE AND I HAD A DISAGREEMENT, AND WE--
IS THAT WHAT YOU CALL IT?
JOHN... WHAT ARE YOU DOING?
KYLE THOUGHT THERE WERE OTHER OPTIONS.
BUT YOU DIDN'T, BECAUSE ONCE AGAIN YOU WERE CERTAIN YOUR WAY WAS THE BEST WAY--THE ONLY WAY.
I'M GRABBING THE DEADLIEST WEAPON AT HAND...
...AND I'M SETTING UP A FIRE POSITION.
JOHN-- STOP!

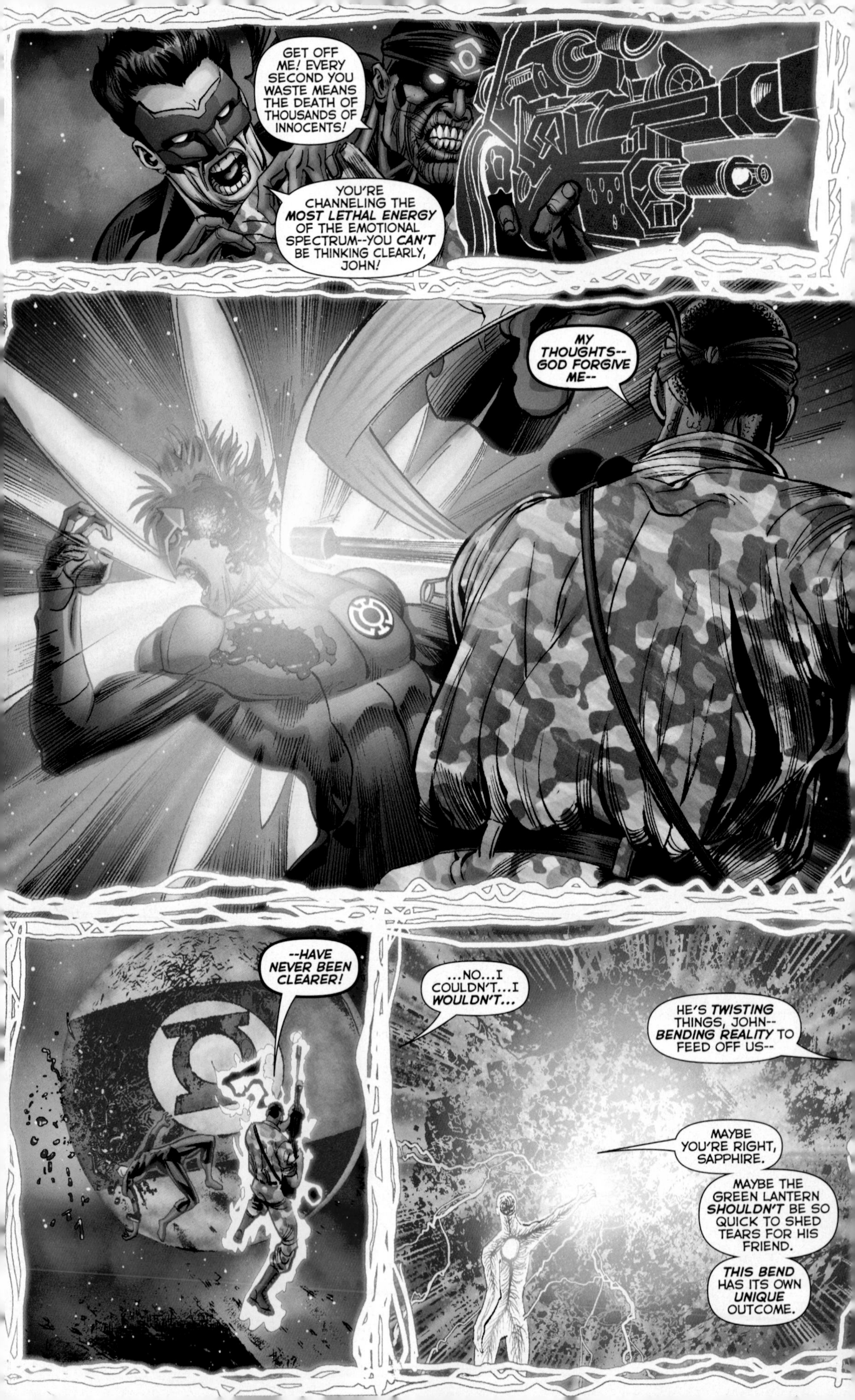
GET OFF ME! EVERY SECOND YOU WASTE MEANS THE DEATH OF THOUSANDS OF INNOCENTS!
YOU'RE CHANNELING THE MOST LETHAL ENERGY OF THE EMOTIONAL SPECTRUM--YOU CAN'T BE THINKING CLEARLY, JOHN!
MY THOUGHTS--GOD FORGIVE ME--
--HAVE NEVER BEEN CLEARER!
...NO...I COULDN'T...I WOULDN'T...
HE'S TWISTING THINGS, JOHN--BENDING REALITY TO FEED OFF US--
MAYBE YOU'RE RIGHT, SAPPHIRE.
MAYBE THE GREEN LANTERN SHOULDN'T BE SO QUICK TO SHED TEARS FOR HIS FRIEND.
THIS BEND HAS ITS OWN UNIQUE OUTCOME.

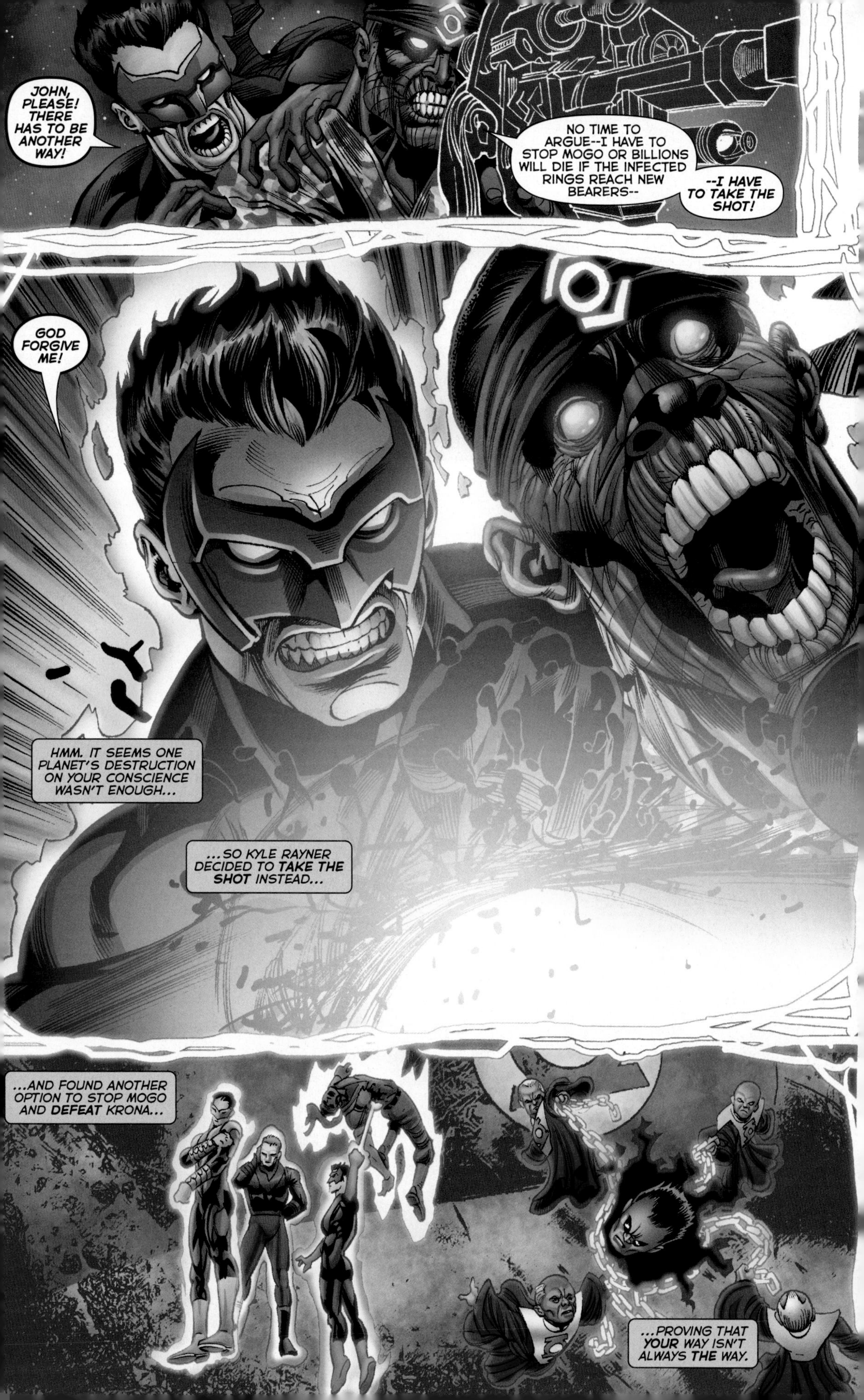

JOHN, PLEASE! THERE HAS TO BE ANOTHER WAY!
NO TIME TO ARGUE--I HAVE TO STOP MOGO OR BILLIONS WILL DIE IF THE INFECTED RINGS REACH NEW BEARERS--
--I HAVE TO TAKE THE SHOT!
GOD FORGIVE ME!
HMM. IT SEEMS ONE PLANET'S DESTRUCTION ON YOUR CONSCIENCE WASN'T ENOUGH...
...SO KYLE RAYNER DECIDED TO TAKE THE SHOT INSTEAD...
...AND FOUND ANOTHER OPTION TO STOP MOGO AND DEFEAT KRONA...
...PROVING THAT YOUR WAY ISN'T ALWAYS THE WAY.

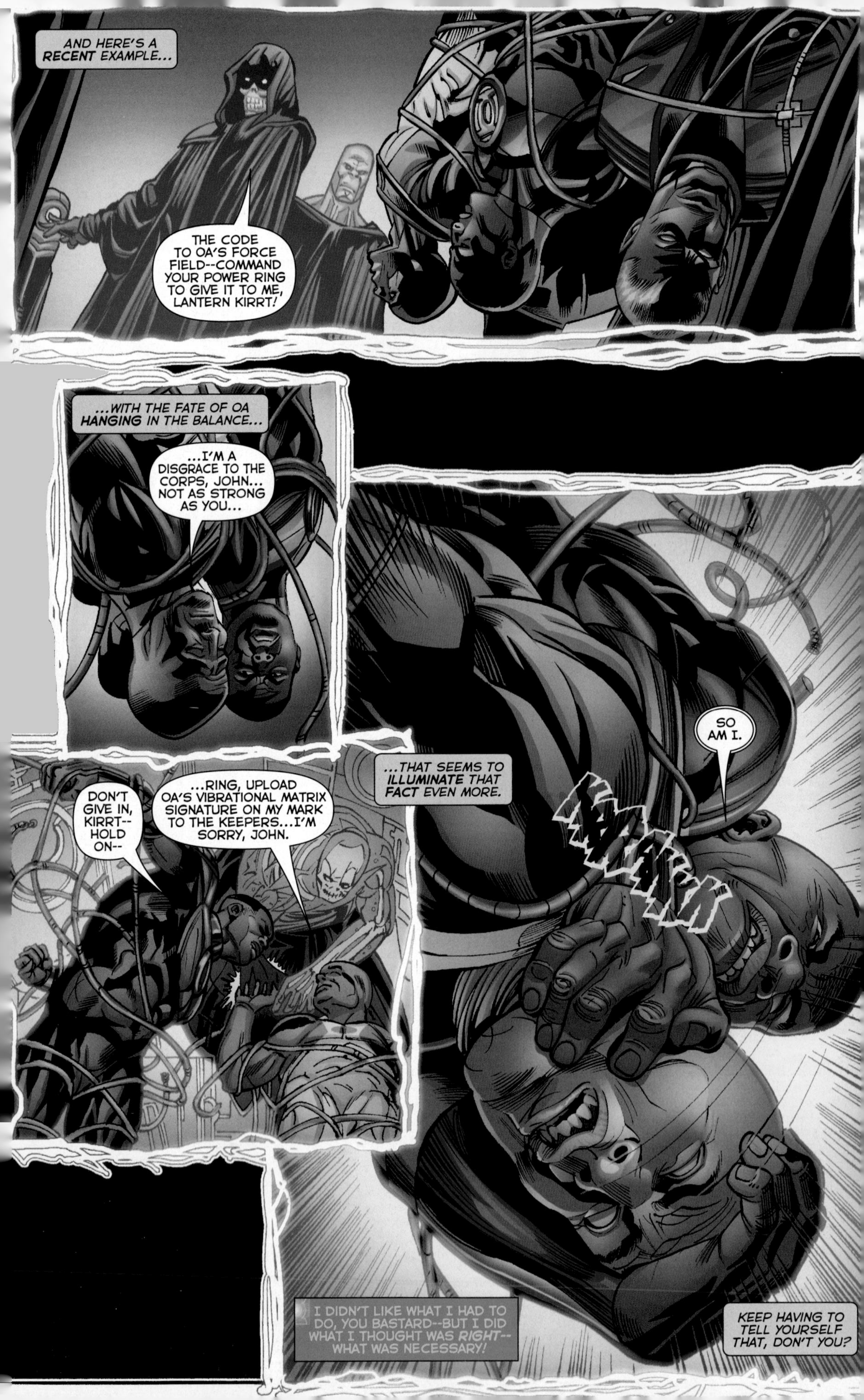
AND HERE'S A RECENT EXAMPLE...
THE CODE TO OA'S FORCE FIELD--COMMAND YOUR POWER RING TO GIVE IT TO ME, LANTERN KIRRT!
...WITH THE FATE OF OA HANGING IN THE BALANCE...
...I'M A DISGRACE TO THE CORPS, JOHN... NOT AS STRONG AS YOU...
DON'T GIVE IN, KIRRT--HOLD ON--
...RING, UPLOAD OA'S VIBRATIONAL MATRIX SIGNATURE ON MY MARK TO THE KEEPERS...I'M SORRY, JOHN.
...THAT SEEMS TO ILLUMINATE THAT FACT EVEN MORE.
SO AM I.
I DIDN'T LIKE WHAT I HAD TO DO, YOU BASTARD--BUT I DID WHAT I THOUGHT WAS RIGHT--WHAT WAS NECESSARY!
KEEP HAVING TO TELL YOURSELF THAT, DON'T YOU?

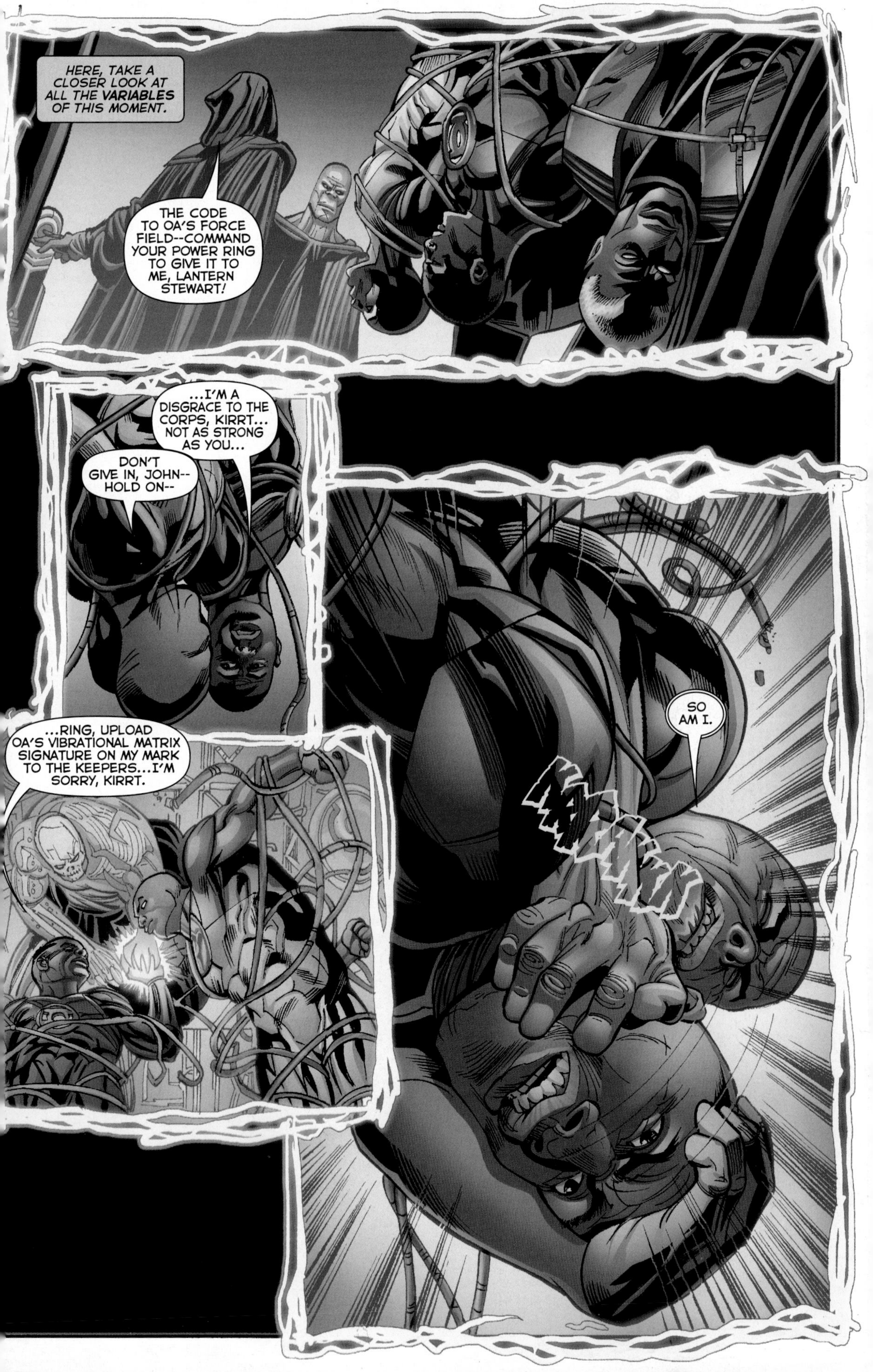
HERE, TAKE A CLOSER LOOK AT ALL THE VARIABLES OF THIS MOMENT.
THE CODE TO OA'S FORCE FIELD--COMMAND YOUR POWER RING TO GIVE IT TO ME, LANTERN STEWART!
...I'M A DISGRACE TO THE CORPS, KIRRT... NOT AS STRONG AS YOU...
DON'T GIVE IN, JOHN-- HOLD ON--
SO AM I.
...RING, UPLOAD OA'S VIBRATIONAL MATRIX SIGNATURE ON MY MARK TO THE KEEPERS...I'M SORRY, KIRRT.

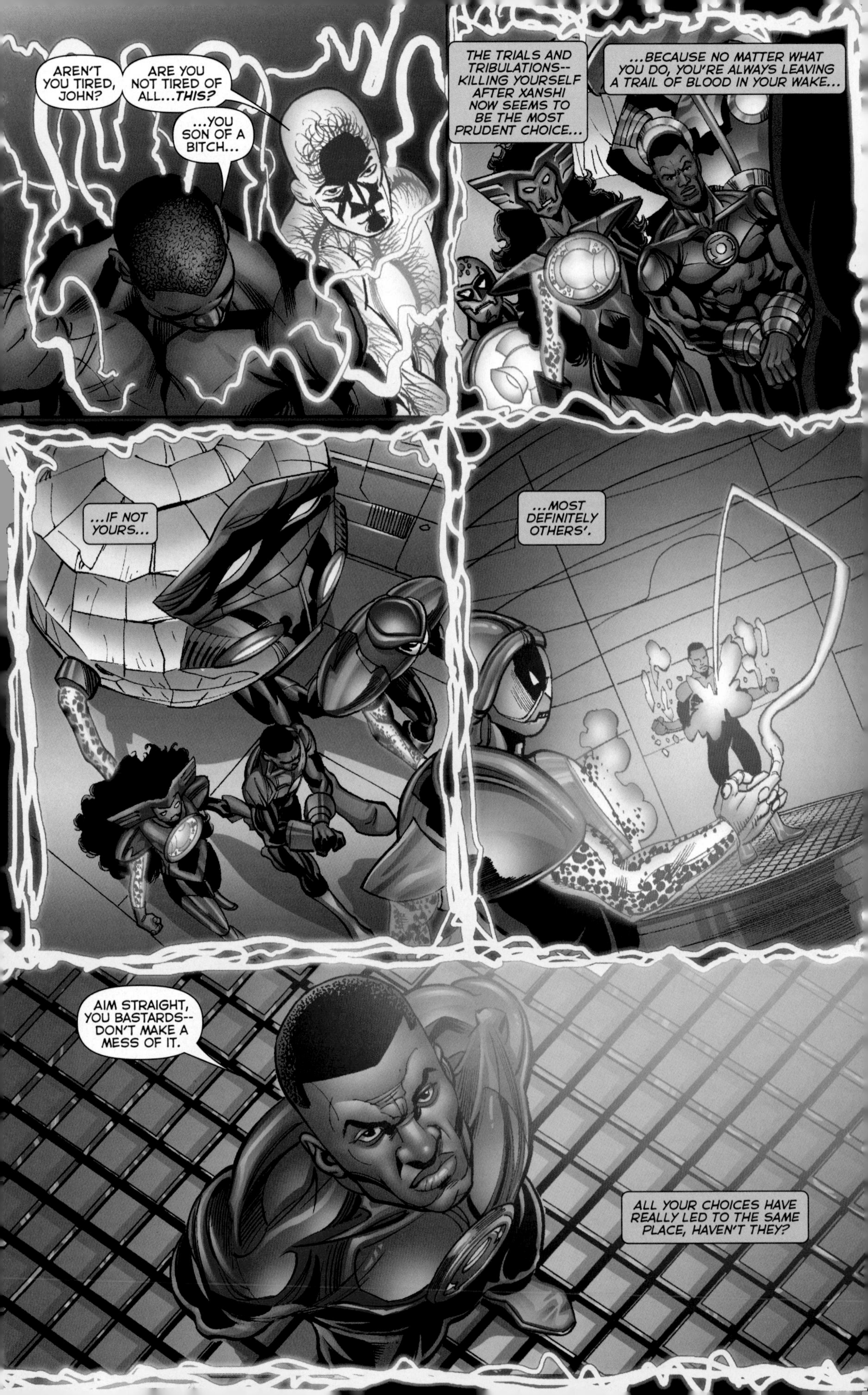
AREN'T YOU TIRED, JOHN?
ARE YOU NOT TIRED OF ALL...THIS?
...YOU SON OF A BITCH...
THE TRIALS AND TRIBULATIONS-- KILLING YOURSELF AFTER XANSHI NOW SEEMS TO BE THE MOST PRUDENT CHOICE...
...BECAUSE NO MATTER WHAT YOU DO, YOU'RE ALWAYS LEAVING A TRAIL OF BLOOD IN YOUR WAKE...
...IF NOT YOURS...
...MOST DEFINITELY OTHERS'.
AIM STRAIGHT, YOU BASTARDS-- DON'T MAKE A MESS OF IT.
ALL YOUR CHOICES HAVE REALLY LED TO THE SAME PLACE, HAVEN'T THEY?

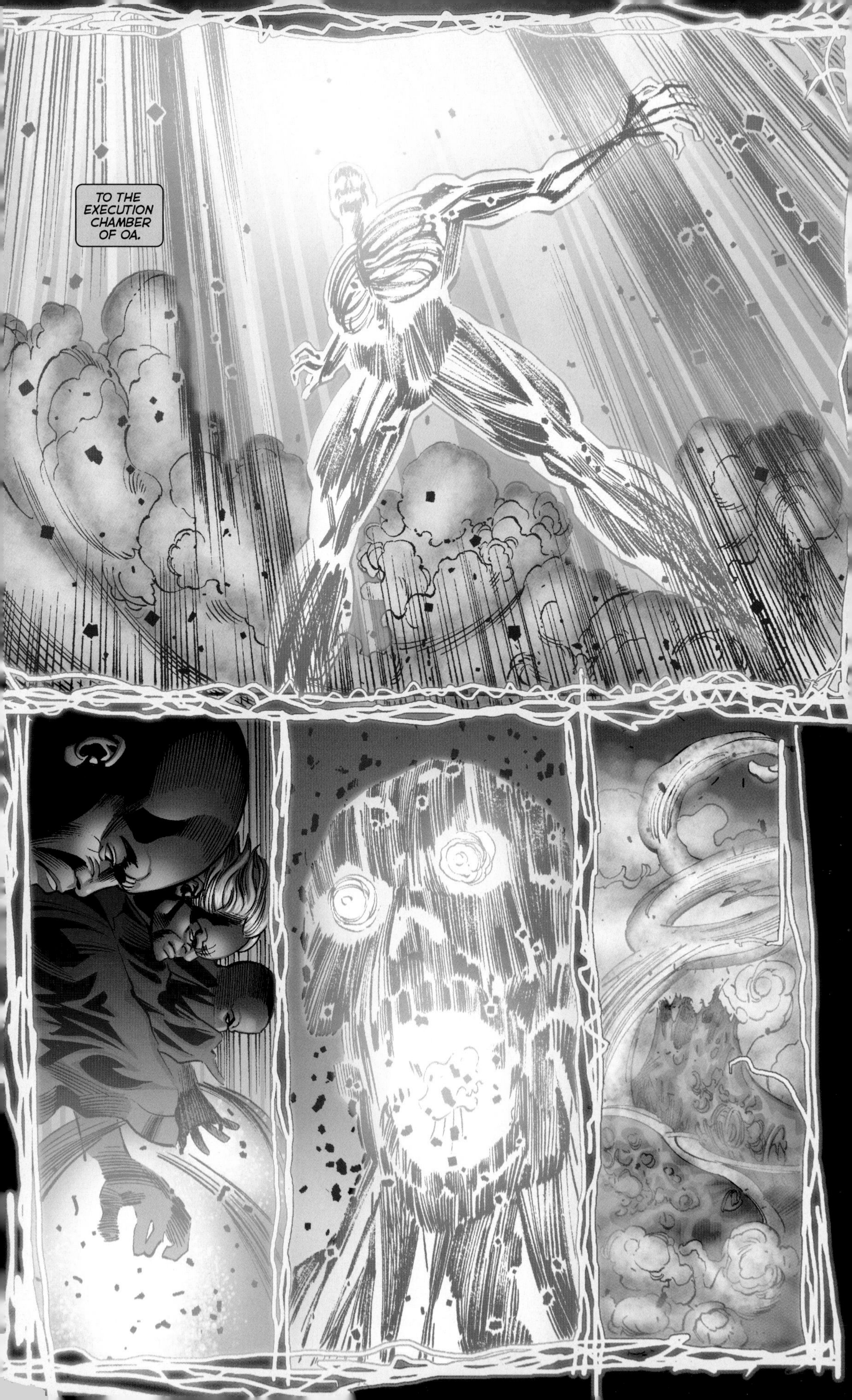
TO THE EXECUTION CHAMBER OF OA.

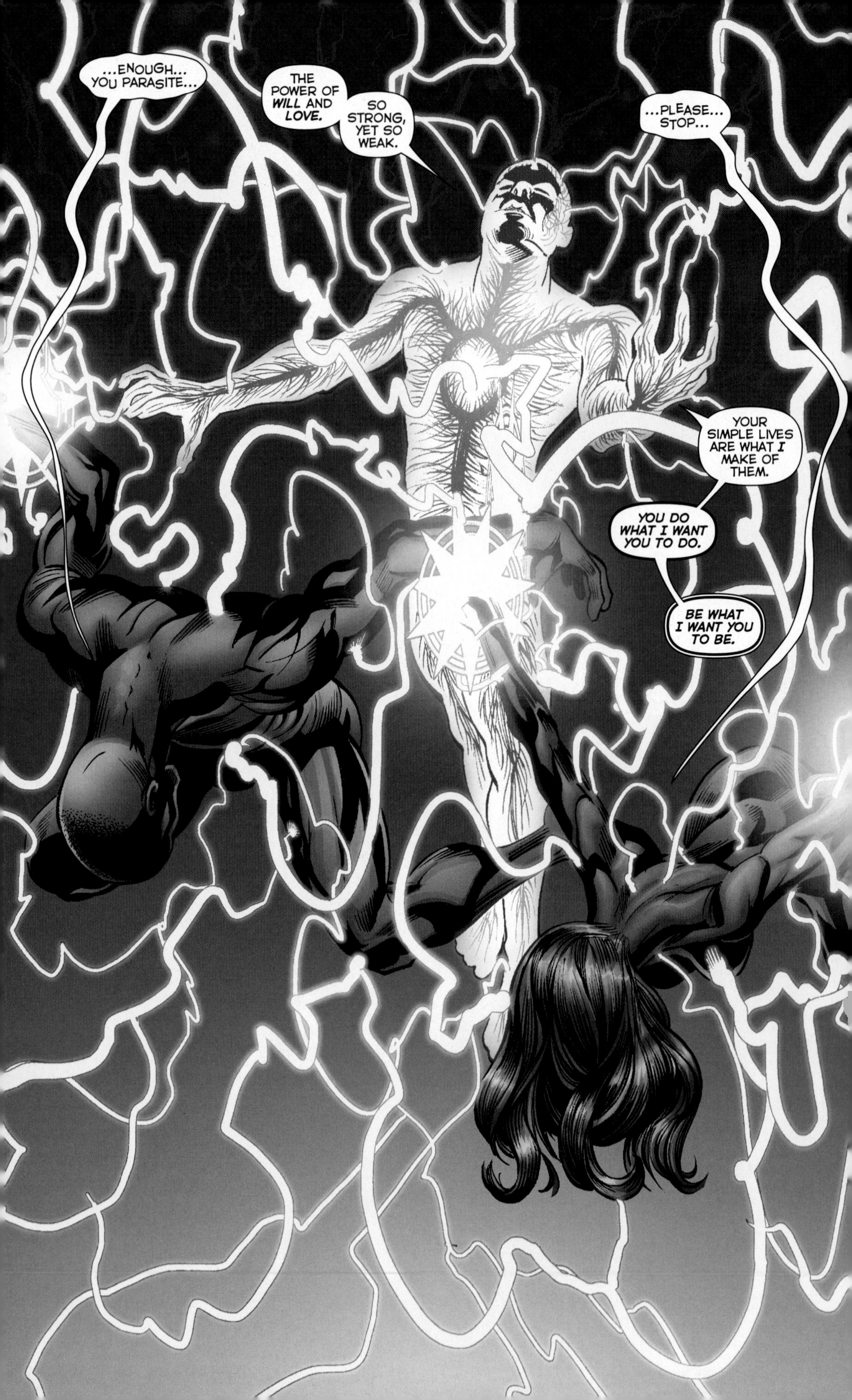
...ENOUGH... YOU PARASITE...
THE POWER OF WILL AND LOVE.
SO STRONG, YET SO WEAK.
...PLEASE... STOP...
YOUR SIMPLE LIVES ARE WHAT I MAKE OF THEM.
YOU DO WHAT I WANT YOU TO DO.
BE WHAT I WANT YOU TO BE.

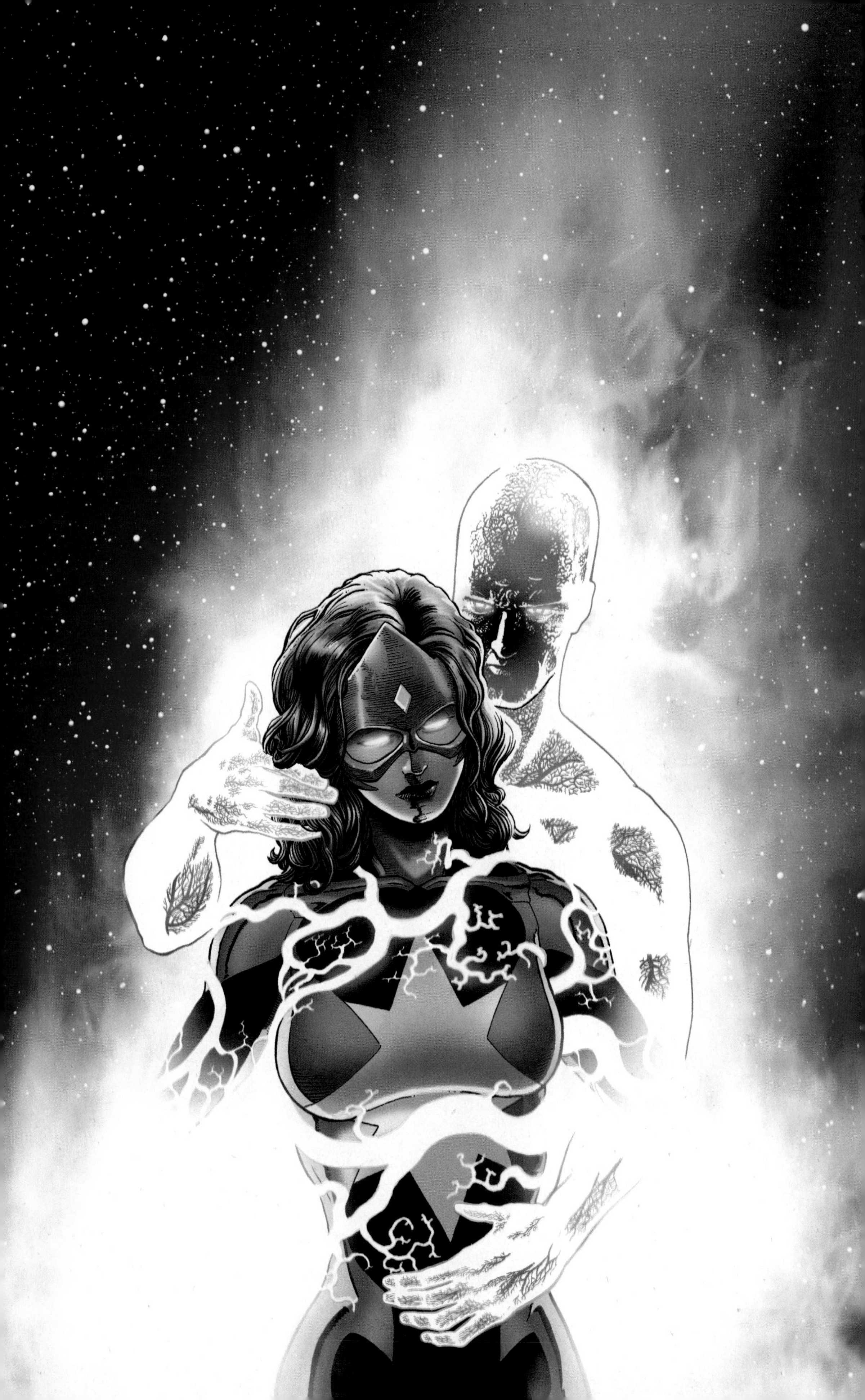

PART SEVEN: PATHS UNTAKEN
HENDRY PRASETYO artist CAROL FERRIS sequence JIM CALAFIORE artist LARFLEEZE sequence
JAVIER PULIDO artist SAINT WALKER sequence

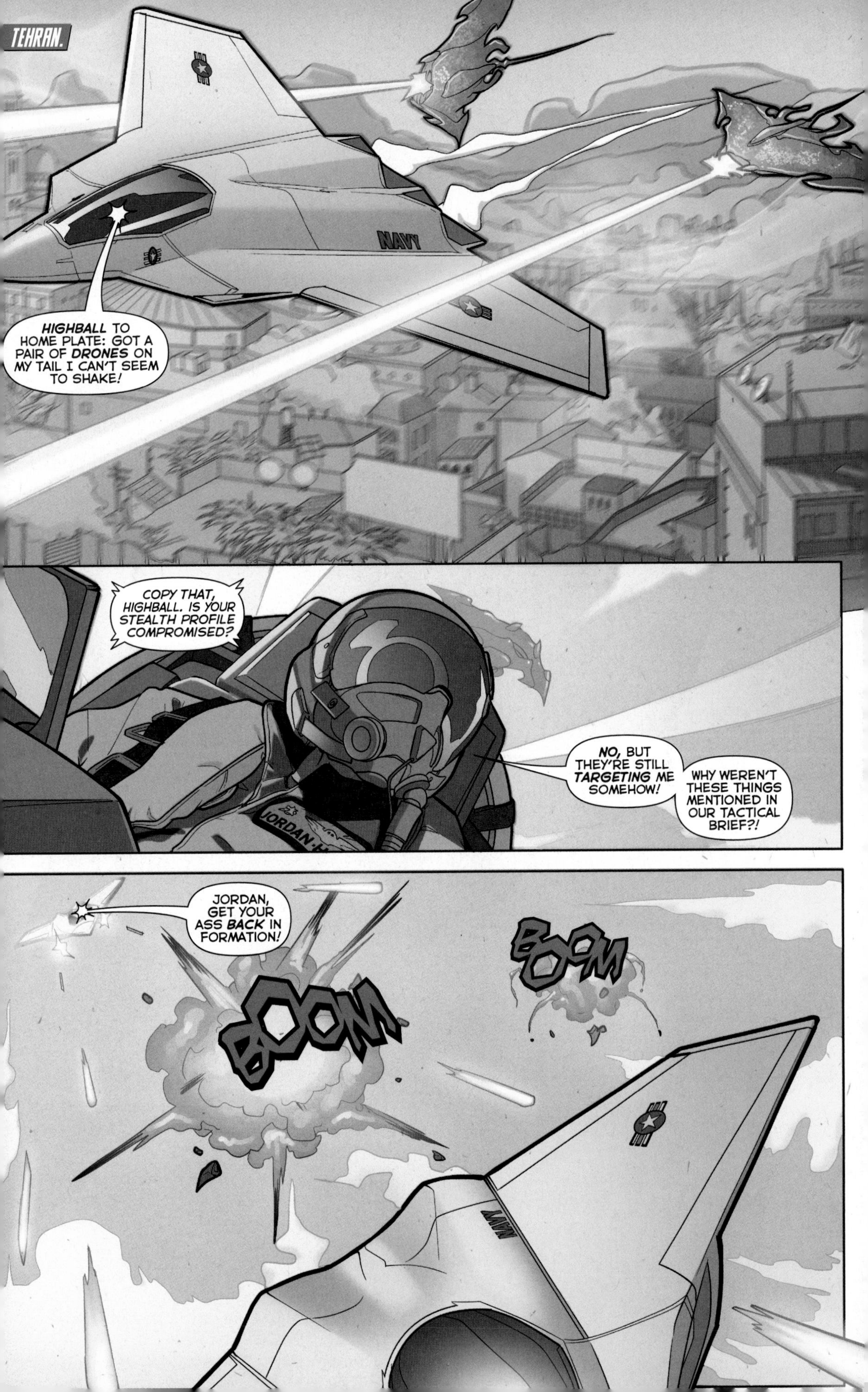
TEHRAN.
HIGHBALL TO HOME PLATE: GOT A PAIR OF DRONES ON MY TAIL I CAN'T SEEM TO SHAKE!
NAVY
COPY THAT, HIGHBALL. IS YOUR STEALTH PROFILE COMPROMISED?
NO, BUT THEY'RE STILL TARGETING ME SOMEHOW!
WHY WEREN'T THESE THINGS MENTIONED IN OUR TACTICAL BRIEF?!
JORDAN, GET YOUR ASS BACK IN FORMATION!
BOOM
BOOM
NAVY

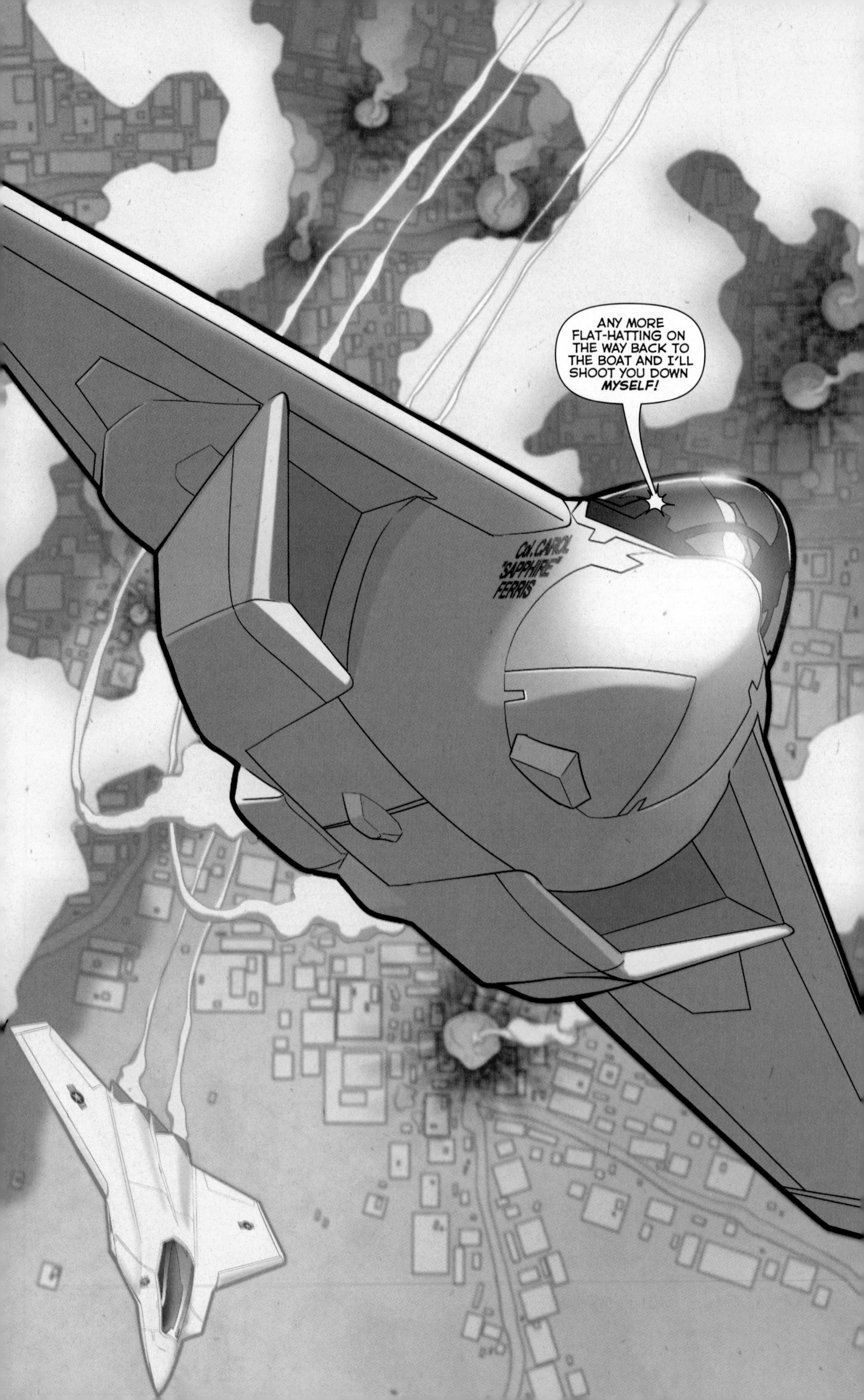
ANY MORE FLAT-HATTING ON THE WAY BACK TO THE BOAT AND I'LL SHOOT YOU DOWN *MYSELF!*
Col. CAROL "SAPPHIRE" FERRIS

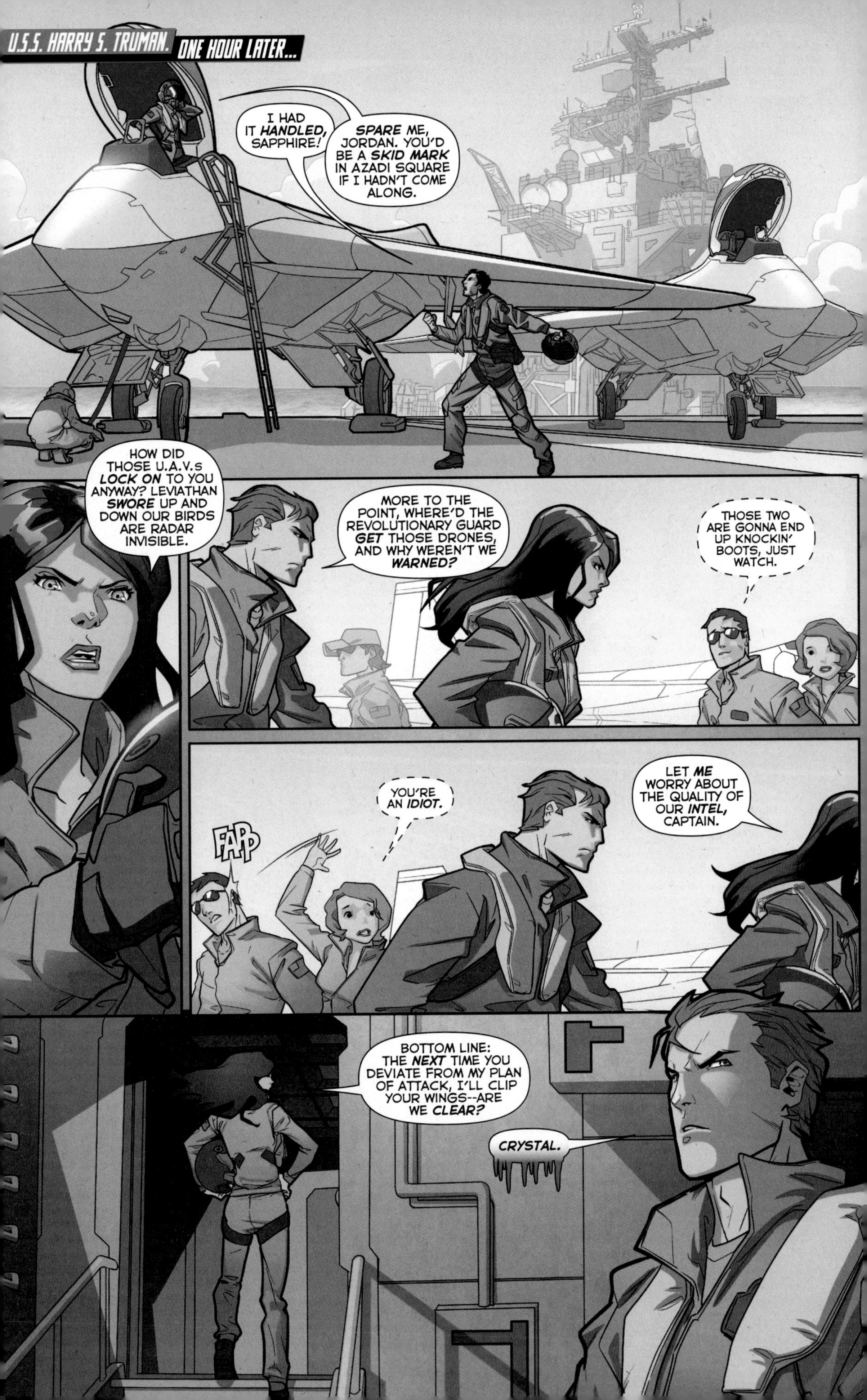
U.S.S. HARRY S. TRUMAN.
ONE HOUR LATER...
I HAD IT HANDLED, SAPPHIRE!
SPARE ME, JORDAN. YOU'D BE A SKID MARK IN AZADI SQUARE IF I HADN'T COME ALONG.
HOW DID THOSE U.A.V.s LOCK ON TO YOU ANYWAY? LEVIATHAN SWORE UP AND DOWN OUR BIRDS ARE RADAR INVISIBLE.
MORE TO THE POINT, WHERE'D THE REVOLUTIONARY GUARD GET THOSE DRONES, AND WHY WEREN'T WE WARNED?
THOSE TWO ARE GONNA END UP KNOCKIN' BOOTS, JUST WATCH.
FAPP
YOU'RE AN IDIOT.
LET ME WORRY ABOUT THE QUALITY OF OUR INTEL, CAPTAIN.
BOTTOM LINE: THE NEXT TIME YOU DEVIATE FROM MY PLAN OF ATTACK, I'LL CLIP YOUR WINGS--ARE WE CLEAR?
CRYSTAL.

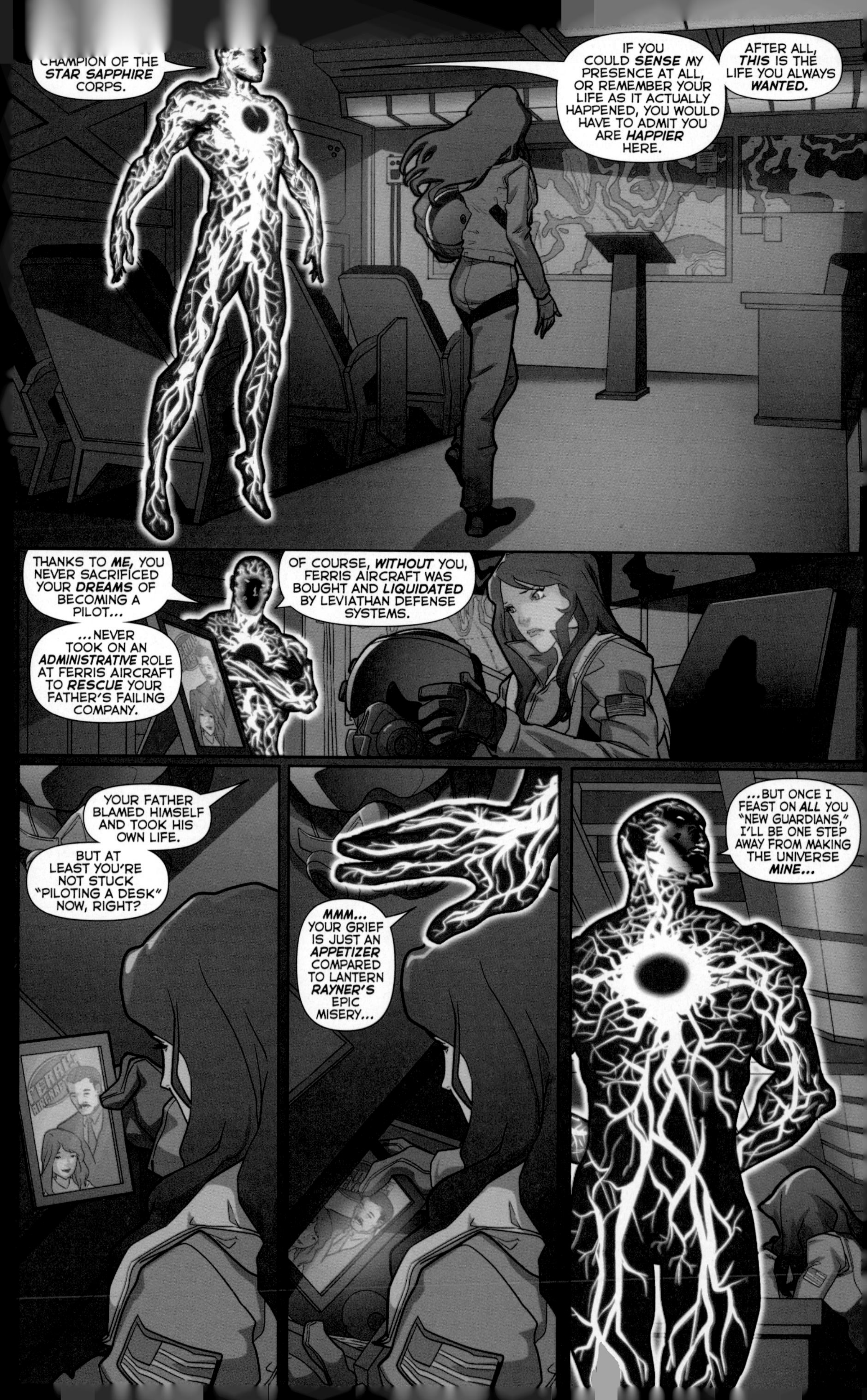
CHAMPION OF THE STAR SAPPHIRE CORPS.
IF YOU COULD SENSE MY PRESENCE AT ALL, OR REMEMBER YOUR LIFE AS IT ACTUALLY HAPPENED, YOU WOULD HAVE TO ADMIT YOU ARE HAPPIER HERE.
AFTER ALL, THIS IS THE LIFE YOU ALWAYS WANTED.
THANKS TO ME, YOU NEVER SACRIFICED YOUR DREAMS OF BECOMING A PILOT...
...NEVER TOOK ON AN ADMINISTRATIVE ROLE AT FERRIS AIRCRAFT TO RESCUE YOUR FATHER'S FAILING COMPANY.
OF COURSE, WITHOUT YOU, FERRIS AIRCRAFT WAS BOUGHT AND LIQUIDATED BY LEVIATHAN DEFENSE SYSTEMS.
YOUR FATHER BLAMED HIMSELF AND TOOK HIS OWN LIFE.
BUT AT LEAST YOU'RE NOT STUCK "PILOTING A DESK" NOW, RIGHT?
MMM... YOUR GRIEF IS JUST AN APPETIZER COMPARED TO LANTERN RAYNER'S EPIC MISERY...
...BUT ONCE I FEAST ON ALL YOU "NEW GUARDIANS," I'LL BE ONE STEP AWAY FROM MAKING THE UNIVERSE MINE...

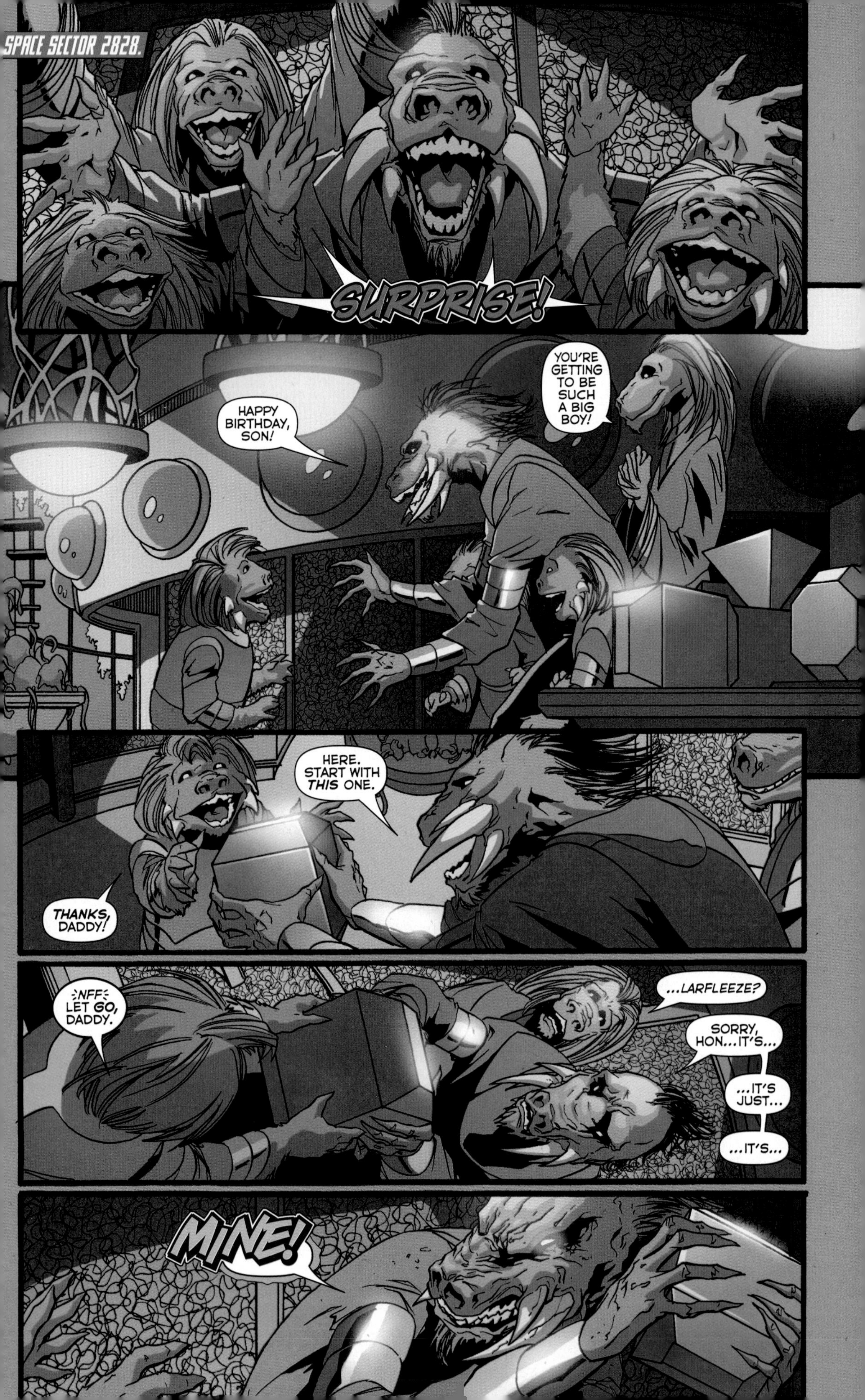
SPACE SECTOR 2828.
SURPRISE!
HAPPY BIRTHDAY, SON!
YOU'RE GETTING TO BE SUCH A BIG BOY!
HERE. START WITH *THIS* ONE.
THANKS, DADDY!
NFF
LET *GO*, DADDY.
...LARFLEEZE?
SORRY, HON...IT'S...
...IT'S JUST...
...IT'S...
MINE!

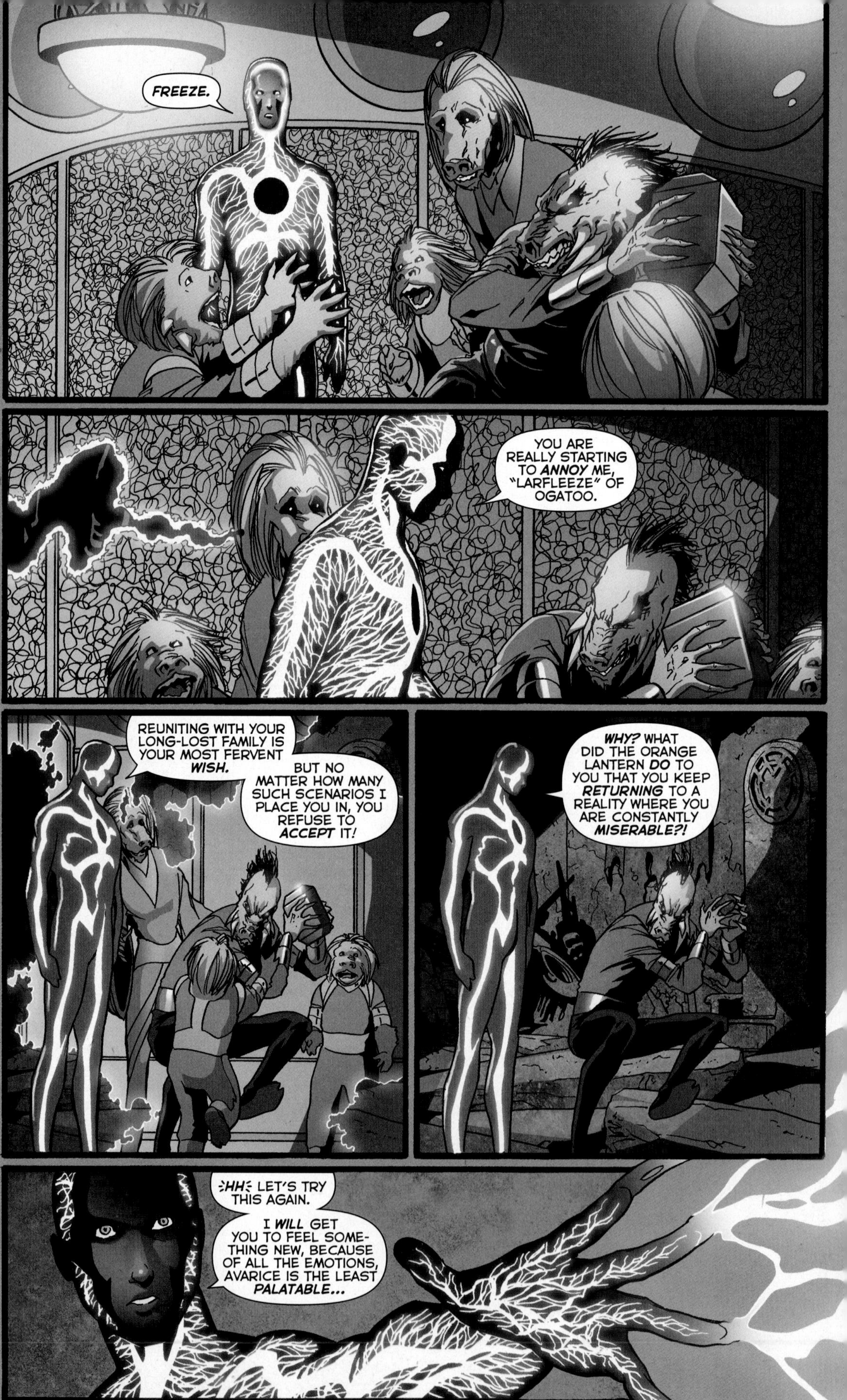
FREEZE.
YOU ARE REALLY STARTING TO ANNOY ME, "LARFLEEZE" OF OGATOO.
REUNITING WITH YOUR LONG-LOST FAMILY IS YOUR MOST FERVENT WISH.
BUT NO MATTER HOW MANY SUCH SCENARIOS I PLACE YOU IN, YOU REFUSE TO ACCEPT IT!
WHY? WHAT DID THE ORANGE LANTERN DO TO YOU THAT YOU KEEP RETURNING TO A REALITY WHERE YOU ARE CONSTANTLY MISERABLE?!
HH LET'S TRY THIS AGAIN.
I WILL GET YOU TO FEEL SOME-THING NEW, BECAUSE OF ALL THE EMOTIONS, AVARICE IS THE LEAST PALATABLE...

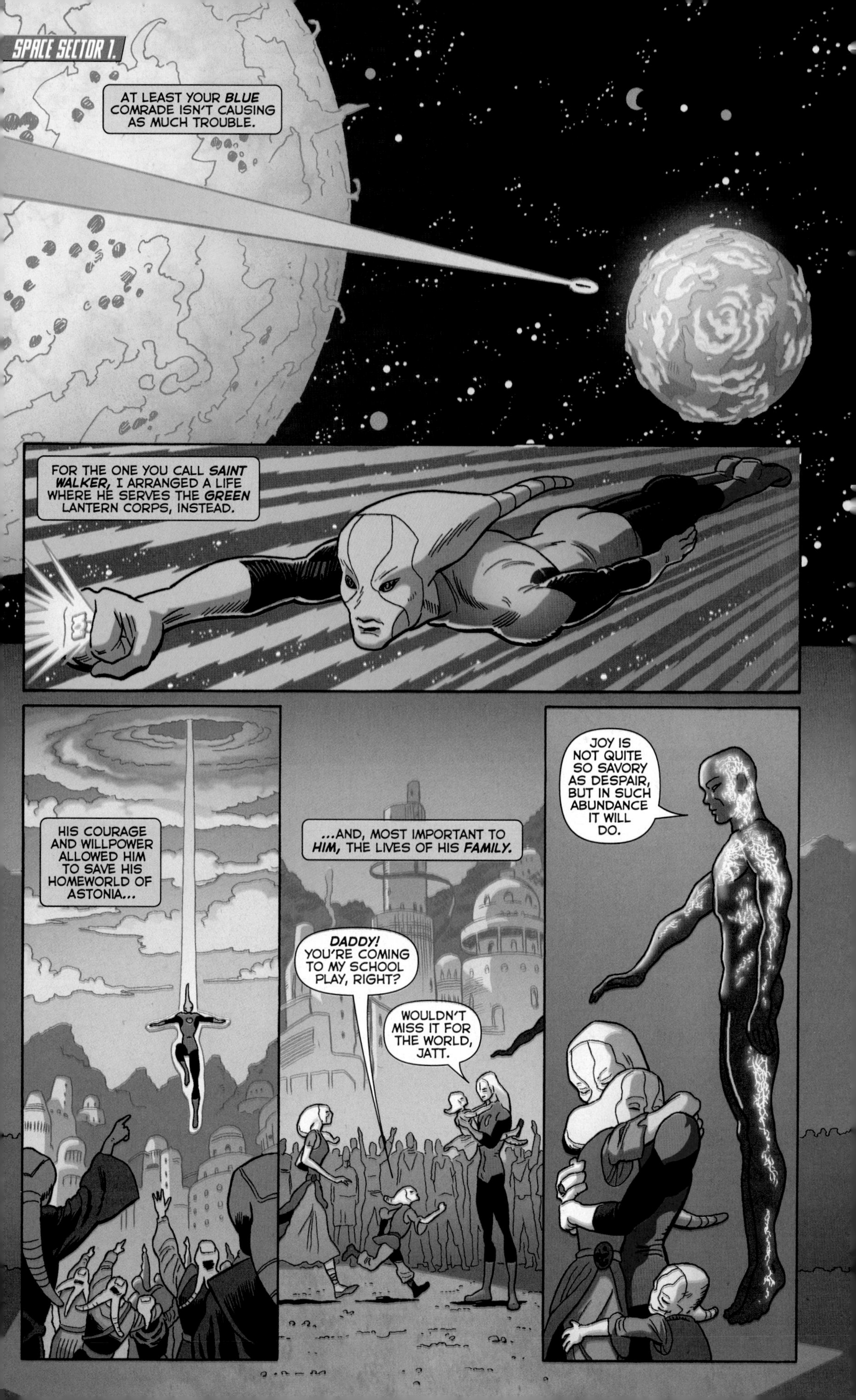
SPACE SECTOR 1.
AT LEAST YOUR BLUE COMRADE ISN'T CAUSING AS MUCH TROUBLE.
FOR THE ONE YOU CALL SAINT WALKER, I ARRANGED A LIFE WHERE HE SERVES THE GREEN LANTERN CORPS, INSTEAD.
HIS COURAGE AND WILLPOWER ALLOWED HIM TO SAVE HIS HOMEWORLD OF ASTONIA...
...AND, MOST IMPORTANT TO HIM, THE LIVES OF HIS FAMILY.
DADDY! YOU'RE COMING TO MY SCHOOL PLAY, RIGHT?
WOULDN'T MISS IT FOR THE WORLD, JATT.
JOY IS NOT QUITE SO SAVORY AS DESPAIR, BUT IN SUCH ABUNDANCE IT WILL DO.

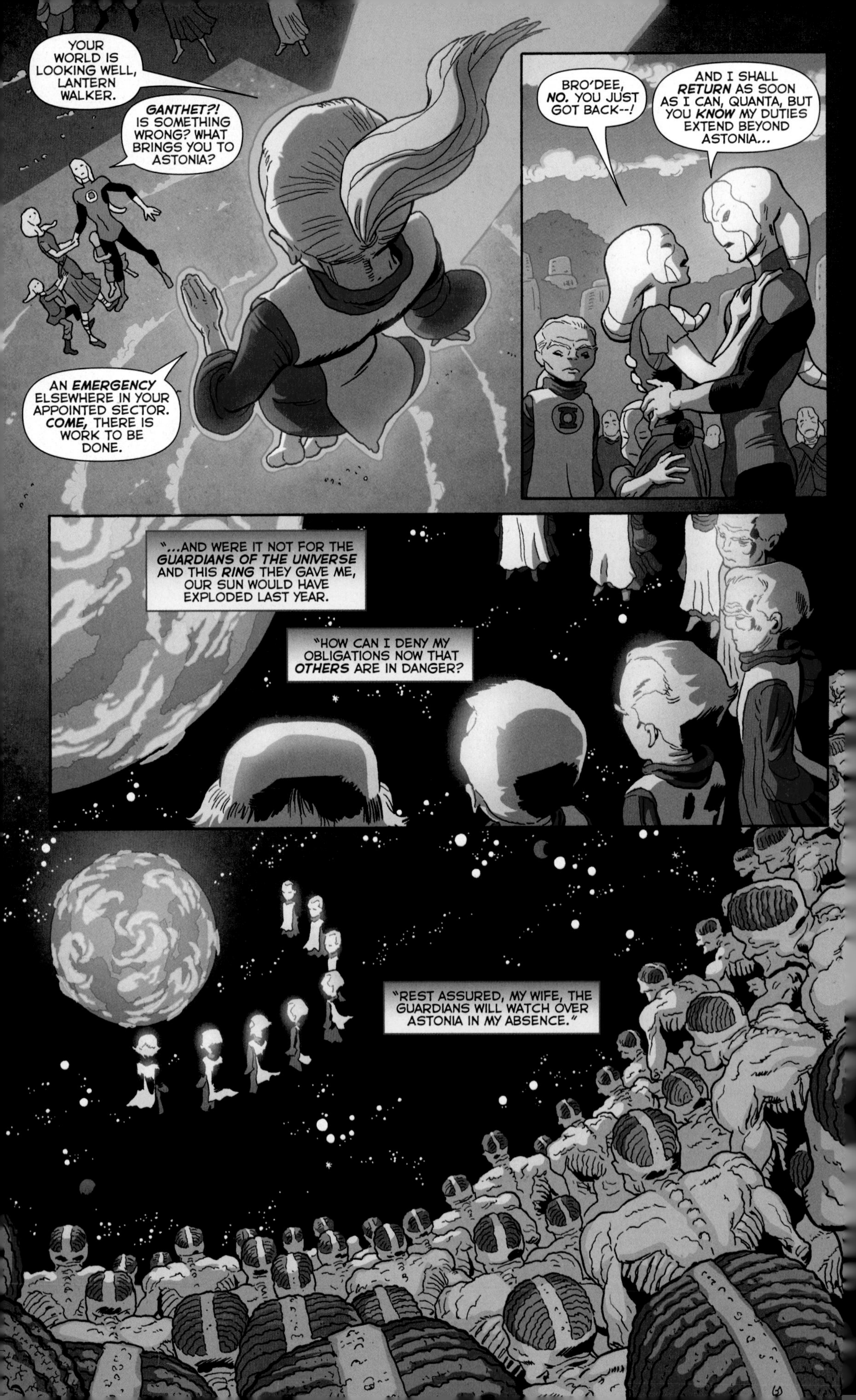
YOUR WORLD IS LOOKING WELL, LANTERN WALKER.
GANTHET?! IS SOMETHING WRONG? WHAT BRINGS YOU TO ASTONIA?
AN EMERGENCY ELSEWHERE IN YOUR APPOINTED SECTOR. COME, THERE IS WORK TO BE DONE.
BRO'DEE, NO. YOU JUST GOT BACK--!
AND I SHALL RETURN AS SOON AS I CAN, QUANTA, BUT YOU KNOW MY DUTIES EXTEND BEYOND ASTONIA...
"...AND WERE IT NOT FOR THE GUARDIANS OF THE UNIVERSE AND THIS RING THEY GAVE ME, OUR SUN WOULD HAVE EXPLODED LAST YEAR.
"HOW CAN I DENY MY OBLIGATIONS NOW THAT OTHERS ARE IN DANGER?
"REST ASSURED, MY WIFE, THE GUARDIANS WILL WATCH OVER ASTONIA IN MY ABSENCE."

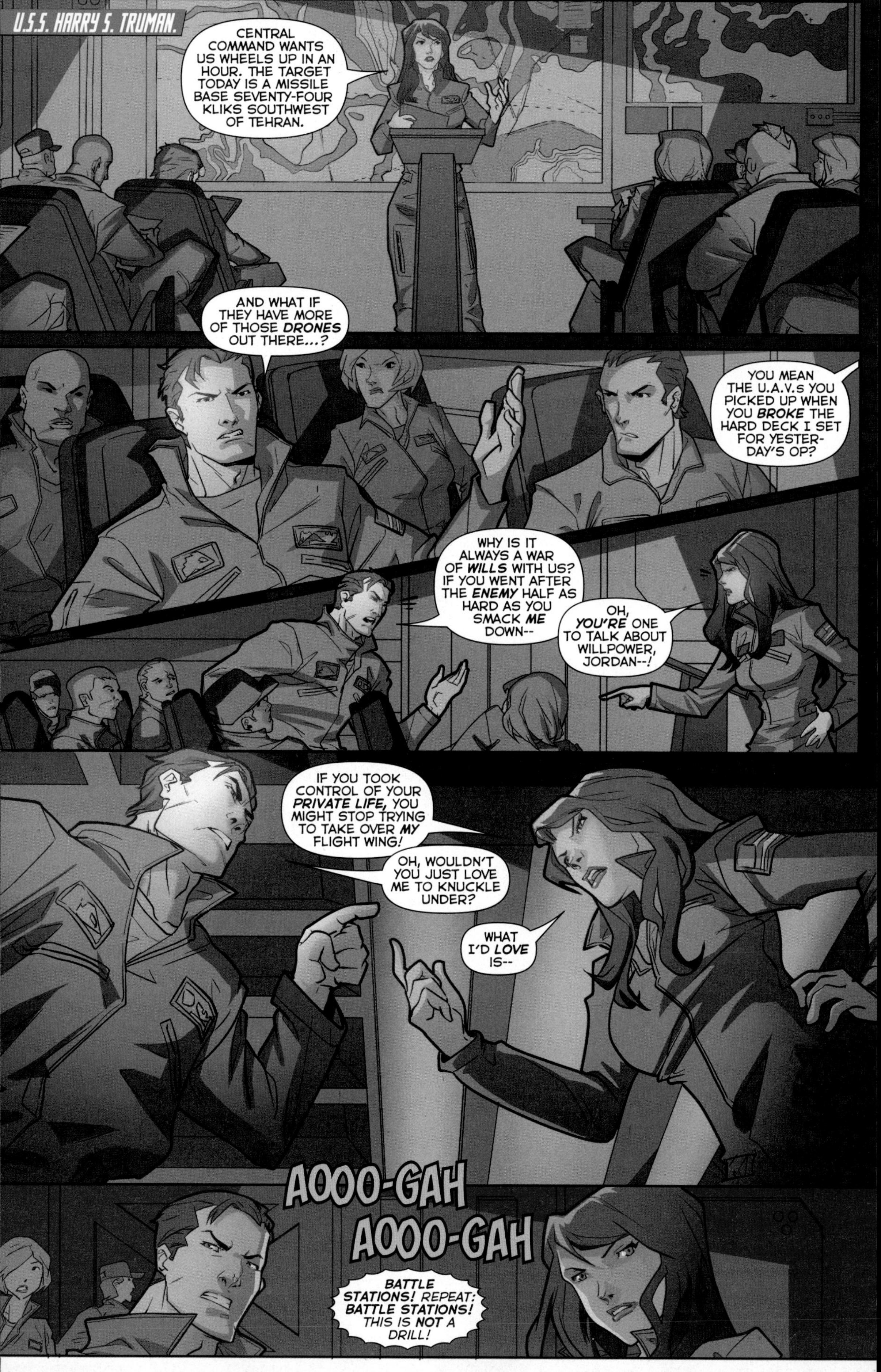
U.S.S. HARRY S. TRUMAN.
CENTRAL COMMAND WANTS US WHEELS UP IN AN HOUR. THE TARGET TODAY IS A MISSILE BASE SEVENTY-FOUR KLIKS SOUTHWEST OF TEHRAN.
AND WHAT IF THEY HAVE MORE OF THOSE DRONES OUT THERE...?
YOU MEAN THE U.A.V.s YOU PICKED UP WHEN YOU BROKE THE HARD DECK I SET FOR YESTER-DAY'S OP?
WHY IS IT ALWAYS A WAR OF WILLS WITH US? IF YOU WENT AFTER THE ENEMY HALF AS HARD AS YOU SMACK ME DOWN--
OH, YOU'RE ONE TO TALK ABOUT WILLPOWER, JORDAN--!
IF YOU TOOK CONTROL OF YOUR PRIVATE LIFE, YOU MIGHT STOP TRYING TO TAKE OVER MY FLIGHT WING!
OH, WOULDN'T YOU JUST LOVE ME TO KNUCKLE UNDER?
WHAT I'D LOVE IS--
AOOO-GAH
AOOO-GAH
BATTLE STATIONS! REPEAT: BATTLE STATIONS! THIS IS NOT A DRILL!

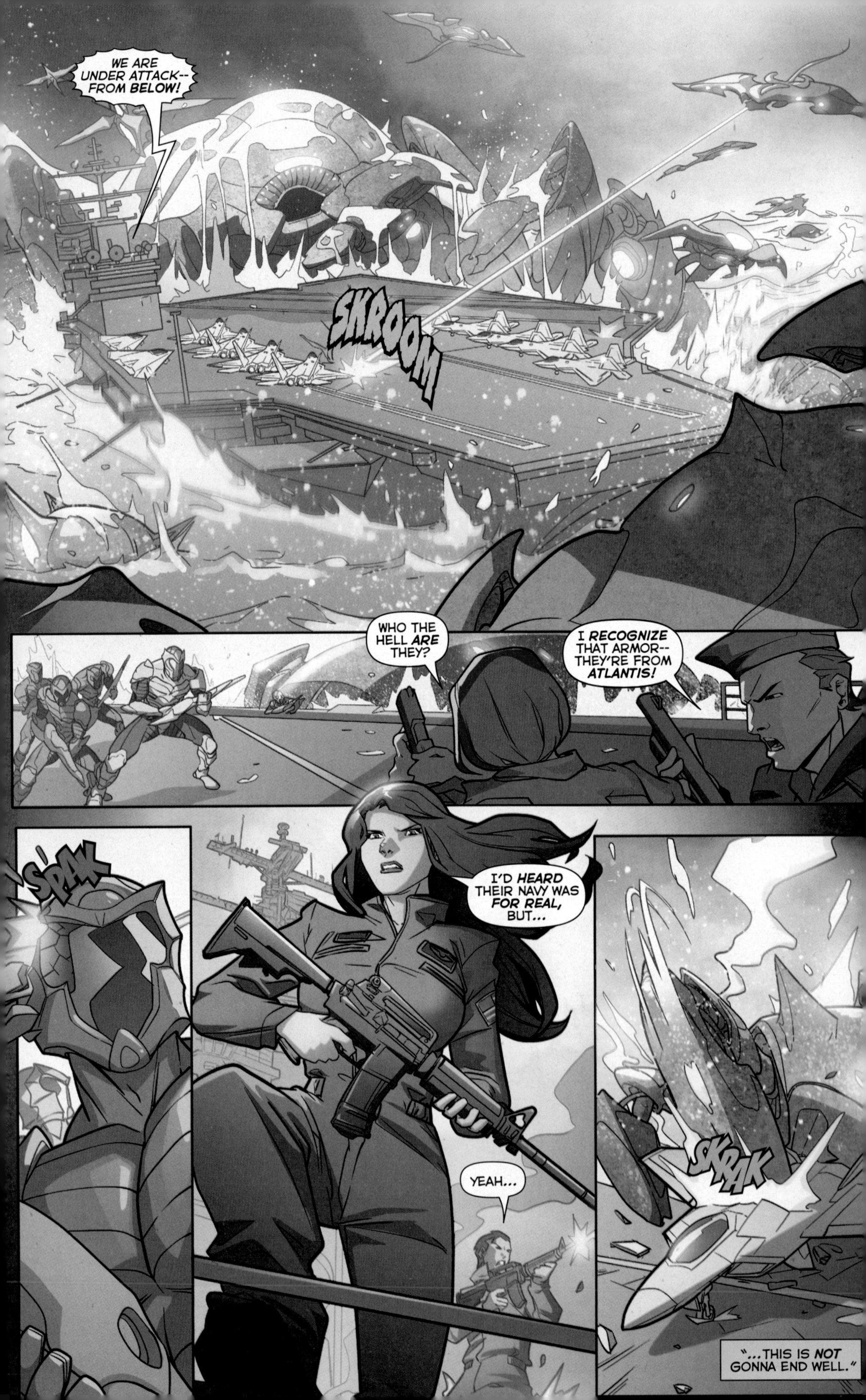
WE ARE UNDER ATTACK-- FROM BELOW!
SKROOM
WHO THE HELL ARE THEY?
I RECOGNIZE THAT ARMOR-- THEY'RE FROM ATLANTIS!
SPAK
I'D HEARD THEIR NAVY WAS FOR REAL, BUT...
YEAH...
SKRAK
"...THIS IS NOT GONNA END WELL."

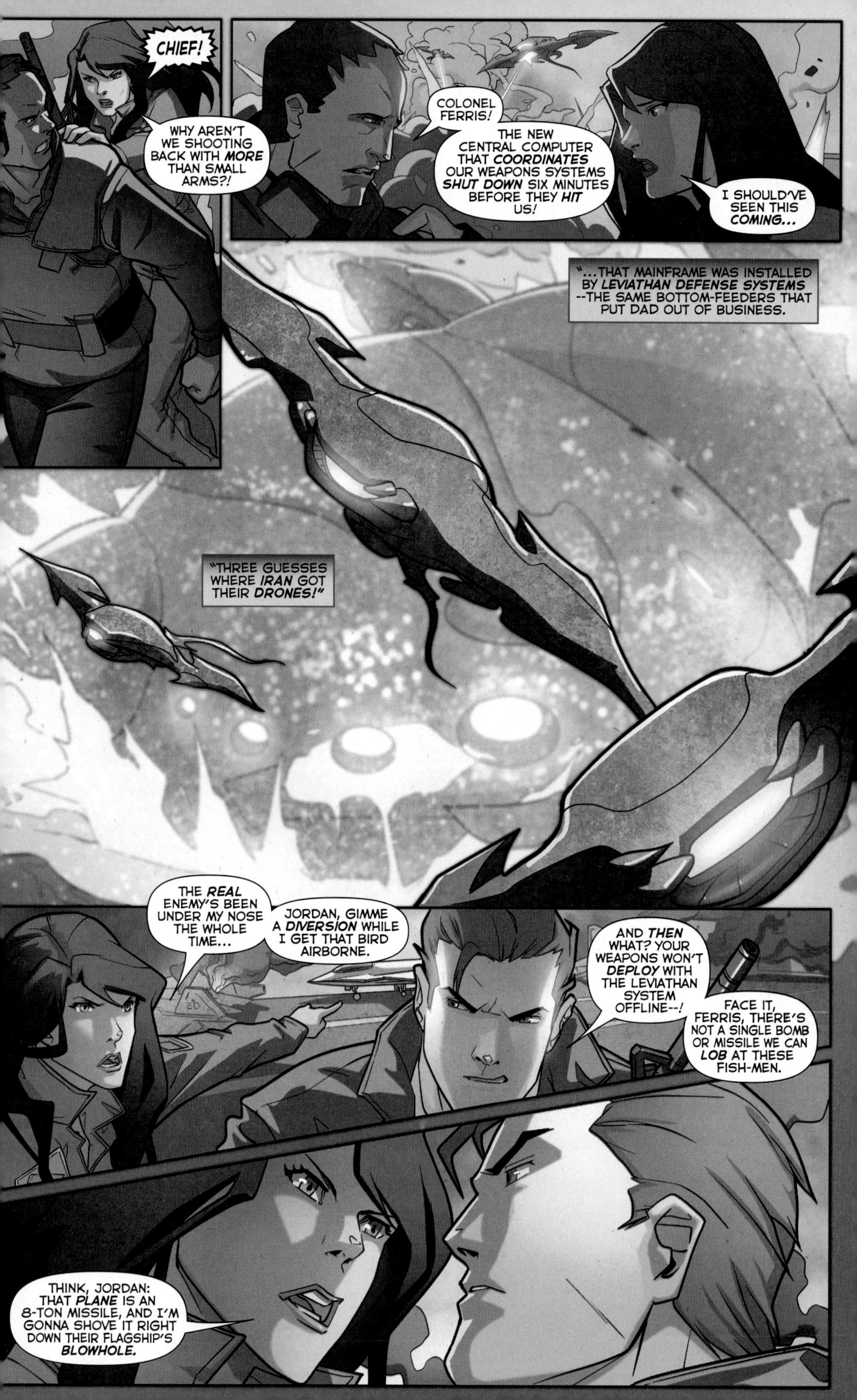
CHIEF!
WHY AREN'T WE SHOOTING BACK WITH MORE THAN SMALL ARMS?!
COLONEL FERRIS!
THE NEW CENTRAL COMPUTER THAT COORDINATES OUR WEAPONS SYSTEMS SHUT DOWN SIX MINUTES BEFORE THEY HIT US!
I SHOULD'VE SEEN THIS COMING...
"...THAT MAINFRAME WAS INSTALLED BY LEVIATHAN DEFENSE SYSTEMS --THE SAME BOTTOM-FEEDERS THAT PUT DAD OUT OF BUSINESS.
"THREE GUESSES WHERE IRAN GOT THEIR DRONES!"
THE REAL ENEMY'S BEEN UNDER MY NOSE THE WHOLE TIME...
JORDAN, GIMME A DIVERSION WHILE I GET THAT BIRD AIRBORNE.
AND THEN WHAT? YOUR WEAPONS WON'T DEPLOY WITH THE LEVIATHAN SYSTEM OFFLINE--!
FACE IT, FERRIS, THERE'S NOT A SINGLE BOMB OR MISSILE WE CAN LOB AT THESE FISH-MEN.
THINK, JORDAN: THAT PLANE IS AN 8-TON MISSILE, AND I'M GONNA SHOVE IT RIGHT DOWN THEIR FLAGSHIP'S BLOWHOLE.

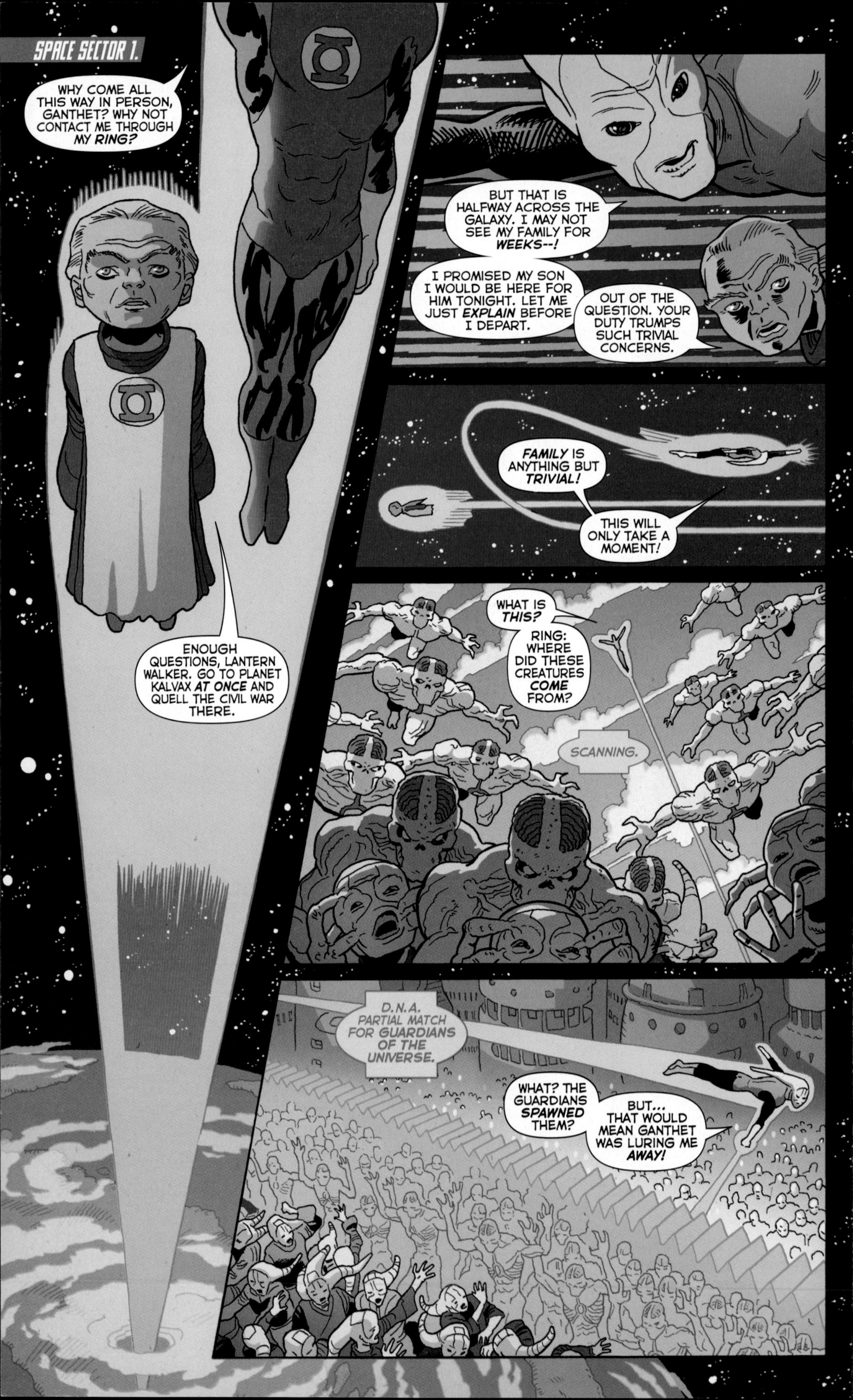
SPACE SECTOR 1.
WHY COME ALL THIS WAY IN PERSON, GANTHET? WHY NOT CONTACT ME THROUGH MY RING?
ENOUGH QUESTIONS, LANTERN WALKER. GO TO PLANET KALVAX AT ONCE AND QUELL THE CIVIL WAR THERE.
BUT THAT IS HALFWAY ACROSS THE GALAXY. I MAY NOT SEE MY FAMILY FOR WEEKS--!
I PROMISED MY SON I WOULD BE HERE FOR HIM TONIGHT. LET ME JUST EXPLAIN BEFORE I DEPART.
OUT OF THE QUESTION. YOUR DUTY TRUMPS SUCH TRIVIAL CONCERNS.
FAMILY IS ANYTHING BUT TRIVIAL!
THIS WILL ONLY TAKE A MOMENT!
WHAT IS THIS?
RING: WHERE DID THESE CREATURES COME FROM?
SCANNING.
D.N.A. PARTIAL MATCH FOR GUARDIANS OF THE UNIVERSE.
WHAT? THE GUARDIANS SPAWNED THEM?
BUT... THAT WOULD MEAN GANTHET WAS LURING ME AWAY!

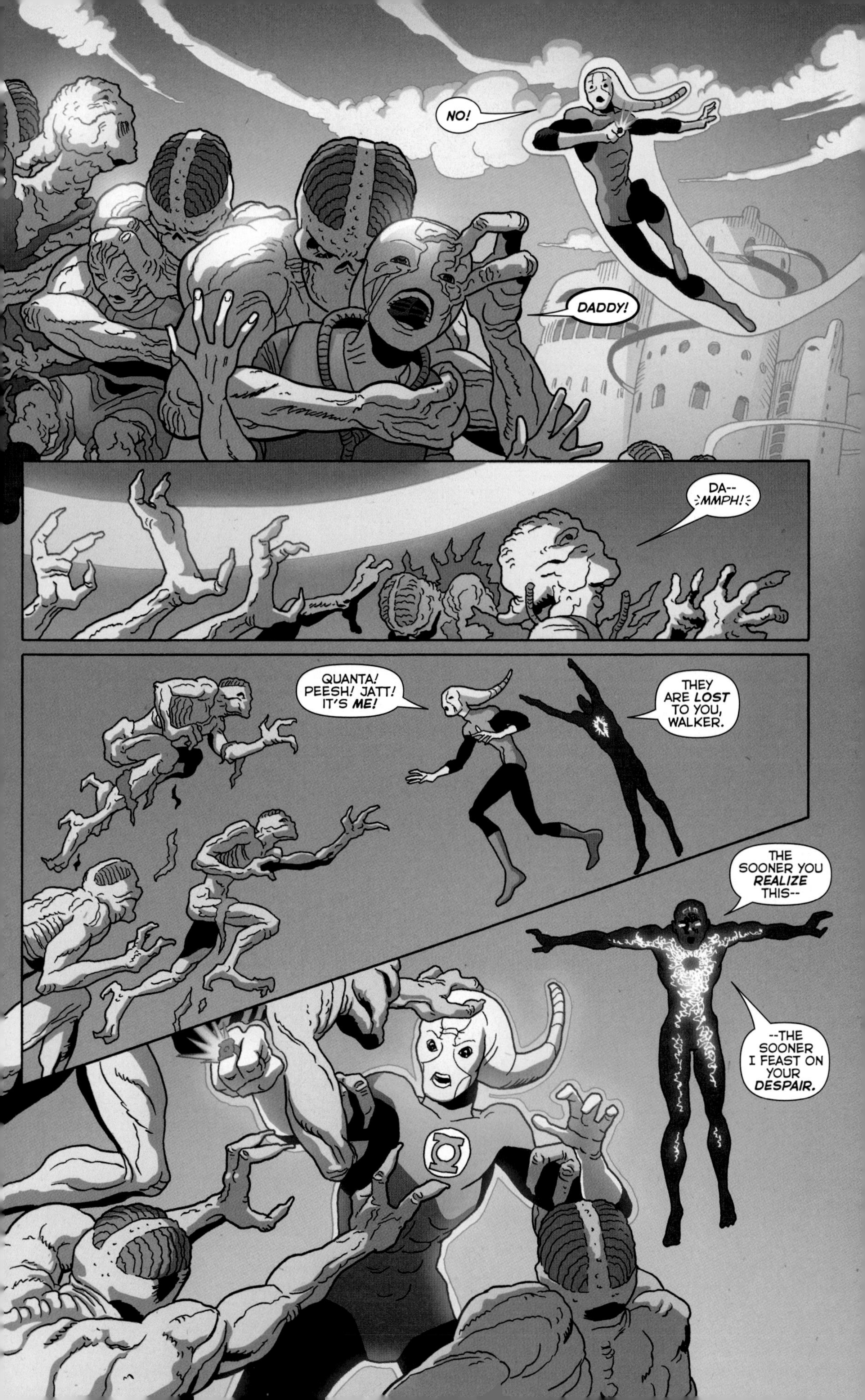
NO!
DADDY!
DA-- MMPH!
QUANTA! PEESH! JATT! IT'S ME!
THEY ARE LOST TO YOU, WALKER.
THE SOONER YOU REALIZE THIS--
--THE SOONER I FEAST ON YOUR DESPAIR.

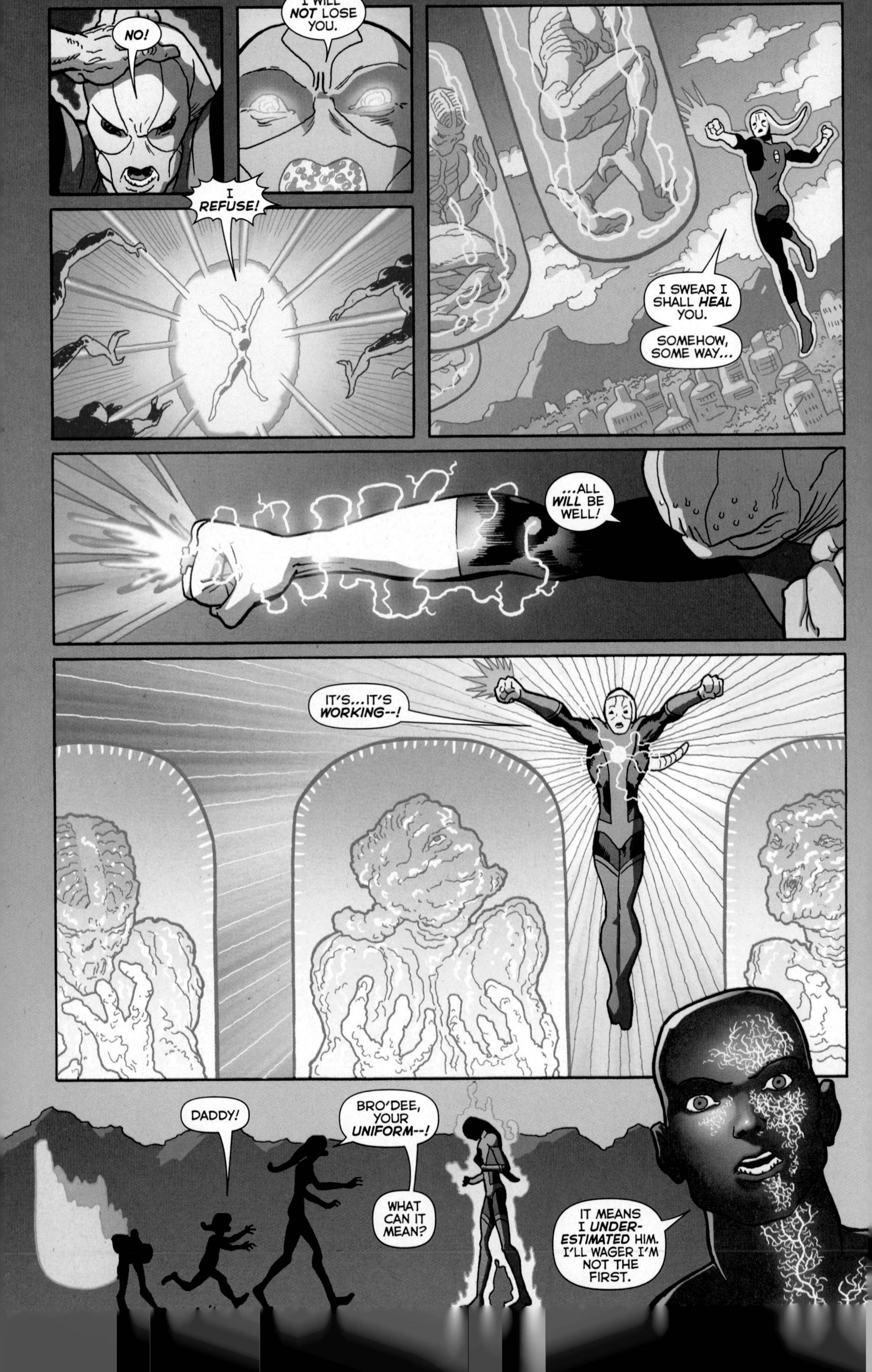
NO!
I WILL NOT LOSE YOU.
I REFUSE!
I SWEAR I SHALL HEAL YOU.
SOMEHOW, SOME WAY...
...ALL WILL BE WELL!
IT'S...IT'S WORKING--!
DADDY!
BRO'DEE, YOUR UNIFORM--!
WHAT CAN IT MEAN?
IT MEANS I UNDER-ESTIMATED HIM. I'LL WAGER I'M NOT THE FIRST.

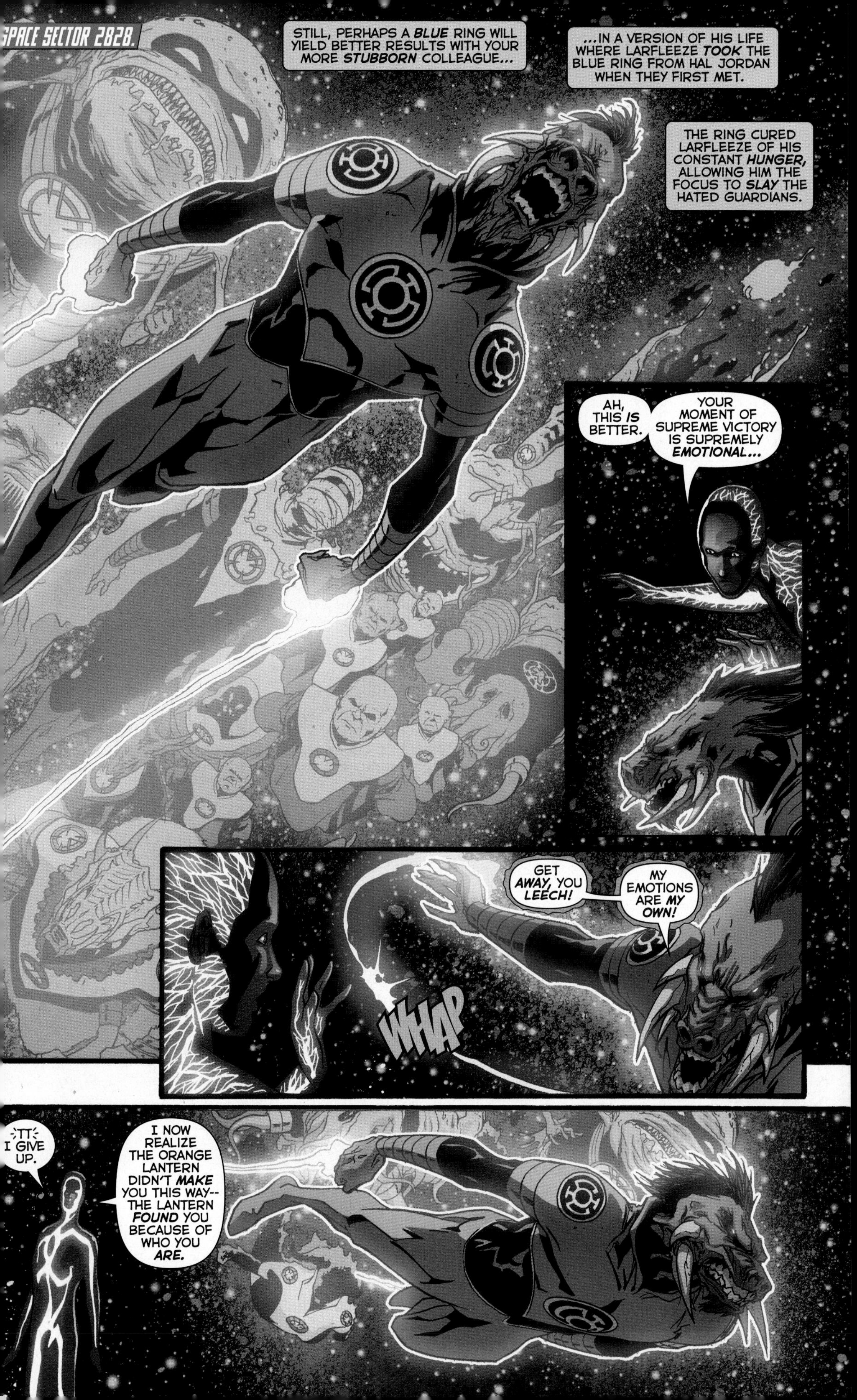
SPACE SECTOR 2828.
STILL, PERHAPS A BLUE RING WILL YIELD BETTER RESULTS WITH YOUR MORE STUBBORN COLLEAGUE...
...IN A VERSION OF HIS LIFE WHERE LARFLEEZE TOOK THE BLUE RING FROM HAL JORDAN WHEN THEY FIRST MET.
THE RING CURED LARFLEEZE OF HIS CONSTANT HUNGER, ALLOWING HIM THE FOCUS TO SLAY THE HATED GUARDIANS.
AH, THIS IS BETTER.
YOUR MOMENT OF SUPREME VICTORY IS SUPREMELY EMOTIONAL...
GET AWAY, YOU LEECH!
MY EMOTIONS ARE MY OWN!
WHAP
TT I GIVE UP.
I NOW REALIZE THE ORANGE LANTERN DIDN'T MAKE YOU THIS WAY-- THE LANTERN FOUND YOU BECAUSE OF WHO YOU ARE.

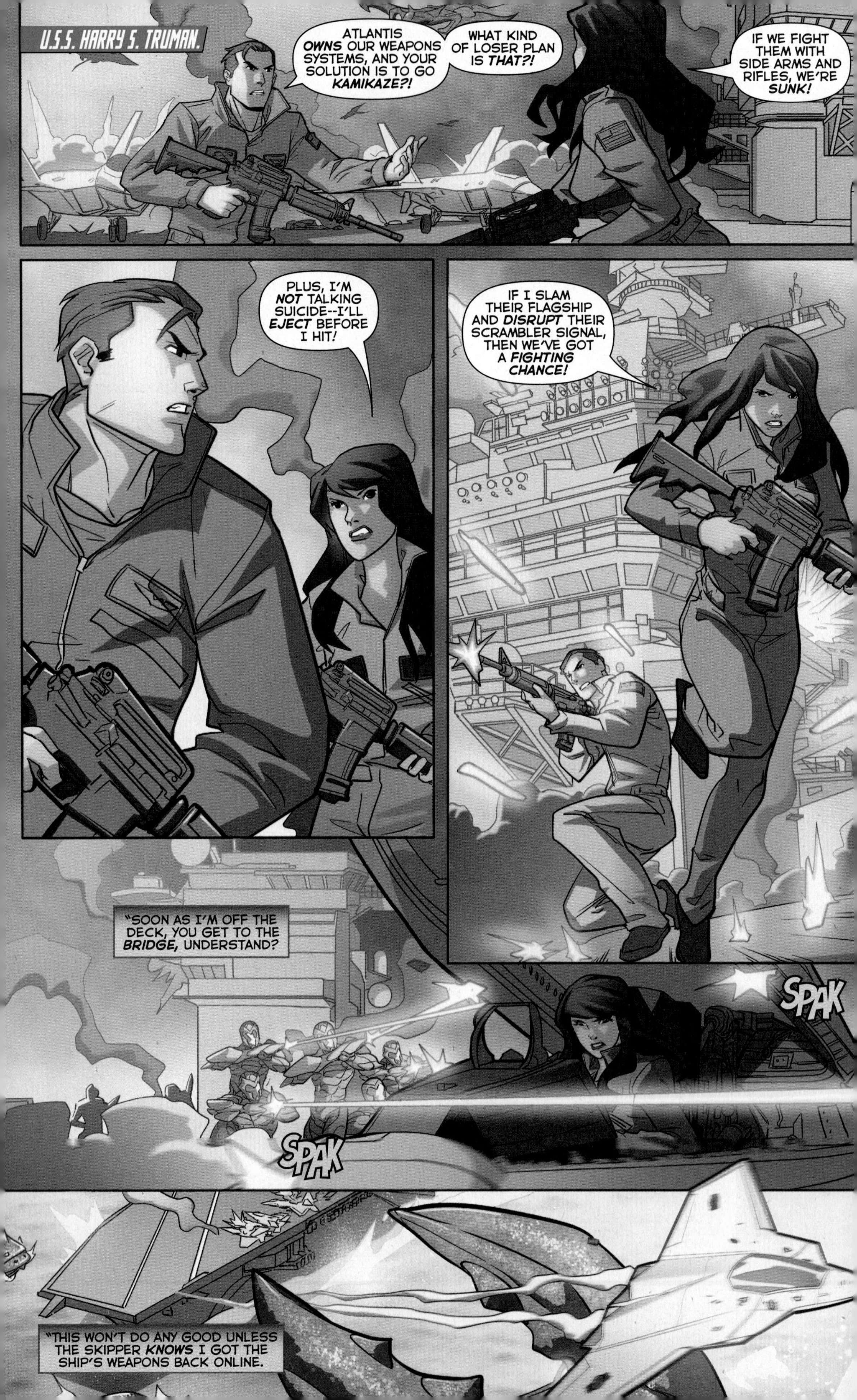
U.S.S. HARRY S. TRUMAN.
ATLANTIS OWNS OUR WEAPONS SYSTEMS, AND YOUR SOLUTION IS TO GO KAMIKAZE?!
WHAT KIND OF LOSER PLAN IS THAT?!
IF WE FIGHT THEM WITH SIDE ARMS AND RIFLES, WE'RE SUNK!
PLUS, I'M NOT TALKING SUICIDE--I'LL EJECT BEFORE I HIT!
IF I SLAM THEIR FLAGSHIP AND DISRUPT THEIR SCRAMBLER SIGNAL, THEN WE'VE GOT A FIGHTING CHANCE!
"SOON AS I'M OFF THE DECK, YOU GET TO THE BRIDGE, UNDERSTAND?
SPAK
SPAK
"THIS WON'T DO ANY GOOD UNLESS THE SKIPPER KNOWS I GOT THE SHIP'S WEAPONS BACK ONLINE.

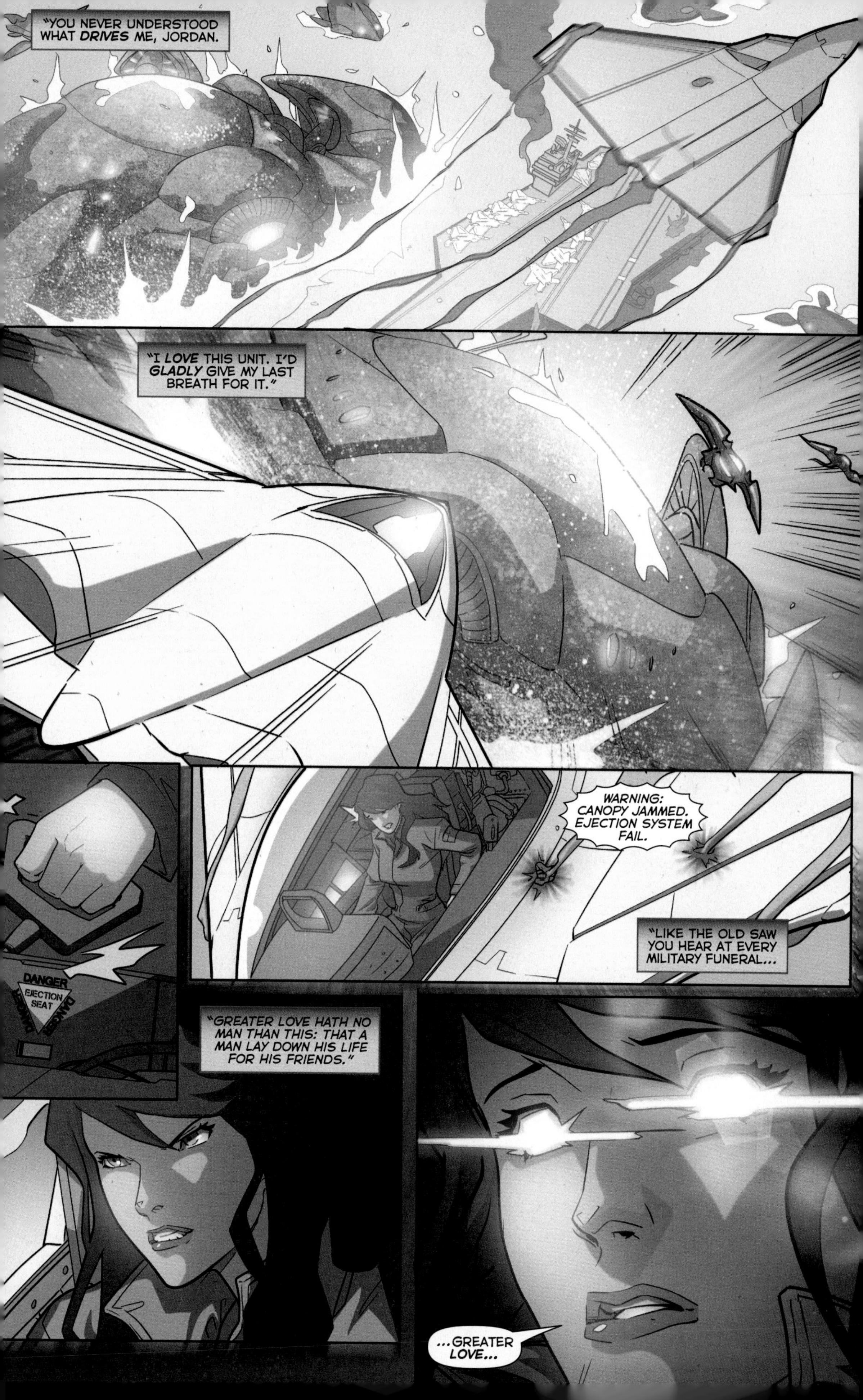
"YOU NEVER UNDERSTOOD WHAT DRIVES ME, JORDAN.
"I LOVE THIS UNIT. I'D GLADLY GIVE MY LAST BREATH FOR IT."
WARNING: CANOPY JAMMED. EJECTION SYSTEM FAIL.
"LIKE THE OLD SAW YOU HEAR AT EVERY MILITARY FUNERAL...
DANGER
EJECTION SEAT
DANGER
DANGER
"GREATER LOVE HATH NO MAN THAN THIS: THAT A MAN LAY DOWN HIS LIFE FOR HIS FRIENDS."
...GREATER LOVE...

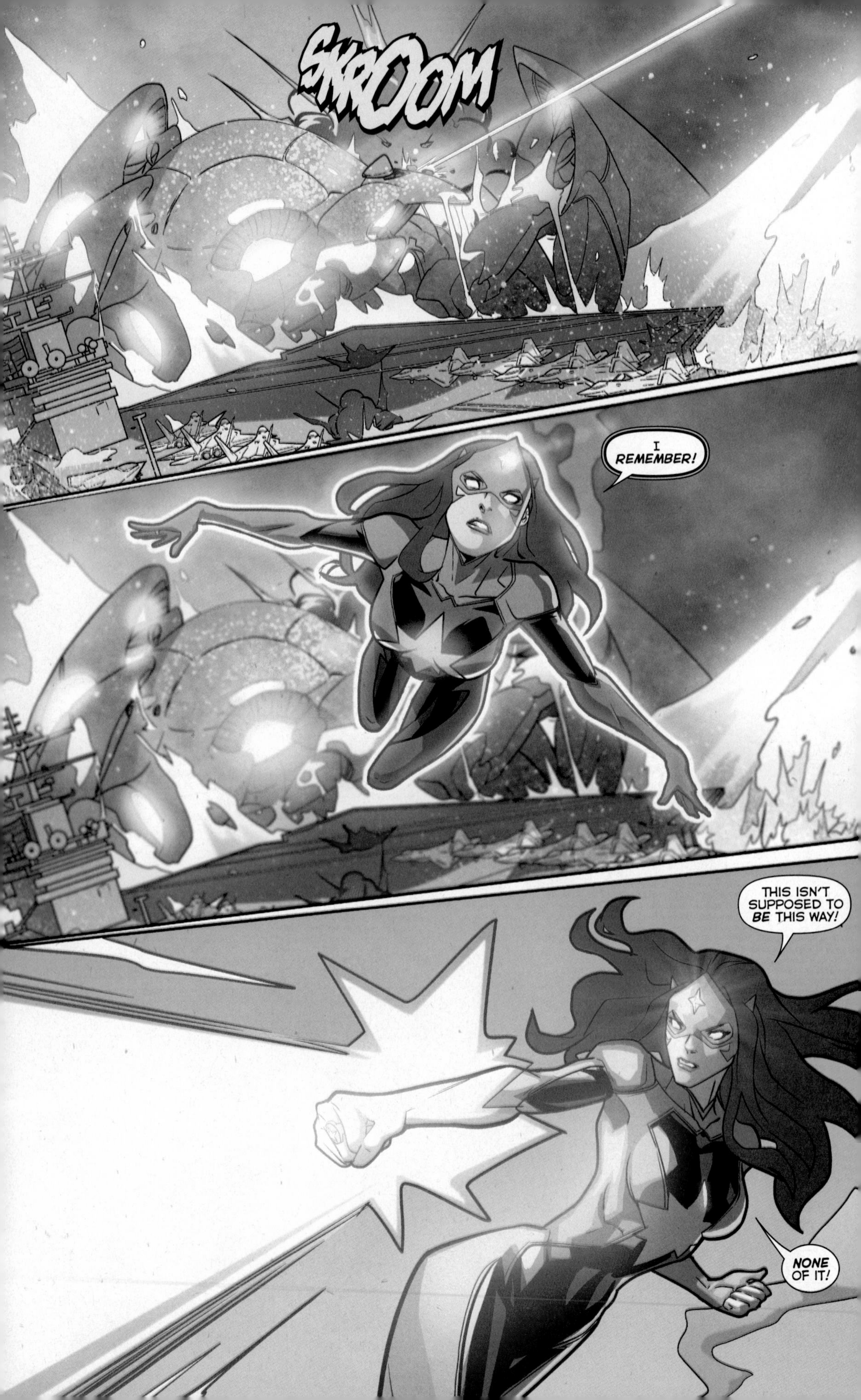
SKROOOM
I REMEMBER!
THIS ISN'T SUPPOSED TO BE THIS WAY!
NONE OF IT!

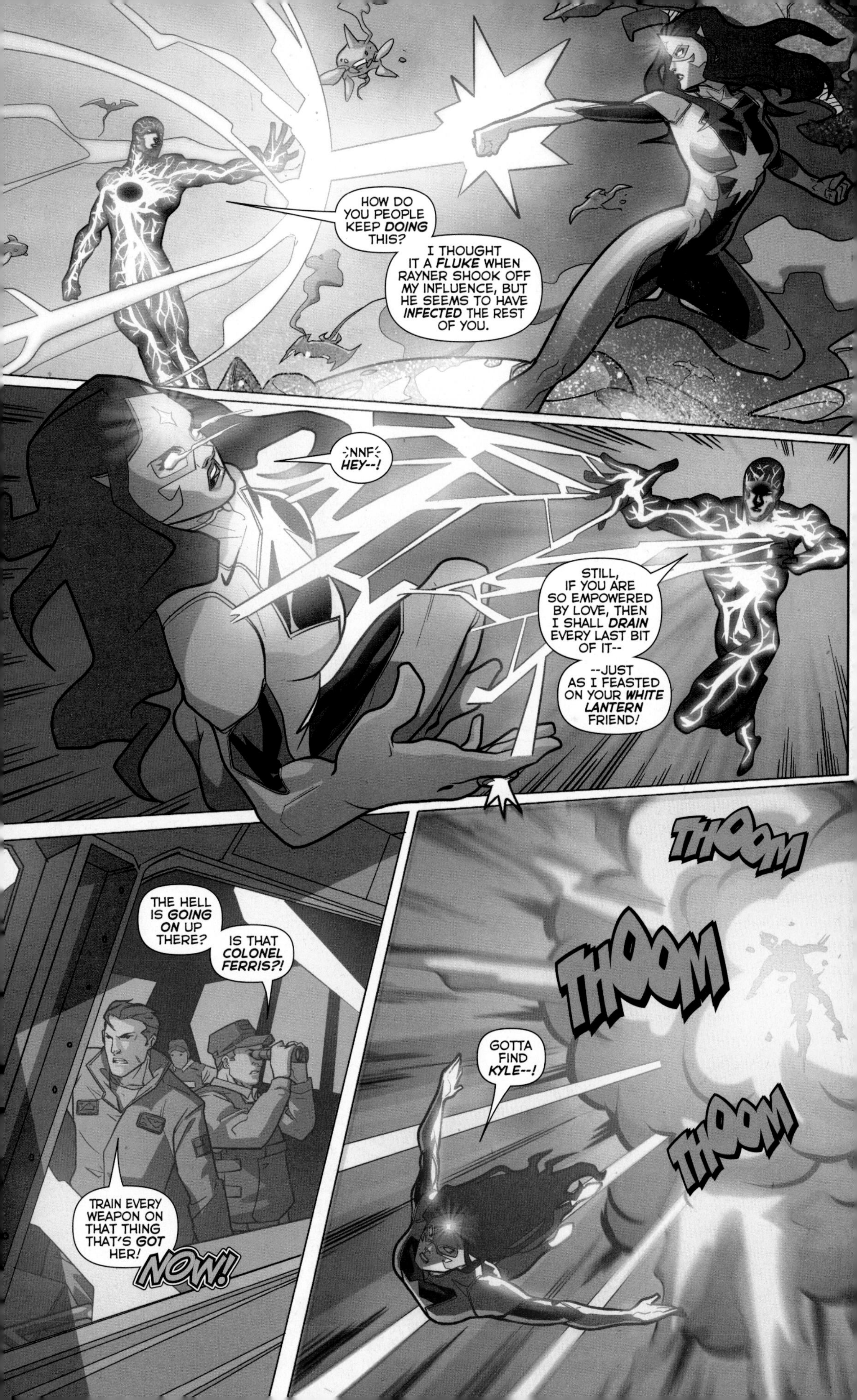
HOW DO YOU PEOPLE KEEP DOING THIS?
I THOUGHT IT A FLUKE WHEN RAYNER SHOOK OFF MY INFLUENCE, BUT HE SEEMS TO HAVE INFECTED THE REST OF YOU.
NNF HEY--!
STILL, IF YOU ARE SO EMPOWERED BY LOVE, THEN I SHALL DRAIN EVERY LAST BIT OF IT--
--JUST AS I FEASTED ON YOUR WHITE LANTERN FRIEND!
THE HELL IS GOING ON UP THERE?
IS THAT COLONEL FERRIS?!
TRAIN EVERY WEAPON ON THAT THING THAT'S GOT HER!
NOW!
THOOM
THOOM
GOTTA FIND KYLE--!
THOOM

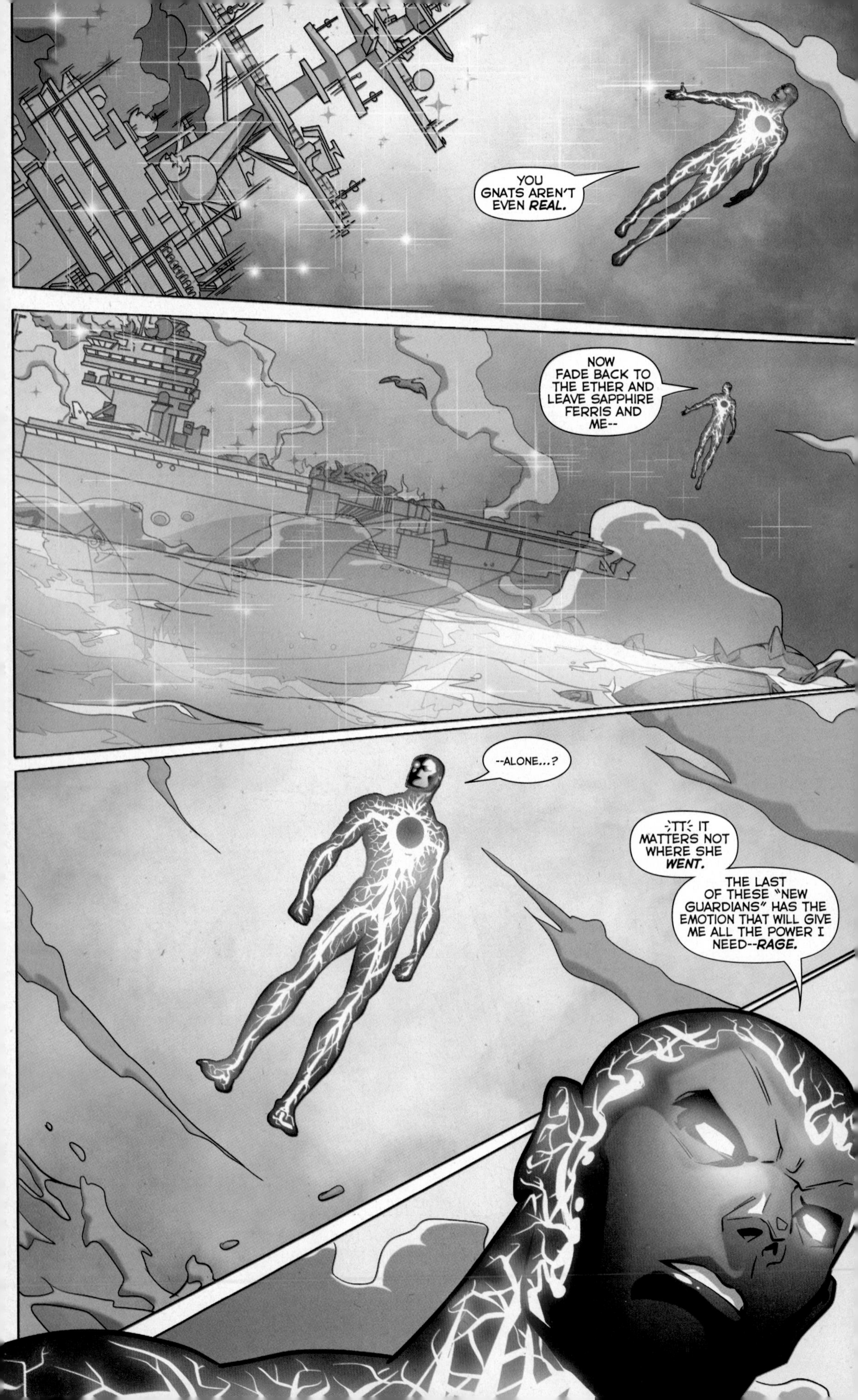
YOU GNATS AREN'T EVEN *REAL.*
NOW FADE BACK TO THE ETHER AND LEAVE SAPPHIRE FERRIS AND ME--
--ALONE...?
TT IT MATTERS NOT WHERE SHE *WENT.*
THE LAST OF THESE "NEW GUARDIANS" HAS THE EMOTION THAT WILL GIVE ME ALL THE POWER I NEED--*RAGE.*

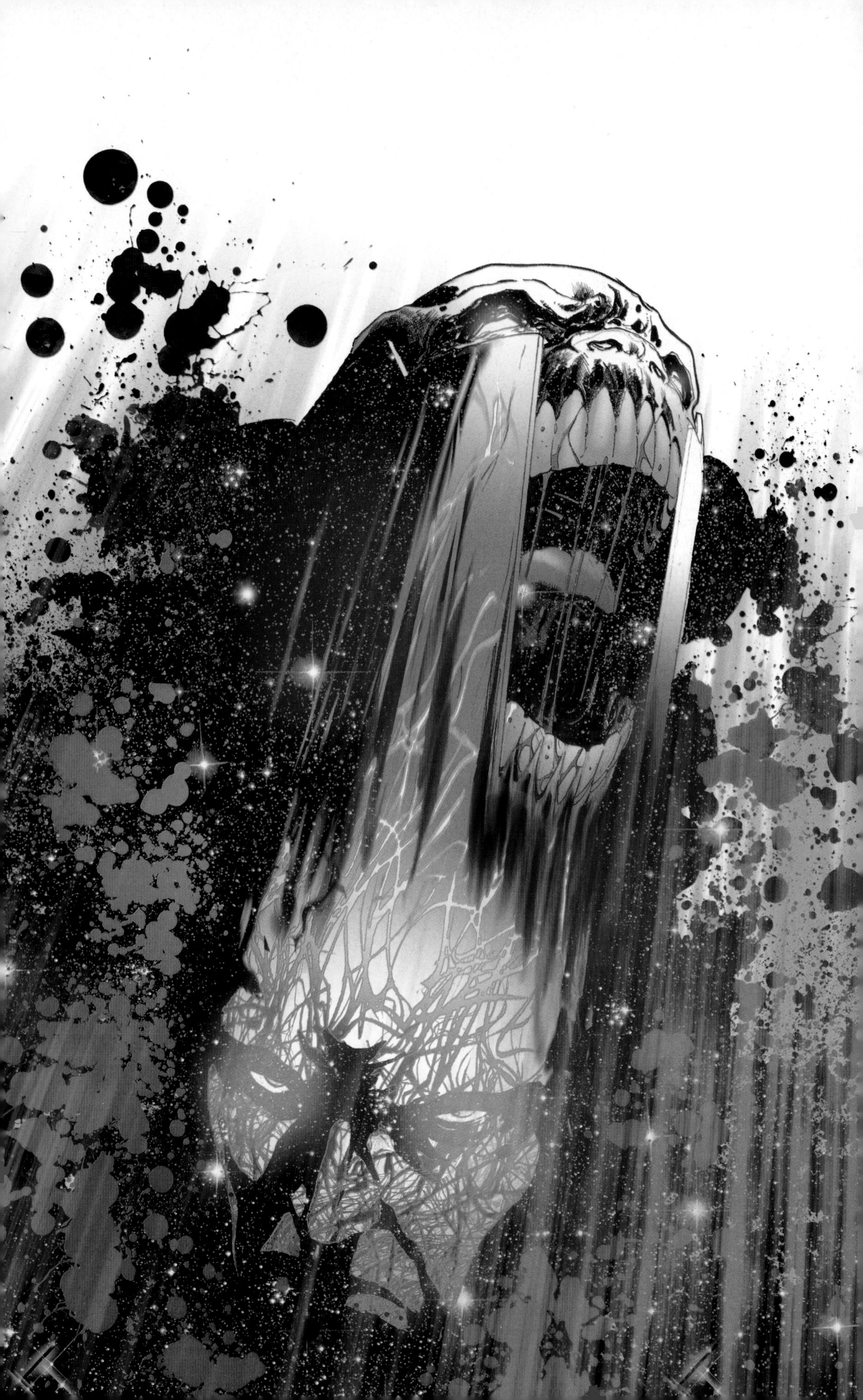

PART EIGHT: THE DECISION

PETER MILLIGAN writer MIGUEL SEPULVEDA artist
cover art by MIGUEL SEPULVEDA & RAIN BEREDO

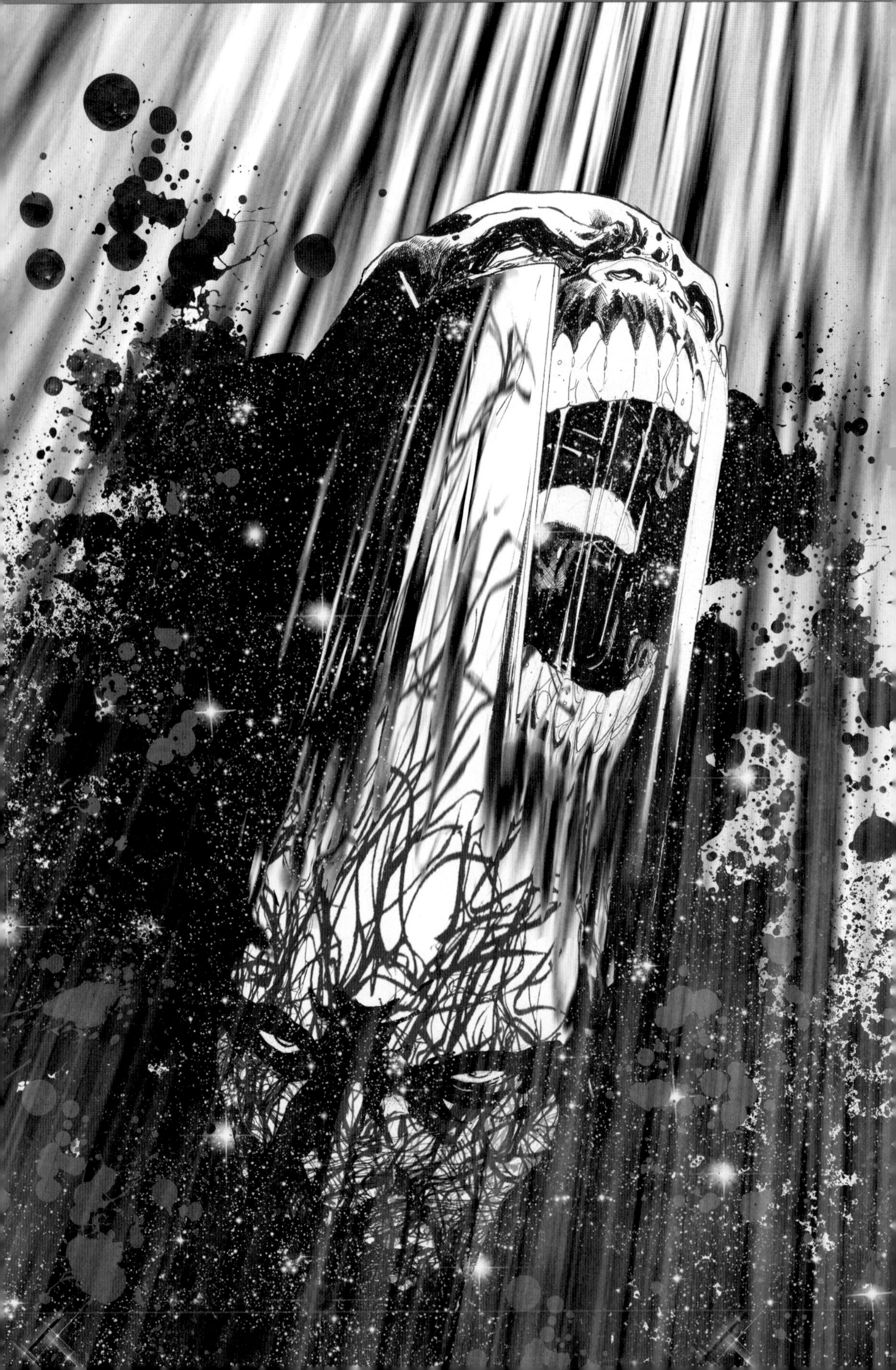

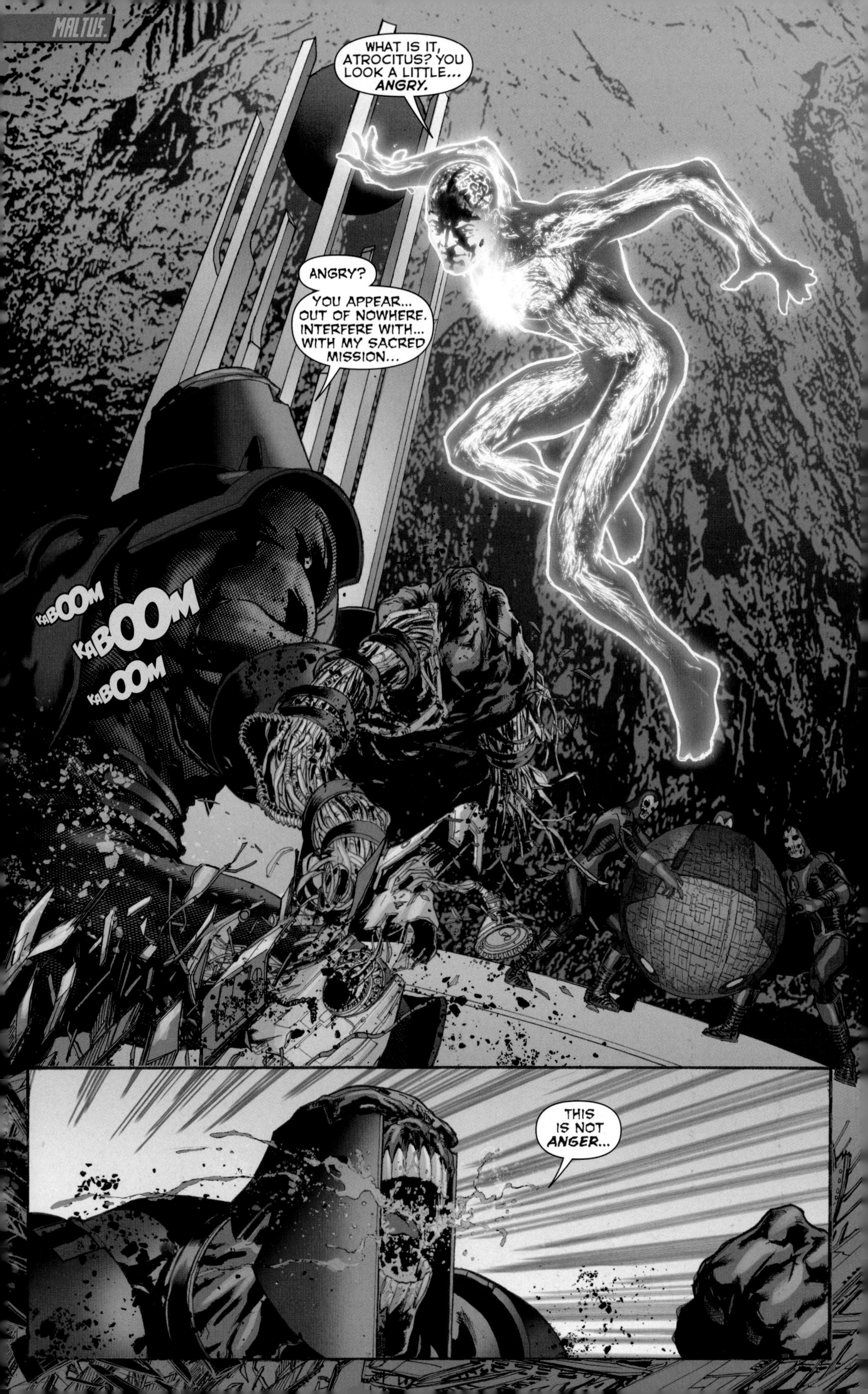
MALTUS.
WHAT IS IT, ATROCITUS? YOU LOOK A LITTLE... ANGRY.
ANGRY?
YOU APPEAR... OUT OF NOWHERE. INTERFERE WITH... WITH MY SACRED MISSION...
KABOOM
KABOOM
KABOOM
THIS IS NOT ANGER...

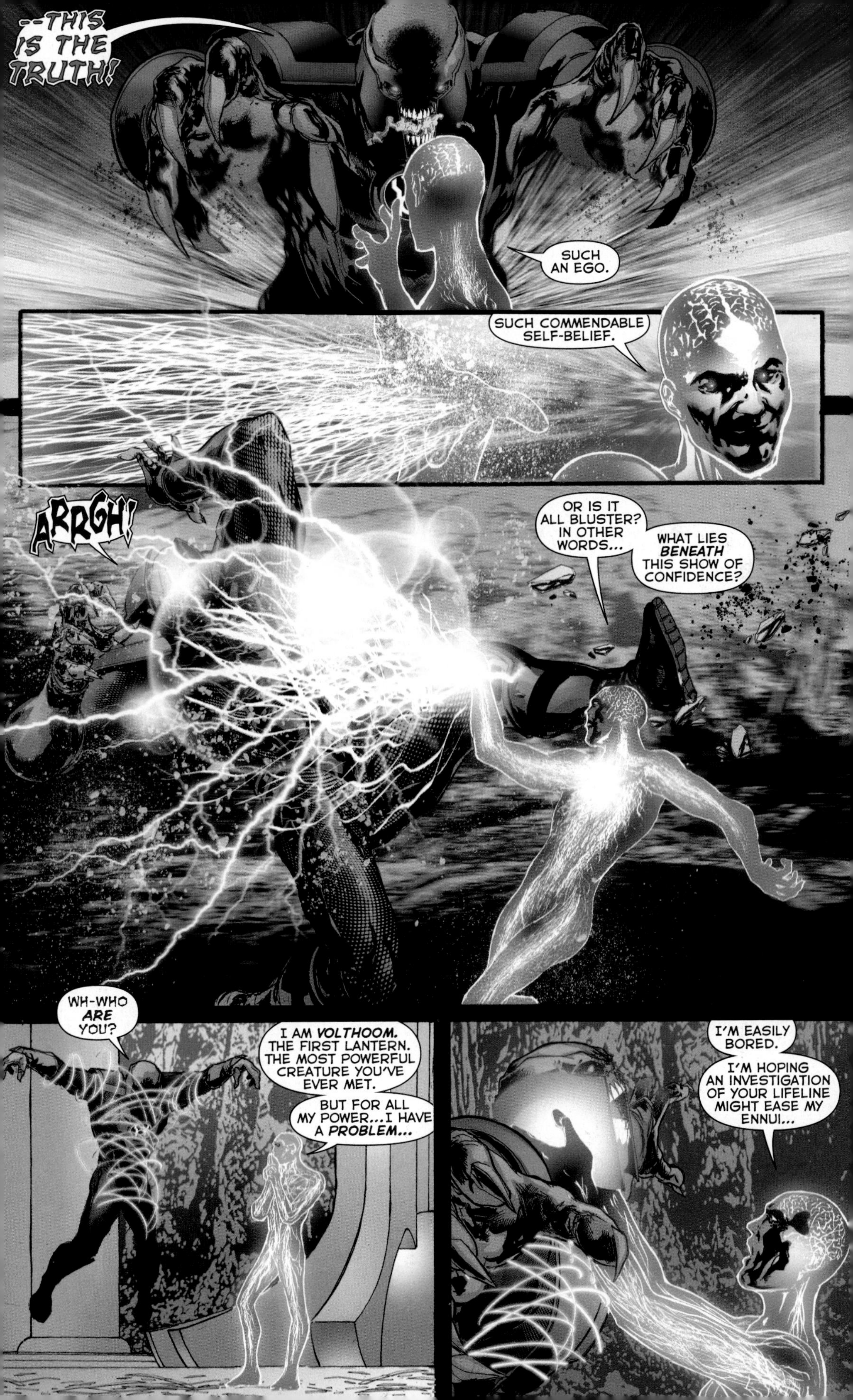
--THIS IS THE TRUTH!
SUCH AN EGO.
SUCH COMMENDABLE SELF-BELIEF.
ARRGH!
OR IS IT ALL BLUSTER? IN OTHER WORDS...
WHAT LIES *BENEATH* THIS SHOW OF CONFIDENCE?
WH-WHO *ARE* YOU?
I AM *VOLTHOOM.* THE FIRST LANTERN. THE MOST POWERFUL CREATURE YOU'VE EVER MET.
BUT FOR ALL MY POWER...I HAVE A *PROBLEM*...
I'M EASILY BORED.
I'M HOPING AN INVESTIGATION OF YOUR LIFELINE MIGHT EASE MY ENNUI...

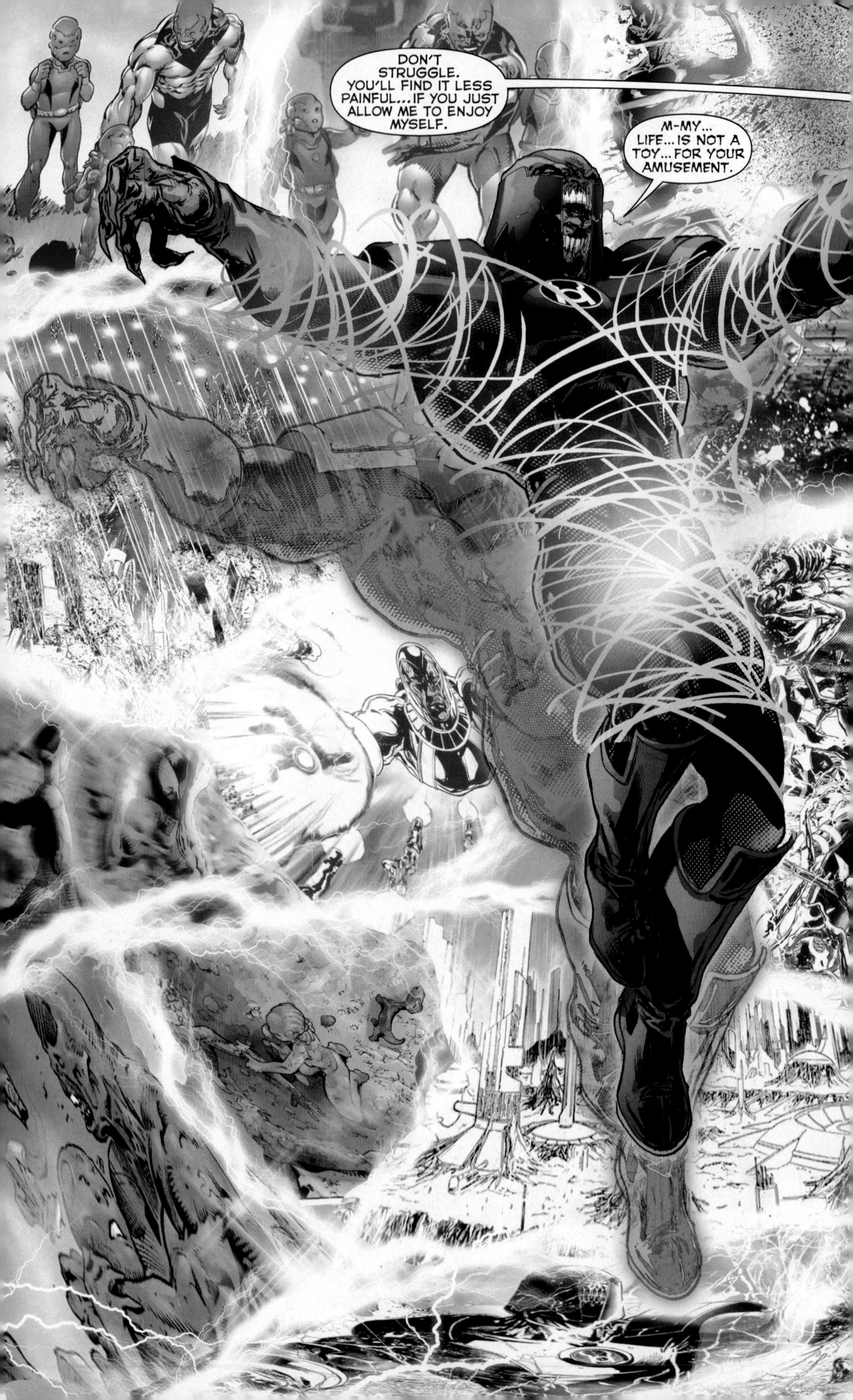
DON'T STRUGGLE. YOU'LL FIND IT LESS PAINFUL...IF YOU JUST ALLOW ME TO ENJOY MYSELF.
M-MY... LIFE...IS NOT A TOY...FOR YOUR AMUSEMENT.

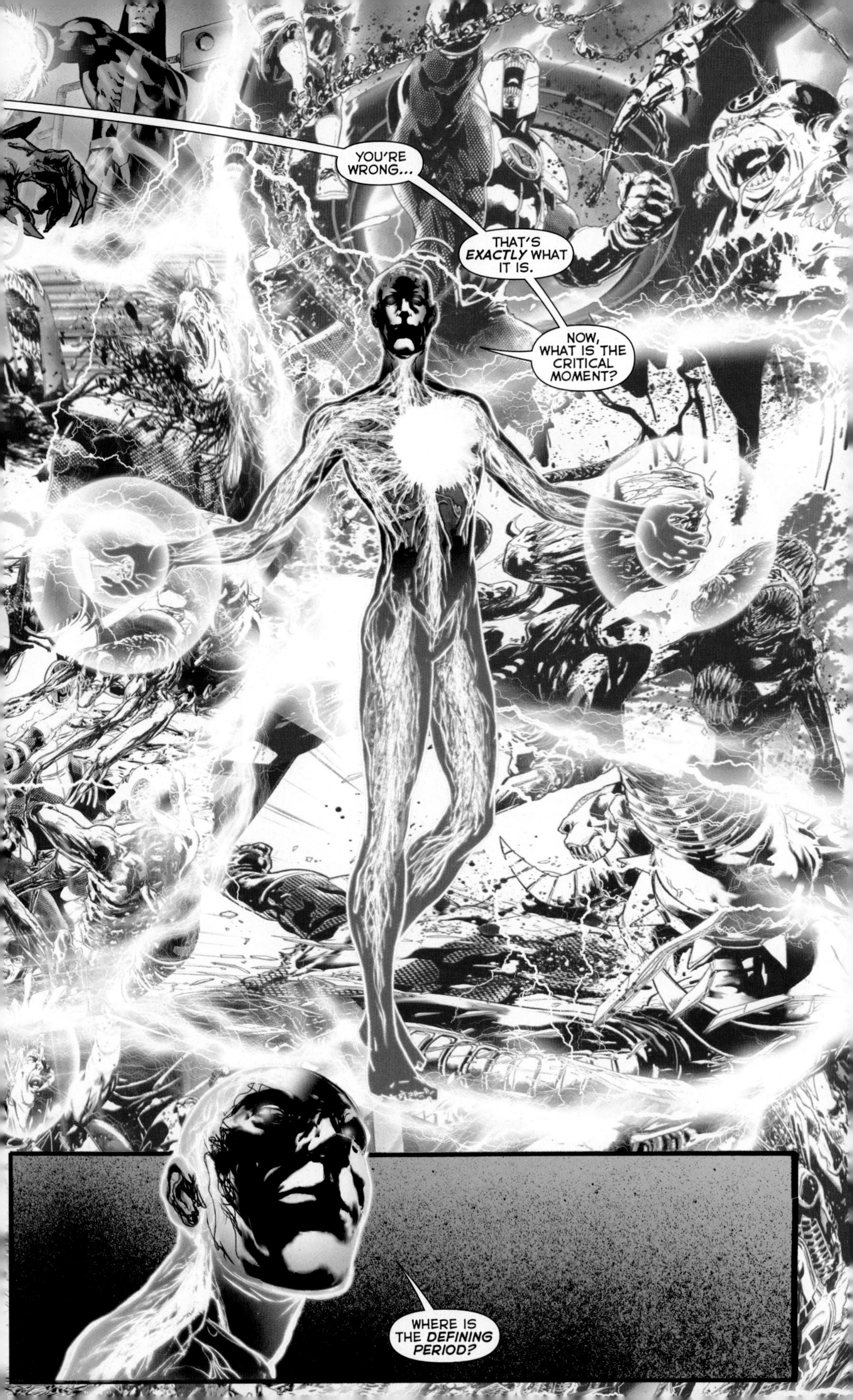
YOU'RE WRONG...
THAT'S *EXACTLY* WHAT IT IS.
NOW, WHAT IS THE CRITICAL MOMENT?
WHERE IS THE *DEFINING PERIOD?*

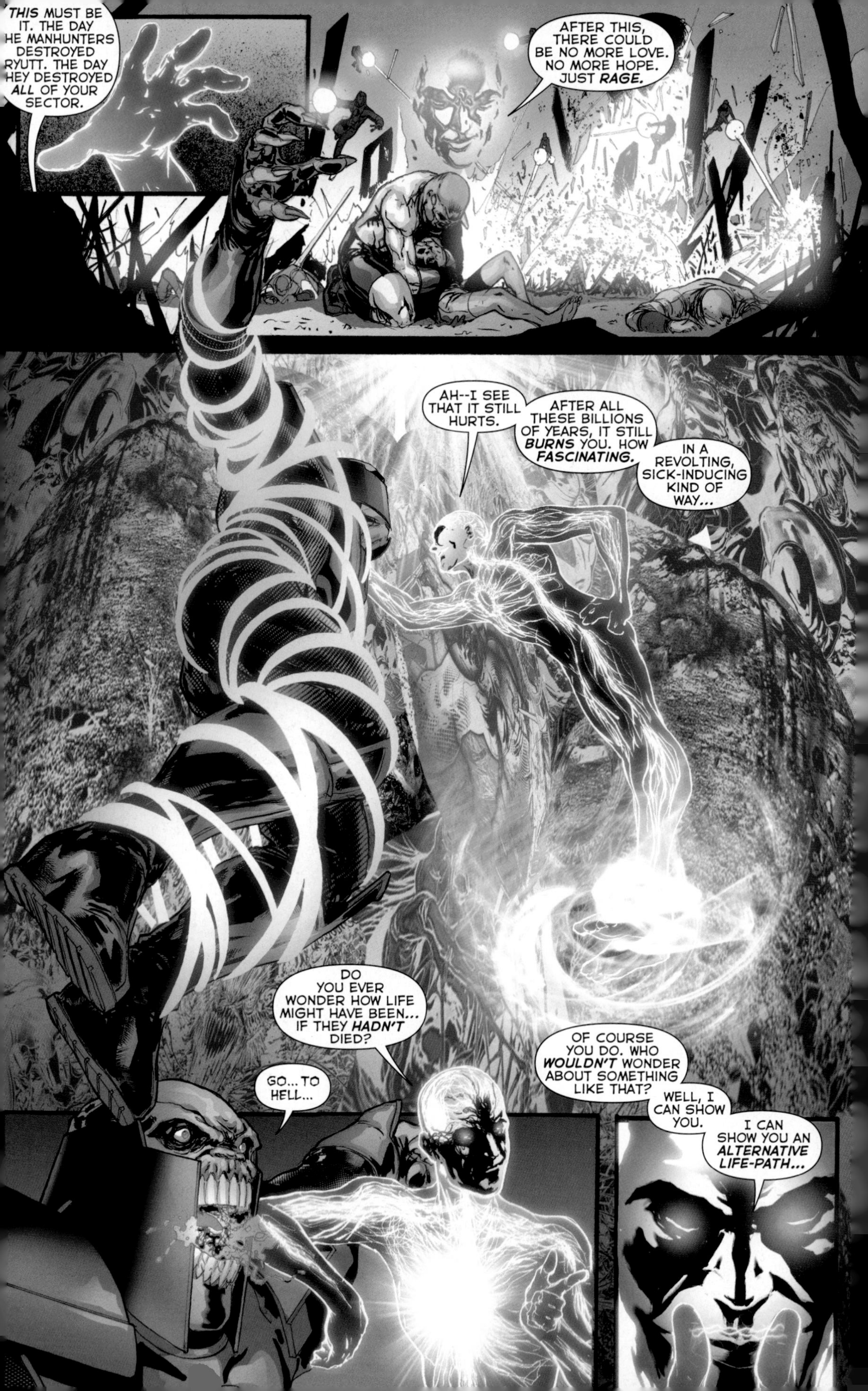
THIS MUST BE IT. THE DAY HE MANHUNTERS DESTROYED RYUTT. THE DAY HEY DESTROYED ALL OF YOUR SECTOR.
AFTER THIS, THERE COULD BE NO MORE LOVE. NO MORE HOPE. JUST RAGE.
AH--I SEE THAT IT STILL HURTS.
AFTER ALL THESE BILLIONS OF YEARS, IT STILL BURNS YOU. HOW FASCINATING.
IN A REVOLTING, SICK-INDUCING KIND OF WAY...
DO YOU EVER WONDER HOW LIFE MIGHT HAVE BEEN... IF THEY HADN'T DIED?
GO... TO HELL...
OF COURSE YOU DO. WHO WOULDN'T WONDER ABOUT SOMETHING LIKE THAT?
WELL, I CAN SHOW YOU.
I CAN SHOW YOU AN ALTERNATIVE LIFE-PATH...

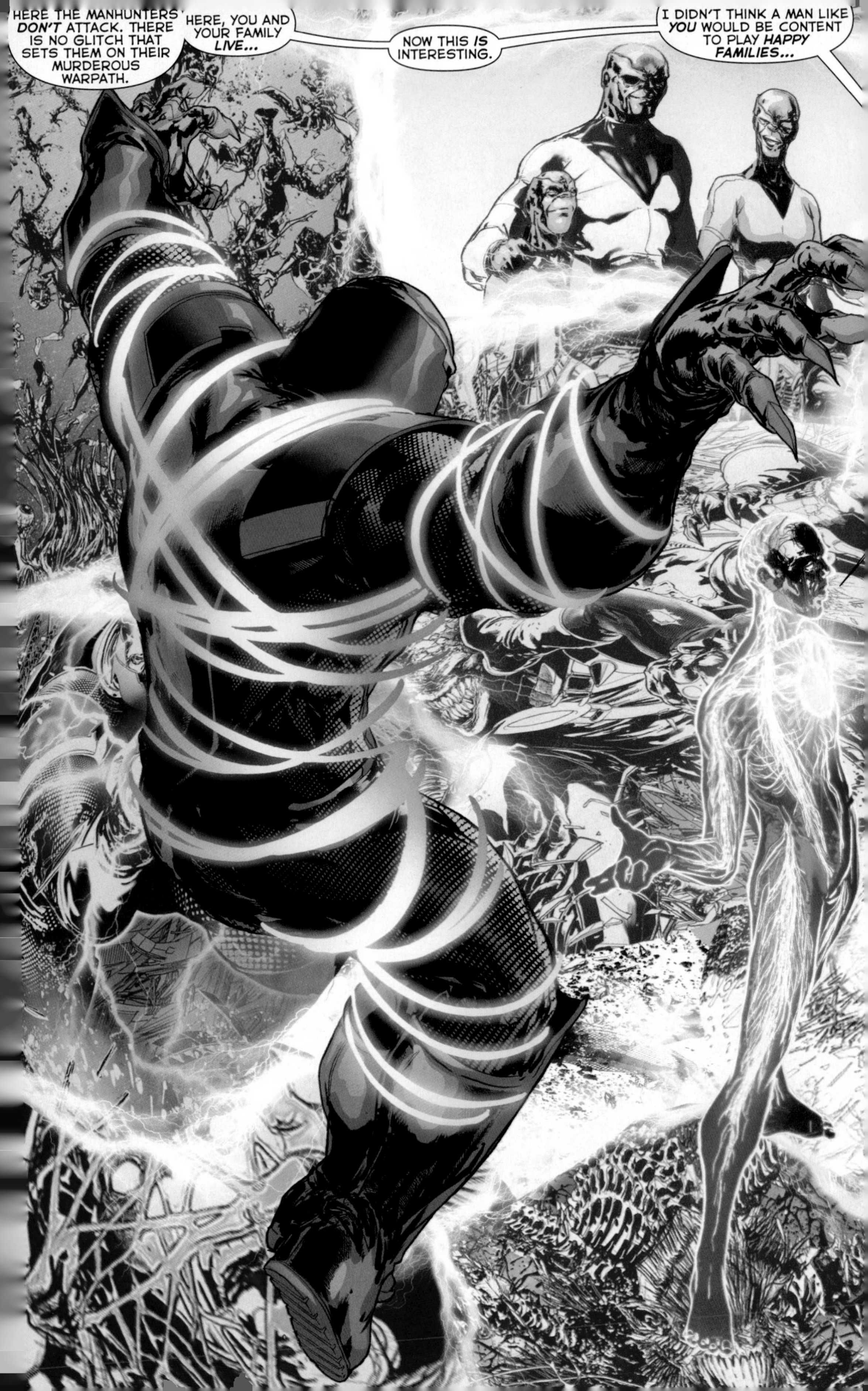
HERE THE MANHUNTERS DON'T ATTACK. THERE IS NO GLITCH THAT SETS THEM ON THEIR MURDEROUS WARPATH.
HERE, YOU AND YOUR FAMILY LIVE...
NOW THIS IS INTERESTING.
I DIDN'T THINK A MAN LIKE YOU WOULD BE CONTENT TO PLAY HAPPY FAMILIES...

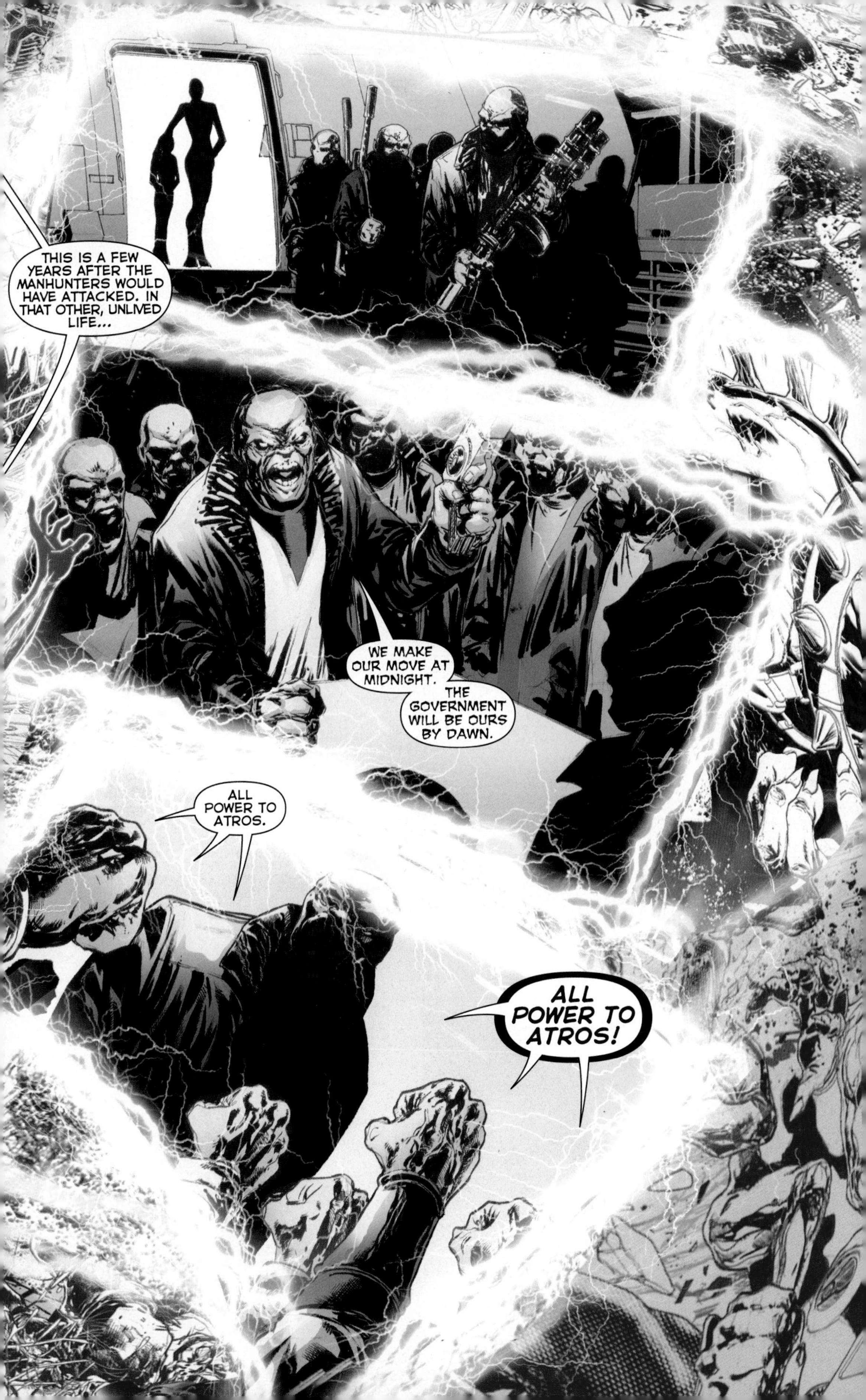
THIS IS A FEW YEARS AFTER THE MANHUNTERS WOULD HAVE ATTACKED. IN THAT OTHER, UNLIVED LIFE...
WE MAKE OUR MOVE AT MIDNIGHT.
THE GOVERNMENT WILL BE OURS BY DAWN.
ALL POWER TO ATROS.
ALL POWER TO ATROS!

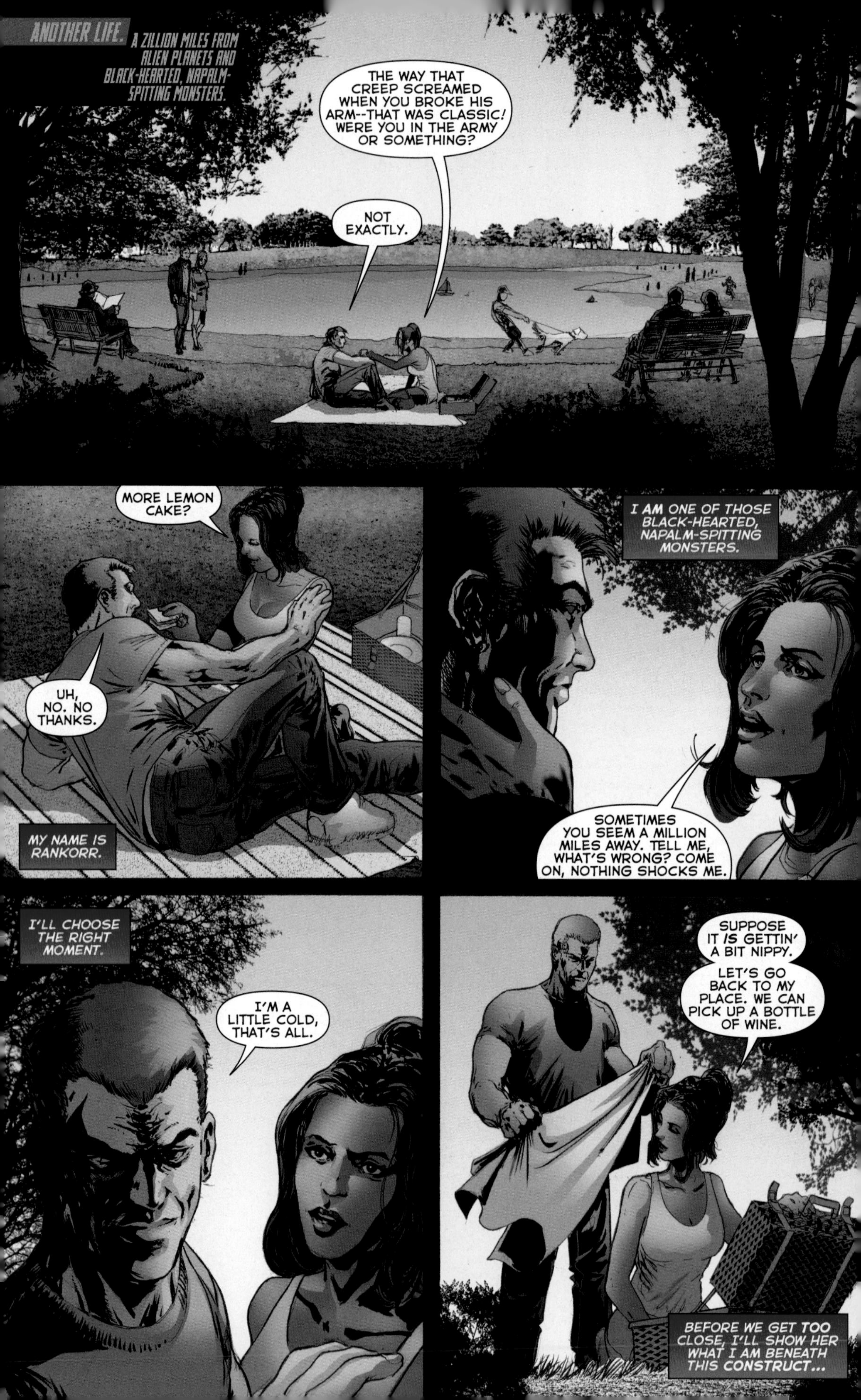
ANOTHER LIFE. A ZILLION MILES FROM ALIEN PLANETS AND BLACK-HEARTED, NAPALM-SPITTING MONSTERS.
THE WAY THAT CREEP SCREAMED WHEN YOU BROKE HIS ARM--THAT WAS CLASSIC! WERE YOU IN THE ARMY OR SOMETHING?
NOT EXACTLY.
MORE LEMON CAKE?
UH, NO. NO THANKS.
MY NAME IS RANKORR.
I AM ONE OF THOSE BLACK-HEARTED, NAPALM-SPITTING MONSTERS.
SOMETIMES YOU SEEM A MILLION MILES AWAY. TELL ME, WHAT'S WRONG? COME ON, NOTHING SHOCKS ME.
I'LL CHOOSE THE RIGHT MOMENT.
I'M A LITTLE COLD, THAT'S ALL.
SUPPOSE IT IS GETTIN' A BIT NIPPY.
LET'S GO BACK TO MY PLACE. WE CAN PICK UP A BOTTLE OF WINE.
BEFORE WE GET TOO CLOSE, I'LL SHOW HER WHAT I AM BENEATH THIS CONSTRUCT...

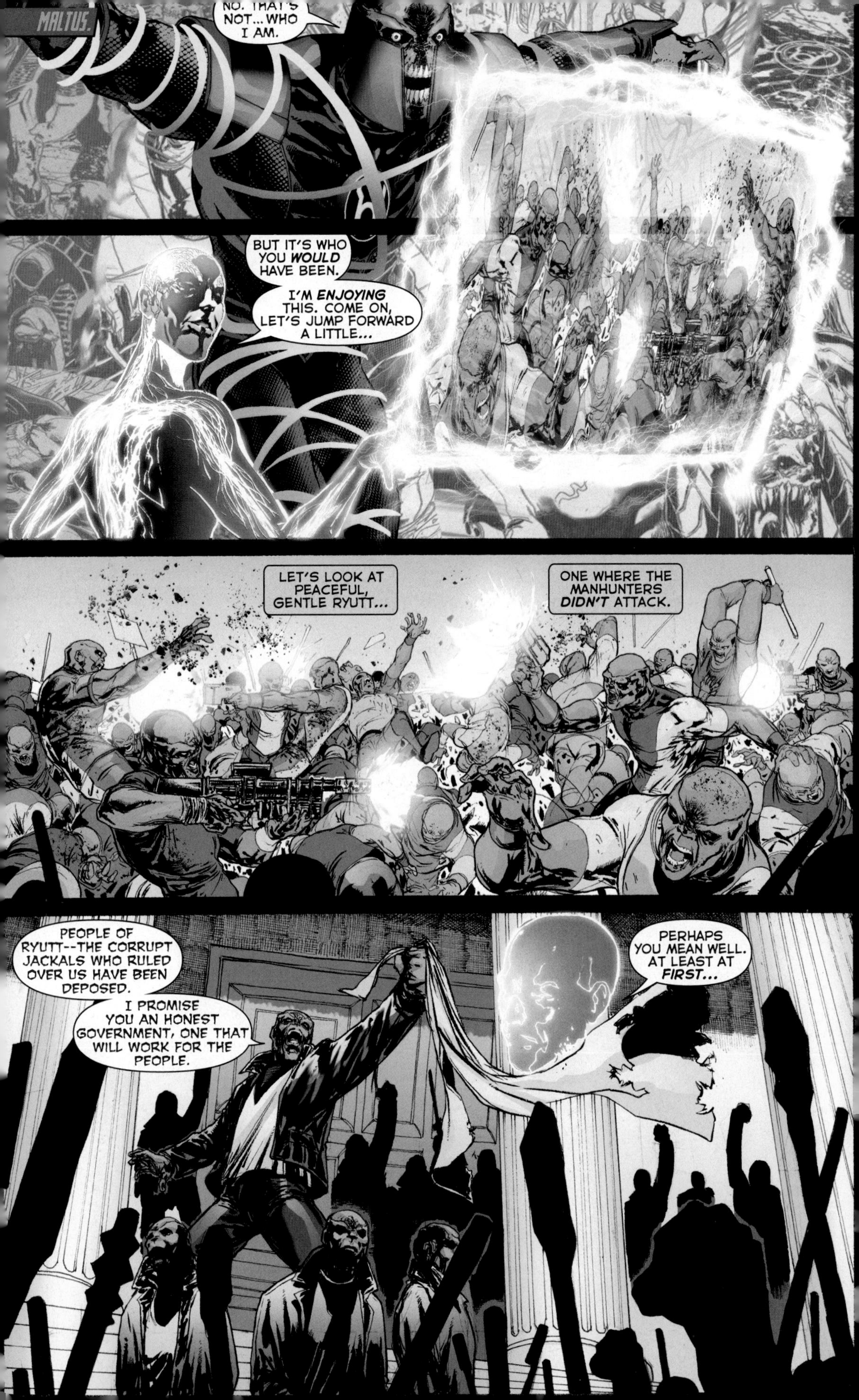
MALTUS.
NO. THAT'S NOT...WHO I AM.
BUT IT'S WHO YOU WOULD HAVE BEEN.
I'M ENJOYING THIS. COME ON, LET'S JUMP FORWARD A LITTLE...
LET'S LOOK AT PEACEFUL, GENTLE RYUTT...
ONE WHERE THE MANHUNTERS DIDN'T ATTACK.
PEOPLE OF RYUTT--THE CORRUPT JACKALS WHO RULED OVER US HAVE BEEN DEPOSED.
I PROMISE YOU AN HONEST GOVERNMENT, ONE THAT WILL WORK FOR THE PEOPLE.
PERHAPS YOU MEAN WELL. AT LEAST AT FIRST...

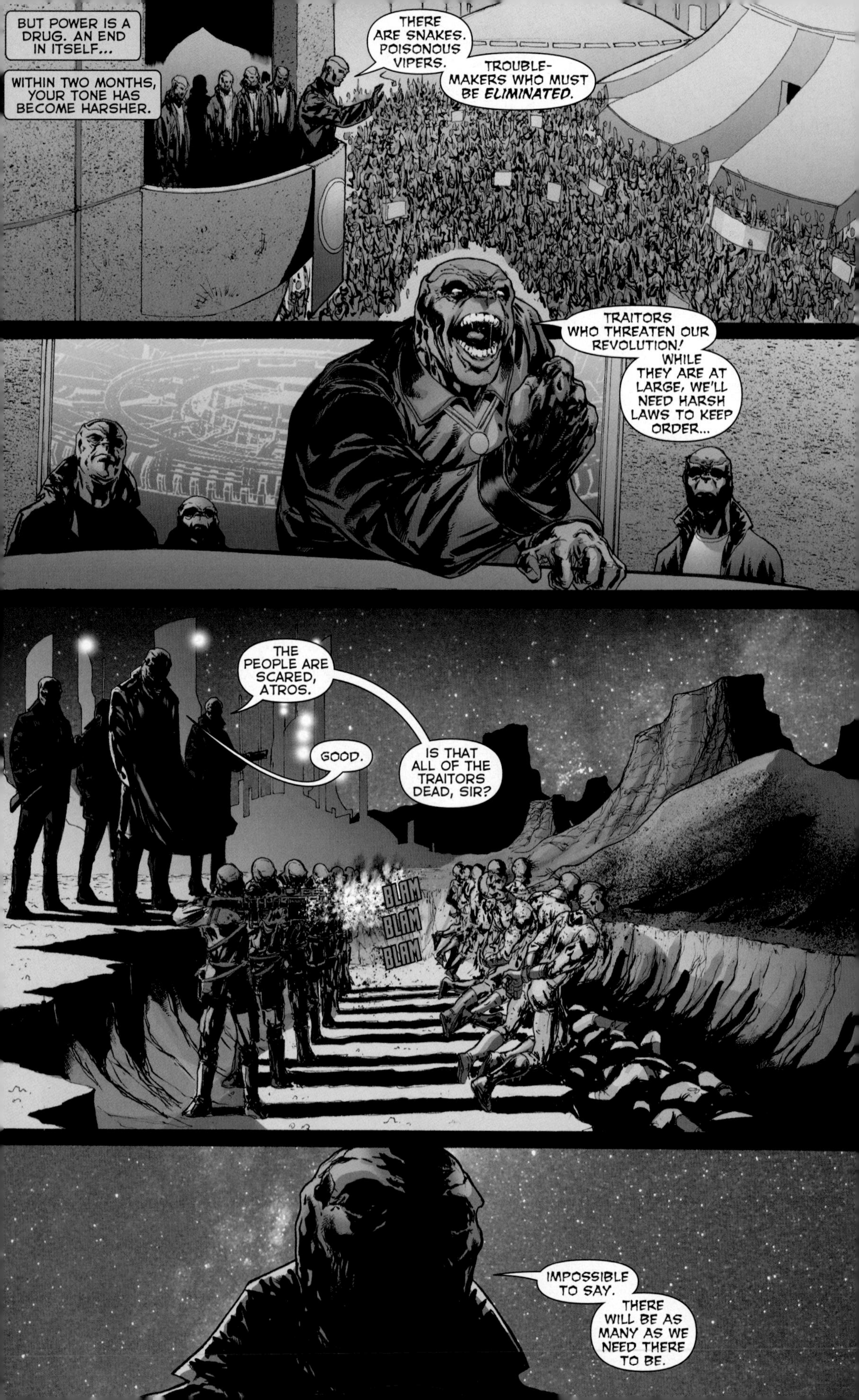
BUT POWER IS A DRUG. AN END IN ITSELF...
WITHIN TWO MONTHS, YOUR TONE HAS BECOME HARSHER.
THERE ARE SNAKES. POISONOUS VIPERS.
TROUBLE-MAKERS WHO MUST BE ELIMINATED.
TRAITORS WHO THREATEN OUR REVOLUTION!
WHILE THEY ARE AT LARGE, WE'LL NEED HARSH LAWS TO KEEP ORDER...
THE PEOPLE ARE SCARED, ATROS.
GOOD.
IS THAT ALL OF THE TRAITORS DEAD, SIR?
BLAM
BLAM
BLAM
IMPOSSIBLE TO SAY.
THERE WILL BE AS MANY AS WE NEED THERE TO BE.

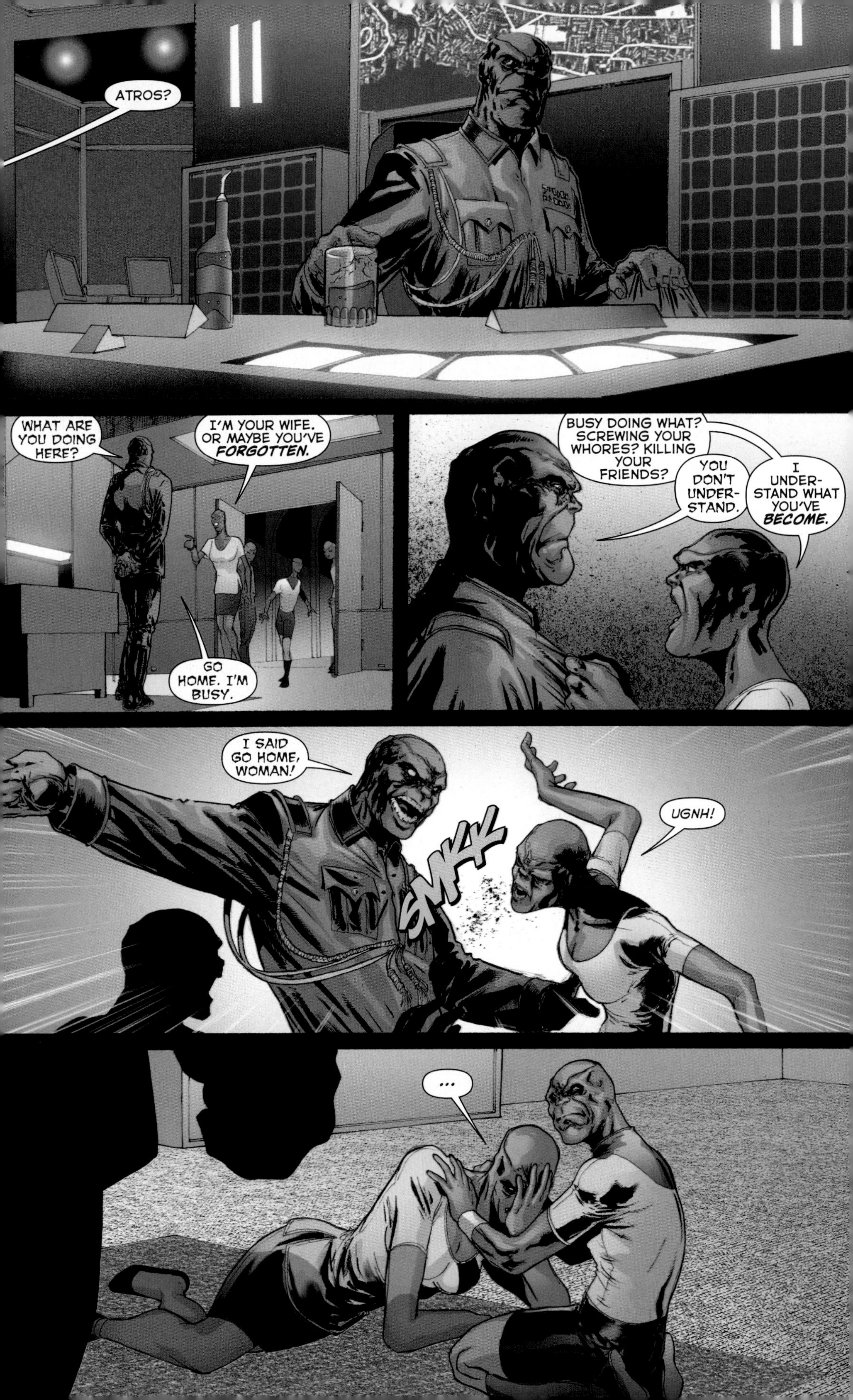
ATROS?
WHAT ARE YOU DOING HERE?
I'M YOUR WIFE. OR MAYBE YOU'VE *FORGOTTEN.*
GO HOME. I'M BUSY.
BUSY DOING WHAT? SCREWING YOUR WHORES? KILLING YOUR FRIENDS?
YOU DON'T UNDER-STAND.
I UNDER-STAND WHAT YOU'VE *BECOME.*
I SAID GO HOME, WOMAN!
SMAK
UGNH!
...

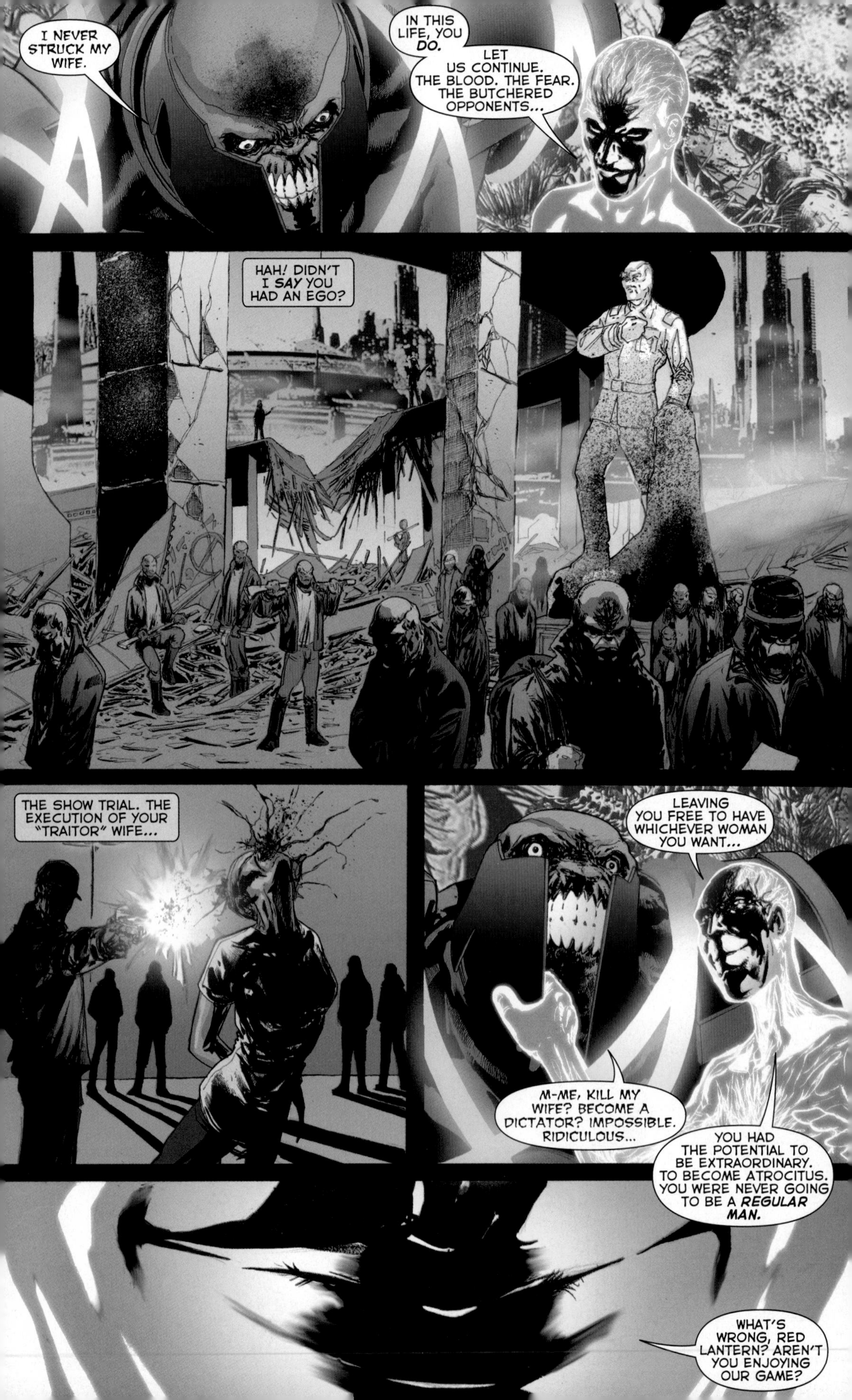
I NEVER STRUCK MY WIFE.
IN THIS LIFE, YOU *DO.*
LET US CONTINUE. THE BLOOD. THE FEAR. THE BUTCHERED OPPONENTS...
HAH! DIDN'T I *SAY* YOU HAD AN EGO?
THE SHOW TRIAL. THE EXECUTION OF YOUR "TRAITOR" WIFE...
LEAVING YOU FREE TO HAVE WHICHEVER WOMAN YOU WANT...
M-ME, KILL MY WIFE? BECOME A DICTATOR? IMPOSSIBLE. RIDICULOUS...
YOU HAD THE POTENTIAL TO BE EXTRAORDINARY. TO BECOME ATROCITUS. YOU WERE NEVER GOING TO BE A *REGULAR MAN.*
WHAT'S WRONG, RED LANTERN? AREN'T YOU ENJOYING OUR GAME?

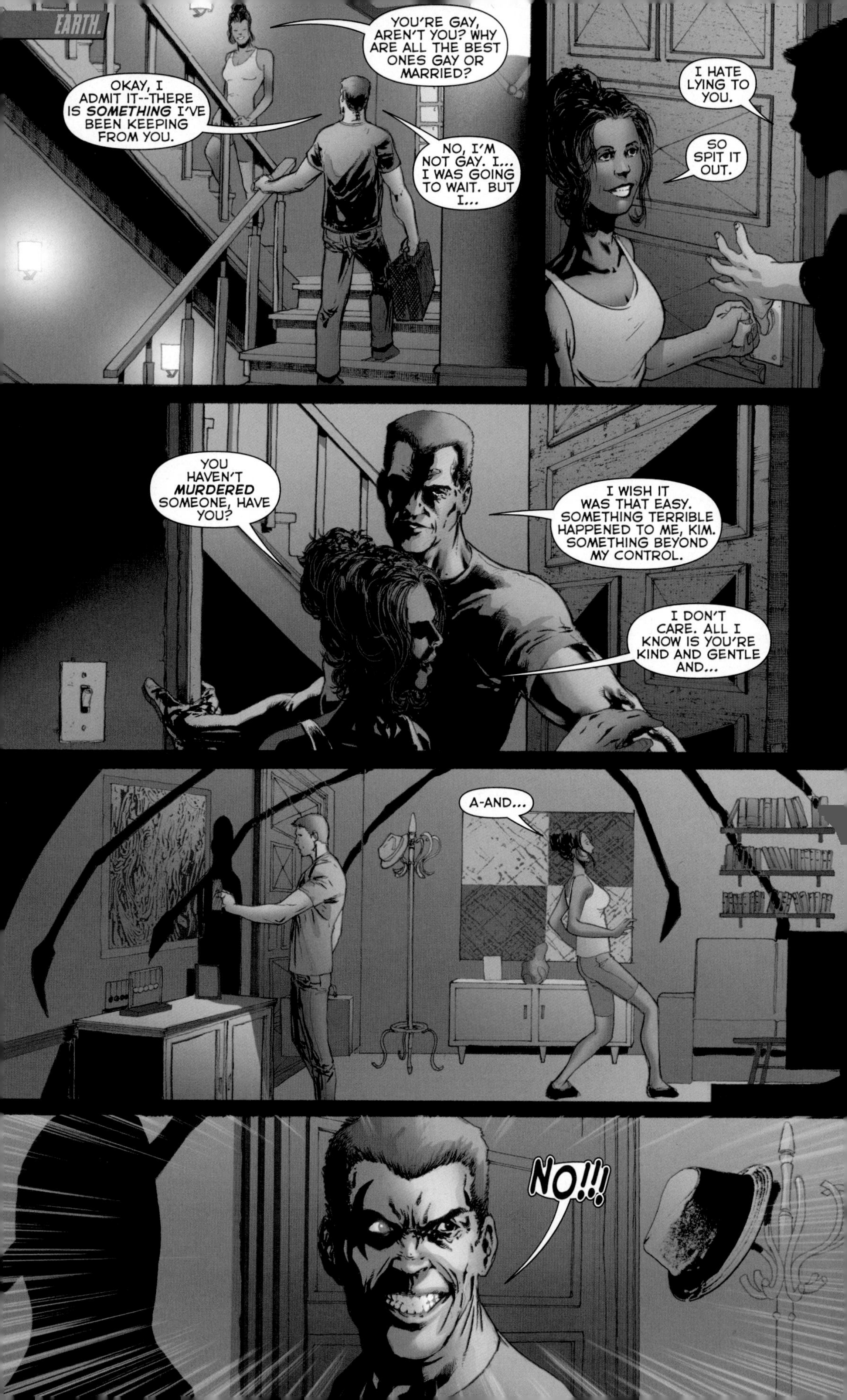
EARTH.
YOU'RE GAY, AREN'T YOU? WHY ARE ALL THE BEST ONES GAY OR MARRIED?
OKAY, I ADMIT IT--THERE IS SOMETHING I'VE BEEN KEEPING FROM YOU.
NO, I'M NOT GAY. I... I WAS GOING TO WAIT. BUT I...
I HATE LYING TO YOU.
SO SPIT IT OUT.
YOU HAVEN'T MURDERED SOMEONE, HAVE YOU?
I WISH IT WAS THAT EASY. SOMETHING TERRIBLE HAPPENED TO ME, KIM. SOMETHING BEYOND MY CONTROL.
I DON'T CARE. ALL I KNOW IS YOU'RE KIND AND GENTLE AND...
A-AND...
NO!!!

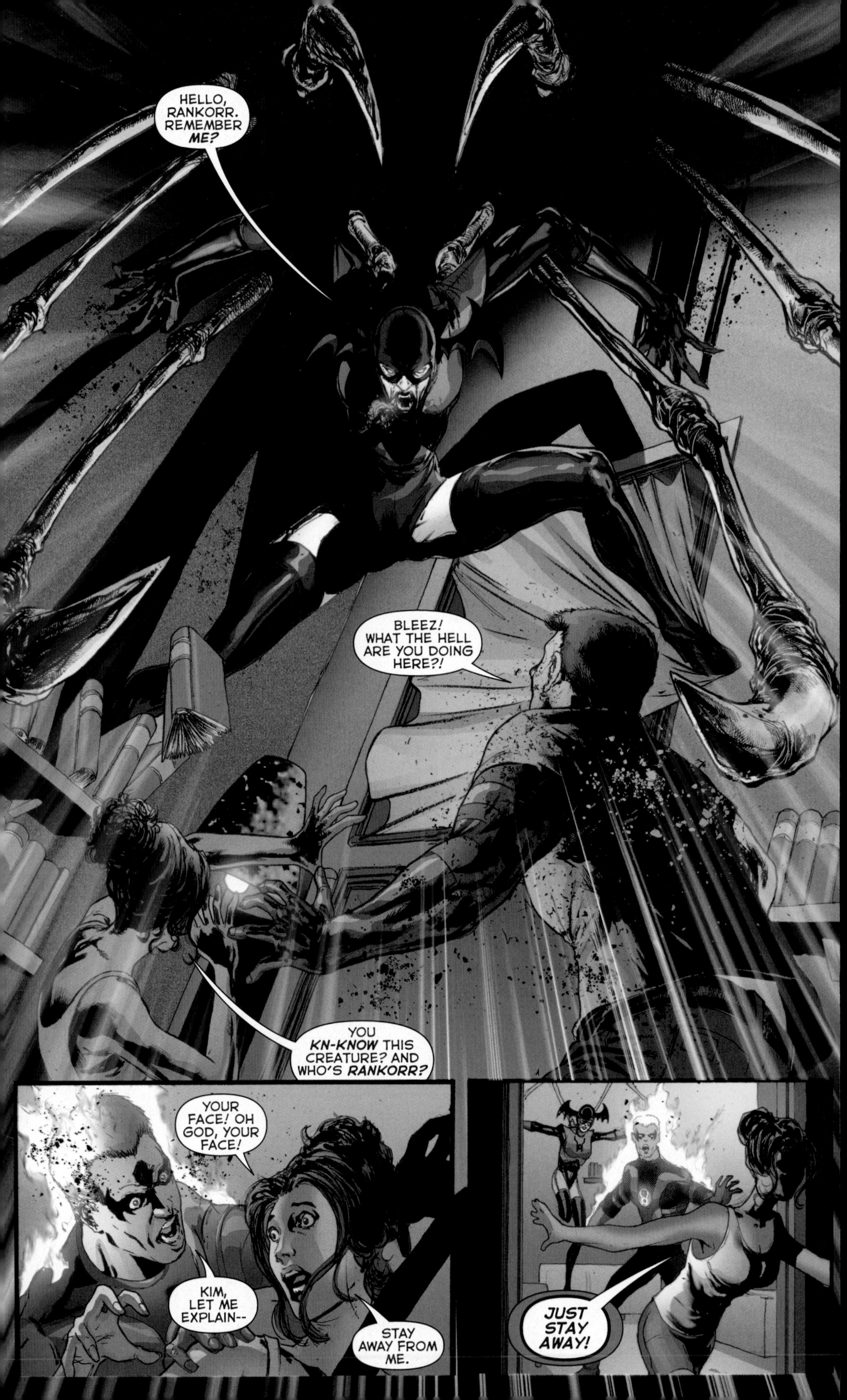
HELLO, RANKORR. REMEMBER *ME?*
BLEEZ! WHAT THE HELL ARE YOU DOING HERE?!
YOU *KN-KNOW* THIS CREATURE? AND WHO'S *RANKORR?*
YOUR FACE! OH GOD, YOUR FACE!
KIM, LET ME EXPLAIN--
STAY AWAY FROM ME.
JUST STAY AWAY!

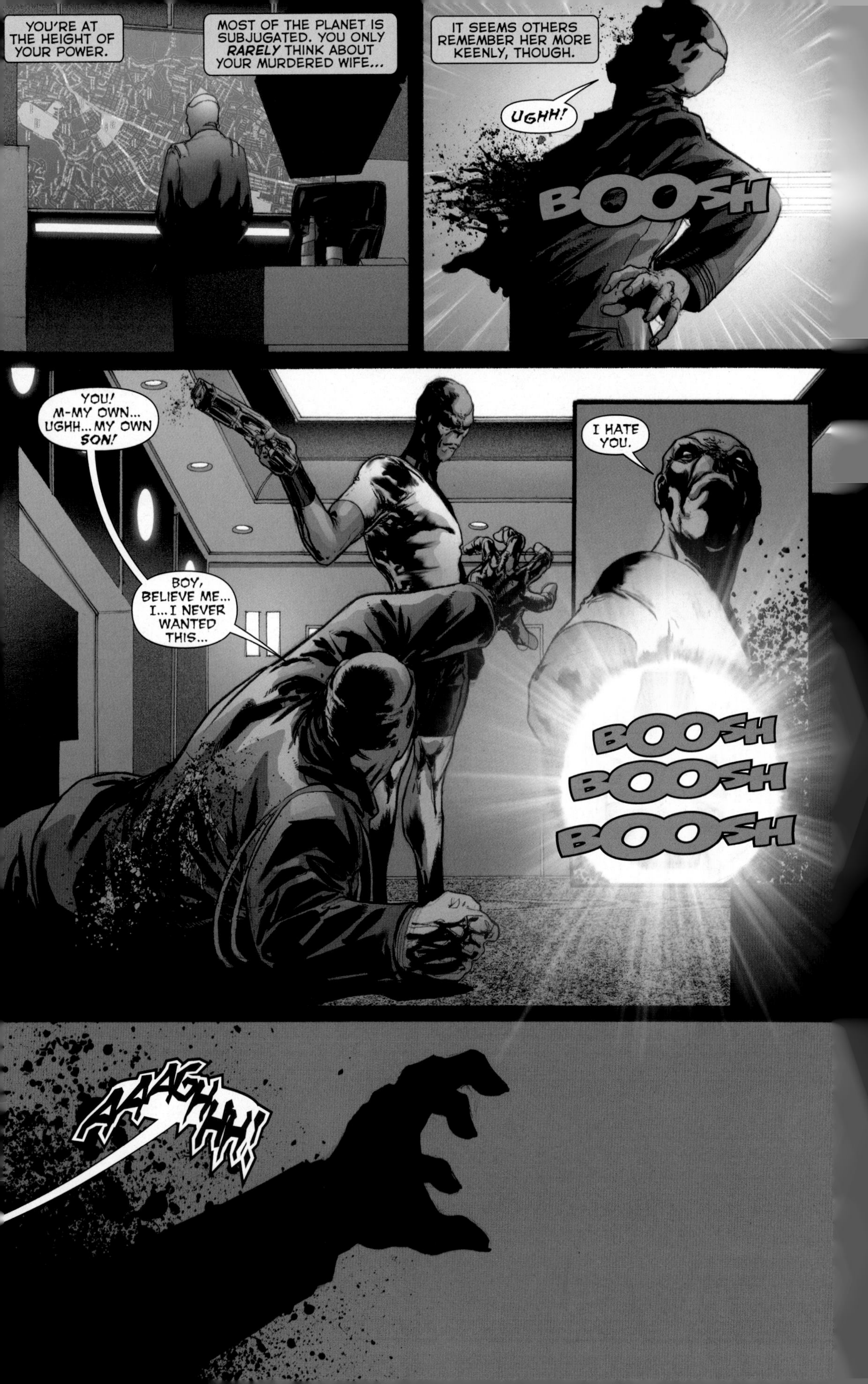

YOU'RE AT THE HEIGHT OF YOUR POWER.
MOST OF THE PLANET IS SUBJUGATED. YOU ONLY RARELY THINK ABOUT YOUR MURDERED WIFE...
IT SEEMS OTHERS REMEMBER HER MORE KEENLY, THOUGH.
UGHH!
BOOSH
YOU! M-MY OWN... UGHH... MY OWN SON!
BOY, BELIEVE ME... I... I NEVER WANTED THIS...
I HATE YOU.
BOOSH
BOOSH
BOOSH
AAAGHHH!

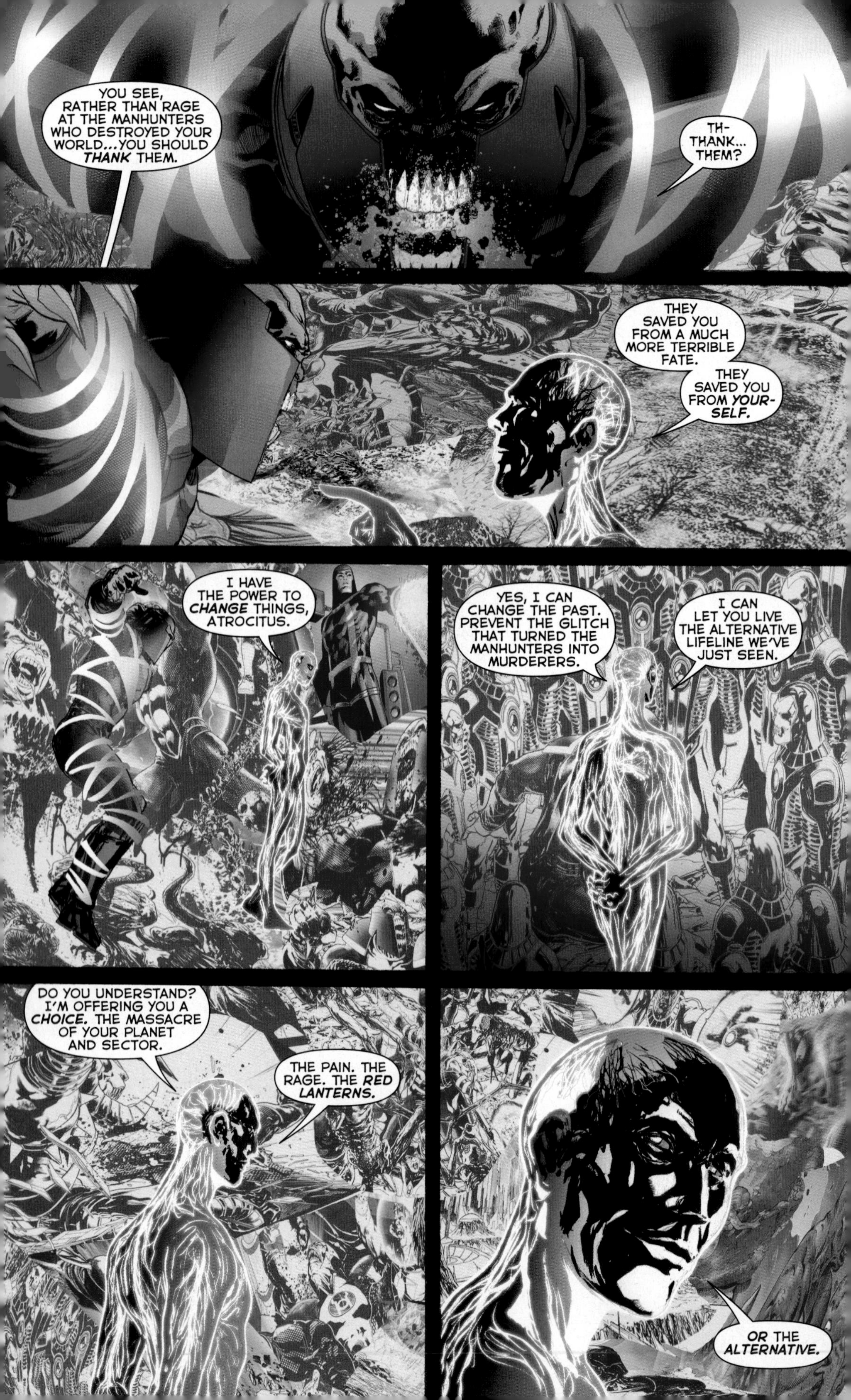
YOU SEE, RATHER THAN RAGE AT THE MANHUNTERS WHO DESTROYED YOUR WORLD...YOU SHOULD *THANK* THEM.
TH-THANK... THEM?
THEY SAVED YOU FROM A MUCH MORE TERRIBLE FATE.
THEY SAVED YOU FROM *YOURSELF.*
I HAVE THE POWER TO *CHANGE* THINGS, ATROCITUS.
YES, I CAN CHANGE THE PAST. PREVENT THE GLITCH THAT TURNED THE MANHUNTERS INTO MURDERERS.
I CAN LET YOU LIVE THE ALTERNATIVE LIFELINE WE'VE JUST SEEN.
DO YOU UNDERSTAND? I'M OFFERING YOU A *CHOICE.* THE MASSACRE OF YOUR PLANET AND SECTOR.
THE PAIN. THE RAGE. THE *RED LANTERNS.*
OR THE ALTERNATIVE.

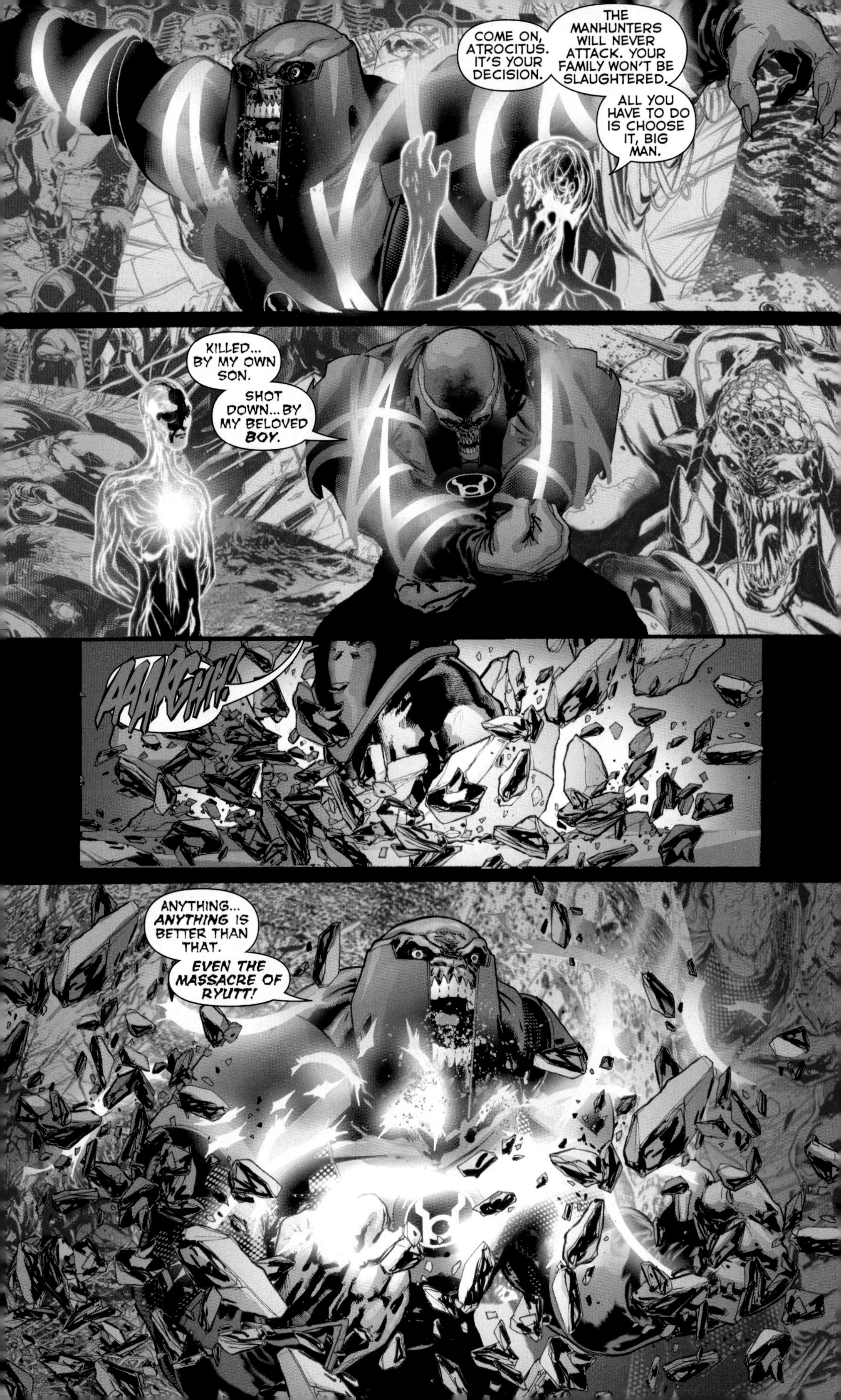
COME ON, ATROCITUS. IT'S YOUR DECISION.
THE MANHUNTERS WILL NEVER ATTACK. YOUR FAMILY WON'T BE SLAUGHTERED.
ALL YOU HAVE TO DO IS CHOOSE IT, BIG MAN.
KILLED... BY MY OWN SON.
SHOT DOWN... BY MY BELOVED BOY.
AAARGHH!
ANYTHING... ANYTHING IS BETTER THAN THAT.
EVEN THE MASSACRE OF RYUTT!

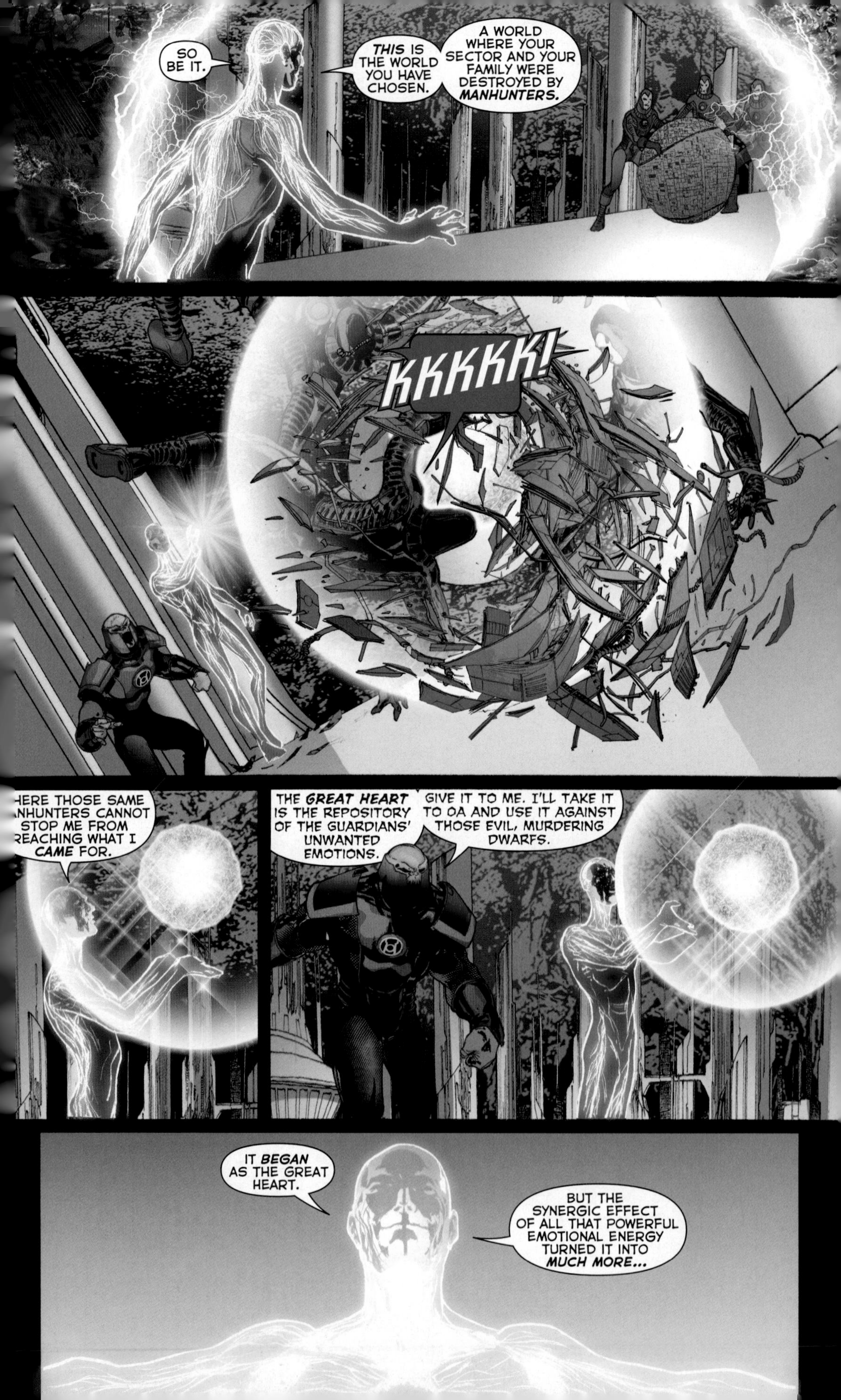

SO BE IT.
THIS IS THE WORLD YOU HAVE CHOSEN.
A WORLD WHERE YOUR SECTOR AND YOUR FAMILY WERE DESTROYED BY MANHUNTERS.
KKKKK!
HERE THOSE SAME ANHUNTERS CANNOT STOP ME FROM REACHING WHAT I CAME FOR.
THE GREAT HEART IS THE REPOSITORY OF THE GUARDIANS' UNWANTED EMOTIONS.
GIVE IT TO ME. I'LL TAKE IT TO OA AND USE IT AGAINST THOSE EVIL, MURDERING DWARFS.
IT BEGAN AS THE GREAT HEART.
BUT THE SYNERGIC EFFECT OF ALL THAT POWERFUL EMOTIONAL ENERGY TURNED IT INTO MUCH MORE...

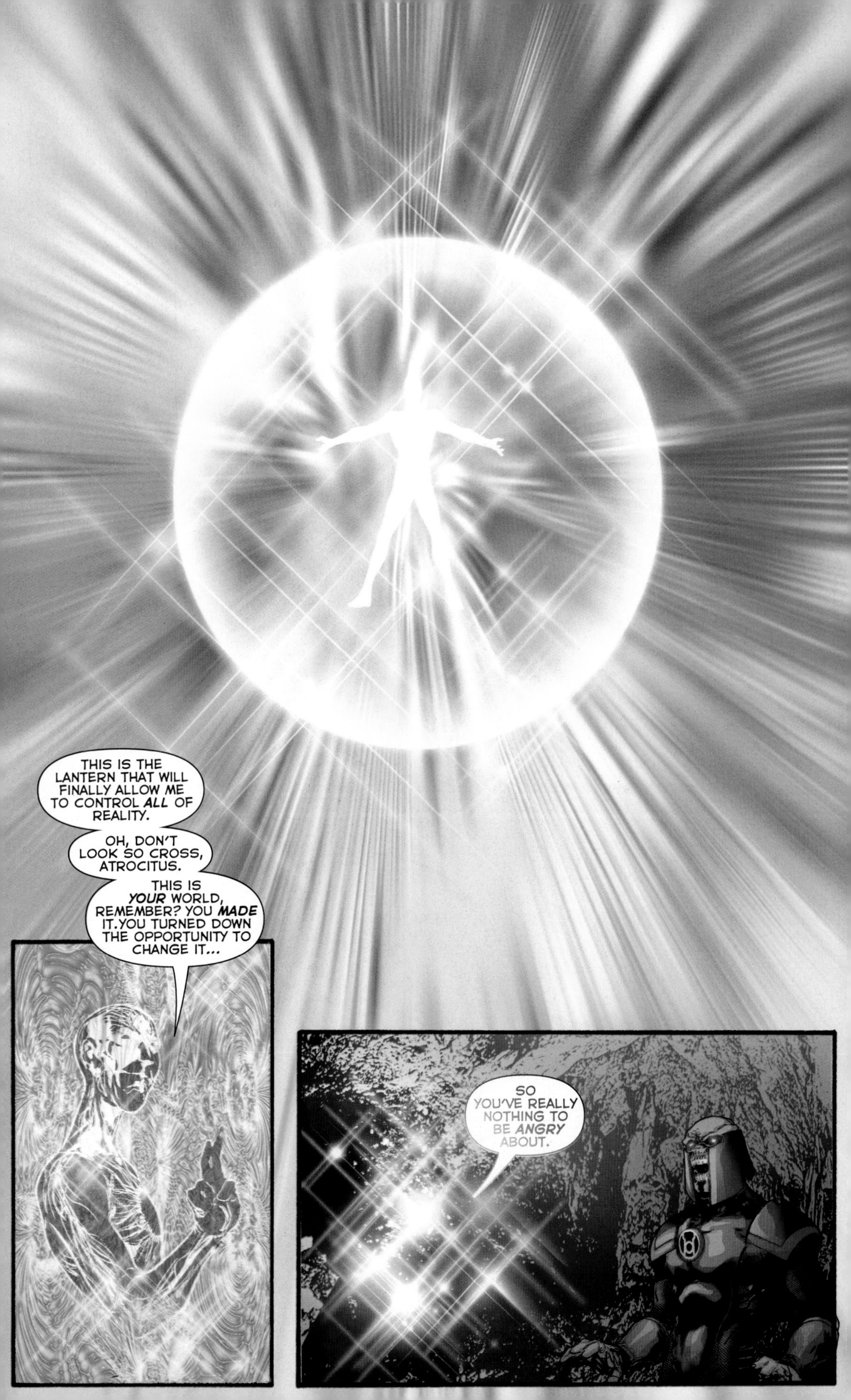
THIS IS THE LANTERN THAT WILL FINALLY ALLOW ME TO CONTROL *ALL* OF REALITY.
OH, DON'T LOOK SO CROSS, ATROCITUS.
THIS IS *YOUR* WORLD, REMEMBER? YOU *MADE* IT. YOU TURNED DOWN THE OPPORTUNITY TO CHANGE IT...
SO YOU'VE REALLY NOTHING TO BE *ANGRY* ABOUT.

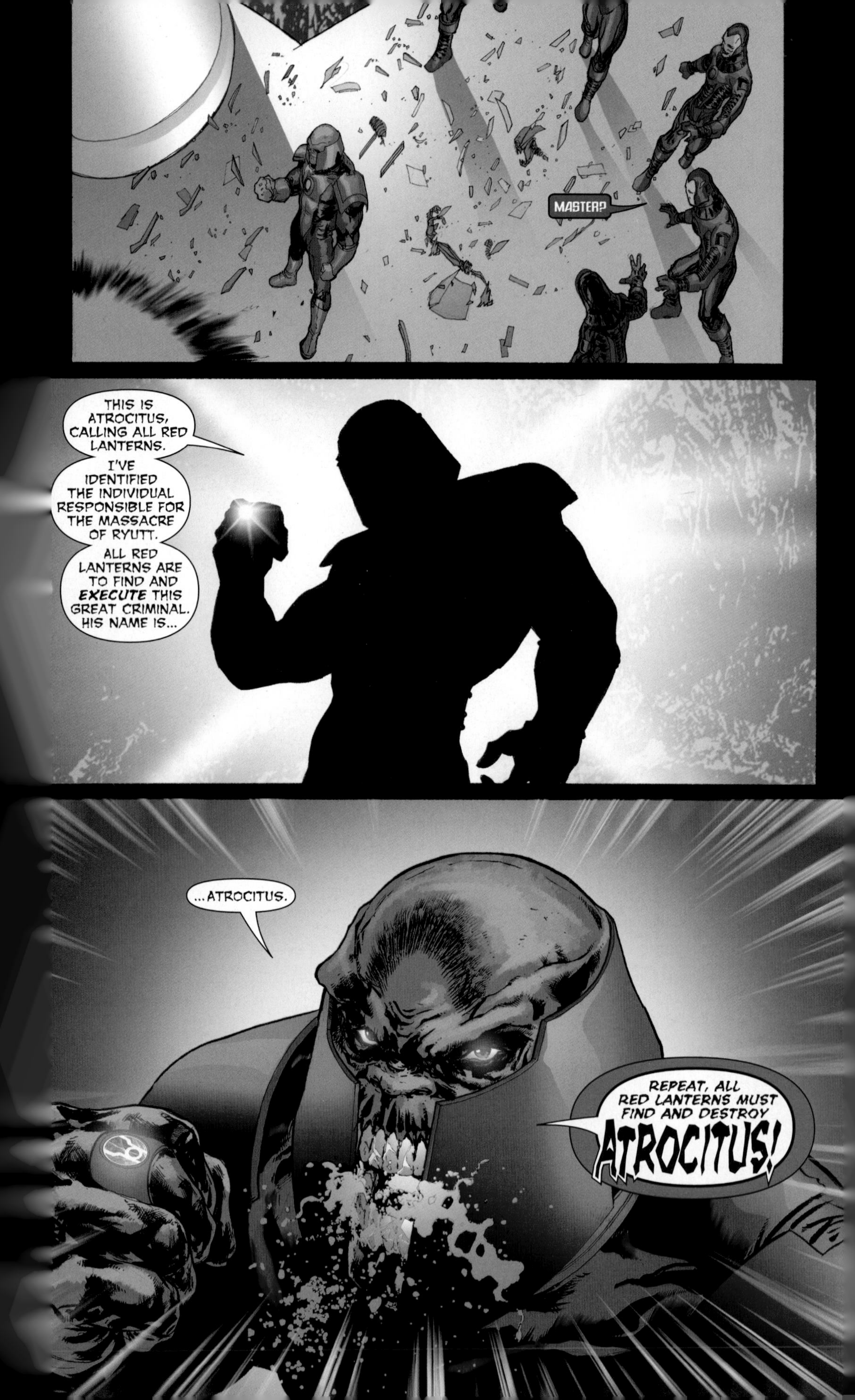
MASTER?
THIS IS ATROCITUS, CALLING ALL RED LANTERNS.
I'VE IDENTIFIED THE INDIVIDUAL RESPONSIBLE FOR THE MASSACRE OF RYUTT.
ALL RED LANTERNS ARE TO FIND AND *EXECUTE* THIS GREAT CRIMINAL. HIS NAME IS...
...ATROCITUS.
REPEAT, ALL RED LANTERNS MUST FIND AND DESTROY ATROCITUS!

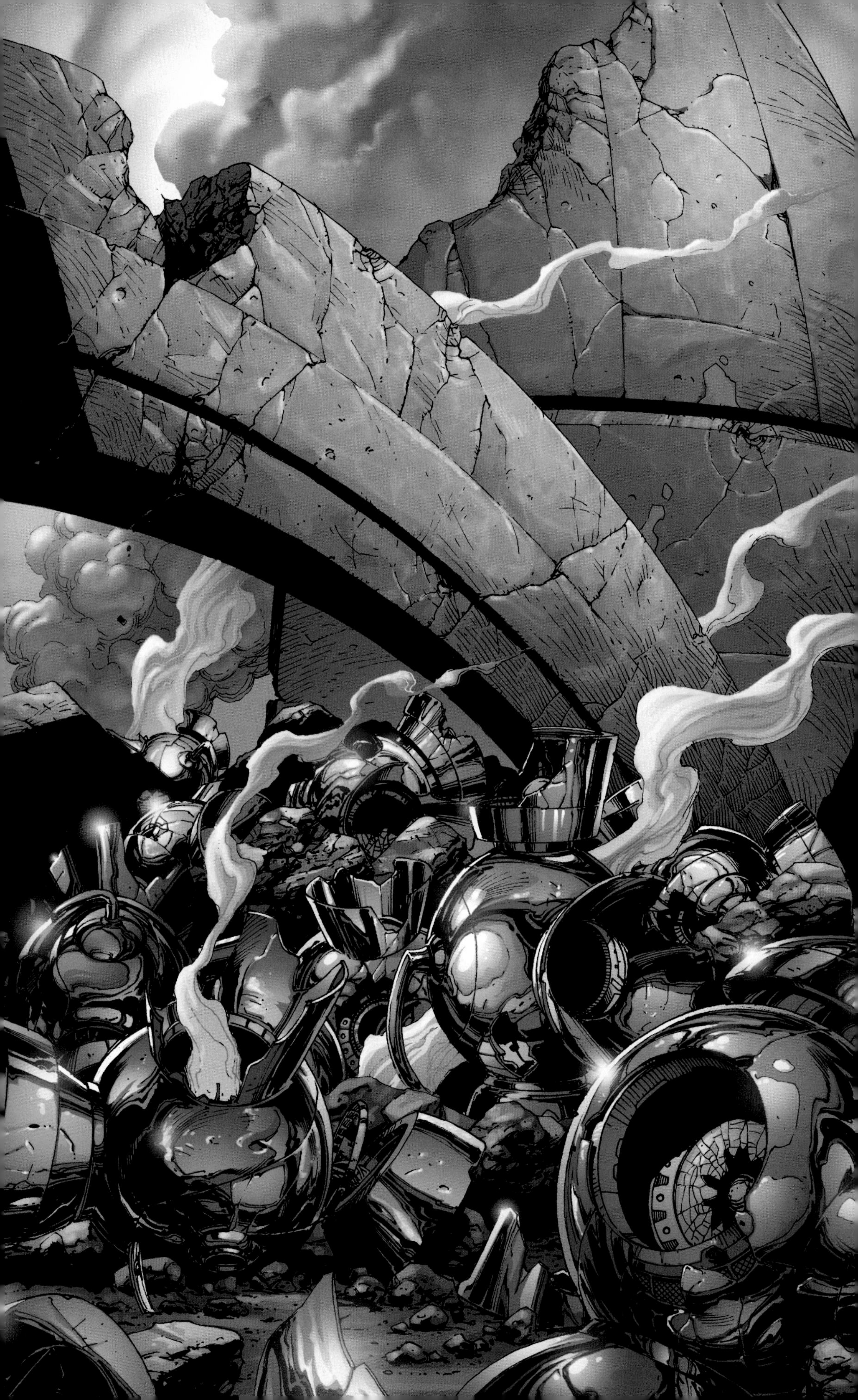

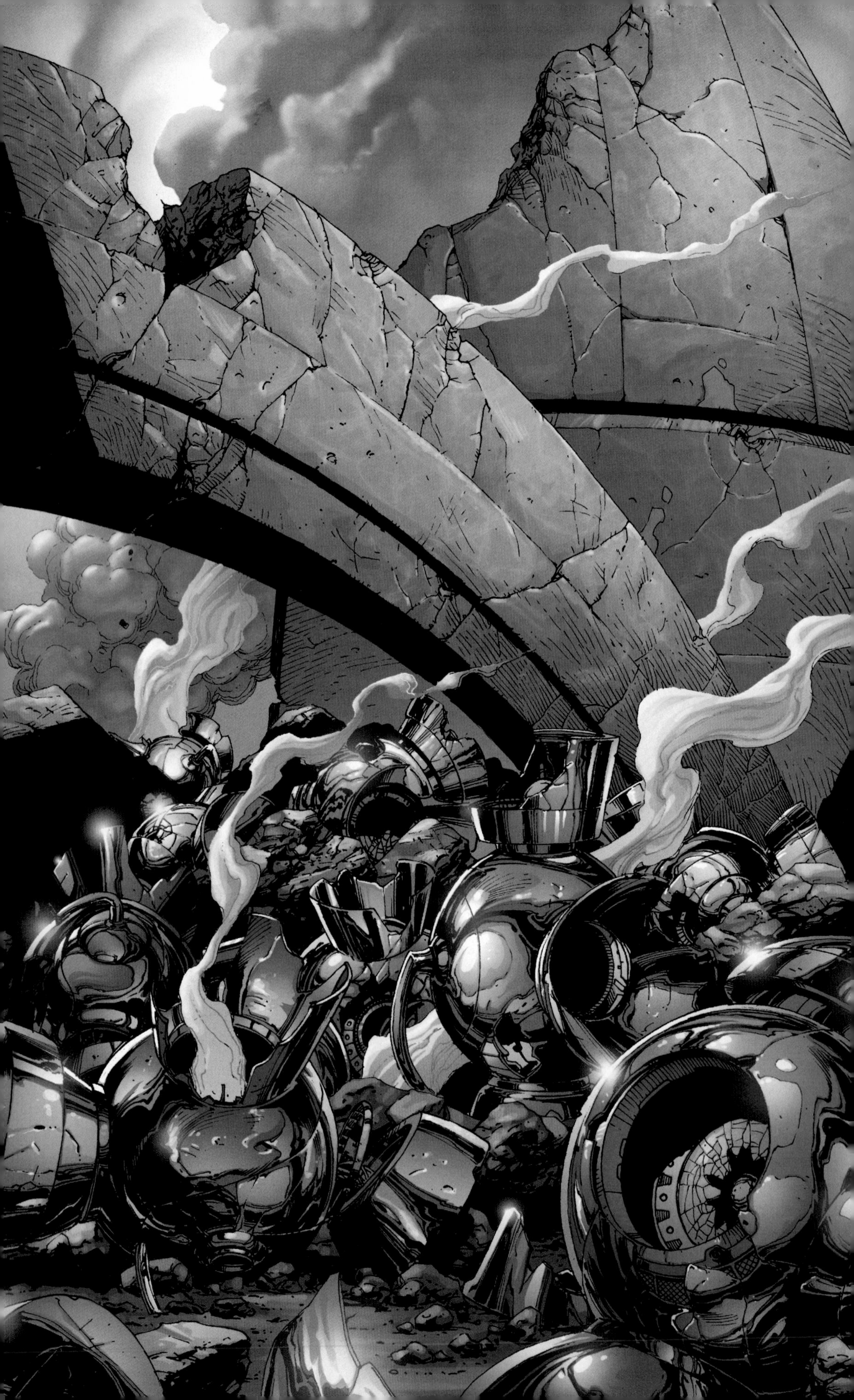

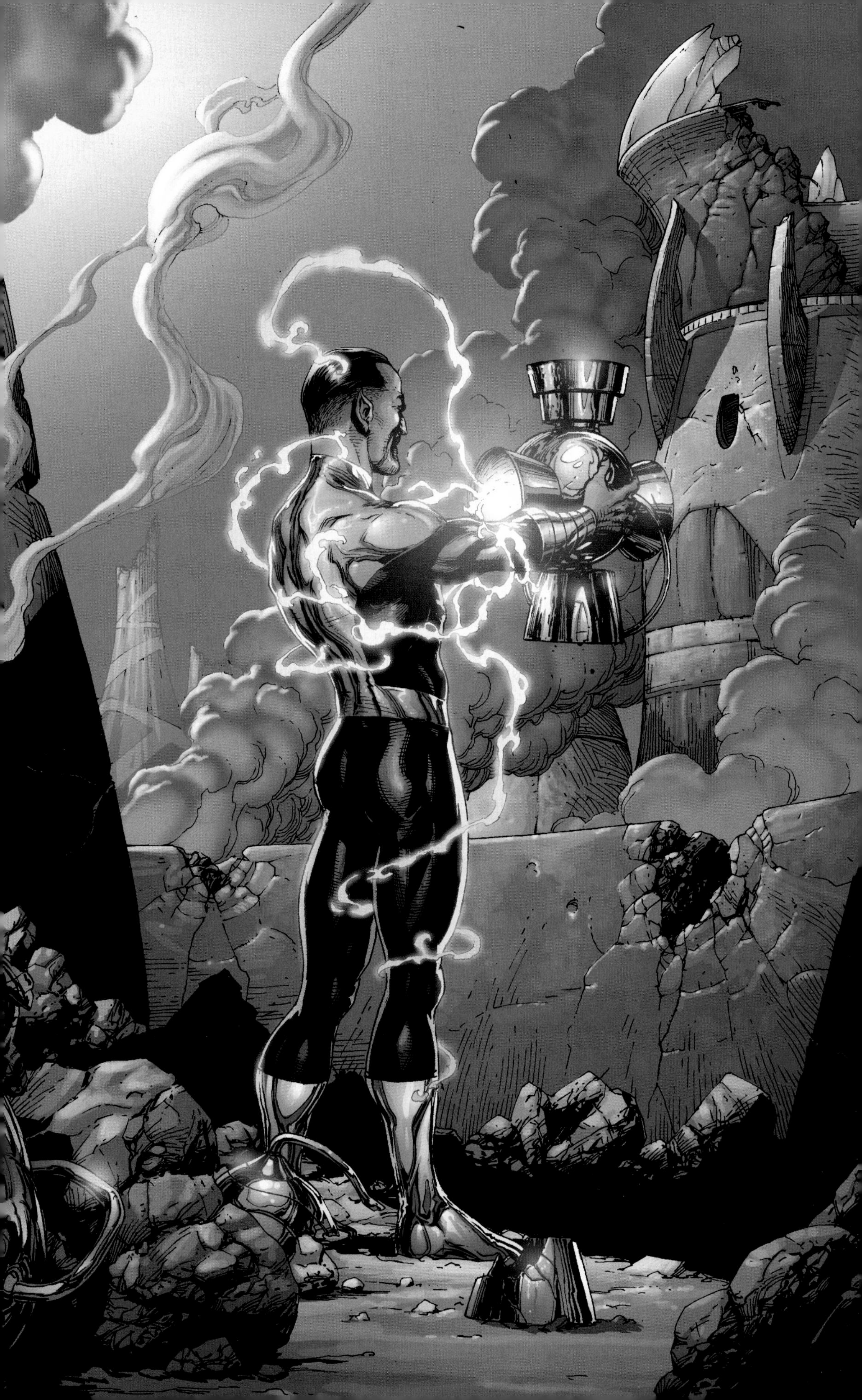

PART NINE

GEOFF JOHNS writer ARDIAN SYAF & SZYMON KUDRANSKI pencillers
MARK IRWIN, GUILLERMO ORTEGO, & SZYMON KUDRANSKI inkers cover art by GARY FRANK & BRAD ANDERSON

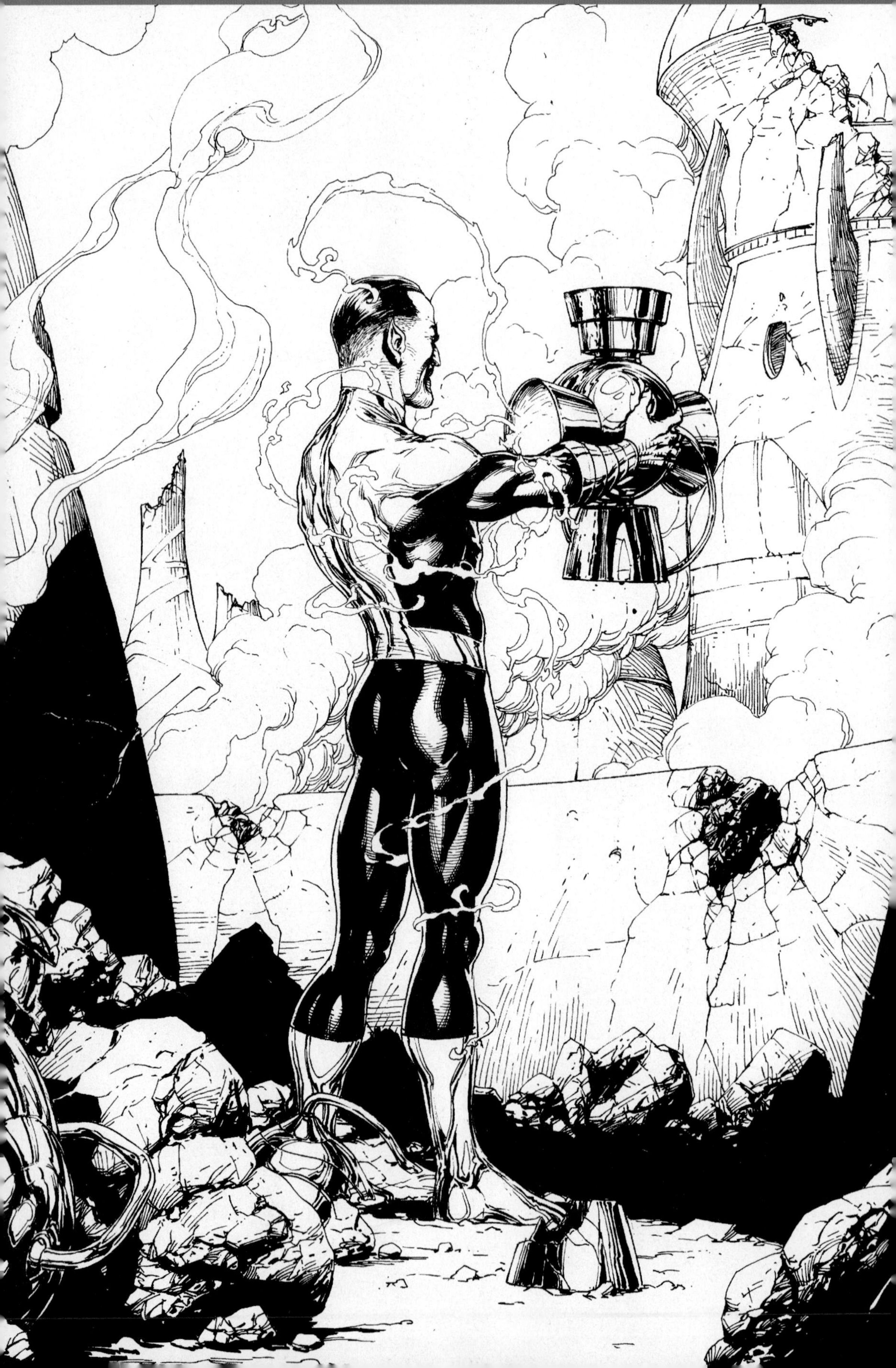

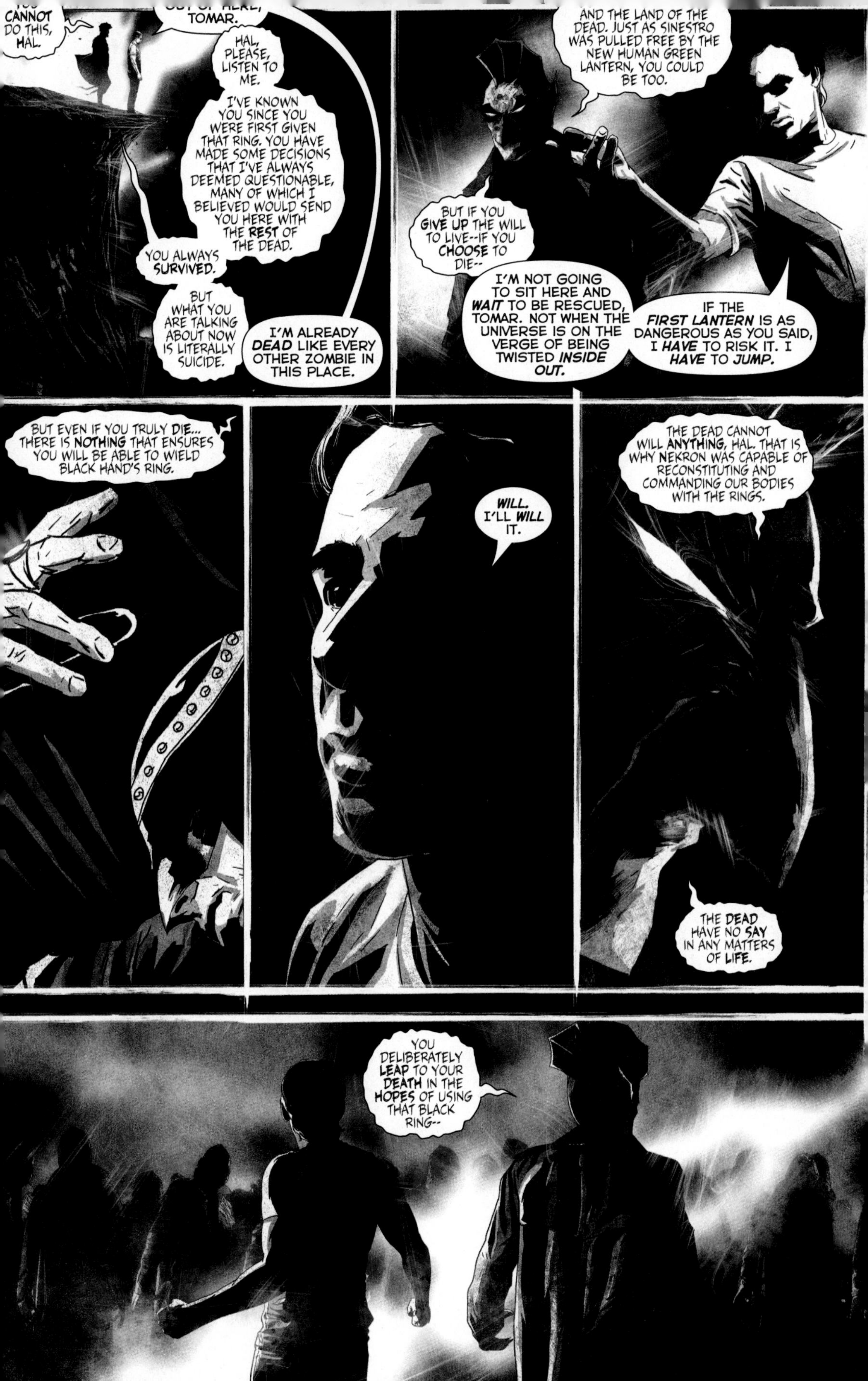
CANNOT DO THIS, HAL.
TOMAR.
HAL, PLEASE, LISTEN TO ME.
I'VE KNOWN YOU SINCE YOU WERE FIRST GIVEN THAT RING. YOU HAVE MADE SOME DECISIONS THAT I'VE ALWAYS DEEMED QUESTIONABLE, MANY OF WHICH I BELIEVED WOULD SEND YOU HERE WITH THE REST OF THE DEAD.
YOU ALWAYS SURVIVED.
BUT WHAT YOU ARE TALKING ABOUT NOW IS LITERALLY SUICIDE.
I'M ALREADY DEAD LIKE EVERY OTHER ZOMBIE IN THIS PLACE.
AND THE LAND OF THE DEAD. JUST AS SINESTRO WAS PULLED FREE BY THE NEW HUMAN GREEN LANTERN, YOU COULD BE TOO.
BUT IF YOU GIVE UP THE WILL TO LIVE--IF YOU CHOOSE TO DIE--
I'M NOT GOING TO SIT HERE AND WAIT TO BE RESCUED, TOMAR. NOT WHEN THE UNIVERSE IS ON THE VERGE OF BEING TWISTED INSIDE OUT.
IF THE FIRST LANTERN IS AS DANGEROUS AS YOU SAID, I HAVE TO RISK IT. I HAVE TO JUMP.
BUT EVEN IF YOU TRULY DIE... THERE IS NOTHING THAT ENSURES YOU WILL BE ABLE TO WIELD BLACK HAND'S RING.
WILL. I'LL WILL IT.
THE DEAD CANNOT WILL ANYTHING, HAL. THAT IS WHY NEKRON WAS CAPABLE OF RECONSTITUTING AND COMMANDING OUR BODIES WITH THE RINGS.
THE DEAD HAVE NO SAY IN ANY MATTERS OF LIFE.
YOU DELIBERATELY LEAP TO YOUR DEATH IN THE HOPES OF USING THAT BLACK RING--

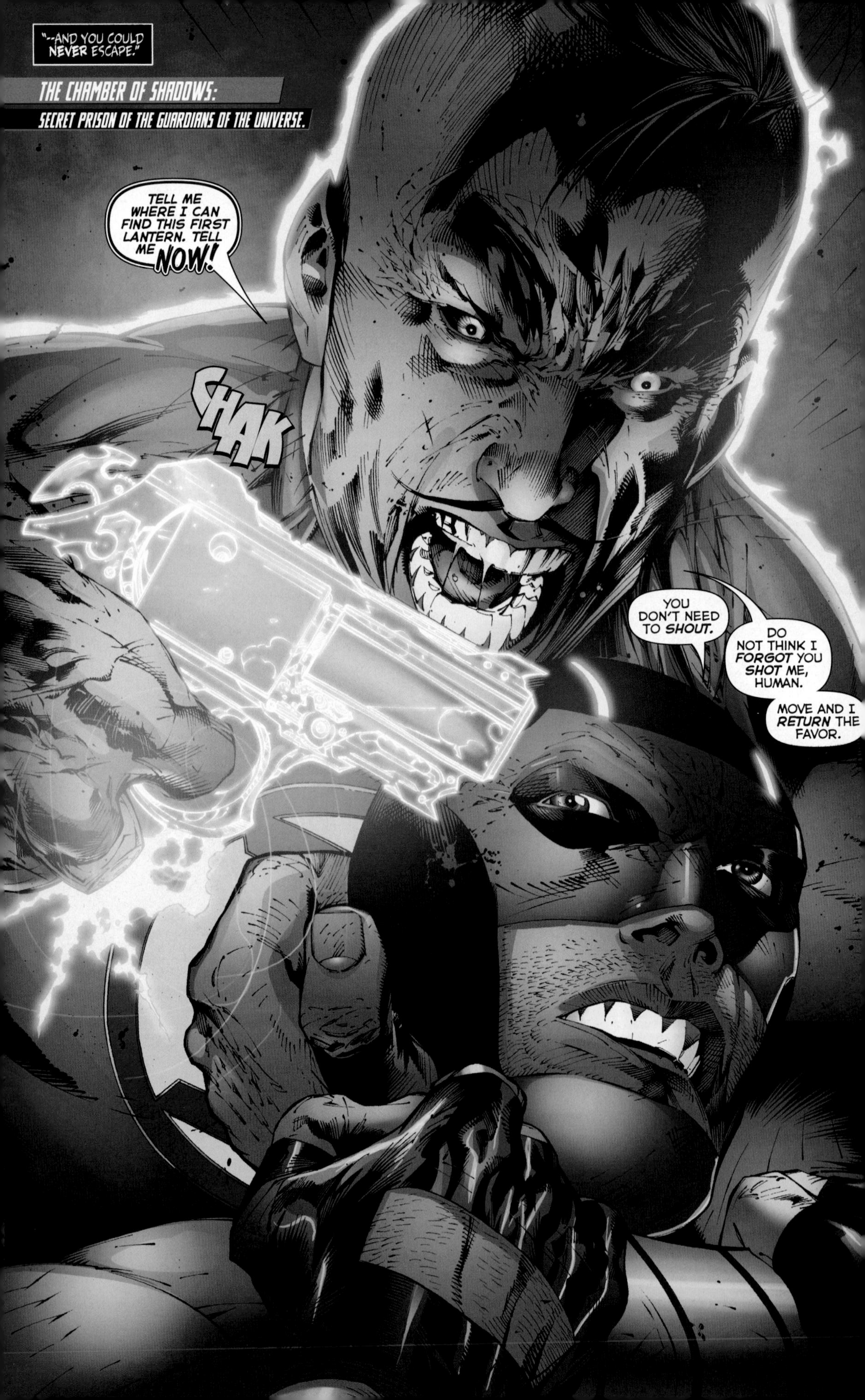
"--AND YOU COULD NEVER ESCAPE."
THE CHAMBER OF SHADOWS:
SECRET PRISON OF THE GUARDIANS OF THE UNIVERSE.
TELL ME WHERE I CAN FIND THIS FIRST LANTERN. TELL ME NOW!
CHAK
YOU DON'T NEED TO SHOUT.
DO NOT THINK I FORGOT YOU SHOT ME, HUMAN.
MOVE AND I RETURN THE FAVOR.

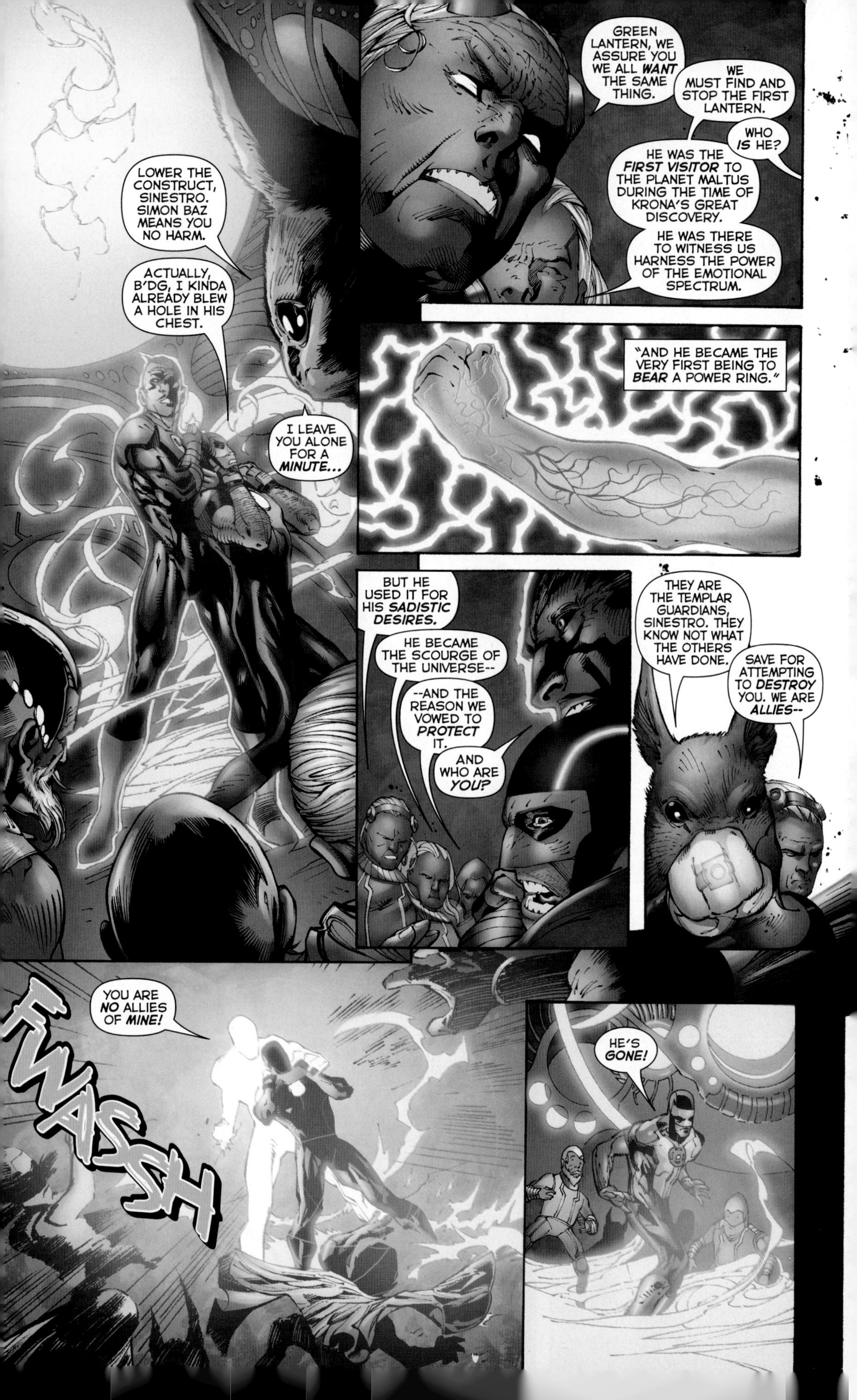
LOWER THE CONSTRUCT, SINESTRO. SIMON BAZ MEANS YOU NO HARM.
ACTUALLY, B'DG, I KINDA ALREADY BLEW A HOLE IN HIS CHEST.
I LEAVE YOU ALONE FOR A MINUTE...
GREEN LANTERN, WE ASSURE YOU WE ALL WANT THE SAME THING.
WE MUST FIND AND STOP THE FIRST LANTERN.
WHO IS HE?
HE WAS THE FIRST VISITOR TO THE PLANET MALTUS DURING THE TIME OF KRONA'S GREAT DISCOVERY.
HE WAS THERE TO WITNESS US HARNESS THE POWER OF THE EMOTIONAL SPECTRUM.
"AND HE BECAME THE VERY FIRST BEING TO BEAR A POWER RING."
BUT HE USED IT FOR HIS SADISTIC DESIRES.
HE BECAME THE SCOURGE OF THE UNIVERSE--
--AND THE REASON WE VOWED TO PROTECT IT.
AND WHO ARE YOU?
THEY ARE THE TEMPLAR GUARDIANS, SINESTRO. THEY KNOW NOT WHAT THE OTHERS HAVE DONE.
SAVE FOR ATTEMPTING TO DESTROY YOU. WE ARE ALLIES--
YOU ARE NO ALLIES OF MINE!
FWASSH
HE'S GONE!

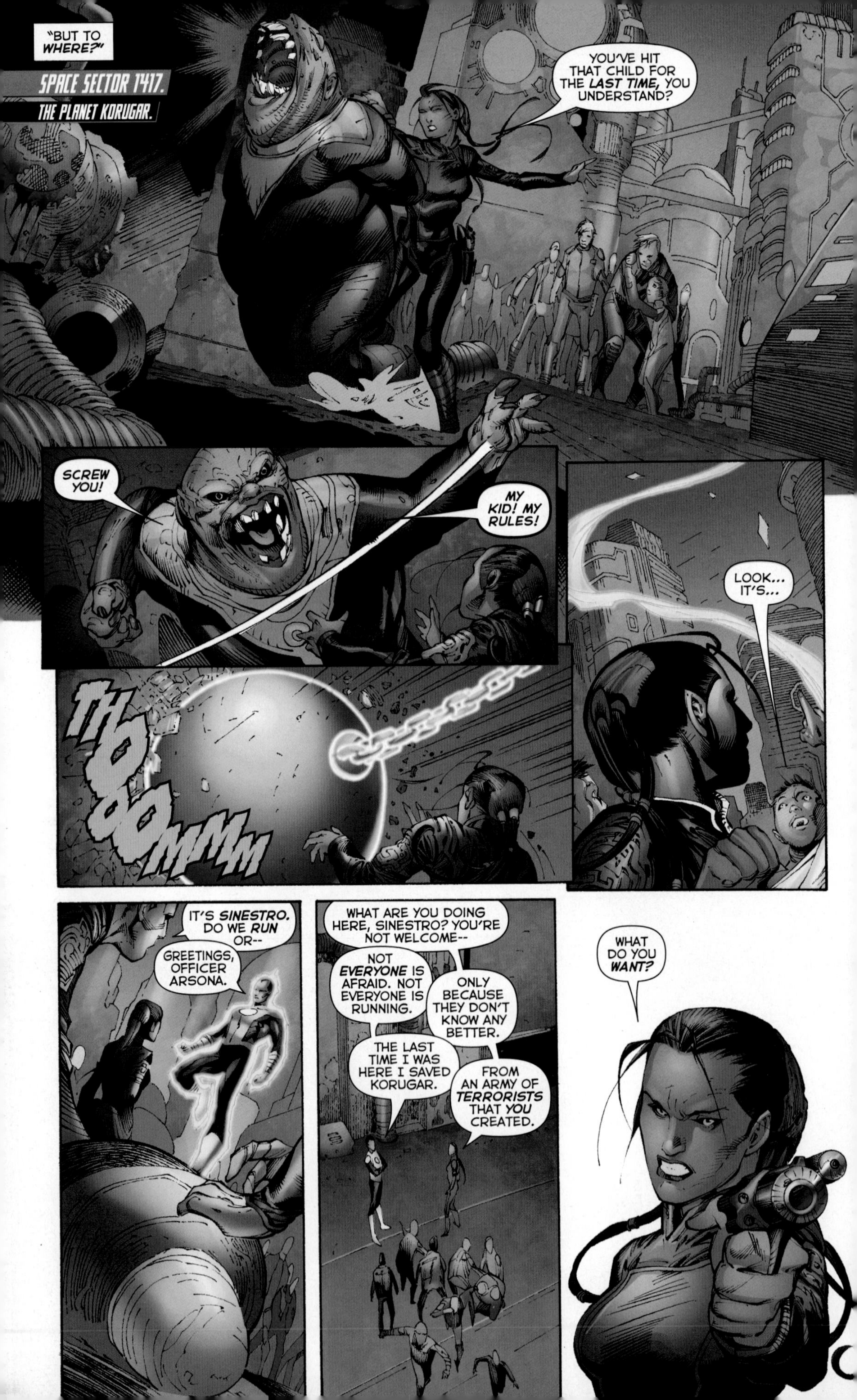

"BUT TO WHERE?"
SPACE SECTOR 1417.
THE PLANET KORUGAR.
YOU'VE HIT THAT CHILD FOR THE LAST TIME, YOU UNDERSTAND?
SCREW YOU!
MY KID! MY RULES!
THOOOMMM
LOOK... IT'S...
IT'S SINESTRO. DO WE RUN OR--
GREETINGS, OFFICER ARSONA.
WHAT ARE YOU DOING HERE, SINESTRO? YOU'RE NOT WELCOME--
NOT EVERYONE IS AFRAID. NOT EVERYONE IS RUNNING.
ONLY BECAUSE THEY DON'T KNOW ANY BETTER.
THE LAST TIME I WAS HERE I SAVED KORUGAR.
FROM AN ARMY OF TERRORISTS THAT YOU CREATED.
WHAT DO YOU WANT?

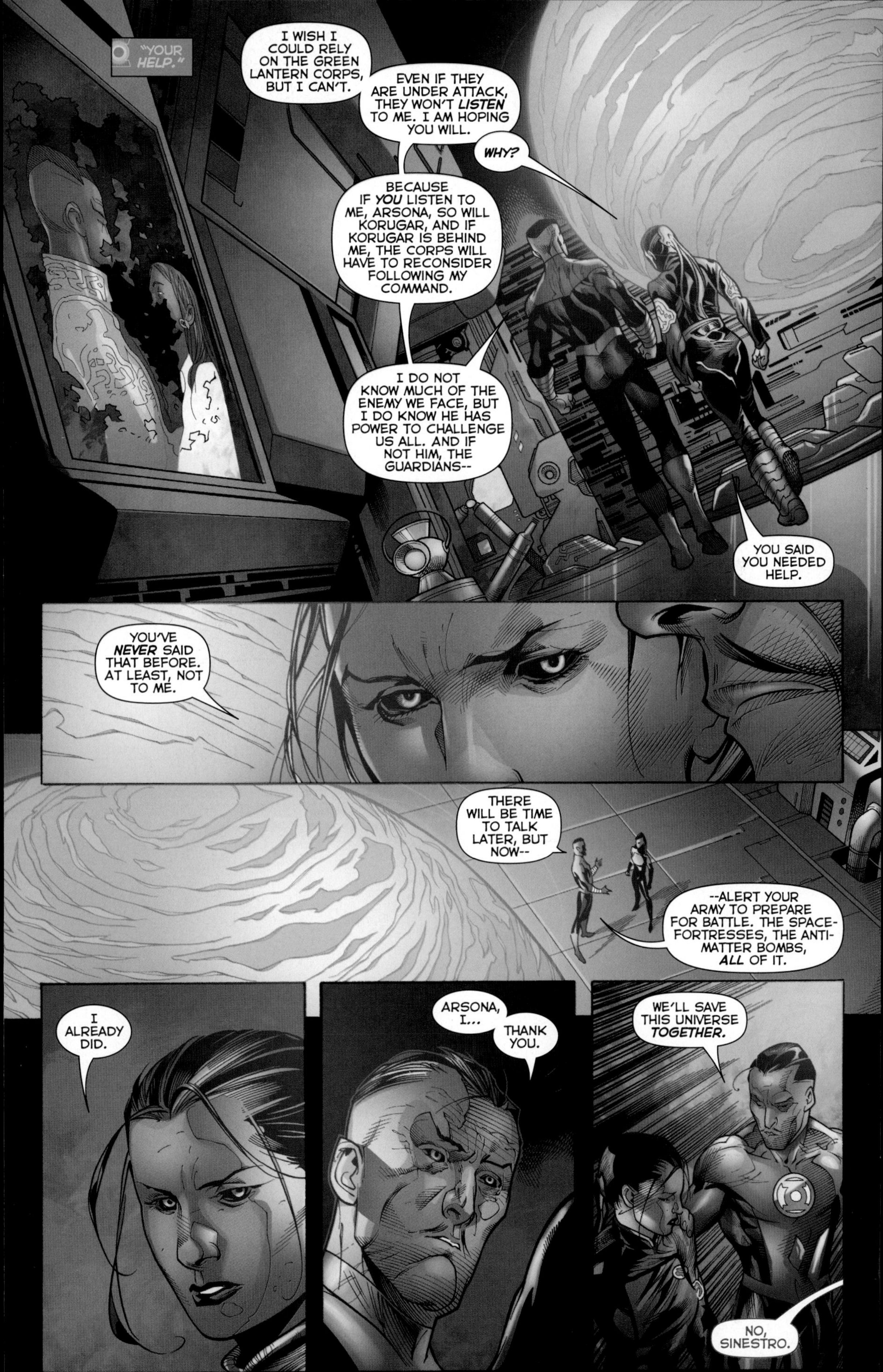
"YOUR HELP."
I WISH I COULD RELY ON THE GREEN LANTERN CORPS, BUT I CAN'T.
EVEN IF THEY ARE UNDER ATTACK, THEY WON'T LISTEN TO ME. I AM HOPING YOU WILL.
WHY?
BECAUSE IF YOU LISTEN TO ME, ARSONA, SO WILL KORUGAR, AND IF KORUGAR IS BEHIND ME, THE CORPS WILL HAVE TO RECONSIDER FOLLOWING MY COMMAND.
I DO NOT KNOW MUCH OF THE ENEMY WE FACE, BUT I DO KNOW HE HAS POWER TO CHALLENGE US ALL. AND IF NOT HIM, THE GUARDIANS--
YOU SAID YOU NEEDED HELP.
YOU'VE NEVER SAID THAT BEFORE. AT LEAST, NOT TO ME.
THERE WILL BE TIME TO TALK LATER, BUT NOW--
--ALERT YOUR ARMY TO PREPARE FOR BATTLE. THE SPACE-FORTRESSES, THE ANTI-MATTER BOMBS, ALL OF IT.
I ALREADY DID.
ARSONA, I...
THANK YOU.
WE'LL SAVE THIS UNIVERSE TOGETHER.
NO, SINESTRO.

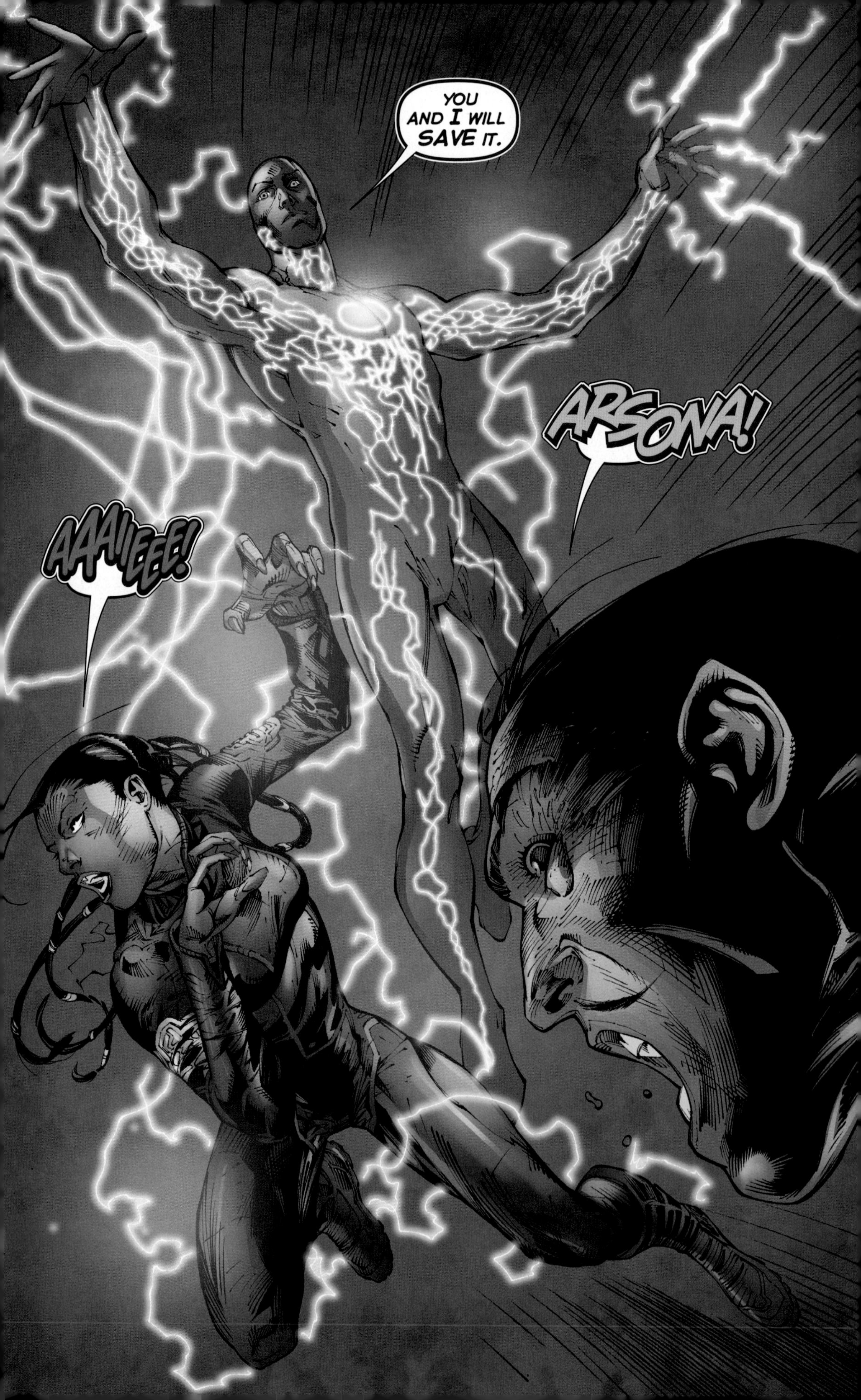
YOU AND I WILL SAVE IT.
ARSONA!
AAAIIEEEE!

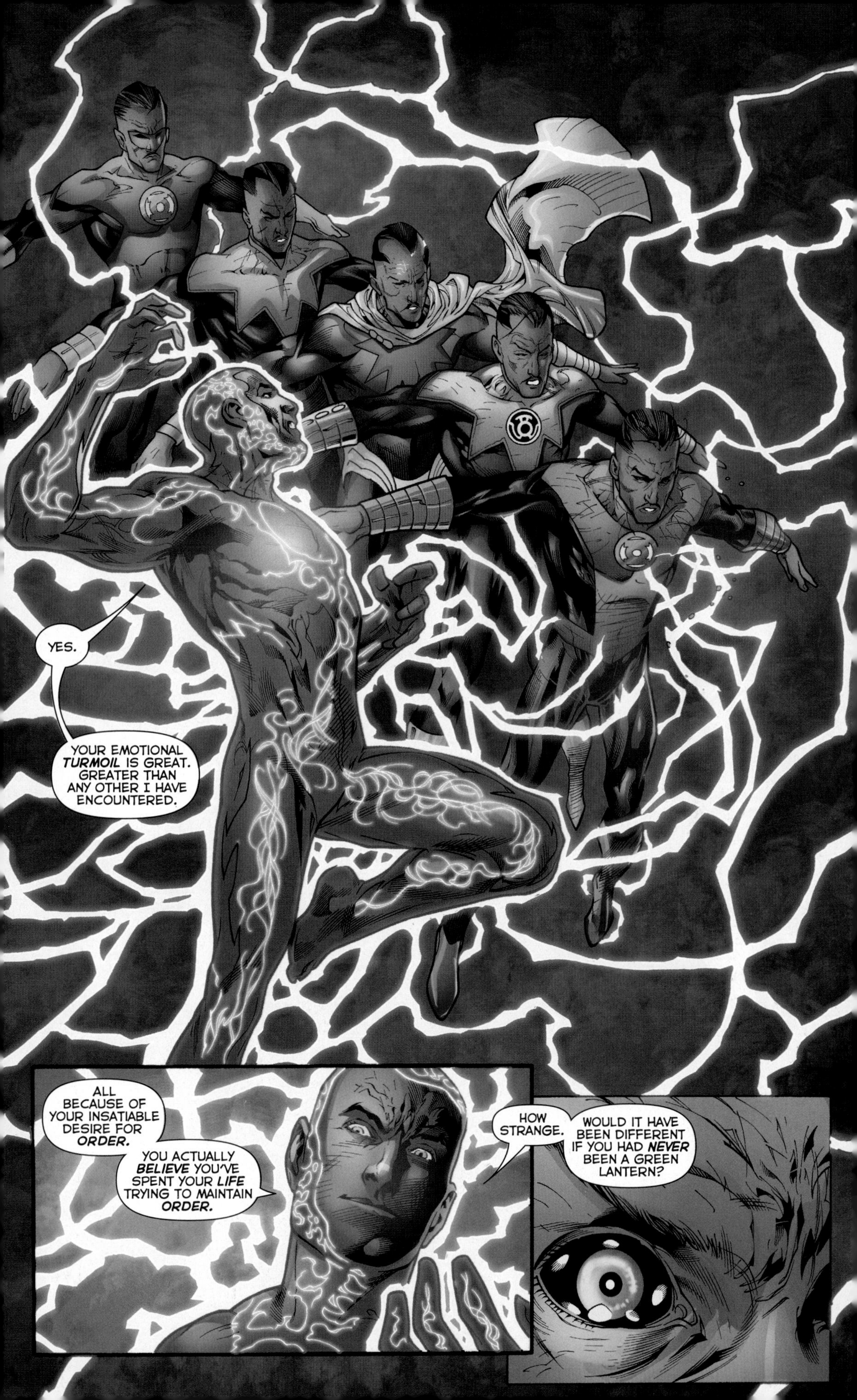
YES.
YOUR EMOTIONAL TURMOIL IS GREAT. GREATER THAN ANY OTHER I HAVE ENCOUNTERED.
ALL BECAUSE OF YOUR INSATIABLE DESIRE FOR ORDER.
YOU ACTUALLY BELIEVE YOU'VE SPENT YOUR LIFE TRYING TO MAINTAIN ORDER.
HOW STRANGE.
WOULD IT HAVE BEEN DIFFERENT IF YOU HAD NEVER BEEN A GREEN LANTERN?

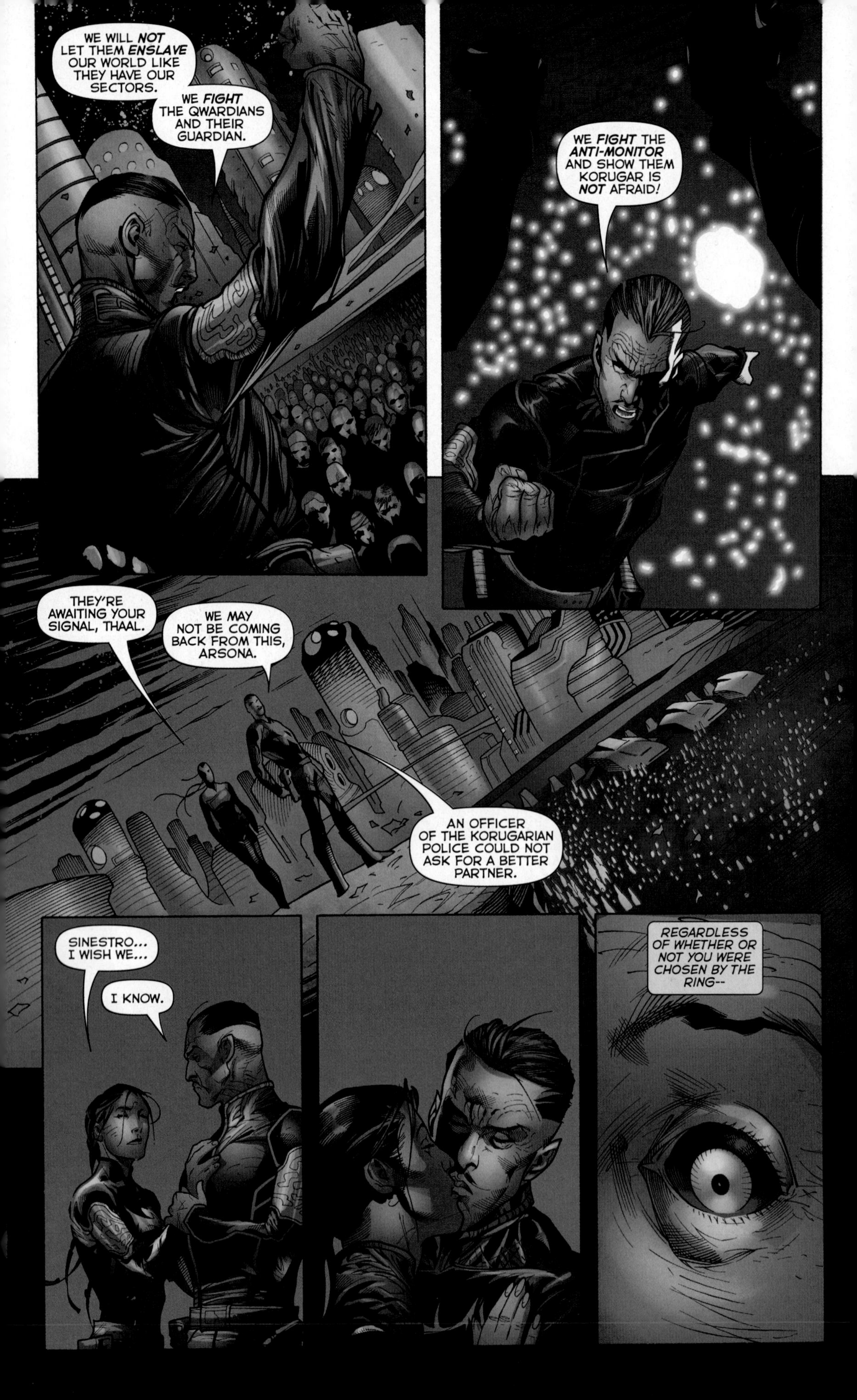

WE WILL NOT LET THEM ENSLAVE OUR WORLD LIKE THEY HAVE OUR SECTORS.
WE FIGHT THE QWARDIANS AND THEIR GUARDIAN.
WE FIGHT THE ANTI-MONITOR AND SHOW THEM KORUGAR IS NOT AFRAID!
THEY'RE AWAITING YOUR SIGNAL, THAAL.
WE MAY NOT BE COMING BACK FROM THIS, ARSONA.
AN OFFICER OF THE KORUGARIAN POLICE COULD NOT ASK FOR A BETTER PARTNER.
SINESTRO... I WISH WE...
I KNOW.
REGARDLESS OF WHETHER OR NOT YOU WERE CHOSEN BY THE RING--

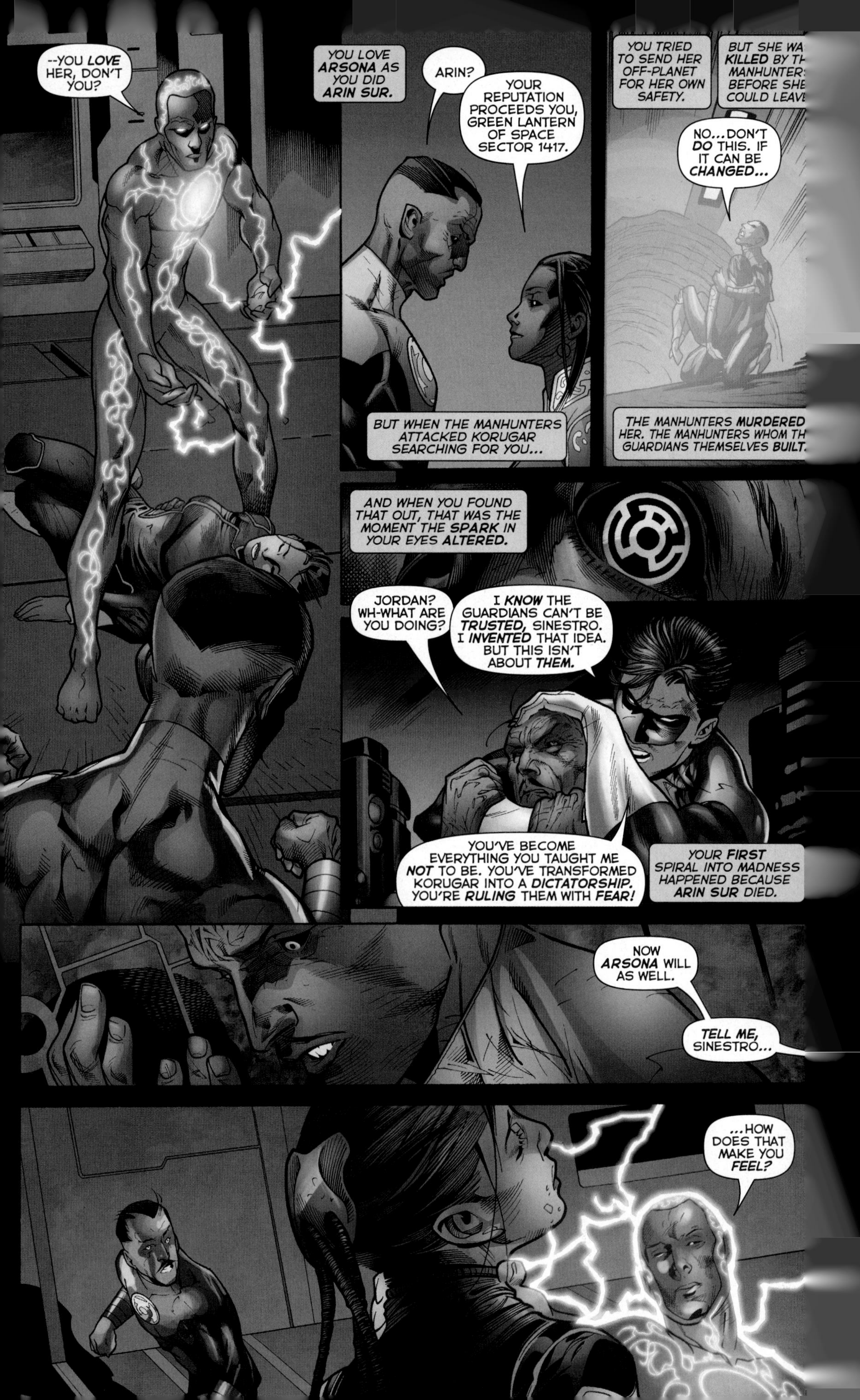
--YOU LOVE HER, DON'T YOU?
YOU LOVE ARSONA AS YOU DID ARIN SUR.
ARIN?
YOUR REPUTATION PROCEEDS YOU, GREEN LANTERN OF SPACE SECTOR 1417.
BUT WHEN THE MANHUNTERS ATTACKED KORUGAR SEARCHING FOR YOU...
YOU TRIED TO SEND HER OFF-PLANET FOR HER OWN SAFETY.
BUT SHE WA KILLED BY TH MANHUNTERS BEFORE SHE COULD LEAVE
NO...DON'T DO THIS. IF IT CAN BE CHANGED...
THE MANHUNTERS MURDERED HER. THE MANHUNTERS WHOM TH GUARDIANS THEMSELVES BUILT.
AND WHEN YOU FOUND THAT OUT, THAT WAS THE MOMENT THE SPARK IN YOUR EYES ALTERED.
JORDAN? WH-WHAT ARE YOU DOING?
I KNOW THE GUARDIANS CAN'T BE TRUSTED, SINESTRO. I INVENTED THAT IDEA. BUT THIS ISN'T ABOUT THEM.
YOU'VE BECOME EVERYTHING YOU TAUGHT ME NOT TO BE. YOU'VE TRANSFORMED KORUGAR INTO A DICTATORSHIP. YOU'RE RULING THEM WITH FEAR!
YOUR FIRST SPIRAL INTO MADNESS HAPPENED BECAUSE ARIN SUR DIED.
NOW ARSONA WILL AS WELL.
TELL ME, SINESTRO...
...HOW DOES THAT MAKE YOU FEEL?

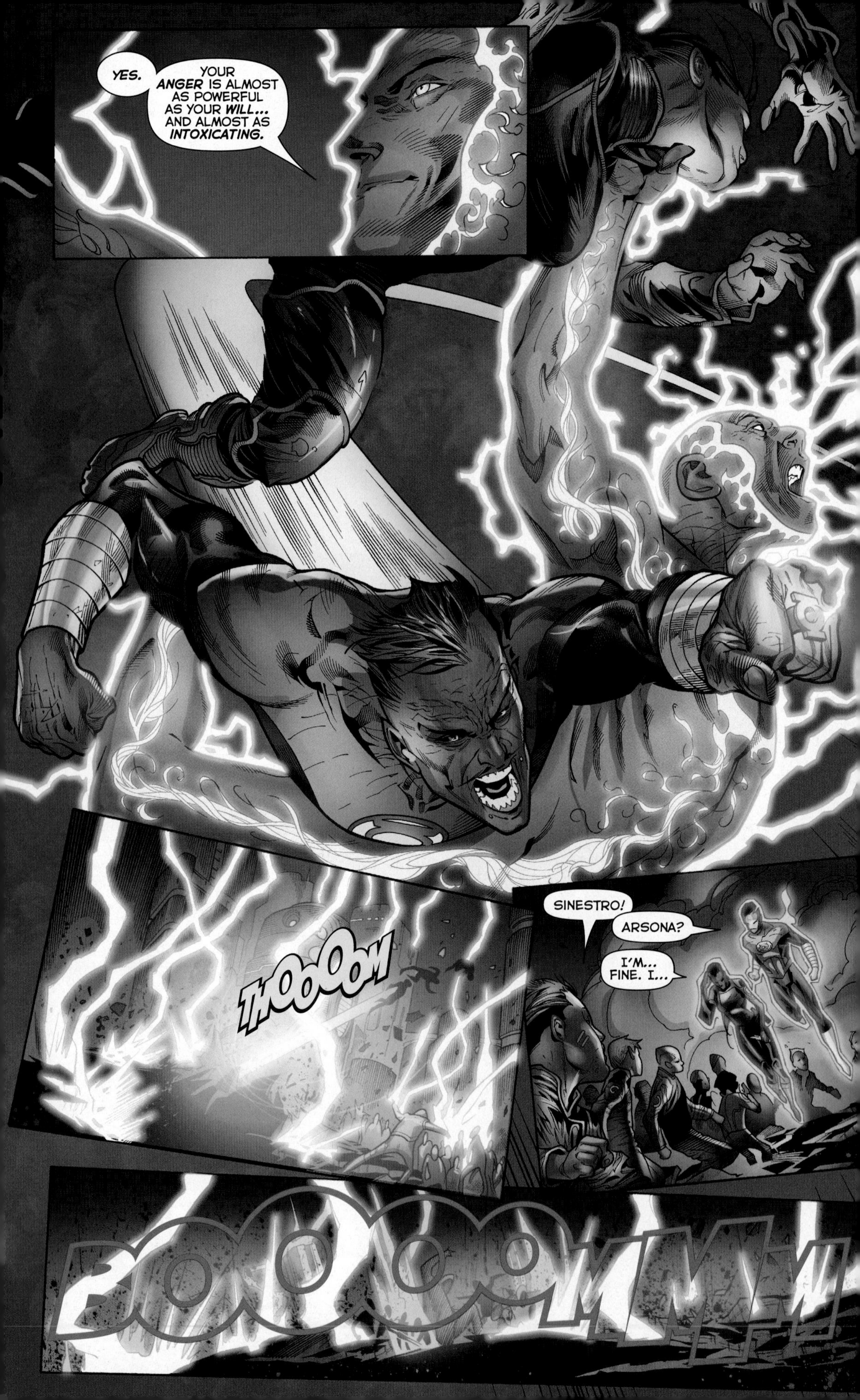
YES.
YOUR ANGER IS ALMOST AS POWERFUL AS YOUR WILL... AND ALMOST AS INTOXICATING.
THOOOOM
SINESTRO!
ARSONA?
I'M... FINE. I...
BOOOOOMMM

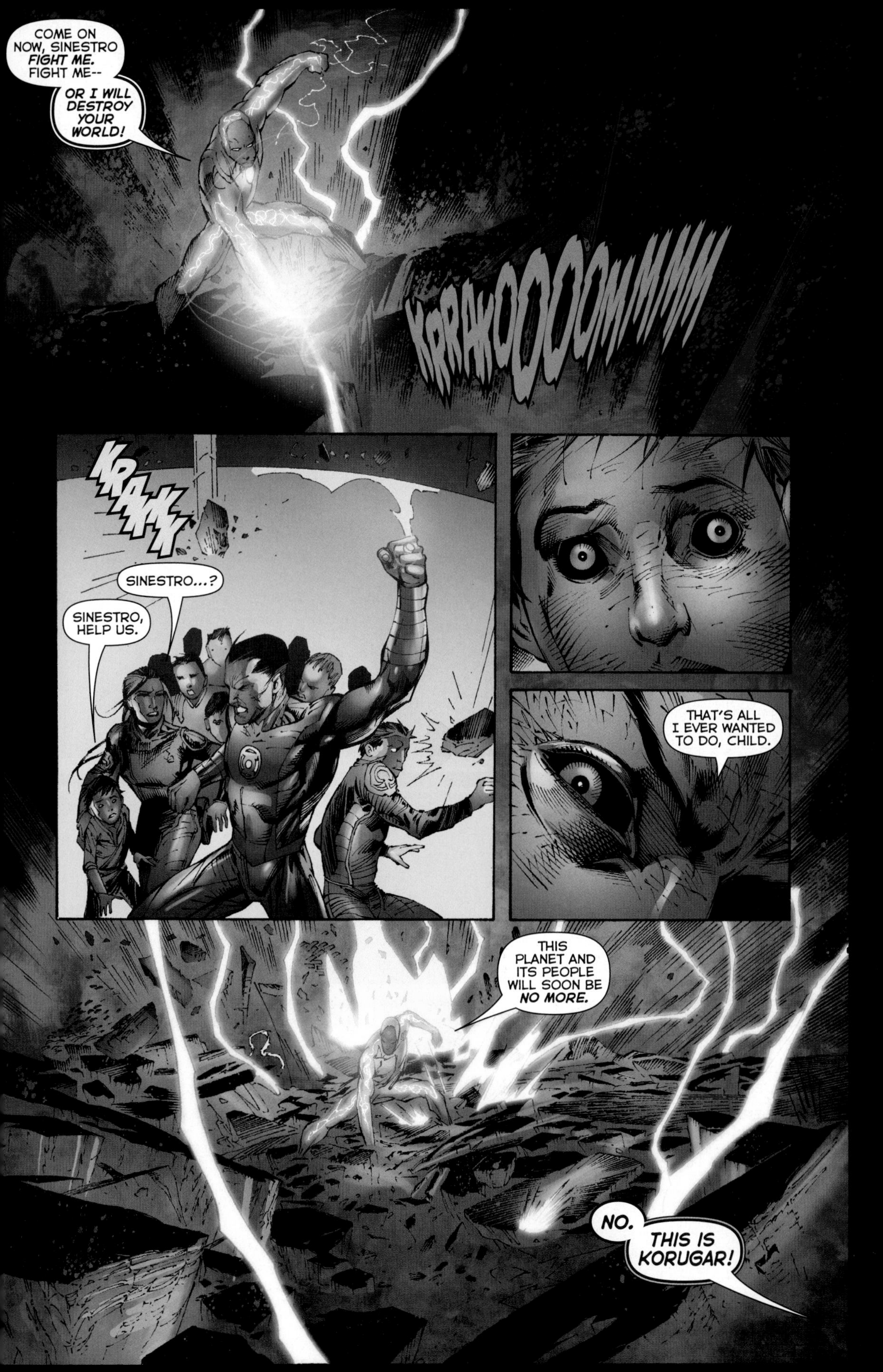
COME ON NOW, SINESTRO FIGHT ME. FIGHT ME--
OR I WILL DESTROY YOUR WORLD!
KRRAKOOOOMMMM
KRAKKK
SINESTRO...?
SINESTRO, HELP US.
THAT'S ALL I EVER WANTED TO DO, CHILD.
THIS PLANET AND ITS PEOPLE WILL SOON BE NO MORE.
NO.
THIS IS KORUGAR!

AND MY OATH ABOVE ALL OTHERS IS TO PROTECT IT!

VZZZZZZ

AAHHH!

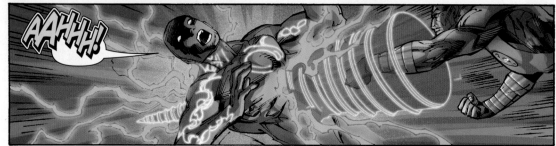

YOU ACTUALLY... *HURT* ME...

BUT YOU'VE ALSO DONE *EXACTLY* WHAT I WISHED. YOU'VE CREATED *SUCH* EMOTION HERE ON KORUGAR OVER THE YEARS.

YOU SEE, I'M NOT REALLY HERE FOR *YOU*, SINESTRO.

I'M HERE FOR *YOUR* WORLD.

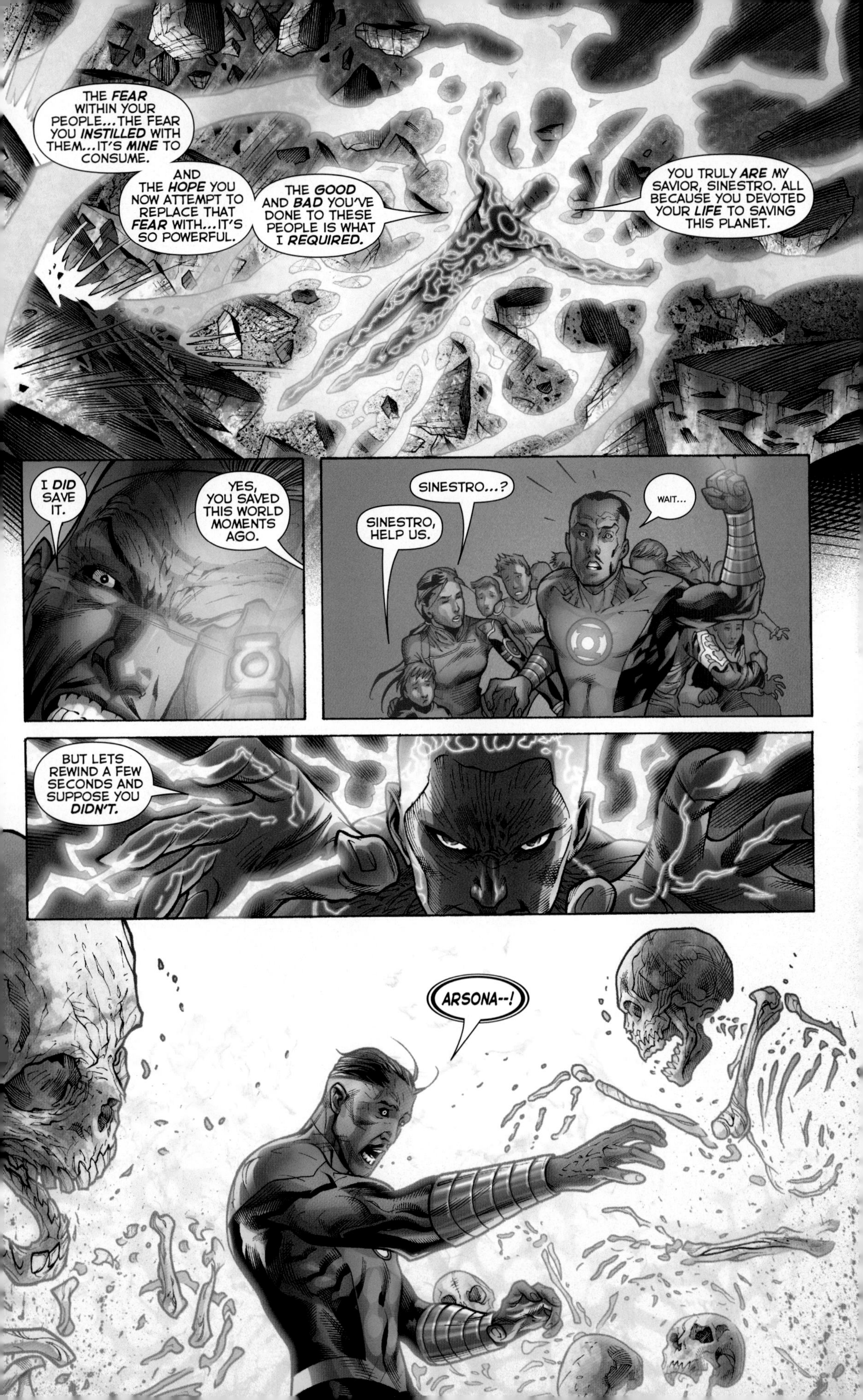
THE FEAR WITHIN YOUR PEOPLE...THE FEAR YOU INSTILLED WITH THEM...IT'S MINE TO CONSUME.
AND THE HOPE YOU NOW ATTEMPT TO REPLACE THAT FEAR WITH...IT'S SO POWERFUL.
THE GOOD AND BAD YOU'VE DONE TO THESE PEOPLE IS WHAT I REQUIRED.
YOU TRULY ARE MY SAVIOR, SINESTRO. ALL BECAUSE YOU DEVOTED YOUR LIFE TO SAVING THIS PLANET.
I DID SAVE IT.
YES, YOU SAVED THIS WORLD MOMENTS AGO.
SINESTRO, HELP US.
SINESTRO...?
WAIT...
BUT LETS REWIND A FEW SECONDS AND SUPPOSE YOU DIDN'T.
ARSONA--!

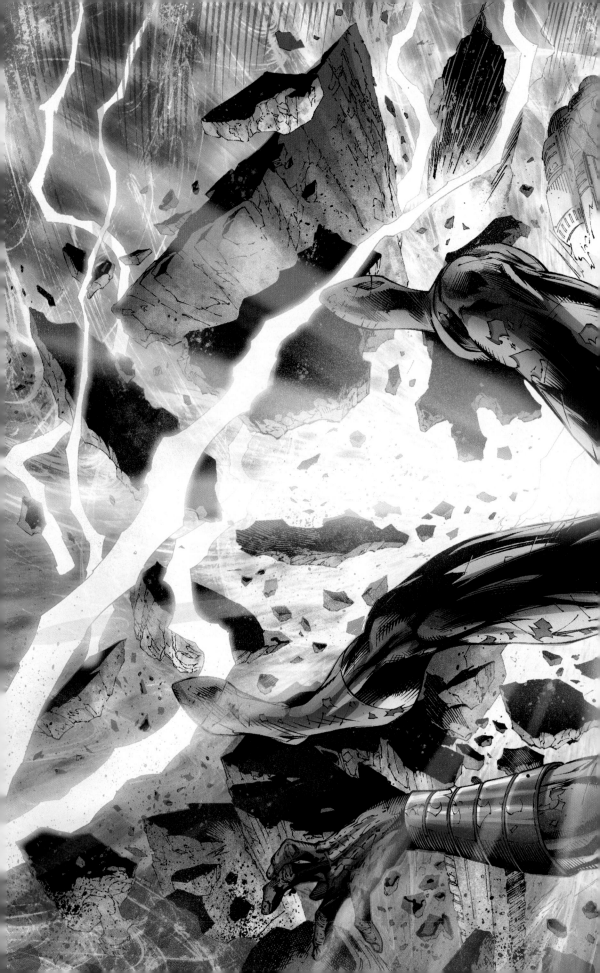

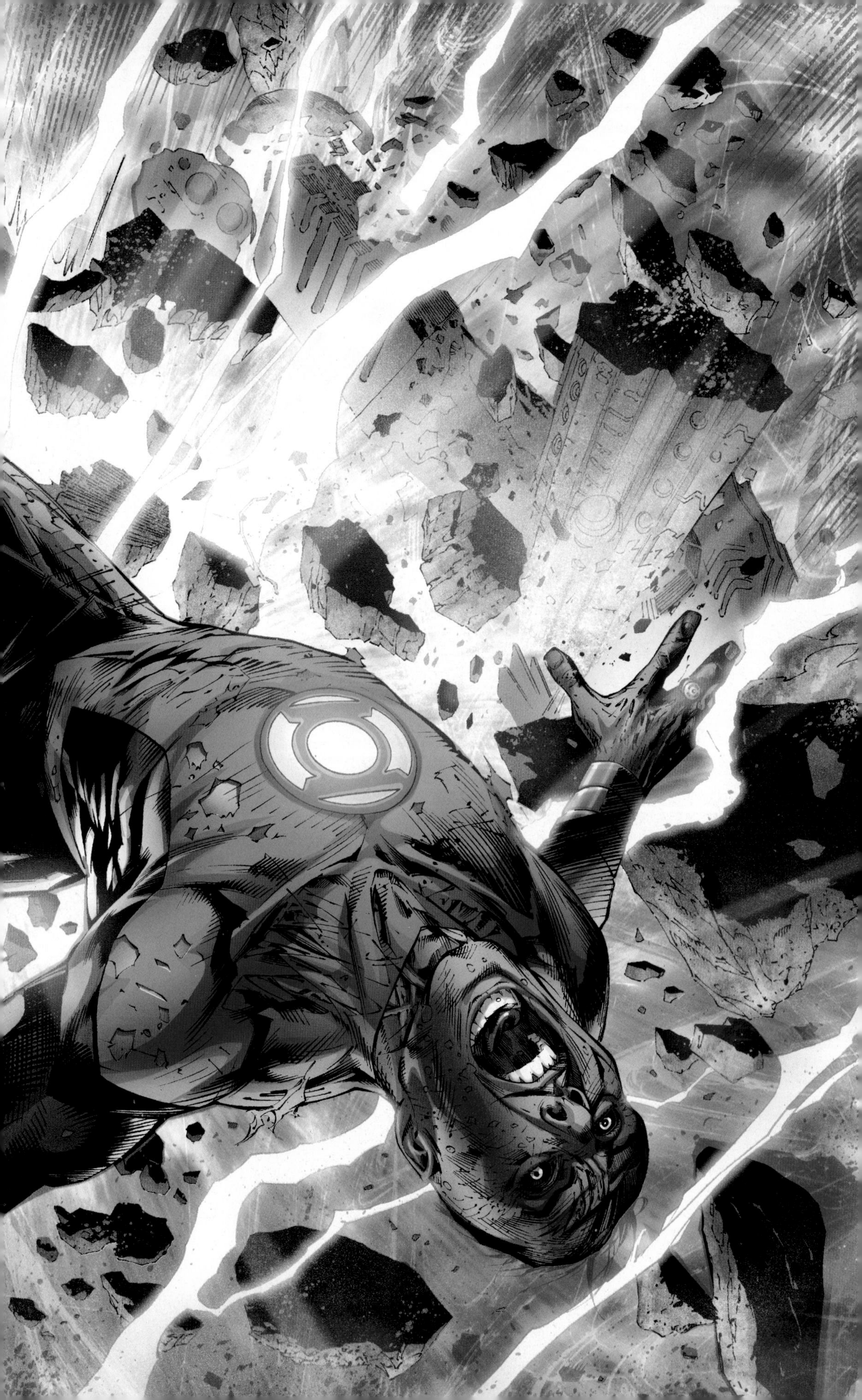

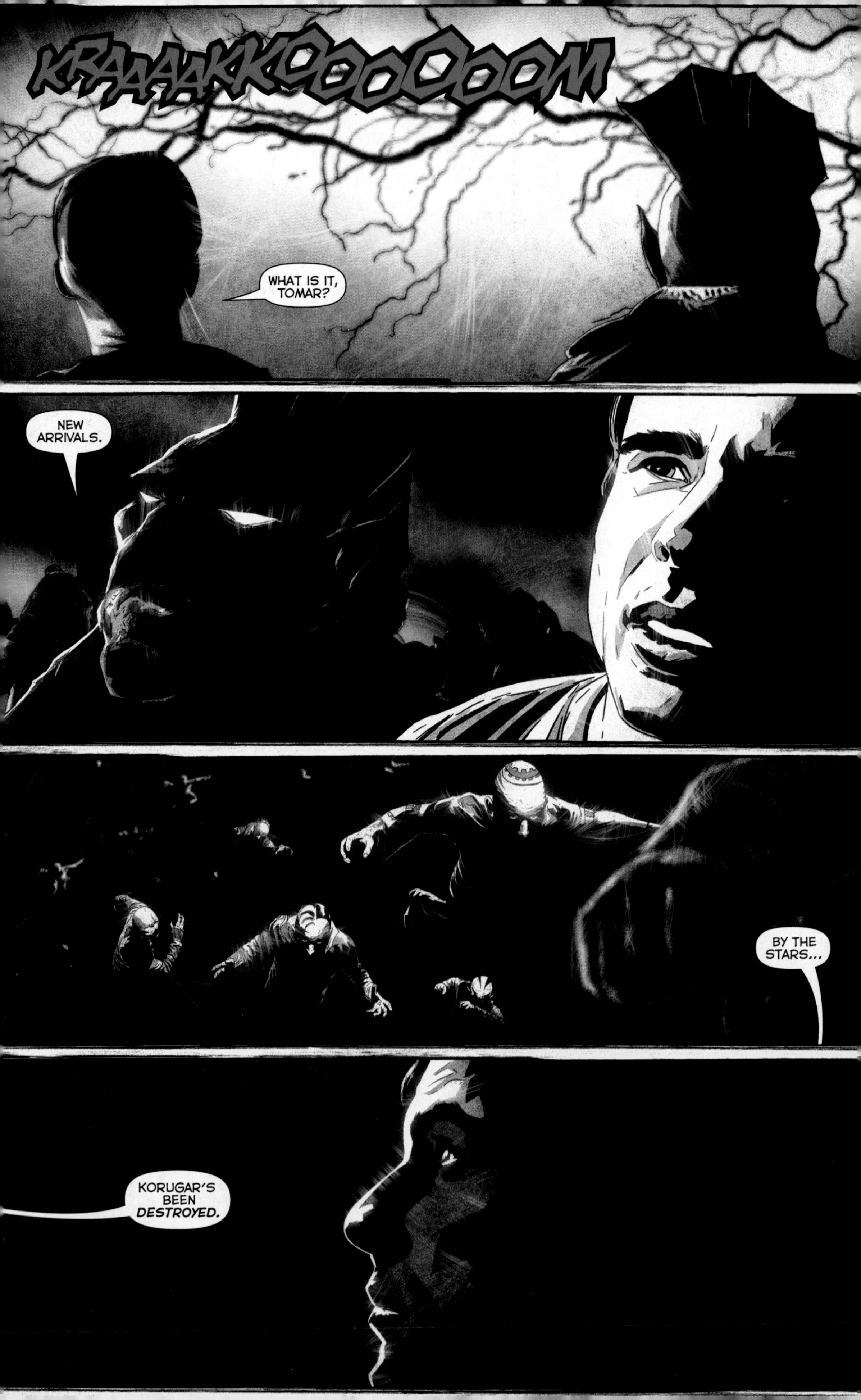
KRAAAKKOOOOOOOM
WHAT IS IT, TOMAR?
NEW ARRIVALS.
BY THE STARS...
KORUGAR'S BEEN *DESTROYED.*

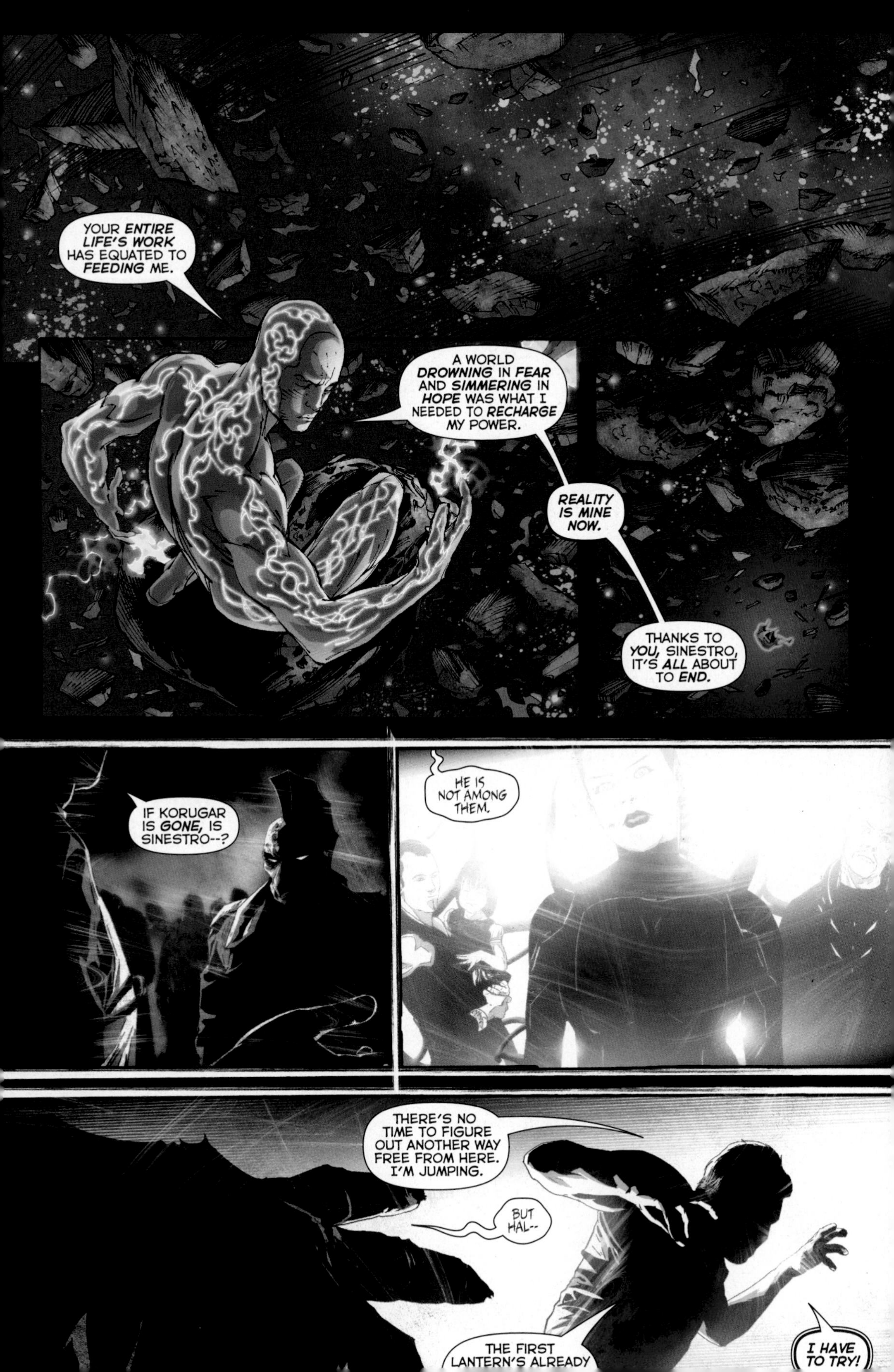
YOUR ENTIRE LIFE'S WORK HAS EQUATED TO FEEDING ME.
A WORLD DROWNING IN FEAR AND SIMMERING IN HOPE WAS WHAT I NEEDED TO RECHARGE MY POWER.
REALITY IS MINE NOW.
THANKS TO YOU, SINESTRO, IT'S ALL ABOUT TO END.
IF KORUGAR IS GONE, IS SINESTRO--?
HE IS NOT AMONG THEM.
THERE'S NO TIME TO FIGURE OUT ANOTHER WAY FREE FROM HERE. I'M JUMPING.
BUT HAL--
THE FIRST LANTERN'S ALREADY
I HAVE TO TRY!

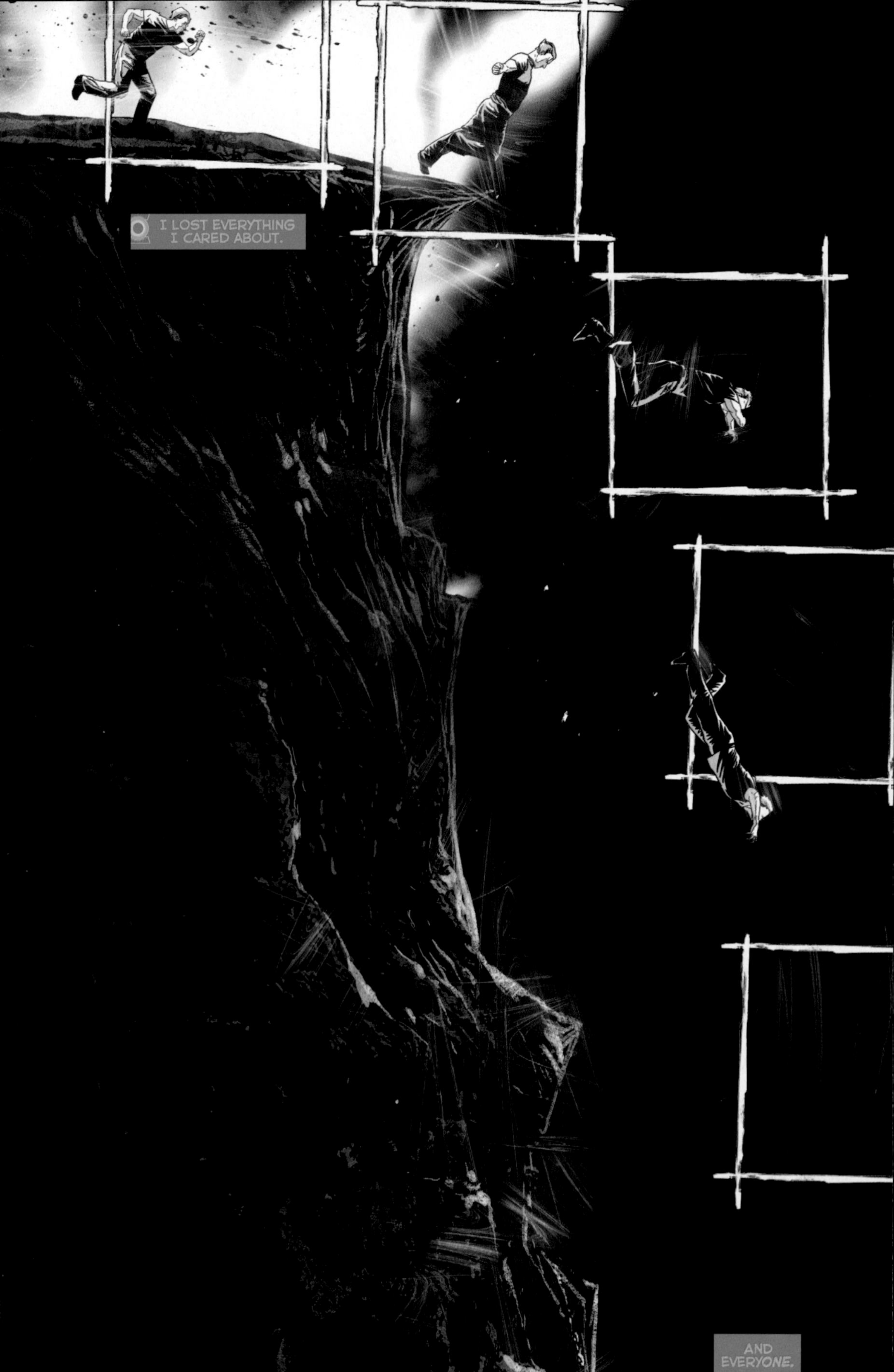
I LOST EVERYTHING I CARED ABOUT.
AND EVERYONE.

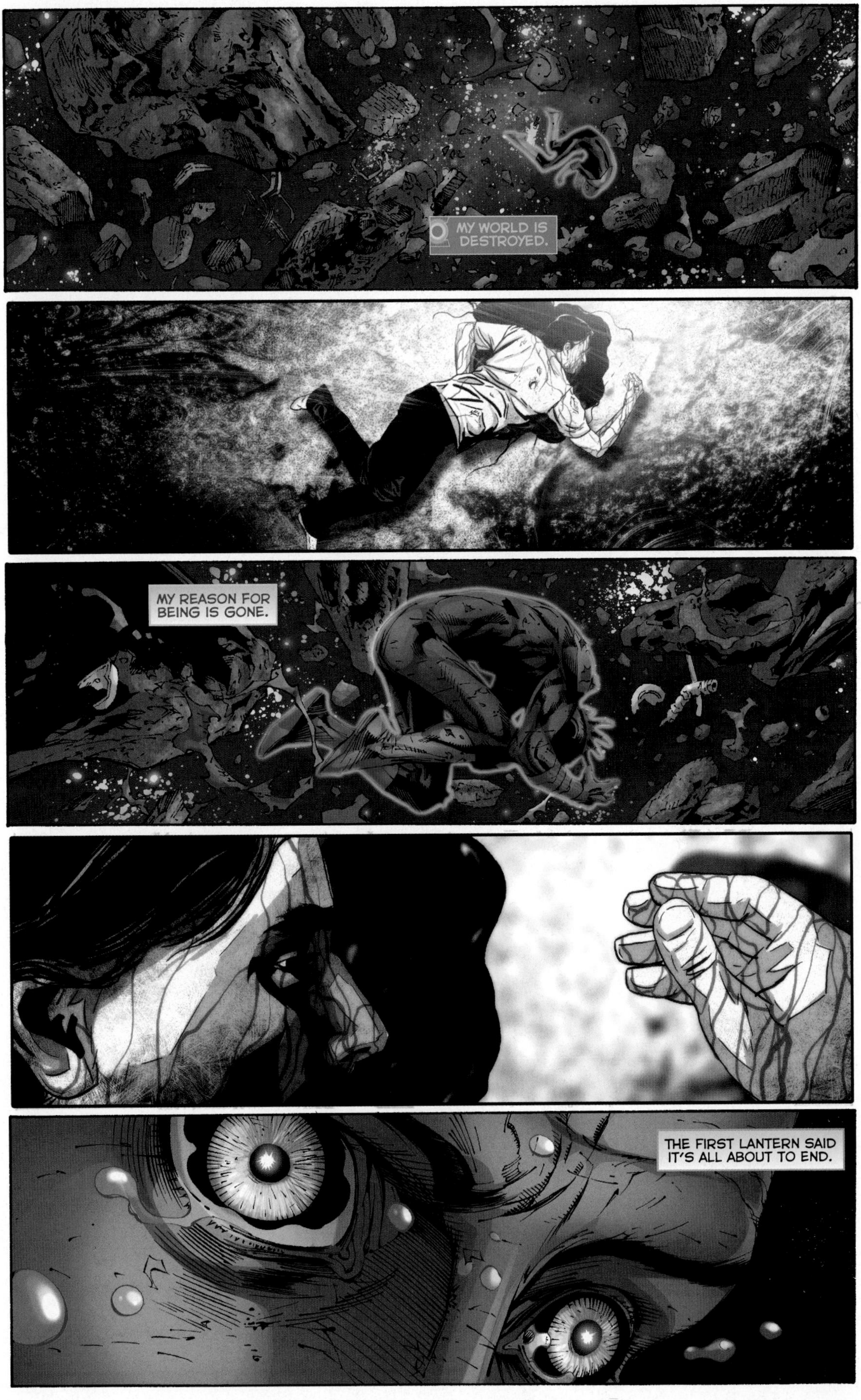
MY WORLD IS DESTROYED.
MY REASON FOR BEING IS GONE.
THE FIRST LANTERN SAID IT'S ALL ABOUT TO END.

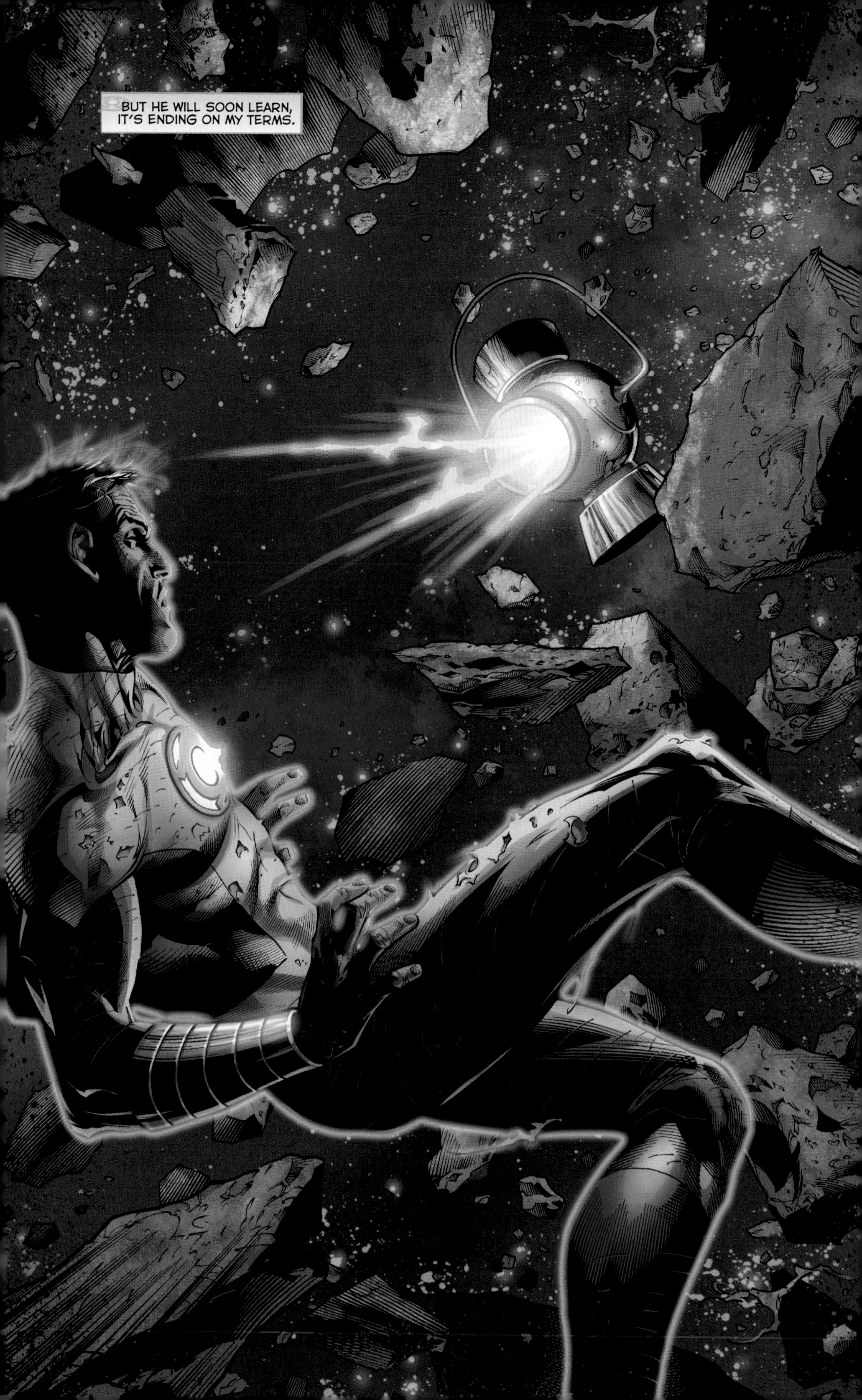
BUT HE WILL SOON LEARN, IT'S ENDING ON MY TERMS.

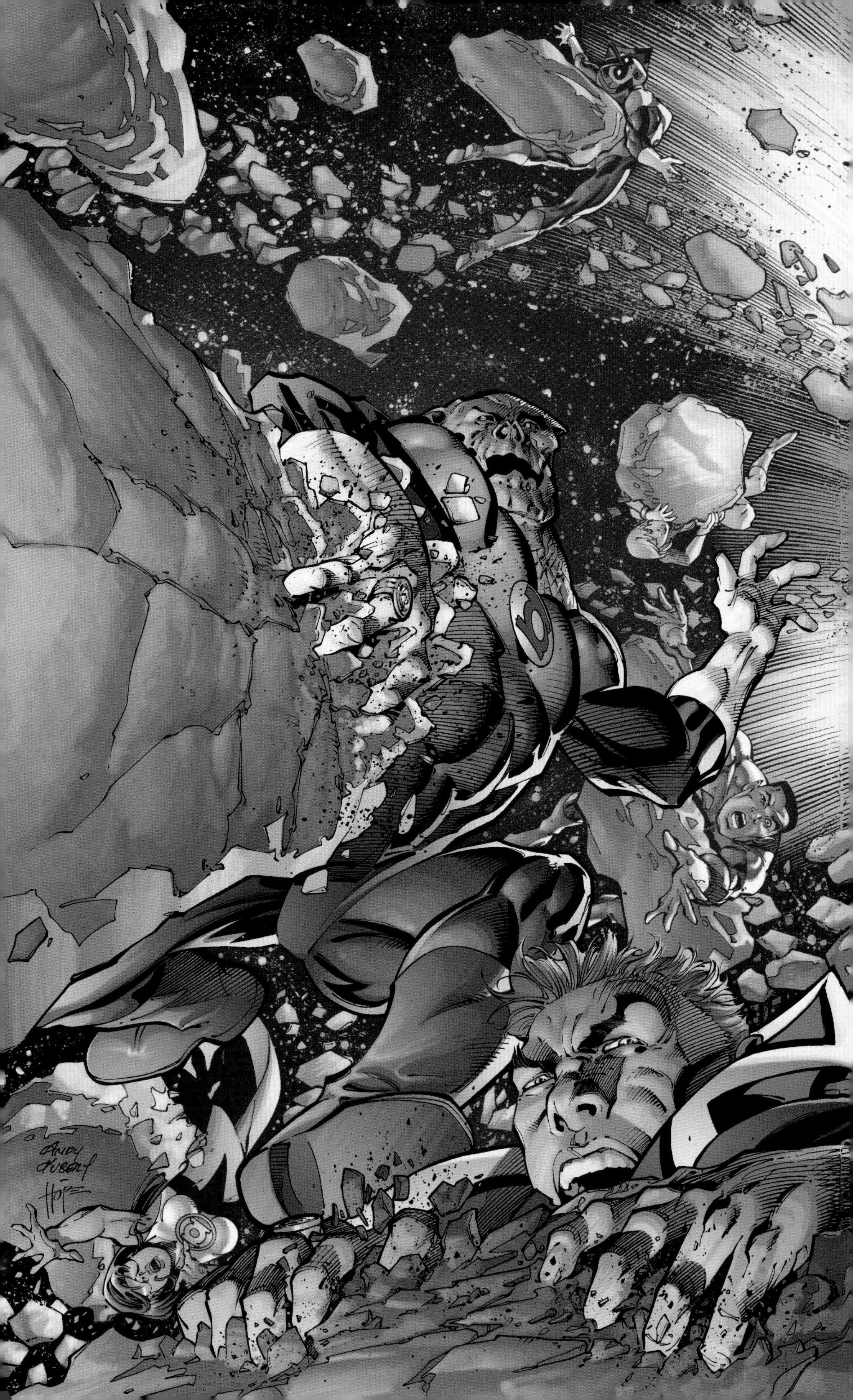
ANDY KUBERT
HOPE

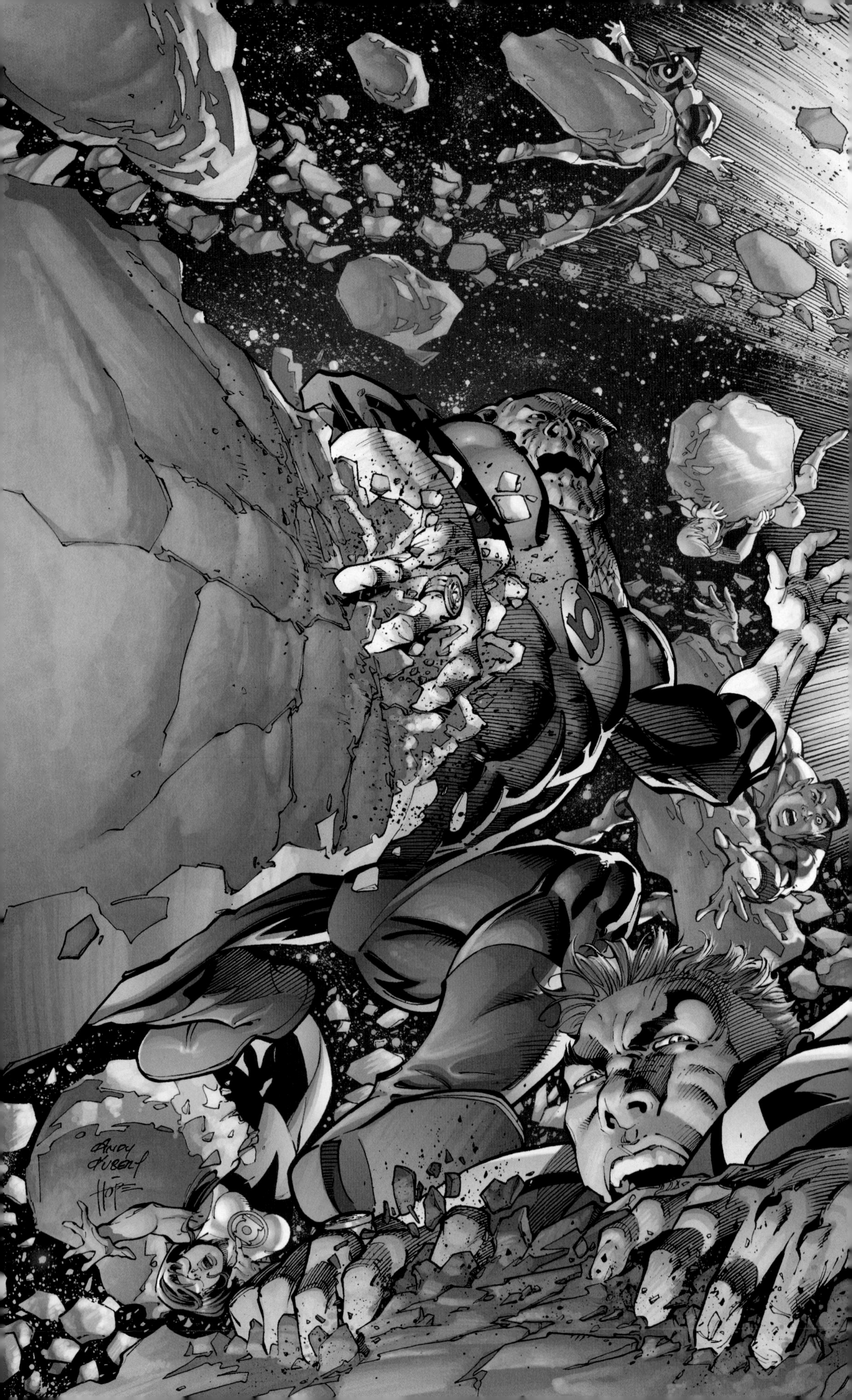
ANDY KUBERT
HOPE

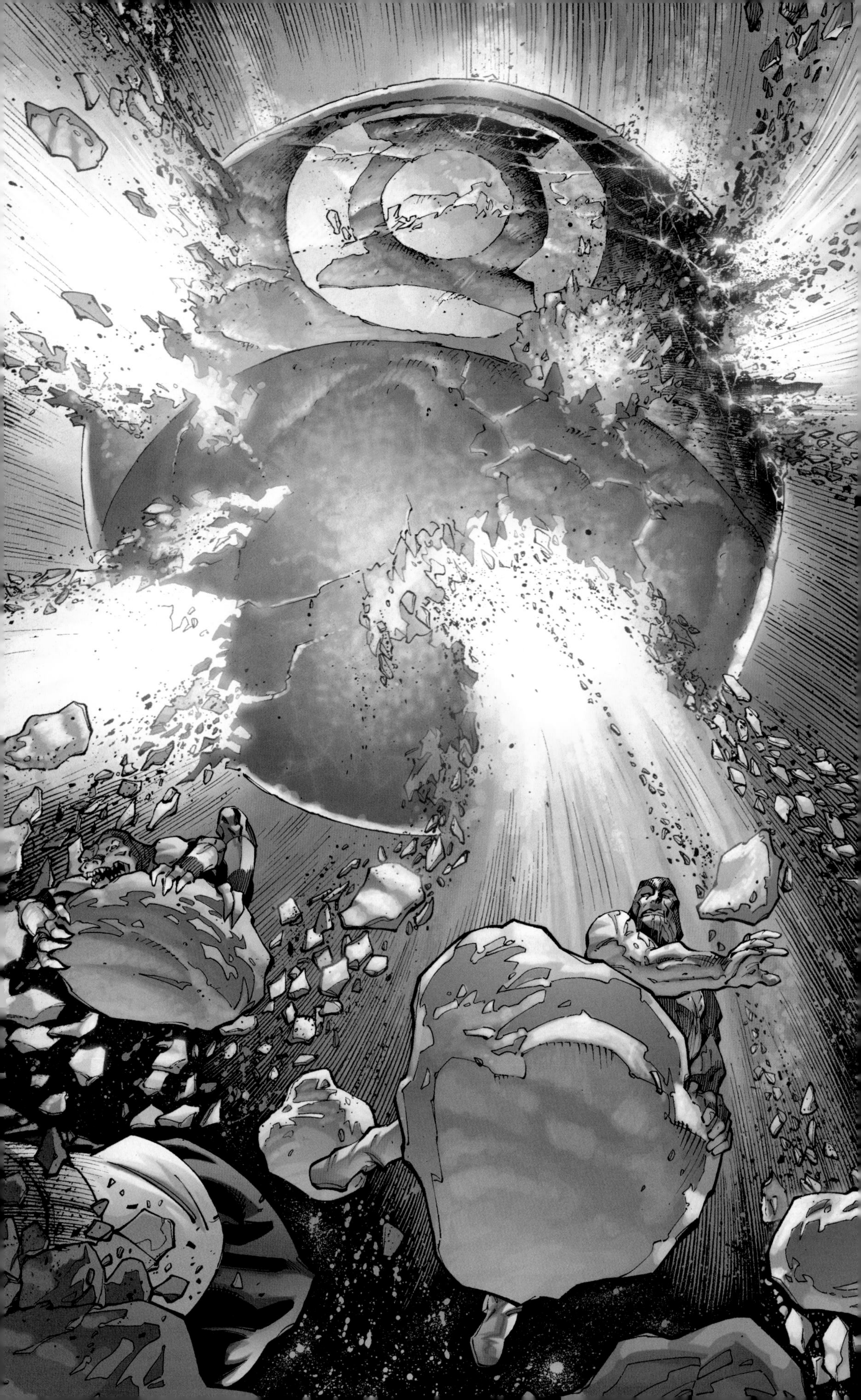

PART TEN: WILLING

PETER J. TOMASI writer **FERNANDO PASARIN** penciller **SCOTT HANNA** with **MARC DEERING** inkers
cover art by **ANDY KUBERT, SANDRA HOPE & BRAD ANDERSON**

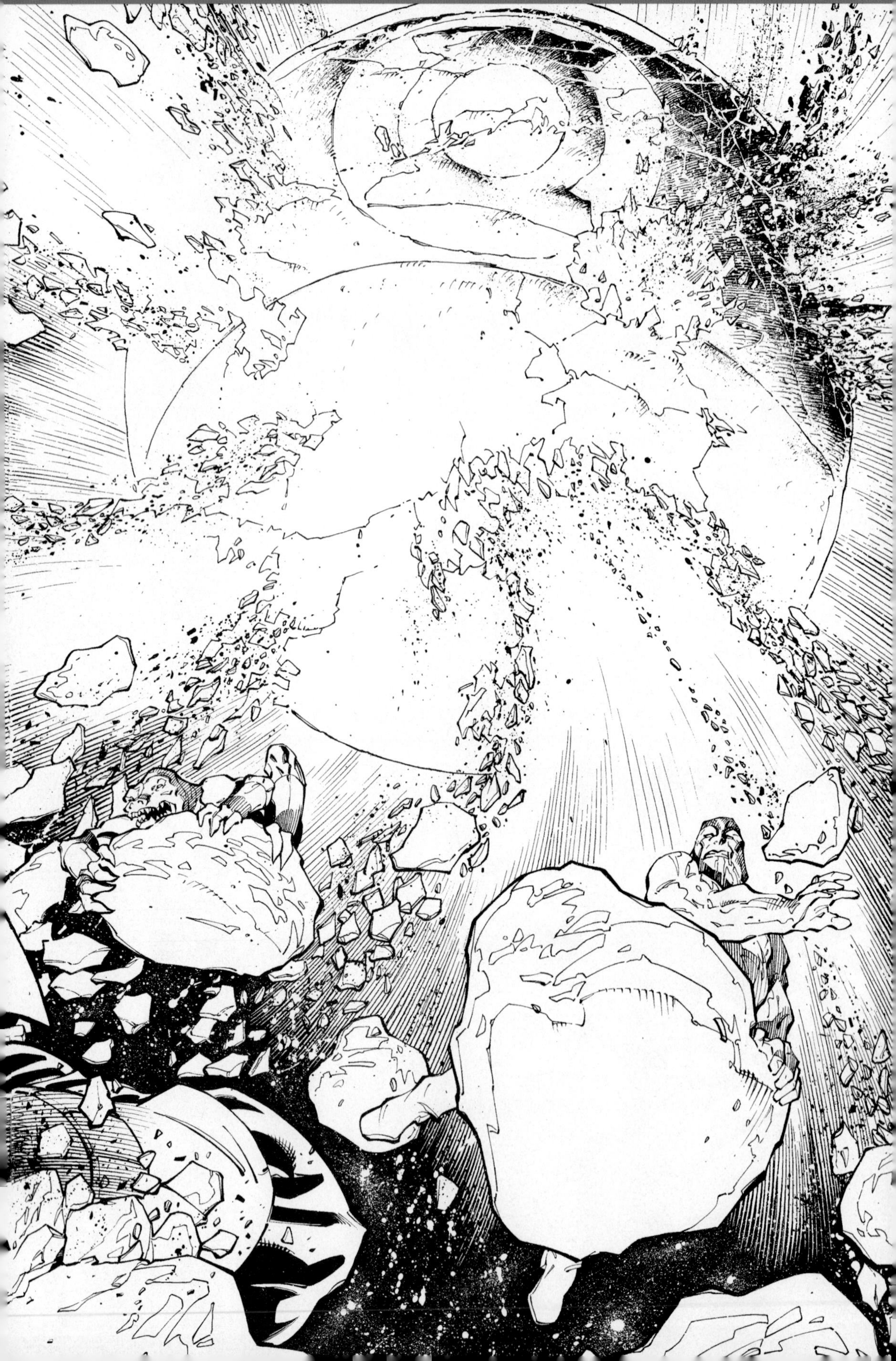

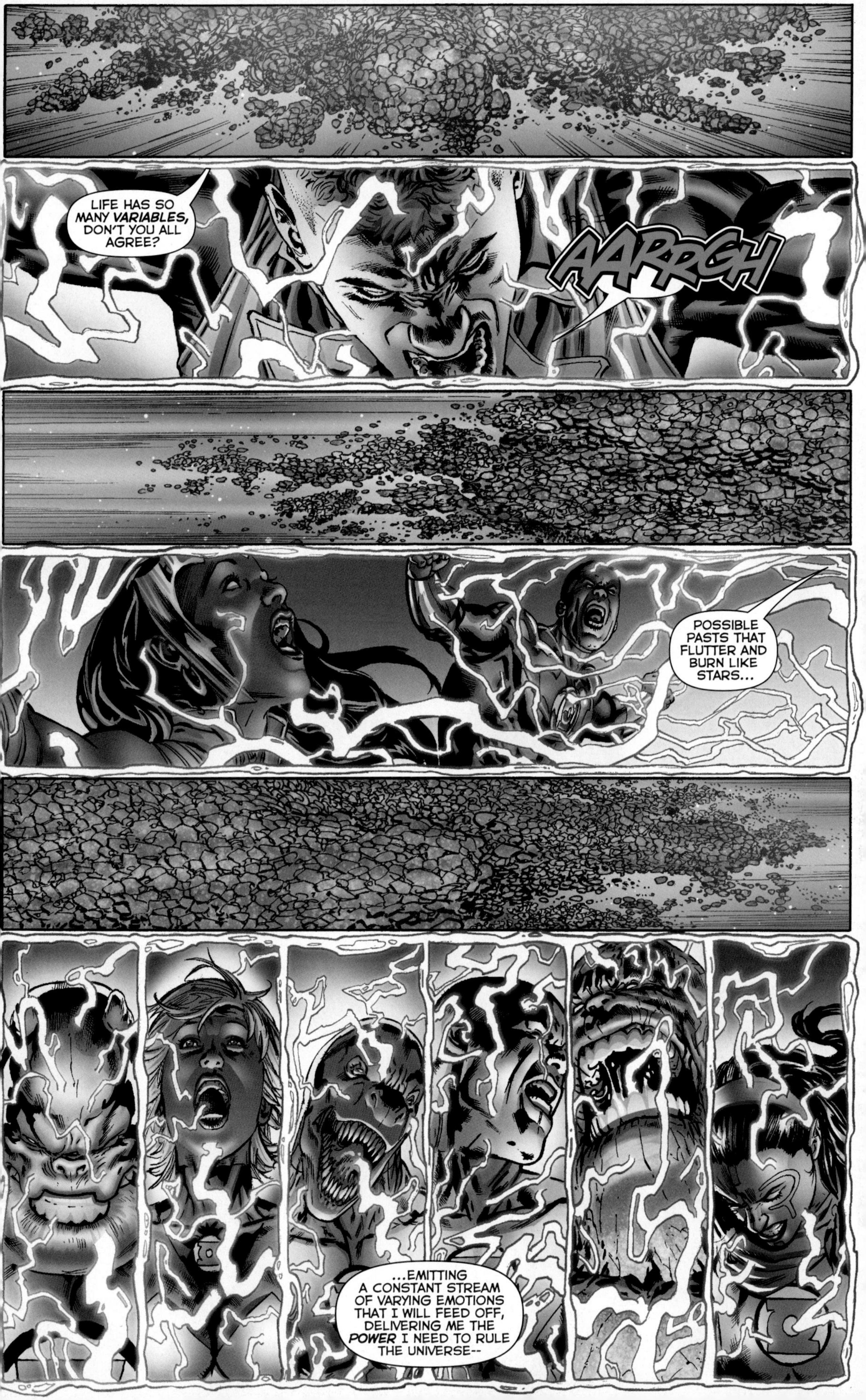
LIFE HAS SO MANY VARIABLES, DON'T YOU ALL AGREE?
AARRGH
POSSIBLE PASTS THAT FLUTTER AND BURN LIKE STARS...
...EMITTING A CONSTANT STREAM OF VARYING EMOTIONS THAT I WILL FEED OFF, DELIVERING ME THE POWER I NEED TO RULE THE UNIVERSE--

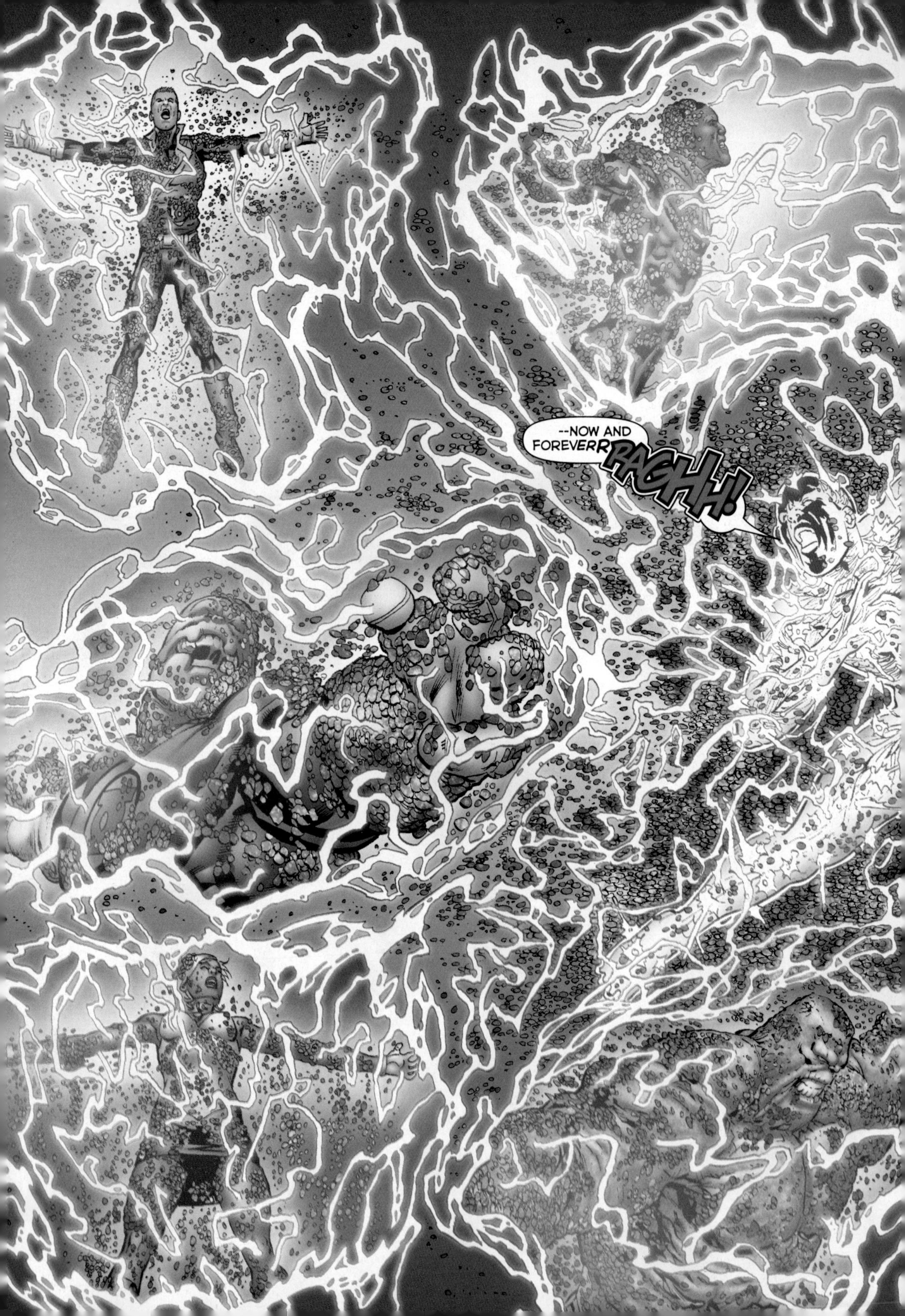
--NOW AND FOREVERRRAGHH!

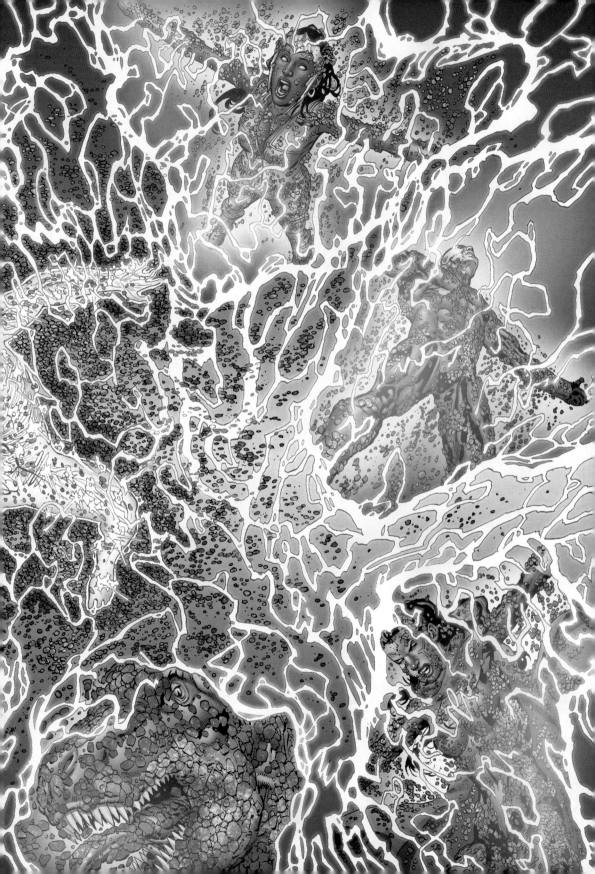

GAHH!
THESE ROCKS--
--CUTTING VOLTHOOM'S LINES--
--BASTARD'S FINALLY OUTTA MY HEAD--
UGNN!
WHO DARES?!?
JOHN!
YRAA, HANG ON!
WHATEVER'S HAPPENING--
"--IS HAPPENING ALL ACROSS OA--"

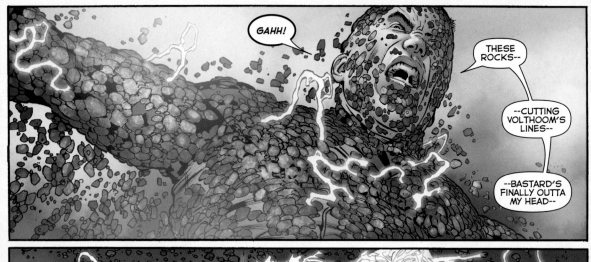

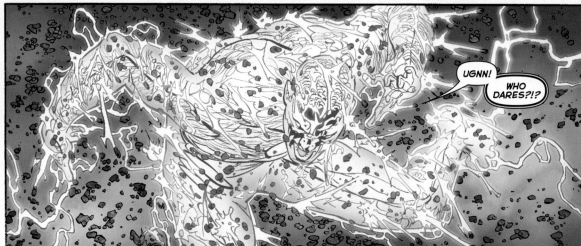

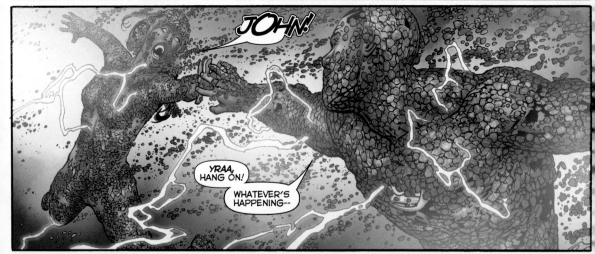

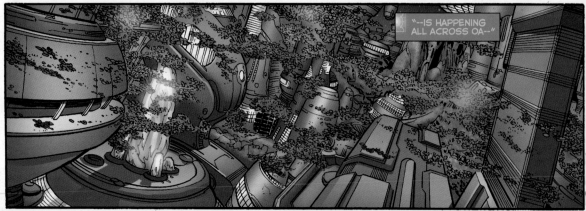

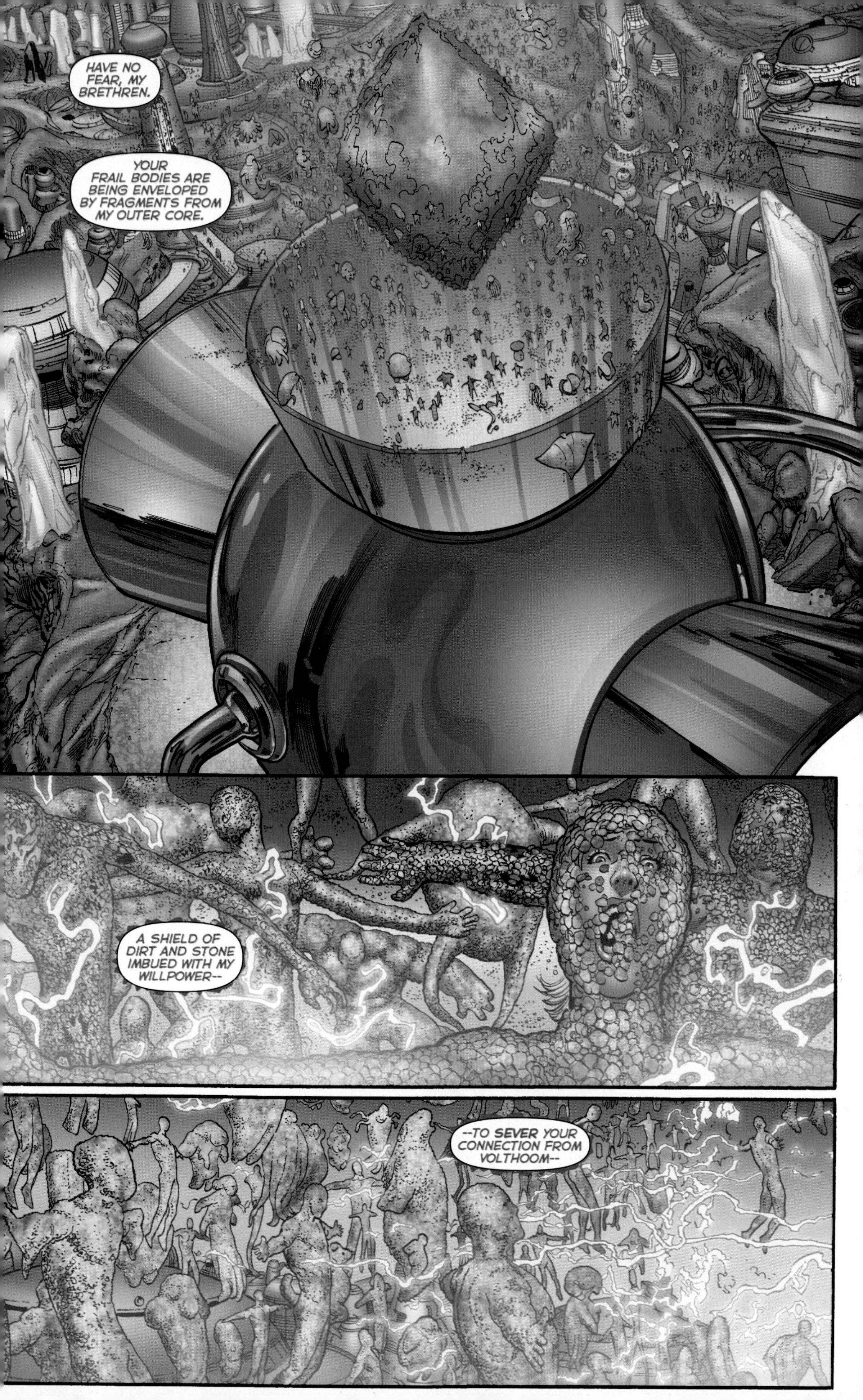
HAVE NO FEAR, MY BRETHREN.
YOUR FRAIL BODIES ARE BEING ENVELOPED BY FRAGMENTS FROM MY OUTER CORE.
A SHIELD OF DIRT AND STONE IMBUED WITH MY WILLPOWER--
--TO SEVER YOUR CONNECTION FROM VOLTHOOM--

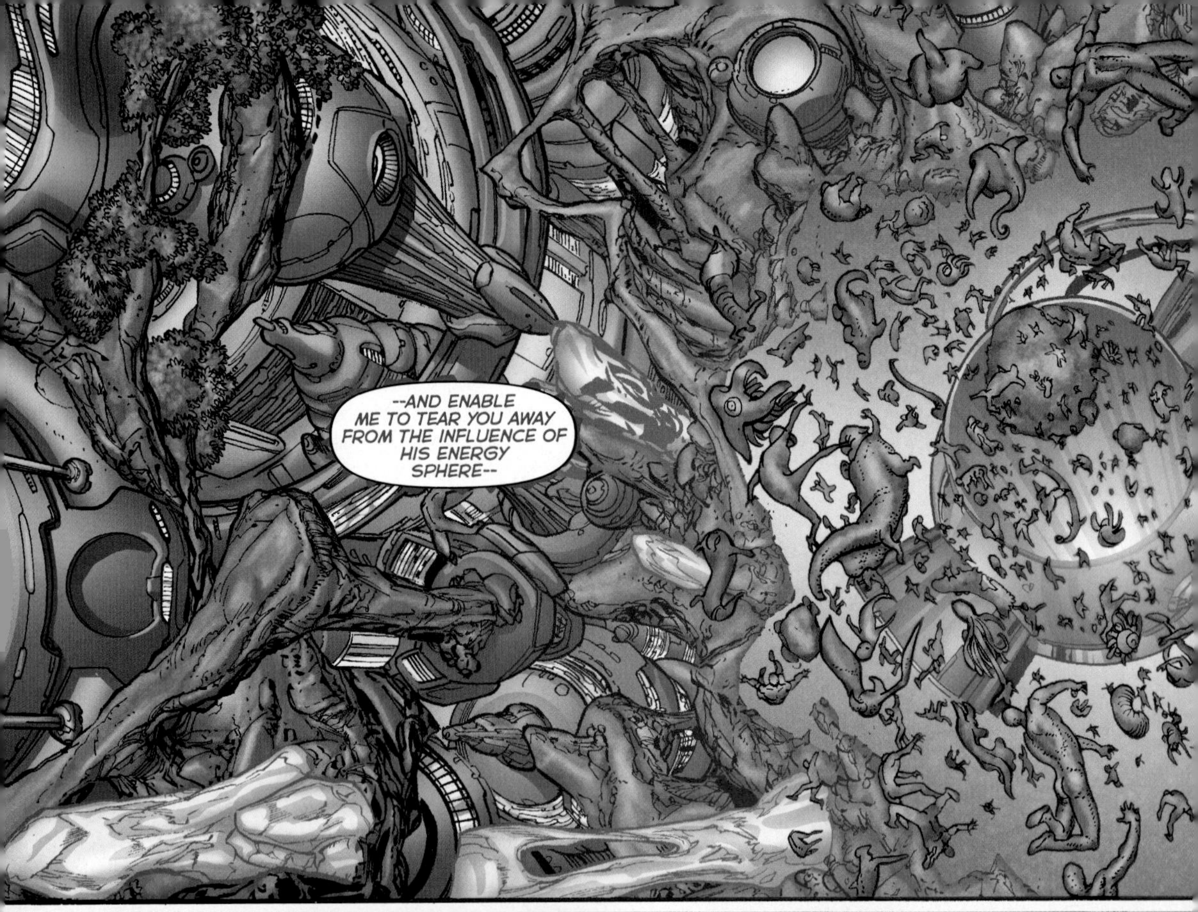
--AND ENABLE ME TO TEAR YOU AWAY FROM THE INFLUENCE OF HIS ENERGY SPHERE--

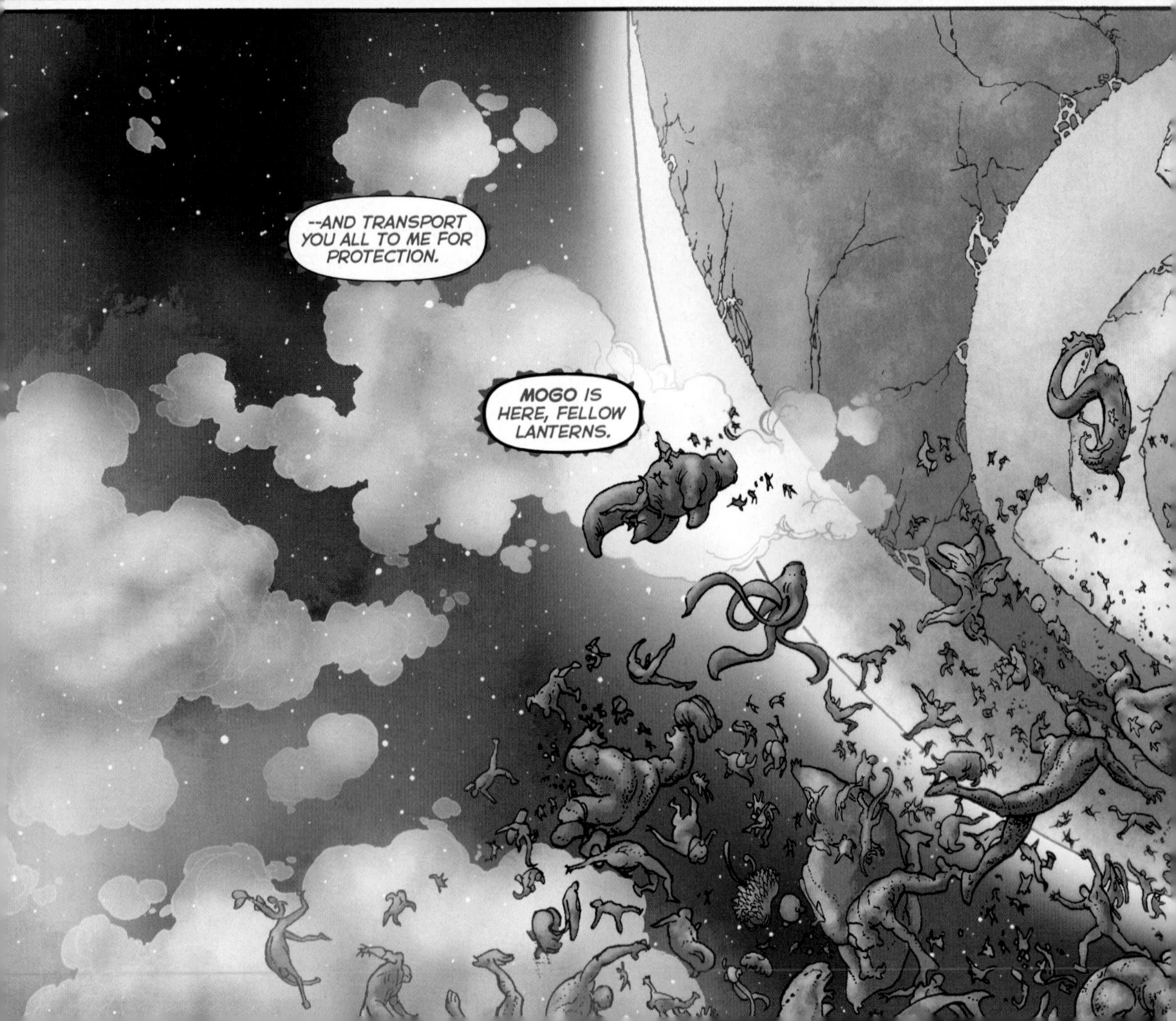
--AND TRANSPORT YOU ALL TO ME FOR PROTECTION.
MOGO IS HERE, FELLOW LANTERNS.

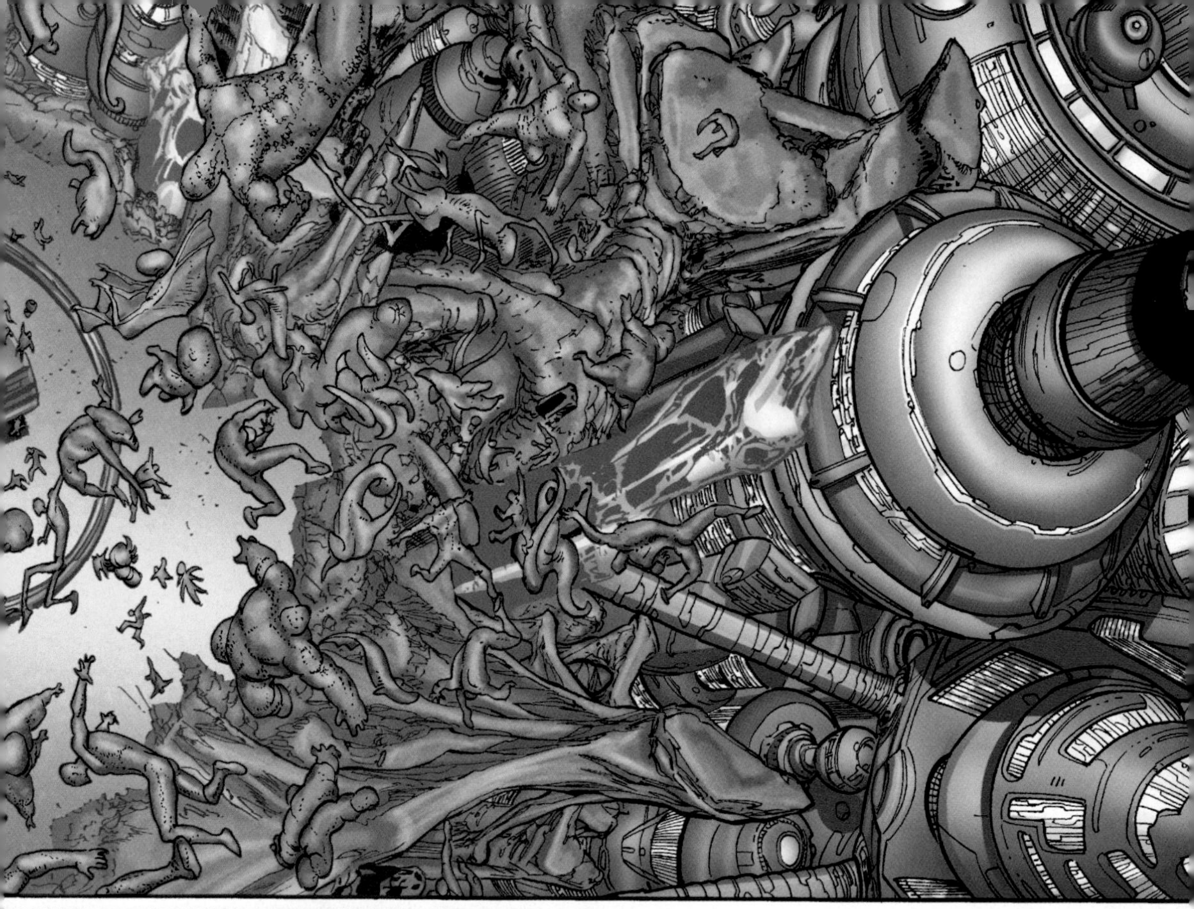
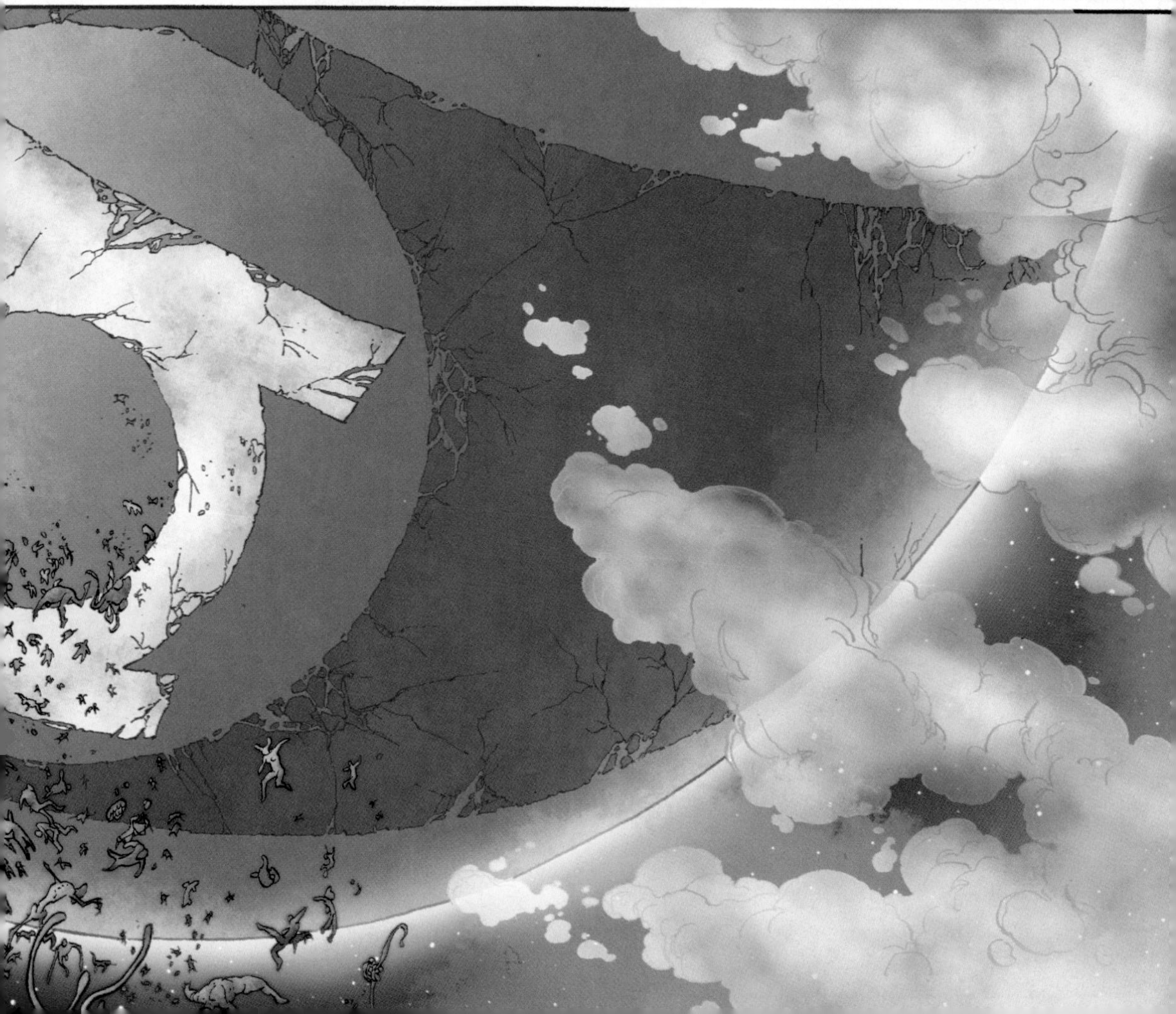

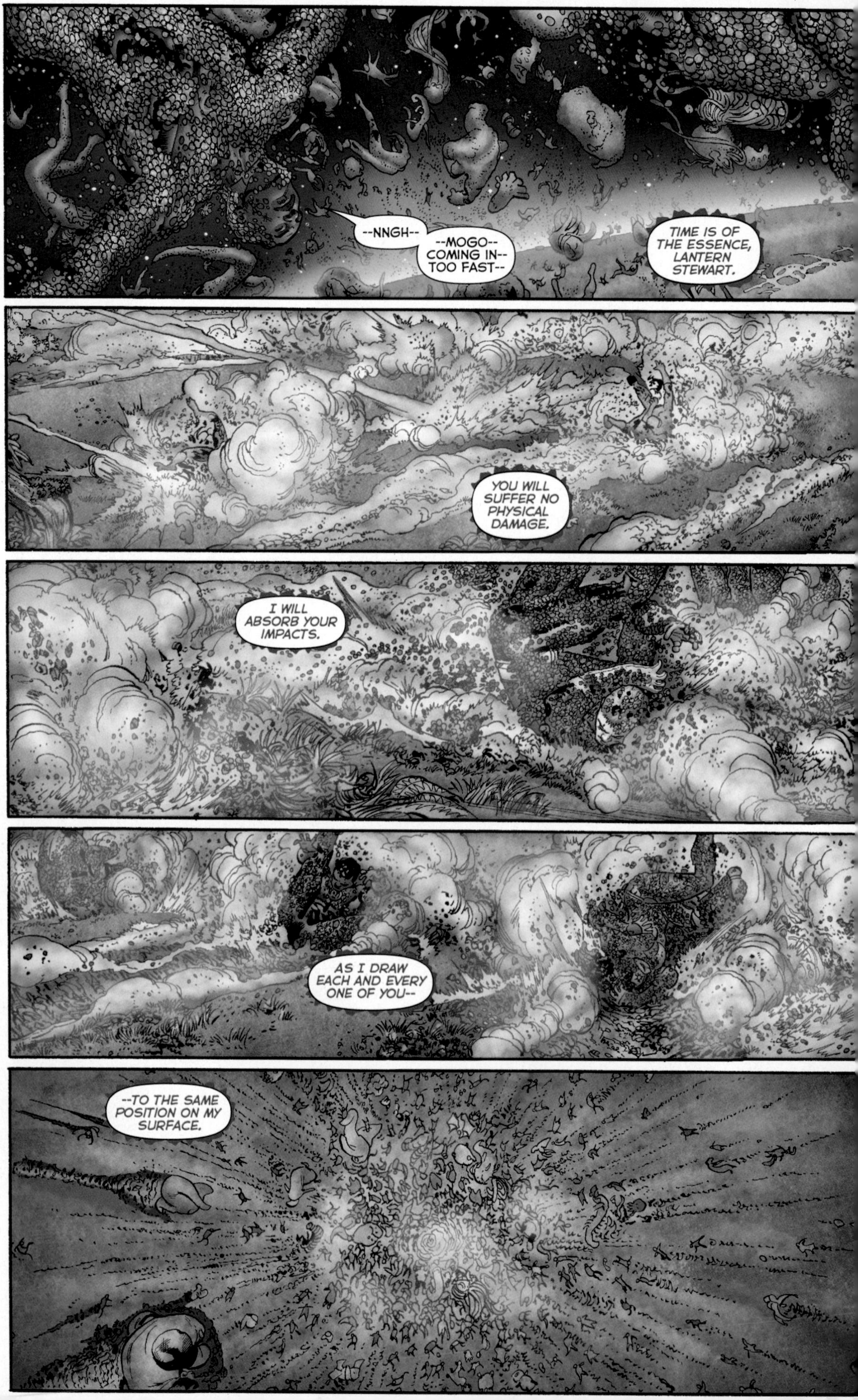
--NNGH--
--MOGO-- COMING IN-- TOO FAST--
TIME IS OF THE ESSENCE, LANTERN STEWART.
YOU WILL SUFFER NO PHYSICAL DAMAGE.
I WILL ABSORB YOUR IMPACTS.
AS I DRAW EACH AND EVERY ONE OF YOU--
--TO THE SAME POSITION ON MY SURFACE.

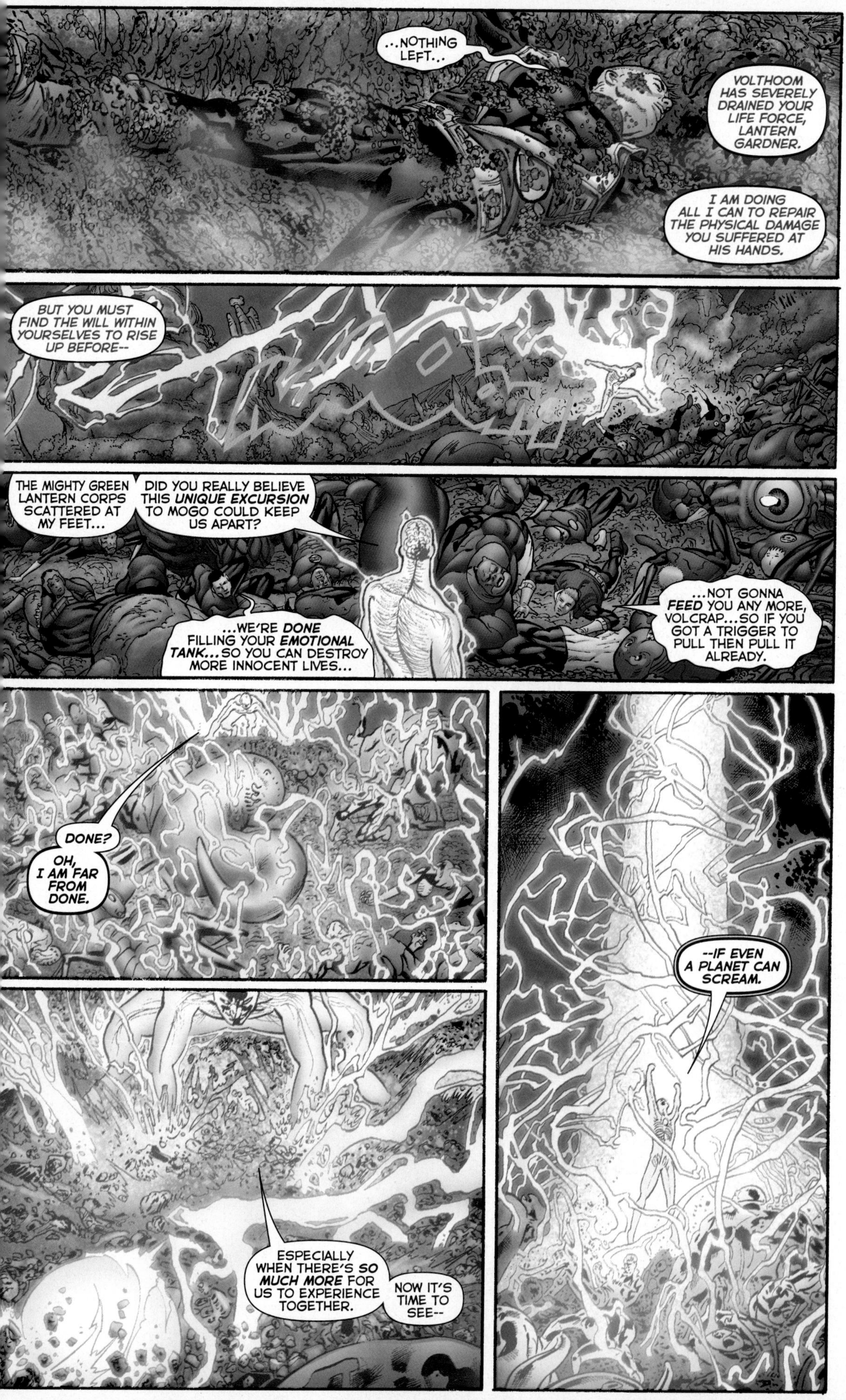
...NOTHING LEFT...
VOLTHOOM HAS SEVERELY DRAINED YOUR LIFE FORCE, LANTERN GARDNER.
I AM DOING ALL I CAN TO REPAIR THE PHYSICAL DAMAGE YOU SUFFERED AT HIS HANDS.
BUT YOU MUST FIND THE WILL WITHIN YOURSELVES TO RISE UP BEFORE--
THE MIGHTY GREEN LANTERN CORPS SCATTERED AT MY FEET...
DID YOU REALLY BELIEVE THIS UNIQUE EXCURSION TO MOGO COULD KEEP US APART?
...WE'RE DONE FILLING YOUR EMOTIONAL TANK...SO YOU CAN DESTROY MORE INNOCENT LIVES...
...NOT GONNA FEED YOU ANY MORE, VOLCRAP...SO IF YOU GOT A TRIGGER TO PULL THEN PULL IT ALREADY.
DONE?
OH, I AM FAR FROM DONE.
ESPECIALLY WHEN THERE'S SO MUCH MORE FOR US TO EXPERIENCE TOGETHER.
NOW IT'S TIME TO SEE--
--IF EVEN A PLANET CAN SCREAM.

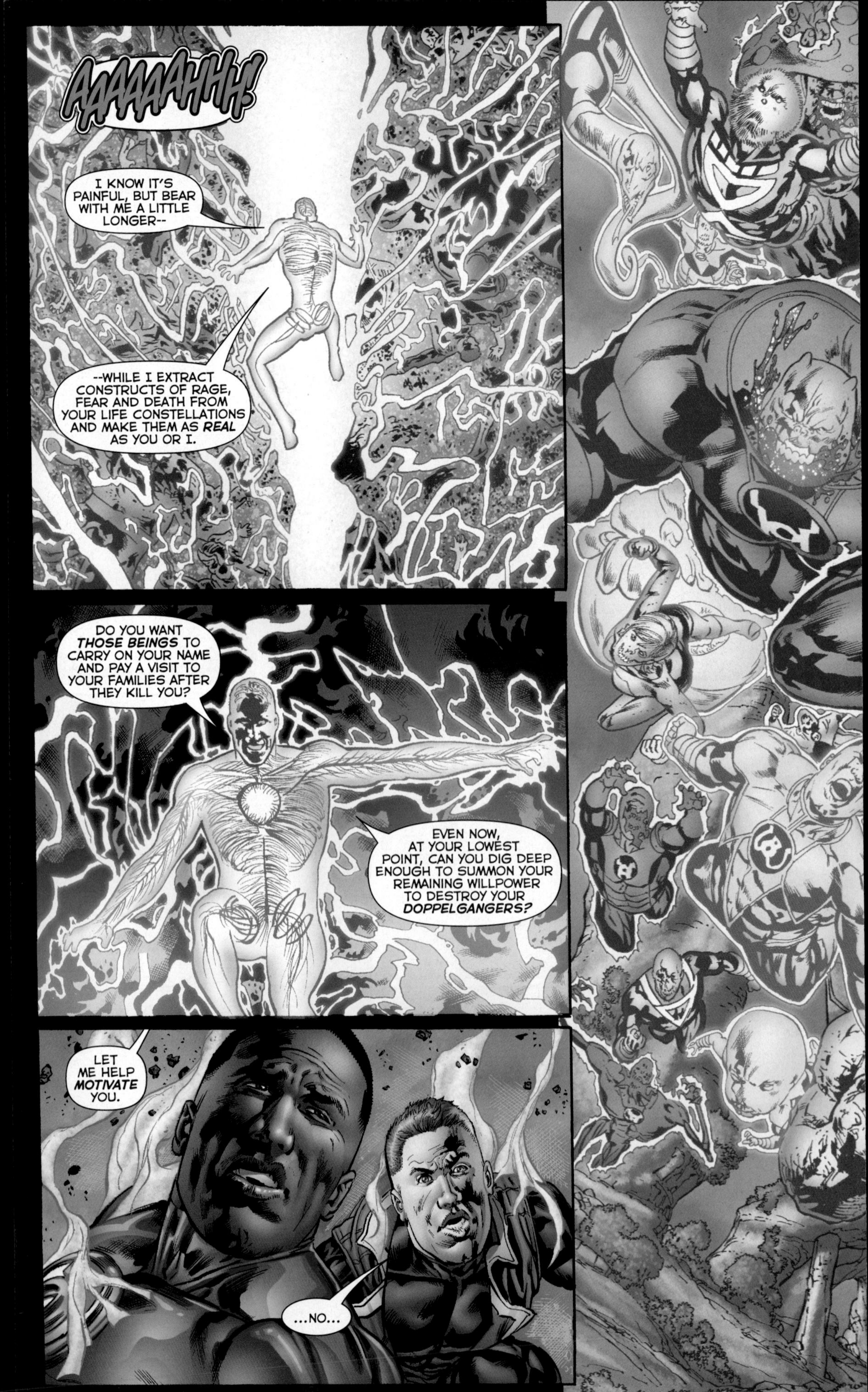
AAAAAAHHH!
I KNOW IT'S PAINFUL, BUT BEAR WITH ME A LITTLE LONGER--
--WHILE I EXTRACT CONSTRUCTS OF RAGE, FEAR AND DEATH FROM YOUR LIFE CONSTELLATIONS AND MAKE THEM AS REAL AS YOU OR I.
DO YOU WANT THOSE BEINGS TO CARRY ON YOUR NAME AND PAY A VISIT TO YOUR FAMILIES AFTER THEY KILL YOU?
EVEN NOW, AT YOUR LOWEST POINT, CAN YOU DIG DEEP ENOUGH TO SUMMON YOUR REMAINING WILLPOWER TO DESTROY YOUR DOPPELGANGERS?
LET ME HELP MOTIVATE YOU.
...NO...

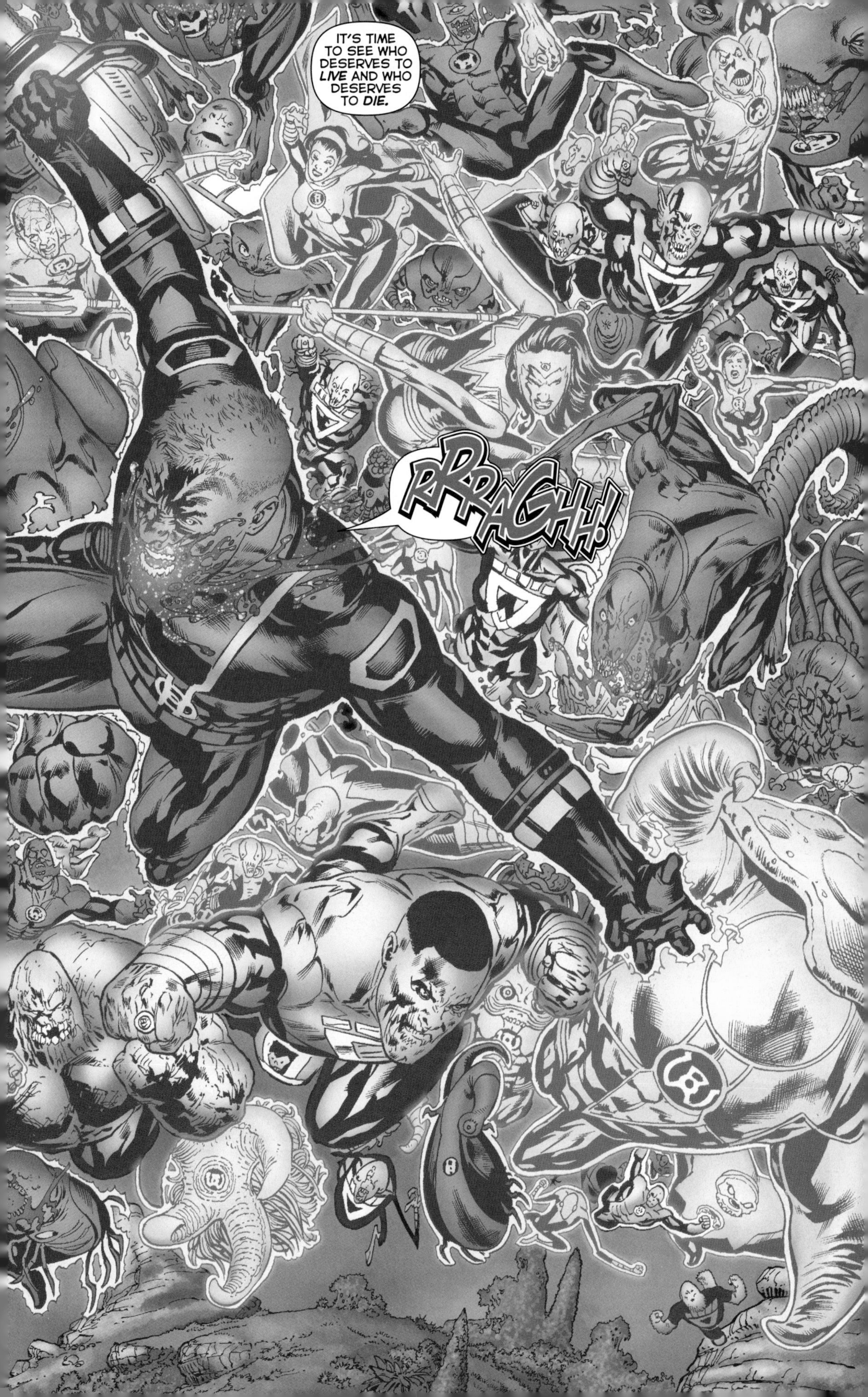
IT'S TIME TO SEE WHO DESERVES TO *LIVE* AND WHO DESERVES TO *DIE.*
RRRAGHH!

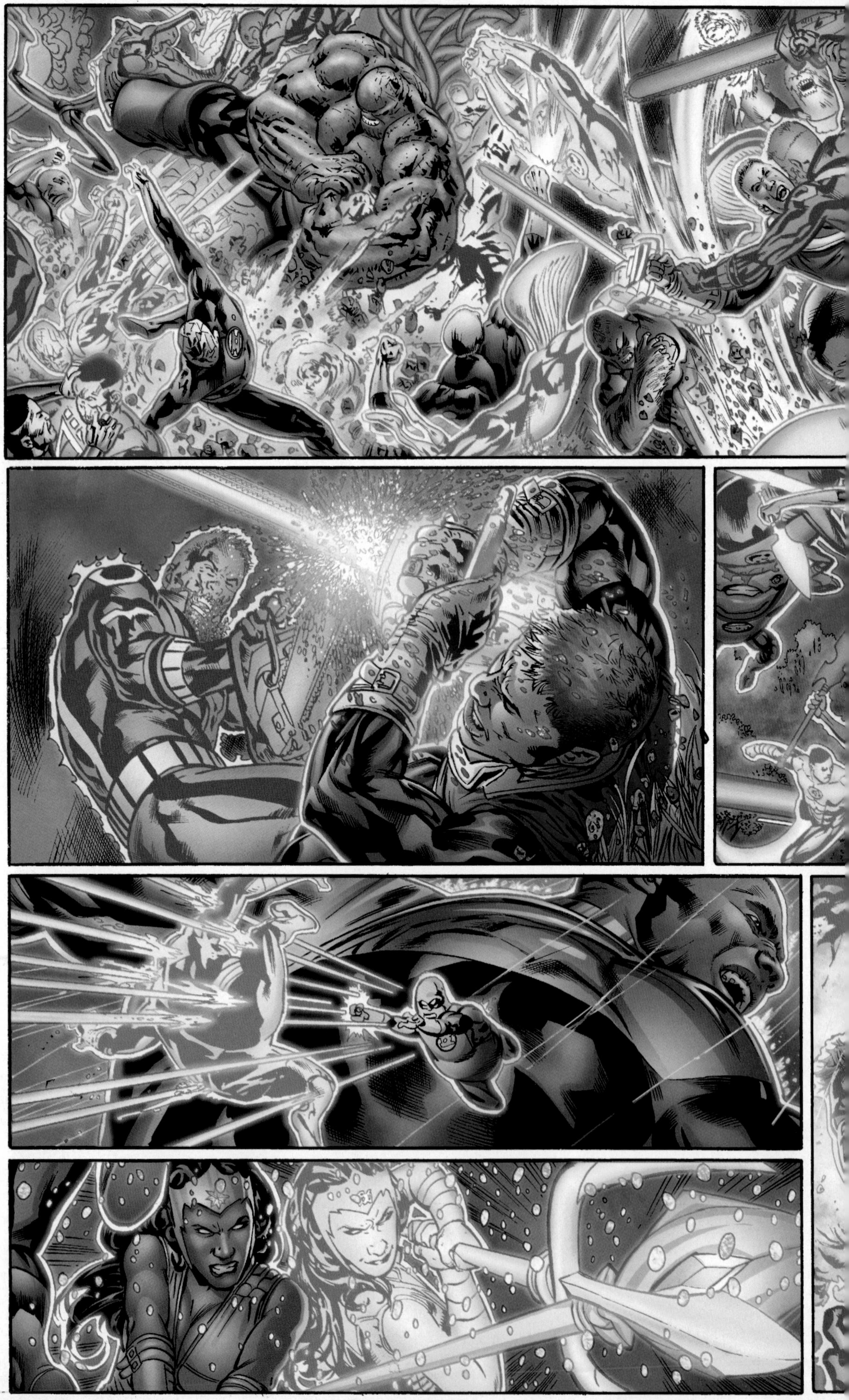

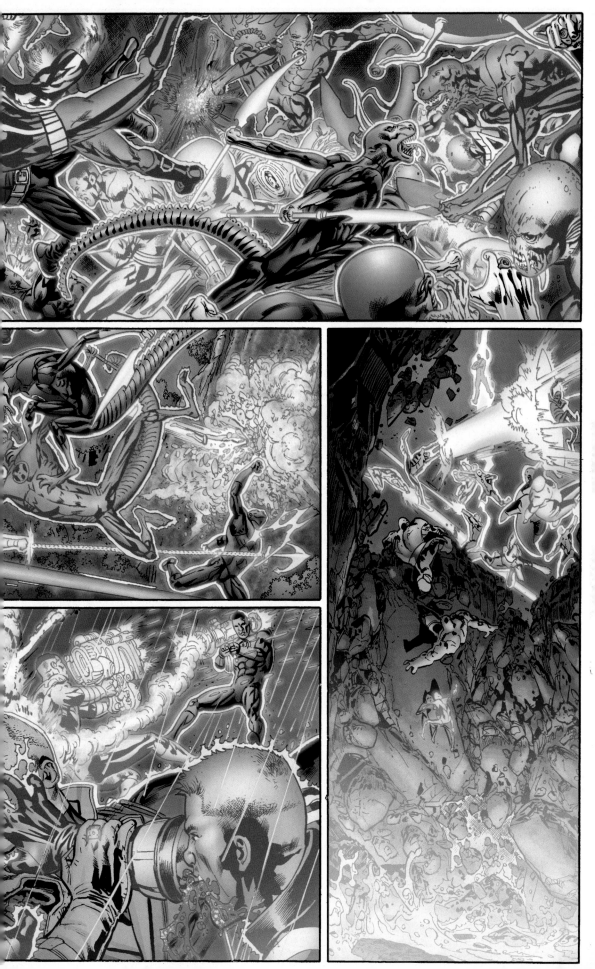

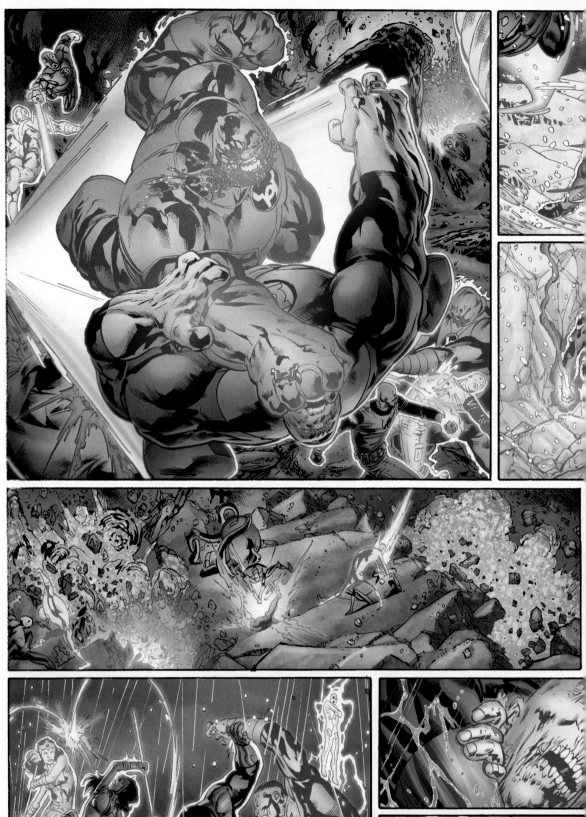

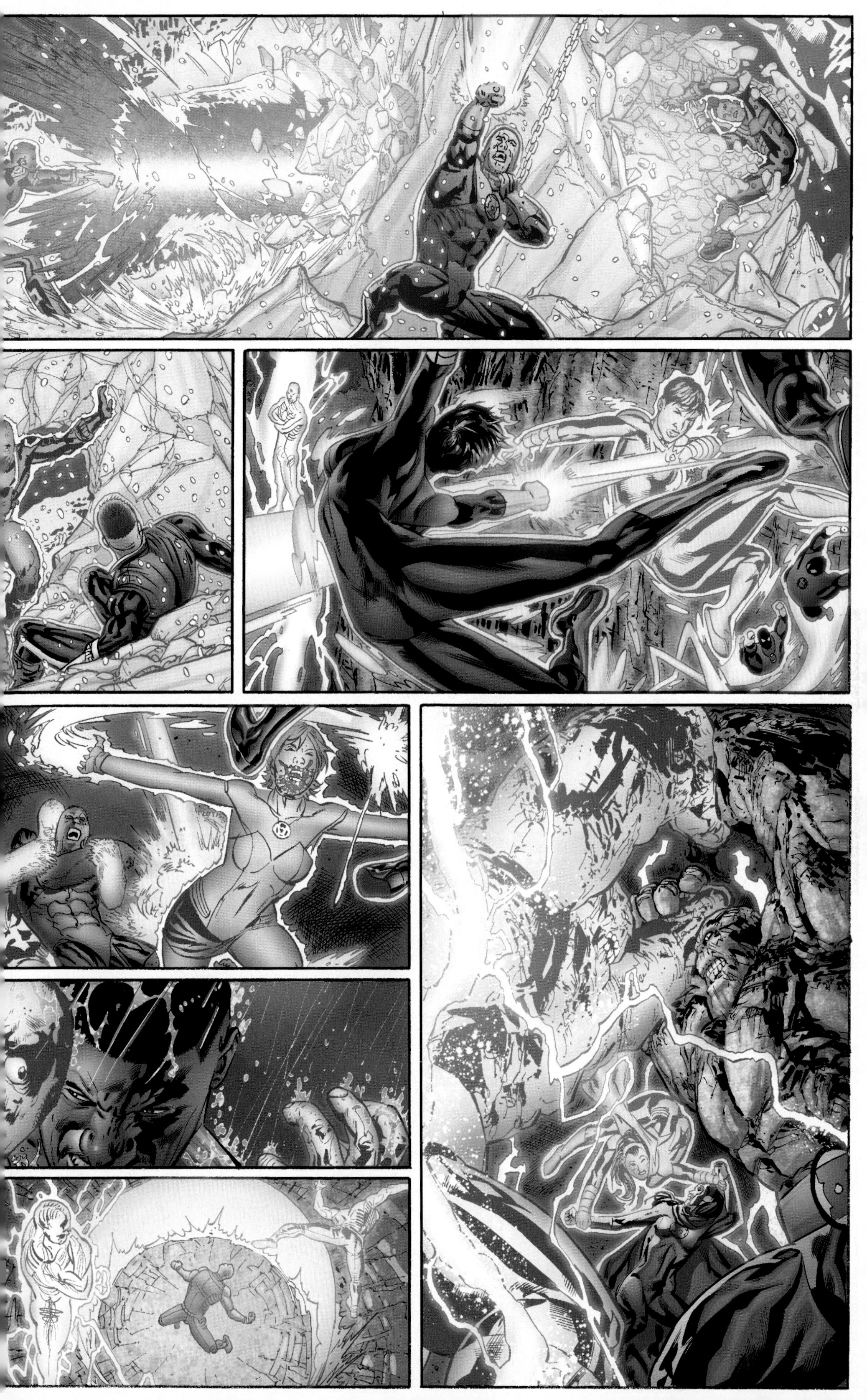

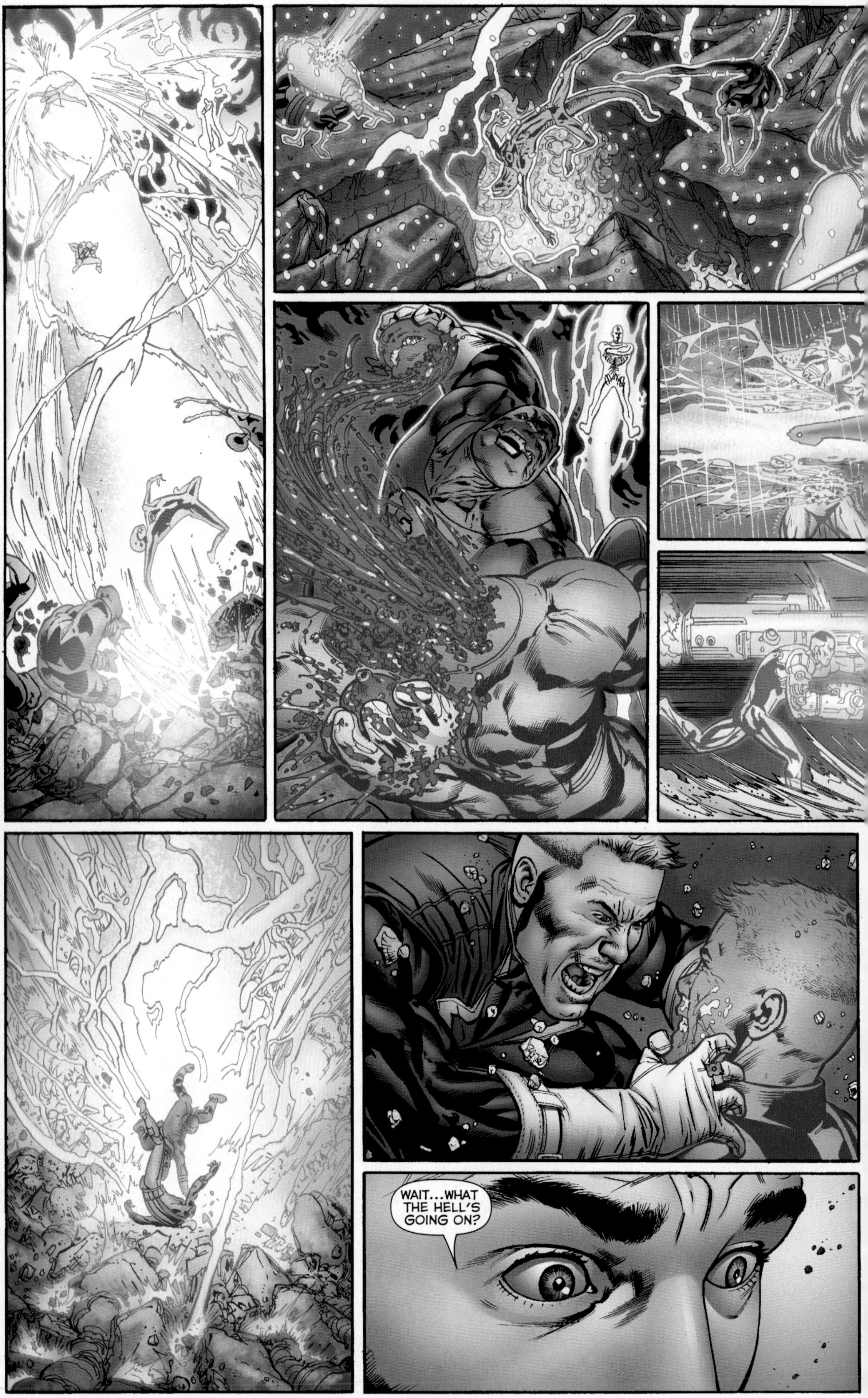
WAIT...WHAT THE HELL'S GOING ON?

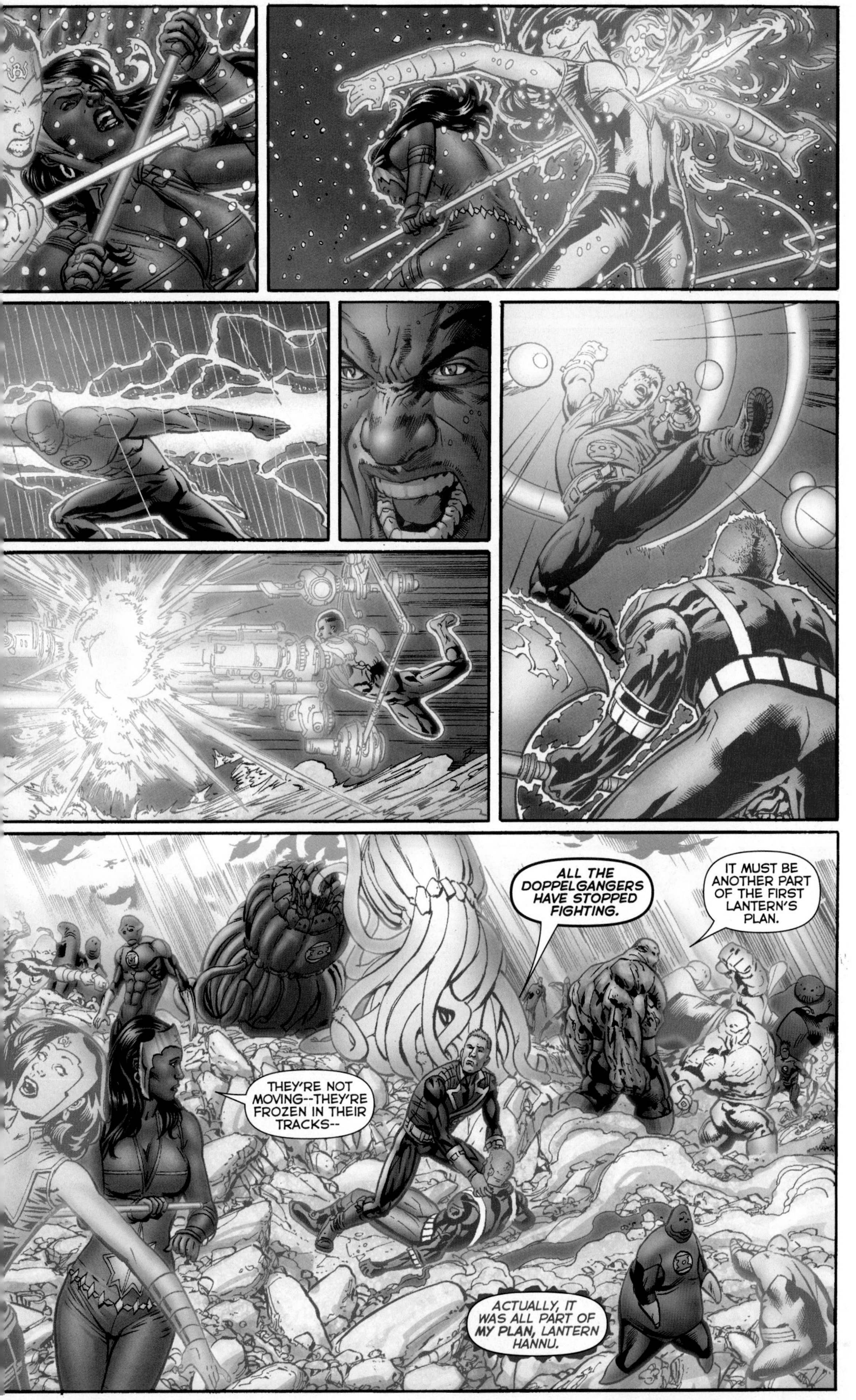
ALL THE DOPPELGANGERS HAVE STOPPED FIGHTING.
IT MUST BE ANOTHER PART OF THE FIRST LANTERN'S PLAN.
THEY'RE NOT MOVING--THEY'RE FROZEN IN THEIR TRACKS--
ACTUALLY, IT WAS ALL PART OF MY PLAN, LANTERN HANNU.

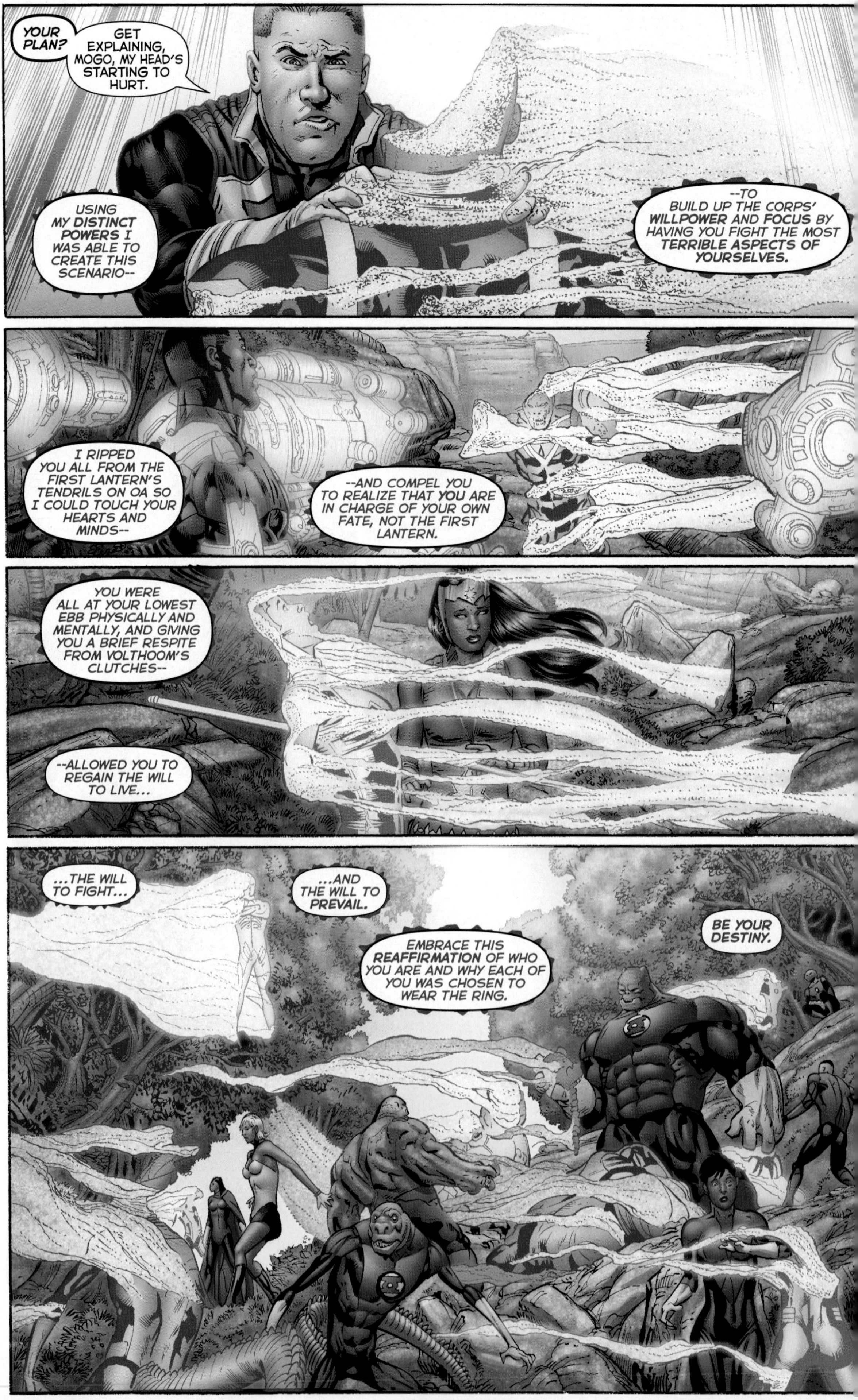
YOUR PLAN?
GET EXPLAINING, MOGO, MY HEAD'S STARTING TO HURT.
USING MY DISTINCT POWERS I WAS ABLE TO CREATE THIS SCENARIO--
--TO BUILD UP THE CORPS' WILLPOWER AND FOCUS BY HAVING YOU FIGHT THE MOST TERRIBLE ASPECTS OF YOURSELVES.
I RIPPED YOU ALL FROM THE FIRST LANTERN'S TENDRILS ON OA SO I COULD TOUCH YOUR HEARTS AND MINDS--
--AND COMPEL YOU TO REALIZE THAT YOU ARE IN CHARGE OF YOUR OWN FATE, NOT THE FIRST LANTERN.
YOU WERE ALL AT YOUR LOWEST EBB PHYSICALLY AND MENTALLY, AND GIVING YOU A BRIEF RESPITE FROM VOLTHOOM'S CLUTCHES--
--ALLOWED YOU TO REGAIN THE WILL TO LIVE...
...THE WILL TO FIGHT...
...AND THE WILL TO PREVAIL.
EMBRACE THIS REAFFIRMATION OF WHO YOU ARE AND WHY EACH OF YOU WAS CHOSEN TO WEAR THE RING.
BE YOUR DESTINY.

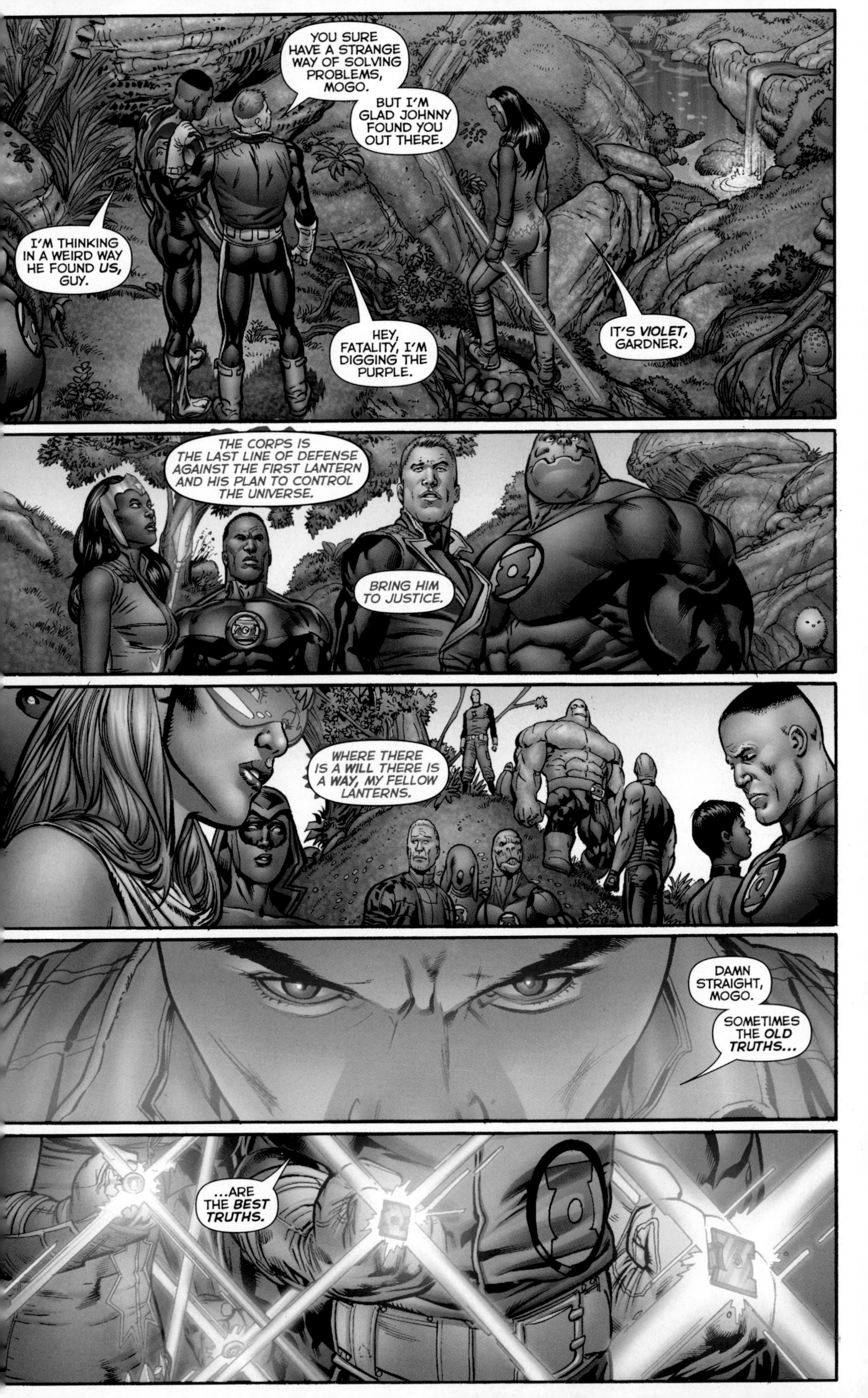
YOU SURE HAVE A STRANGE WAY OF SOLVING PROBLEMS, MOGO.
BUT I'M GLAD JOHNNY FOUND YOU OUT THERE.
I'M THINKING IN A WEIRD WAY HE FOUND *US*, GUY.
HEY, FATALITY, I'M DIGGING THE PURPLE.
IT'S *VIOLET*, GARDNER.
THE CORPS IS THE LAST LINE OF DEFENSE AGAINST THE FIRST LANTERN AND HIS PLAN TO CONTROL THE UNIVERSE.
BRING HIM TO JUSTICE.
WHERE THERE IS A *WILL* THERE IS A *WAY*, MY FELLOW LANTERNS.
DAMN STRAIGHT, MOGO.
SOMETIMES THE *OLD TRUTHS*...
...ARE THE *BEST TRUTHS*.

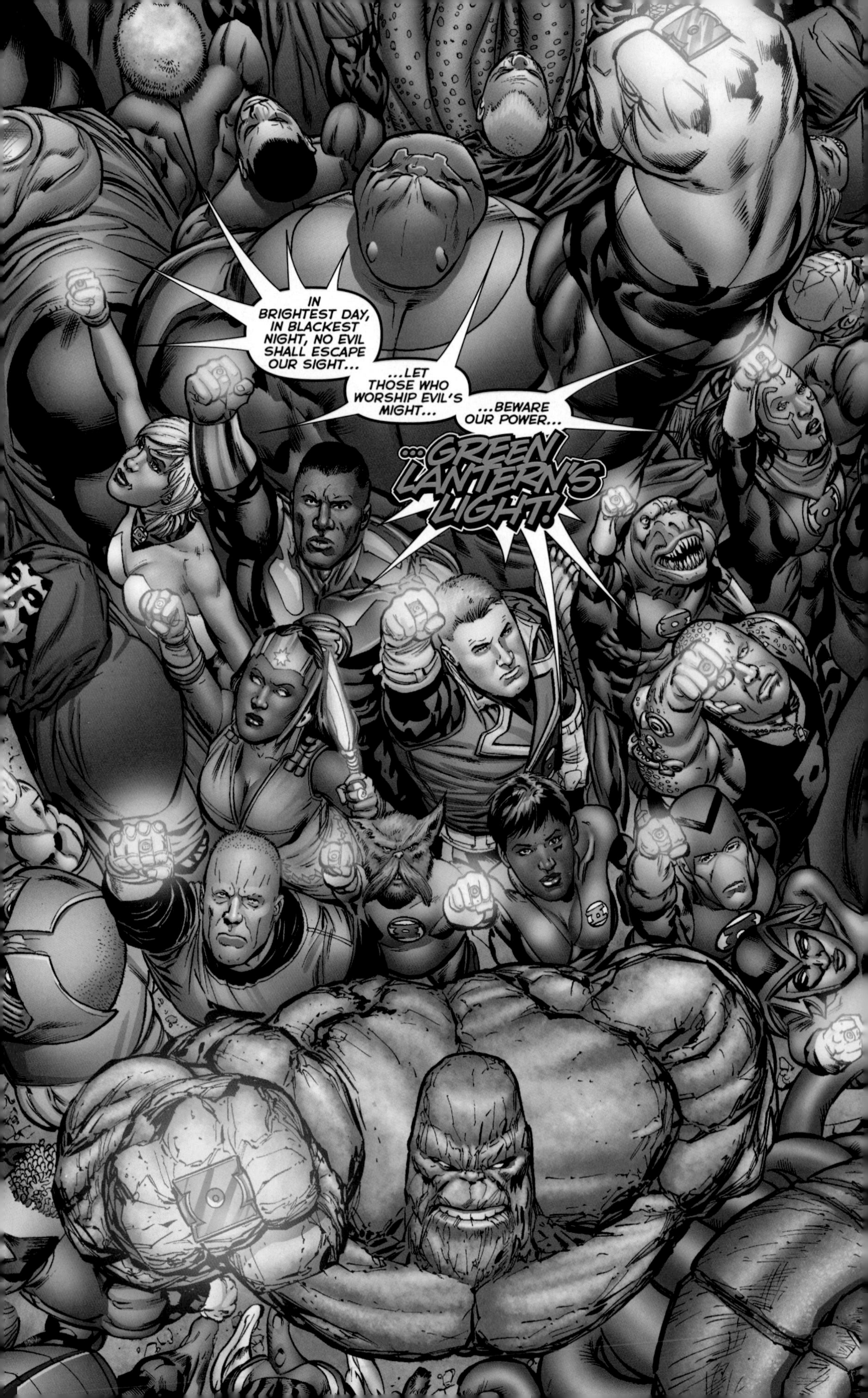
IN BRIGHTEST DAY, IN BLACKEST NIGHT, NO EVIL SHALL ESCAPE OUR SIGHT...
...LET THOSE WHO WORSHIP EVIL'S MIGHT...
...BEWARE OUR POWER...
...GREEN LANTERN'S LIGHT!

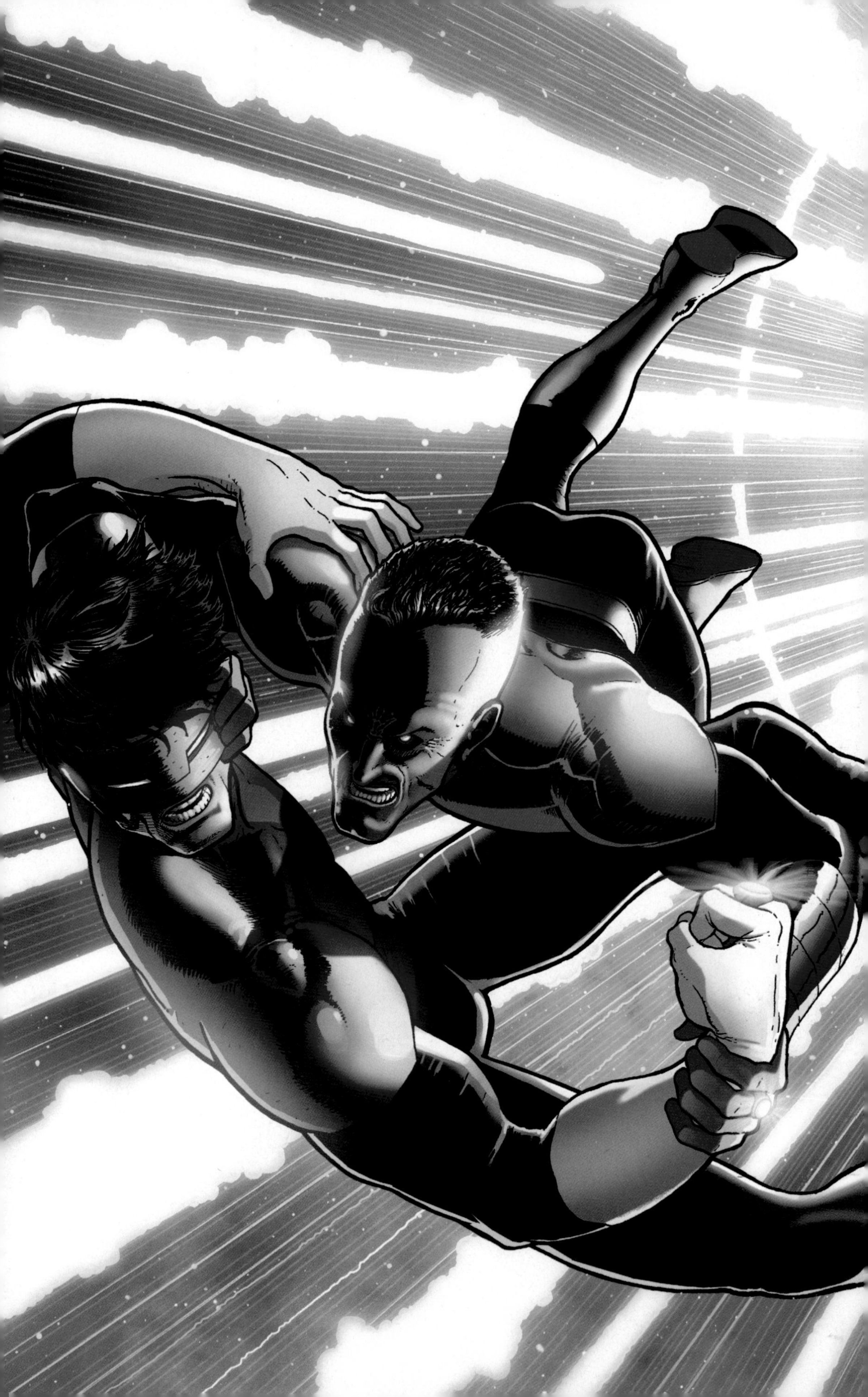

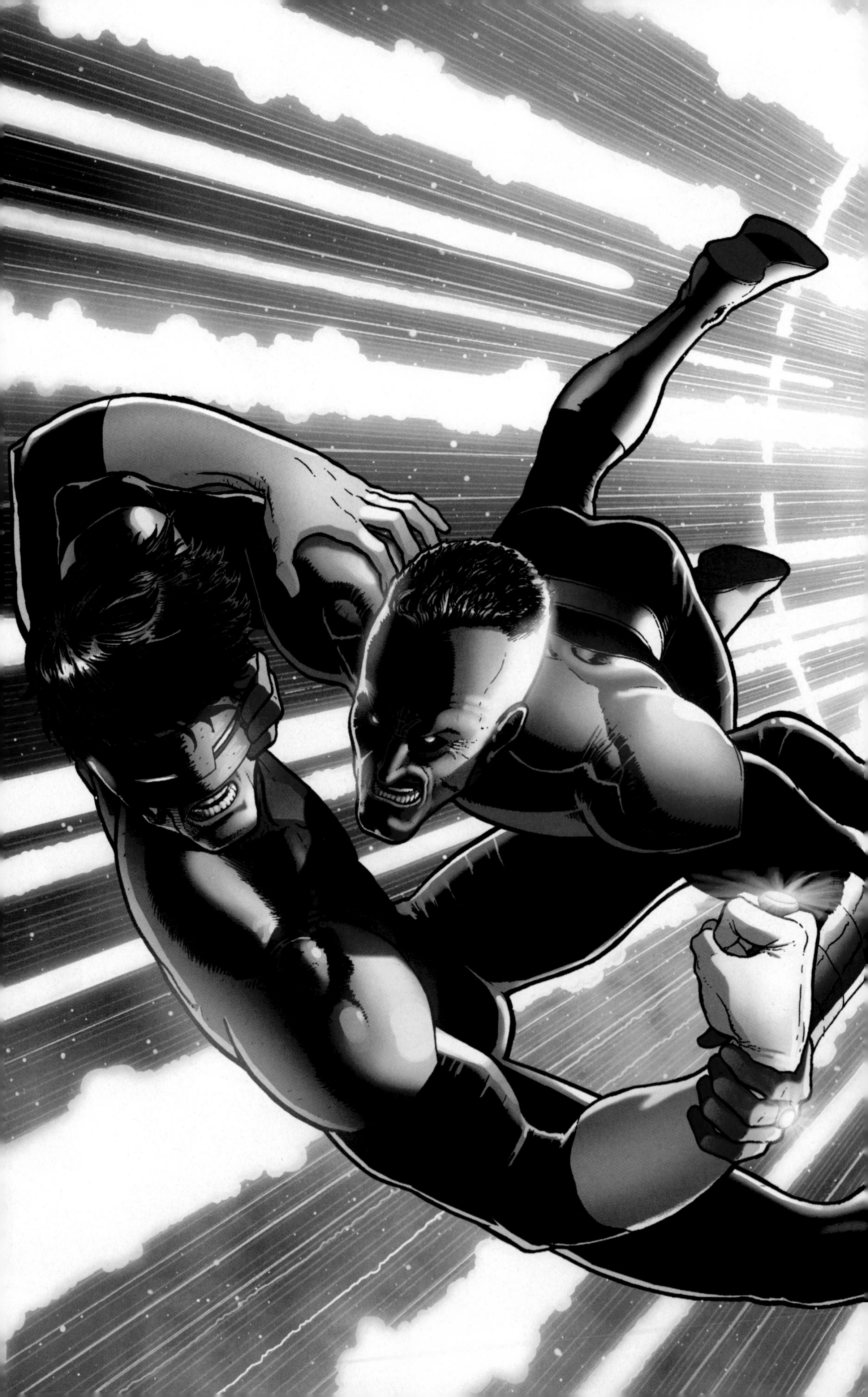

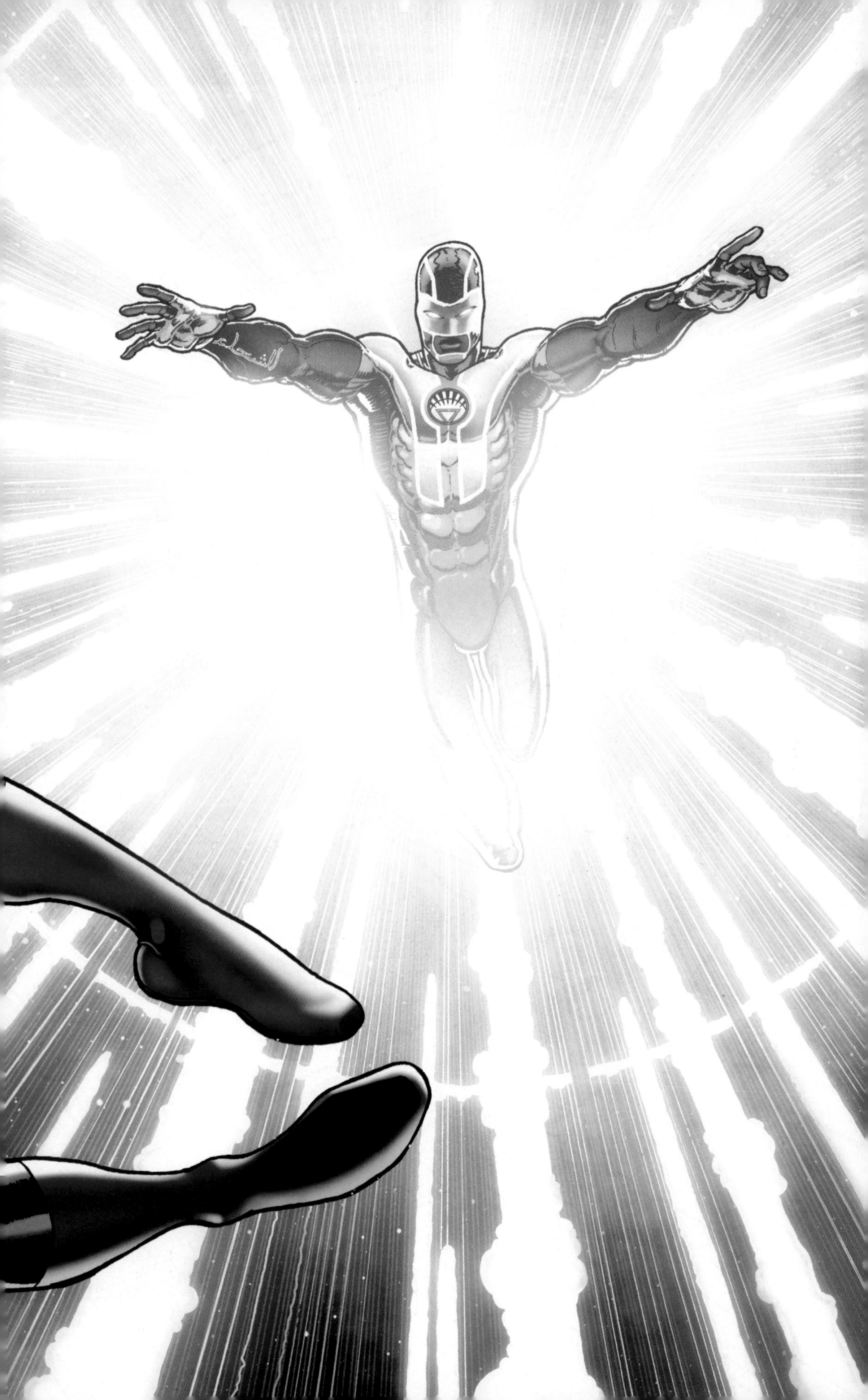

الشجاعة

PART ELEVEN: SHADOW OF DEATH

TONY BEDARD writer **ANDRES GUINALDO** penciller **RAUL FERNANDEZ** inker
cover art by **AARON KUDER & WIL QUINTANA**

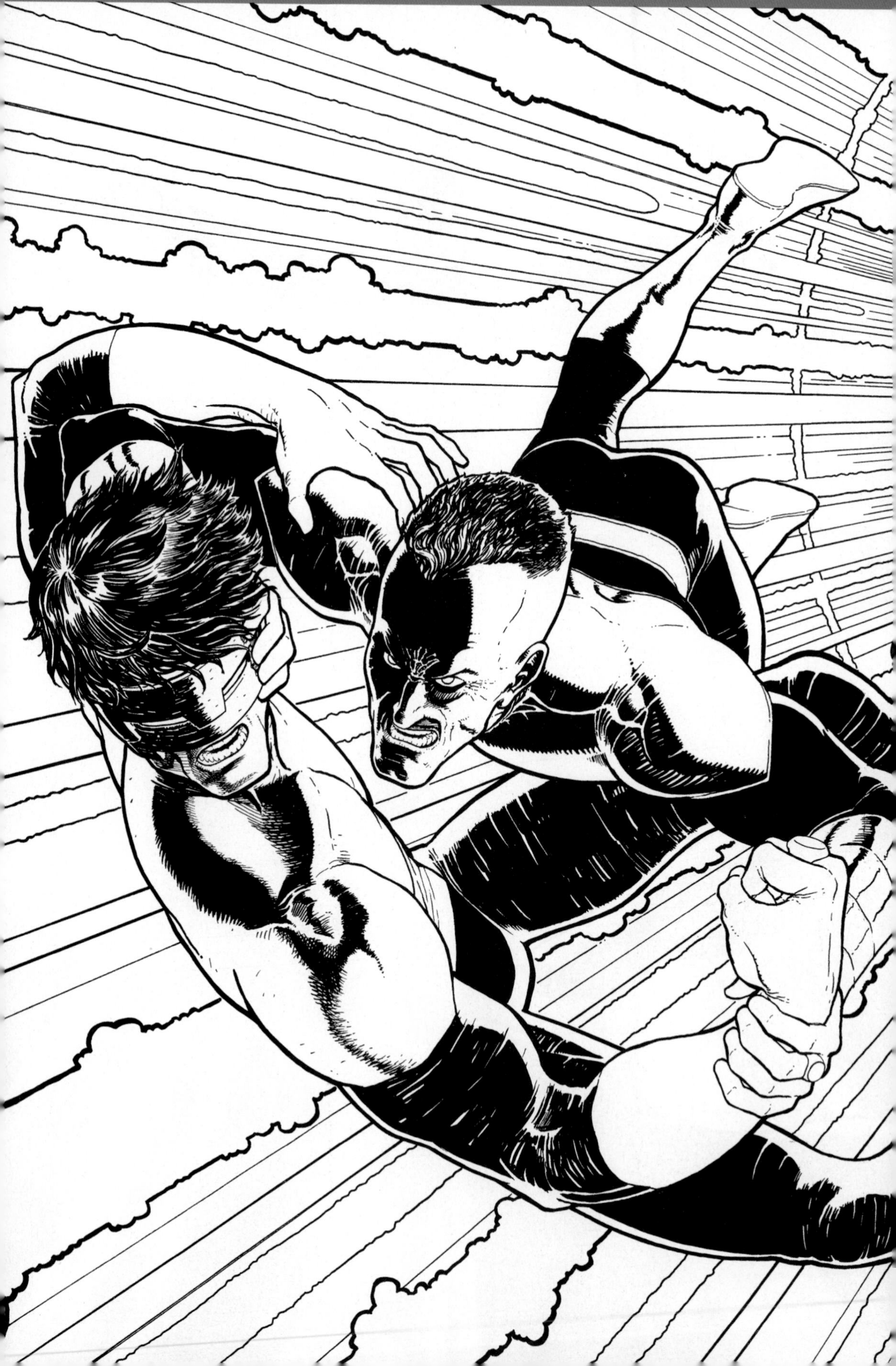

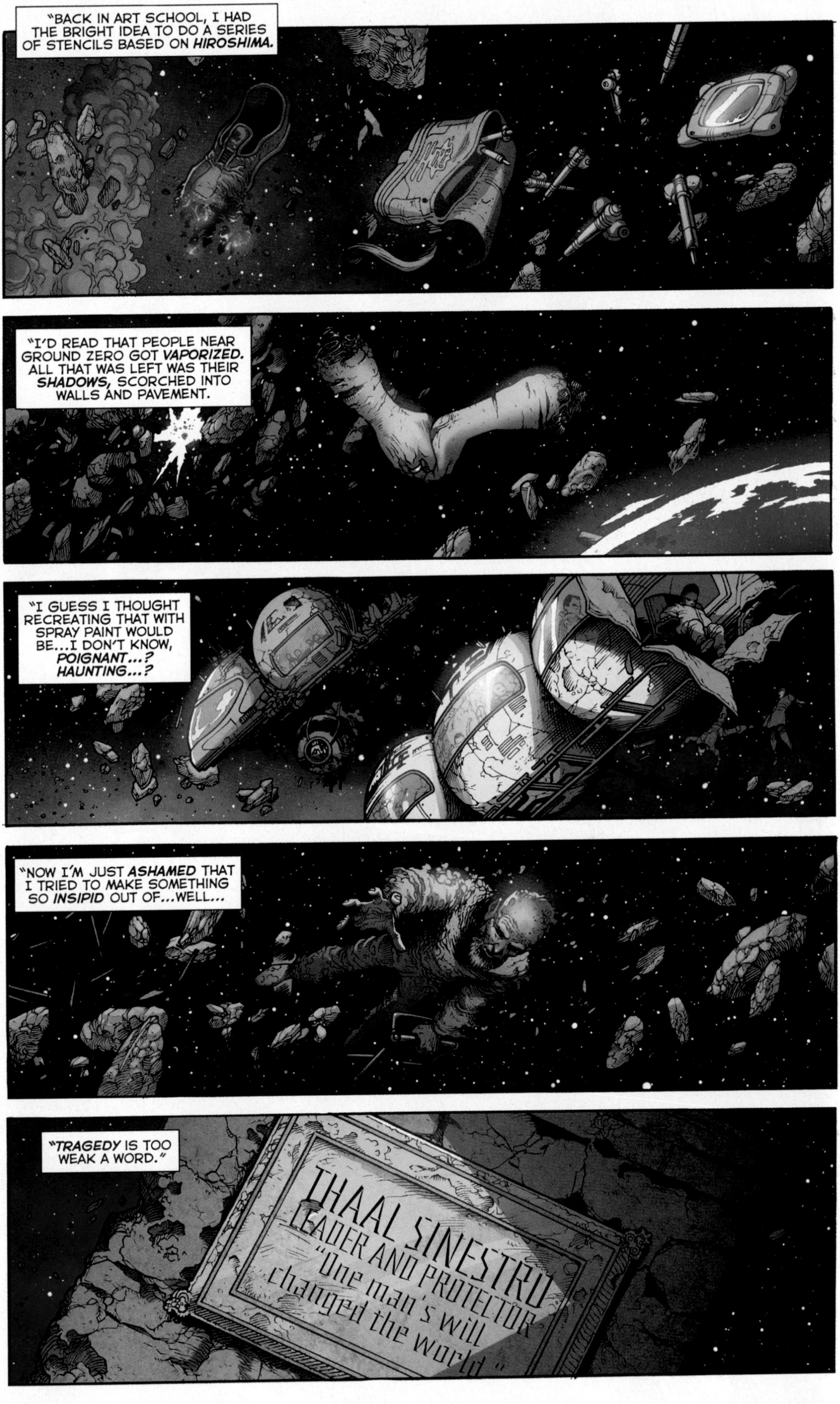
"BACK IN ART SCHOOL, I HAD THE BRIGHT IDEA TO DO A SERIES OF STENCILS BASED ON HIROSHIMA.
"I'D READ THAT PEOPLE NEAR GROUND ZERO GOT VAPORIZED. ALL THAT WAS LEFT WAS THEIR SHADOWS, SCORCHED INTO WALLS AND PAVEMENT.
"I GUESS I THOUGHT RECREATING THAT WITH SPRAY PAINT WOULD BE...I DON'T KNOW, POIGNANT...? HAUNTING...?
"NOW I'M JUST ASHAMED THAT I TRIED TO MAKE SOMETHING SO INSIPID OUT OF...WELL...
"TRAGEDY IS TOO WEAK A WORD."
THAAL SINESTRO
LEADER AND PROTECTOR
"One man's will changed the world."

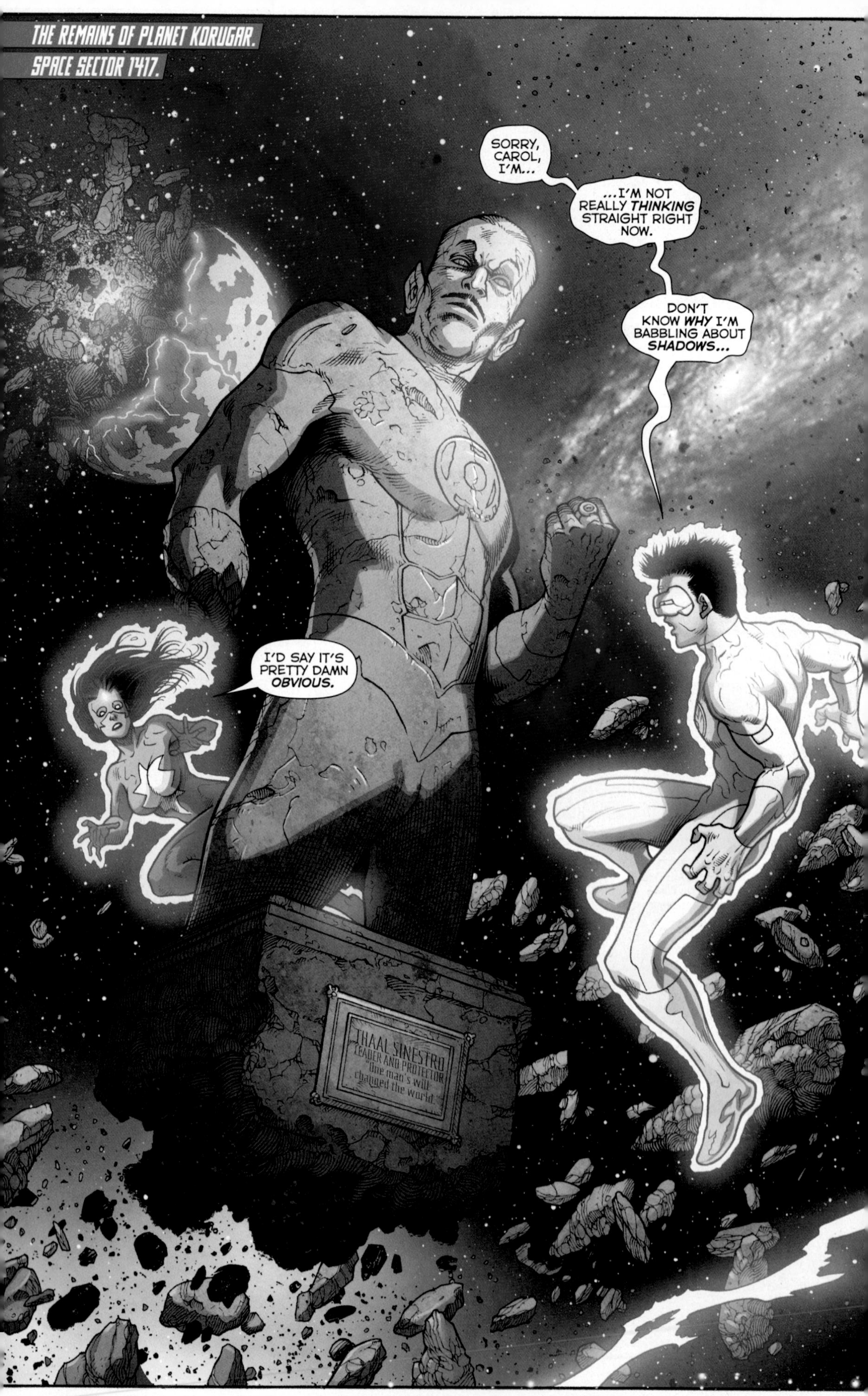
THE REMAINS OF PLANET KORUGAR.
SPACE SECTOR 1417.
SORRY, CAROL, I'M...
...I'M NOT REALLY THINKING STRAIGHT RIGHT NOW.
DON'T KNOW WHY I'M BABBLING ABOUT SHADOWS...
I'D SAY IT'S PRETTY DAMN OBVIOUS.
THAAL SINESTRO
LEADER AND PROTECTOR
"One man's will changed the world."

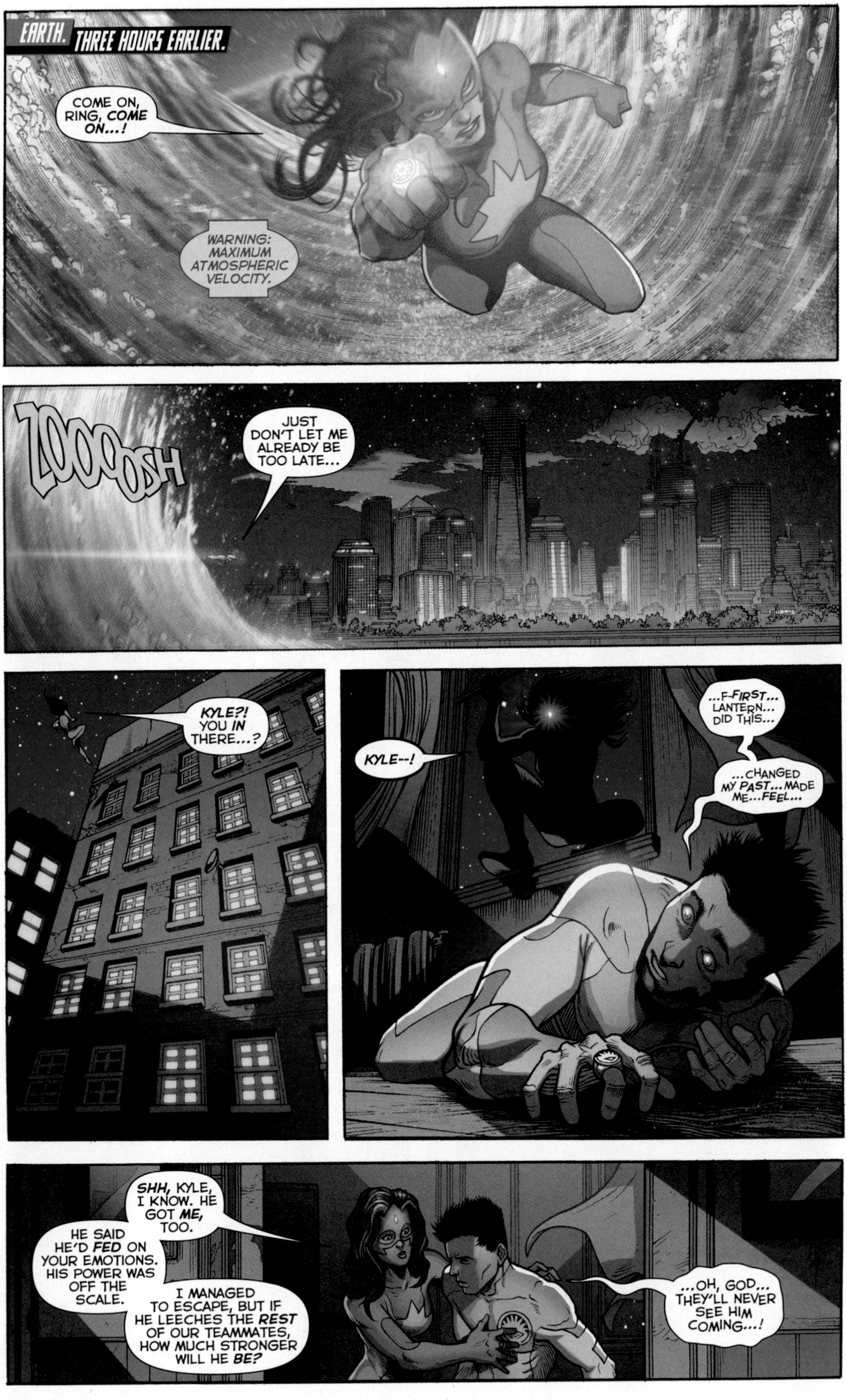
EARTH. THREE HOURS EARLIER.
COME ON, RING, COME ON...!
WARNING: MAXIMUM ATMOSPHERIC VELOCITY.
ZOOOOOSH
JUST DON'T LET ME ALREADY BE TOO LATE...
KYLE?! YOU IN THERE...?
KYLE--!
...F-FIRST... LANTERN... DID THIS...
...CHANGED MY PAST...MADE ME...FEEL...
SHH, KYLE, I KNOW. HE GOT ME, TOO.
HE SAID HE'D FED ON YOUR EMOTIONS. HIS POWER WAS OFF THE SCALE.
I MANAGED TO ESCAPE, BUT IF HE LEECHES THE REST OF OUR TEAMMATES, HOW MUCH STRONGER WILL HE BE?
...OH, GOD... THEY'LL NEVER SEE HIM COMING...!

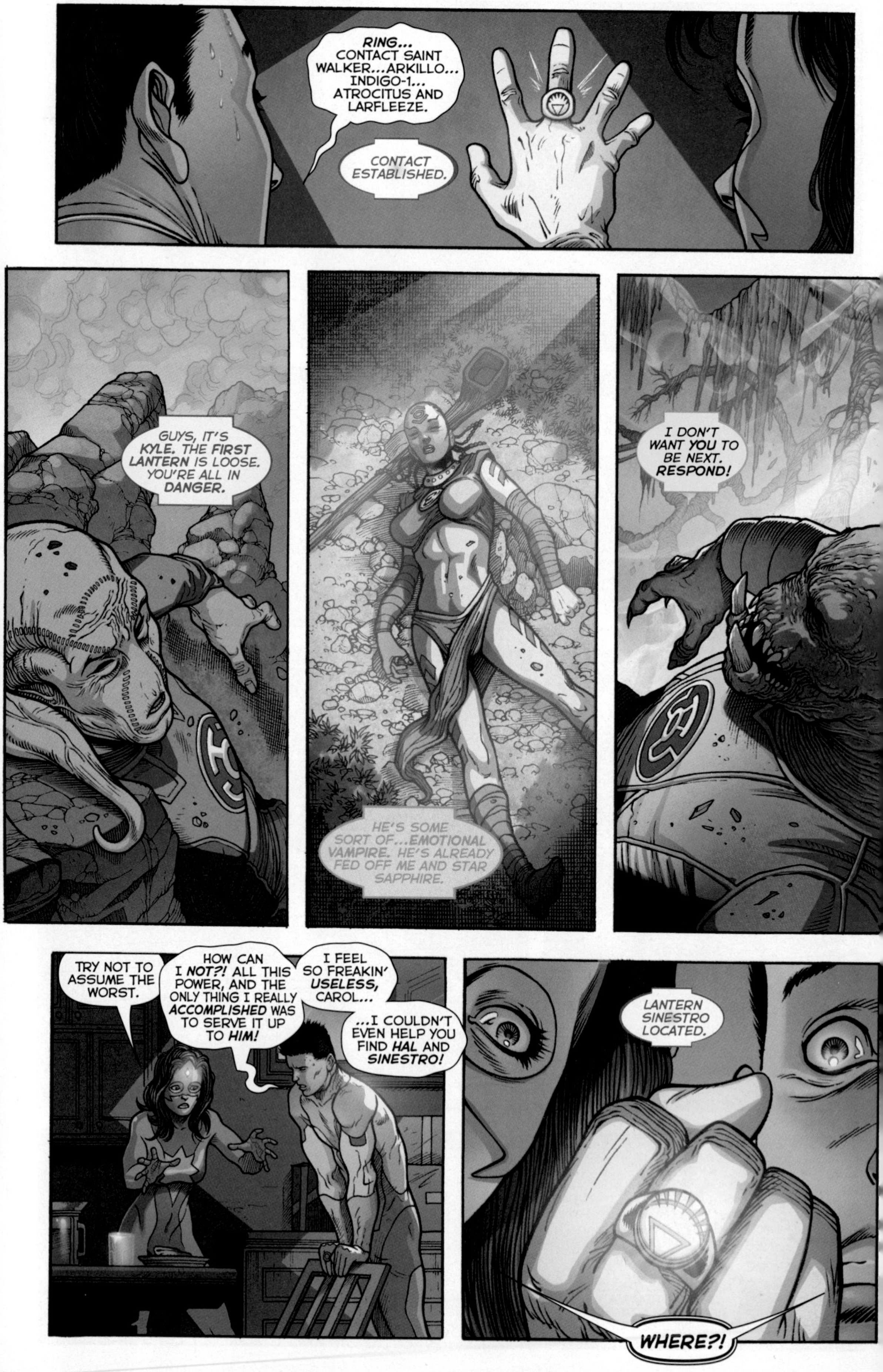
RING... CONTACT SAINT WALKER...ARKILLO... INDIGO-1... ATROCITUS AND LARFLEEZE.
CONTACT ESTABLISHED.
GUYS, IT'S KYLE. THE FIRST LANTERN IS LOOSE. YOU'RE ALL IN DANGER.
HE'S SOME SORT OF...EMOTIONAL VAMPIRE. HE'S ALREADY FED OFF ME AND STAR SAPPHIRE.
I DON'T WANT YOU TO BE NEXT. RESPOND!
TRY NOT TO ASSUME THE WORST.
HOW CAN I NOT?! ALL THIS POWER, AND THE ONLY THING I REALLY ACCOMPLISHED WAS TO SERVE IT UP TO HIM!
I FEEL SO FREAKIN' USELESS, CAROL...
...I COULDN'T EVEN HELP YOU FIND HAL AND SINESTRO!
LANTERN SINESTRO LOCATED.
WHERE?!

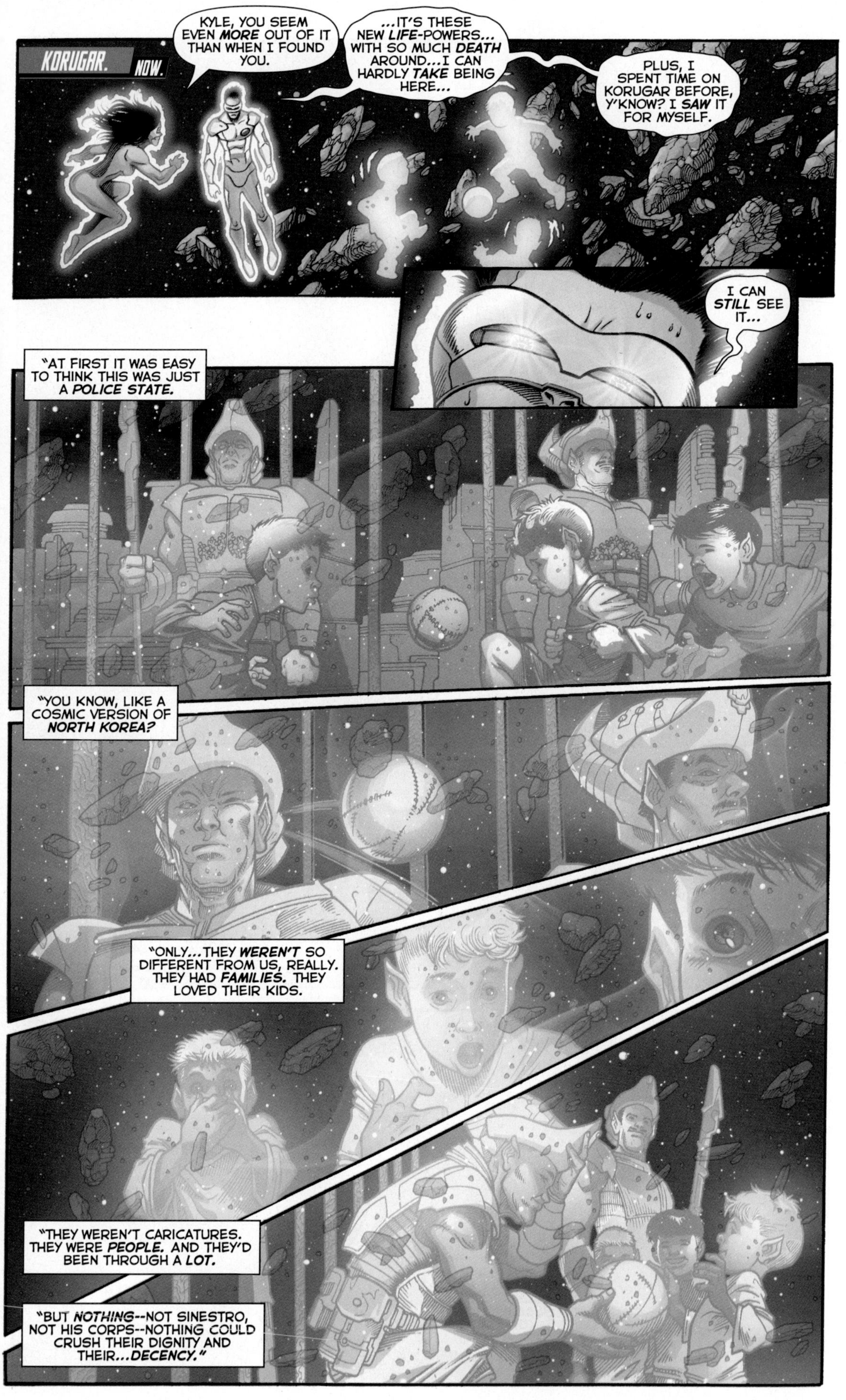
KORUGAR. NOW.
KYLE, YOU SEEM EVEN MORE OUT OF IT THAN WHEN I FOUND YOU.
...IT'S THESE NEW LIFE-POWERS... WITH SO MUCH DEATH AROUND...I CAN HARDLY TAKE BEING HERE...
PLUS, I SPENT TIME ON KORUGAR BEFORE, Y'KNOW? I SAW IT FOR MYSELF.
I CAN STILL SEE IT...
"AT FIRST IT WAS EASY TO THINK THIS WAS JUST A POLICE STATE.
"YOU KNOW, LIKE A COSMIC VERSION OF NORTH KOREA?
"ONLY...THEY WEREN'T SO DIFFERENT FROM US, REALLY. THEY HAD FAMILIES. THEY LOVED THEIR KIDS.
"THEY WEREN'T CARICATURES. THEY WERE PEOPLE. AND THEY'D BEEN THROUGH A LOT.
"BUT NOTHING--NOT SINESTRO, NOT HIS CORPS--NOTHING COULD CRUSH THEIR DIGNITY AND THEIR...DECENCY."

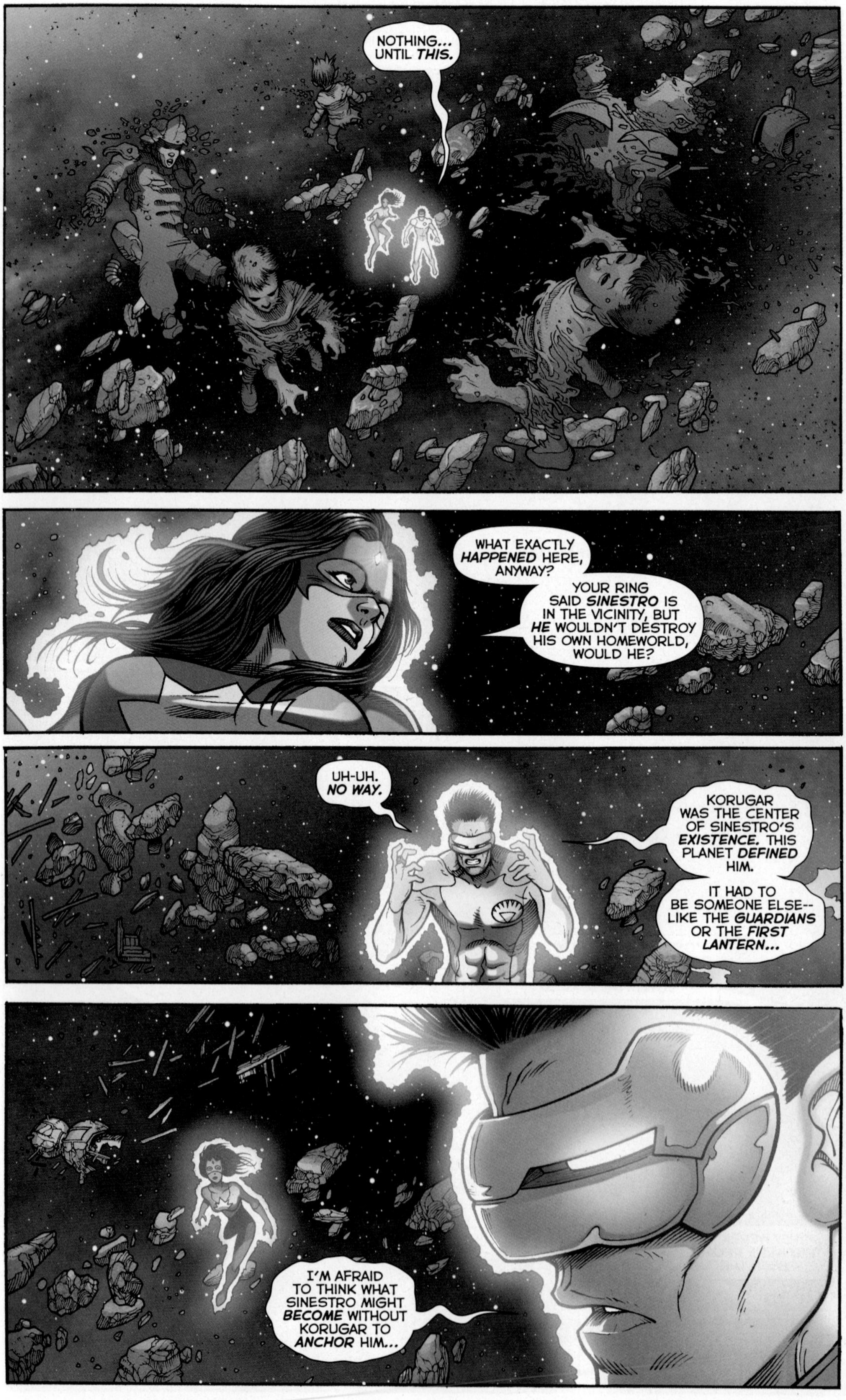
NOTHING... UNTIL *THIS.*
WHAT EXACTLY *HAPPENED* HERE, ANYWAY?
YOUR RING SAID *SINESTRO* IS IN THE VICINITY, BUT *HE* WOULDN'T DESTROY HIS OWN HOMEWORLD, WOULD HE?
UH-UH. *NO WAY.*
KORUGAR WAS THE CENTER OF SINESTRO'S *EXISTENCE.* THIS PLANET *DEFINED* HIM.
IT HAD TO BE SOMEONE ELSE-- LIKE THE *GUARDIANS* OR THE *FIRST LANTERN...*
I'M AFRAID TO THINK WHAT SINESTRO MIGHT *BECOME* WITHOUT KORUGAR TO *ANCHOR* HIM...

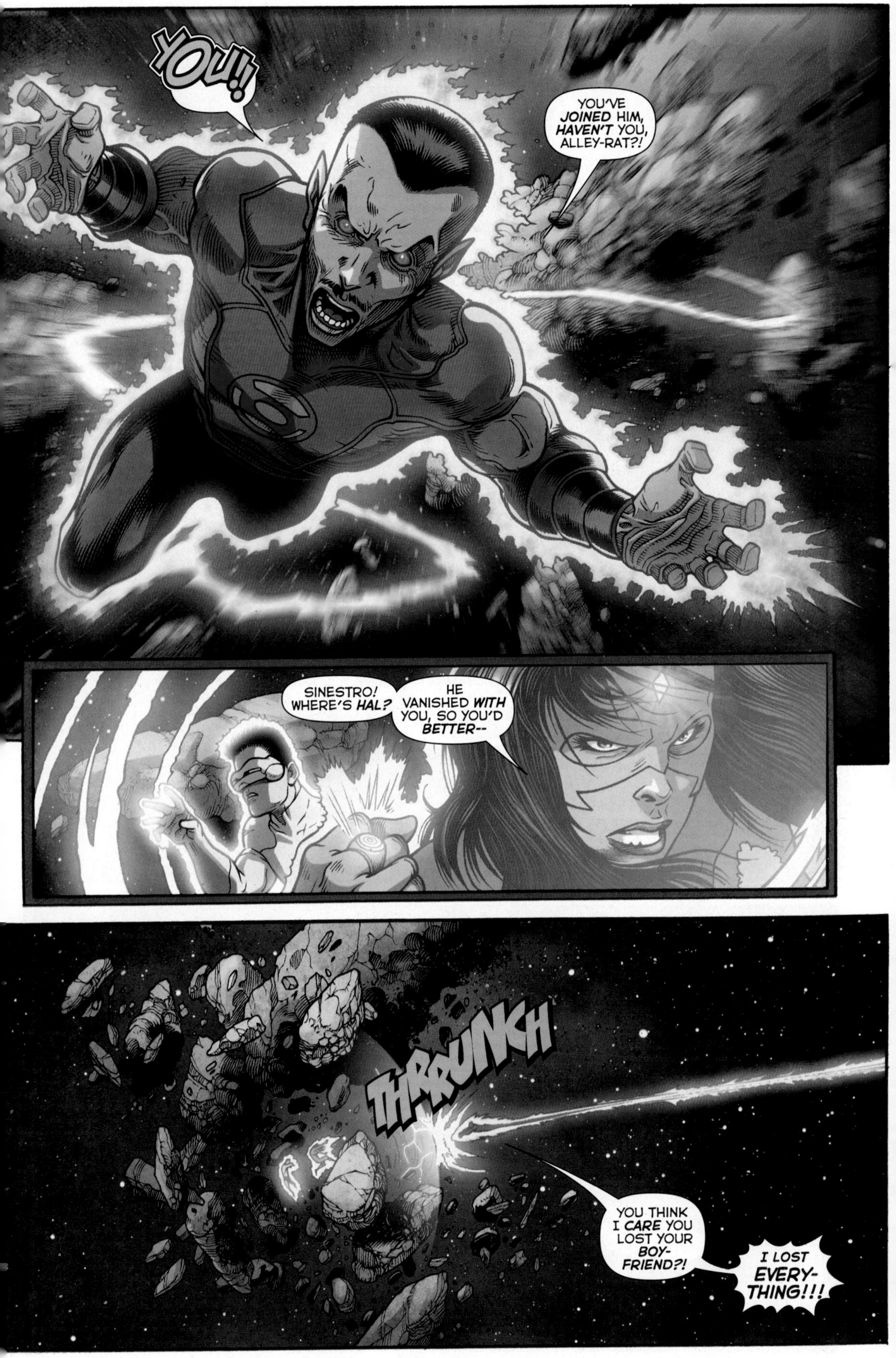
YOU!!
YOU'VE JOINED HIM, HAVEN'T YOU, ALLEY-RAT?!
SINESTRO! WHERE'S HAL?
HE VANISHED WITH YOU, SO YOU'D BETTER--
THRRUNCH
YOU THINK I CARE YOU LOST YOUR BOY-FRIEND?!
I LOST EVERY-THING!!!

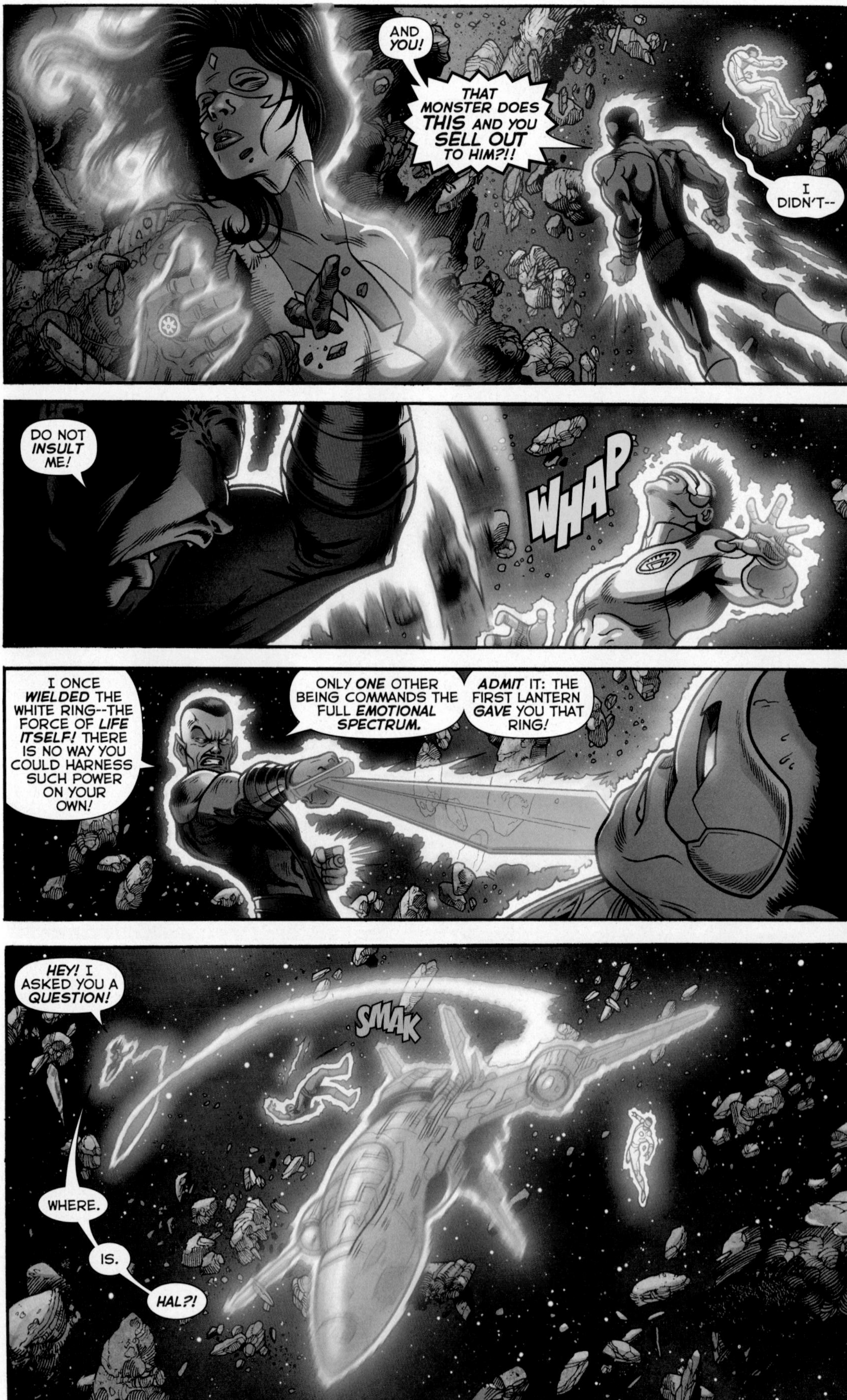
AND YOU!
THAT MONSTER DOES THIS AND YOU SELL OUT TO HIM?!!
I DIDN'T--
DO NOT INSULT ME!
WHAP
I ONCE WIELDED THE WHITE RING--THE FORCE OF LIFE ITSELF! THERE IS NO WAY YOU COULD HARNESS SUCH POWER ON YOUR OWN!
ONLY ONE OTHER BEING COMMANDS THE FULL EMOTIONAL SPECTRUM.
ADMIT IT: THE FIRST LANTERN GAVE YOU THAT RING!
HEY! I ASKED YOU A QUESTION!
SMAK
WHERE.
IS.
HAL?!

ENOUGH OF YOUR *WHINING!*
JORDAN IS *DEAD!* AND THIS TIME HE'S *NOT* COMING BACK!
YOU...
YOU'RE *LYING!* I'LL...
I'LL RIP THE *TRUTH* OUT OF YOU!
NO.
YOU'LL GET OUT OF *MY WAY.*

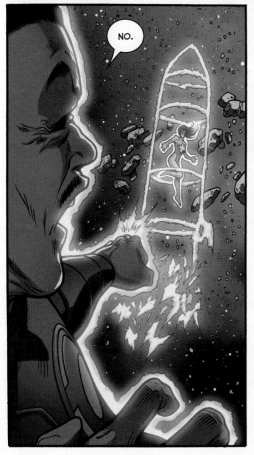

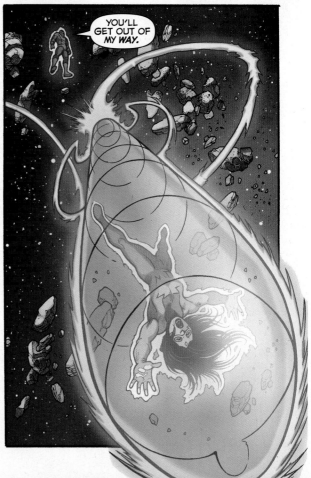

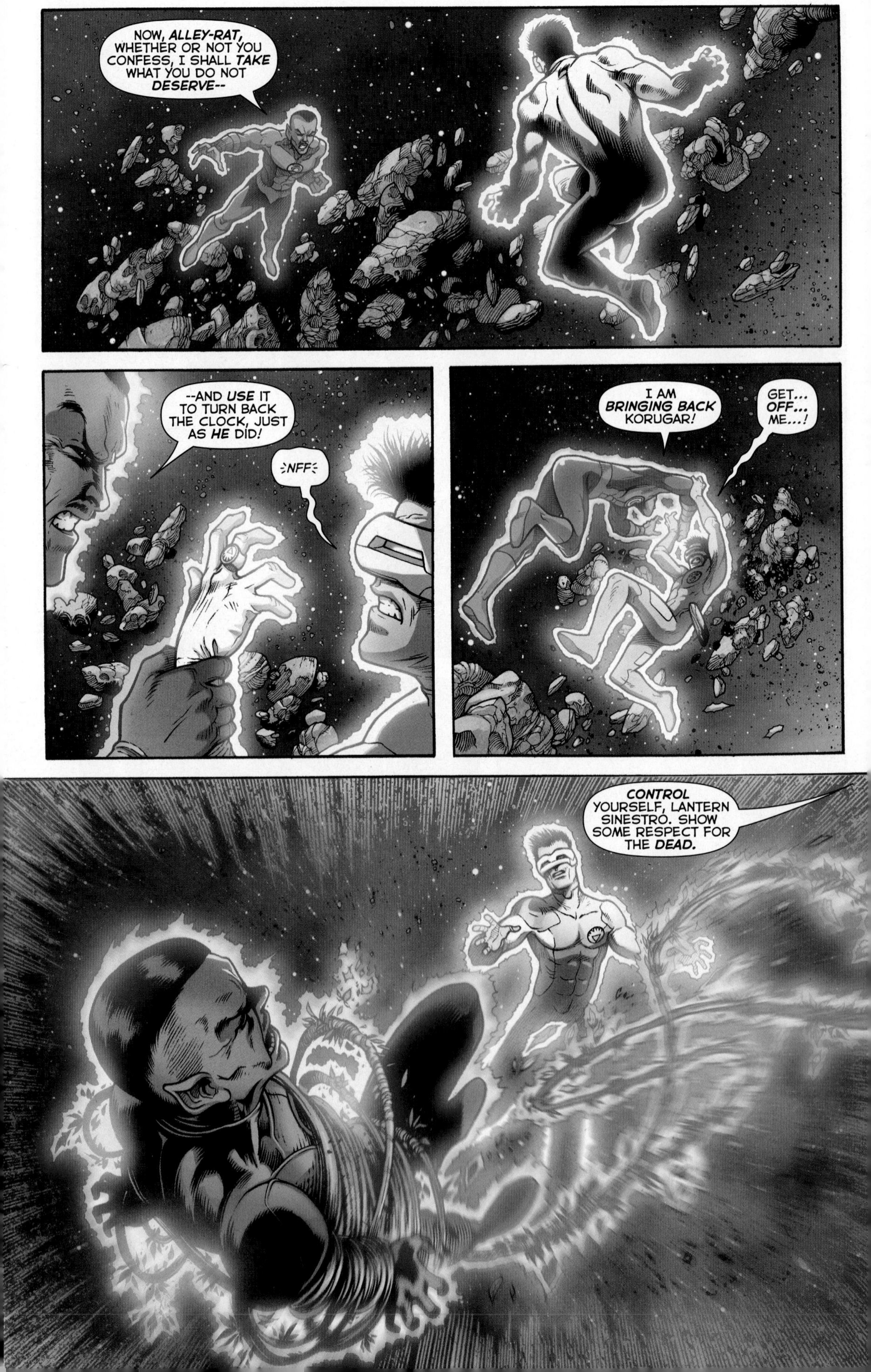
NOW, ALLEY-RAT, WHETHER OR NOT YOU CONFESS, I SHALL TAKE WHAT YOU DO NOT DESERVE--
--AND USE IT TO TURN BACK THE CLOCK, JUST AS HE DID!
NFF
I AM BRINGING BACK KORUGAR!
GET... OFF... ME...!
CONTROL YOURSELF, LANTERN SINESTRO. SHOW SOME RESPECT FOR THE DEAD.

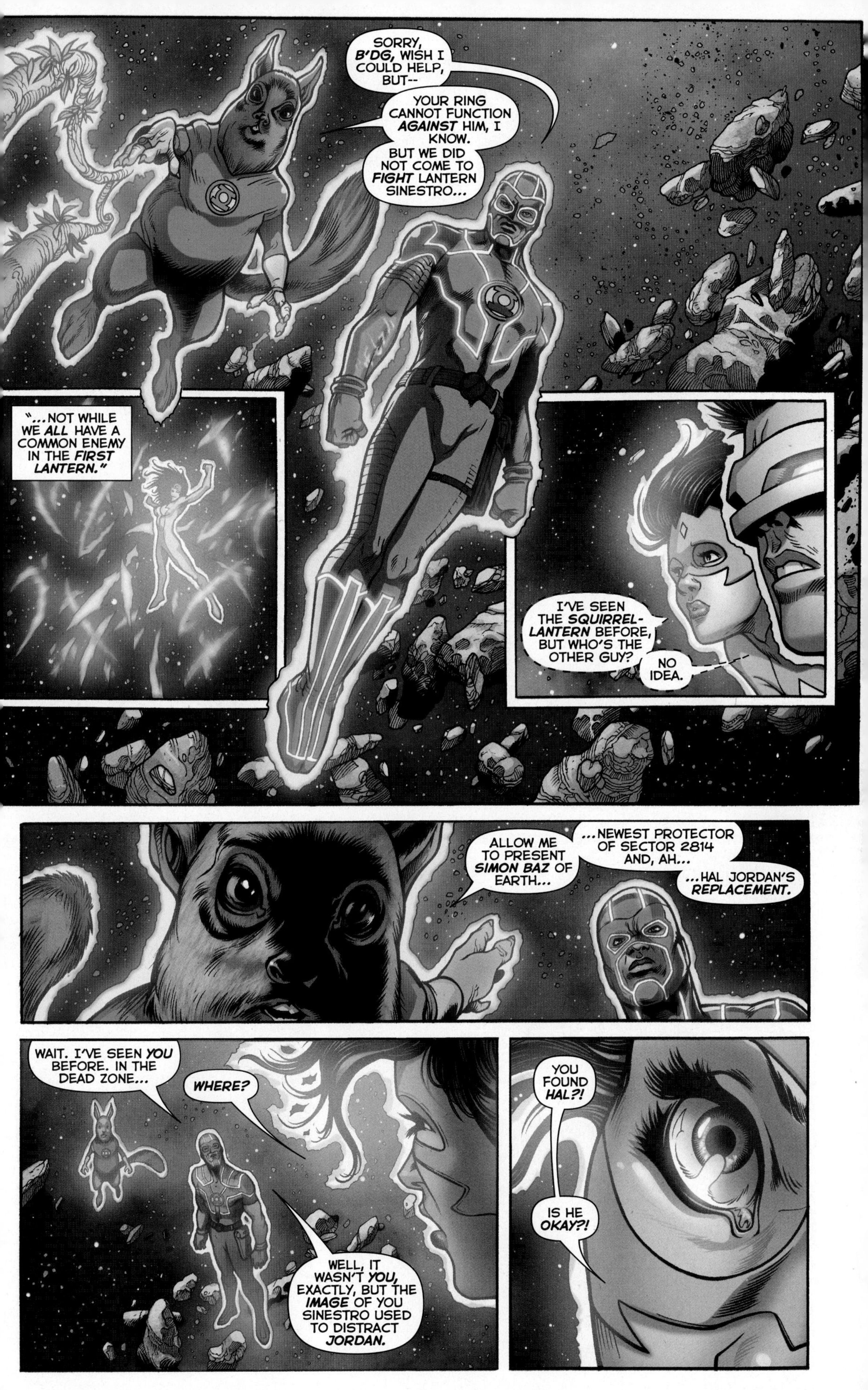
SORRY, B'DG, WISH I COULD HELP, BUT--
YOUR RING CANNOT FUNCTION AGAINST HIM, I KNOW.
BUT WE DID NOT COME TO FIGHT LANTERN SINESTRO...
"...NOT WHILE WE ALL HAVE A COMMON ENEMY IN THE FIRST LANTERN."
I'VE SEEN THE SQUIRREL-LANTERN BEFORE, BUT WHO'S THE OTHER GUY?
NO IDEA.
ALLOW ME TO PRESENT SIMON BAZ OF EARTH...
...NEWEST PROTECTOR OF SECTOR 2814 AND, AH...
...HAL JORDAN'S REPLACEMENT.
WAIT. I'VE SEEN YOU BEFORE. IN THE DEAD ZONE...
WHERE?
WELL, IT WASN'T YOU, EXACTLY, BUT THE IMAGE OF YOU SINESTRO USED TO DISTRACT JORDAN.
YOU FOUND HAL?!
IS HE OKAY?!

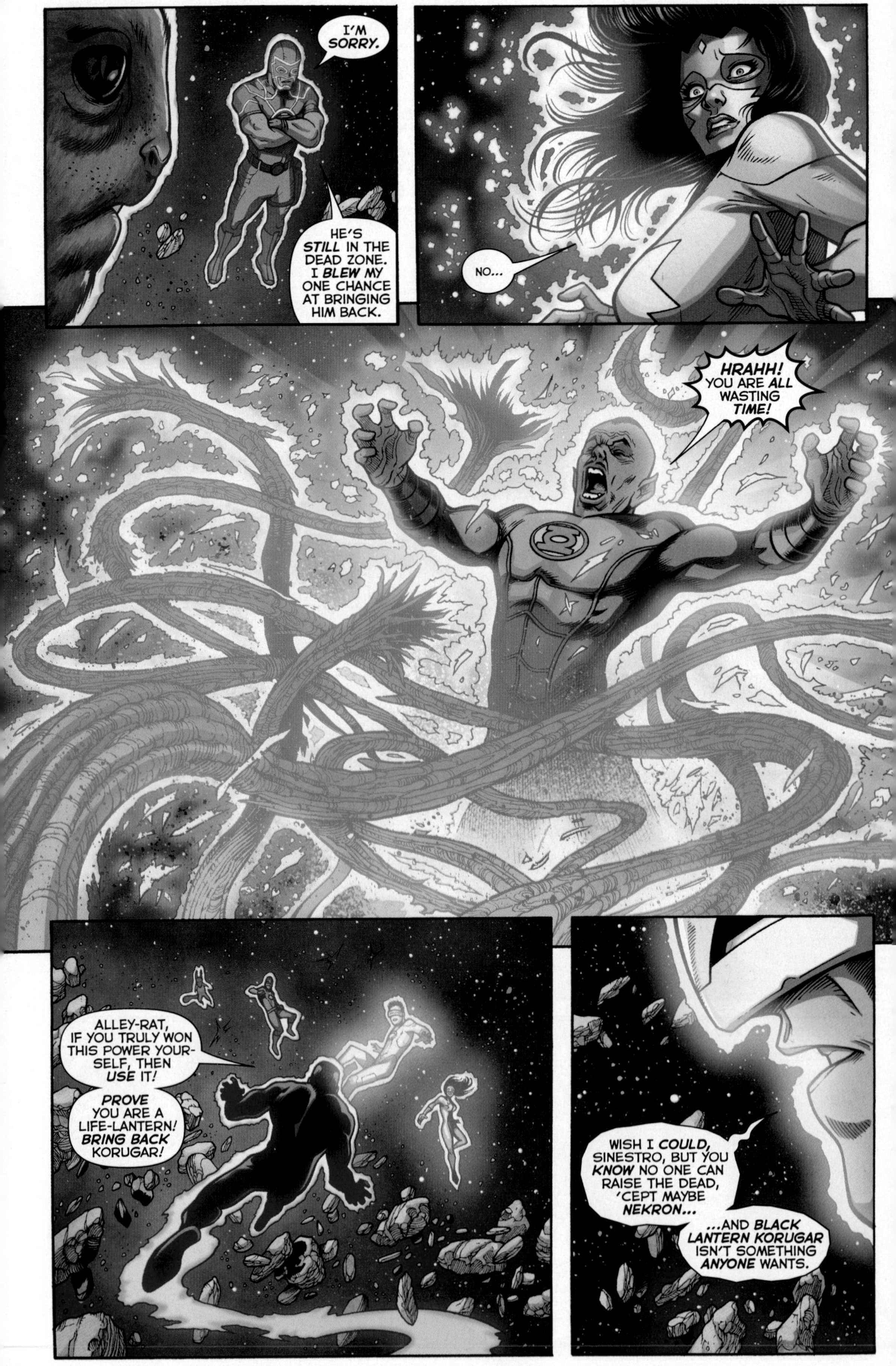

I'M SORRY.
HE'S STILL IN THE DEAD ZONE. I BLEW MY ONE CHANCE AT BRINGING HIM BACK.
NO...
HRAHH! YOU ARE ALL WASTING TIME!
ALLEY-RAT, IF YOU TRULY WON THIS POWER YOURSELF, THEN USE IT!
PROVE YOU ARE A LIFE-LANTERN! BRING BACK KORUGAR!
WISH I COULD, SINESTRO, BUT YOU KNOW NO ONE CAN RAISE THE DEAD, 'CEPT MAYBE NEKRON...
...AND BLACK LANTERN KORUGAR ISN'T SOMETHING ANYONE WANTS.

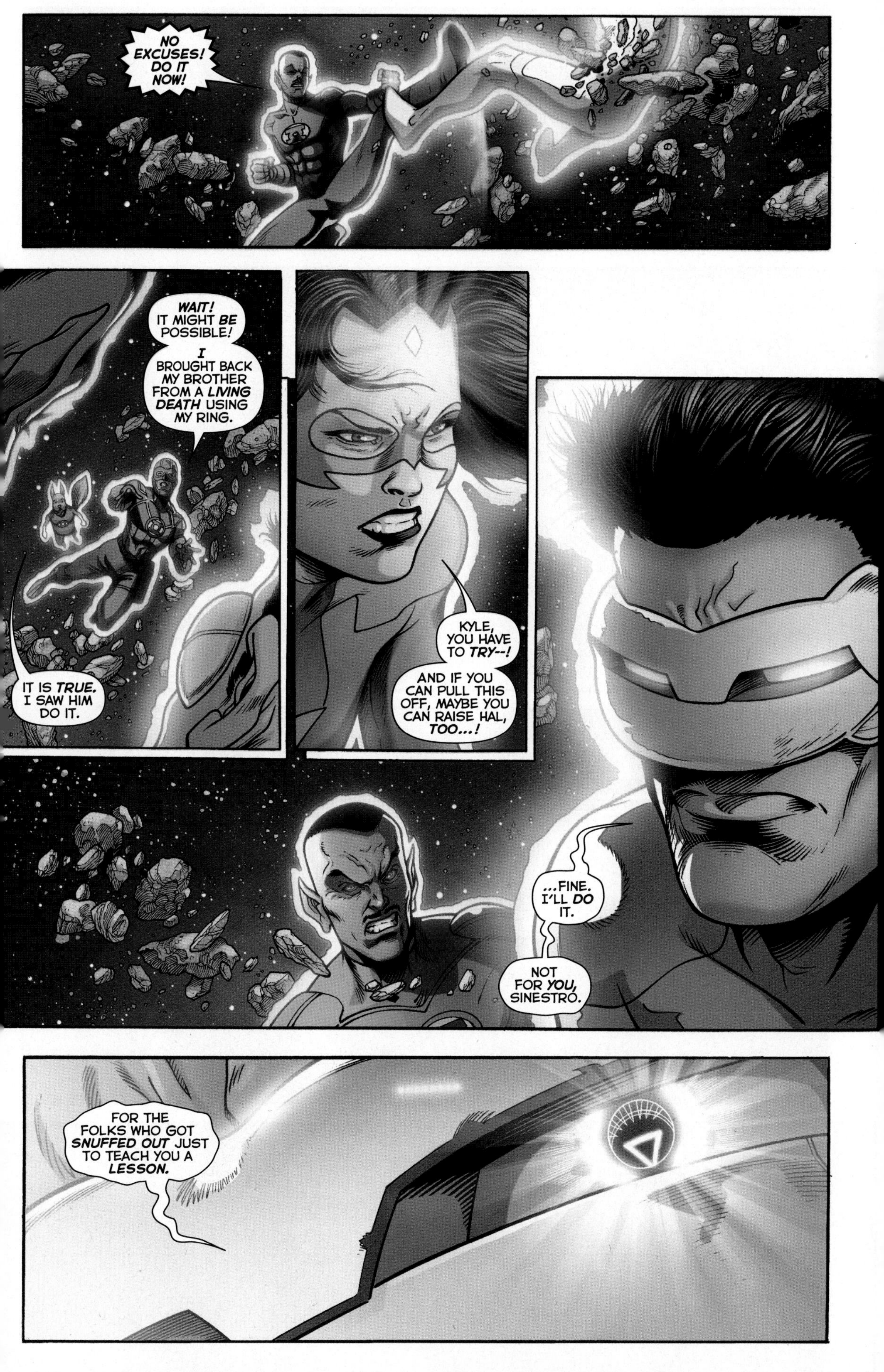
NO EXCUSES! DO IT NOW!
WAIT! IT MIGHT BE POSSIBLE!
I BROUGHT BACK MY BROTHER FROM A LIVING DEATH USING MY RING.
IT IS TRUE. I SAW HIM DO IT.
KYLE, YOU HAVE TO TRY--!
AND IF YOU CAN PULL THIS OFF, MAYBE YOU CAN RAISE HAL, TOO...!
...FINE. I'LL DO IT.
NOT FOR YOU, SINESTRO.
FOR THE FOLKS WHO GOT SNUFFED OUT JUST TO TEACH YOU A LESSON.

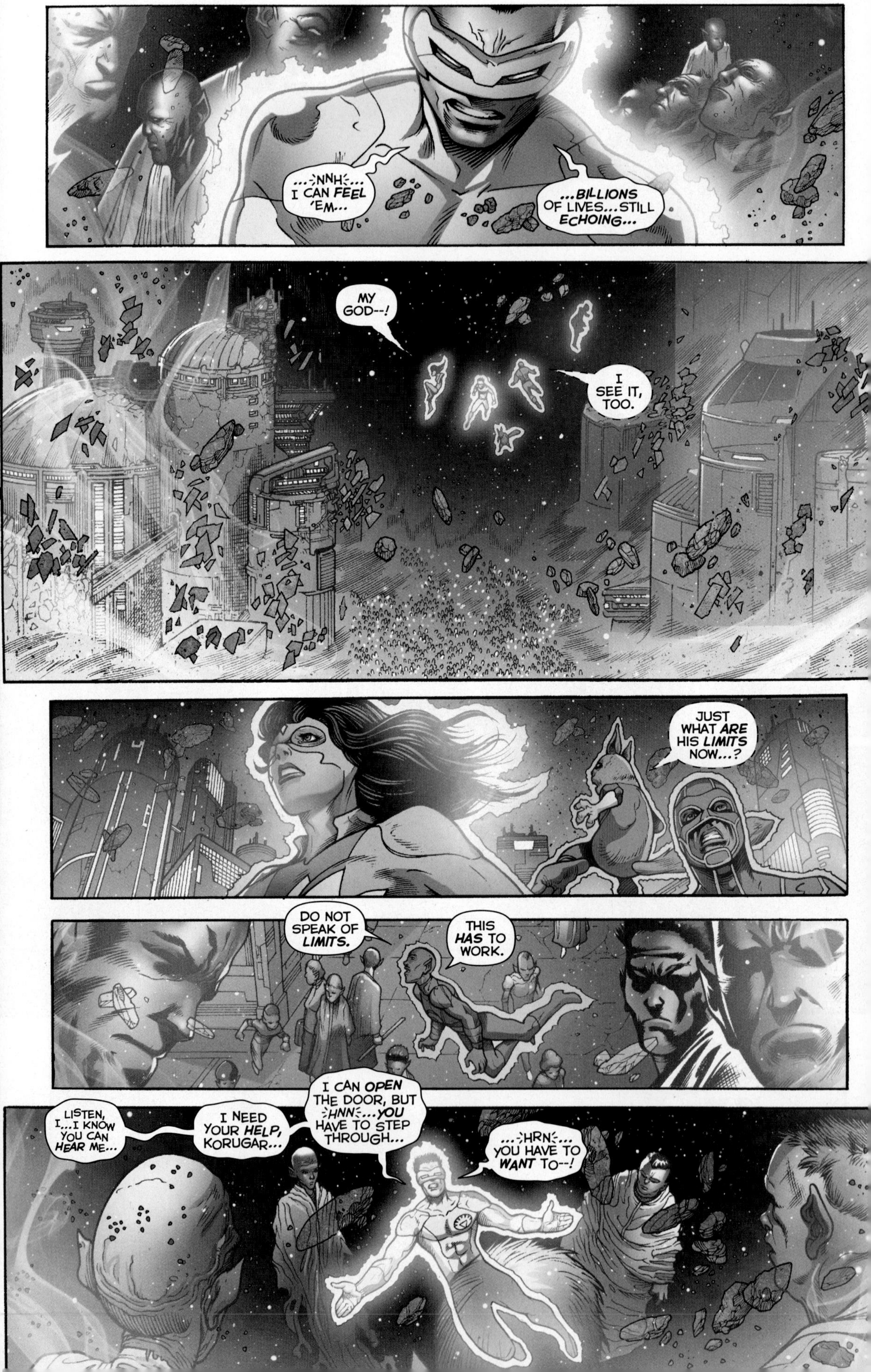
...NNH... I CAN FEEL 'EM...
...BILLIONS OF LIVES...STILL ECHOING...
MY GOD--!
I SEE IT, TOO.
JUST WHAT ARE HIS LIMITS NOW...?
DO NOT SPEAK OF LIMITS.
THIS HAS TO WORK.
LISTEN, I...I KNOW YOU CAN HEAR ME...
I NEED YOUR HELP, KORUGAR...
I CAN OPEN THE DOOR, BUT HNN...YOU HAVE TO STEP THROUGH...
...HRN... YOU HAVE TO WANT TO--!

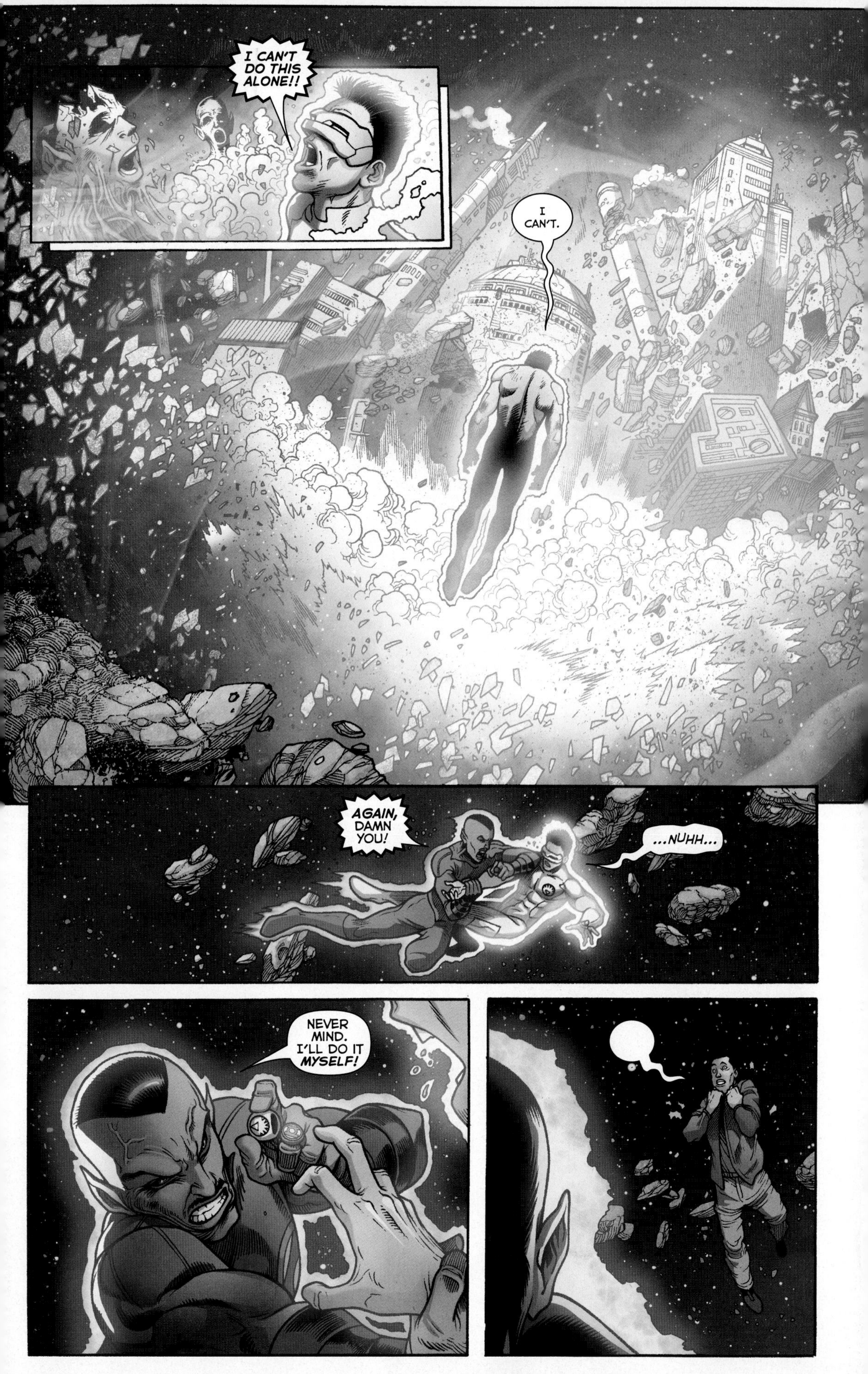
I CAN'T DO THIS ALONE!!
I CAN'T.
AGAIN, DAMN YOU!
...NUHH...
NEVER MIND. I'LL DO IT *MYSELF!*

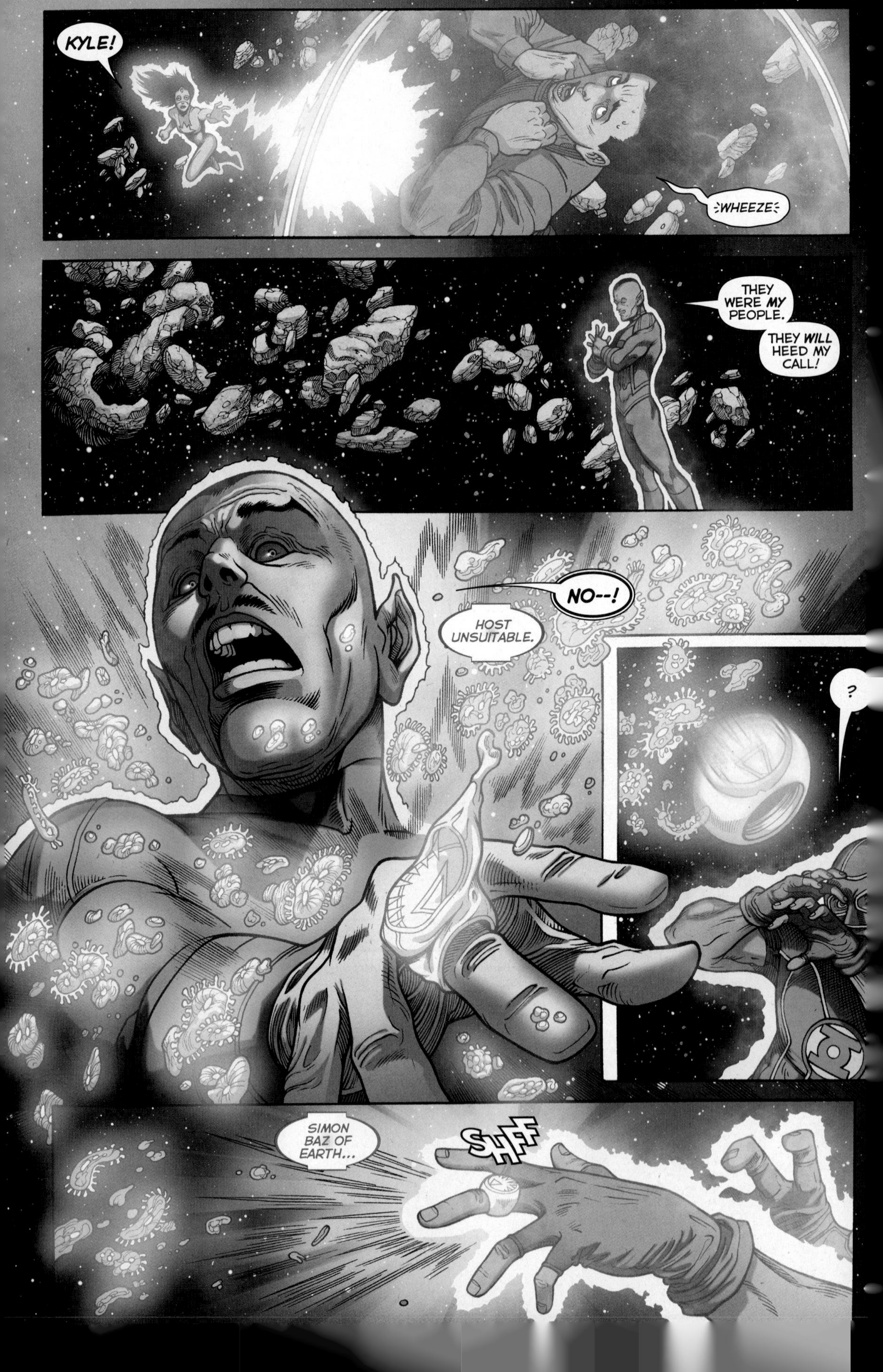
KYLE!
WHEEZE
THEY WERE MY PEOPLE.
THEY WILL HEED MY CALL!
NO--!
HOST UNSUITABLE.
?
SIMON BAZ OF EARTH...
SHFF

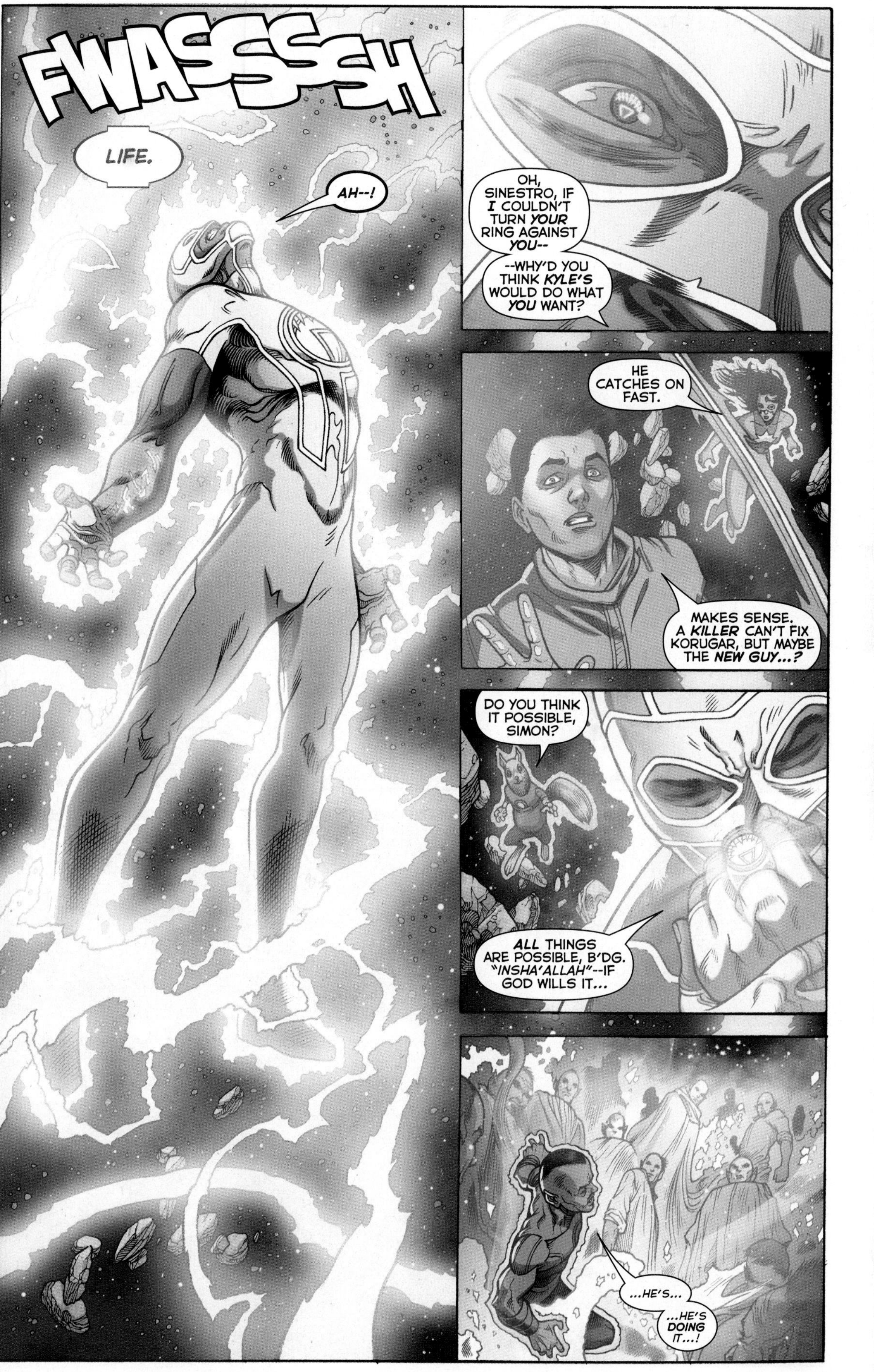
FWASSSSH
LIFE.
AH--!
OH, SINESTRO, IF I COULDN'T TURN YOUR RING AGAINST YOU--
--WHY'D YOU THINK KYLE'S WOULD DO WHAT YOU WANT?
HE CATCHES ON FAST.
MAKES SENSE. A KILLER CAN'T FIX KORUGAR, BUT MAYBE THE NEW GUY...?
DO YOU THINK IT POSSIBLE, SIMON?
ALL THINGS ARE POSSIBLE, B'DG. "INSHA'ALLAH"--IF GOD WILLS IT...
...HE'S...
...HE'S DOING IT...!

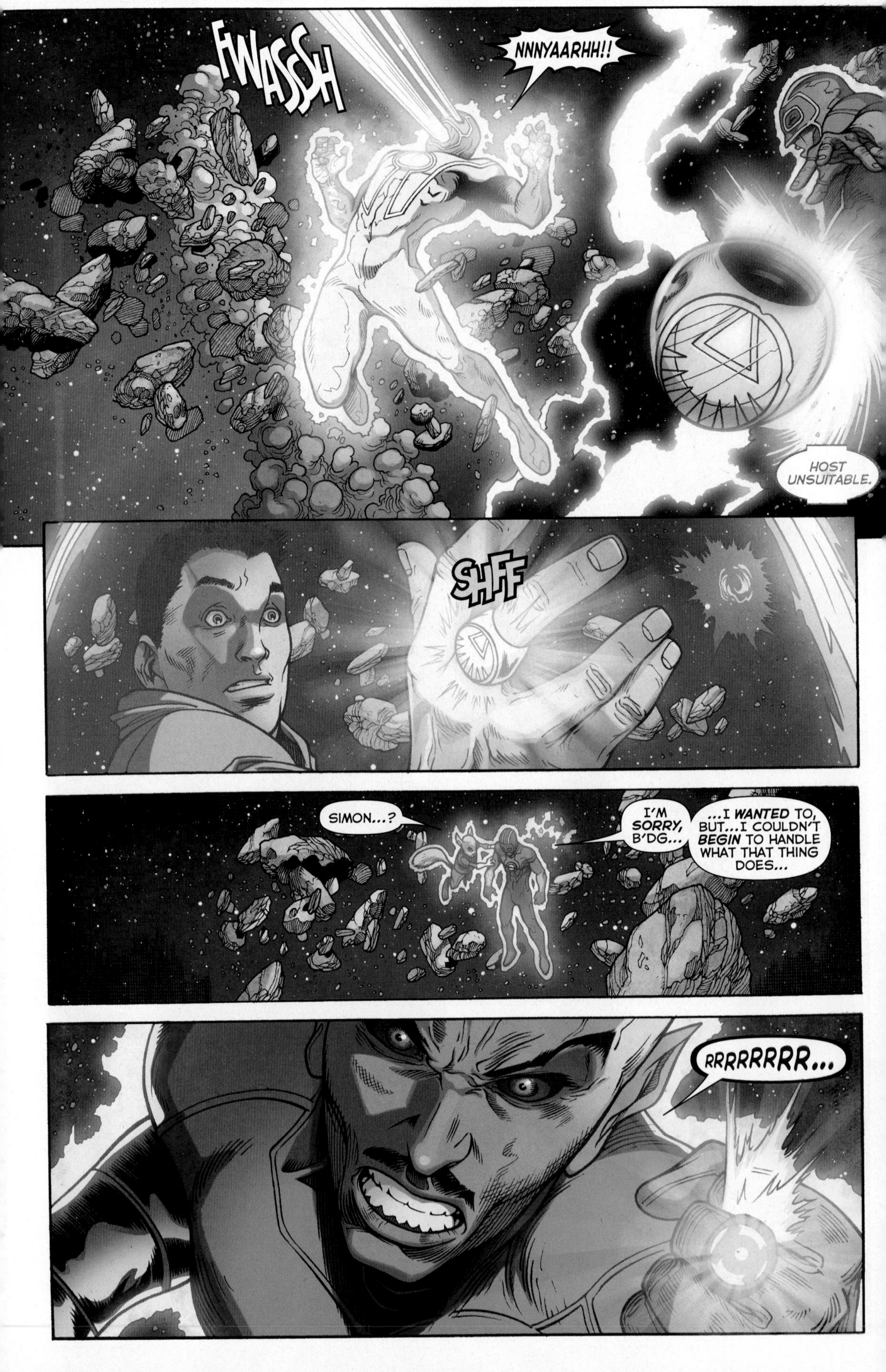
FWASSSH
NNNYAARHH!!
HOST UNSUITABLE.
SHFF
SIMON...?
I'M SORRY, B'DG...
...I WANTED TO, BUT...I COULDN'T BEGIN TO HANDLE WHAT THAT THING DOES...
RRRRRRRR...

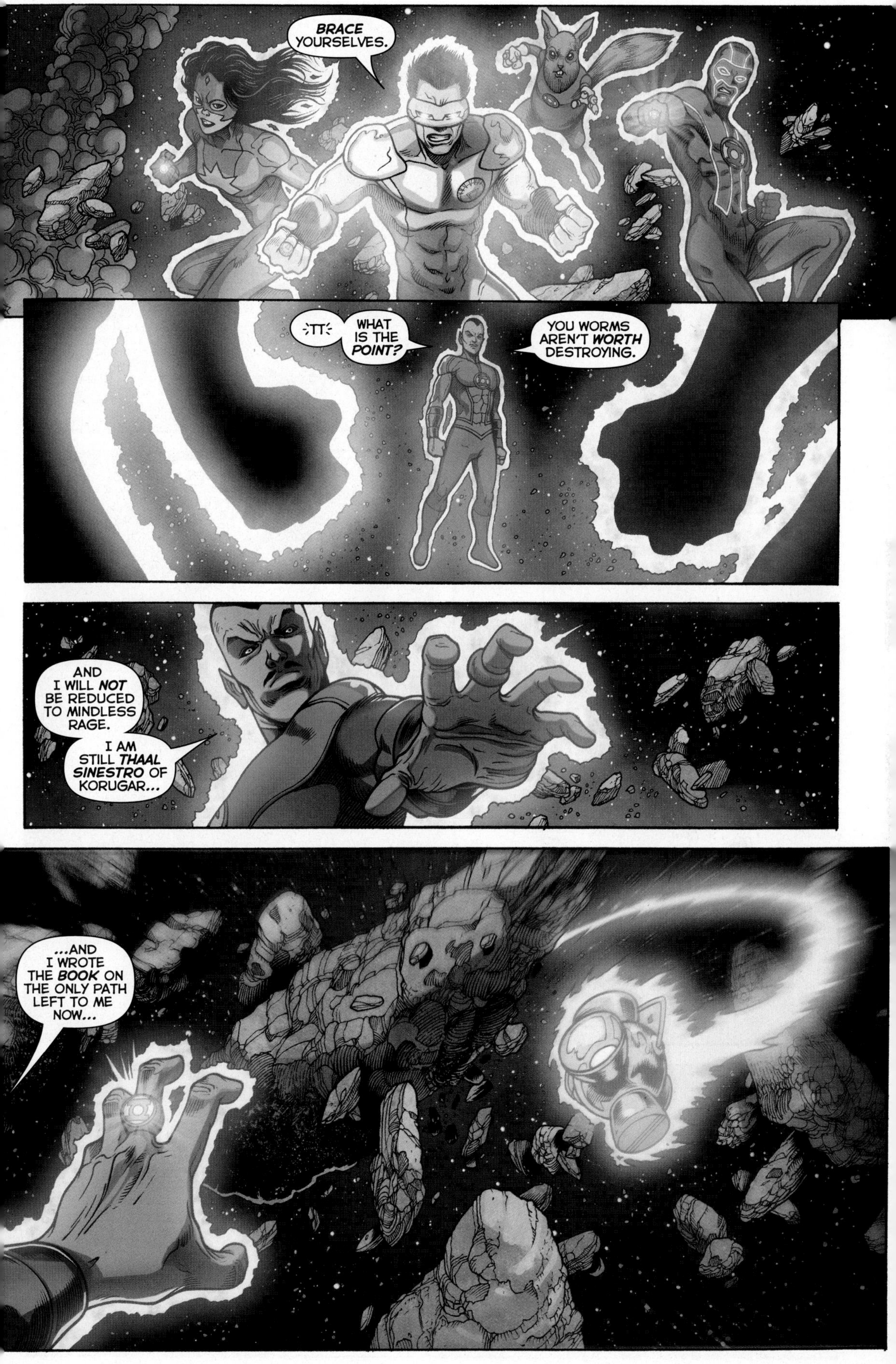
BRACE YOURSELVES.
TT
WHAT IS THE POINT?
YOU WORMS AREN'T WORTH DESTROYING.
AND I WILL NOT BE REDUCED TO MINDLESS RAGE.
I AM STILL THAAL SINESTRO OF KORUGAR...
...AND I WROTE THE BOOK ON THE ONLY PATH LEFT TO ME NOW...

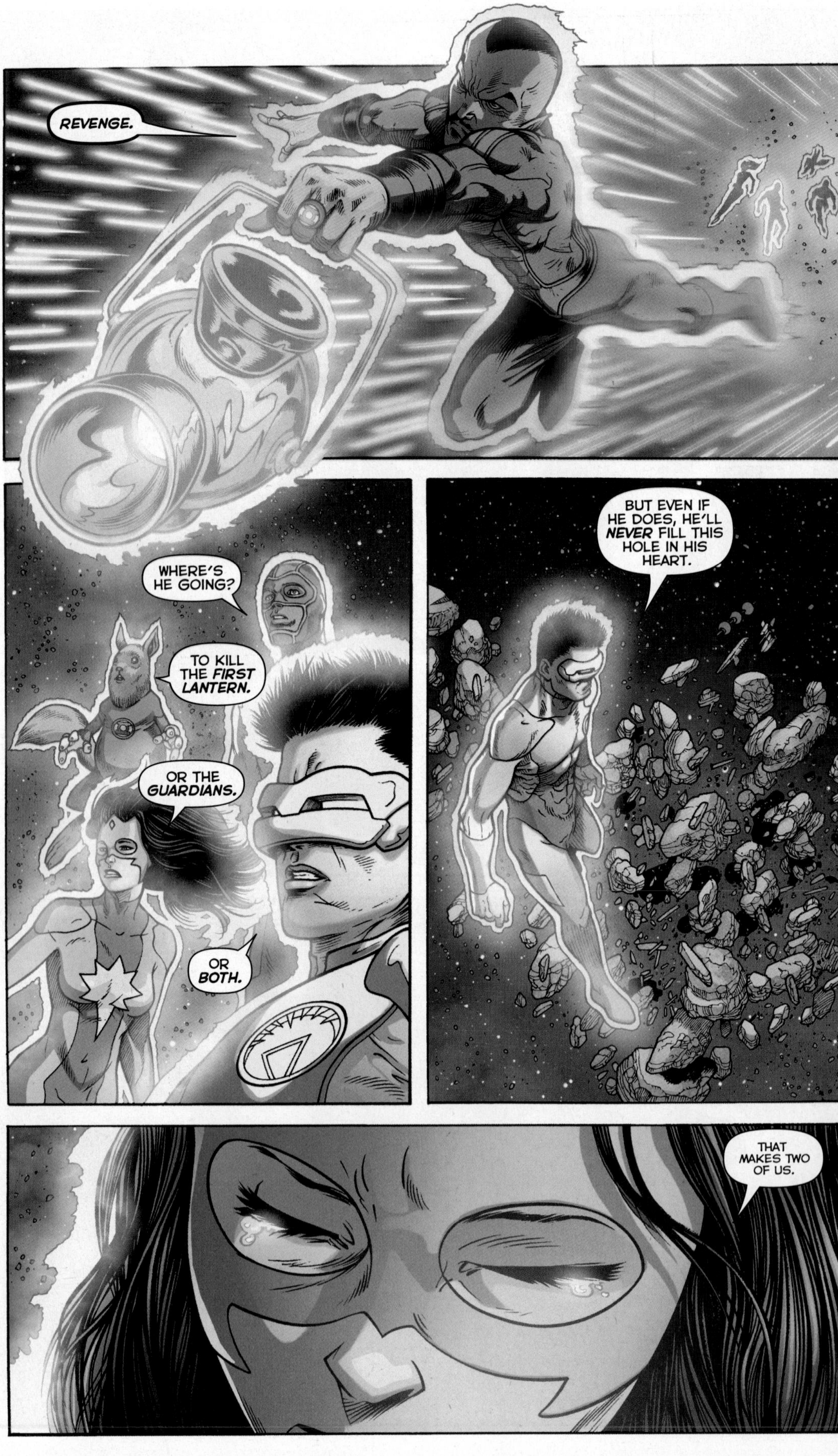
REVENGE.
WHERE'S HE GOING?
TO KILL THE FIRST LANTERN.
OR THE GUARDIANS.
OR BOTH.
BUT EVEN IF HE DOES, HE'LL NEVER FILL THIS HOLE IN HIS HEART.
THAT MAKES TWO OF US.

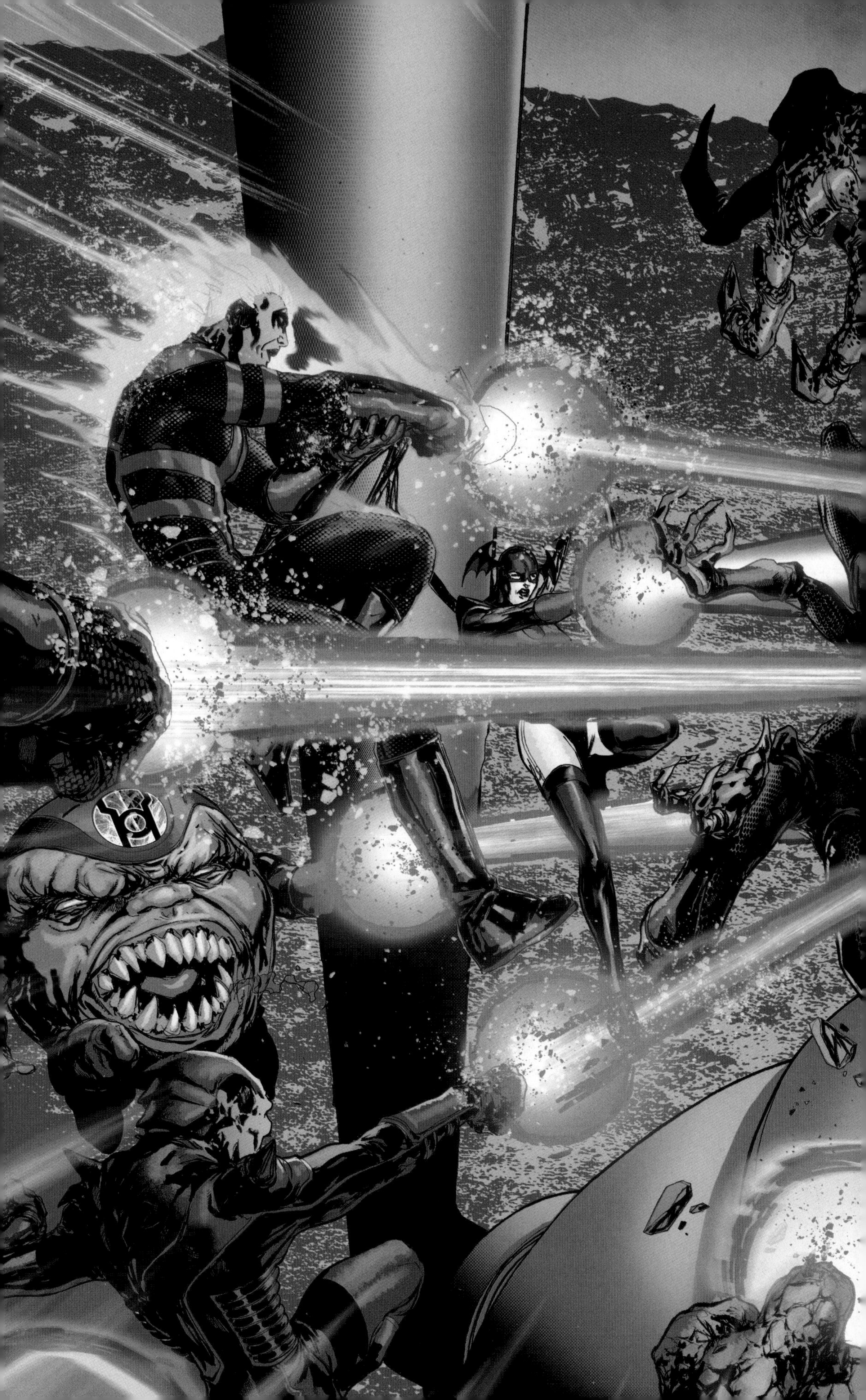

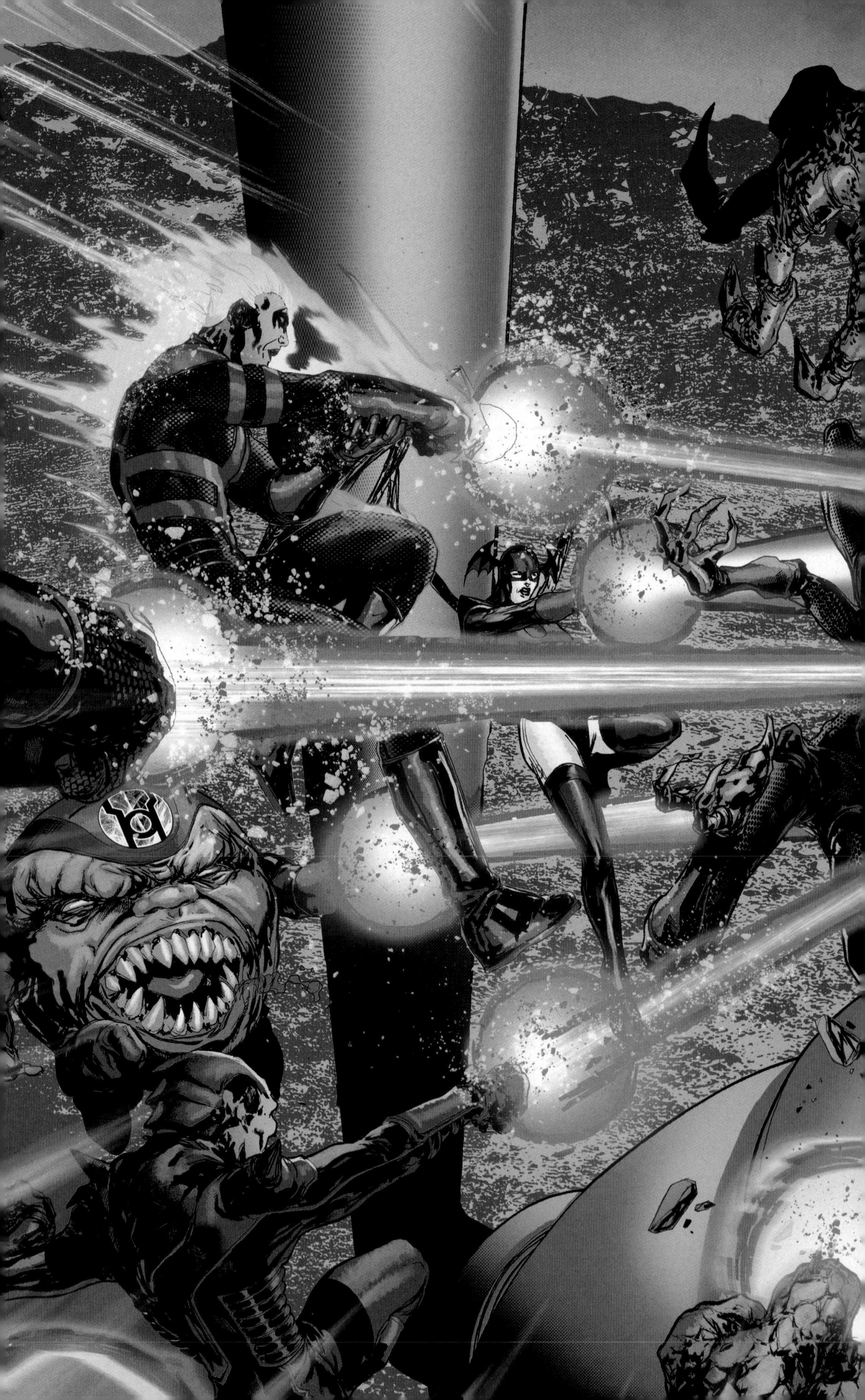

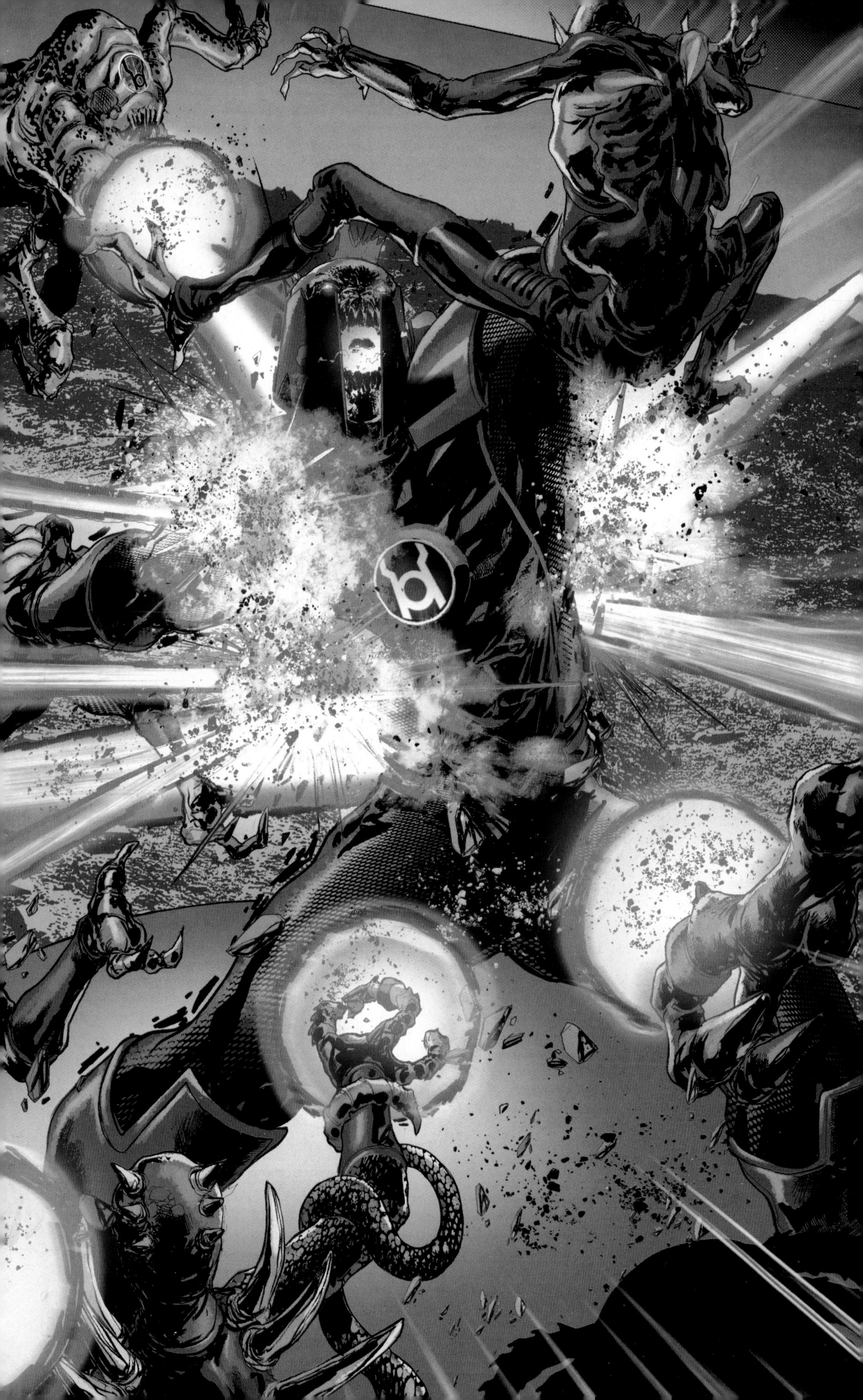

PART TWELVE: THE DEATH OF ATROCITUS

PETER MILLIGAN writer WILL CONRAD artist
cover art by MIGUEL SEPULVEDA & RAIN BEREDO

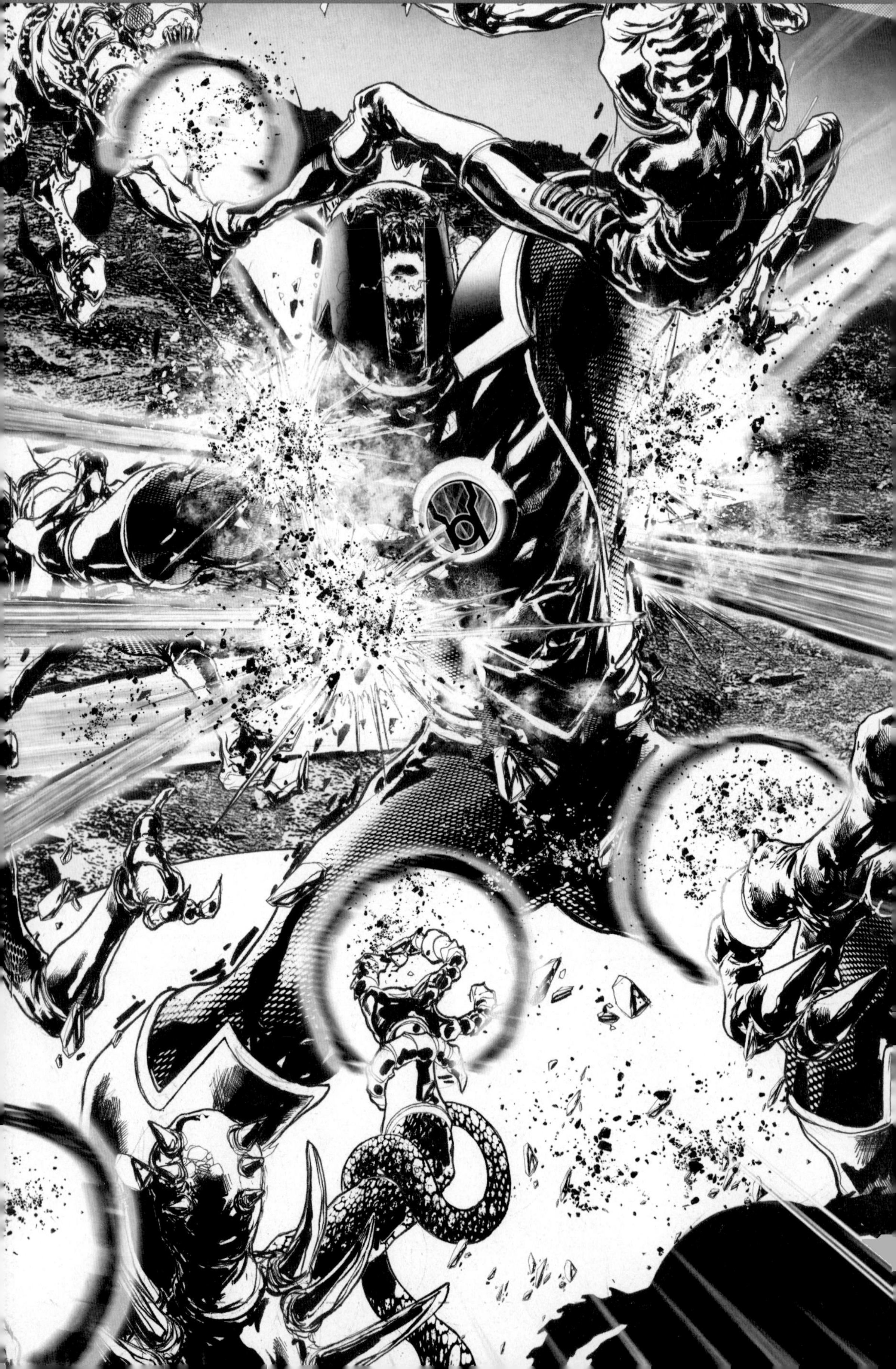

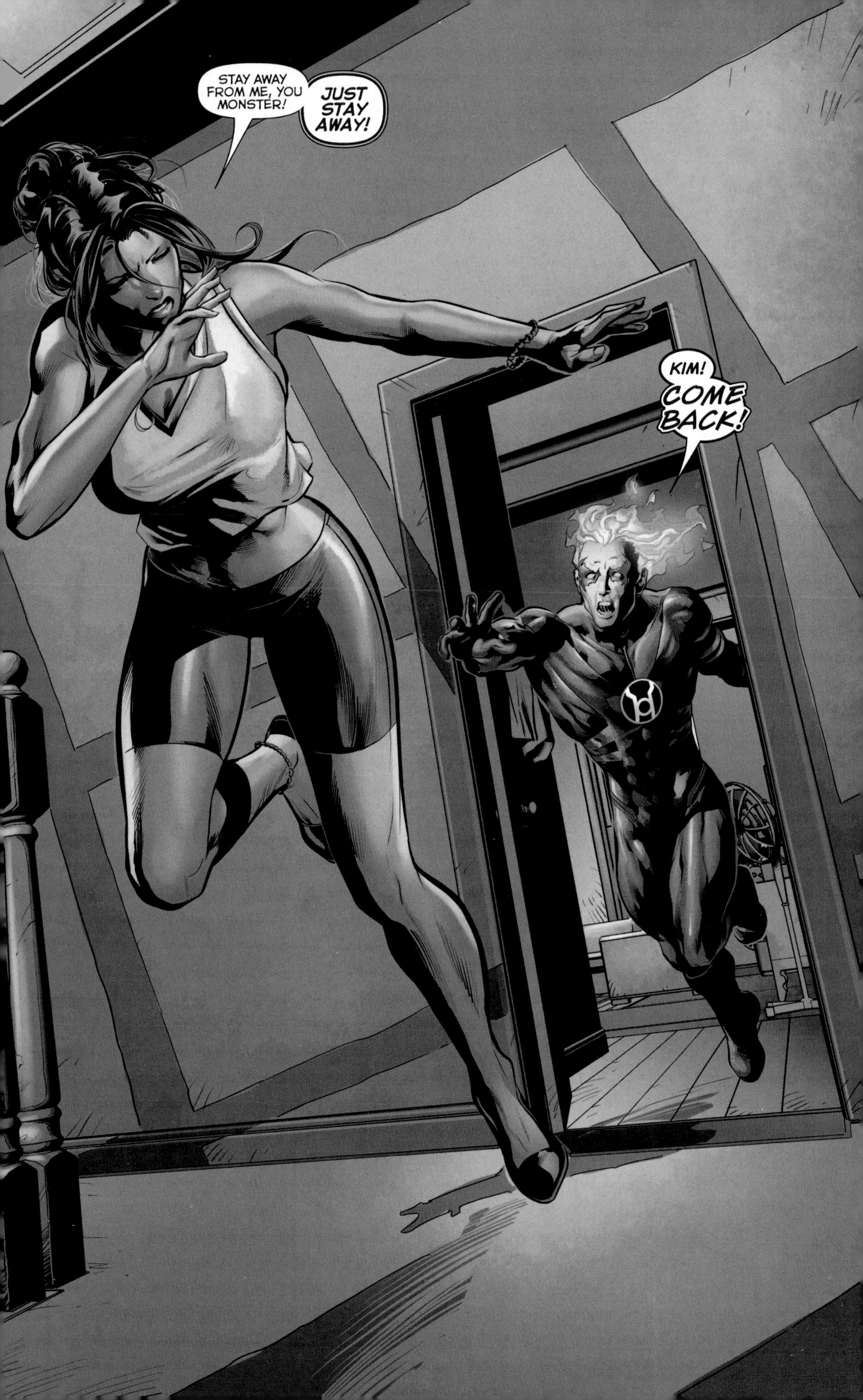
STAY AWAY FROM ME, YOU MONSTER!
JUST STAY AWAY!
KIM! COME BACK!

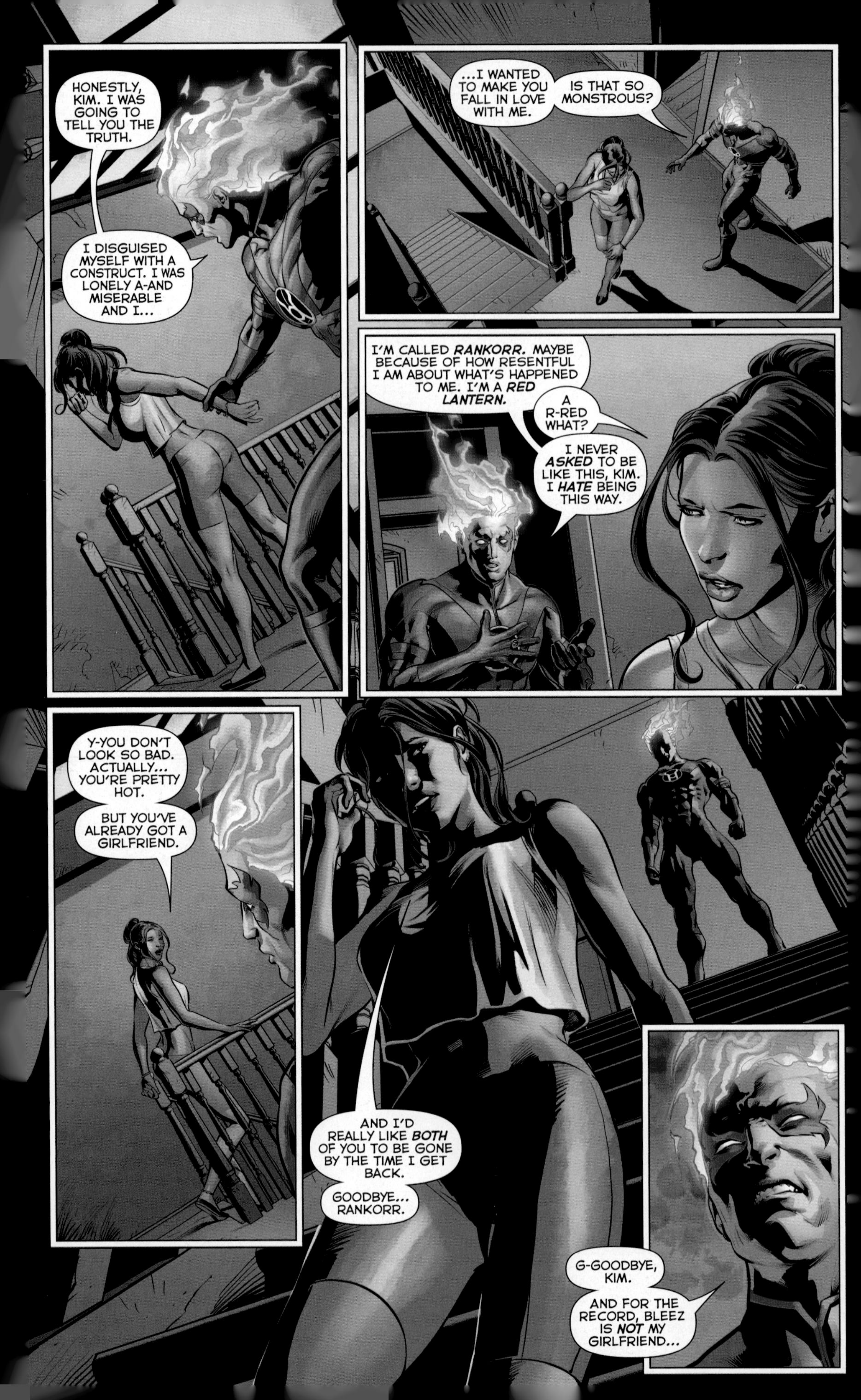
HONESTLY, KIM. I WAS GOING TO TELL YOU THE TRUTH.
I DISGUISED MYSELF WITH A CONSTRUCT. I WAS LONELY A-AND MISERABLE AND I...
...I WANTED TO MAKE YOU FALL IN LOVE WITH ME.
IS THAT SO MONSTROUS?
I'M CALLED RANKORR. MAYBE BECAUSE OF HOW RESENTFUL I AM ABOUT WHAT'S HAPPENED TO ME. I'M A RED LANTERN.
A R-RED WHAT?
I NEVER ASKED TO BE LIKE THIS, KIM. I HATE BEING THIS WAY.
Y-YOU DON'T LOOK SO BAD. ACTUALLY... YOU'RE PRETTY HOT.
BUT YOU'VE ALREADY GOT A GIRLFRIEND.
AND I'D REALLY LIKE BOTH OF YOU TO BE GONE BY THE TIME I GET BACK.
GOODBYE... RANKORR.
G-GOODBYE, KIM.
AND FOR THE RECORD, BLEEZ IS NOT MY GIRLFRIEND...

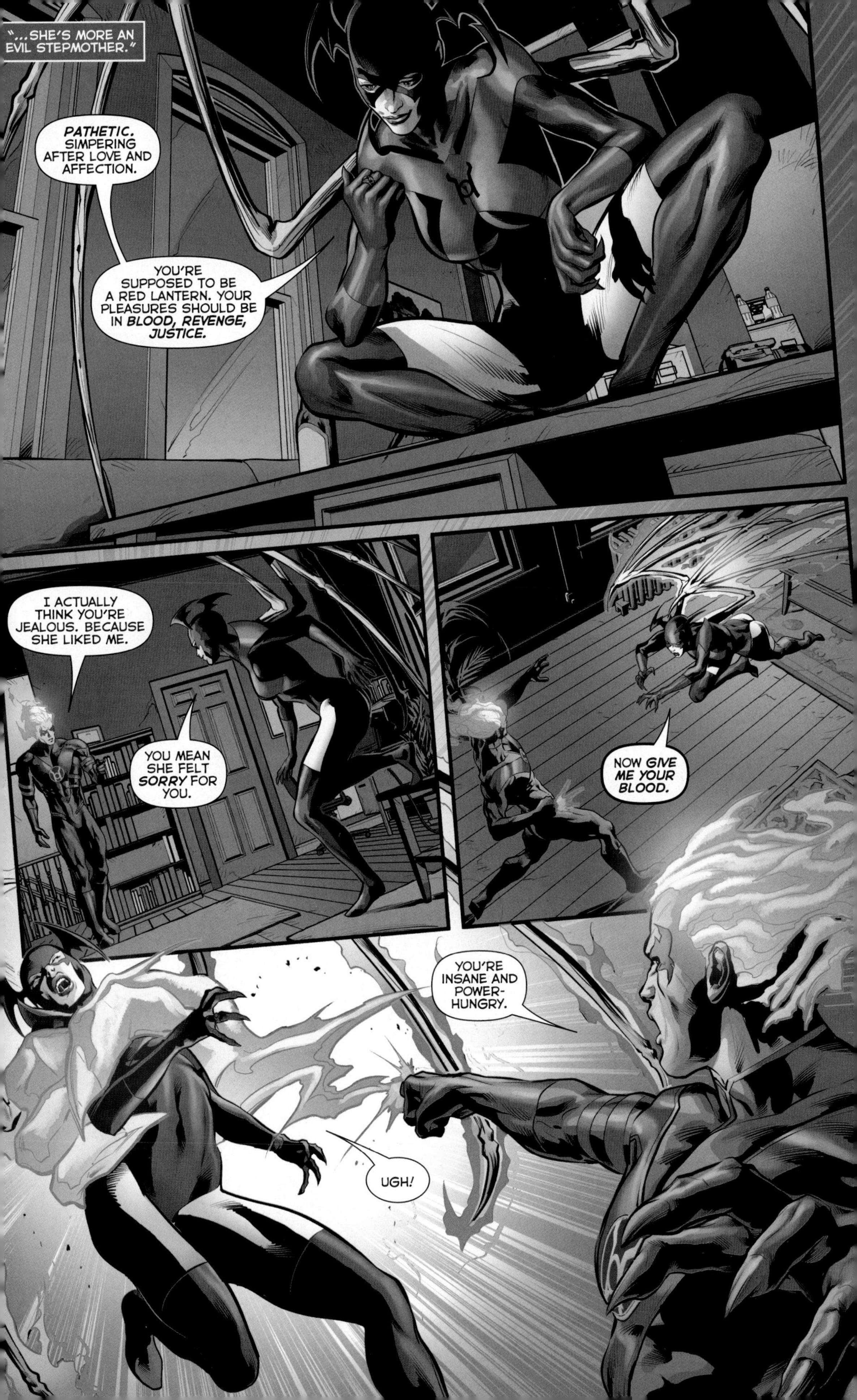
"...SHE'S MORE AN EVIL STEPMOTHER."
PATHETIC. SIMPERING AFTER LOVE AND AFFECTION.
YOU'RE SUPPOSED TO BE A RED LANTERN. YOUR PLEASURES SHOULD BE IN BLOOD, REVENGE, JUSTICE.
I ACTUALLY THINK YOU'RE JEALOUS. BECAUSE SHE LIKED ME.
YOU MEAN SHE FELT SORRY FOR YOU.
NOW GIVE ME YOUR BLOOD.
YOU'RE INSANE AND POWER-HUNGRY.
UGH!

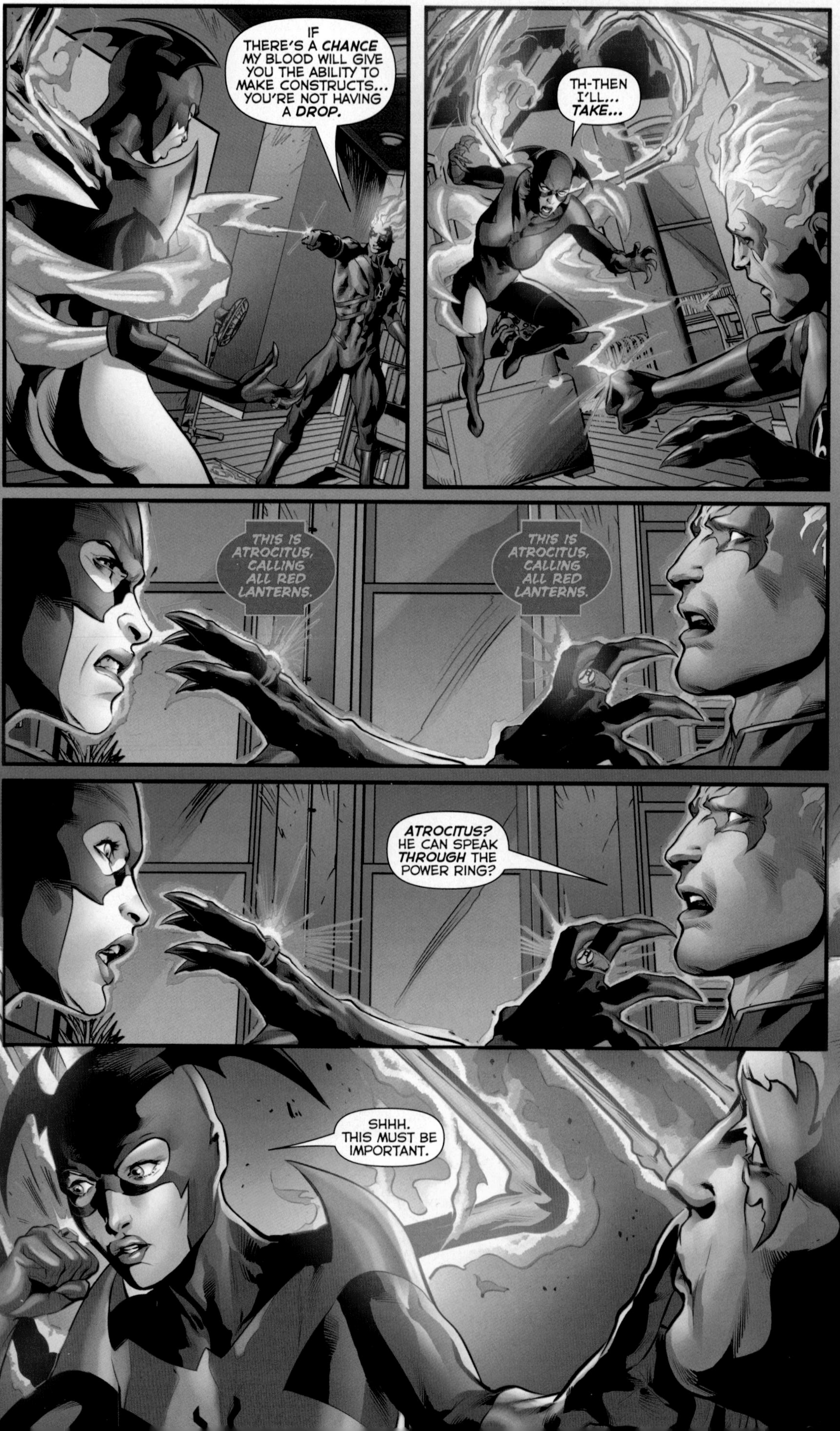
IF THERE'S A CHANCE MY BLOOD WILL GIVE YOU THE ABILITY TO MAKE CONSTRUCTS... YOU'RE NOT HAVING A DROP.
TH-THEN I'LL... TAKE...
THIS IS ATROCITUS, CALLING ALL RED LANTERNS.
THIS IS ATROCITUS, CALLING ALL RED LANTERNS.
ATROCITUS? HE CAN SPEAK THROUGH THE POWER RING?
SHHH. THIS MUST BE IMPORTANT.

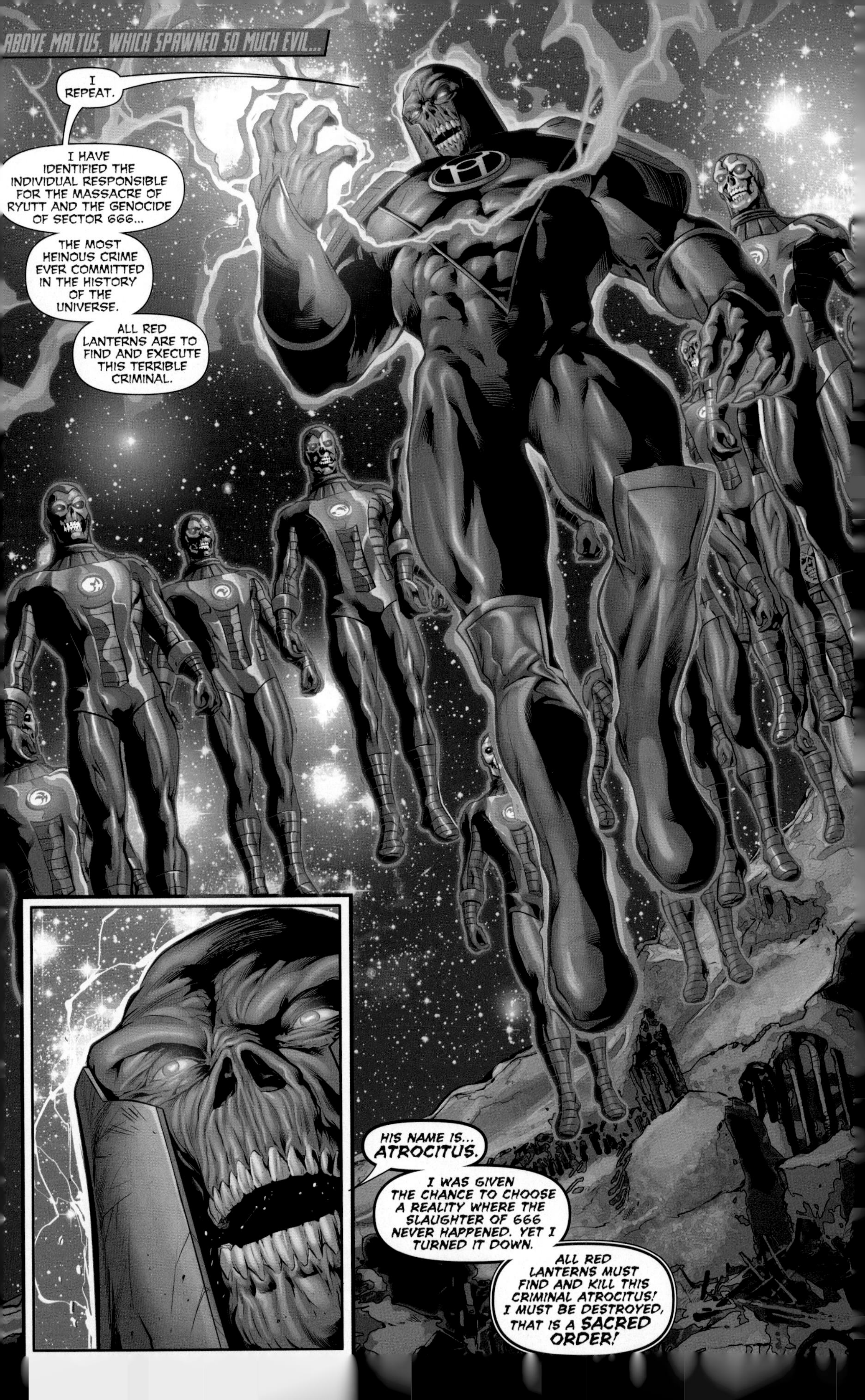

ABOVE MALTUS, WHICH SPAWNED SO MUCH EVIL...
I REPEAT.
I HAVE IDENTIFIED THE INDIVIDUAL RESPONSIBLE FOR THE MASSACRE OF RYUTT AND THE GENOCIDE OF SECTOR 666...
THE MOST HEINOUS CRIME EVER COMMITTED IN THE HISTORY OF THE UNIVERSE.
ALL RED LANTERNS ARE TO FIND AND EXECUTE THIS TERRIBLE CRIMINAL.
HIS NAME IS... ATROCITUS.
I WAS GIVEN THE CHANCE TO CHOOSE A REALITY WHERE THE SLAUGHTER OF 666 NEVER HAPPENED. YET I TURNED IT DOWN.
ALL RED LANTERNS MUST FIND AND KILL THIS CRIMINAL ATROCITUS! I MUST BE DESTROYED, THAT IS A SACRED ORDER!

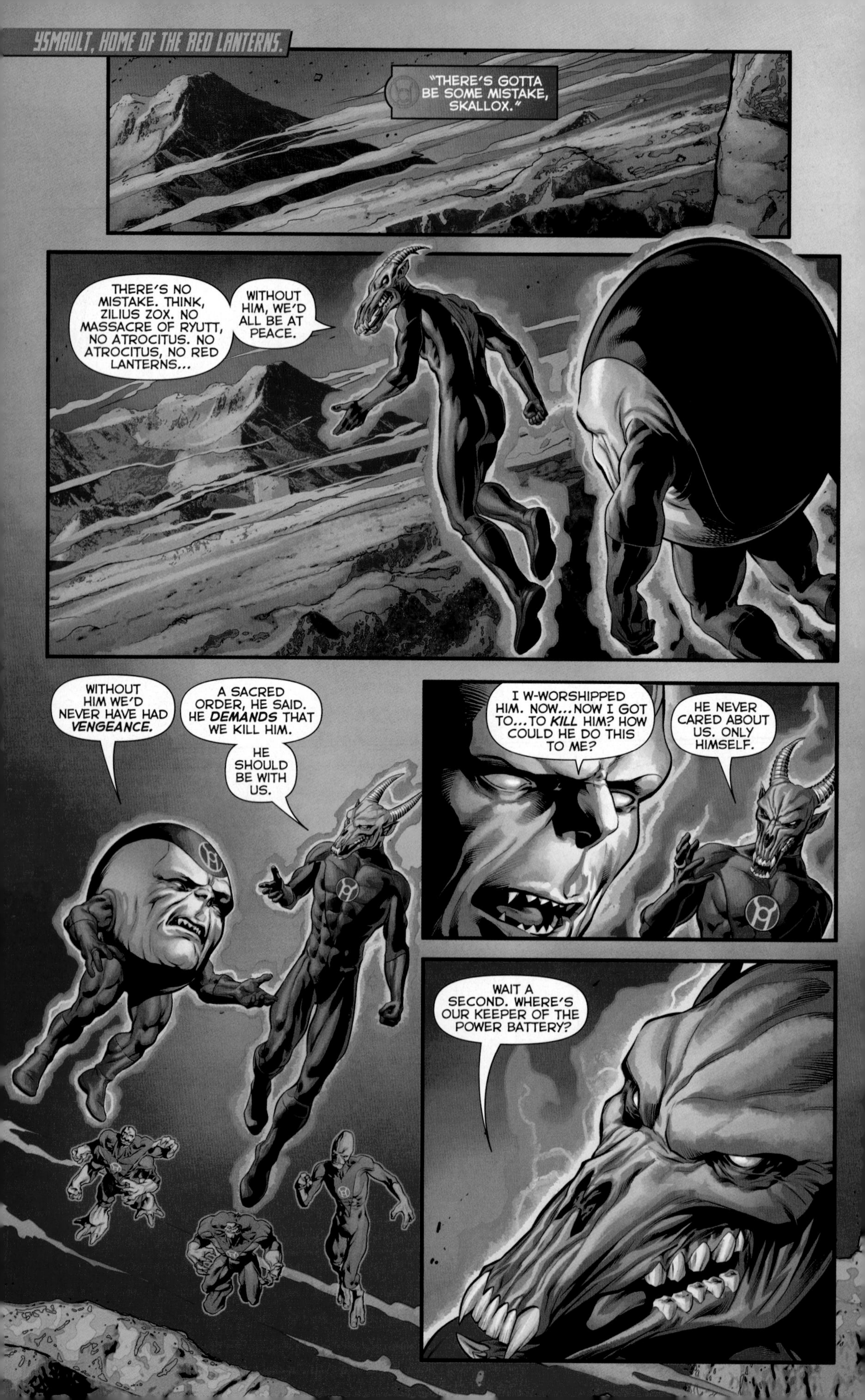
YSMAULT, HOME OF THE RED LANTERNS.
"THERE'S GOTTA BE SOME MISTAKE, SKALLOX."
THERE'S NO MISTAKE. THINK, ZILIUS ZOX. NO MASSACRE OF RYUTT, NO ATROCITUS. NO ATROCITUS, NO RED LANTERNS...
WITHOUT HIM, WE'D ALL BE AT PEACE.
WITHOUT HIM WE'D NEVER HAVE HAD *VENGEANCE.*
A SACRED ORDER, HE SAID. HE *DEMANDS* THAT WE KILL HIM.
HE SHOULD BE WITH US.
I W-WORSHIPPED HIM. NOW...NOW I GOT TO...TO *KILL* HIM? HOW COULD HE DO THIS TO ME?
HE NEVER CARED ABOUT US. ONLY HIMSELF.
WAIT A SECOND. WHERE'S OUR KEEPER OF THE POWER BATTERY?

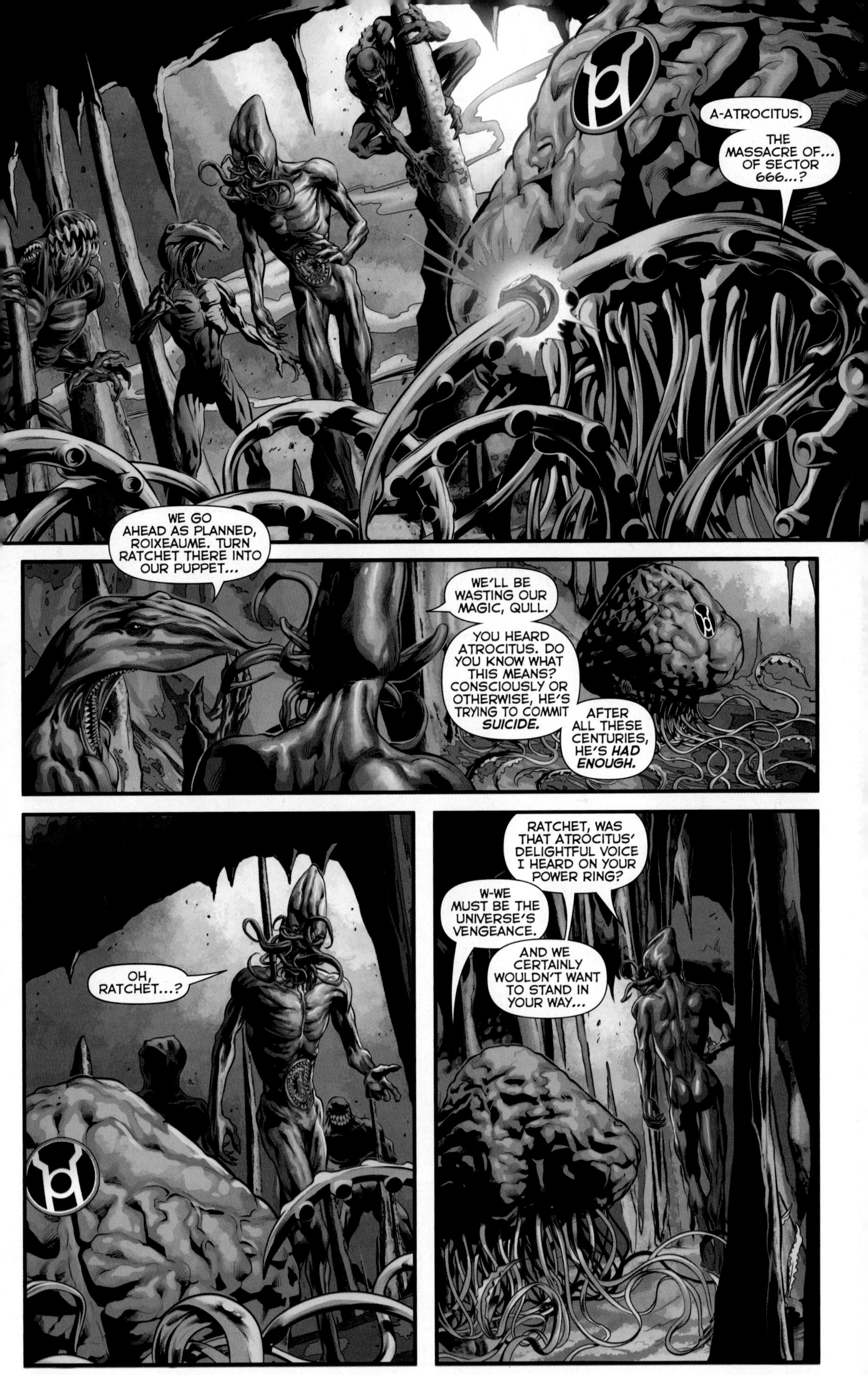
A-ATROCITUS.
THE MASSACRE OF... OF SECTOR 666...?
WE GO AHEAD AS PLANNED, ROIXEAUME. TURN RATCHET THERE INTO OUR PUPPET...
WE'LL BE WASTING OUR MAGIC, QULL.
YOU HEARD ATROCITUS. DO YOU KNOW WHAT THIS MEANS? CONSCIOUSLY OR OTHERWISE, HE'S TRYING TO COMMIT SUICIDE.
AFTER ALL THESE CENTURIES, HE'S HAD ENOUGH.
OH, RATCHET...?
RATCHET, WAS THAT ATROCITUS' DELIGHTFUL VOICE I HEARD ON YOUR POWER RING?
W-WE MUST BE THE UNIVERSE'S VENGEANCE.
AND WE CERTAINLY WOULDN'T WANT TO STAND IN YOUR WAY...

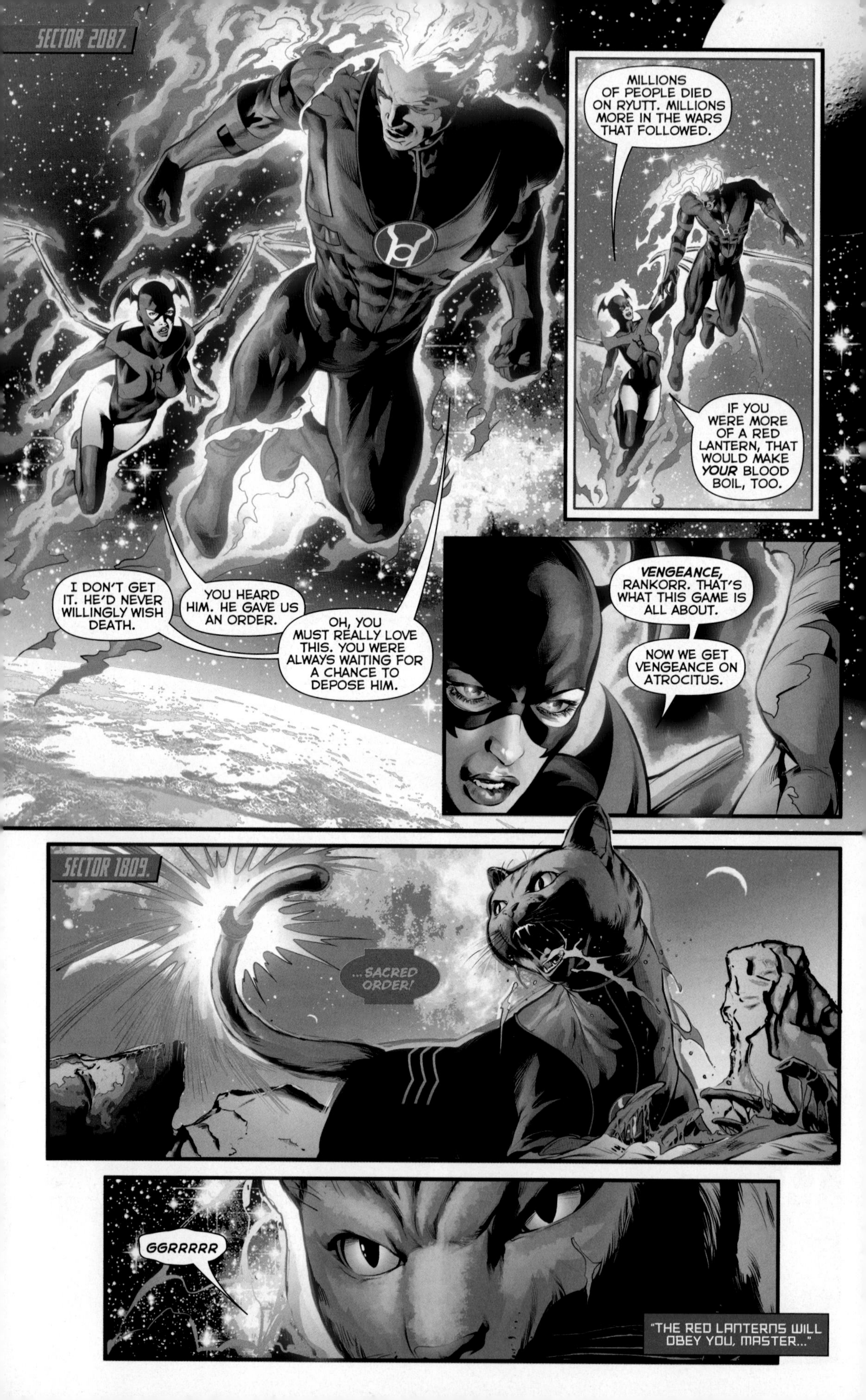

SECTOR 2087.
MILLIONS OF PEOPLE DIED ON RYUTT. MILLIONS MORE IN THE WARS THAT FOLLOWED.
IF YOU WERE MORE OF A RED LANTERN, THAT WOULD MAKE YOUR BLOOD BOIL, TOO.
I DON'T GET IT. HE'D NEVER WILLINGLY WISH DEATH.
YOU HEARD HIM. HE GAVE US AN ORDER.
OH, YOU MUST REALLY LOVE THIS. YOU WERE ALWAYS WAITING FOR A CHANCE TO DEPOSE HIM.
VENGEANCE, RANKORR. THAT'S WHAT THIS GAME IS ALL ABOUT.
NOW WE GET VENGEANCE ON ATROCITUS.
SECTOR 1809.
...SACRED ORDER!
GGRRRRR
"THE RED LANTERNS WILL OBEY YOU, MASTER..."

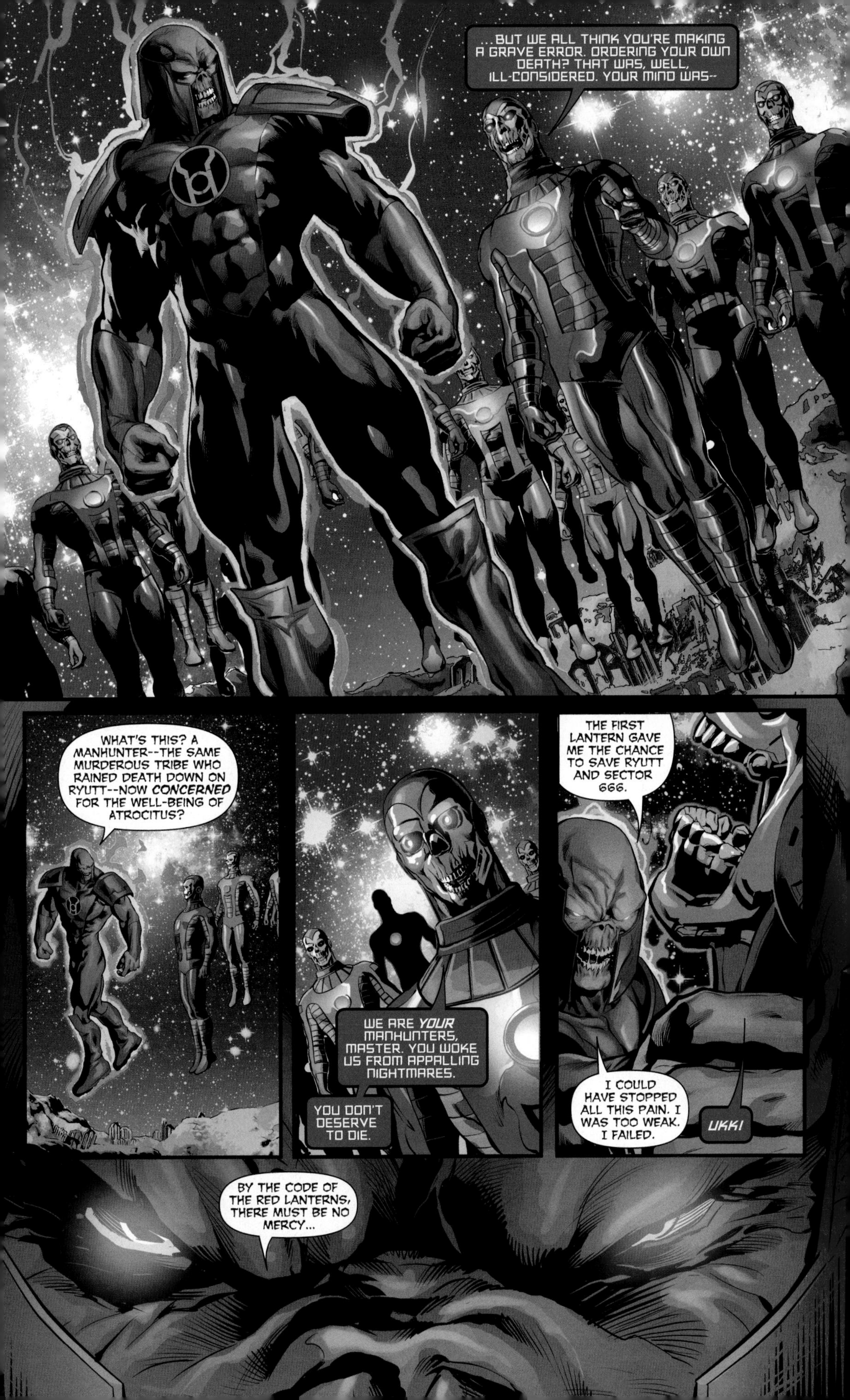
...BUT WE ALL THINK YOU'RE MAKING A GRAVE ERROR. ORDERING YOUR OWN DEATH? THAT WAS, WELL, ILL-CONSIDERED. YOUR MIND WAS--
WHAT'S THIS? A MANHUNTER--THE SAME MURDEROUS TRIBE WHO RAINED DEATH DOWN ON RYUTT--NOW CONCERNED FOR THE WELL-BEING OF ATROCITUS?
WE ARE YOUR MANHUNTERS, MASTER. YOU WOKE US FROM APPALLING NIGHTMARES.
YOU DON'T DESERVE TO DIE.
THE FIRST LANTERN GAVE ME THE CHANCE TO SAVE RYUTT AND SECTOR 666.
I COULD HAVE STOPPED ALL THIS PAIN. I WAS TOO WEAK. I FAILED.
UKK!
BY THE CODE OF THE RED LANTERNS, THERE MUST BE NO MERCY...

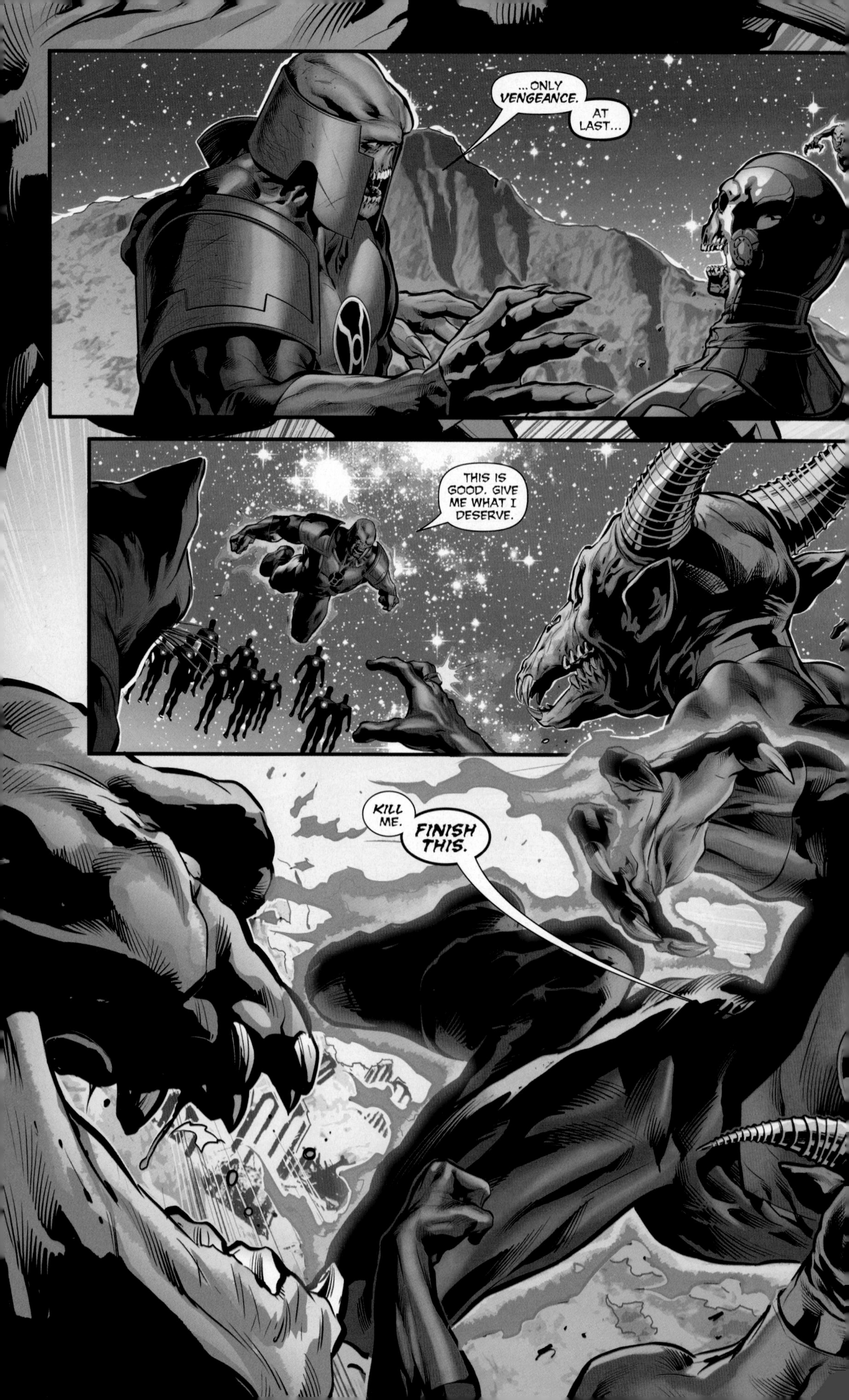
...ONLY VENGEANCE.
AT LAST...
THIS IS GOOD. GIVE ME WHAT I DESERVE.
KILL ME.
FINISH THIS.

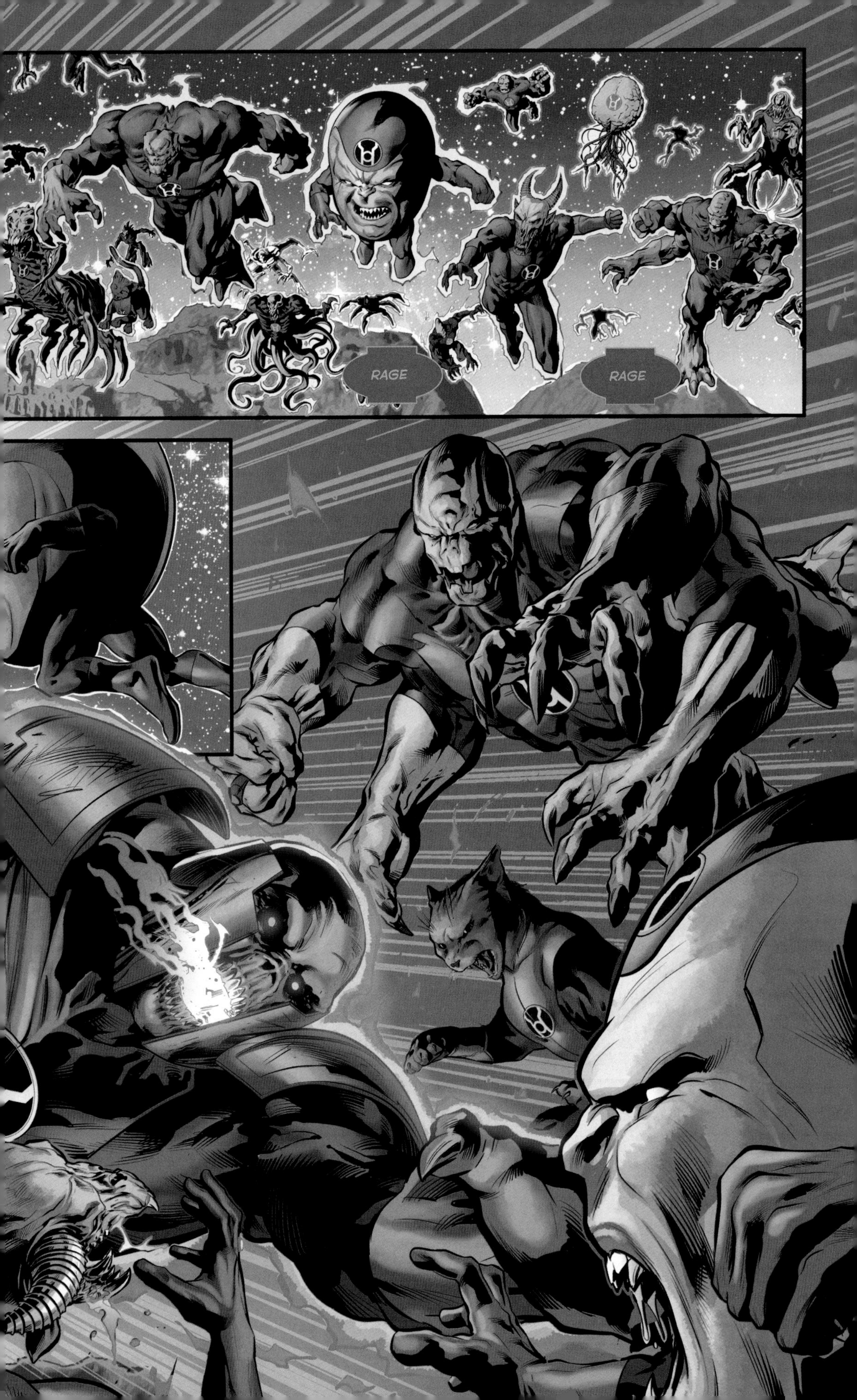
RAGE
RAGE

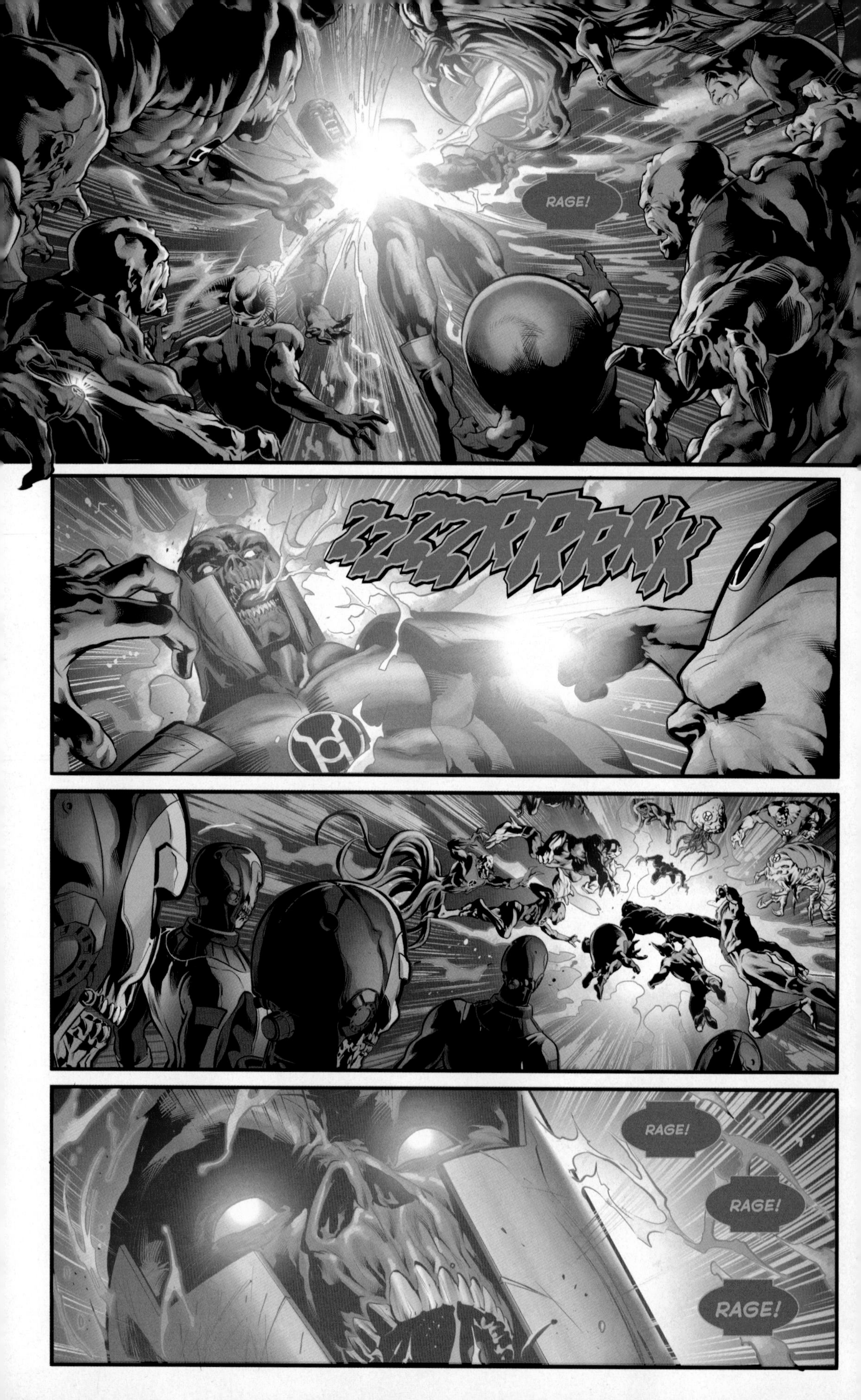
RAGE!
ZZZZRRRRKK
RAGE!
RAGE!
RAGE!

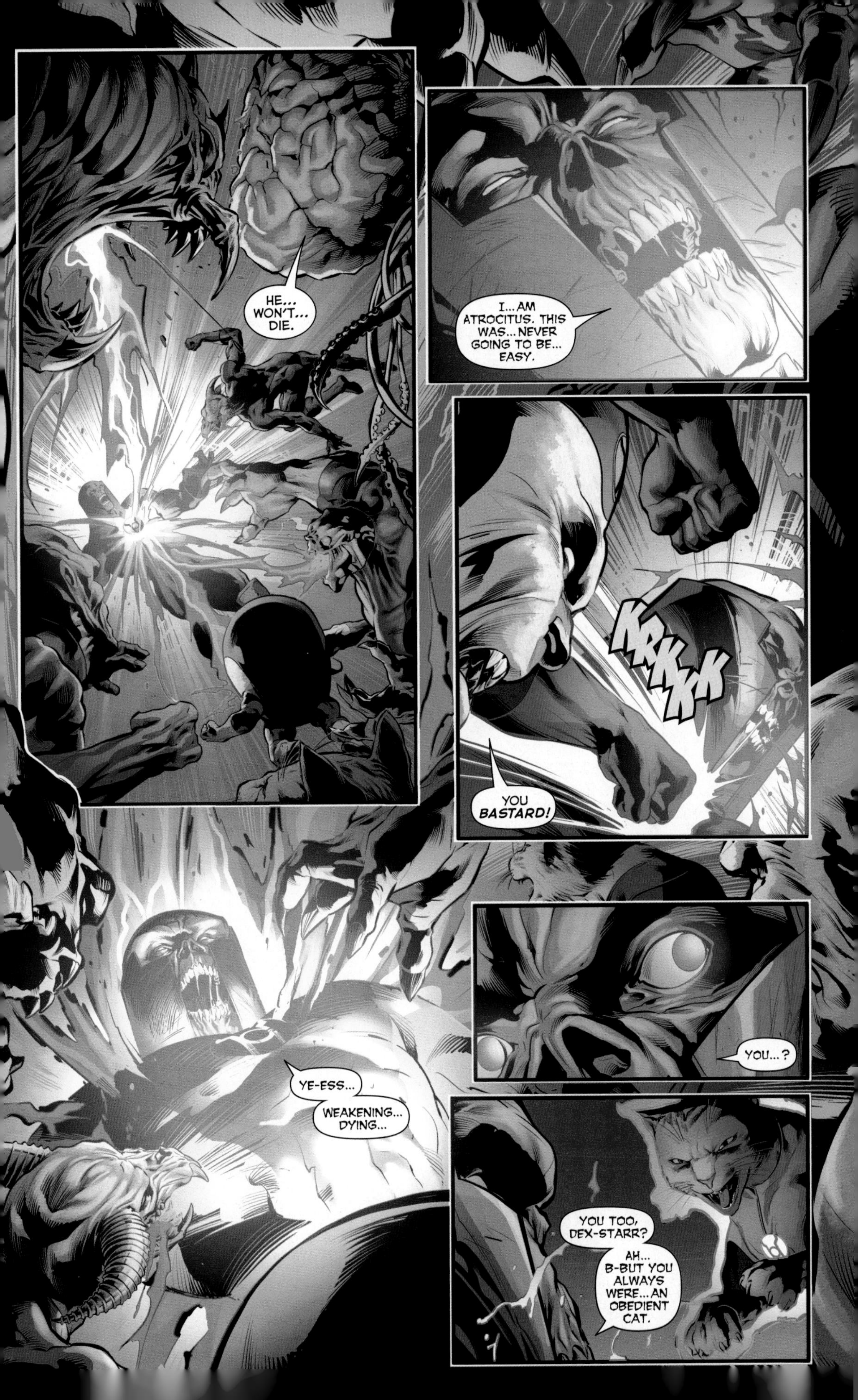
HE... WON'T... DIE.
I...AM ATROCITUS. THIS WAS...NEVER GOING TO BE... EASY.
KRKKK
YOU BASTARD!
YE-ESS...
WEAKENING... DYING...
YOU...?
YOU TOO, DEX-STARR?
AH... B-BUT YOU ALWAYS WERE...AN OBEDIENT CAT.

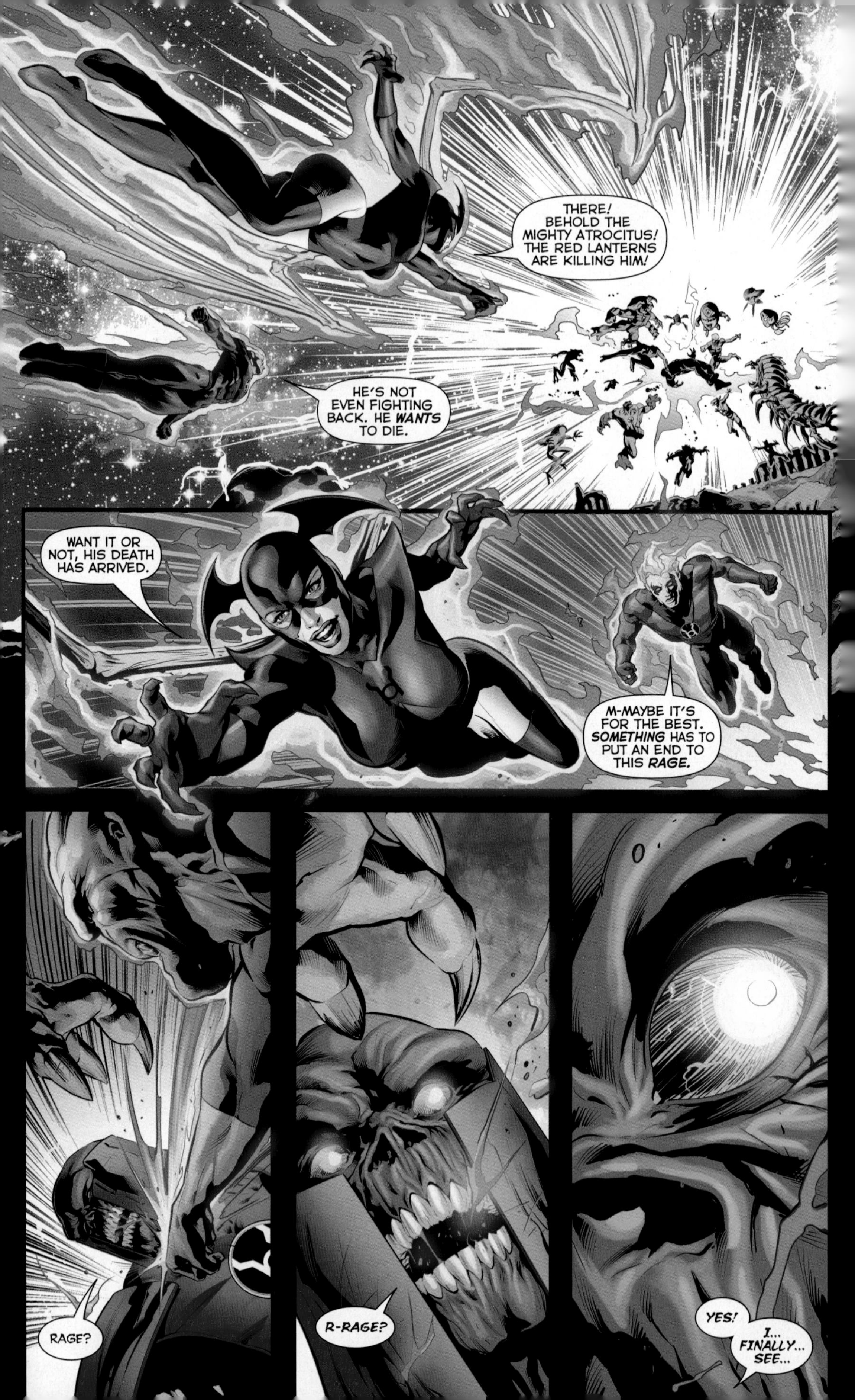
THERE! BEHOLD THE MIGHTY ATROCITUS! THE RED LANTERNS ARE KILLING HIM!
HE'S NOT EVEN FIGHTING BACK. HE *WANTS* TO DIE.
WANT IT OR NOT, HIS DEATH HAS ARRIVED.
M-MAYBE IT'S FOR THE BEST. *SOMETHING* HAS TO PUT AN END TO THIS *RAGE.*
RAGE?
R-RAGE?
YES!
I... FINALLY... SEE...

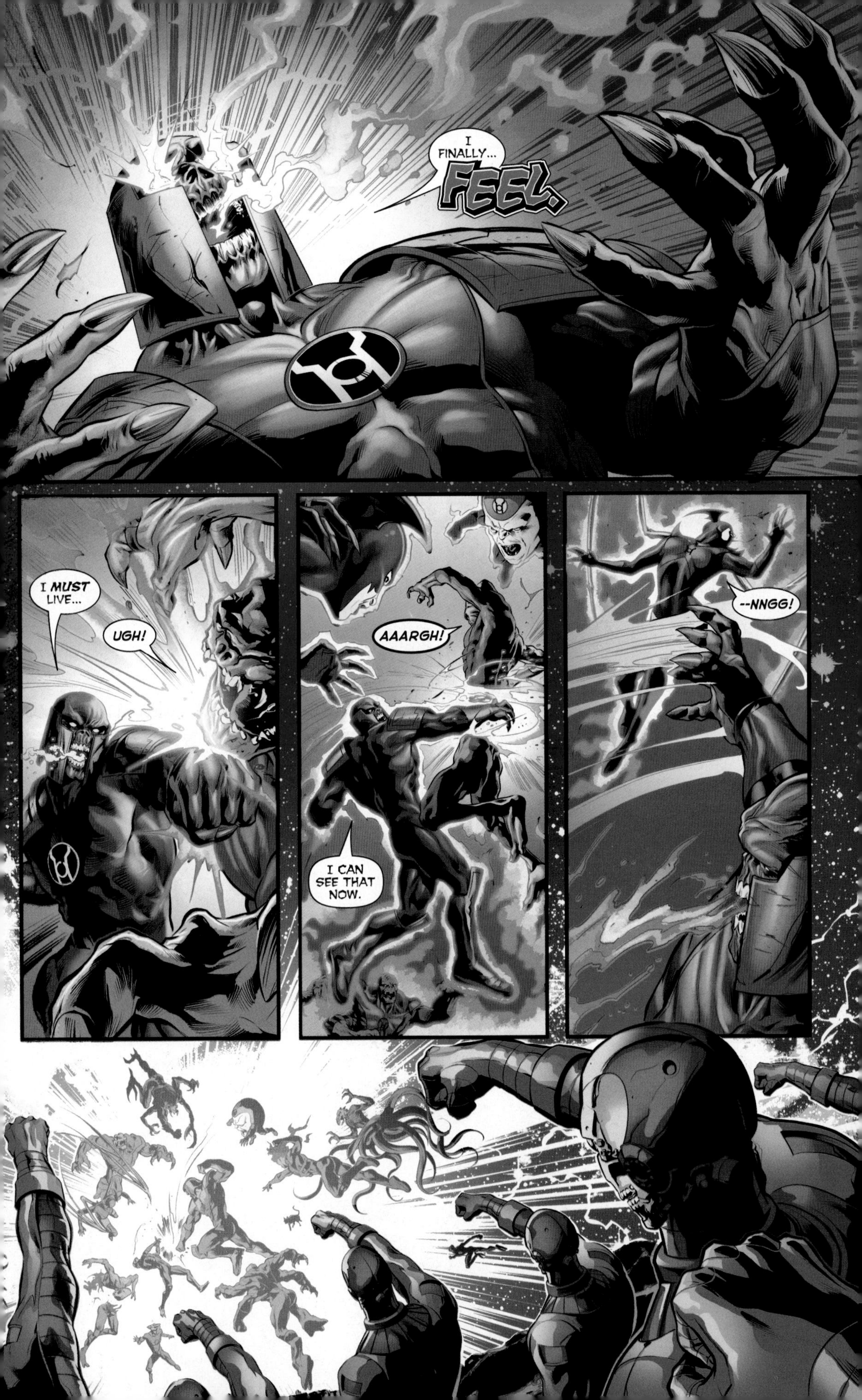
I FINALLY...
FEEL.
I MUST LIVE...
UGH!
AAARGH!
I CAN SEE THAT NOW.
--NNGG!

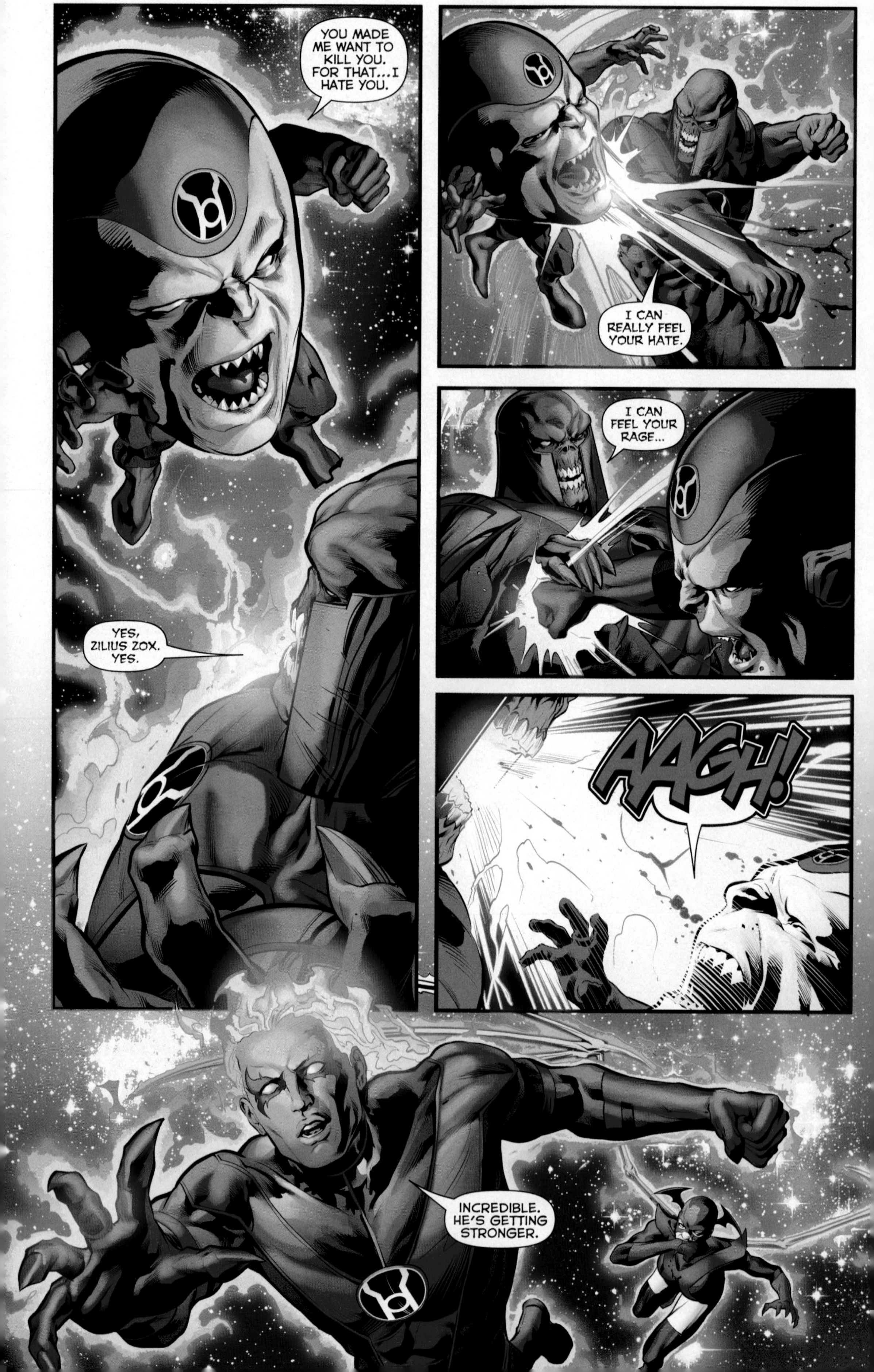
YOU MADE ME WANT TO KILL YOU. FOR THAT...I HATE YOU.
YES, ZILIUS ZOX. YES.
I CAN REALLY FEEL YOUR HATE.
I CAN FEEL YOUR RAGE...
AAGH!
INCREDIBLE. HE'S GETTING STRONGER.

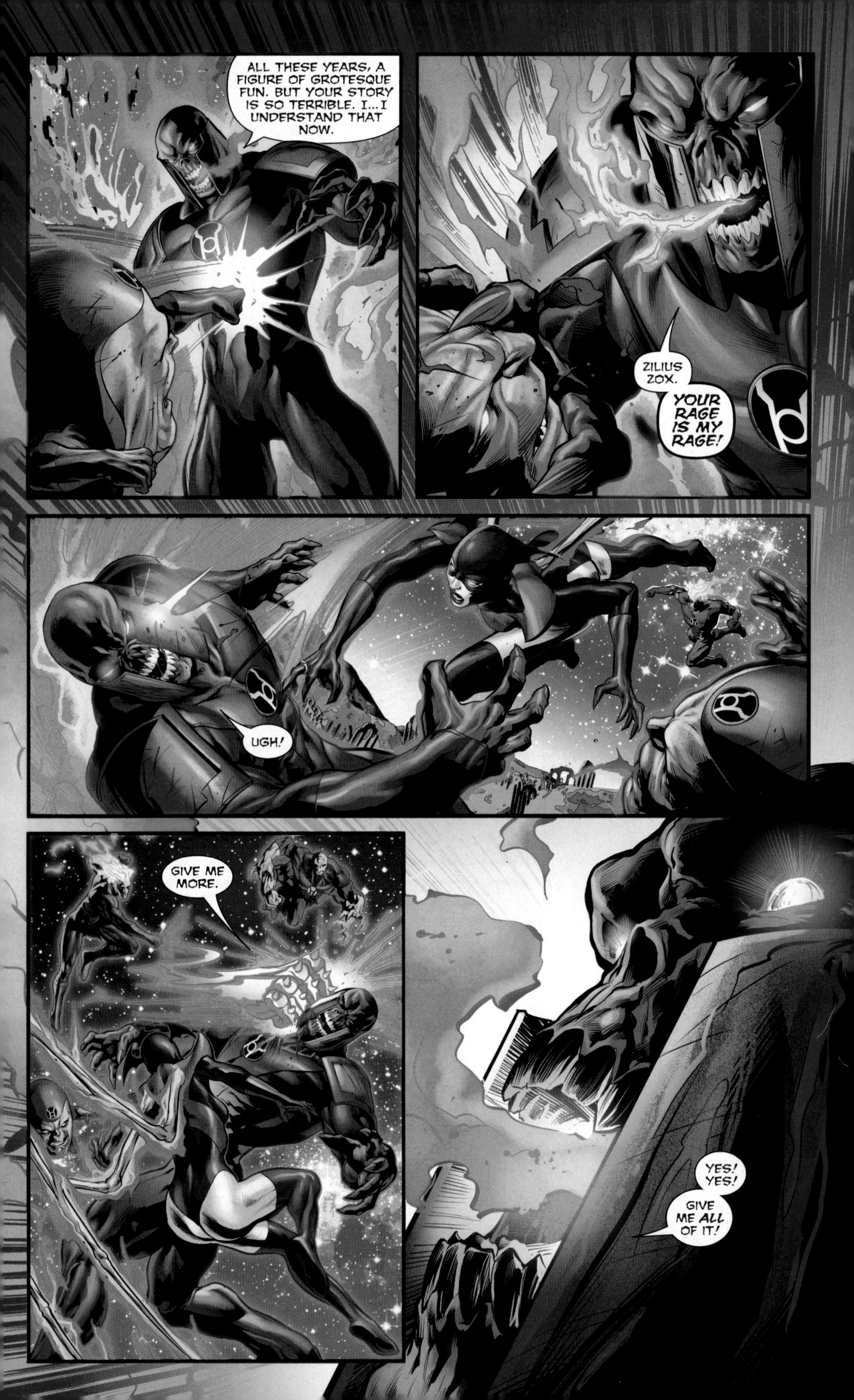
ALL THESE YEARS, A FIGURE OF GROTESQUE FUN. BUT YOUR STORY IS SO TERRIBLE. I...I UNDERSTAND THAT NOW.
ZILIUS ZOX.
YOUR RAGE IS MY RAGE!
UGH!
GIVE ME MORE.
YES! YES!
GIVE ME ALL OF IT!

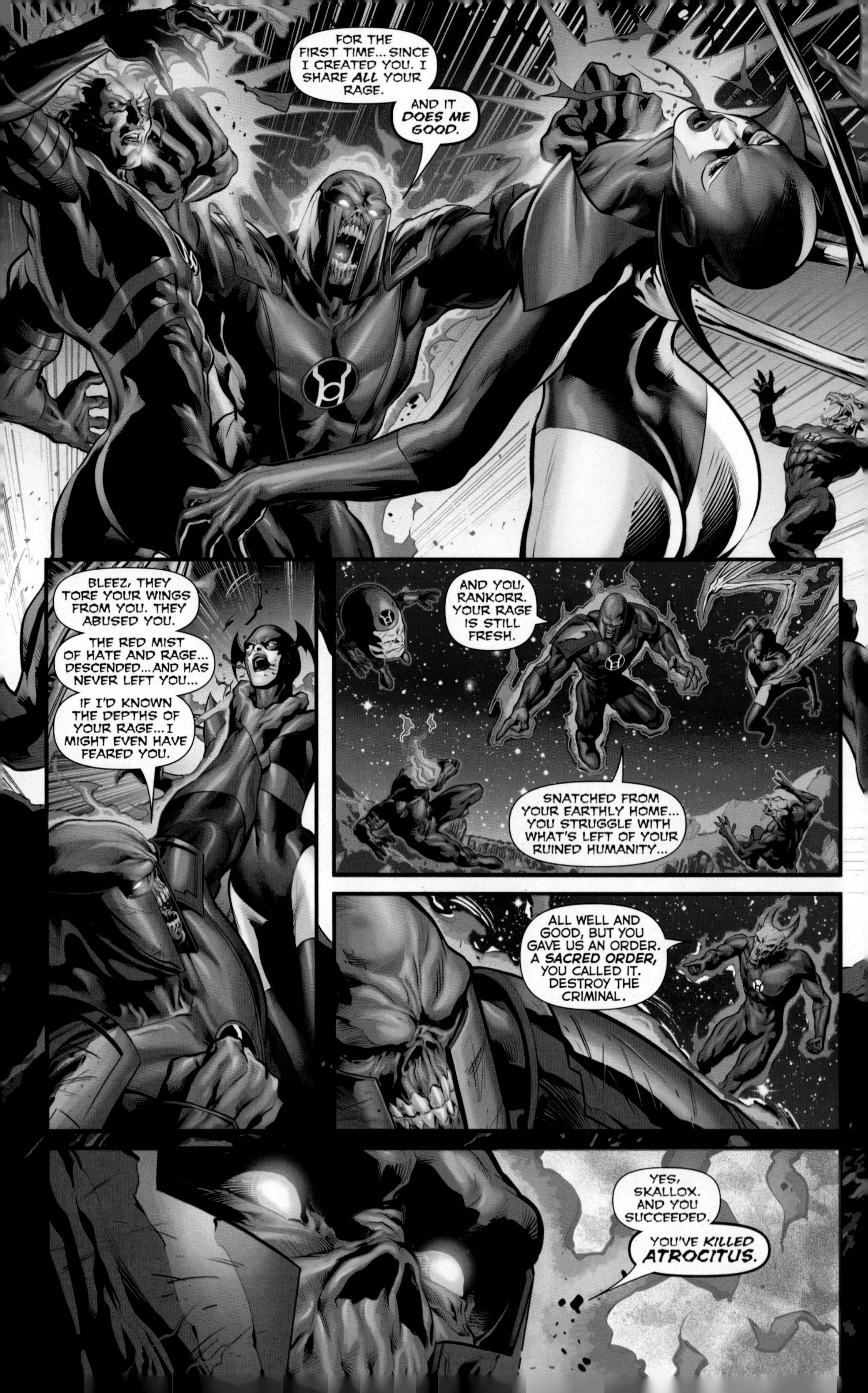
FOR THE FIRST TIME... SINCE I CREATED YOU. I SHARE ALL YOUR RAGE.
AND IT DOES ME GOOD.
BLEEZ, THEY TORE YOUR WINGS FROM YOU. THEY ABUSED YOU.
THE RED MIST OF HATE AND RAGE... DESCENDED... AND HAS NEVER LEFT YOU...
IF I'D KNOWN THE DEPTHS OF YOUR RAGE... I MIGHT EVEN HAVE FEARED YOU.
AND YOU, RANKORR. YOUR RAGE IS STILL FRESH.
SNATCHED FROM YOUR EARTHLY HOME... YOU STRUGGLE WITH WHAT'S LEFT OF YOUR RUINED HUMANITY...
ALL WELL AND GOOD, BUT YOU GAVE US AN ORDER. A SACRED ORDER, YOU CALLED IT. DESTROY THE CRIMINAL.
YES, SKALLOX. AND YOU SUCCEEDED.
YOU'VE KILLED ATROCITUS.

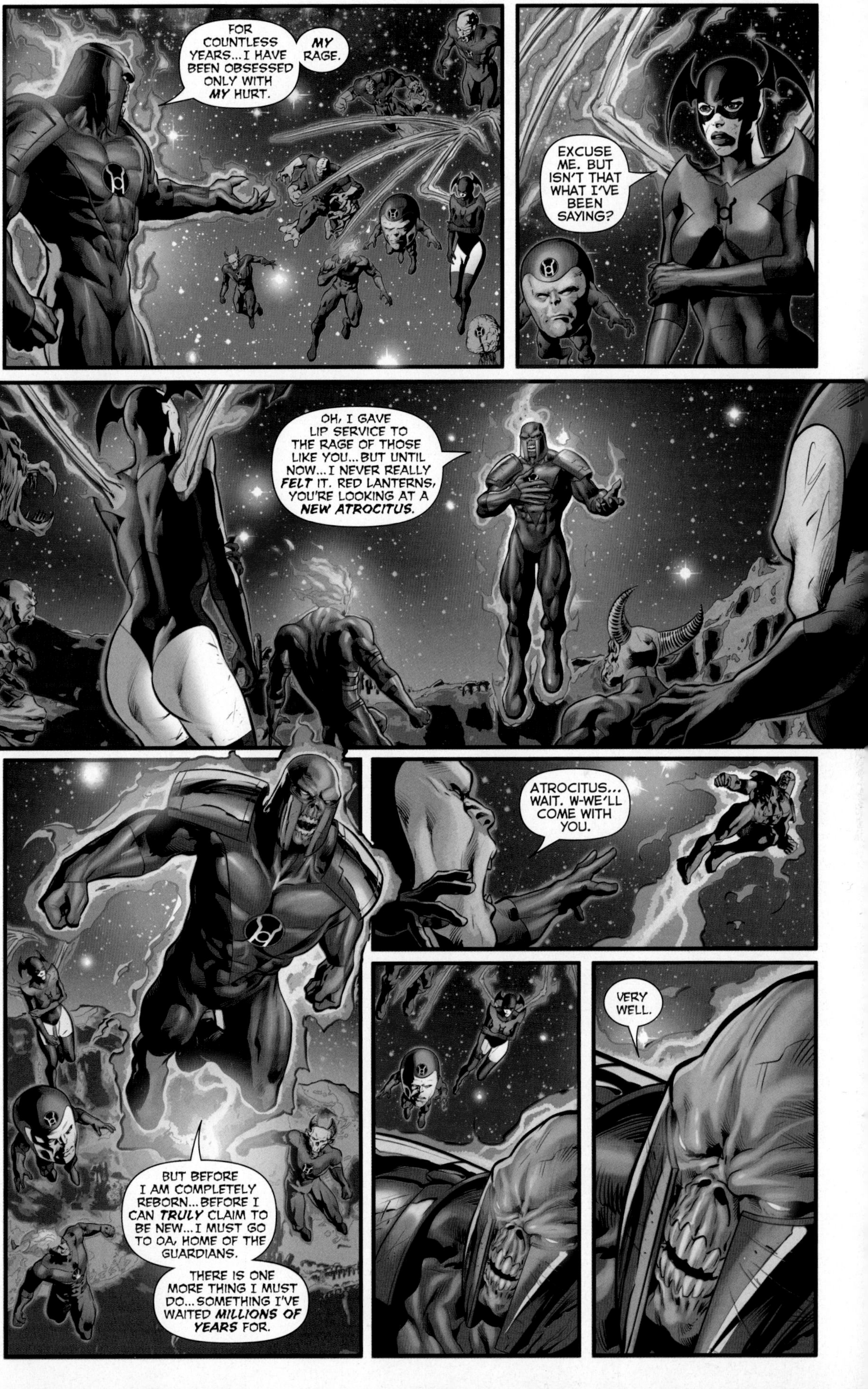

FOR COUNTLESS YEARS... I HAVE BEEN OBSESSED ONLY WITH *MY* HURT.
MY RAGE.
EXCUSE ME. BUT ISN'T THAT WHAT I'VE BEEN SAYING?
OH, I GAVE LIP SERVICE TO THE RAGE OF THOSE LIKE YOU... BUT UNTIL NOW... I NEVER REALLY *FELT* IT. RED LANTERNS, YOU'RE LOOKING AT A *NEW ATROCITUS*.
BUT BEFORE I AM COMPLETELY REBORN... BEFORE I CAN *TRULY* CLAIM TO BE NEW... I MUST GO TO OA, HOME OF THE GUARDIANS.
THERE IS ONE MORE THING I MUST DO... SOMETHING I'VE WAITED *MILLIONS OF YEARS* FOR.
ATROCITUS... WAIT. W-WE'LL COME WITH YOU.
VERY WELL.

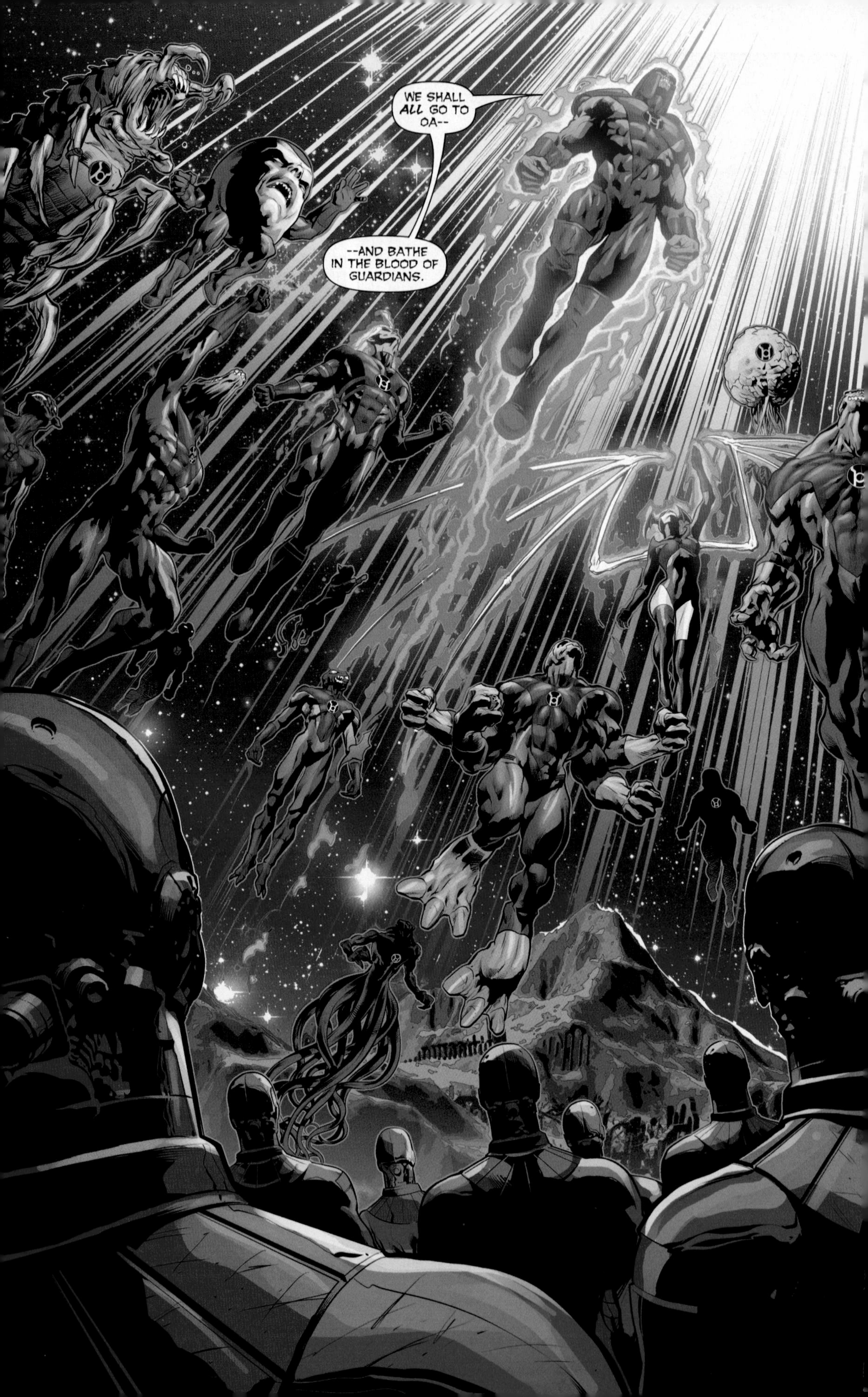
WE SHALL ALL GO TO OA--
--AND BATHE IN THE BLOOD OF GUARDIANS.

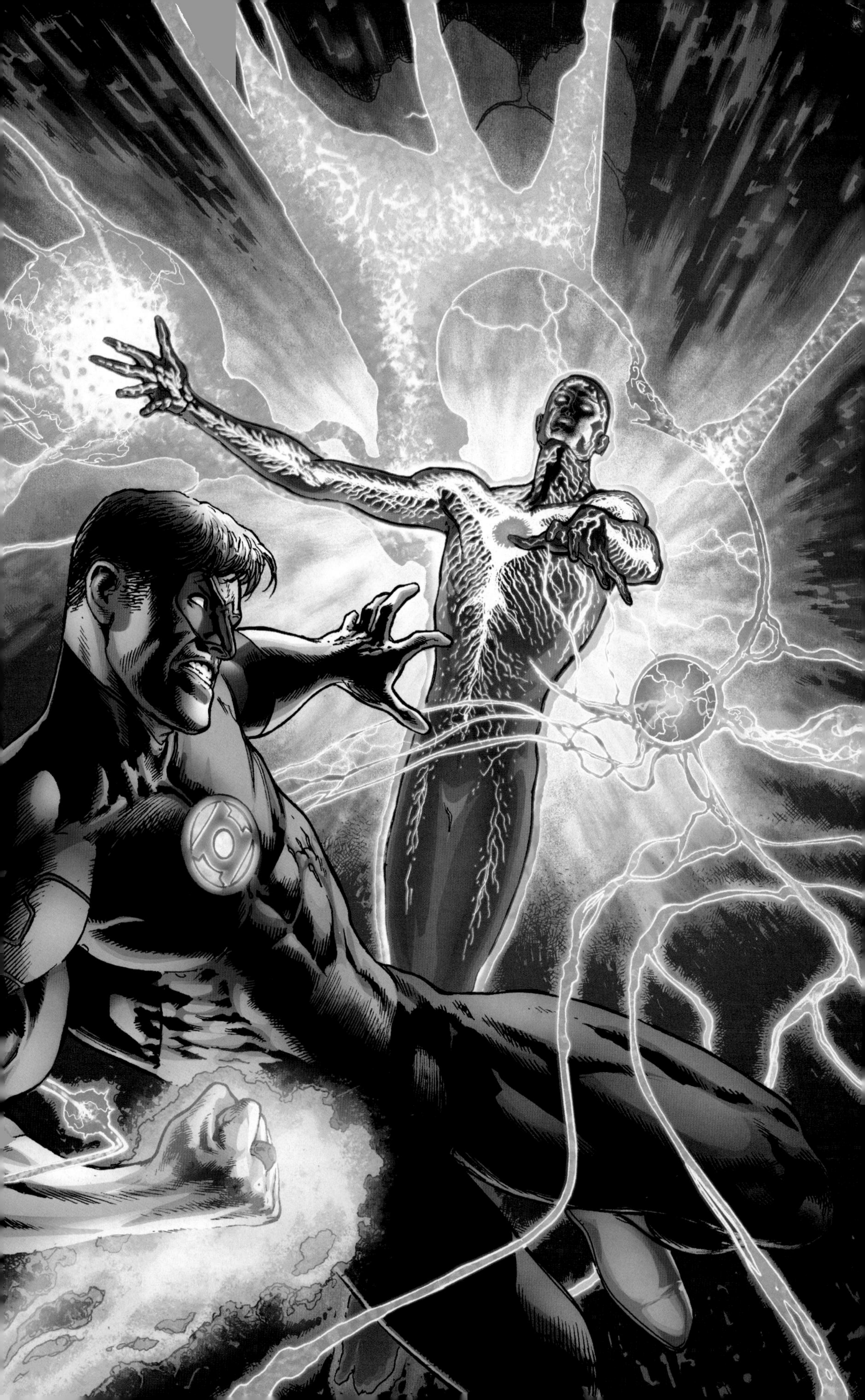

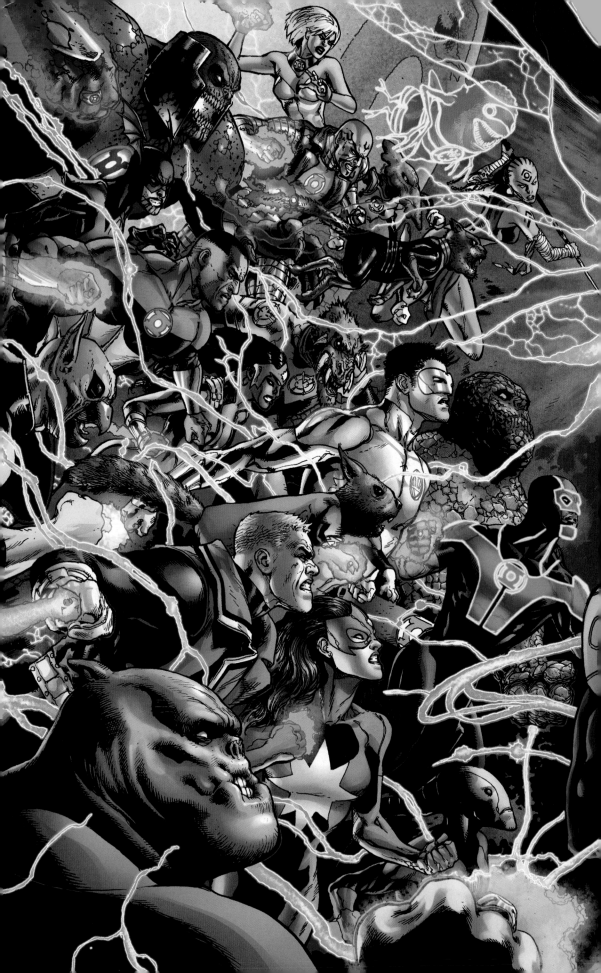

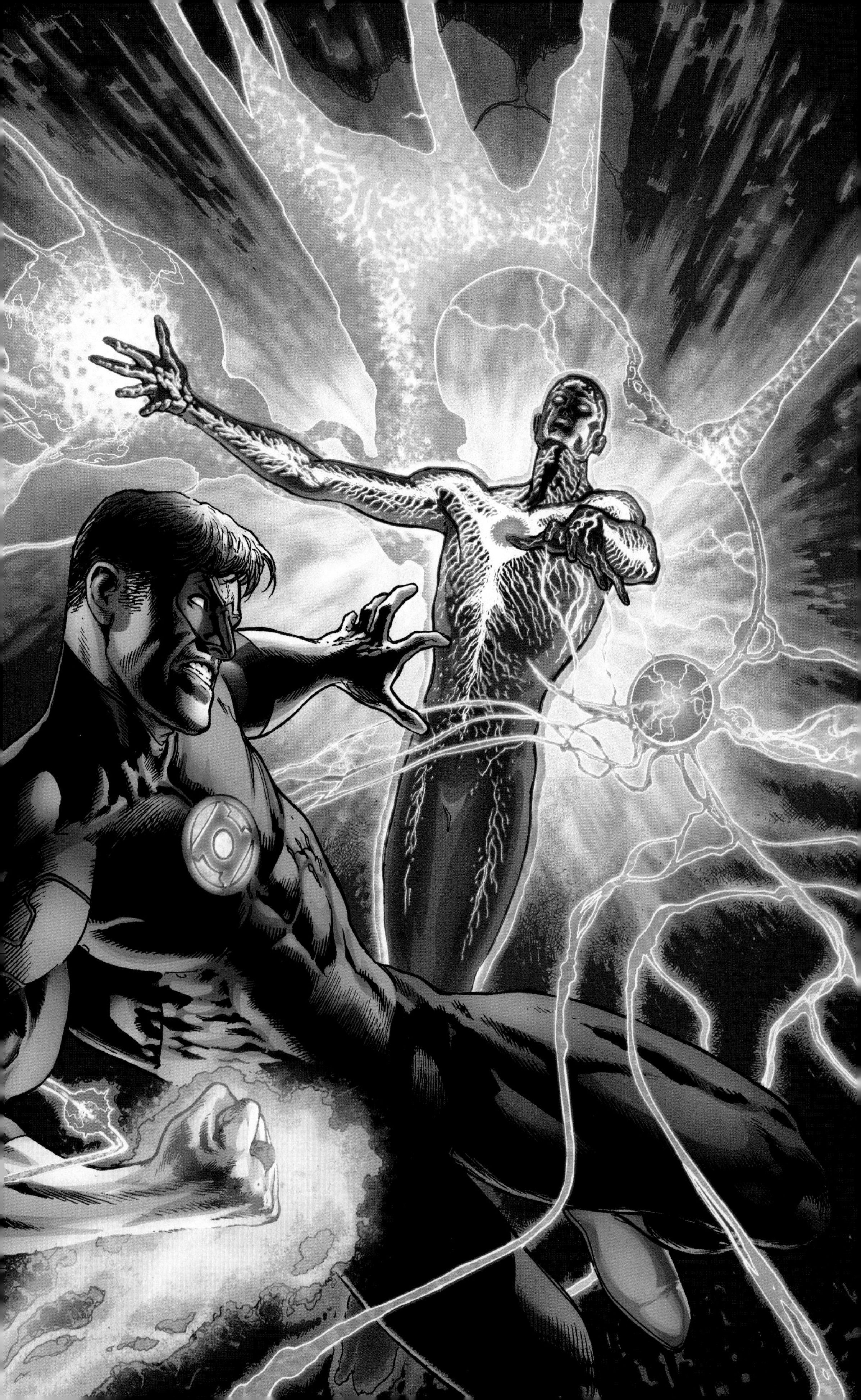

THE WRATH OF THE FIRST LANTERN FINALE: THE END

GEOFF JOHNS writer DOUG MAHNKE, PATRICK GLEASON, CULLY HAMNER, AARON KUDER, JERRY ORDWAY, ETHAN VAN SCIVER, IVAN REIS with OCLAIR ALBERT & JOE PRADO pencillers CHRISTIAN ALAMY, KEITH CHAMPAGNE, MARC DEERING, MARK IRWIN, WADE VON GRAWBADGER, TOM NGUYEN & DOUG MAHNKE inkers cover art by DOUG MAHNKE with ALEX SINCLAIR

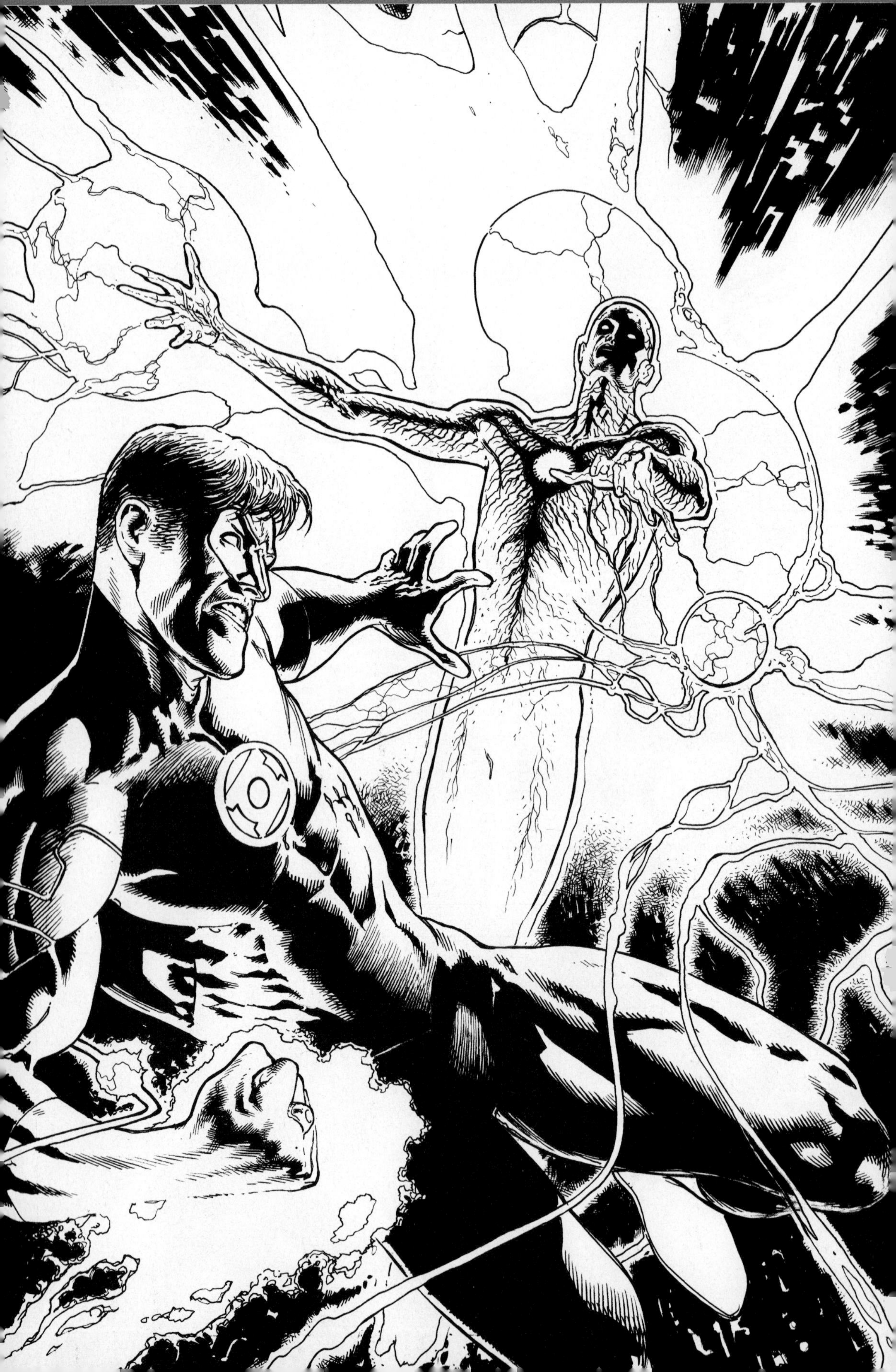

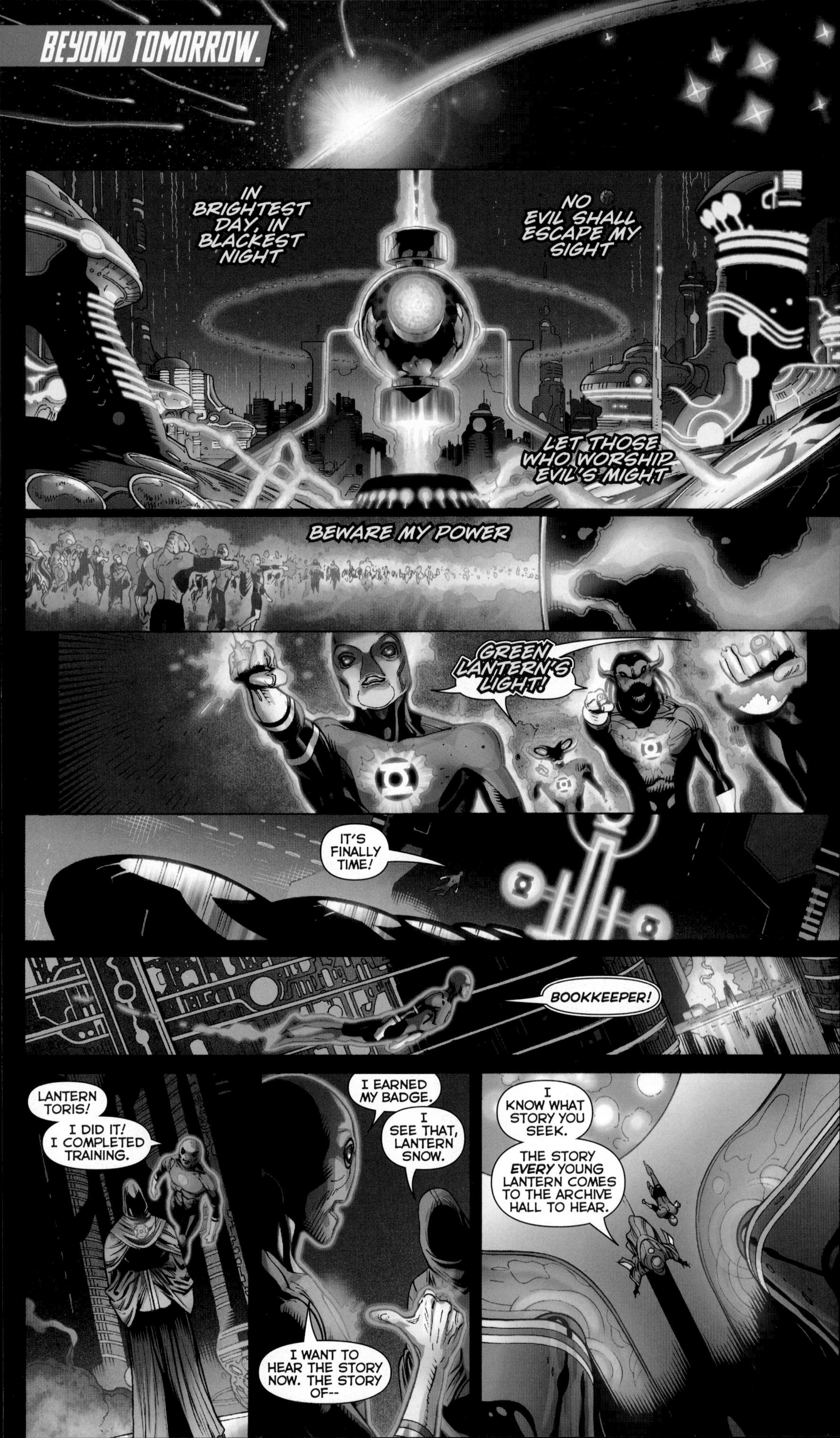
BEYOND TOMORROW.
IN BRIGHTEST DAY, IN BLACKEST NIGHT
NO EVIL SHALL ESCAPE MY SIGHT
LET THOSE WHO WORSHIP EVIL'S MIGHT
BEWARE MY POWER
GREEN LANTERN'S LIGHT!
IT'S FINALLY TIME!
BOOKKEEPER!
LANTERN TORIS!
I DID IT! I COMPLETED TRAINING.
I EARNED MY BADGE.
I SEE THAT, LANTERN SNOW.
I WANT TO HEAR THE STORY NOW. THE STORY OF--
I KNOW WHAT STORY YOU SEEK.
THE STORY EVERY YOUNG LANTERN COMES TO THE ARCHIVE HALL TO HEAR.

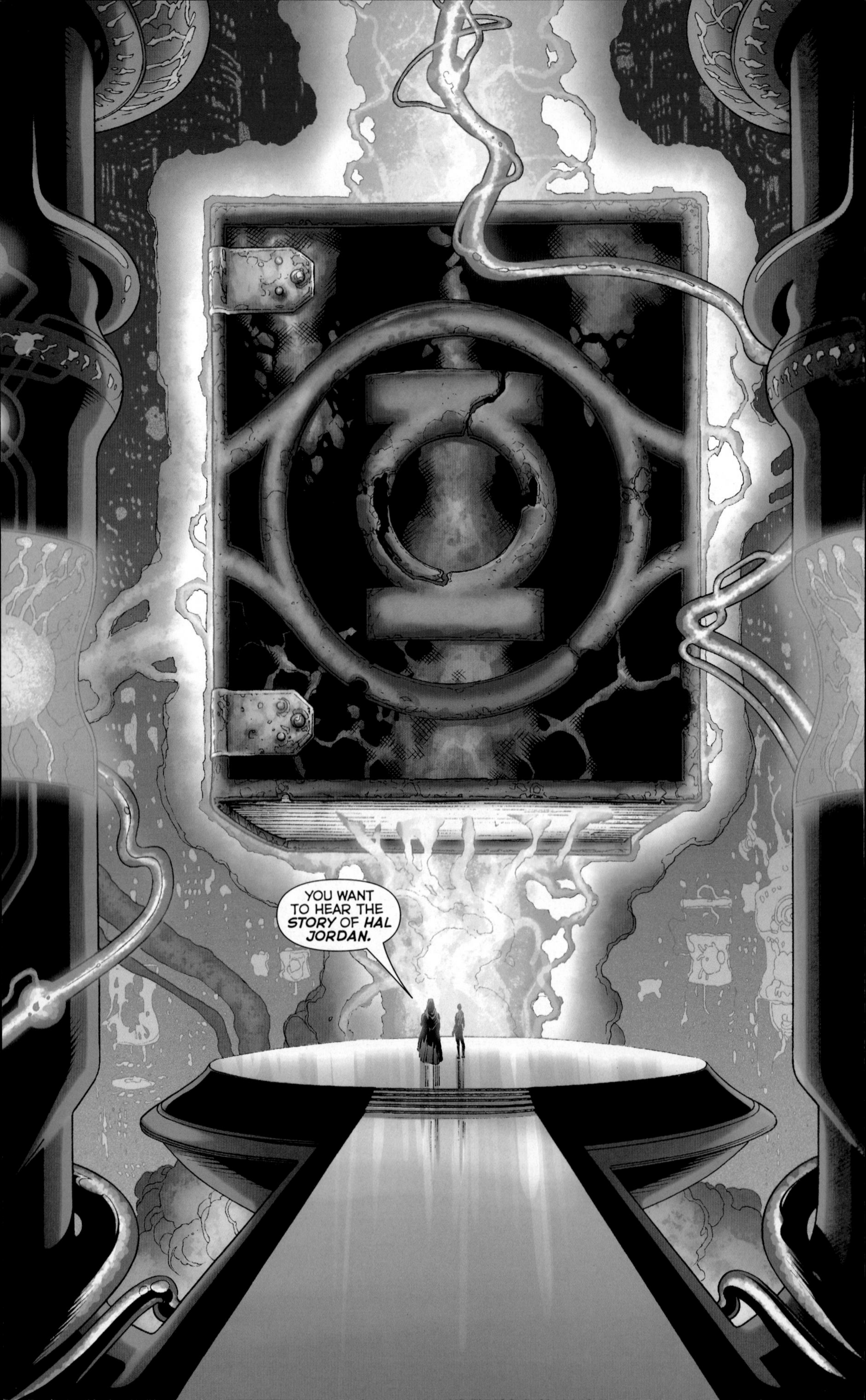
YOU WANT TO HEAR THE STORY OF HAL JORDAN.

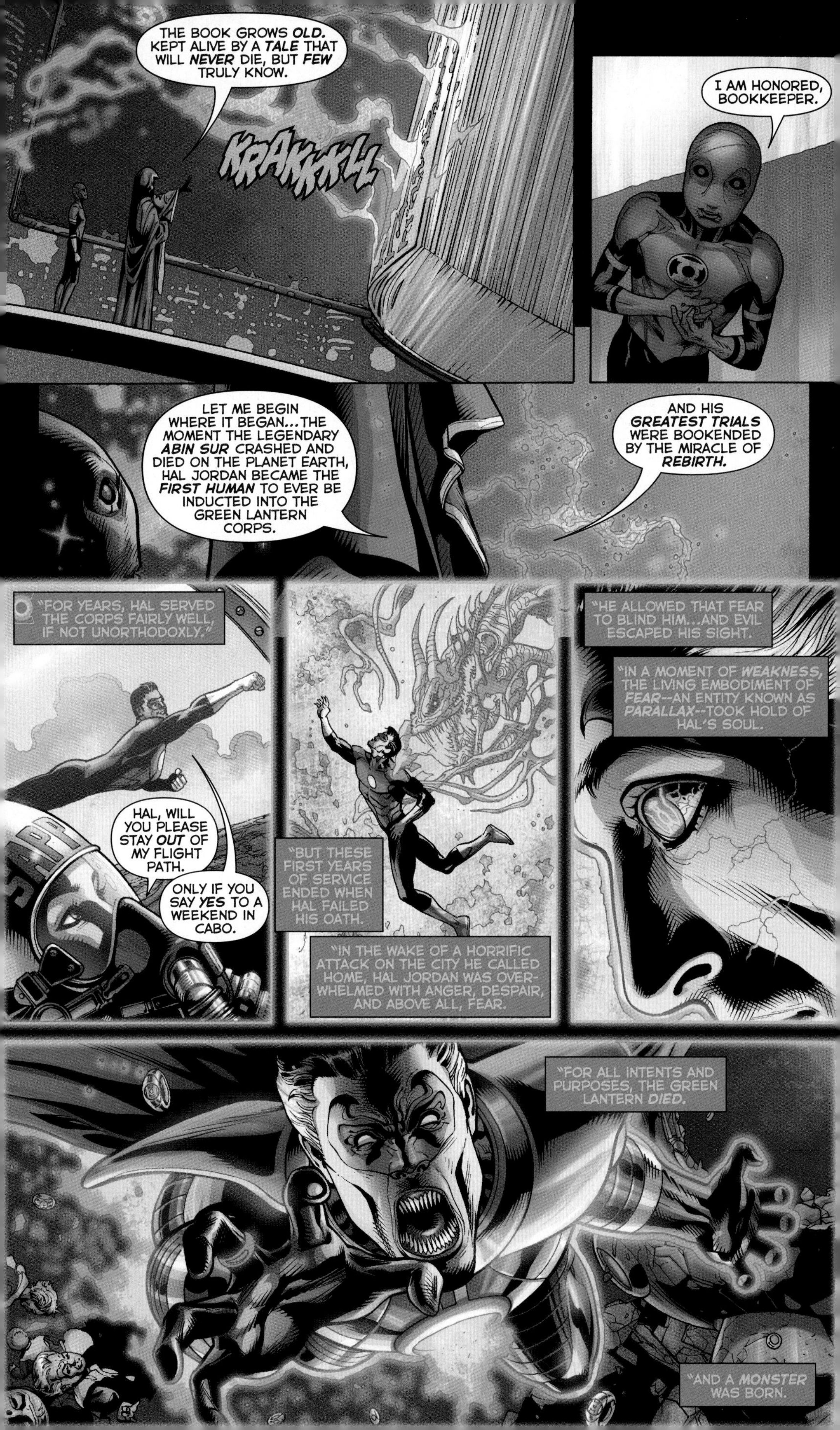
THE BOOK GROWS OLD. KEPT ALIVE BY A TALE THAT WILL NEVER DIE, BUT FEW TRULY KNOW.
KRAKKKLL
I AM HONORED, BOOKKEEPER.
LET ME BEGIN WHERE IT BEGAN... THE MOMENT THE LEGENDARY ABIN SUR CRASHED AND DIED ON THE PLANET EARTH, HAL JORDAN BECAME THE FIRST HUMAN TO EVER BE INDUCTED INTO THE GREEN LANTERN CORPS.
AND HIS GREATEST TRIALS WERE BOOKENDED BY THE MIRACLE OF REBIRTH.
"FOR YEARS, HAL SERVED THE CORPS FAIRLY WELL, IF NOT UNORTHODOXLY."
HAL, WILL YOU PLEASE STAY OUT OF MY FLIGHT PATH.
ONLY IF YOU SAY YES TO A WEEKEND IN CABO.
"BUT THESE FIRST YEARS OF SERVICE ENDED WHEN HAL FAILED HIS OATH.
"IN THE WAKE OF A HORRIFIC ATTACK ON THE CITY HE CALLED HOME, HAL JORDAN WAS OVER-WHELMED WITH ANGER, DESPAIR, AND ABOVE ALL, FEAR.
"HE ALLOWED THAT FEAR TO BLIND HIM...AND EVIL ESCAPED HIS SIGHT.
"IN A MOMENT OF WEAKNESS, THE LIVING EMBODIMENT OF FEAR--AN ENTITY KNOWN AS PARALLAX--TOOK HOLD OF HAL'S SOUL.
"FOR ALL INTENTS AND PURPOSES, THE GREEN LANTERN DIED.
"AND A MONSTER WAS BORN.

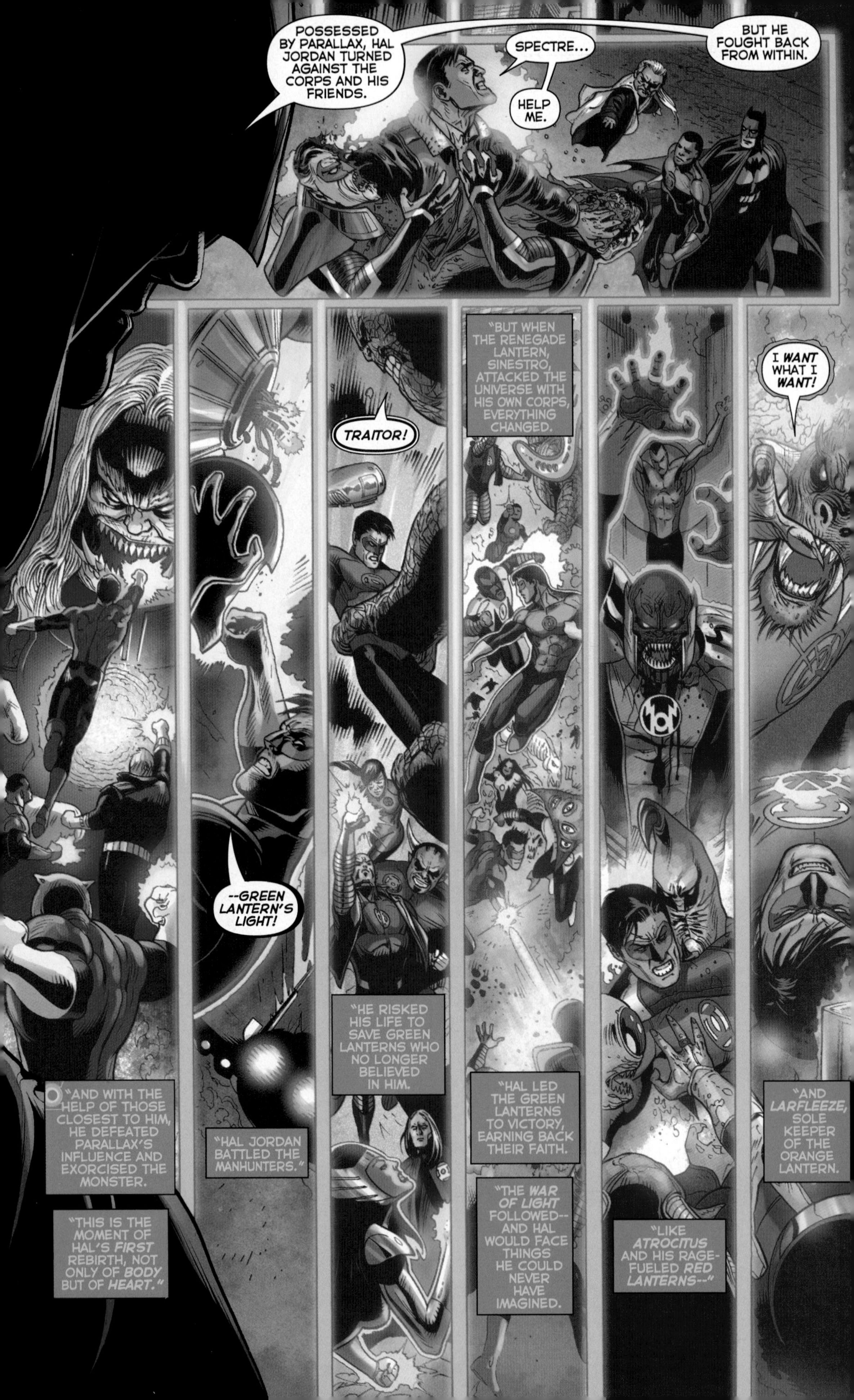
POSSESSED BY PARALLAX, HAL JORDAN TURNED AGAINST THE CORPS AND HIS FRIENDS.
SPECTRE...
HELP ME.
BUT HE FOUGHT BACK FROM WITHIN.
"AND WITH THE HELP OF THOSE CLOSEST TO HIM, HE DEFEATED PARALLAX'S INFLUENCE AND EXORCISED THE MONSTER.
"THIS IS THE MOMENT OF HAL'S *FIRST* REBIRTH, NOT ONLY OF *BODY* BUT OF *HEART*."
--GREEN LANTERN'S LIGHT!
"HAL JORDAN BATTLED THE MANHUNTERS."
TRAITOR!
"HE RISKED HIS LIFE TO SAVE GREEN LANTERNS WHO NO LONGER BELIEVED IN HIM.
"BUT WHEN THE RENEGADE LANTERN, SINESTRO, ATTACKED THE UNIVERSE WITH HIS OWN CORPS, EVERYTHING CHANGED.
"HAL LED THE GREEN LANTERNS TO VICTORY, EARNING BACK THEIR FAITH.
"THE *WAR OF LIGHT* FOLLOWED--AND HAL WOULD FACE THINGS HE COULD NEVER HAVE IMAGINED.
"LIKE *ATROCITUS* AND HIS RAGE-FUELED *RED LANTERNS*--"
I *WANT* WHAT I *WANT*!
"AND *LARFLEEZE*, SOLE KEEPER OF THE ORANGE LANTERN.

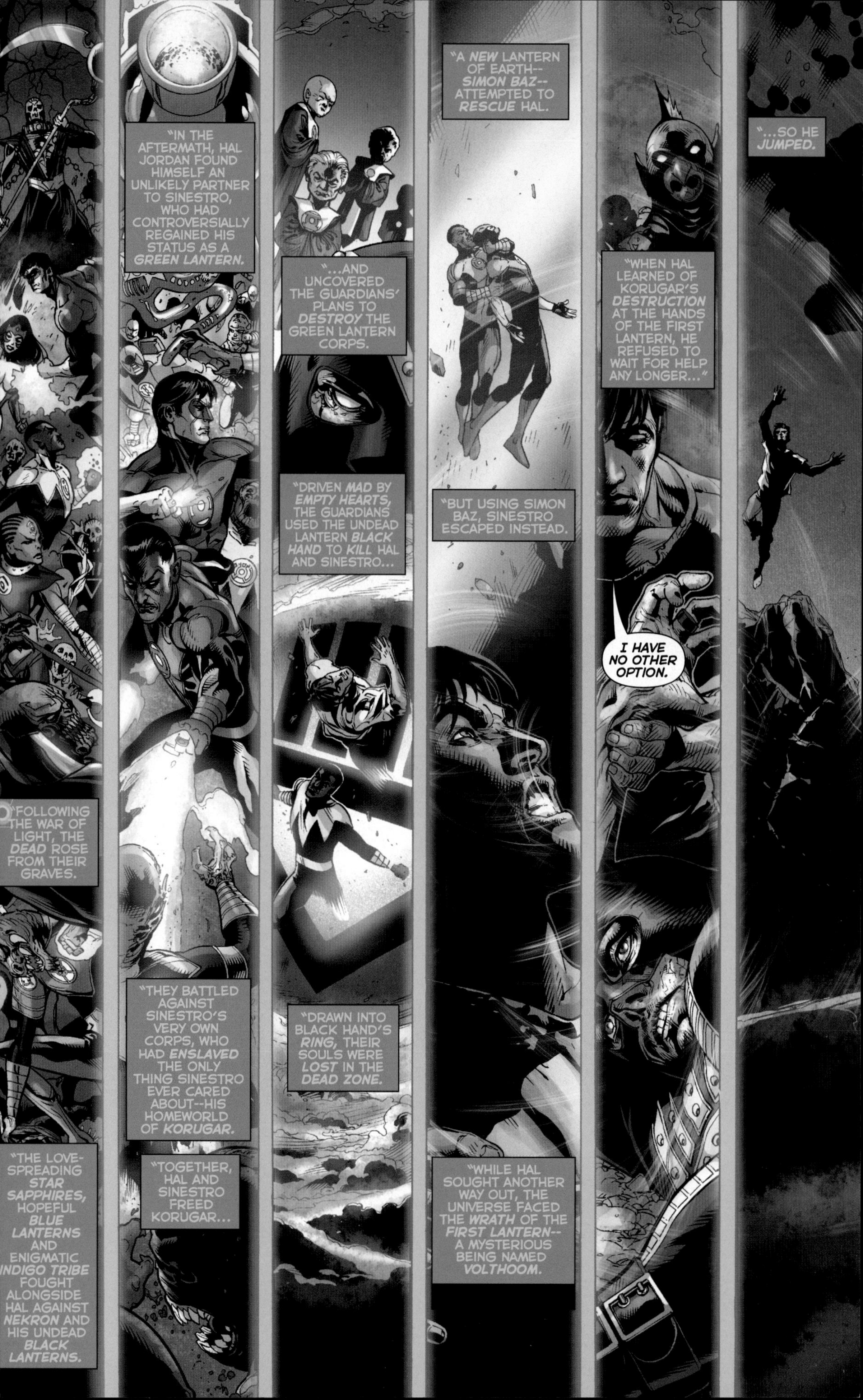
"FOLLOWING THE WAR OF LIGHT, THE DEAD ROSE FROM THEIR GRAVES.
"THE LOVE-SPREADING STAR SAPPHIRES, HOPEFUL BLUE LANTERNS AND ENIGMATIC INDIGO TRIBE FOUGHT ALONGSIDE HAL AGAINST NEKRON AND HIS UNDEAD BLACK LANTERNS.
"IN THE AFTERMATH, HAL JORDAN FOUND HIMSELF AN UNLIKELY PARTNER TO SINESTRO, WHO HAD CONTROVERSIALLY REGAINED HIS STATUS AS A GREEN LANTERN.
"THEY BATTLED AGAINST SINESTRO'S VERY OWN CORPS, WHO HAD ENSLAVED THE ONLY THING SINESTRO EVER CARED ABOUT--HIS HOMEWORLD OF KORUGAR.
"TOGETHER, HAL AND SINESTRO FREED KORUGAR...
"...AND UNCOVERED THE GUARDIANS' PLANS TO DESTROY THE GREEN LANTERN CORPS.
"DRIVEN MAD BY EMPTY HEARTS, THE GUARDIANS USED THE UNDEAD LANTERN BLACK HAND TO KILL HAL AND SINESTRO...
"DRAWN INTO BLACK HAND'S RING, THEIR SOULS WERE LOST IN THE DEAD ZONE.
"A NEW LANTERN OF EARTH--SIMON BAZ--ATTEMPTED TO RESCUE HAL.
"BUT USING SIMON BAZ, SINESTRO ESCAPED INSTEAD.
"WHILE HAL SOUGHT ANOTHER WAY OUT, THE UNIVERSE FACED THE WRATH OF THE FIRST LANTERN--A MYSTERIOUS BEING NAMED VOLTHOOM.
"WHEN HAL LEARNED OF KORUGAR'S DESTRUCTION AT THE HANDS OF THE FIRST LANTERN, HE REFUSED TO WAIT FOR HELP ANY LONGER..."
I HAVE NO OTHER OPTION.
"...SO HE JUMPED.

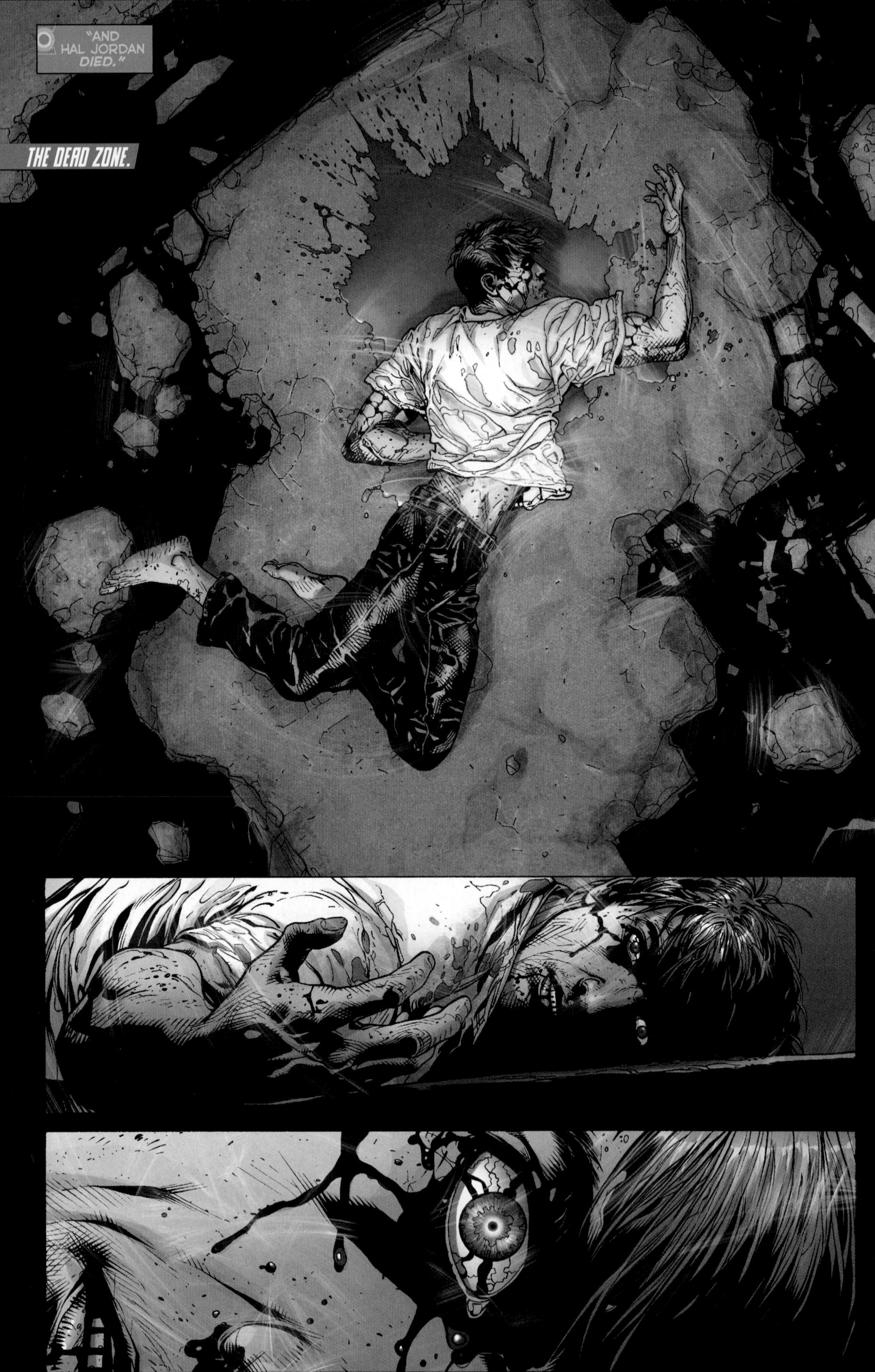
"AND HAL JORDAN DIED."
THE DEAD ZONE.

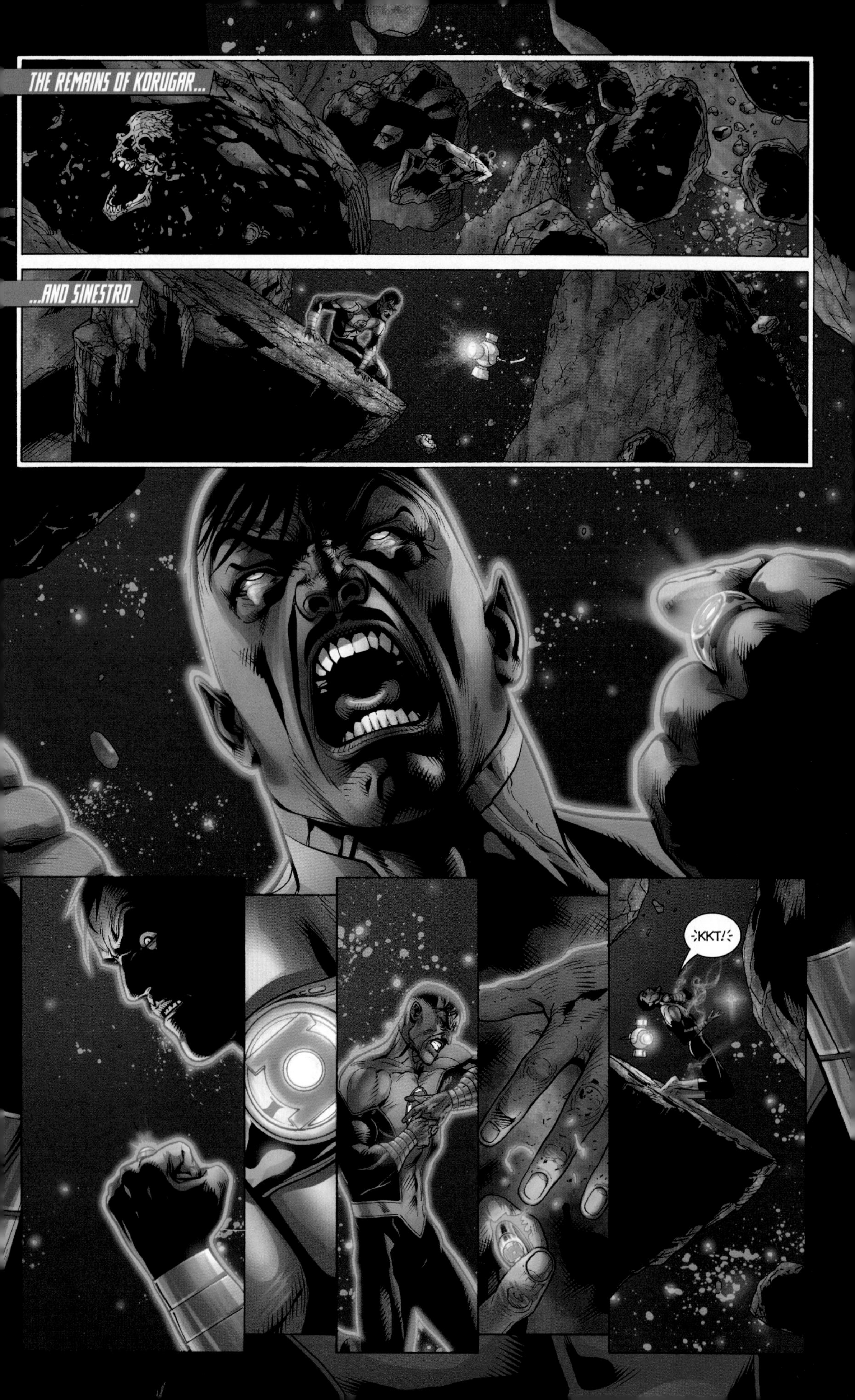
THE REMAINS OF KORUGAR...
...AND SINESTRO.
KKT!

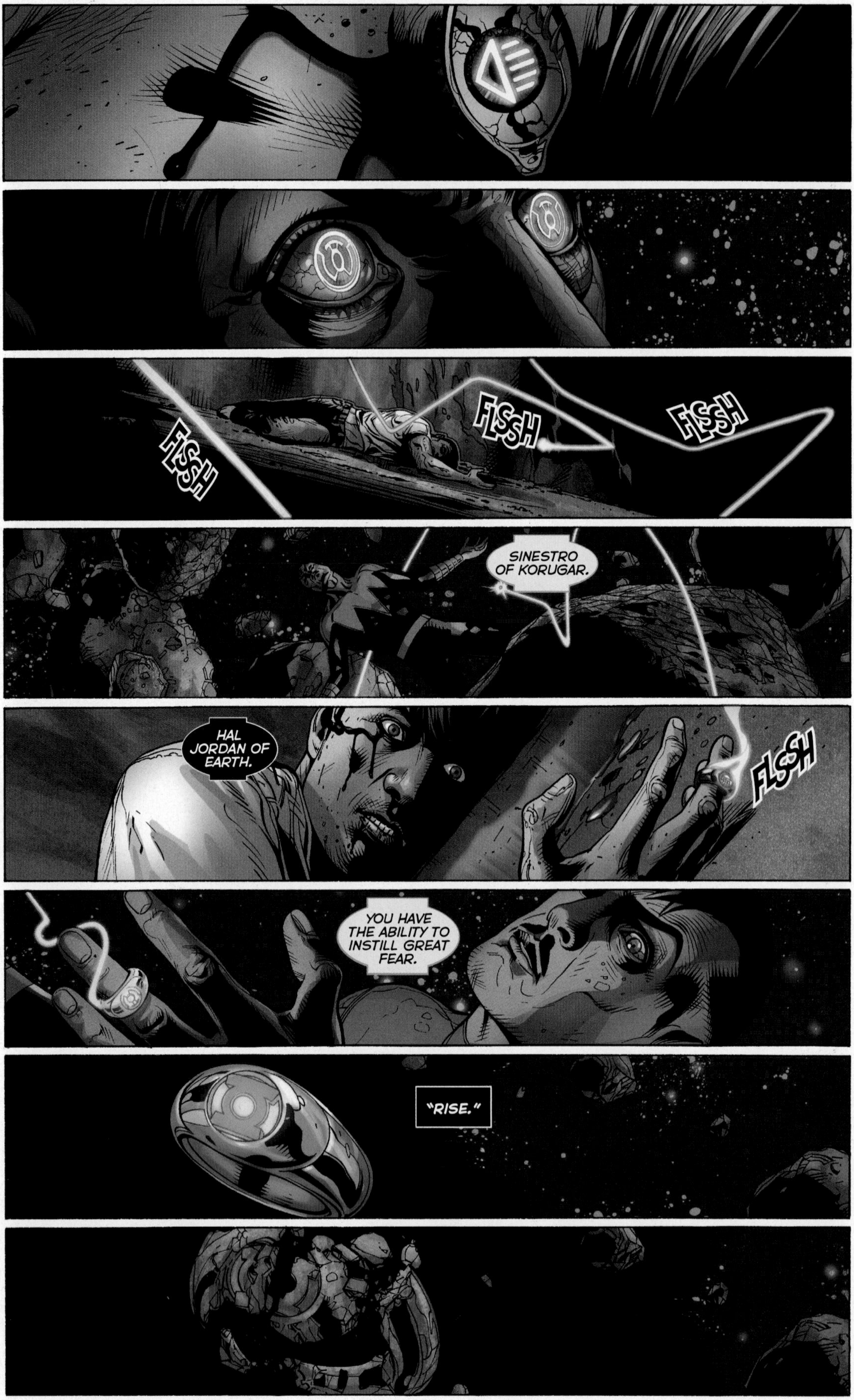
FLSSH
FLSSH
FLSSH
SINESTRO OF KORUGAR.
HAL JORDAN OF EARTH.
FLSSH
YOU HAVE THE ABILITY TO INSTILL GREAT FEAR.
"RISE."

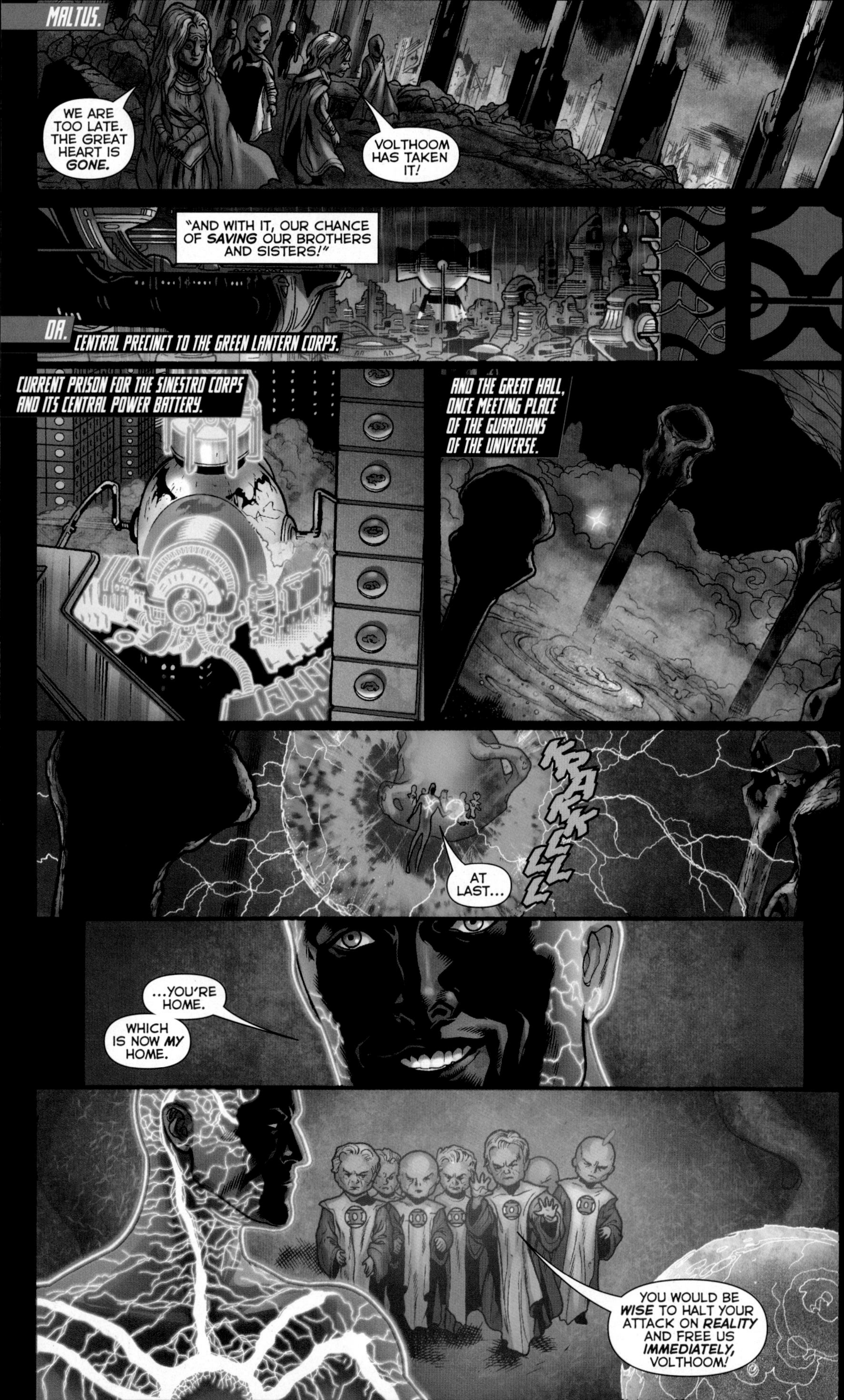
MALTUS.
WE ARE TOO LATE. THE GREAT HEART IS GONE.
VOLTHOOM HAS TAKEN IT!
"AND WITH IT, OUR CHANCE OF SAVING OUR BROTHERS AND SISTERS!"
OA.
CENTRAL PRECINCT TO THE GREEN LANTERN CORPS.
CURRENT PRISON FOR THE SINESTRO CORPS AND ITS CENTRAL POWER BATTERY.
AND THE GREAT HALL, ONCE MEETING PLACE OF THE GUARDIANS OF THE UNIVERSE.
KRAKKLLL
AT LAST...
...YOU'RE HOME.
WHICH IS NOW MY HOME.
YOU WOULD BE WISE TO HALT YOUR ATTACK ON REALITY AND FREE US IMMEDIATELY, VOLTHOOM!

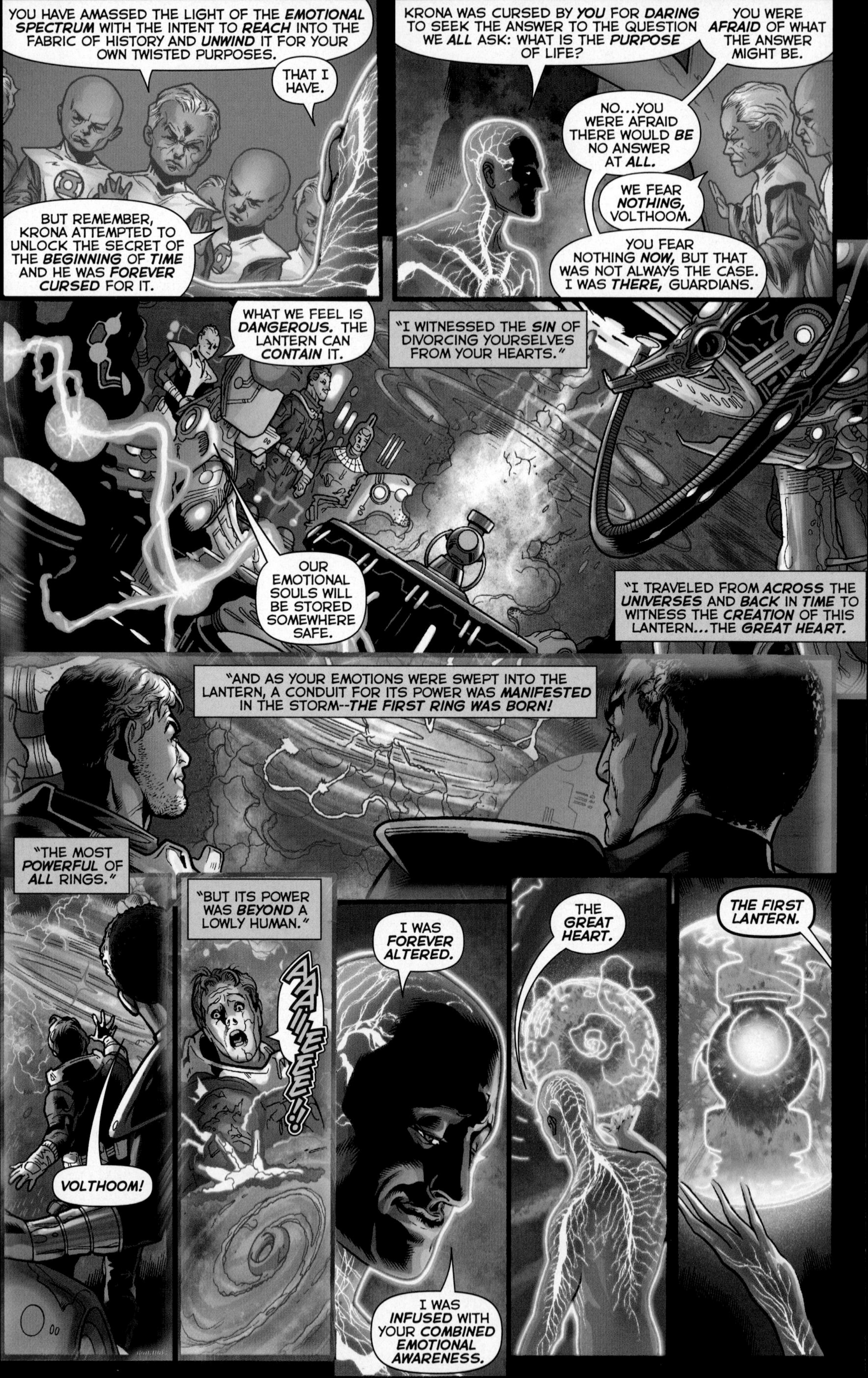
YOU HAVE AMASSED THE LIGHT OF THE EMOTIONAL SPECTRUM WITH THE INTENT TO REACH INTO THE FABRIC OF HISTORY AND UNWIND IT FOR YOUR OWN TWISTED PURPOSES.
THAT I HAVE.
BUT REMEMBER, KRONA ATTEMPTED TO UNLOCK THE SECRET OF THE BEGINNING OF TIME AND HE WAS FOREVER CURSED FOR IT.
KRONA WAS CURSED BY YOU FOR DARING TO SEEK THE ANSWER TO THE QUESTION WE ALL ASK: WHAT IS THE PURPOSE OF LIFE?
YOU WERE AFRAID OF WHAT THE ANSWER MIGHT BE.
NO...YOU WERE AFRAID THERE WOULD BE NO ANSWER AT ALL.
WE FEAR NOTHING, VOLTHOOM.
YOU FEAR NOTHING NOW, BUT THAT WAS NOT ALWAYS THE CASE. I WAS THERE, GUARDIANS.
WHAT WE FEEL IS DANGEROUS. THE LANTERN CAN CONTAIN IT.
"I WITNESSED THE SIN OF DIVORCING YOURSELVES FROM YOUR HEARTS."
OUR EMOTIONAL SOULS WILL BE STORED SOMEWHERE SAFE.
"I TRAVELED FROM ACROSS THE UNIVERSES AND BACK IN TIME TO WITNESS THE CREATION OF THIS LANTERN...THE GREAT HEART.
"AND AS YOUR EMOTIONS WERE SWEPT INTO THE LANTERN, A CONDUIT FOR ITS POWER WAS MANIFESTED IN THE STORM--THE FIRST RING WAS BORN!
"THE MOST POWERFUL OF ALL RINGS."
VOLTHOOM!
"BUT ITS POWER WAS BEYOND A LOWLY HUMAN."
AAAIIEEEE!!
I WAS FOREVER ALTERED.
I WAS INFUSED WITH YOUR COMBINED EMOTIONAL AWARENESS.
THE GREAT HEART.
THE FIRST LANTERN.

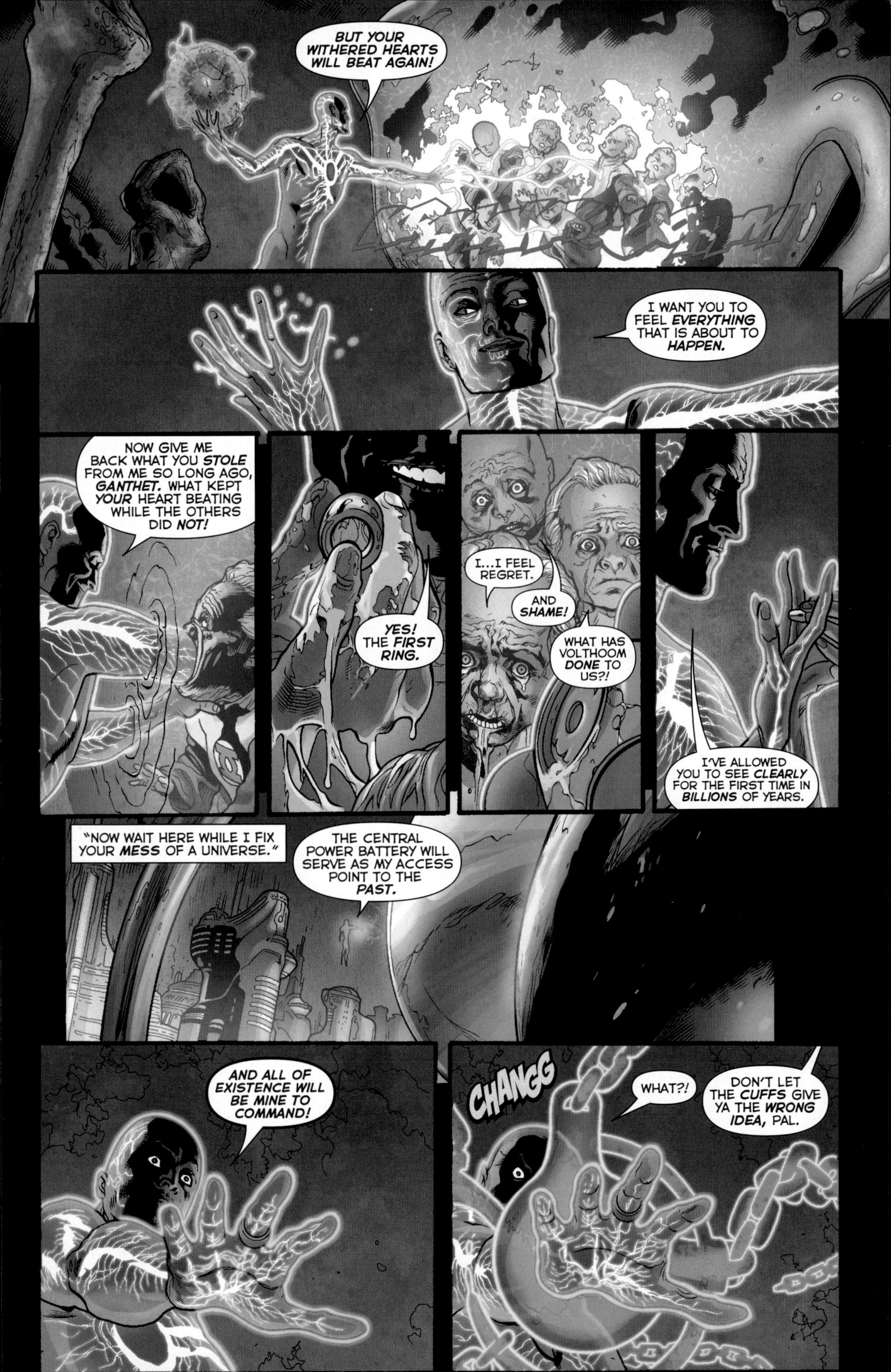

BUT YOUR WITHERED HEARTS WILL BEAT AGAIN!
I WANT YOU TO FEEL EVERYTHING THAT IS ABOUT TO HAPPEN.
NOW GIVE ME BACK WHAT YOU STOLE FROM ME SO LONG AGO, GANTHET. WHAT KEPT YOUR HEART BEATING WHILE THE OTHERS DID NOT!
YES! THE FIRST RING.
I...I FEEL REGRET.
AND SHAME!
WHAT HAS VOLTHOOM DONE TO US?!
I'VE ALLOWED YOU TO SEE CLEARLY FOR THE FIRST TIME IN BILLIONS OF YEARS.
"NOW WAIT HERE WHILE I FIX YOUR MESS OF A UNIVERSE."
THE CENTRAL POWER BATTERY WILL SERVE AS MY ACCESS POINT TO THE PAST.
AND ALL OF EXISTENCE WILL BE MINE TO COMMAND!
CHANGG
WHAT?!
DON'T LET THE CUFFS GIVE YA THE WRONG IDEA, PAL.

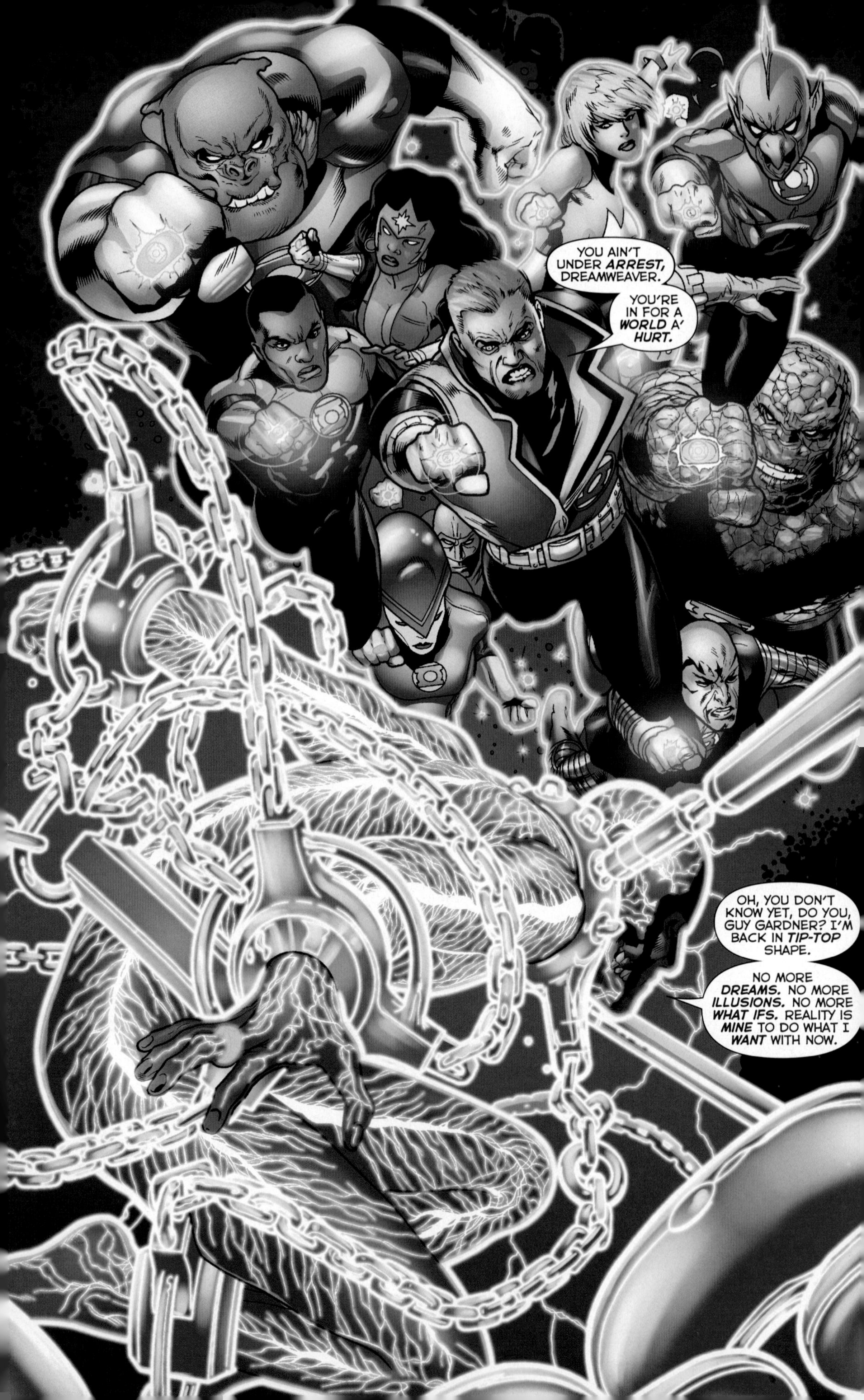
YOU AIN'T UNDER **ARREST,** DREAMWEAVER.
YOU'RE IN FOR A **WORLD** A' **HURT.**
OH, YOU DON'T KNOW YET, DO YOU, GUY GARDNER? I'M BACK IN **TIP-TOP** SHAPE.
NO MORE **DREAMS.** NO MORE **ILLUSIONS.** NO MORE **WHAT IFS.** REALITY IS **MINE** TO DO WHAT I **WANT** WITH NOW.

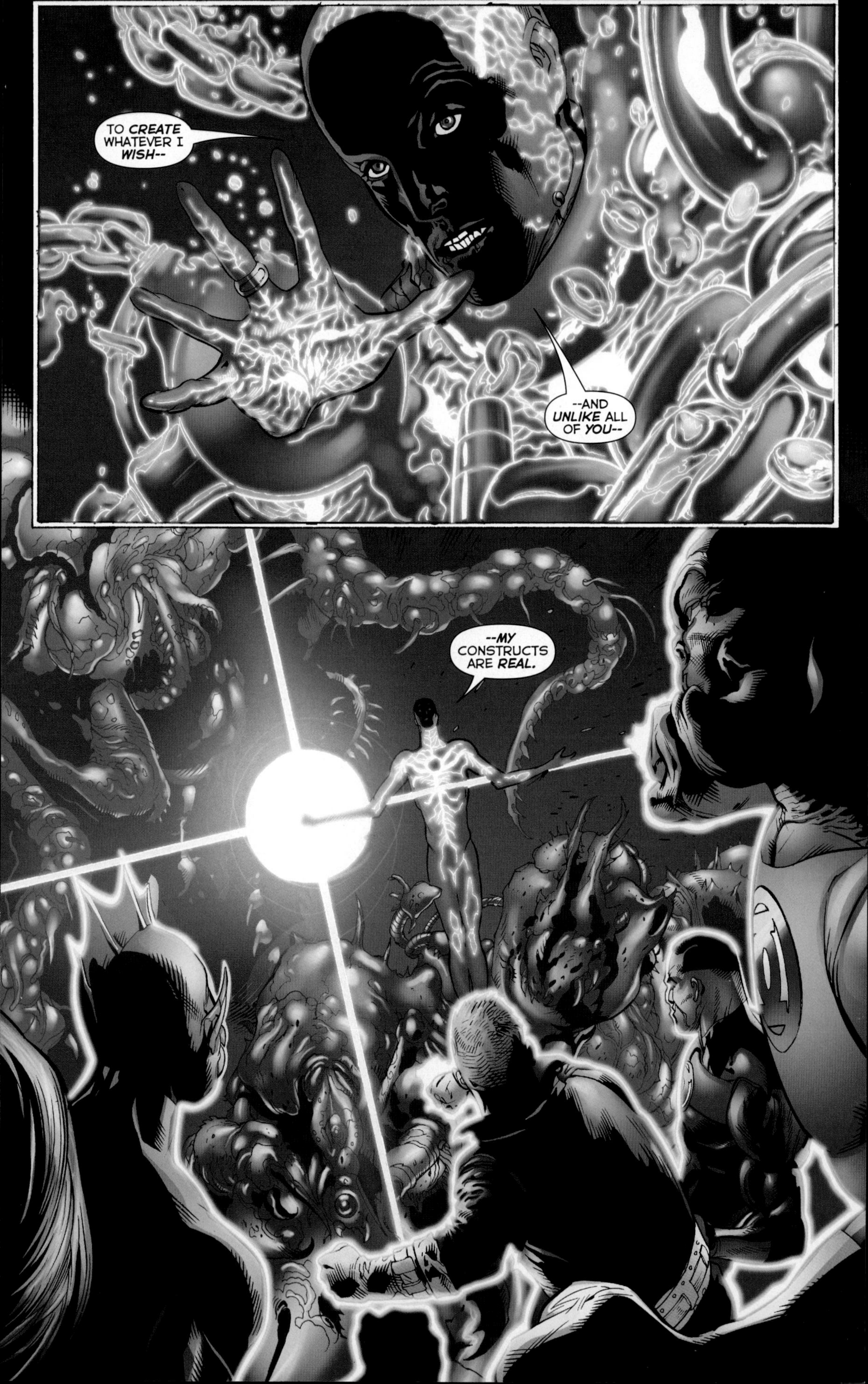
TO CREATE WHATEVER I WISH--
--AND UNLIKE ALL OF YOU--
--MY CONSTRUCTS ARE REAL.

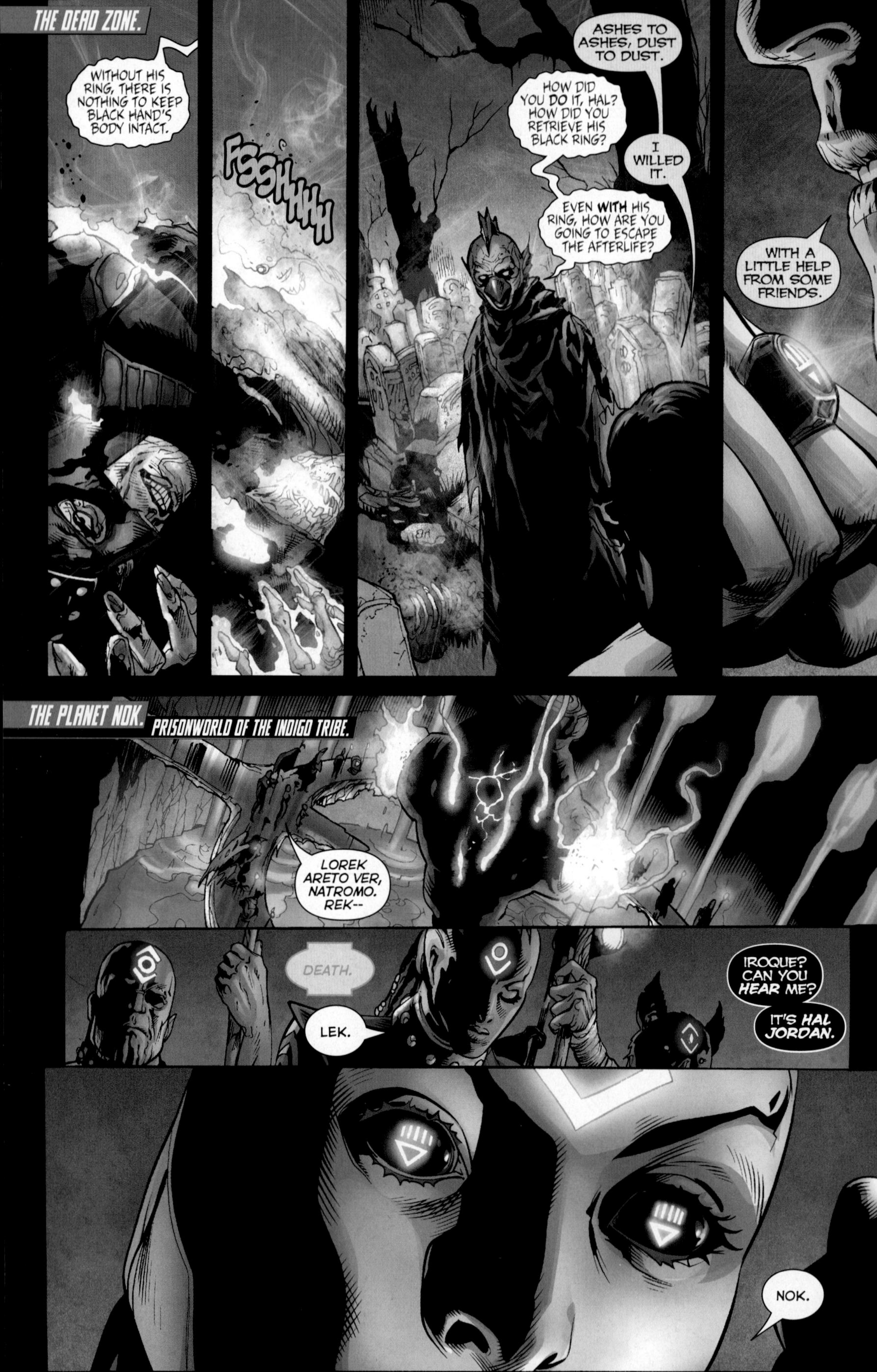
THE DEAD ZONE.
WITHOUT HIS RING, THERE IS NOTHING TO KEEP BLACK HAND'S BODY INTACT.
FSSHHHH
ASHES TO ASHES, DUST TO DUST.
HOW DID YOU DO IT, HAL? HOW DID YOU RETRIEVE HIS BLACK RING?
I WILLED IT.
EVEN WITH HIS RING, HOW ARE YOU GOING TO ESCAPE THE AFTERLIFE?
WITH A LITTLE HELP FROM SOME FRIENDS.
THE PLANET NOK.
PRISONWORLD OF THE INDIGO TRIBE.
LOREK ARETO VER, NATROMO. REK--
DEATH.
LEK.
IROQUE? CAN YOU HEAR ME?
IT'S HAL JORDAN.
NOK.

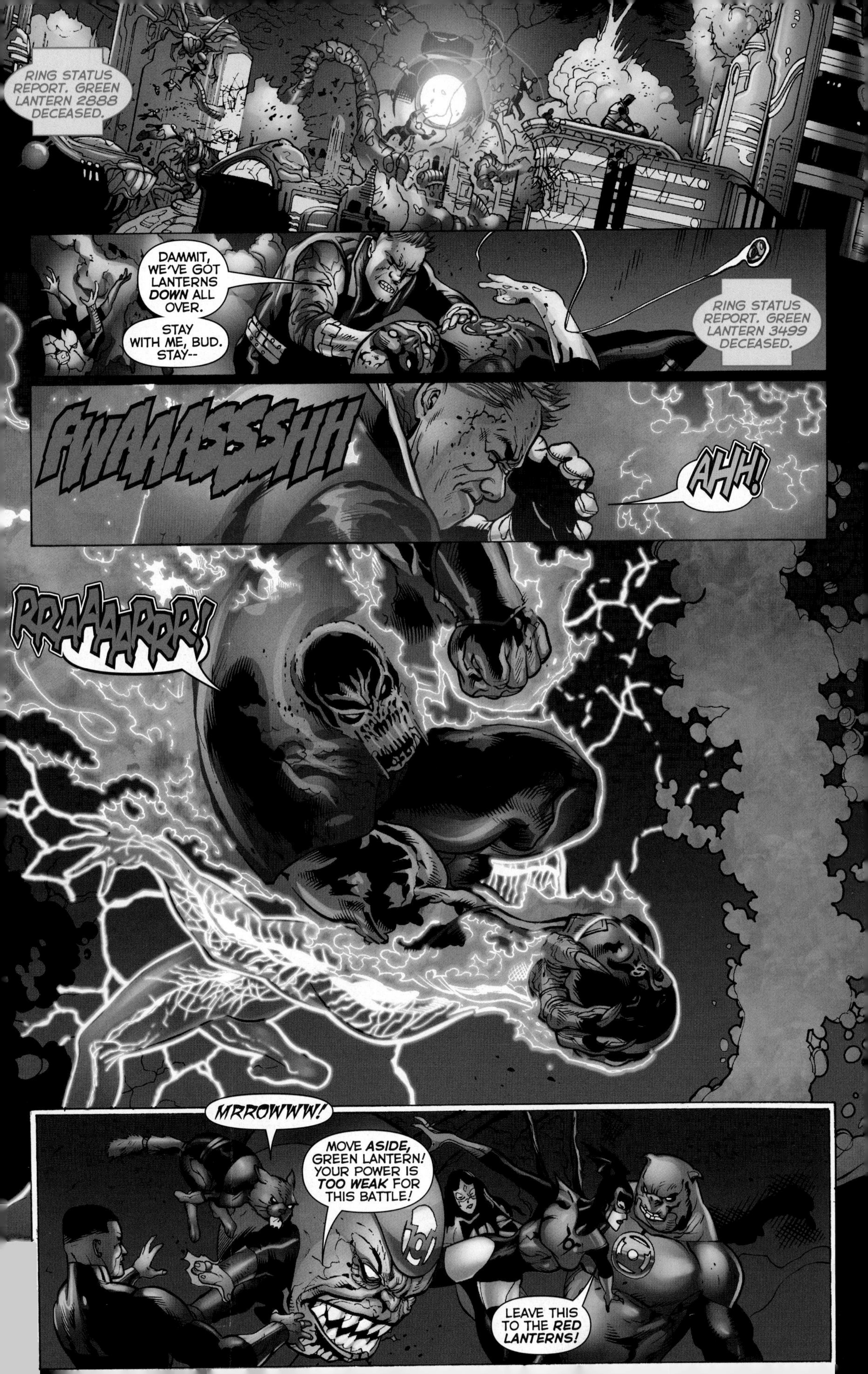
RING STATUS REPORT. GREEN LANTERN 2888 DECEASED.
DAMMIT, WE'VE GOT LANTERNS DOWN ALL OVER.
STAY WITH ME, BUD. STAY--
RING STATUS REPORT. GREEN LANTERN 3499 DECEASED.
FWAAAASSSHH
AHH!
RRAAAARRR!
MRROWWW!
MOVE ASIDE, GREEN LANTERN! YOUR POWER IS TOO WEAK FOR THIS BATTLE!
LEAVE THIS TO THE RED LANTERNS!

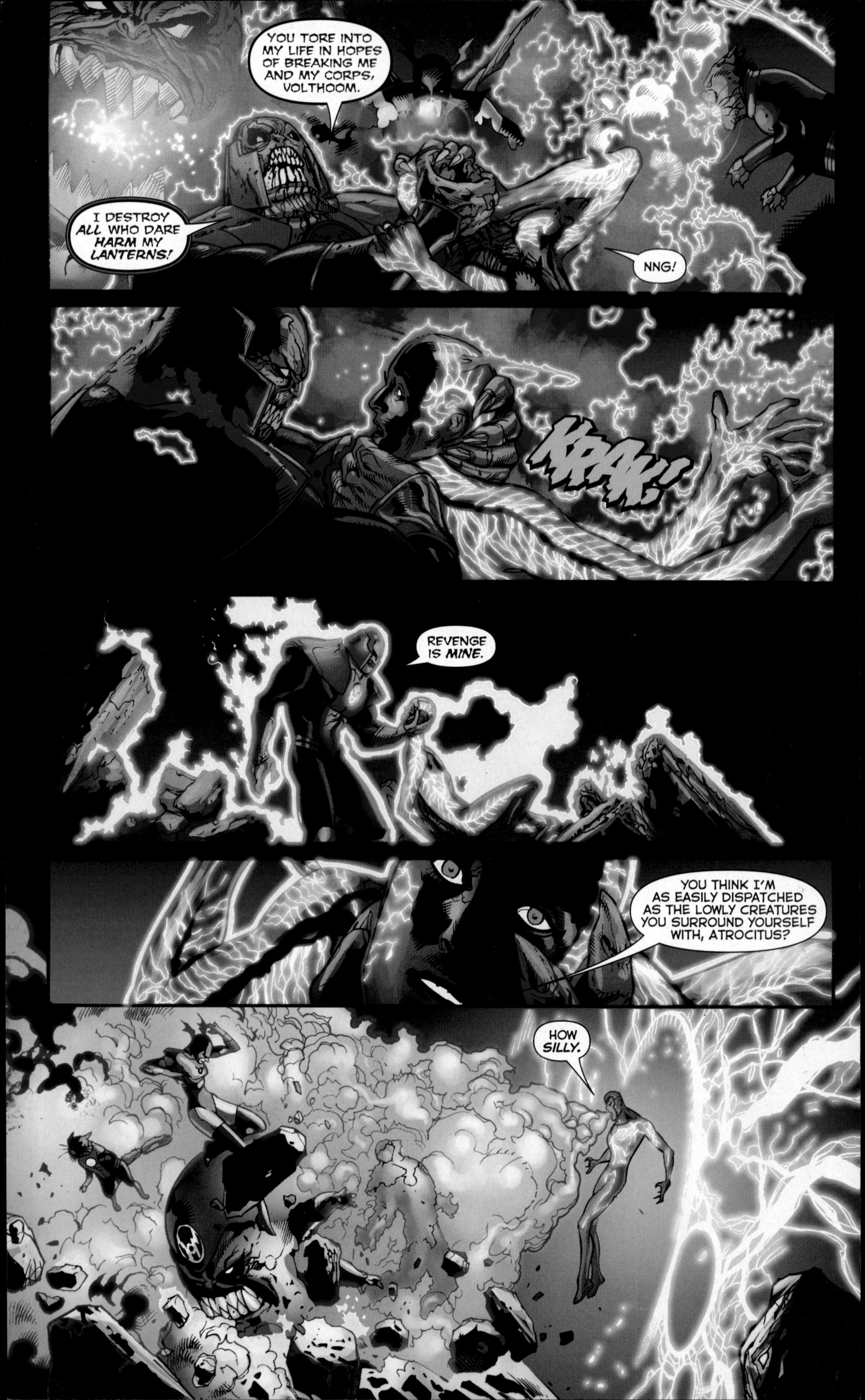
YOU TORE INTO MY LIFE IN HOPES OF BREAKING ME AND MY CORPS, VOLTHOOM.
I DESTROY ALL WHO DARE HARM MY LANTERNS!
NNG!
KRAK!
REVENGE IS MINE.
YOU THINK I'M AS EASILY DISPATCHED AS THE LOWLY CREATURES YOU SURROUND YOURSELF WITH, ATROCITUS?
HOW SILLY.

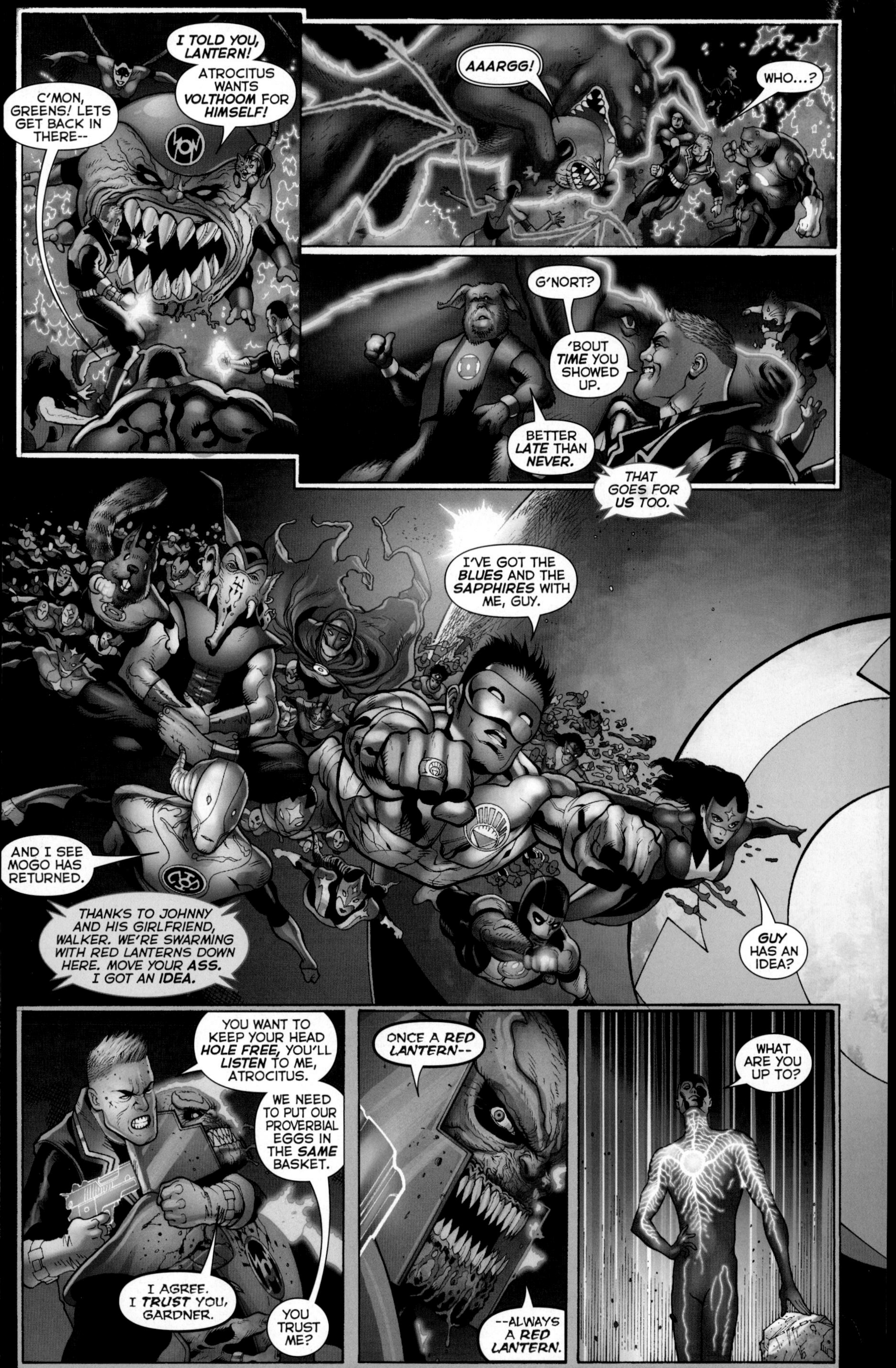
I TOLD YOU, LANTERN!
ATROCITUS WANTS VOLTHOOM FOR HIMSELF!
C'MON, GREENS! LETS GET BACK IN THERE--
AAARGG!
WHO...?
G'NORT?
'BOUT TIME YOU SHOWED UP.
BETTER LATE THAN NEVER.
THAT GOES FOR US TOO.
I'VE GOT THE BLUES AND THE SAPPHIRES WITH ME, GUY.
AND I SEE MOGO HAS RETURNED.
THANKS TO JOHNNY AND HIS GIRLFRIEND, WALKER. WE'RE SWARMING WITH RED LANTERNS DOWN HERE. MOVE YOUR ASS. I GOT AN IDEA.
GUY HAS AN IDEA?
YOU WANT TO KEEP YOUR HEAD HOLE FREE, YOU'LL LISTEN TO ME, ATROCITUS.
WE NEED TO PUT OUR PROVERBIAL EGGS IN THE SAME BASKET.
I AGREE. I TRUST YOU, GARDNER.
YOU TRUST ME?
ONCE A RED LANTERN--
--ALWAYS A RED LANTERN.
WHAT ARE YOU UP TO?

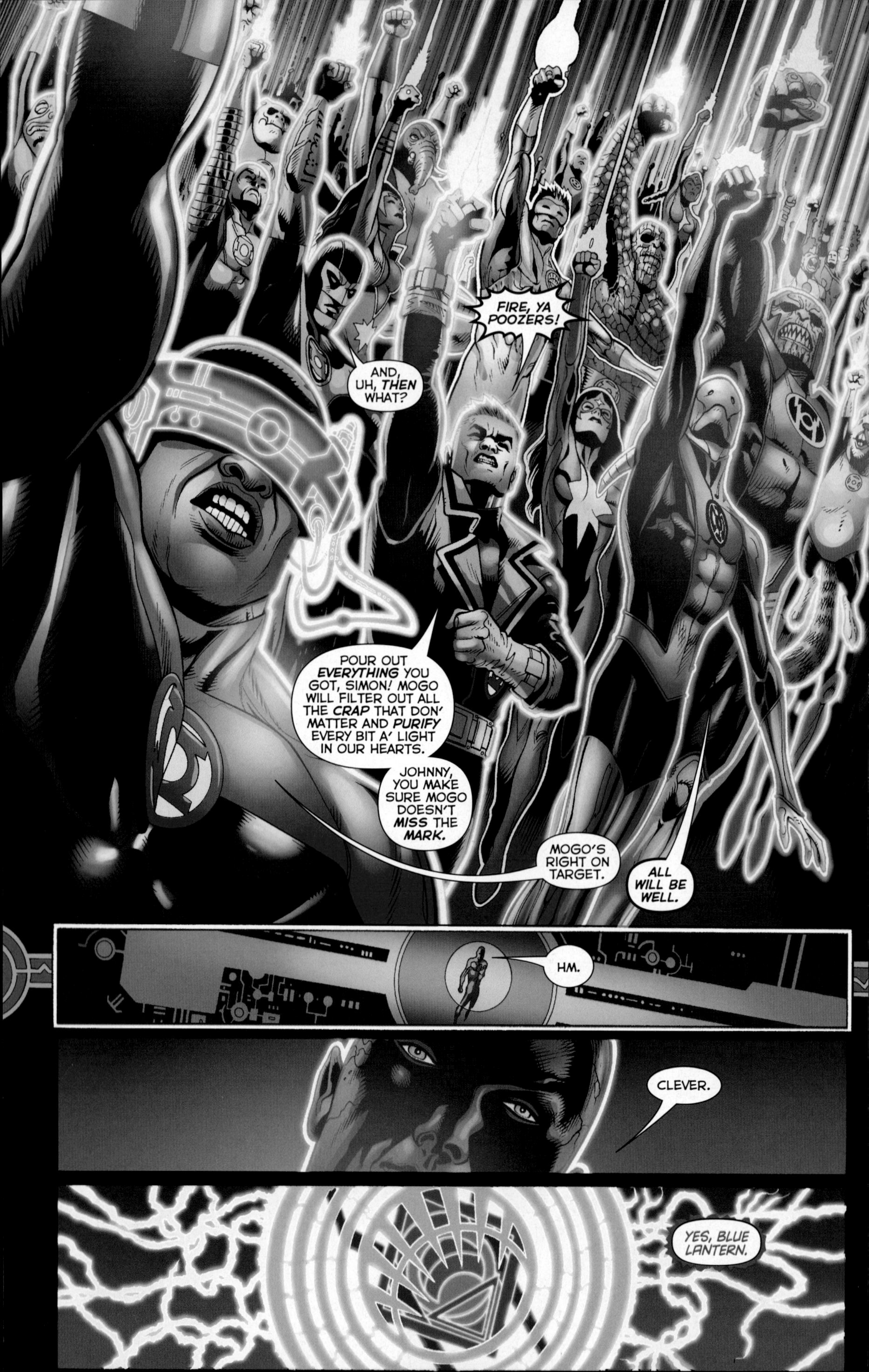
FIRE, YA POOZERS!
AND, UH, *THEN* WHAT?
POUR OUT *EVERYTHING* YOU GOT, SIMON! MOGO WILL FILTER OUT ALL THE *CRAP* THAT DON' MATTER AND *PURIFY* EVERY BIT A' LIGHT IN OUR HEARTS.
JOHNNY, YOU MAKE SURE MOGO DOESN'T *MISS* THE *MARK.*
MOGO'S RIGHT ON TARGET.
ALL WILL BE WELL.
HM.
CLEVER.
YES, BLUE LANTERN.

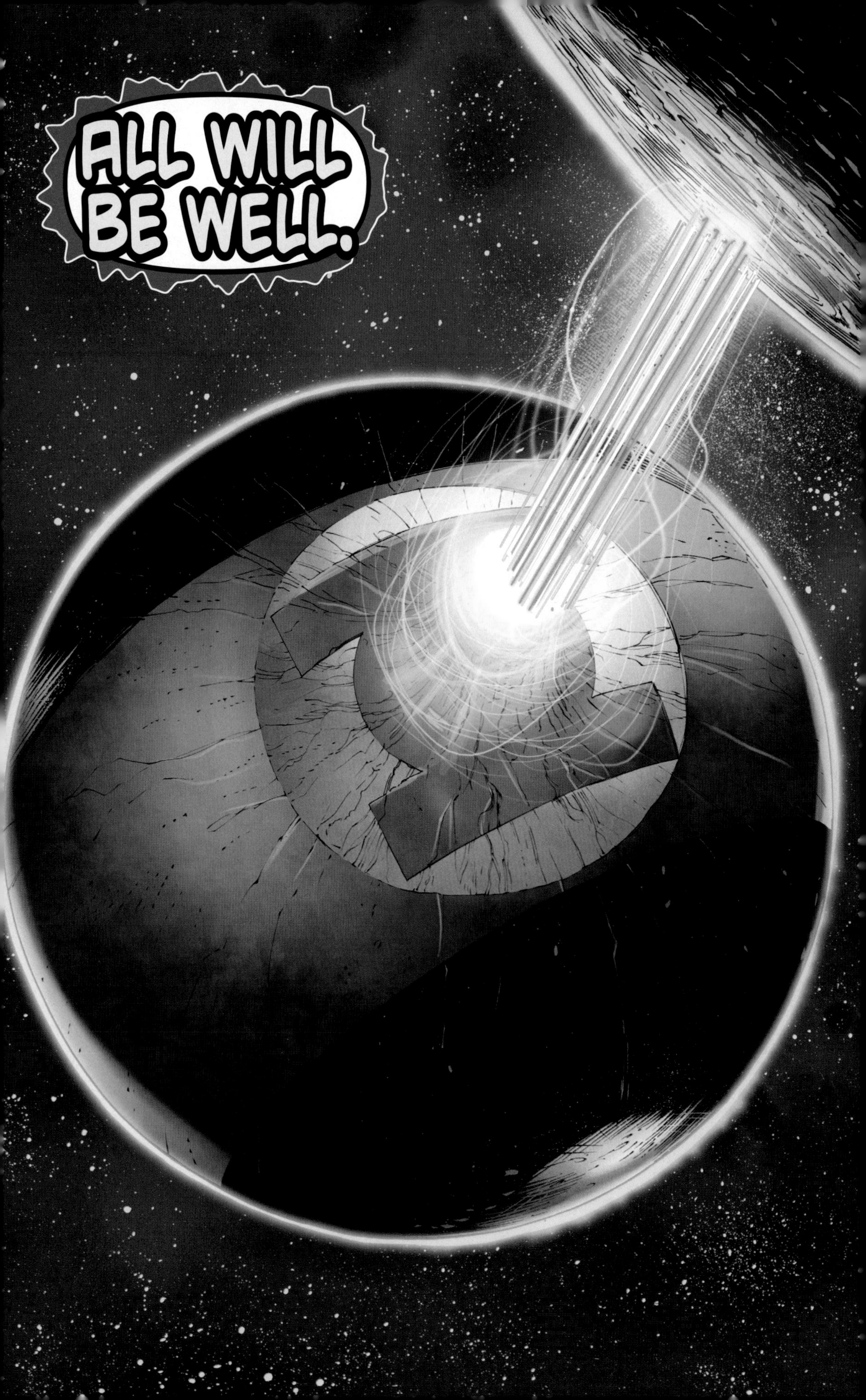
ALL WILL BE WELL.

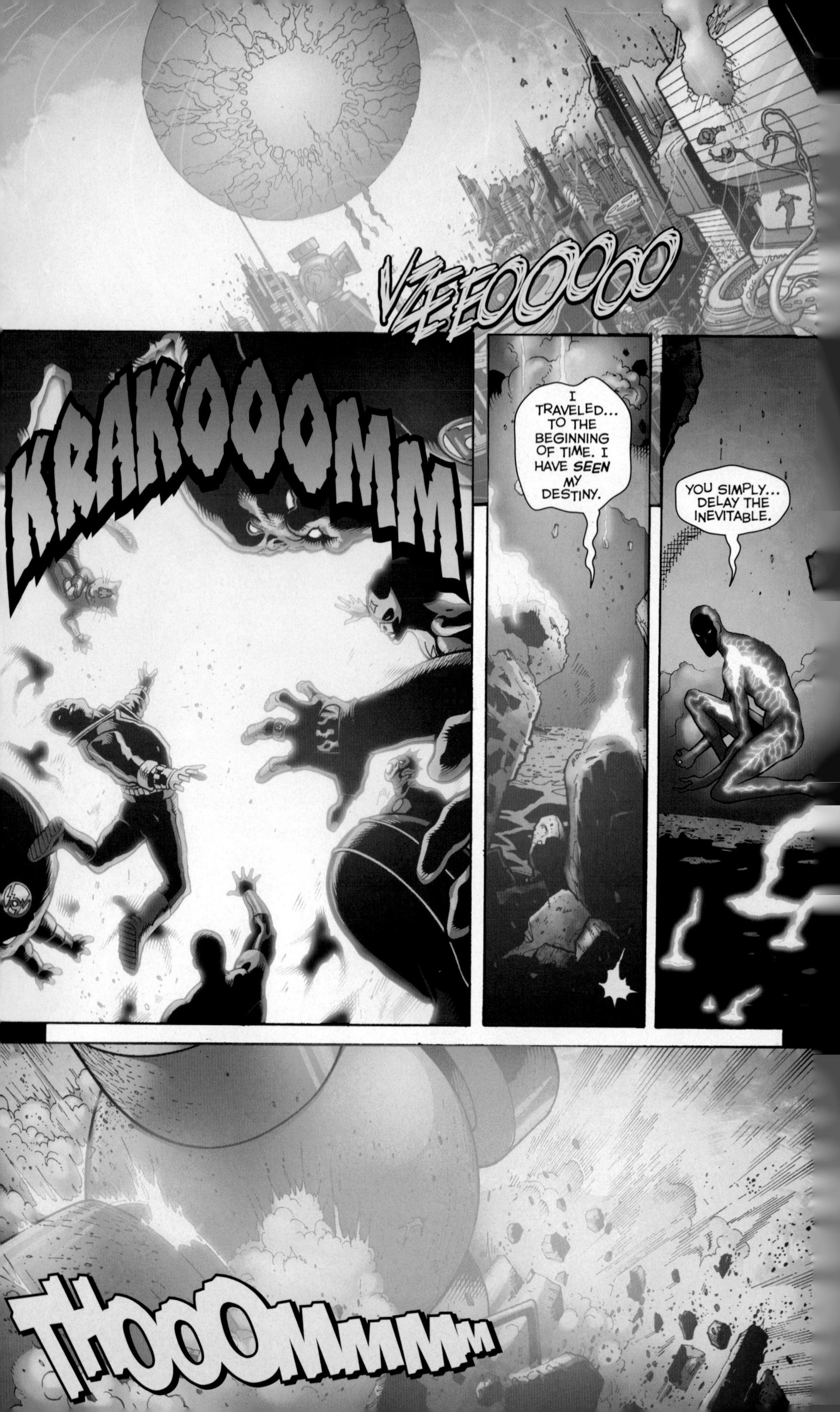
VZEEOOOOOO
KRAKOOOMMM
I TRAVELED... TO THE BEGINNING OF TIME. I HAVE SEEN MY DESTINY.
YOU SIMPLY... DELAY THE INEVITABLE.
THOOOMMMMM

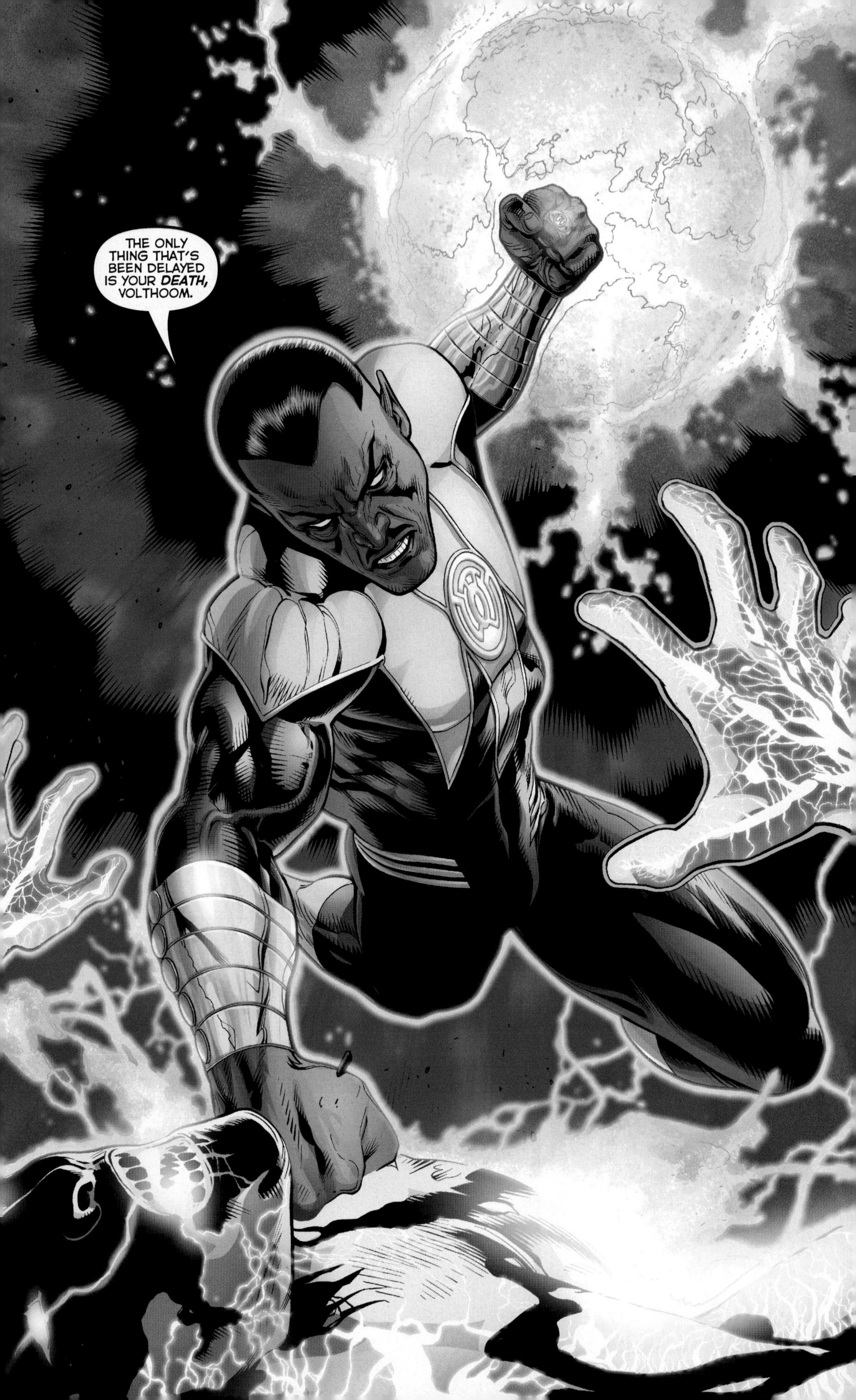
THE ONLY THING THAT'S BEEN DELAYED IS YOUR *DEATH,* VOLTHOOM.

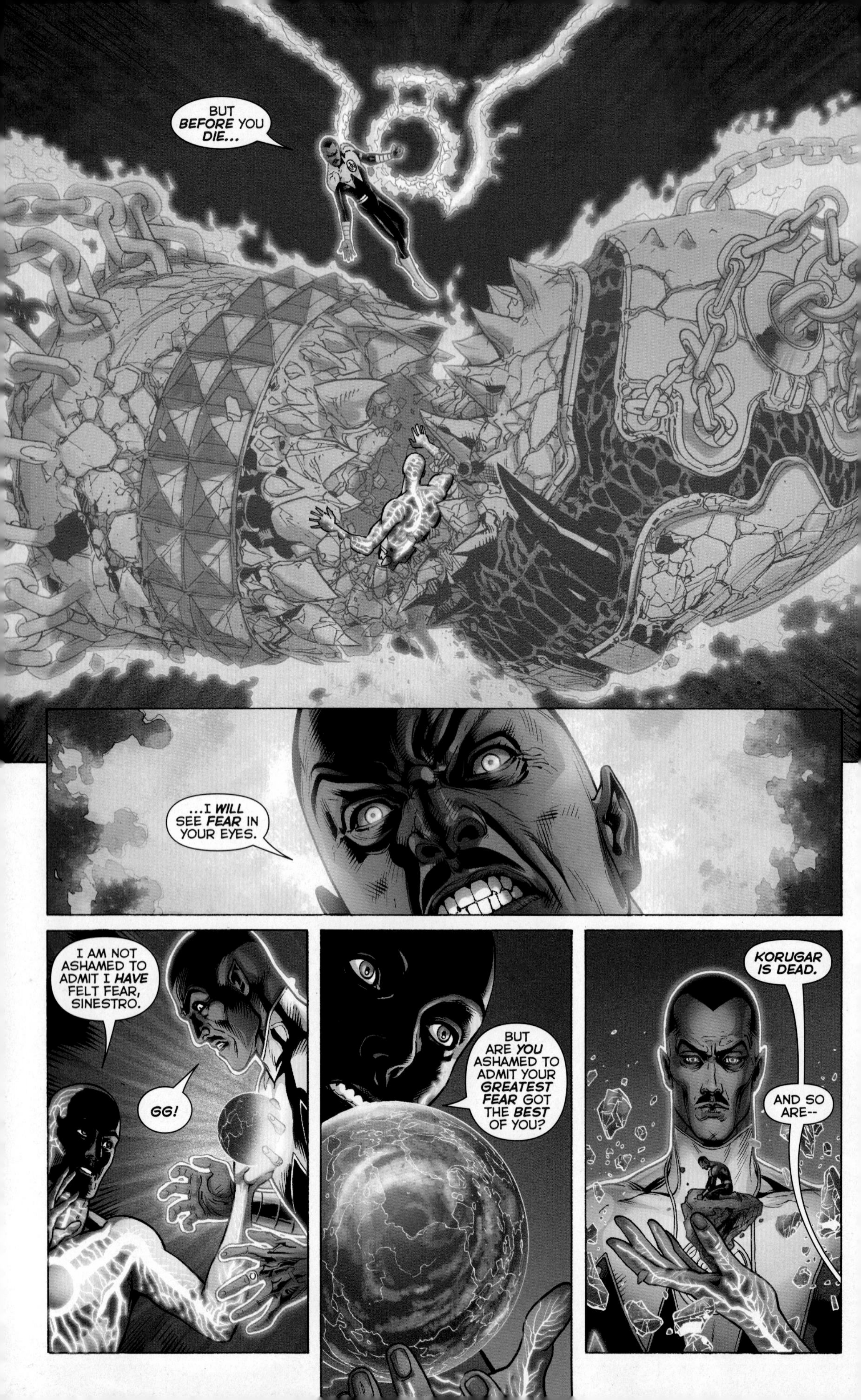
BUT *BEFORE* YOU *DIE*...
...I *WILL* SEE *FEAR* IN YOUR EYES.
I AM NOT ASHAMED TO ADMIT I *HAVE* FELT FEAR, SINESTRO.
GG!
BUT ARE *YOU* ASHAMED TO ADMIT YOUR *GREATEST FEAR* GOT THE *BEST* OF YOU?
KORUGAR IS DEAD.
AND SO ARE--

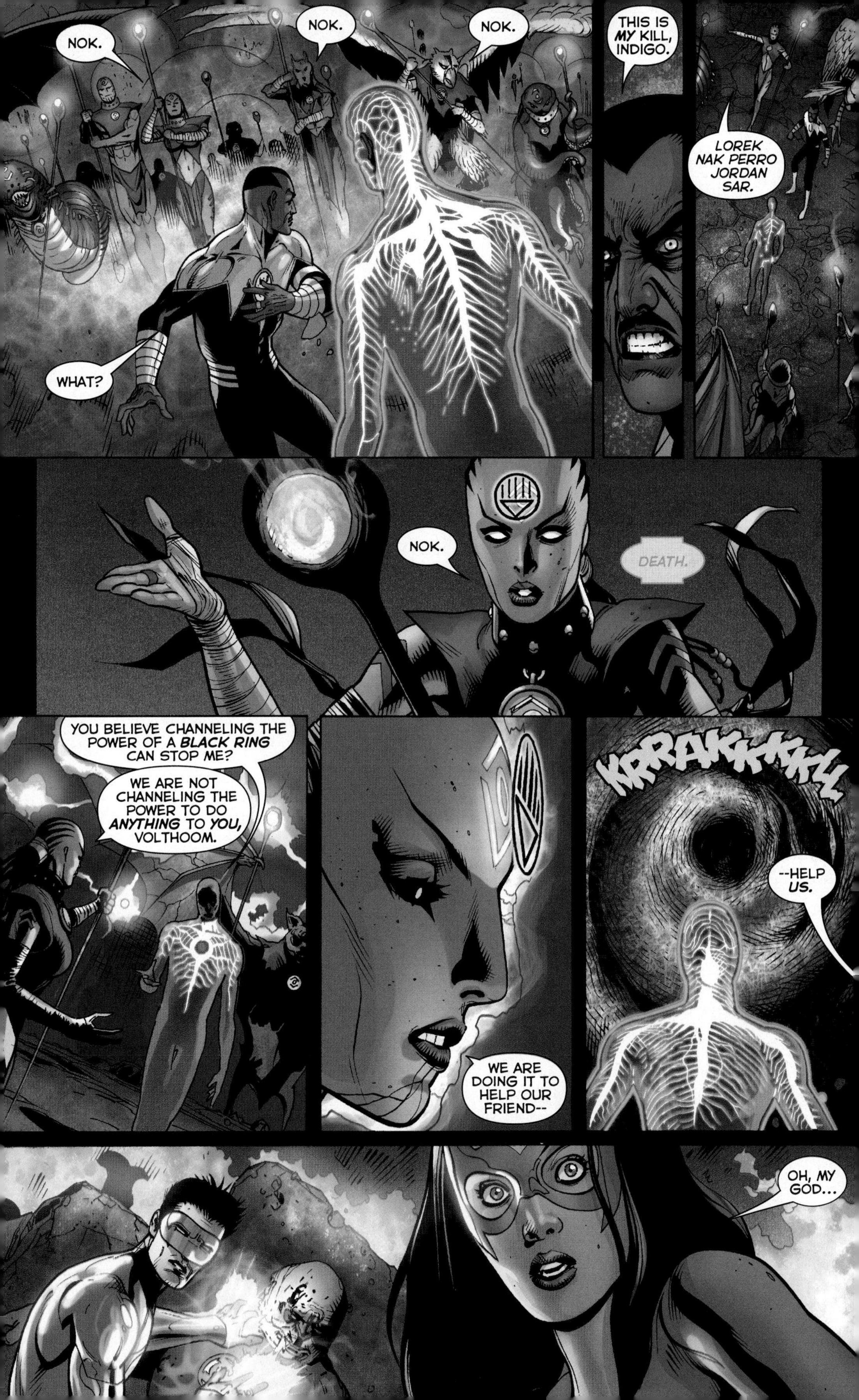
NOK.
NOK.
NOK.
WHAT?
THIS IS *MY* KILL, INDIGO.
LOREK NAK PERRO JORDAN SAR.
NOK.
DEATH.
YOU BELIEVE CHANNELING THE POWER OF A *BLACK RING* CAN STOP ME?
WE ARE NOT CHANNELING THE POWER TO DO *ANYTHING* TO *YOU,* VOLTHOOM.
WE ARE DOING IT TO HELP OUR FRIEND--
KRRAKKKKL
--HELP *US.*
OH, MY GOD...

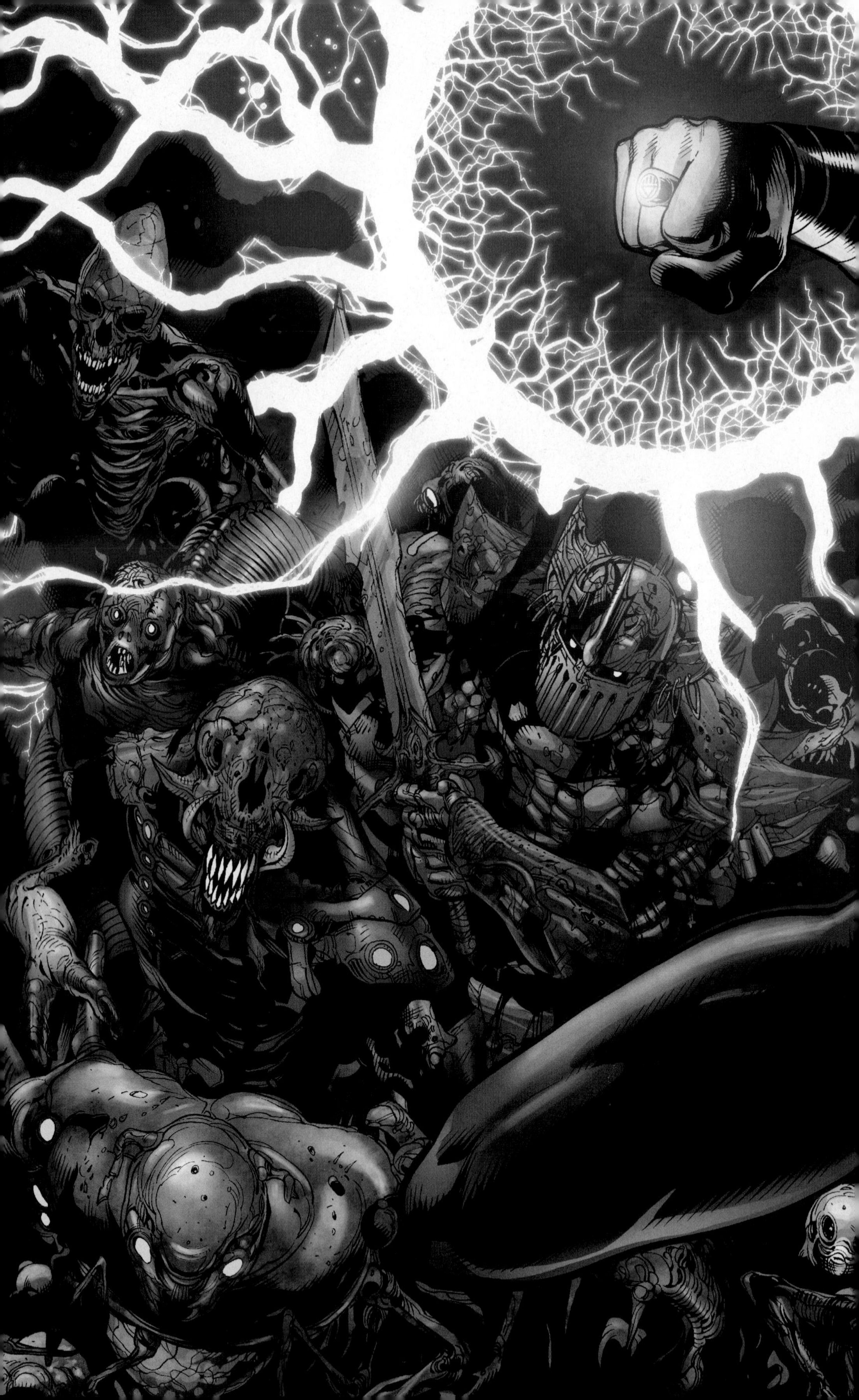

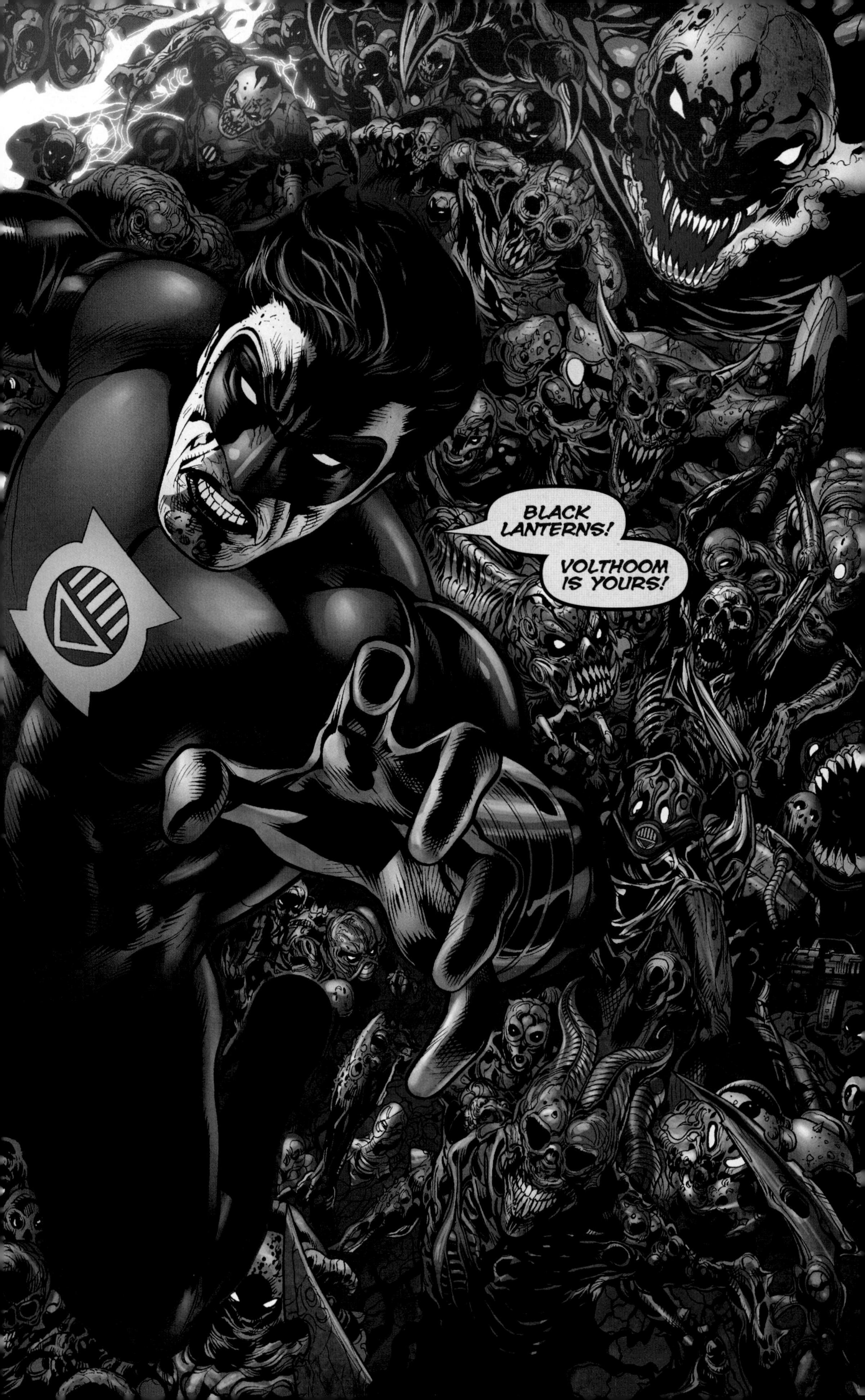
BLACK LANTERNS!
VOLTHOOM IS YOURS!

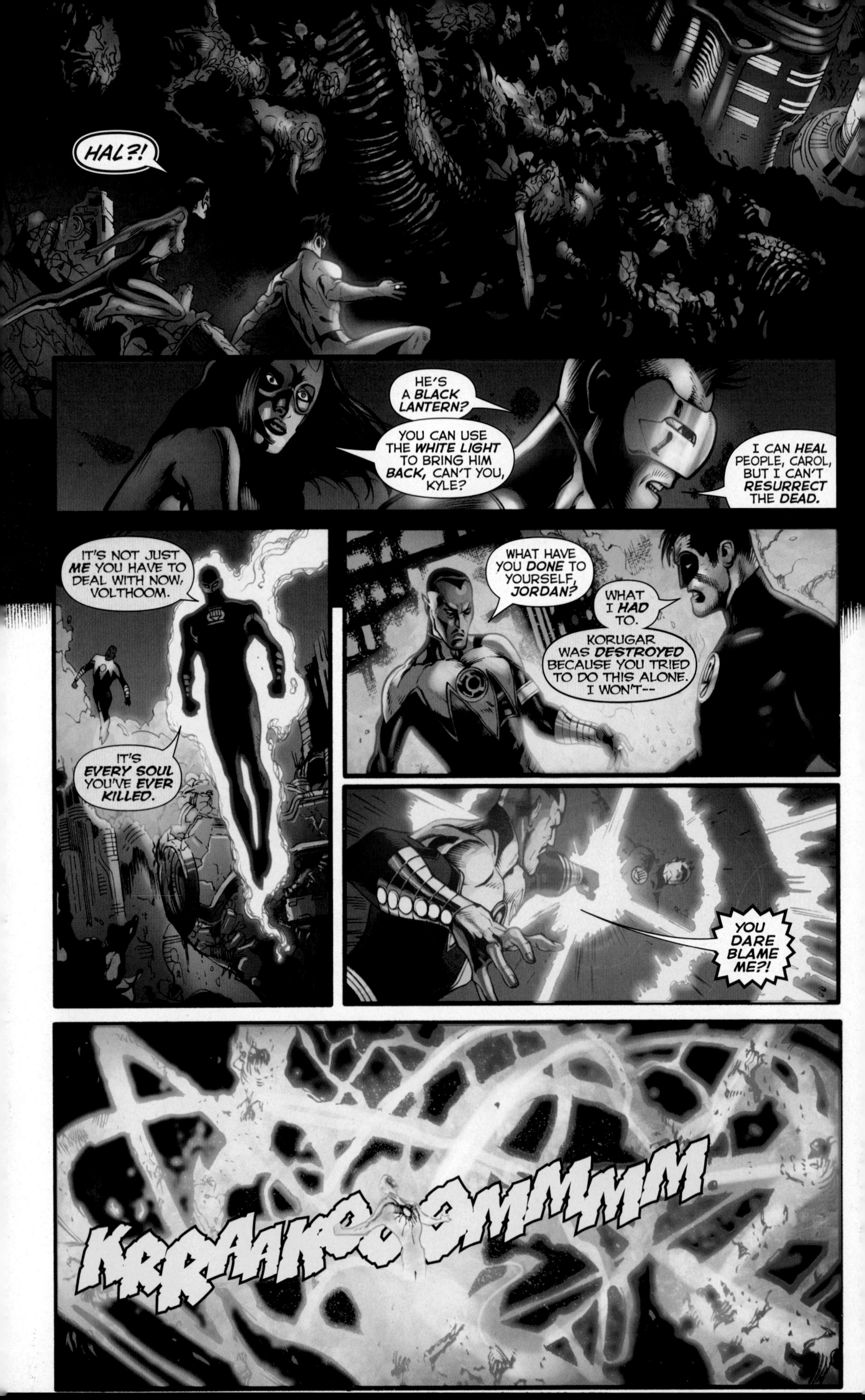
HAL?!
HE'S A BLACK LANTERN?
YOU CAN USE THE WHITE LIGHT TO BRING HIM BACK, CAN'T YOU, KYLE?
I CAN HEAL PEOPLE, CAROL, BUT I CAN'T RESURRECT THE DEAD.
IT'S NOT JUST ME YOU HAVE TO DEAL WITH NOW, VOLTHOOM.
IT'S EVERY SOUL YOU'VE EVER KILLED.
WHAT HAVE YOU DONE TO YOURSELF, JORDAN?
WHAT I HAD TO.
KORUGAR WAS DESTROYED BECAUSE YOU TRIED TO DO THIS ALONE. I WON'T--
YOU DARE BLAME ME?!
KRRAAKOOOMMMMM

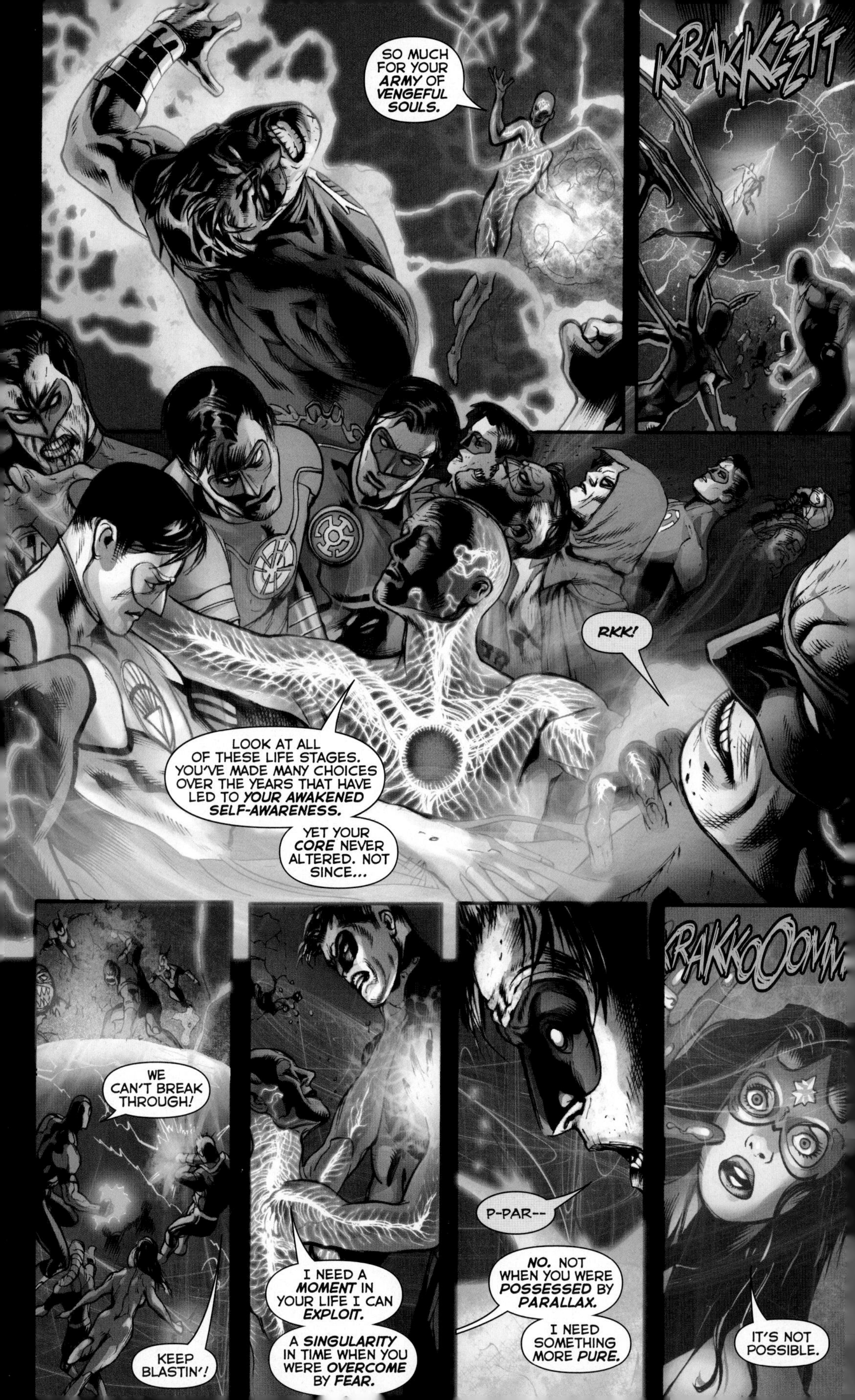

SO MUCH FOR YOUR ARMY OF VENGEFUL SOULS.
KRAKKZZTT
RKK!
LOOK AT ALL OF THESE LIFE STAGES. YOU'VE MADE MANY CHOICES OVER THE YEARS THAT HAVE LED TO YOUR AWAKENED SELF-AWARENESS.
YET YOUR CORE NEVER ALTERED. NOT SINCE...
WE CAN'T BREAK THROUGH!
KEEP BLASTIN'!
I NEED A MOMENT IN YOUR LIFE I CAN EXPLOIT.
A SINGULARITY IN TIME WHEN YOU WERE OVERCOME BY FEAR.
P-PAR--
NO. NOT WHEN YOU WERE POSSESSED BY PARALLAX.
I NEED SOMETHING MORE PURE.
KRAKKOOOMM
IT'S NOT POSSIBLE.

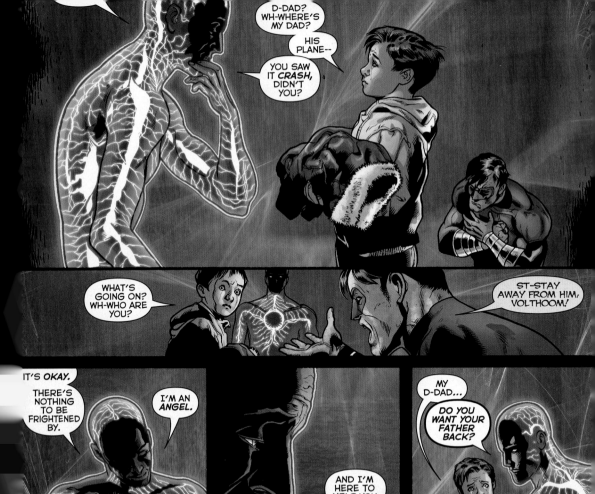

D-DAD? WH-WHERE'S MY DAD?

HIS PLANE--

YOU SAW IT *CRASH,* DIDN'T YOU?

WHAT'S GOING ON? WH-WHO ARE YOU?

ST-STAY AWAY FROM HIM, VOLTHOOM!

IT'S *OKAY.*

THERE'S NOTHING TO BE FRIGHTENED BY.

I'M AN *ANGEL.*

AND I'M HERE TO *HELP* YOU.

MY D-DAD...

DO YOU WANT YOUR FATHER BACK?

WISH FOR IT.

WISH *HARDER* THAN YOU EVER HAVE IN YOUR *LIFE,* AND I CAN BRING HIM HERE FOR YOU, HAL.

I...I WISH--

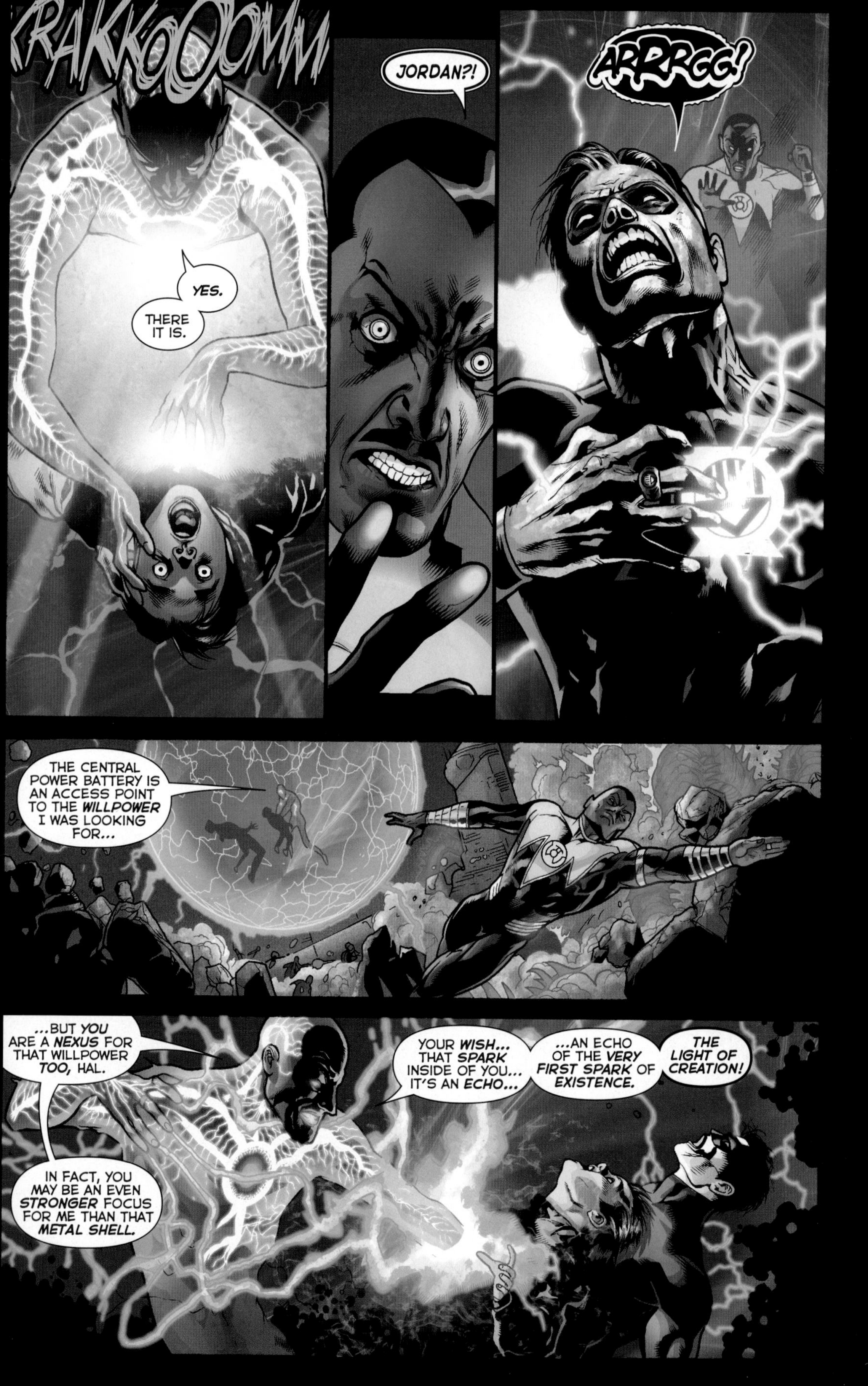
KRAKKOOOMM
YES.
THERE IT IS.
JORDAN?!
ARRRGG!
THE CENTRAL POWER BATTERY IS AN ACCESS POINT TO THE *WILLPOWER* I WAS LOOKING FOR...
...BUT *YOU* ARE A *NEXUS* FOR THAT WILLPOWER *TOO,* HAL.
IN FACT, YOU MAY BE AN EVEN *STRONGER* FOCUS FOR ME THAN THAT *METAL SHELL.*
YOUR *WISH*... THAT *SPARK* INSIDE OF YOU... IT'S AN *ECHO*...
...AN ECHO OF THE *VERY FIRST SPARK* OF *EXISTENCE.*
THE LIGHT OF CREATION!

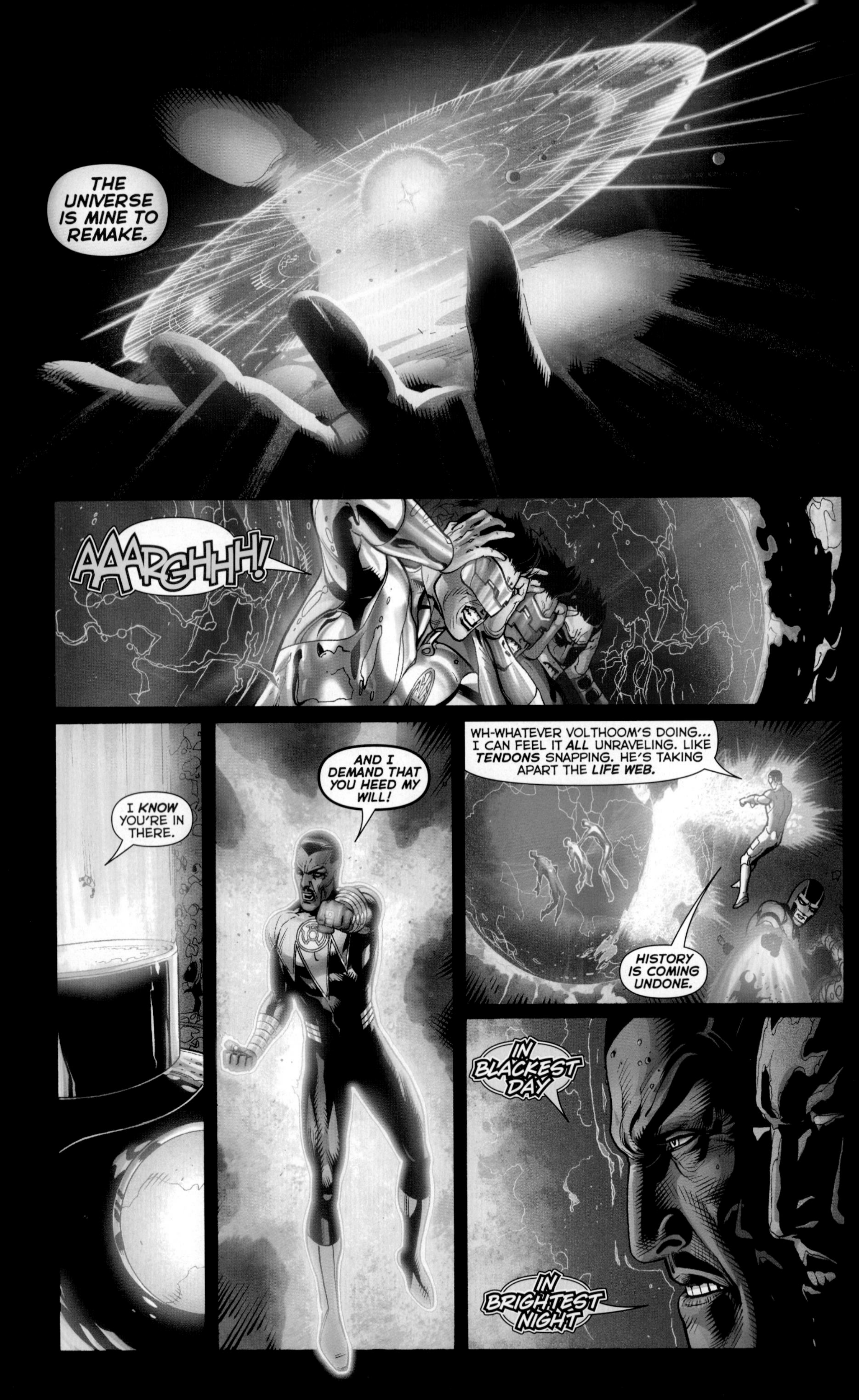
THE UNIVERSE IS MINE TO REMAKE.
AAARGHHH!
I KNOW YOU'RE IN THERE.
AND I DEMAND THAT YOU HEED MY WILL!
WH-WHATEVER VOLTHOOM'S DOING... I CAN FEEL IT ALL UNRAVELING. LIKE TENDONS SNAPPING. HE'S TAKING APART THE LIFE WEB.
HISTORY IS COMING UNDONE.
IN BLACKEST DAY
IN BRIGHTEST NIGHT

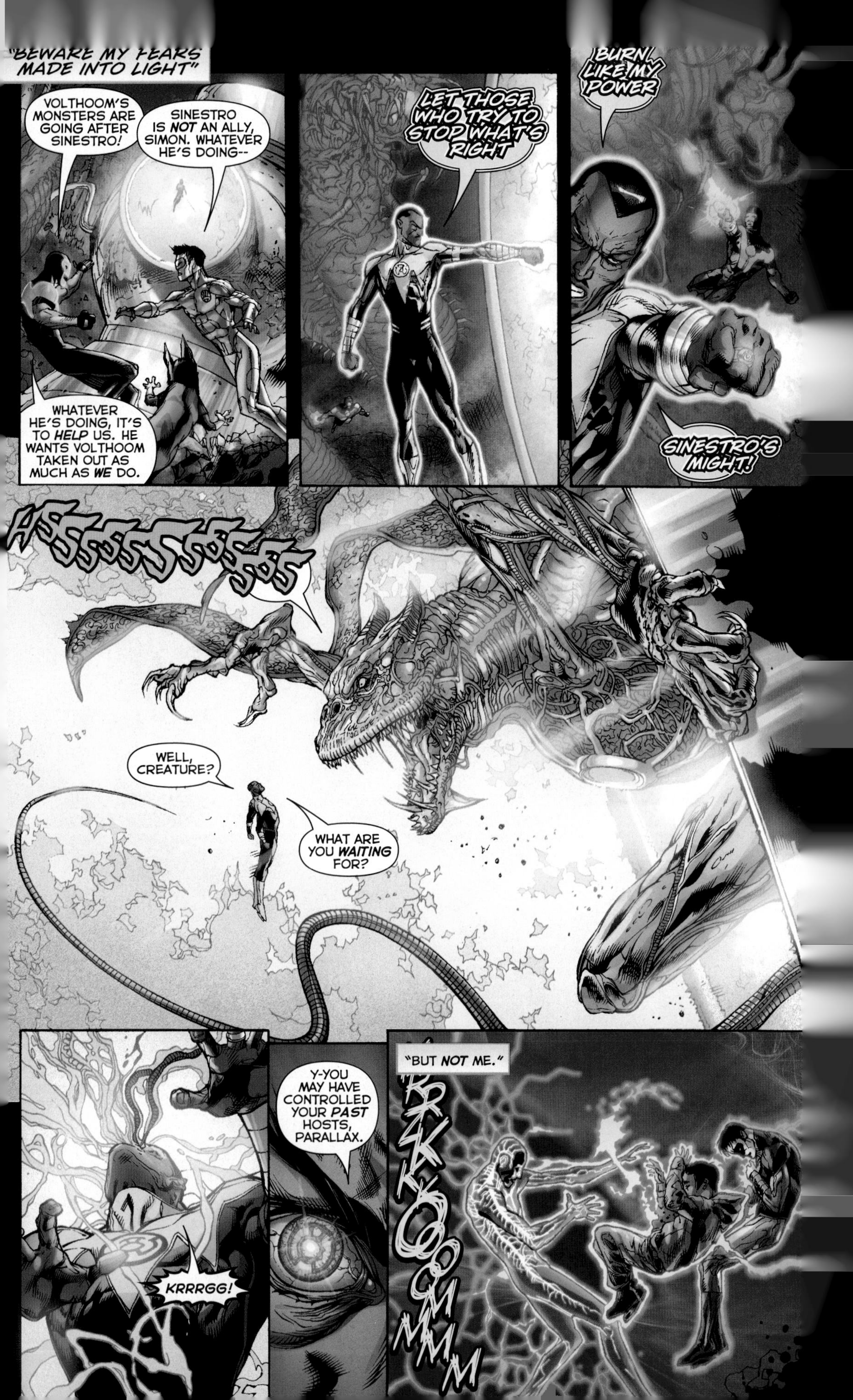
"BEWARE MY FEARS MADE INTO LIGHT"
VOLTHOOM'S MONSTERS ARE GOING AFTER SINESTRO!
SINESTRO IS NOT AN ALLY, SIMON. WHATEVER HE'S DOING--
WHATEVER HE'S DOING, IT'S TO HELP US. HE WANTS VOLTHOOM TAKEN OUT AS MUCH AS WE DO.
LET THOSE WHO TRY TO STOP WHAT'S RIGHT
BURN LIKE MY POWER
SINESTRO'S MIGHT!
HSSSSSSSSSS
WELL, CREATURE?
WHAT ARE YOU WAITING FOR?
KRRRGG!
Y-YOU MAY HAVE CONTROLLED YOUR PAST HOSTS, PARALLAX.
"BUT NOT ME."
KRAKOOOMMMM

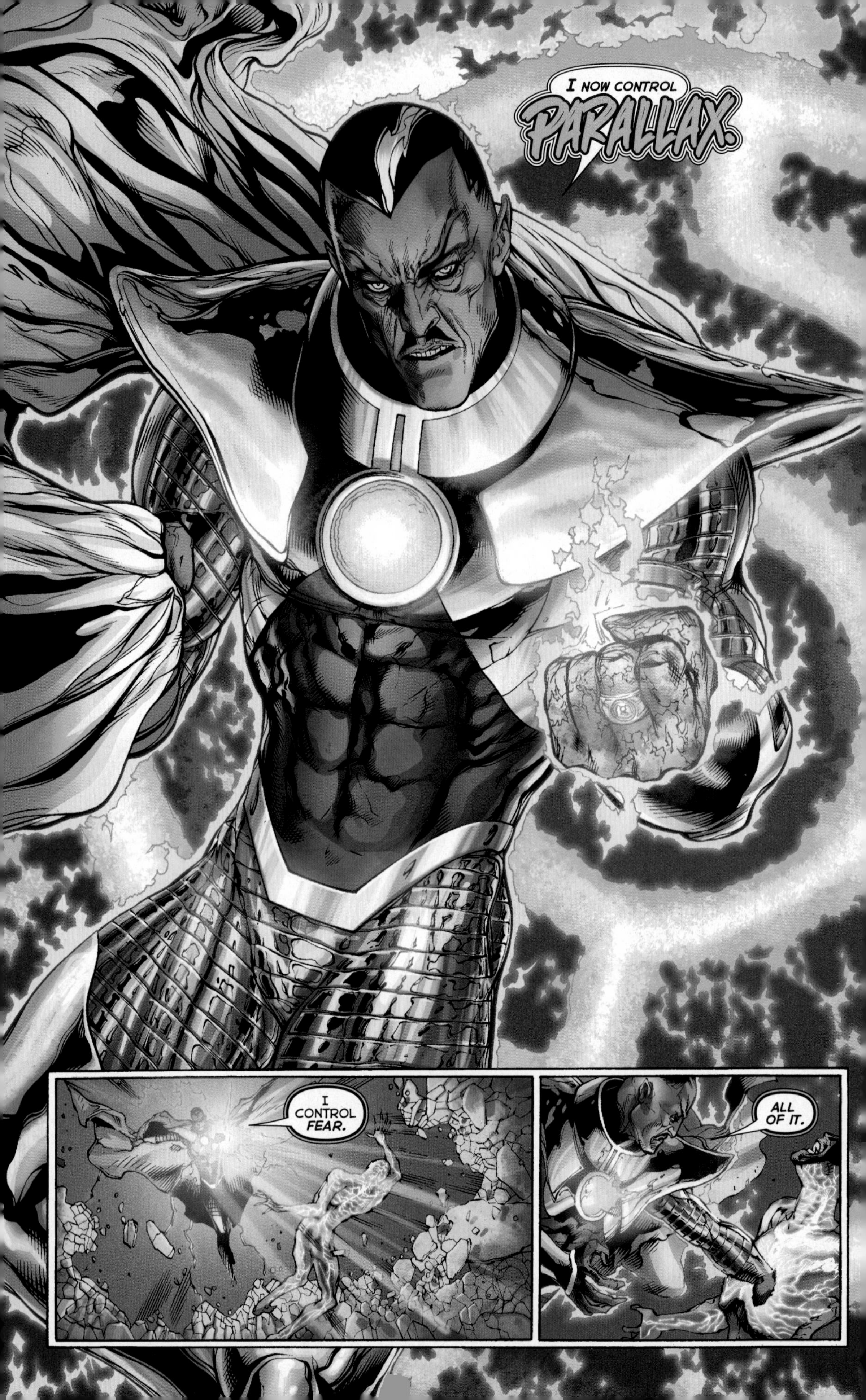
I NOW CONTROL
PARALLAX.
I CONTROL FEAR.
ALL OF IT.

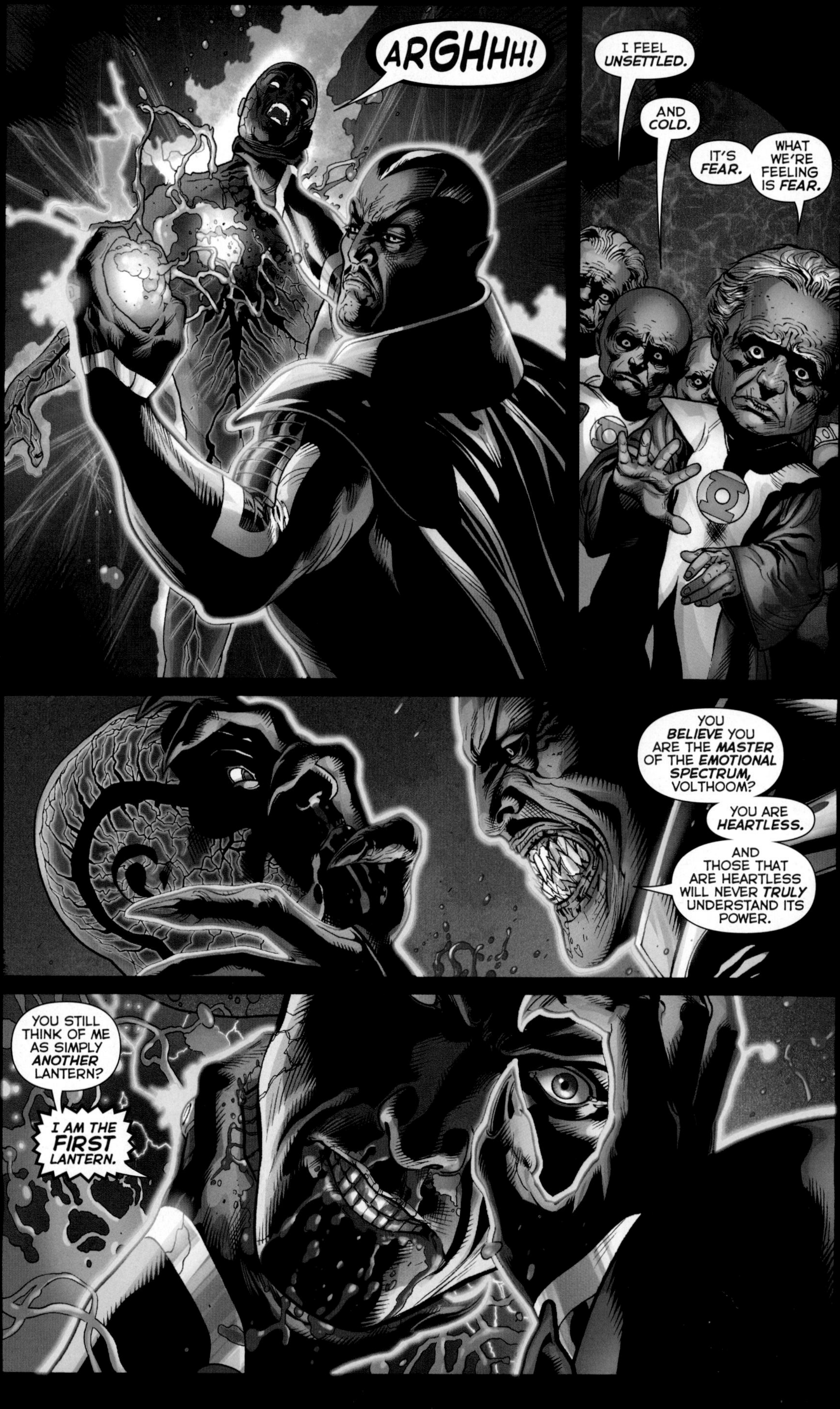
ARGHHH!
I FEEL UNSETTLED.
AND COLD.
IT'S FEAR.
WHAT WE'RE FEELING IS FEAR.
YOU BELIEVE YOU ARE THE MASTER OF THE EMOTIONAL SPECTRUM, VOLTHOOM?
YOU ARE HEARTLESS.
AND THOSE THAT ARE HEARTLESS WILL NEVER TRULY UNDERSTAND ITS POWER.
YOU STILL THINK OF ME AS SIMPLY ANOTHER LANTERN?
I AM THE FIRST LANTERN.

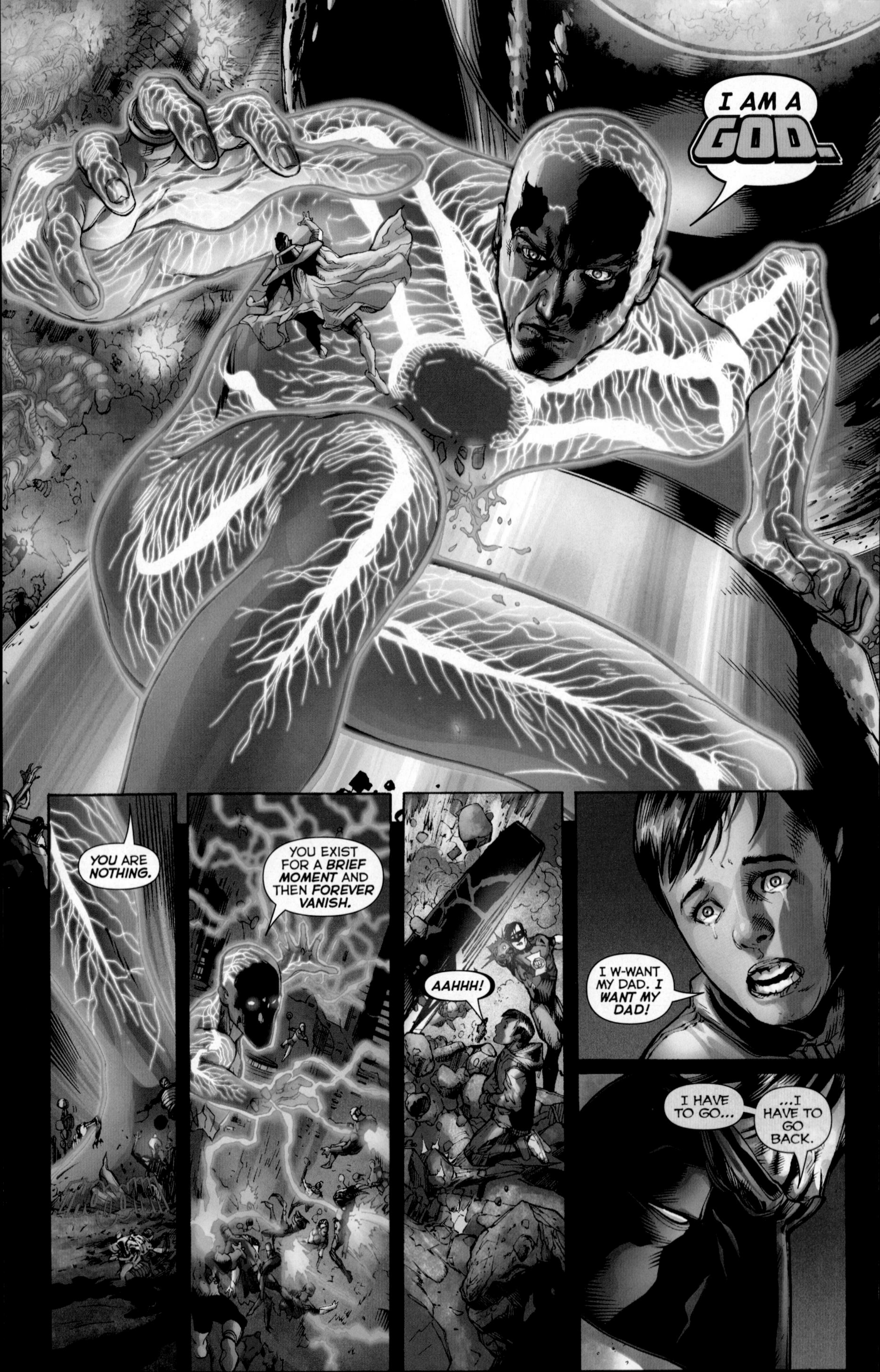

I AM A GOD...
YOU ARE NOTHING.
YOU EXIST FOR A BRIEF MOMENT AND THEN FOREVER VANISH.
AAHHH!
I W-WANT MY DAD. I WANT MY DAD!
I HAVE TO GO...
...I HAVE TO GO BACK.

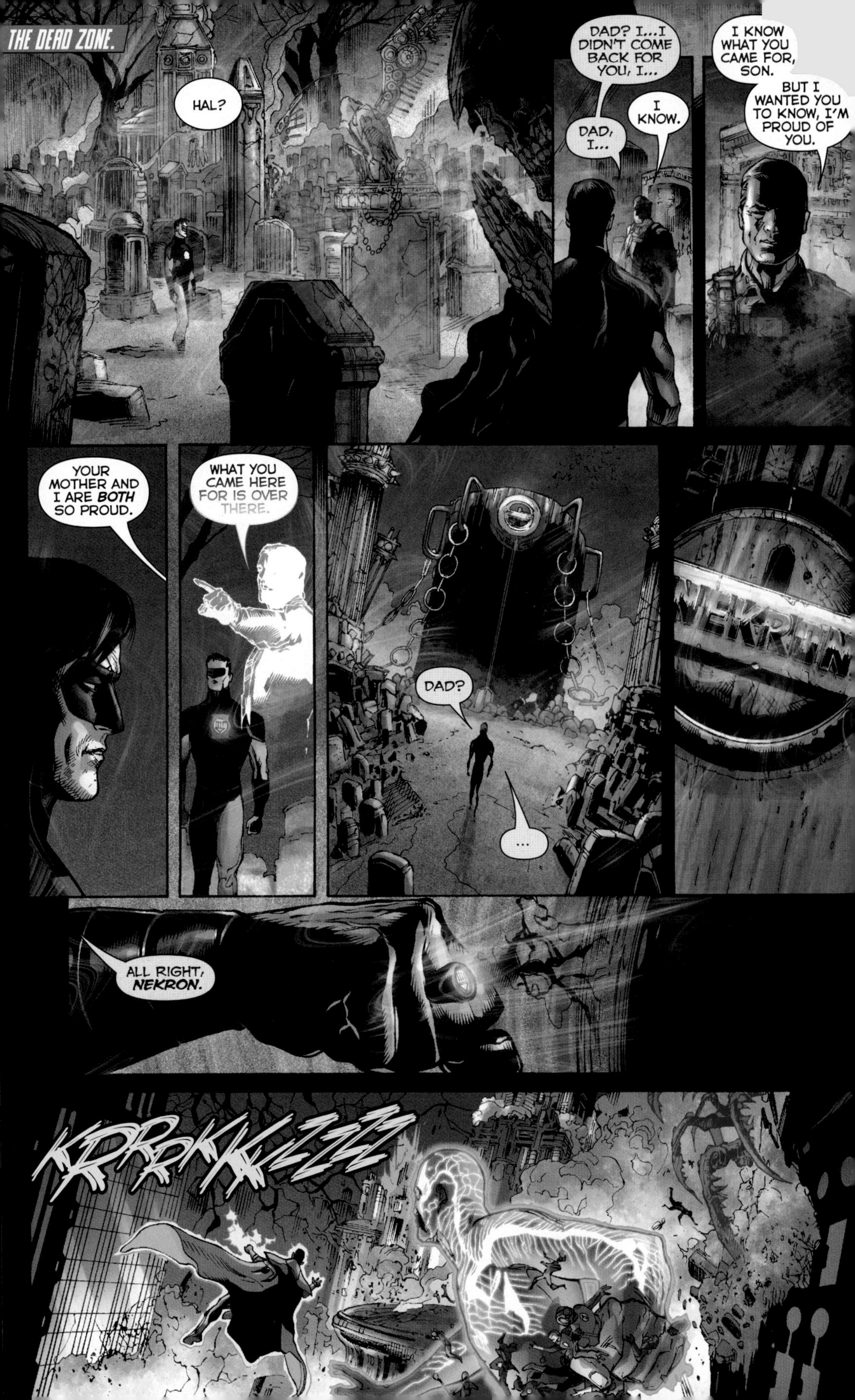
THE DEAD ZONE.
HAL?
DAD? I...I DIDN'T COME BACK FOR YOU, I...
DAD, I...
I KNOW.
I KNOW WHAT YOU CAME FOR, SON.
BUT I WANTED YOU TO KNOW, I'M PROUD OF YOU.
YOUR MOTHER AND I ARE BOTH SO PROUD.
WHAT YOU CAME HERE FOR IS OVER THERE.
DAD?
...
NEKRON
ALL RIGHT, NEKRON.
KRRKKZZZ

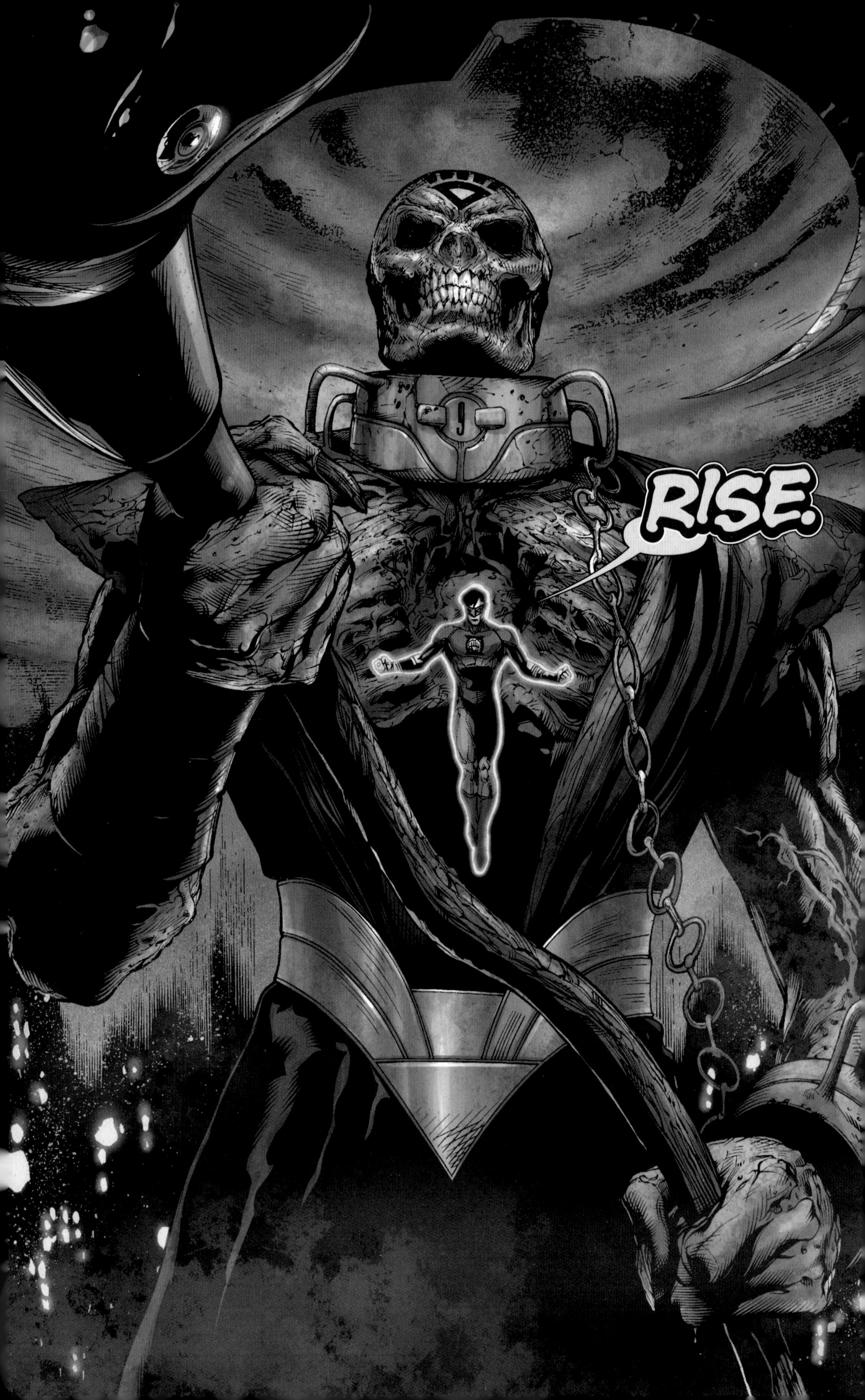
RISE.

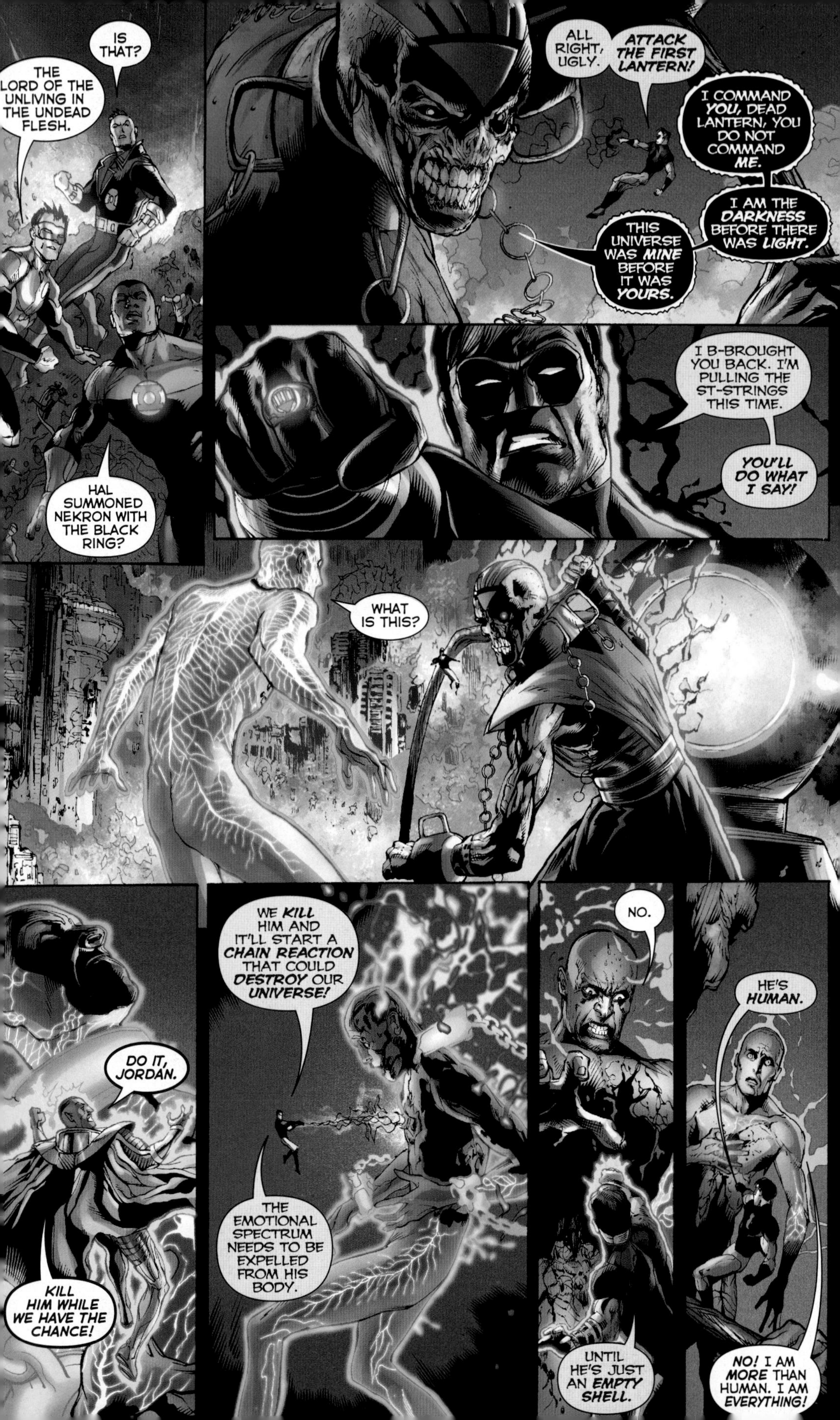

IS THAT?
THE LORD OF THE UNLIVING IN THE UNDEAD FLESH.
HAL SUMMONED NEKRON WITH THE BLACK RING?
ALL RIGHT, UGLY.
ATTACK THE FIRST LANTERN!
I COMMAND YOU, DEAD LANTERN, YOU DO NOT COMMAND ME.
I AM THE DARKNESS BEFORE THERE WAS LIGHT.
THIS UNIVERSE WAS MINE BEFORE IT WAS YOURS.
I B-BROUGHT YOU BACK. I'M PULLING THE ST-STRINGS THIS TIME.
YOU'LL DO WHAT I SAY!
WHAT IS THIS?
DO IT, JORDAN.
KILL HIM WHILE WE HAVE THE CHANCE!
WE KILL HIM AND IT'LL START A CHAIN REACTION THAT COULD DESTROY OUR UNIVERSE!
THE EMOTIONAL SPECTRUM NEEDS TO BE EXPELLED FROM HIS BODY.
NO.
UNTIL HE'S JUST AN EMPTY SHELL.
HE'S HUMAN.
NO! I AM MORE THAN HUMAN. I AM EVERYTHING!

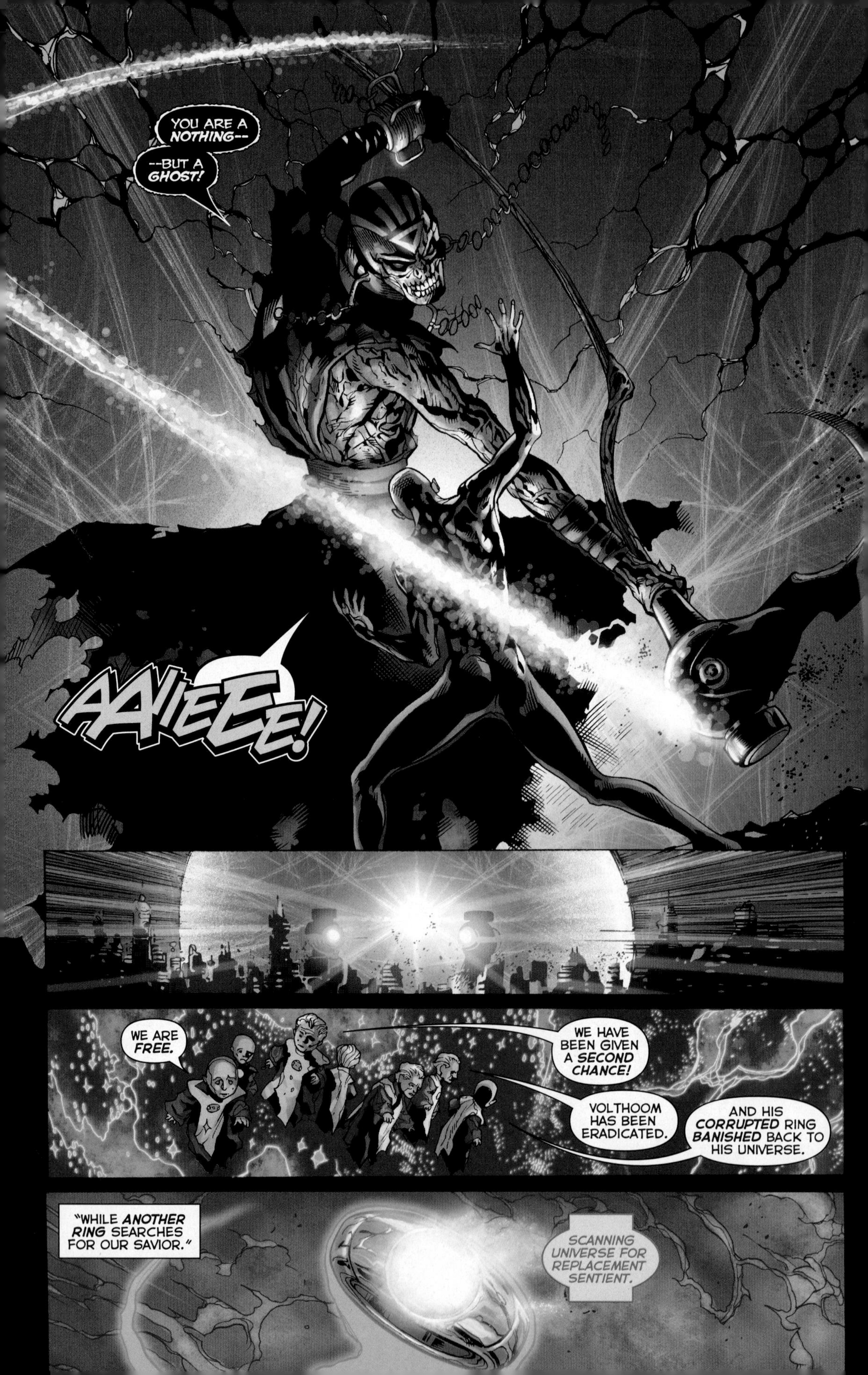
YOU ARE A NOTHING--
--BUT A GHOST!
AAIIEEE!
WE ARE FREE.
WE HAVE BEEN GIVEN A SECOND CHANCE!
VOLTHOOM HAS BEEN ERADICATED.
AND HIS CORRUPTED RING BANISHED BACK TO HIS UNIVERSE.
"WHILE ANOTHER RING SEARCHES FOR OUR SAVIOR."
SCANNING UNIVERSE FOR REPLACEMENT SENTIENT.

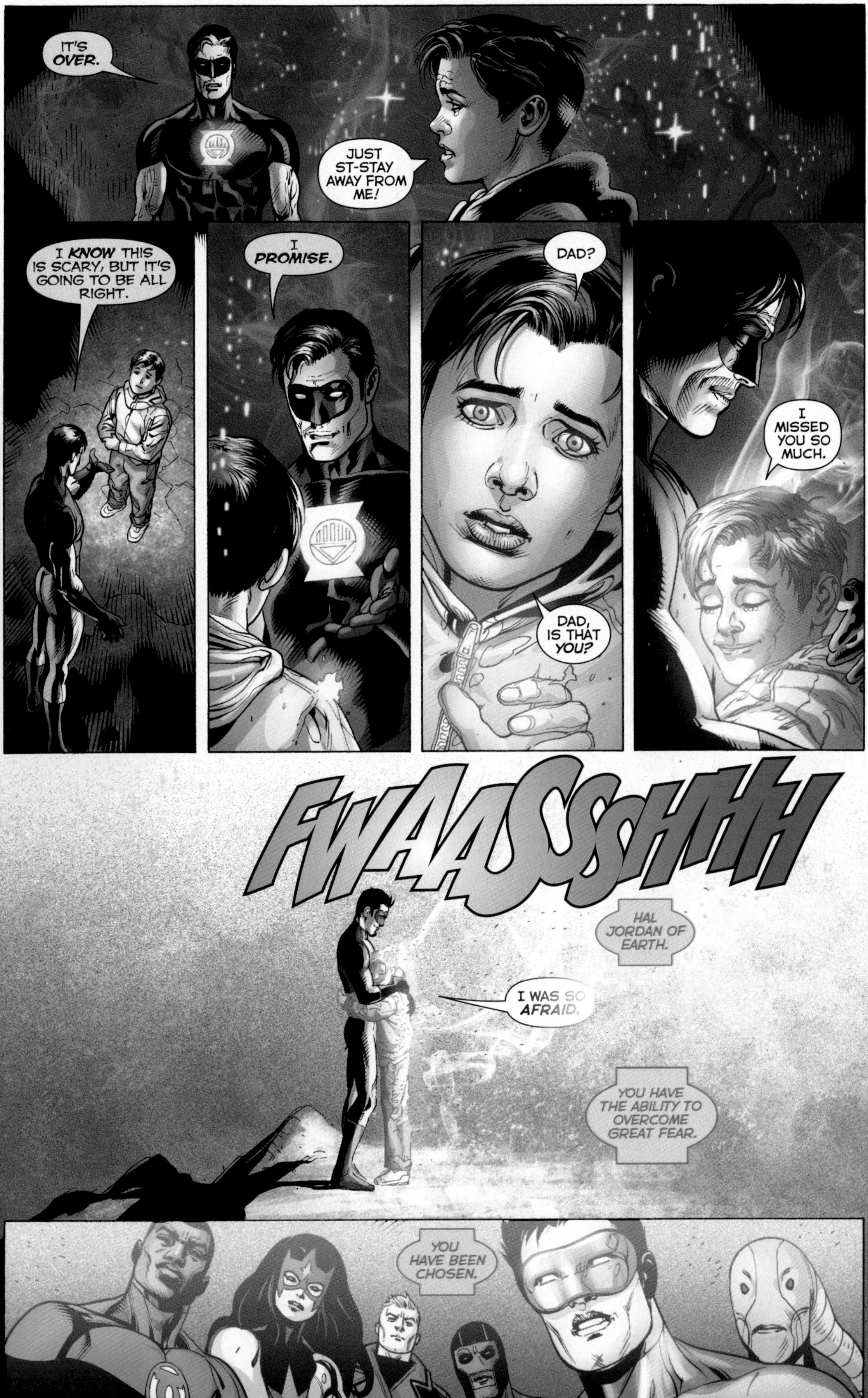
IT'S OVER.
JUST ST-STAY AWAY FROM ME!
I KNOW THIS IS SCARY, BUT IT'S GOING TO BE ALL RIGHT.
I PROMISE.
DAD?
DAD, IS THAT YOU?
I MISSED YOU SO MUCH.
FWAASSHHH
HAL JORDAN OF EARTH.
I WAS SO AFRAID.
YOU HAVE THE ABILITY TO OVERCOME GREAT FEAR.
YOU HAVE BEEN CHOSEN.

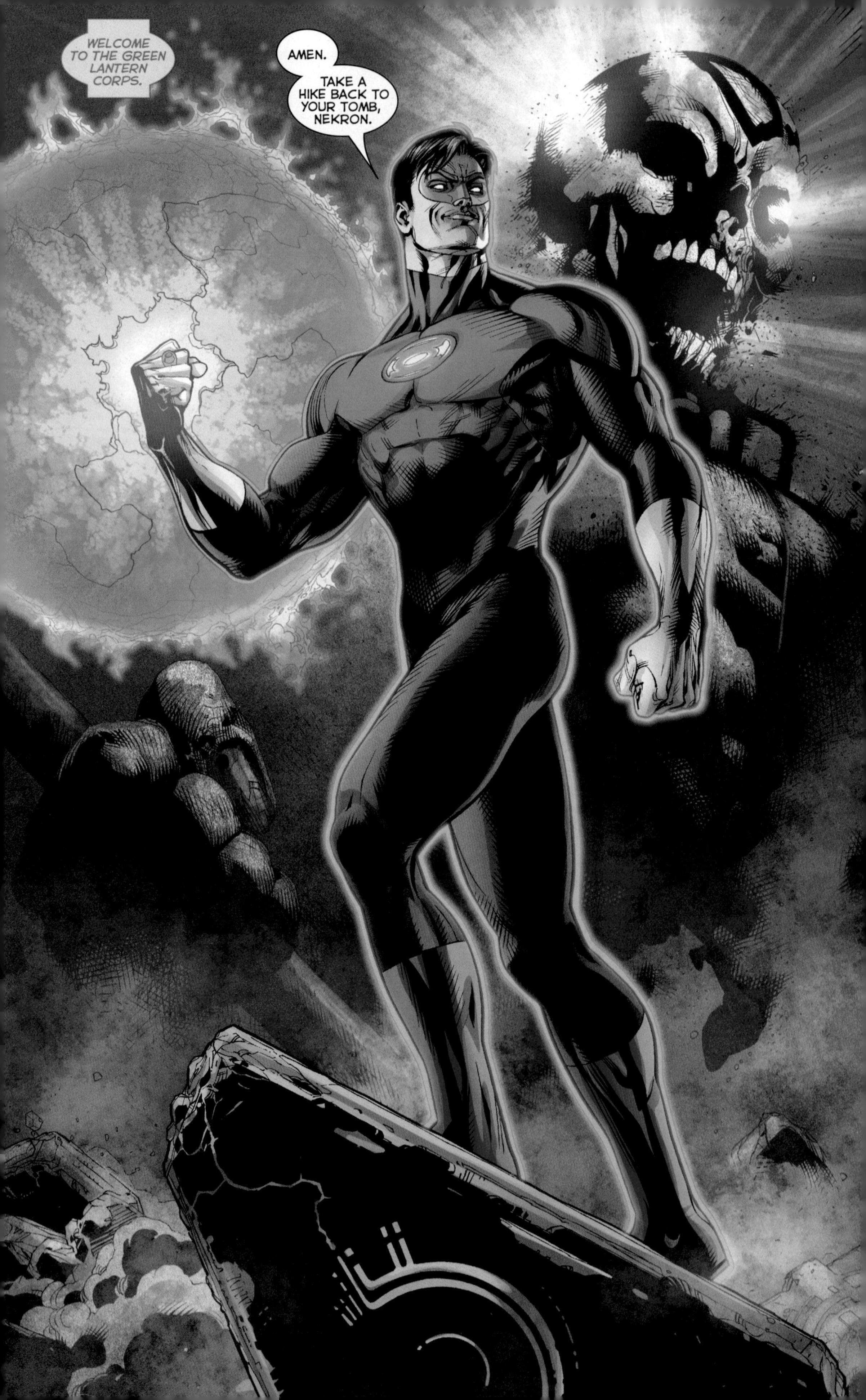
WELCOME TO THE GREEN LANTERN CORPS.
AMEN.
TAKE A HIKE BACK TO YOUR TOMB, NEKRON.

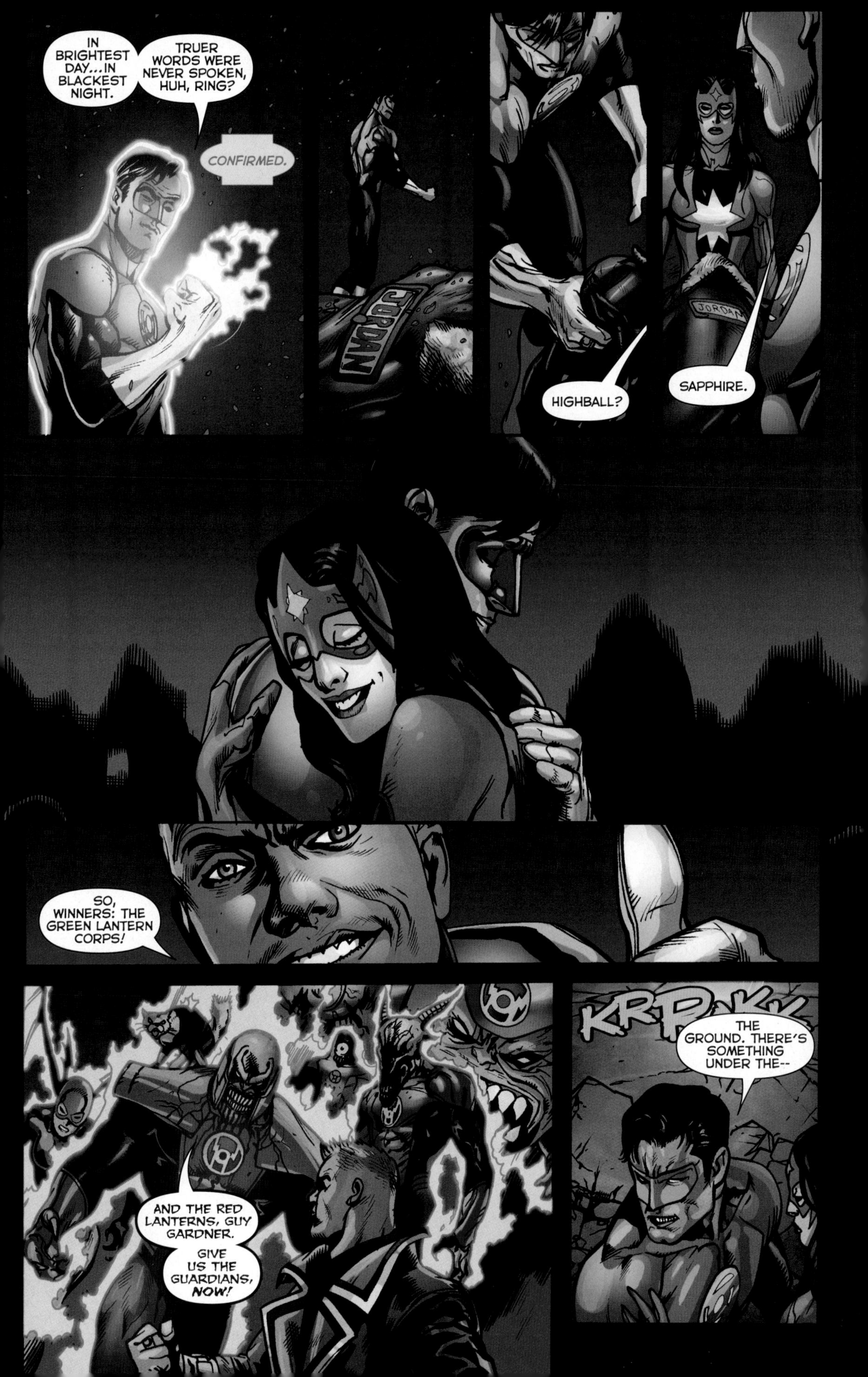
IN BRIGHTEST DAY...IN BLACKEST NIGHT.
TRUER WORDS WERE NEVER SPOKEN, HUH, RING?
CONFIRMED.
JORDAN
JORDAN
HIGHBALL?
SAPPHIRE.
SO, WINNERS: THE GREEN LANTERN CORPS!
AND THE RED LANTERNS, GUY GARDNER.
GIVE US THE GUARDIANS, NOW!
KRRKK
THE GROUND. THERE'S SOMETHING UNDER THE--

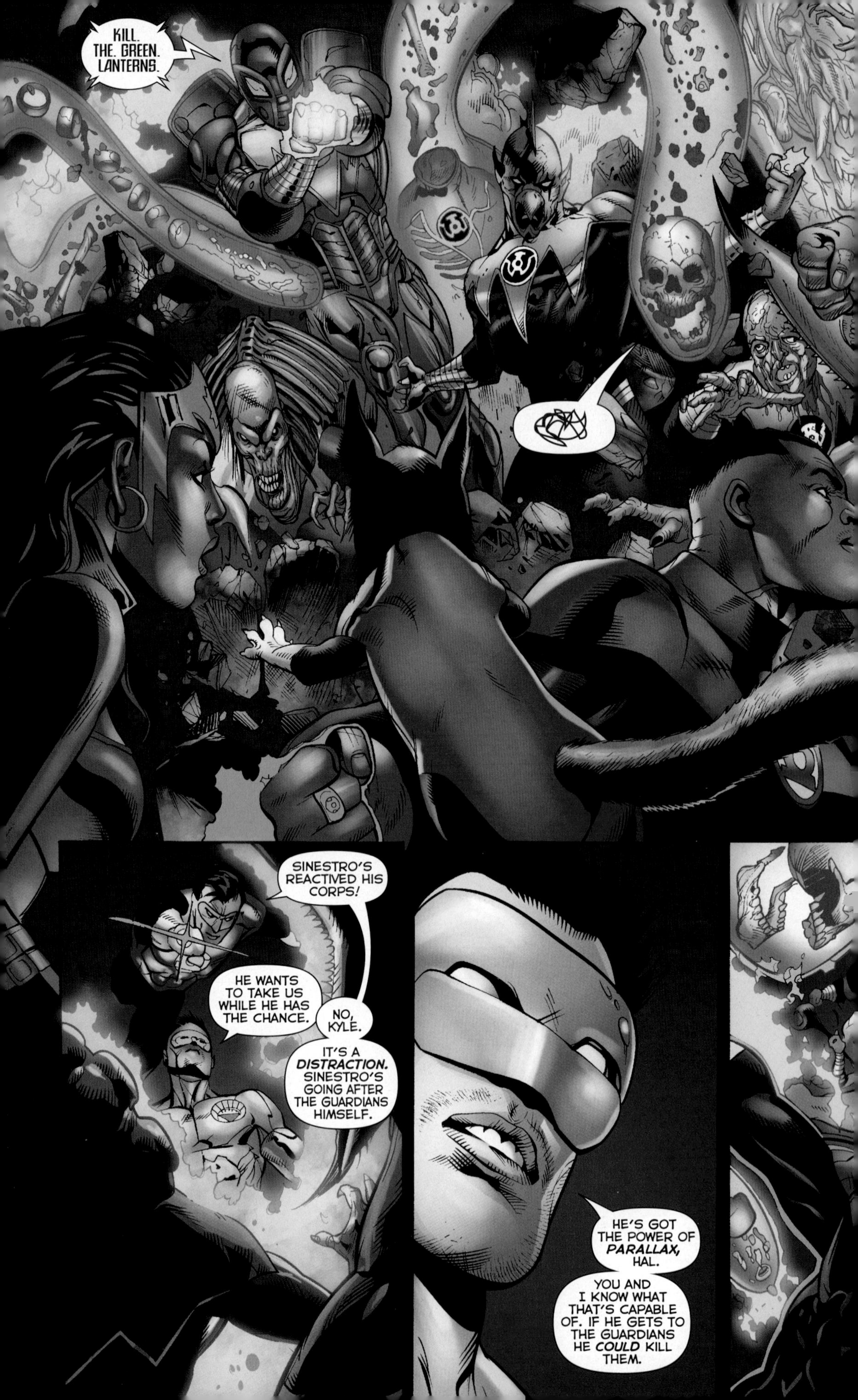
KILL. THE. GREEN. LANTERNS.
SINESTRO'S REACTIVED HIS CORPS!
HE WANTS TO TAKE US WHILE HE HAS THE CHANCE.
NO, KYLE.
IT'S A *DISTRACTION.* SINESTRO'S GOING AFTER THE GUARDIANS HIMSELF.
HE'S GOT THE POWER OF *PARALLAX,* HAL.
YOU AND I KNOW WHAT THAT'S CAPABLE OF. IF HE GETS TO THE GUARDIANS HE *COULD* KILL THEM.

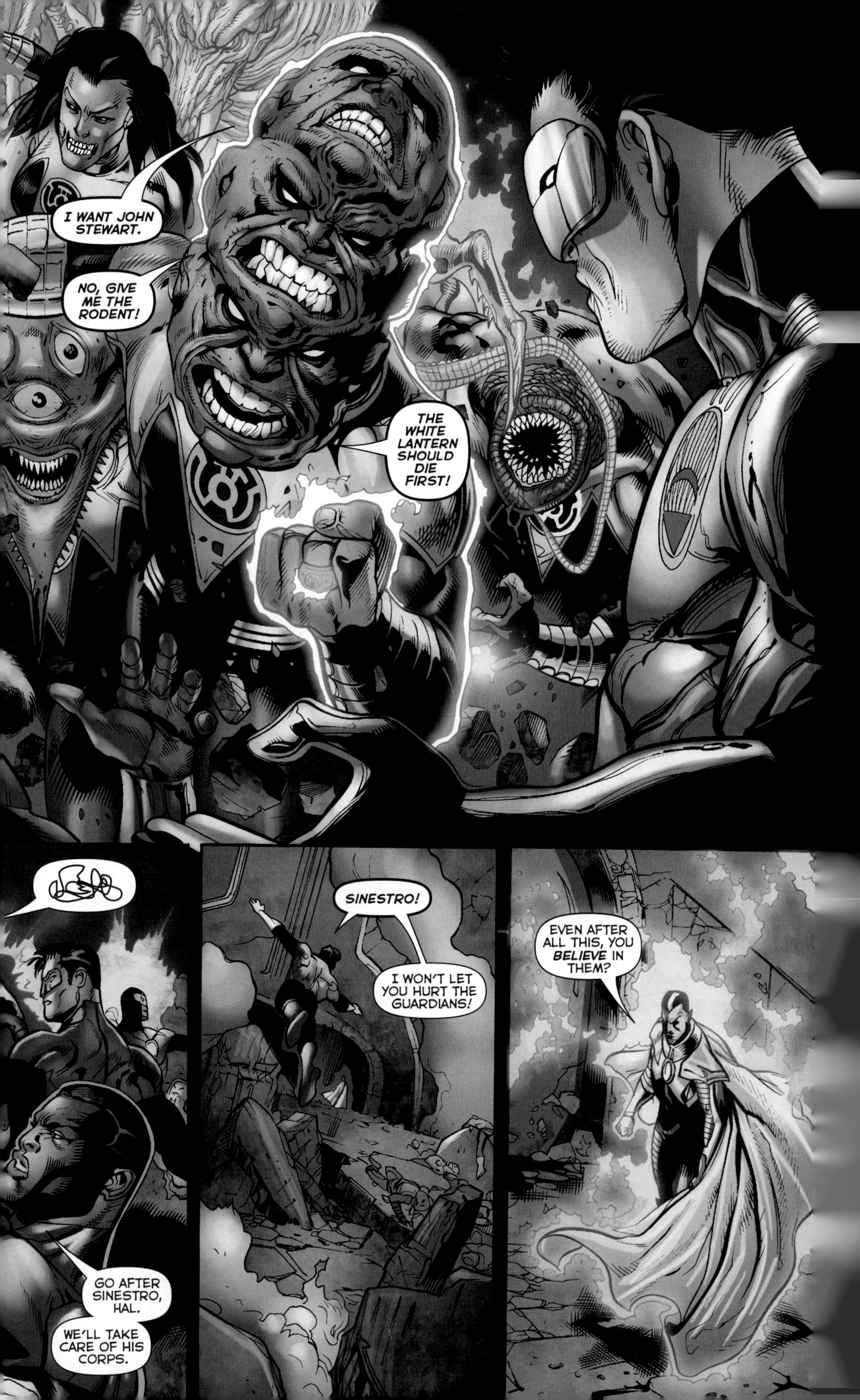
I WANT JOHN STEWART.
NO, GIVE ME THE RODENT!
THE WHITE LANTERN SHOULD DIE FIRST!
SINESTRO!
I WON'T LET YOU HURT THE GUARDIANS!
EVEN AFTER ALL THIS, YOU *BELIEVE* IN THEM?
GO AFTER SINESTRO, HAL.
WE'LL TAKE CARE OF HIS CORPS.

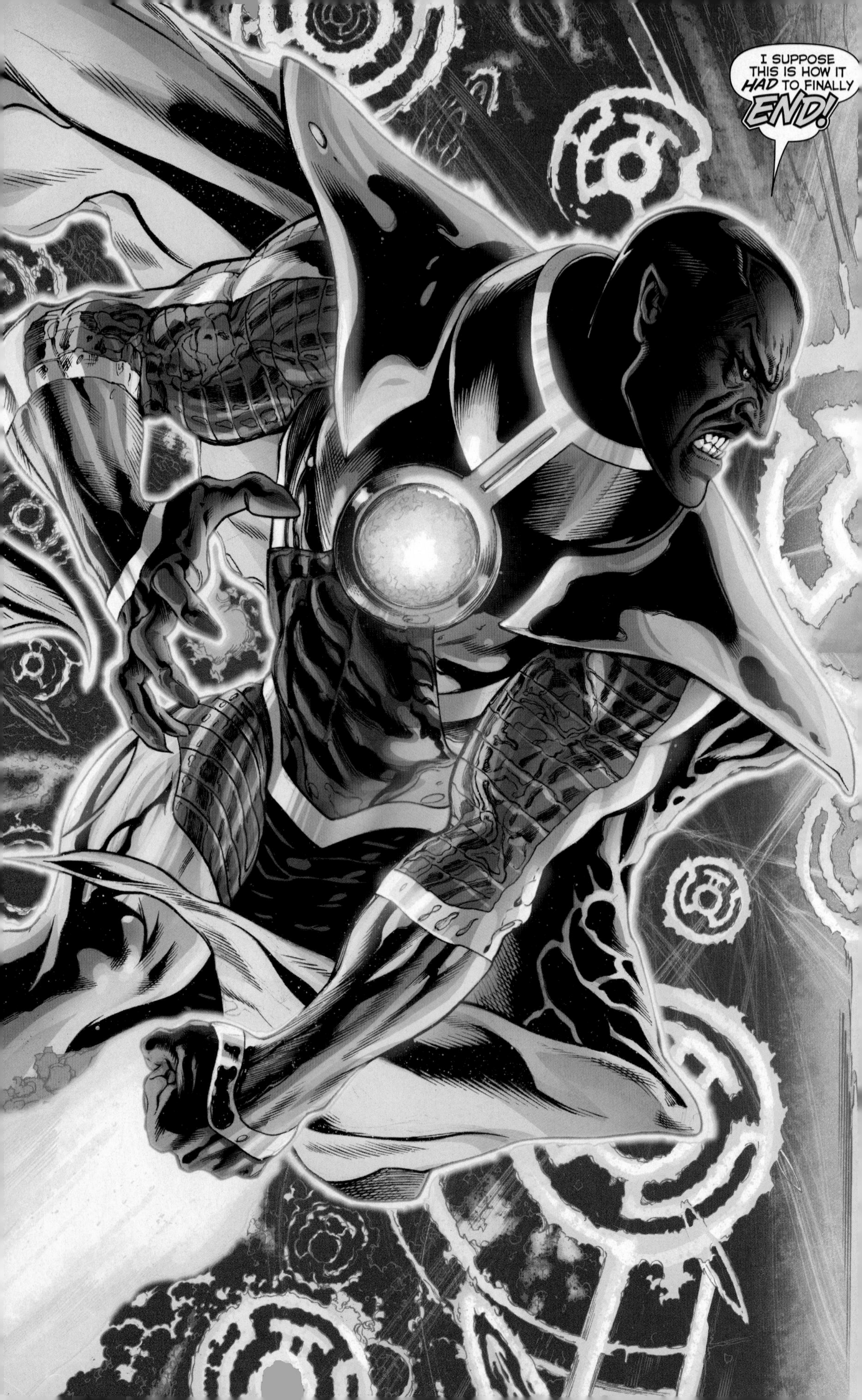
I SUPPOSE THIS IS HOW IT HAD TO FINALLY END!

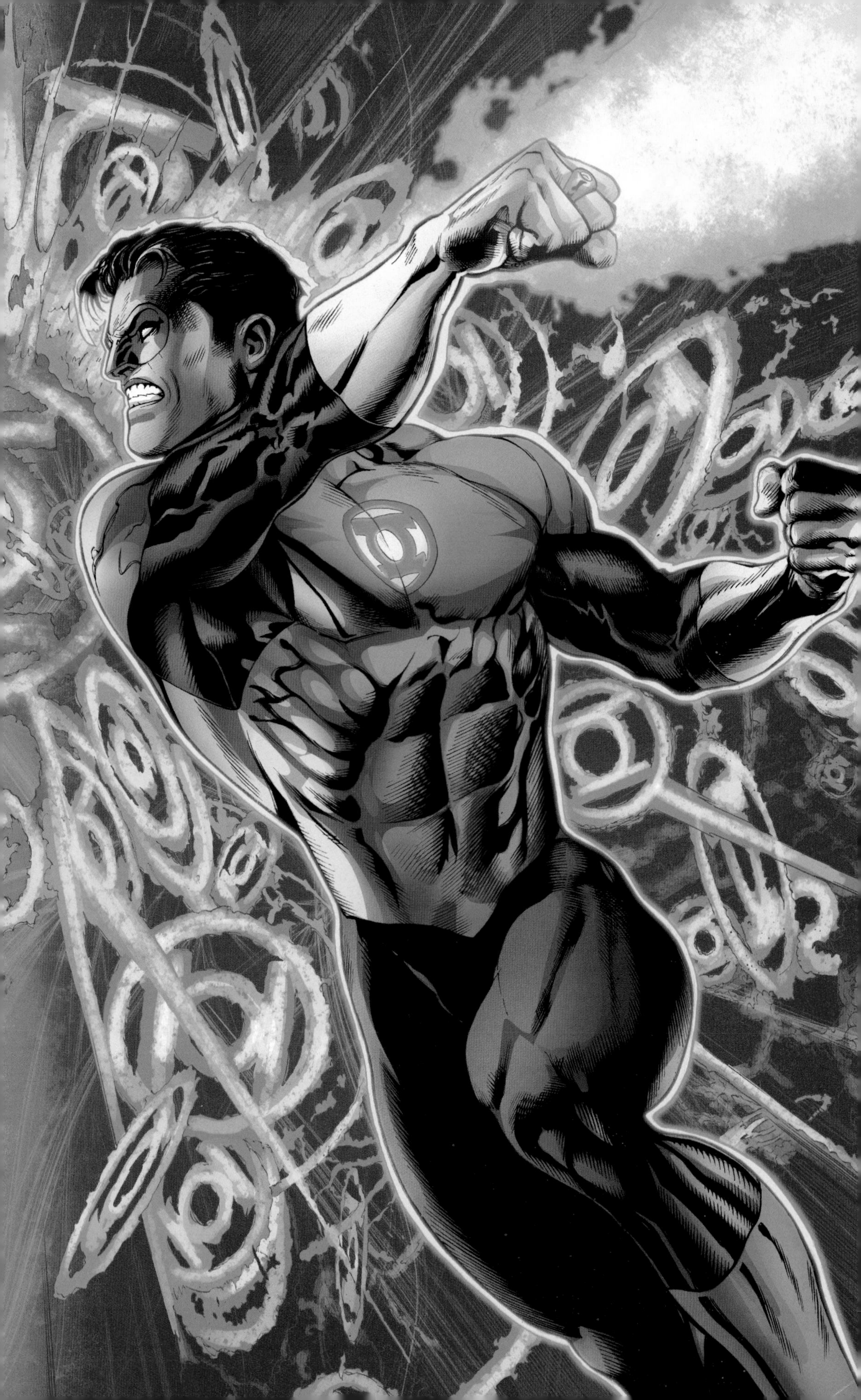

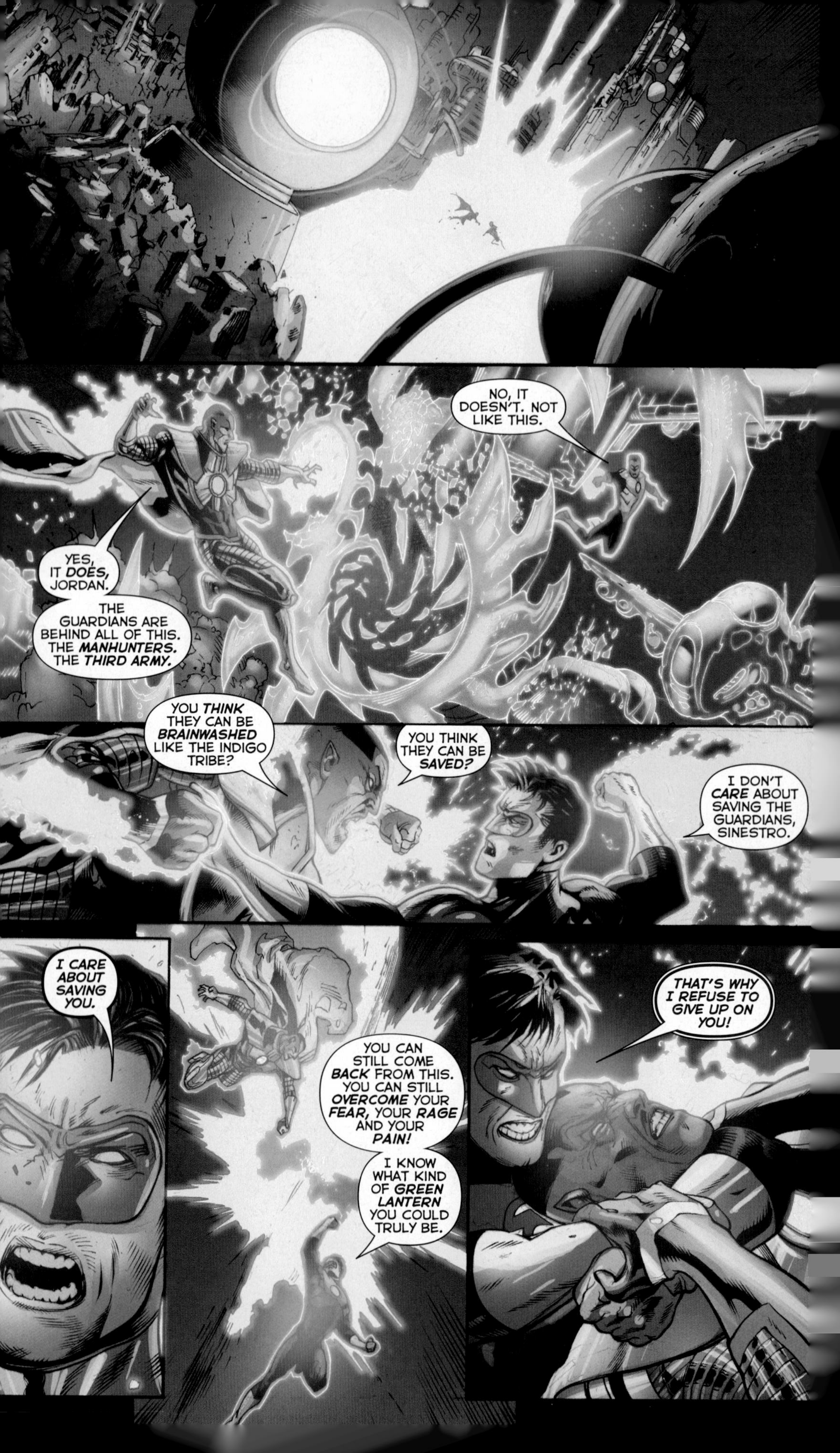

NO, IT DOESN'T. NOT LIKE THIS.
YES, IT DOES, JORDAN.
THE GUARDIANS ARE BEHIND ALL OF THIS. THE MANHUNTERS. THE THIRD ARMY.
YOU THINK THEY CAN BE BRAINWASHED LIKE THE INDIGO TRIBE?
YOU THINK THEY CAN BE SAVED?
I DON'T CARE ABOUT SAVING THE GUARDIANS, SINESTRO.
I CARE ABOUT SAVING YOU.
YOU CAN STILL COME BACK FROM THIS. YOU CAN STILL OVERCOME YOUR FEAR, YOUR RAGE AND YOUR PAIN!
I KNOW WHAT KIND OF GREEN LANTERN YOU COULD TRULY BE.
THAT'S WHY I REFUSE TO GIVE UP ON YOU!

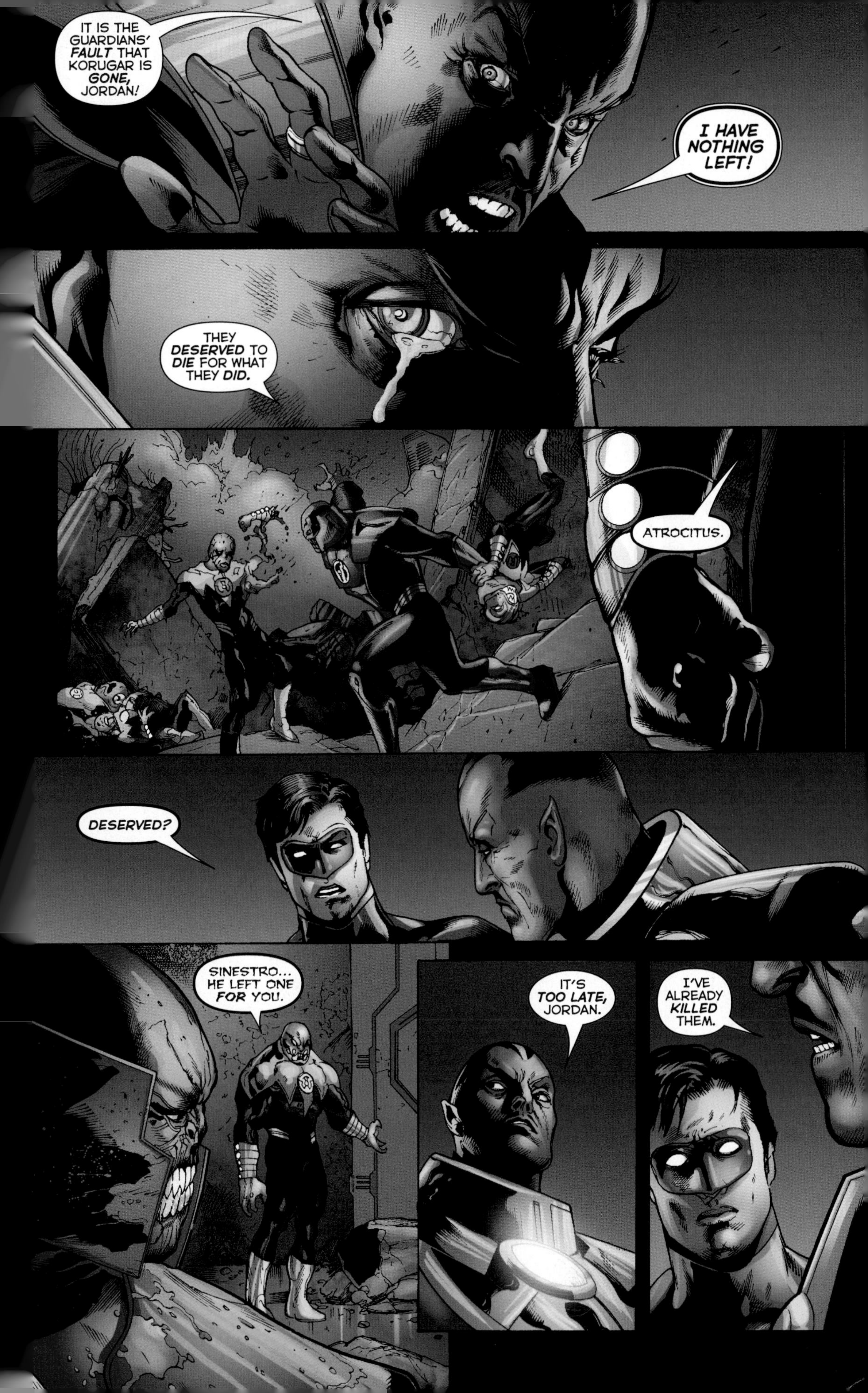
IT IS THE GUARDIANS' FAULT THAT KORUGAR IS GONE, JORDAN!
I HAVE NOTHING LEFT!
THEY DESERVED TO DIE FOR WHAT THEY DID.
ATROCITUS.
DESERVED?
SINESTRO... HE LEFT ONE FOR YOU.
IT'S TOO LATE, JORDAN.
I'VE ALREADY KILLED THEM.

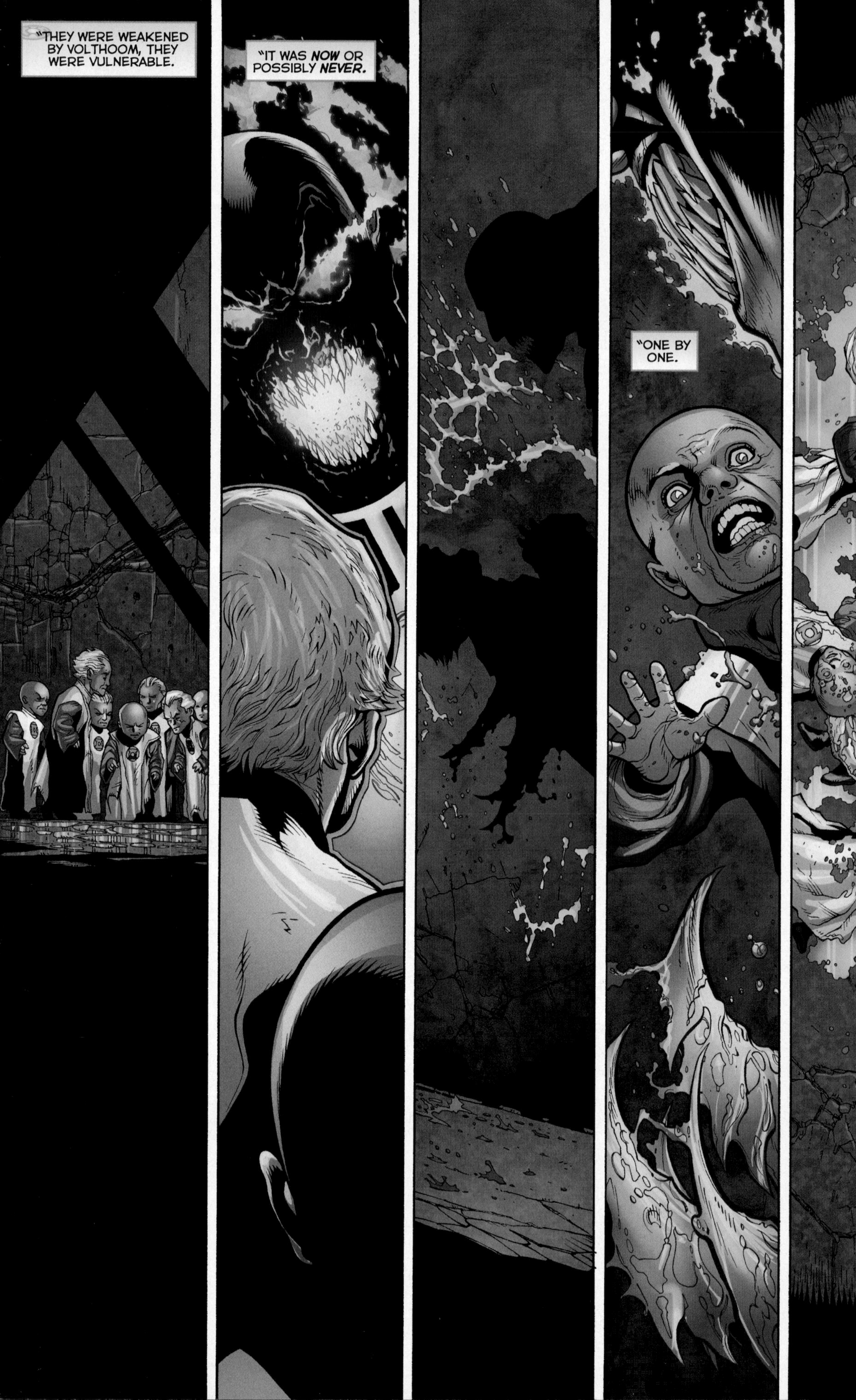
"THEY WERE WEAKENED BY VOLTHOOM, THEY WERE VULNERABLE.
"IT WAS NOW OR POSSIBLY NEVER.
"ONE BY ONE.

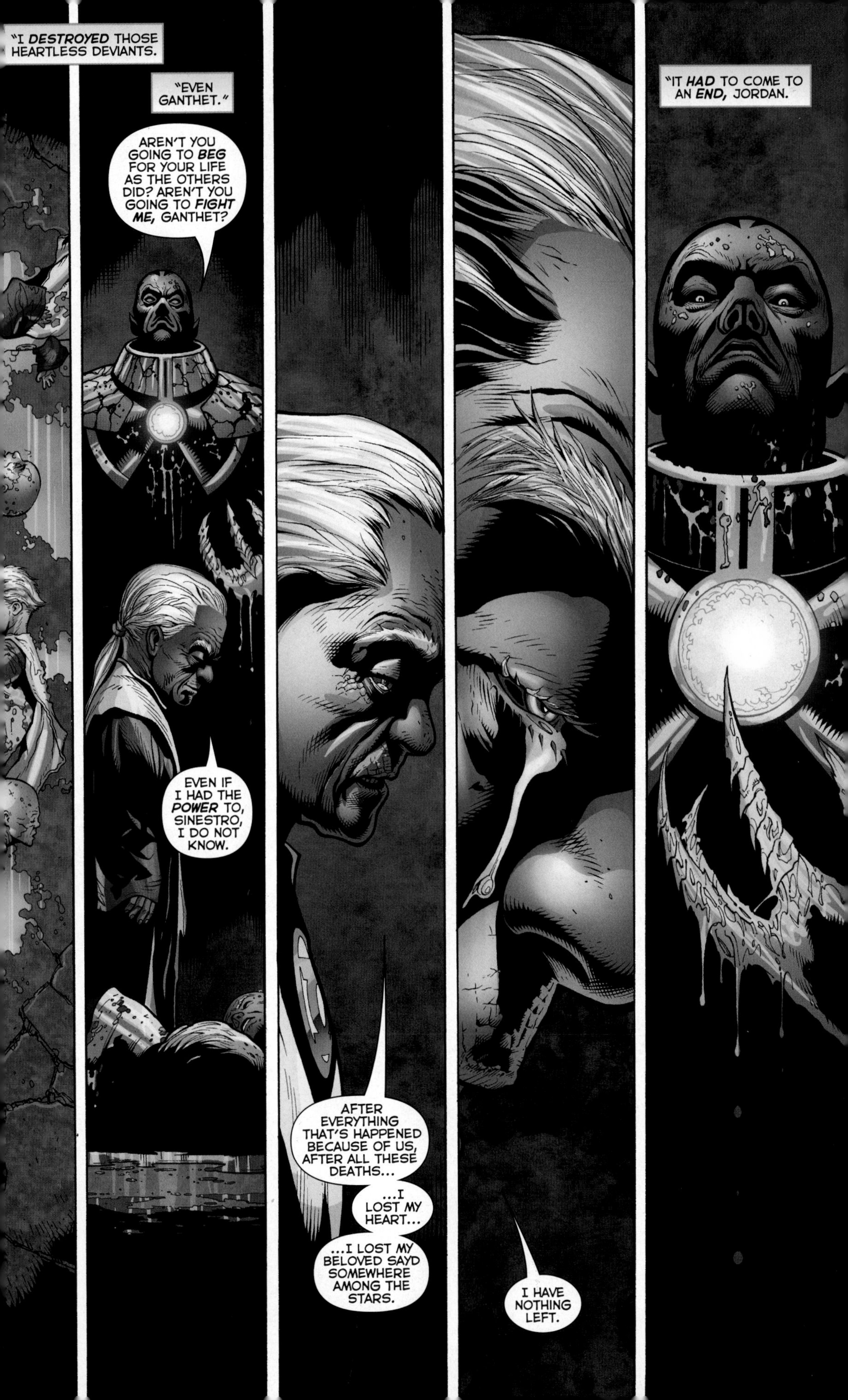
"I DESTROYED THOSE HEARTLESS DEVIANTS.
"EVEN GANTHET."
AREN'T YOU GOING TO BEG FOR YOUR LIFE AS THE OTHERS DID? AREN'T YOU GOING TO FIGHT ME, GANTHET?
EVEN IF I HAD THE POWER TO, SINESTRO, I DO NOT KNOW.
AFTER EVERYTHING THAT'S HAPPENED BECAUSE OF US, AFTER ALL THESE DEATHS...
...I LOST MY HEART...
...I LOST MY BELOVED SAYD SOMEWHERE AMONG THE STARS.
I HAVE NOTHING LEFT.
"IT HAD TO COME TO AN END, JORDAN.

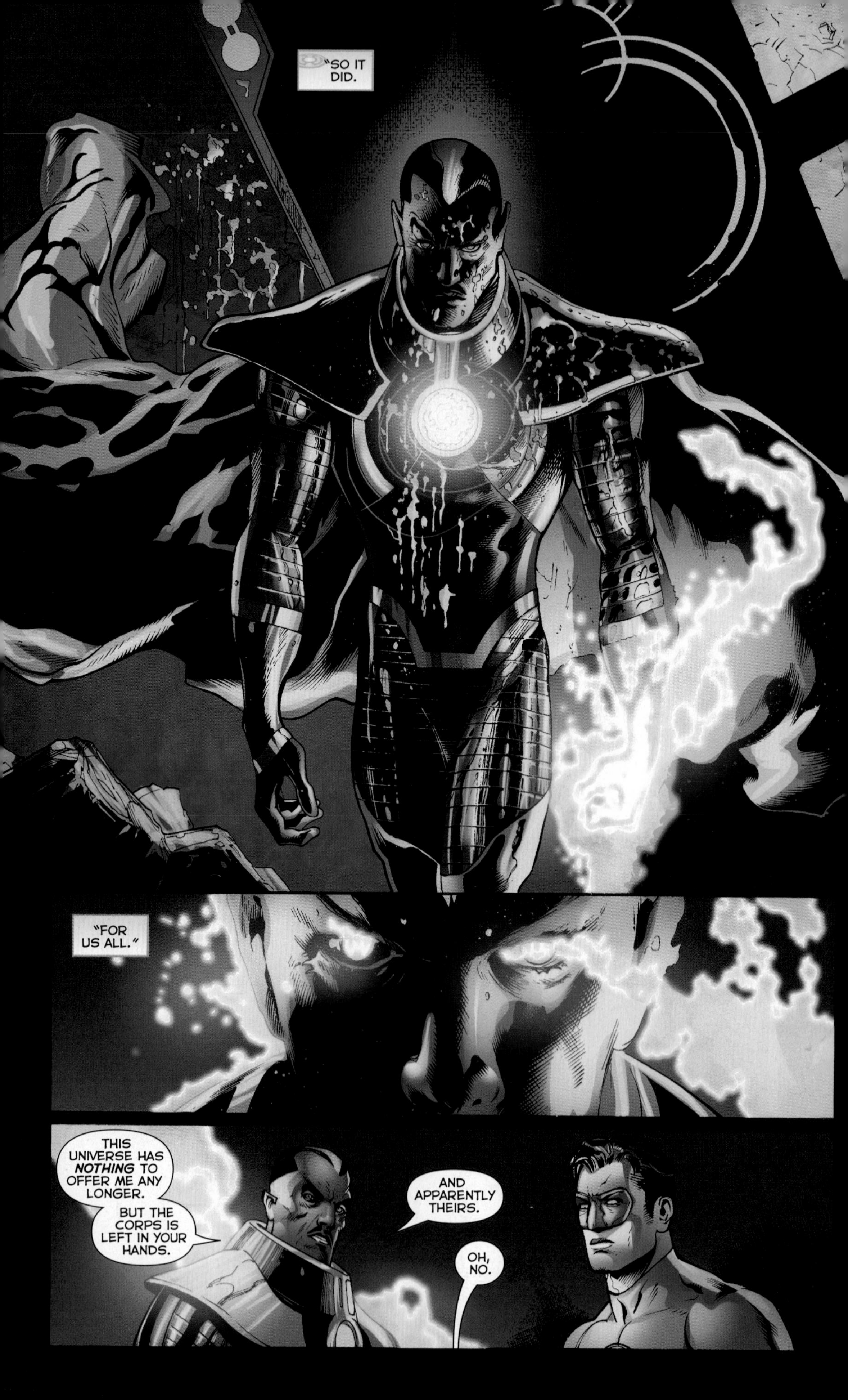
"SO IT DID.
"FOR US ALL."
THIS UNIVERSE HAS NOTHING TO OFFER ME ANY LONGER.
BUT THE CORPS IS LEFT IN YOUR HANDS.
AND APPARENTLY THEIRS.
OH, NO.

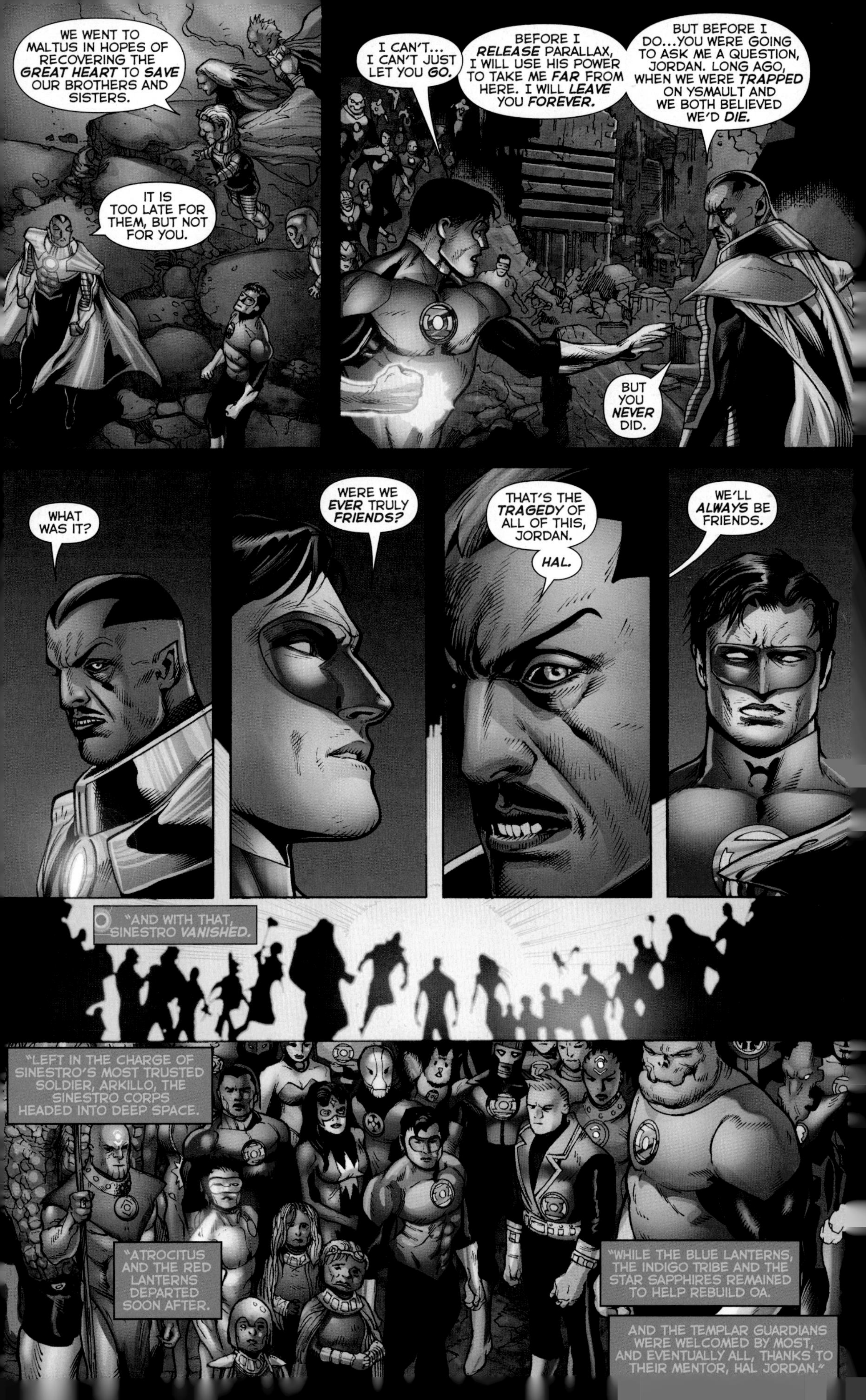
WE WENT TO MALTUS IN HOPES OF RECOVERING THE GREAT HEART TO SAVE OUR BROTHERS AND SISTERS.
IT IS TOO LATE FOR THEM, BUT NOT FOR YOU.
I CAN'T... I CAN'T JUST LET YOU GO.
BEFORE I RELEASE PARALLAX, I WILL USE HIS POWER TO TAKE ME FAR FROM HERE. I WILL LEAVE YOU FOREVER.
BUT BEFORE I DO...YOU WERE GOING TO ASK ME A QUESTION, JORDAN. LONG AGO, WHEN WE WERE TRAPPED ON YSMAULT AND WE BOTH BELIEVED WE'D DIE.
BUT YOU NEVER DID.
WHAT WAS IT?
WERE WE EVER TRULY FRIENDS?
THAT'S THE TRAGEDY OF ALL OF THIS, JORDAN.
HAL.
WE'LL ALWAYS BE FRIENDS.
"AND WITH THAT, SINESTRO VANISHED.
"LEFT IN THE CHARGE OF SINESTRO'S MOST TRUSTED SOLDIER, ARKILLO, THE SINESTRO CORPS HEADED INTO DEEP SPACE.
"ATROCITUS AND THE RED LANTERNS DEPARTED SOON AFTER.
"WHILE THE BLUE LANTERNS, THE INDIGO TRIBE AND THE STAR SAPPHIRES REMAINED TO HELP REBUILD OA.
AND THE TEMPLAR GUARDIANS WERE WELCOMED BY MOST, AND EVENTUALLY ALL, THANKS TO THEIR MENTOR, HAL JORDAN."

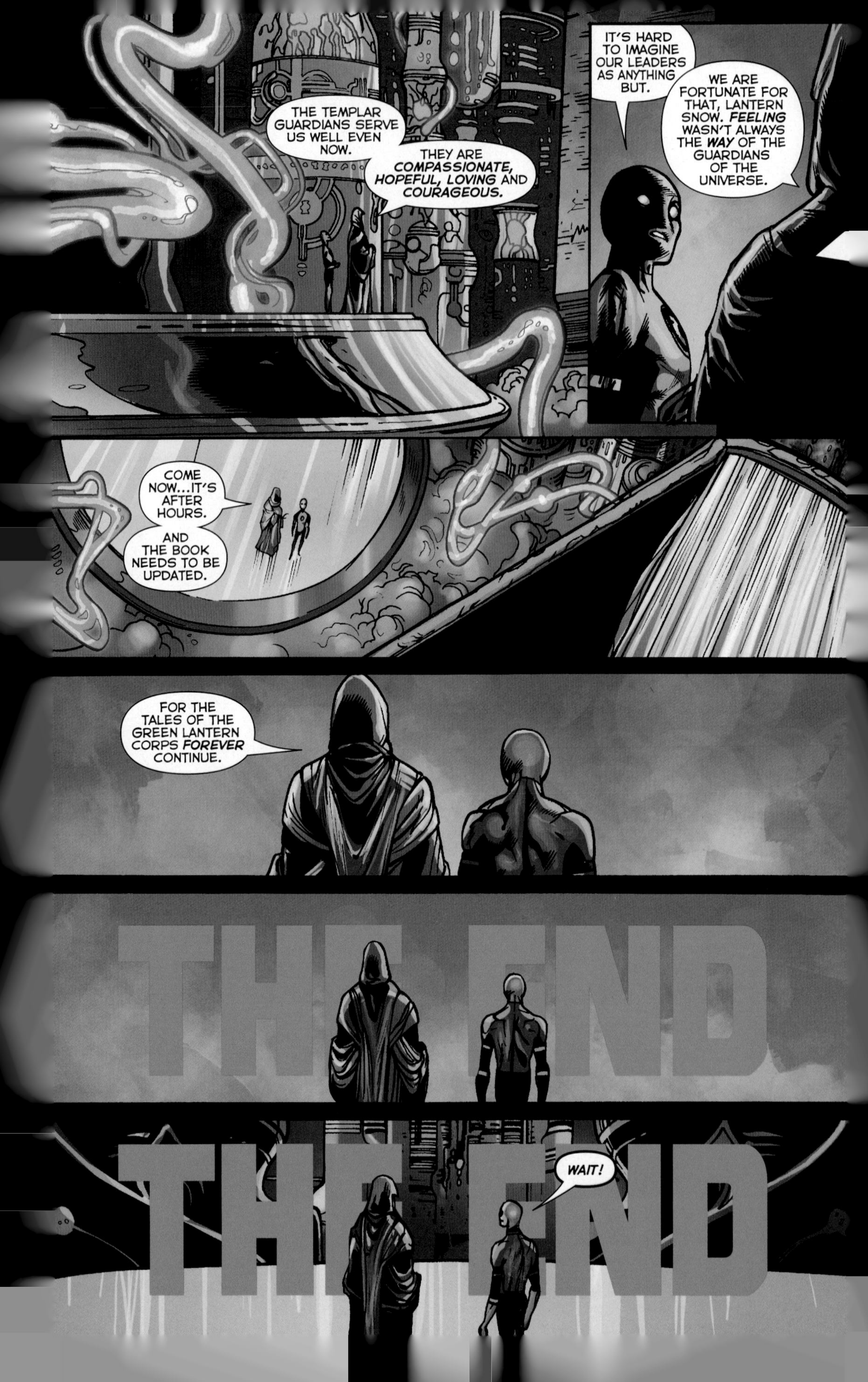
THE TEMPLAR GUARDIANS SERVE US WELL EVEN NOW.
THEY ARE COMPASSIONATE, HOPEFUL, LOVING AND COURAGEOUS.
IT'S HARD TO IMAGINE OUR LEADERS AS ANYTHING BUT.
WE ARE FORTUNATE FOR THAT, LANTERN SNOW. FEELING WASN'T ALWAYS THE WAY OF THE GUARDIANS OF THE UNIVERSE.
COME NOW...IT'S AFTER HOURS.
AND THE BOOK NEEDS TO BE UPDATED.
FOR THE TALES OF THE GREEN LANTERN CORPS FOREVER CONTINUE.
THE END
WAIT!

WHAT HAPPENED TO EVERYONE? I MEAN, IN THE END?

WHAT HAPPENED TO EVERYONE IN *THE END?*

YOU ASK OF THEIR *FUTURES?*

OF HOW THEY *DIED?*

YES.

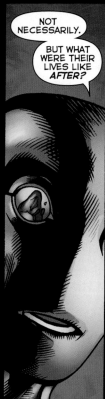

NOT NECESSARILY.

BUT WHAT WERE THEIR LIVES LIKE *AFTER?*

AFTER THEIR MOST CHALLENGING AND ADVENTUROUS YEARS?

YES. AFTER THE *BOOKENDS* OF REBIRTH.

LET ME OPEN THE BOOK OF OA AGAIN, THEN...

...AND I'LL SHOW YOU...

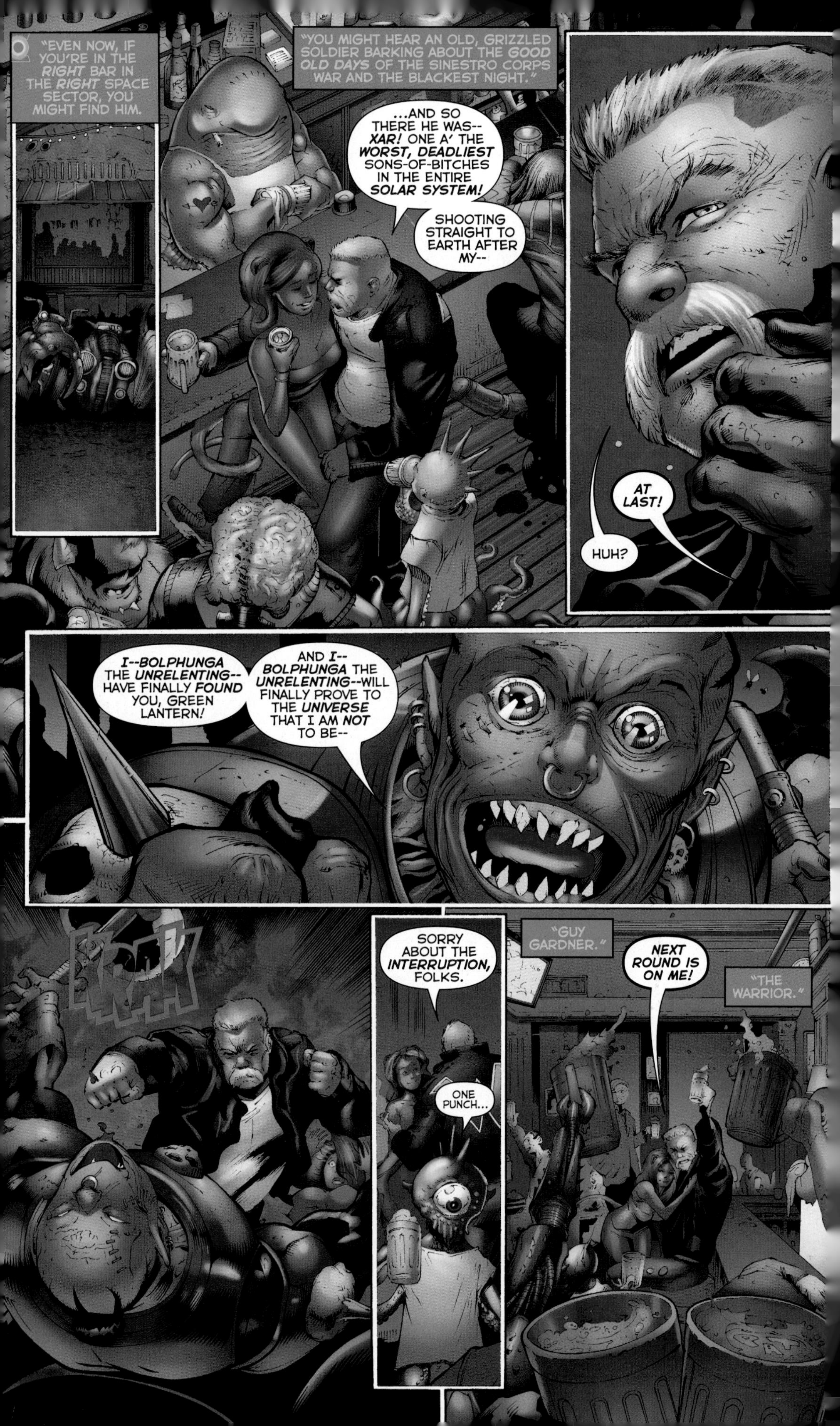
"EVEN NOW, IF YOU'RE IN THE RIGHT BAR IN THE RIGHT SPACE SECTOR, YOU MIGHT FIND HIM.
"YOU MIGHT HEAR AN OLD, GRIZZLED SOLDIER BARKING ABOUT THE GOOD OLD DAYS OF THE SINESTRO CORPS WAR AND THE BLACKEST NIGHT."
...AND SO THERE HE WAS-- XAR! ONE A' THE WORST, DEADLIEST SONS-OF-BITCHES IN THE ENTIRE SOLAR SYSTEM!
SHOOTING STRAIGHT TO EARTH AFTER MY--
HUH?
AT LAST!
I--BOLPHUNGA THE UNRELENTING--HAVE FINALLY FOUND YOU, GREEN LANTERN!
AND I--BOLPHUNGA THE UNRELENTING--WILL FINALLY PROVE TO THE UNIVERSE THAT I AM NOT TO BE--
SORRY ABOUT THE INTERRUPTION, FOLKS.
ONE PUNCH...
"GUY GARDNER."
NEXT ROUND IS ON ME!
"THE WARRIOR."

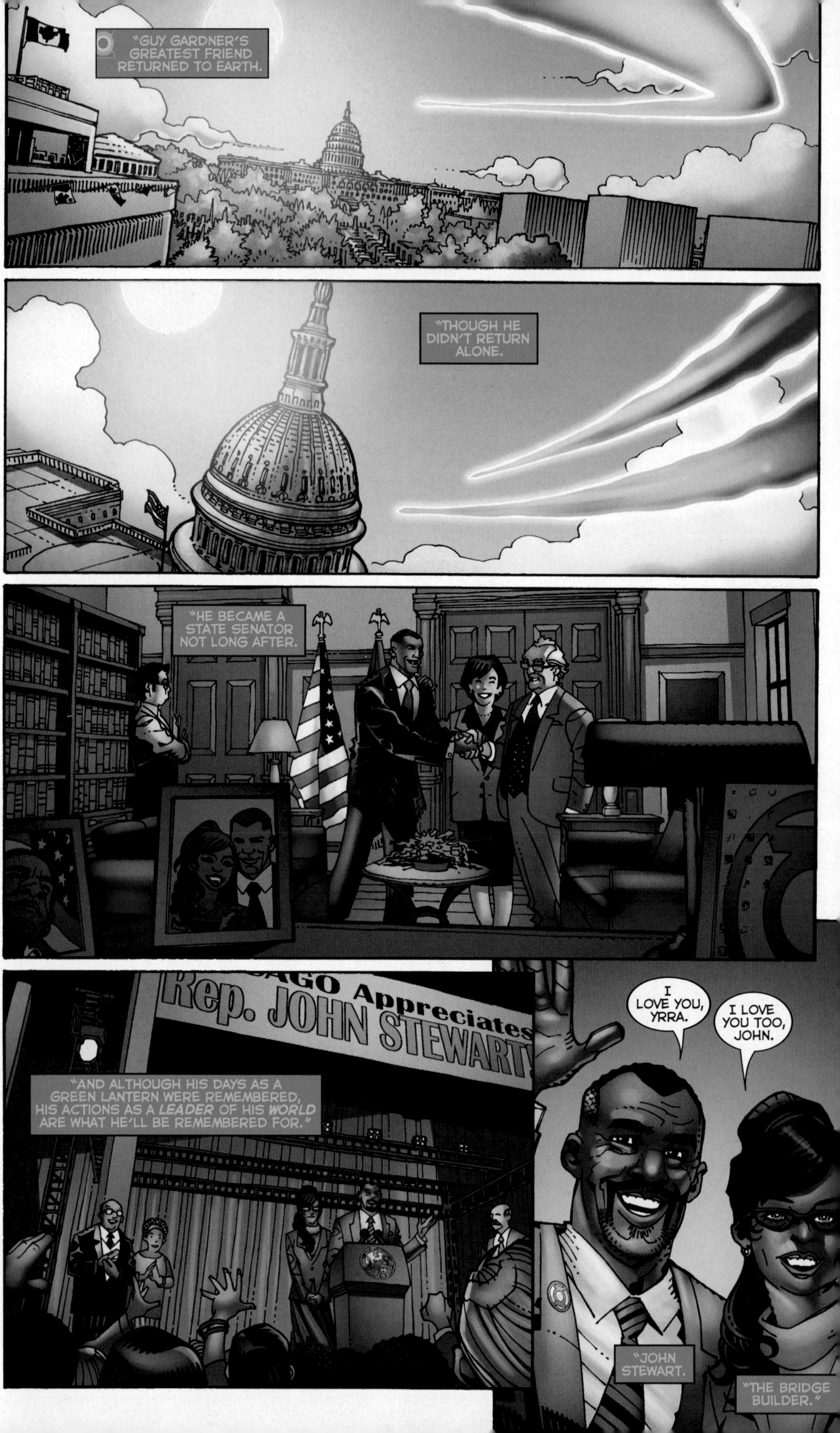
"GUY GARDNER'S GREATEST FRIEND RETURNED TO EARTH.
"THOUGH HE DIDN'T RETURN ALONE.
"HE BECAME A STATE SENATOR NOT LONG AFTER.
Rep. JOHN STEWART
"AND ALTHOUGH HIS DAYS AS A GREEN LANTERN WERE REMEMBERED, HIS ACTIONS AS A *LEADER* OF HIS *WORLD* ARE WHAT HE'LL BE REMEMBERED FOR."
I LOVE YOU, YRRA.
I LOVE YOU TOO, JOHN.
"JOHN STEWART.
"THE BRIDGE BUILDER."

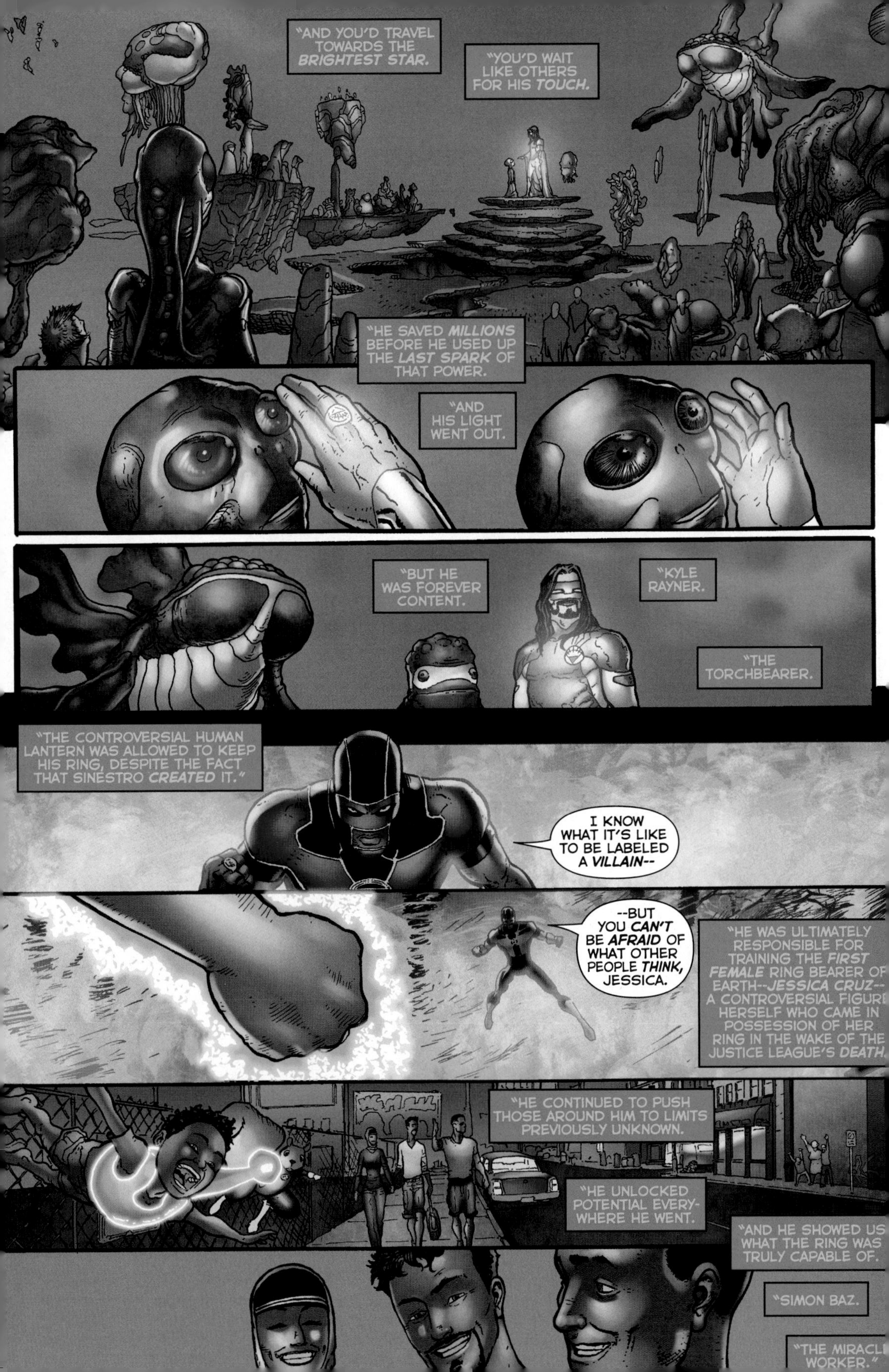
"AND YOU'D TRAVEL TOWARDS THE *BRIGHTEST STAR.*
"YOU'D WAIT LIKE OTHERS FOR HIS *TOUCH.*
"HE SAVED *MILLIONS* BEFORE HE USED UP THE *LAST SPARK* OF THAT POWER.
"AND HIS LIGHT WENT OUT.
"BUT HE WAS FOREVER CONTENT.
"KYLE RAYNER.
"THE TORCHBEARER.
"THE CONTROVERSIAL HUMAN LANTERN WAS ALLOWED TO KEEP HIS RING, DESPITE THE FACT THAT SINESTRO *CREATED* IT."
I KNOW WHAT IT'S LIKE TO BE LABELED A *VILLAIN*--
--BUT YOU *CAN'T* BE *AFRAID* OF WHAT OTHER PEOPLE *THINK,* JESSICA.
"HE WAS ULTIMATELY RESPONSIBLE FOR TRAINING THE *FIRST FEMALE* RING BEARER OF EARTH--*JESSICA CRUZ*--A CONTROVERSIAL FIGURE HERSELF WHO CAME IN POSSESSION OF HER RING IN THE WAKE OF THE JUSTICE LEAGUE'S *DEATH.*
"HE CONTINUED TO PUSH THOSE AROUND HIM TO LIMITS PREVIOUSLY UNKNOWN.
"HE UNLOCKED POTENTIAL EVERY-WHERE HE WENT.
"AND HE SHOWED US WHAT THE RING WAS TRULY CAPABLE OF.
"SIMON BAZ.
"THE MIRACLE WORKER."

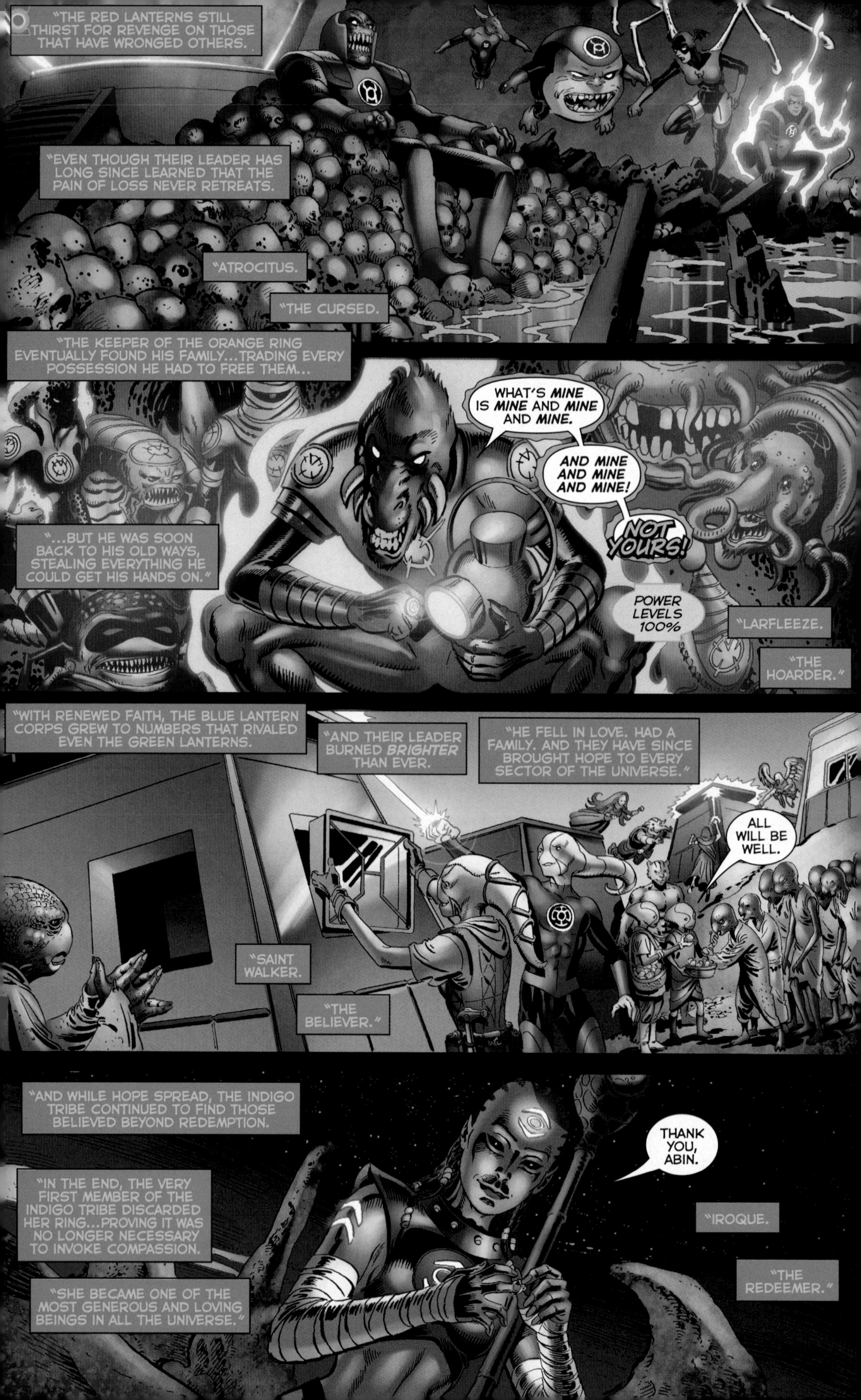
"THE RED LANTERNS STILL THIRST FOR REVENGE ON THOSE THAT HAVE WRONGED OTHERS.
"EVEN THOUGH THEIR LEADER HAS LONG SINCE LEARNED THAT THE PAIN OF LOSS NEVER RETREATS.
"ATROCITUS.
"THE CURSED.
"THE KEEPER OF THE ORANGE RING EVENTUALLY FOUND HIS FAMILY...TRADING EVERY POSSESSION HE HAD TO FREE THEM...
WHAT'S MINE IS MINE AND MINE AND MINE.
AND MINE AND MINE AND MINE!
NOT YOURS!
"...BUT HE WAS SOON BACK TO HIS OLD WAYS, STEALING EVERYTHING HE COULD GET HIS HANDS ON."
POWER LEVELS 100%
"LARFLEEZE.
"THE HOARDER."
"WITH RENEWED FAITH, THE BLUE LANTERN CORPS GREW TO NUMBERS THAT RIVALED EVEN THE GREEN LANTERNS.
"AND THEIR LEADER BURNED BRIGHTER THAN EVER.
"HE FELL IN LOVE. HAD A FAMILY. AND THEY HAVE SINCE BROUGHT HOPE TO EVERY SECTOR OF THE UNIVERSE."
ALL WILL BE WELL.
"SAINT WALKER.
"THE BELIEVER."
"AND WHILE HOPE SPREAD, THE INDIGO TRIBE CONTINUED TO FIND THOSE BELIEVED BEYOND REDEMPTION.
THANK YOU, ABIN.
"IN THE END, THE VERY FIRST MEMBER OF THE INDIGO TRIBE DISCARDED HER RING...PROVING IT WAS NO LONGER NECESSARY TO INVOKE COMPASSION.
"SHE BECAME ONE OF THE MOST GENEROUS AND LOVING BEINGS IN ALL THE UNIVERSE."
"IROQUE.
"THE REDEEMER."

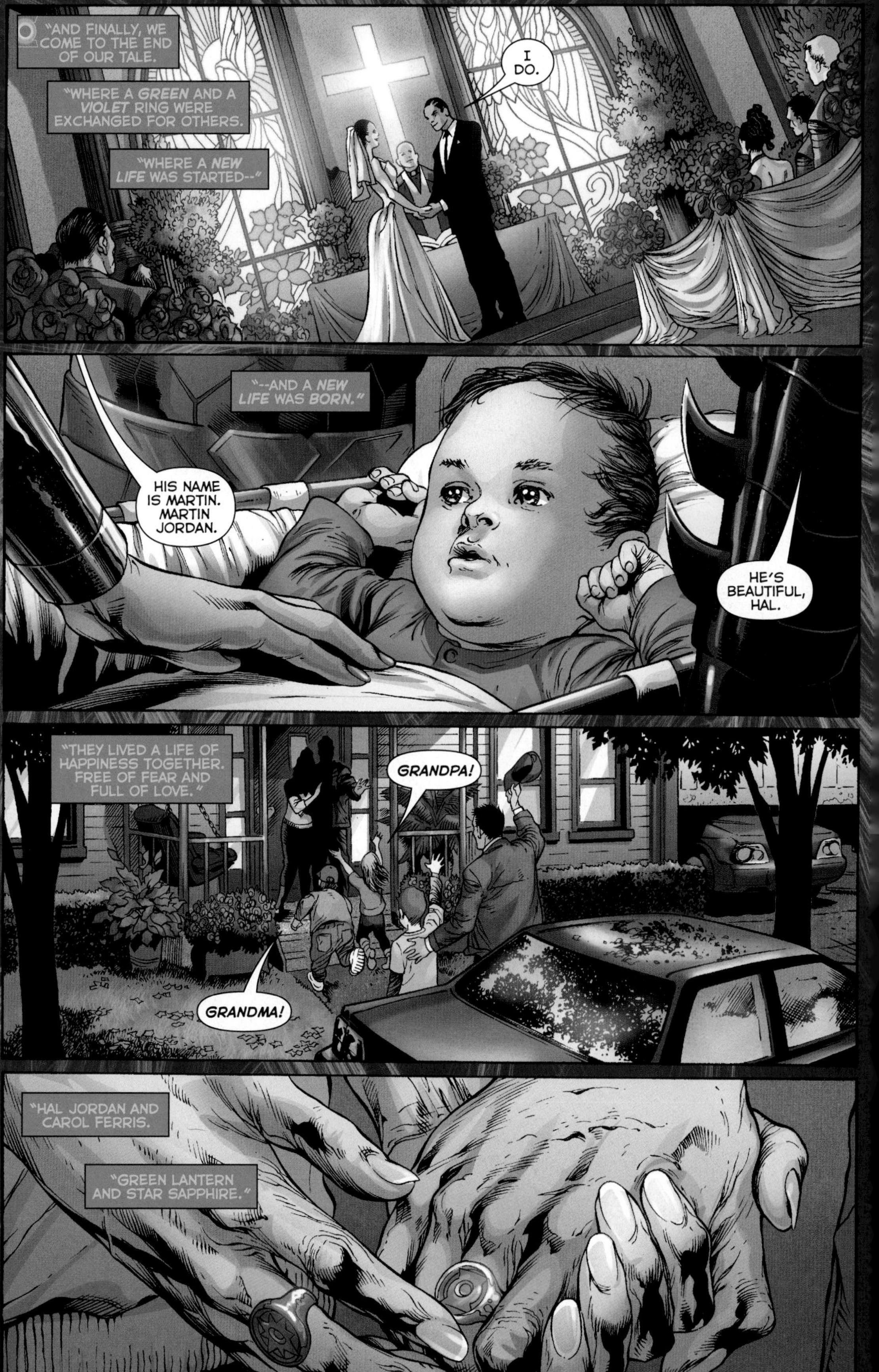
"AND FINALLY, WE COME TO THE END OF OUR TALE.
"WHERE A GREEN AND A VIOLET RING WERE EXCHANGED FOR OTHERS.
"WHERE A NEW LIFE WAS STARTED--"
I DO.
"--AND A NEW LIFE WAS BORN."
HIS NAME IS MARTIN. MARTIN JORDAN.
HE'S BEAUTIFUL, HAL.
"THEY LIVED A LIFE OF HAPPINESS TOGETHER. FREE OF FEAR AND FULL OF LOVE."
GRANDPA!
GRANDMA!
"HAL JORDAN AND CAROL FERRIS.
"GREEN LANTERN AND STAR SAPPHIRE."

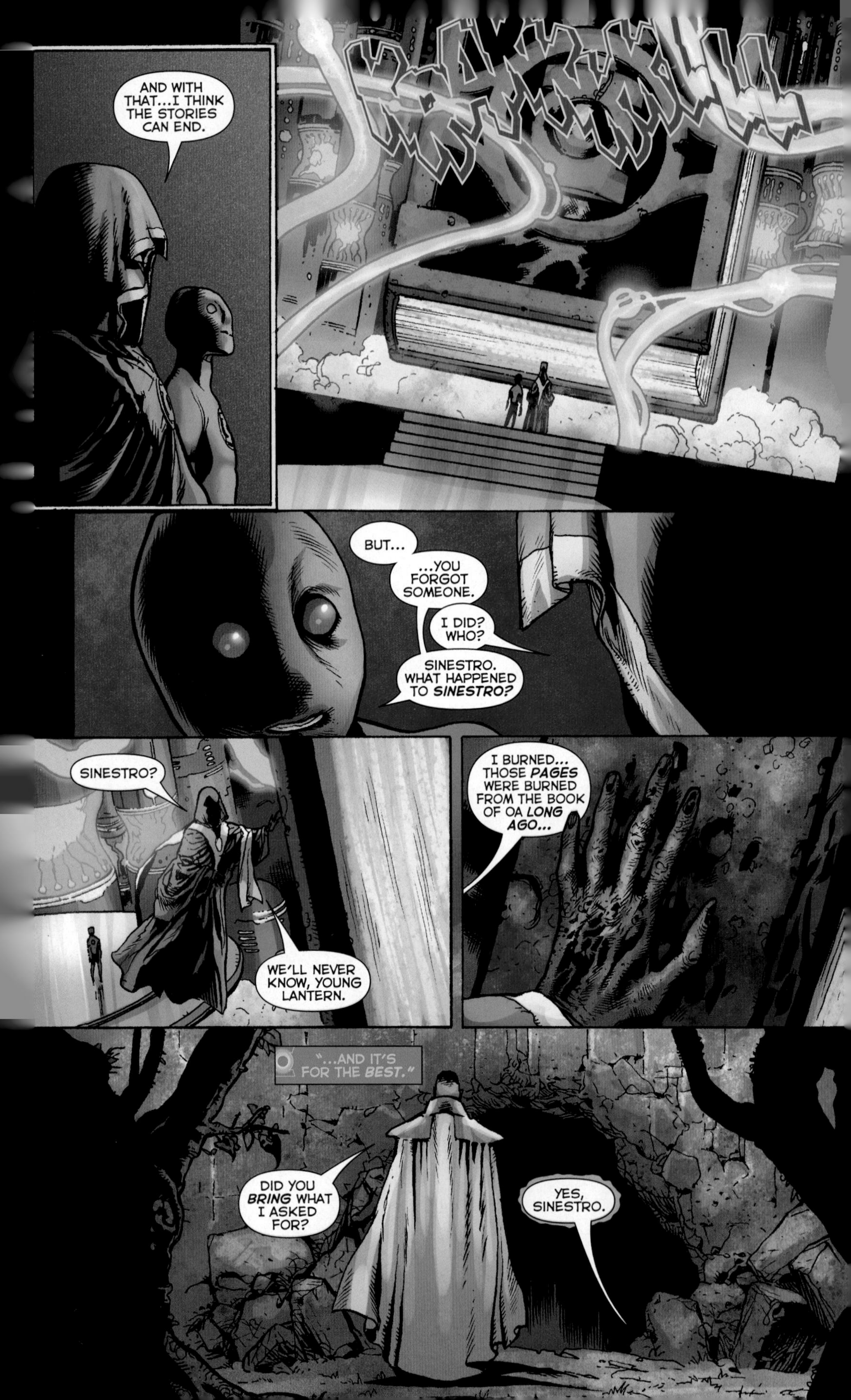
AND WITH THAT...I THINK THE STORIES CAN END.
BUT...
...YOU FORGOT SOMEONE.
I DID? WHO?
SINESTRO. WHAT HAPPENED TO SINESTRO?
SINESTRO?
WE'LL NEVER KNOW, YOUNG LANTERN.
I BURNED... THOSE PAGES WERE BURNED FROM THE BOOK OF OA LONG AGO...
"...AND IT'S FOR THE BEST."
DID YOU BRING WHAT I ASKED FOR?
YES, SINESTRO.

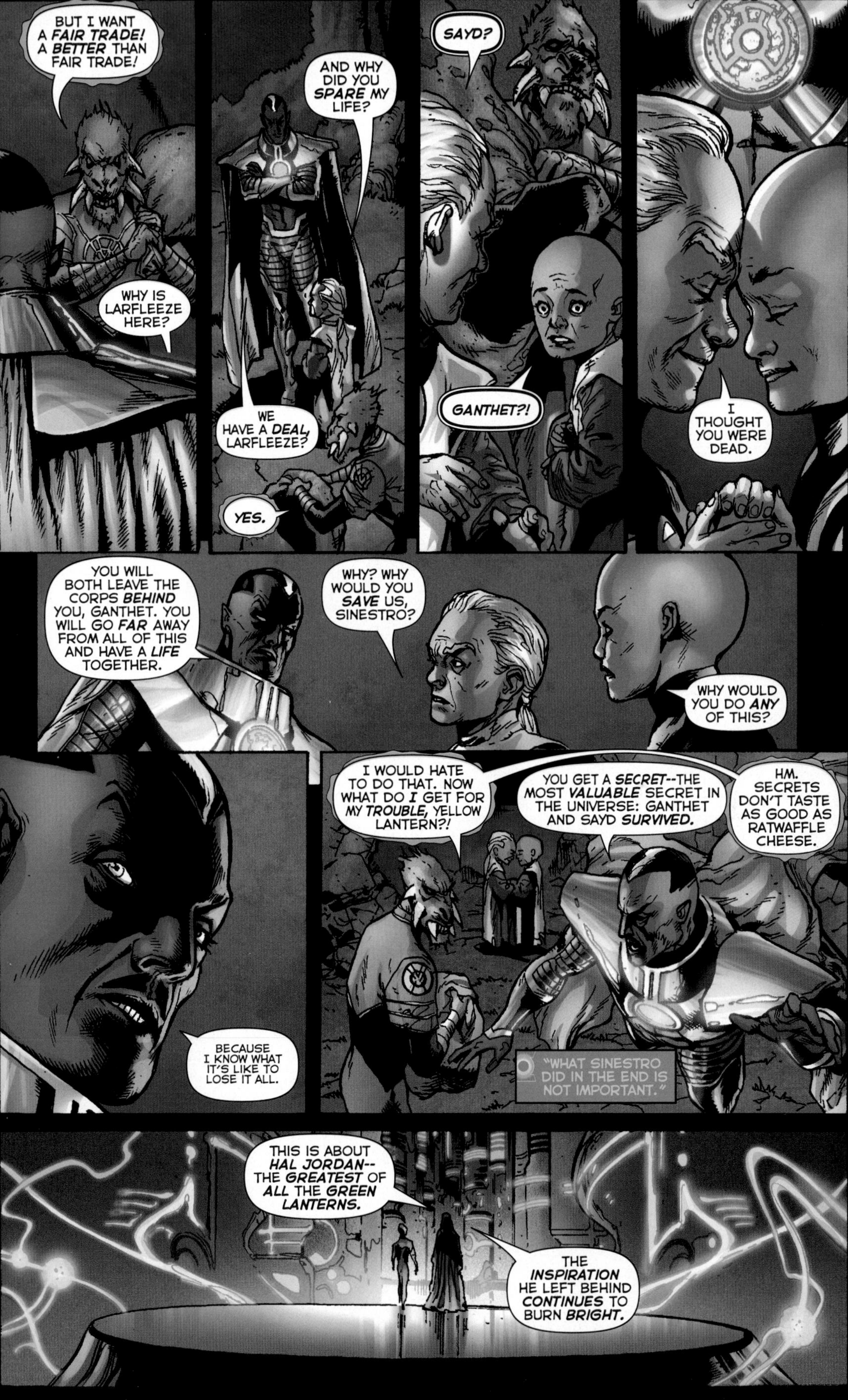

BUT I WANT A FAIR TRADE! A BETTER THAN FAIR TRADE!
WHY IS LARFLEEZE HERE?
AND WHY DID YOU SPARE MY LIFE?
WE HAVE A DEAL, LARFLEEZE?
YES.
SAYD?
GANTHET?!
I THOUGHT YOU WERE DEAD.
YOU WILL BOTH LEAVE THE CORPS BEHIND YOU, GANTHET. YOU WILL GO FAR AWAY FROM ALL OF THIS AND HAVE A LIFE TOGETHER.
WHY? WHY WOULD YOU SAVE US, SINESTRO?
WHY WOULD YOU DO ANY OF THIS?
BECAUSE I KNOW WHAT IT'S LIKE TO LOSE IT ALL.
I WOULD HATE TO DO THAT. NOW WHAT DO I GET FOR MY TROUBLE, YELLOW LANTERN?!
YOU GET A SECRET--THE MOST VALUABLE SECRET IN THE UNIVERSE: GANTHET AND SAYD SURVIVED.
HM. SECRETS DON'T TASTE AS GOOD AS RATWAFFLE CHEESE.
"WHAT SINESTRO DID IN THE END IS NOT IMPORTANT."
THIS IS ABOUT HAL JORDAN-- THE GREATEST OF ALL THE GREEN LANTERNS.
THE INSPIRATION HE LEFT BEHIND CONTINUES TO BURN BRIGHT.

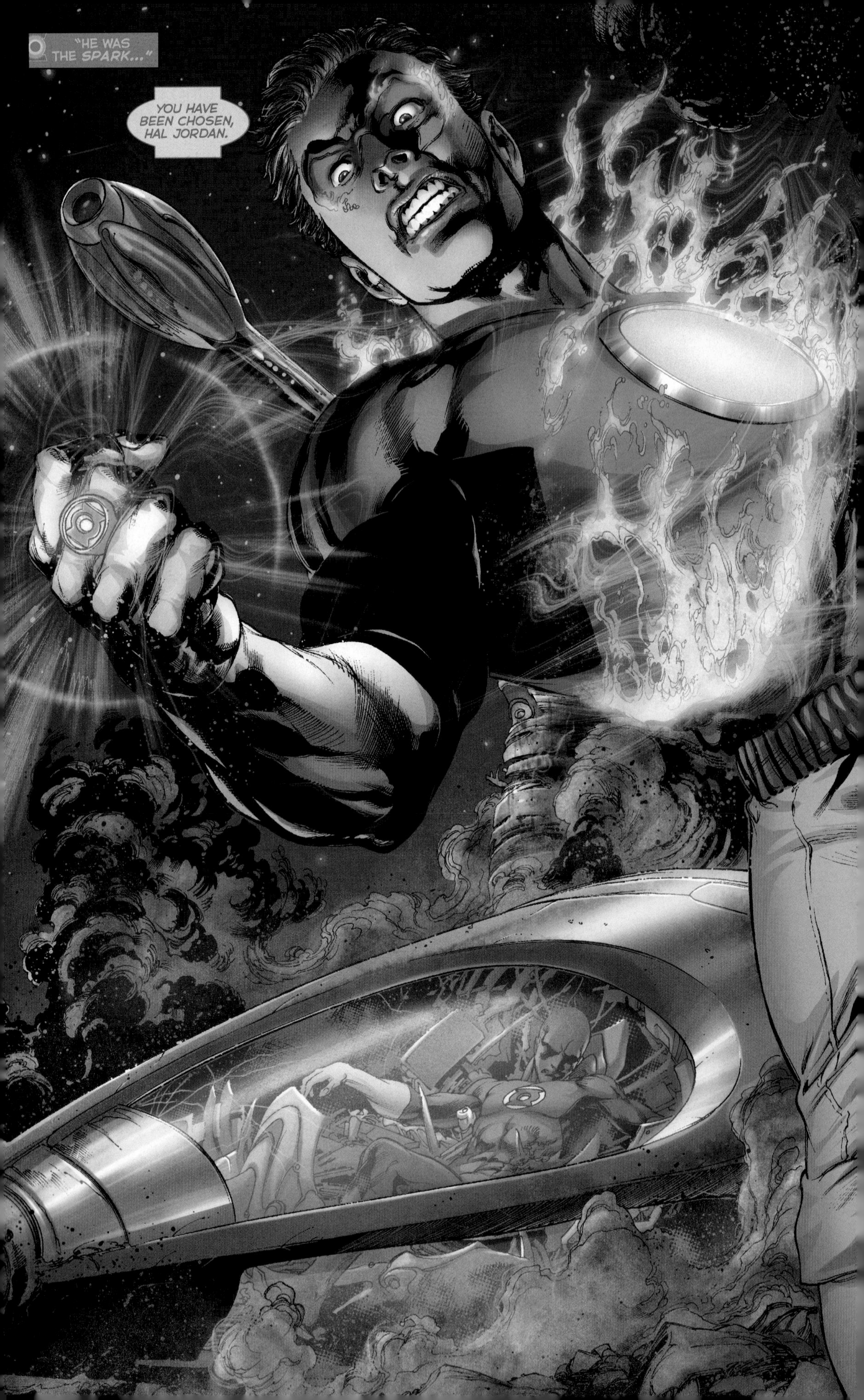
"HE WAS THE SPARK..."
YOU HAVE BEEN CHOSEN, HAL JORDAN.

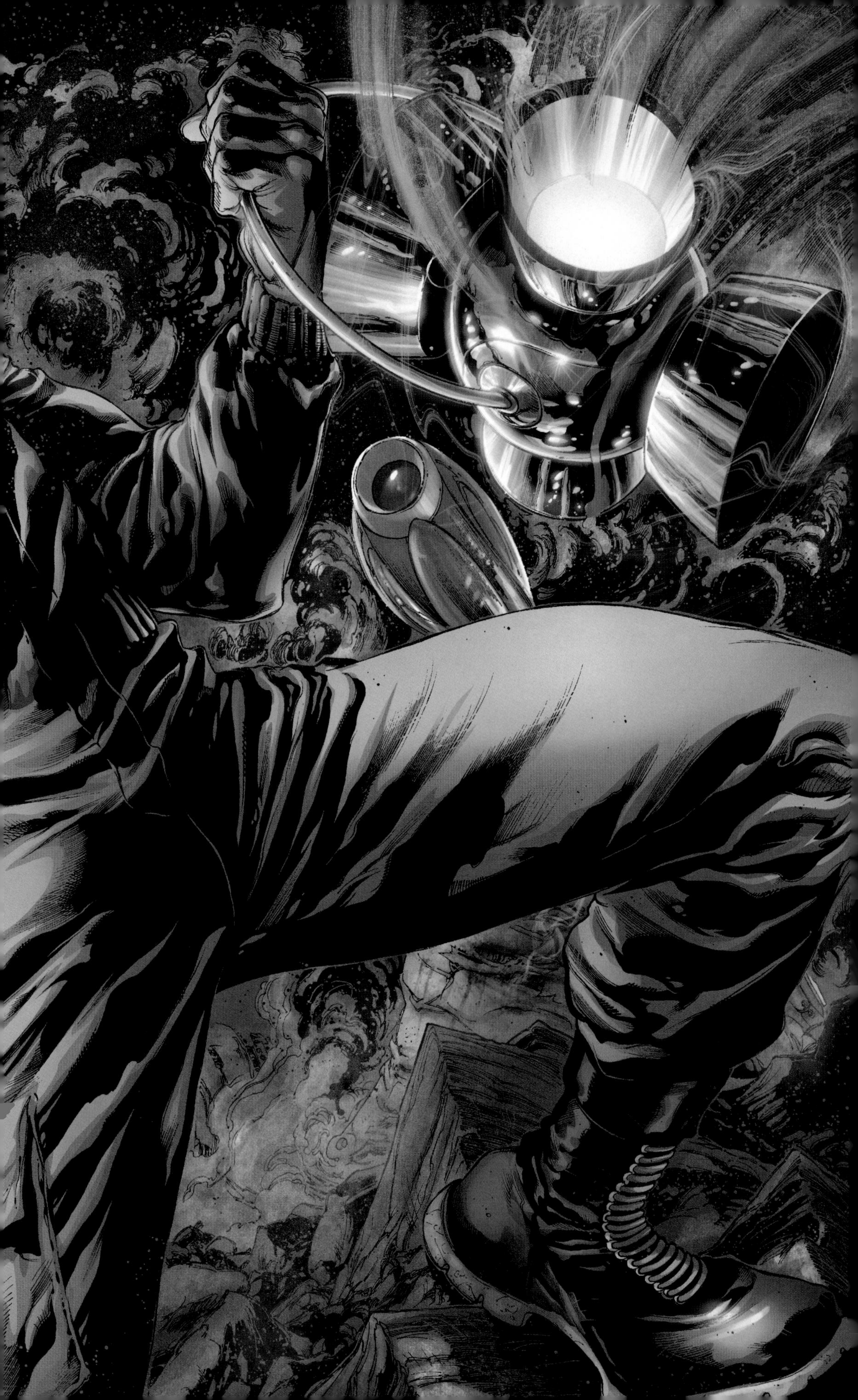

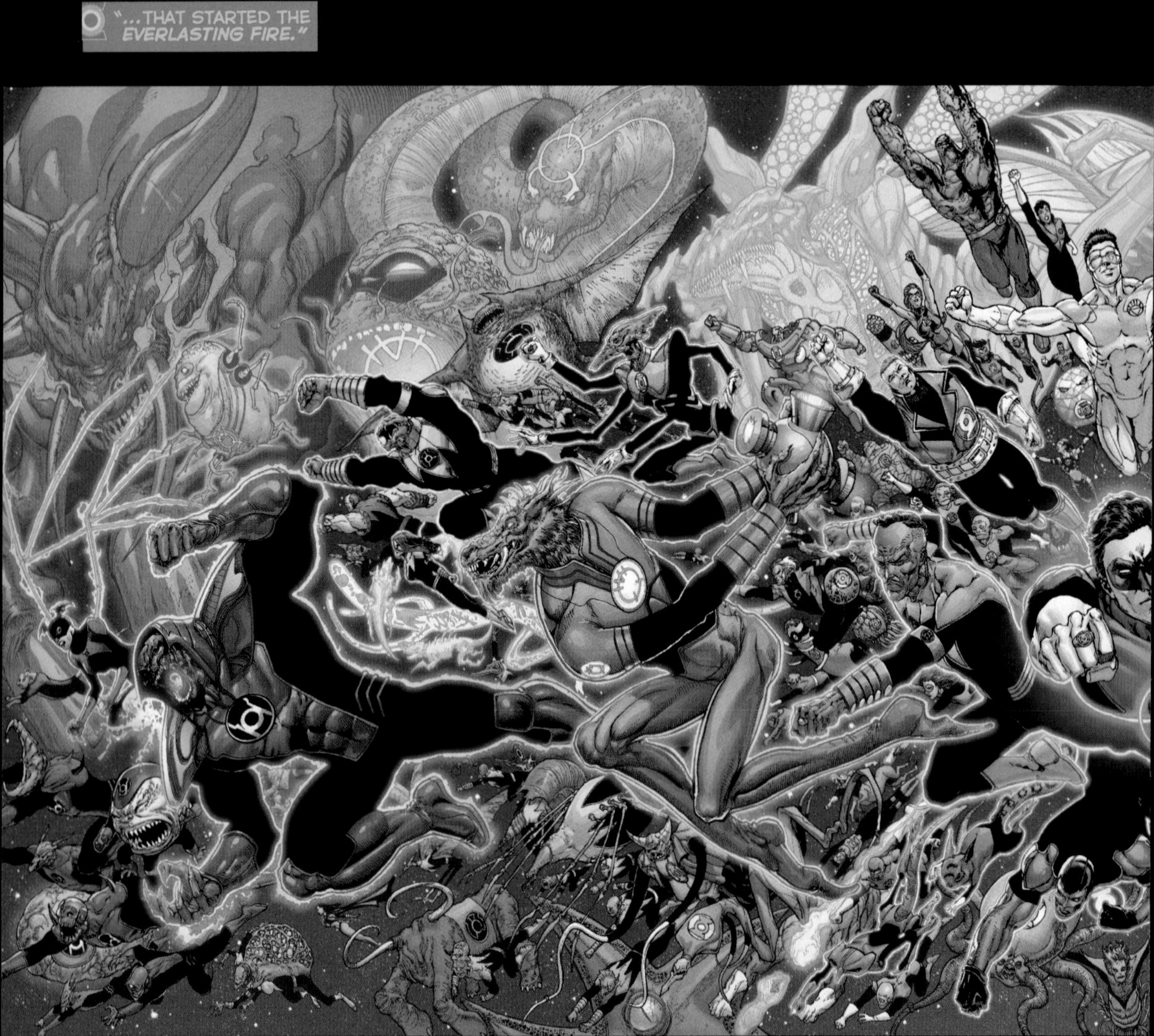
"...THAT STARTED THE EVERLASTING FIRE."

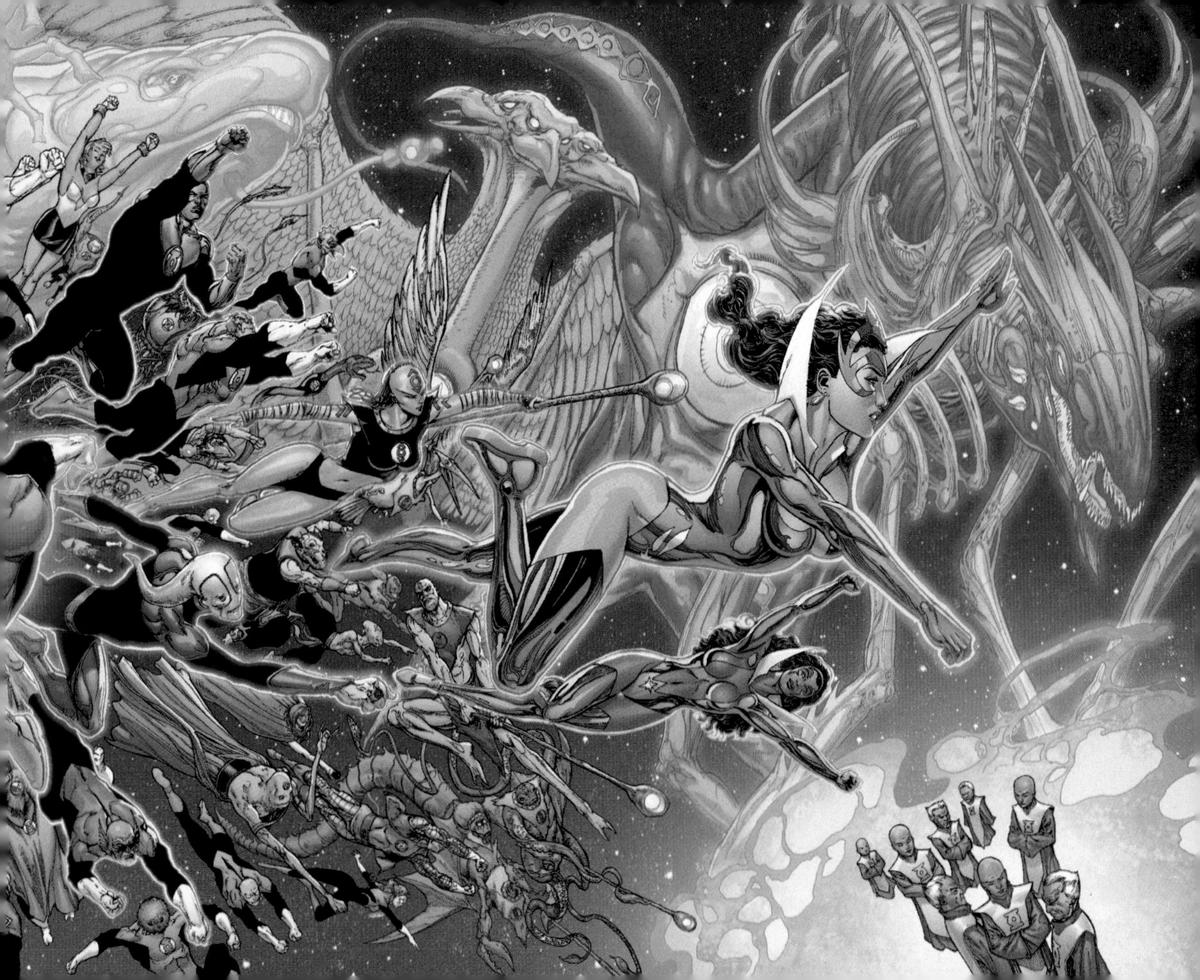

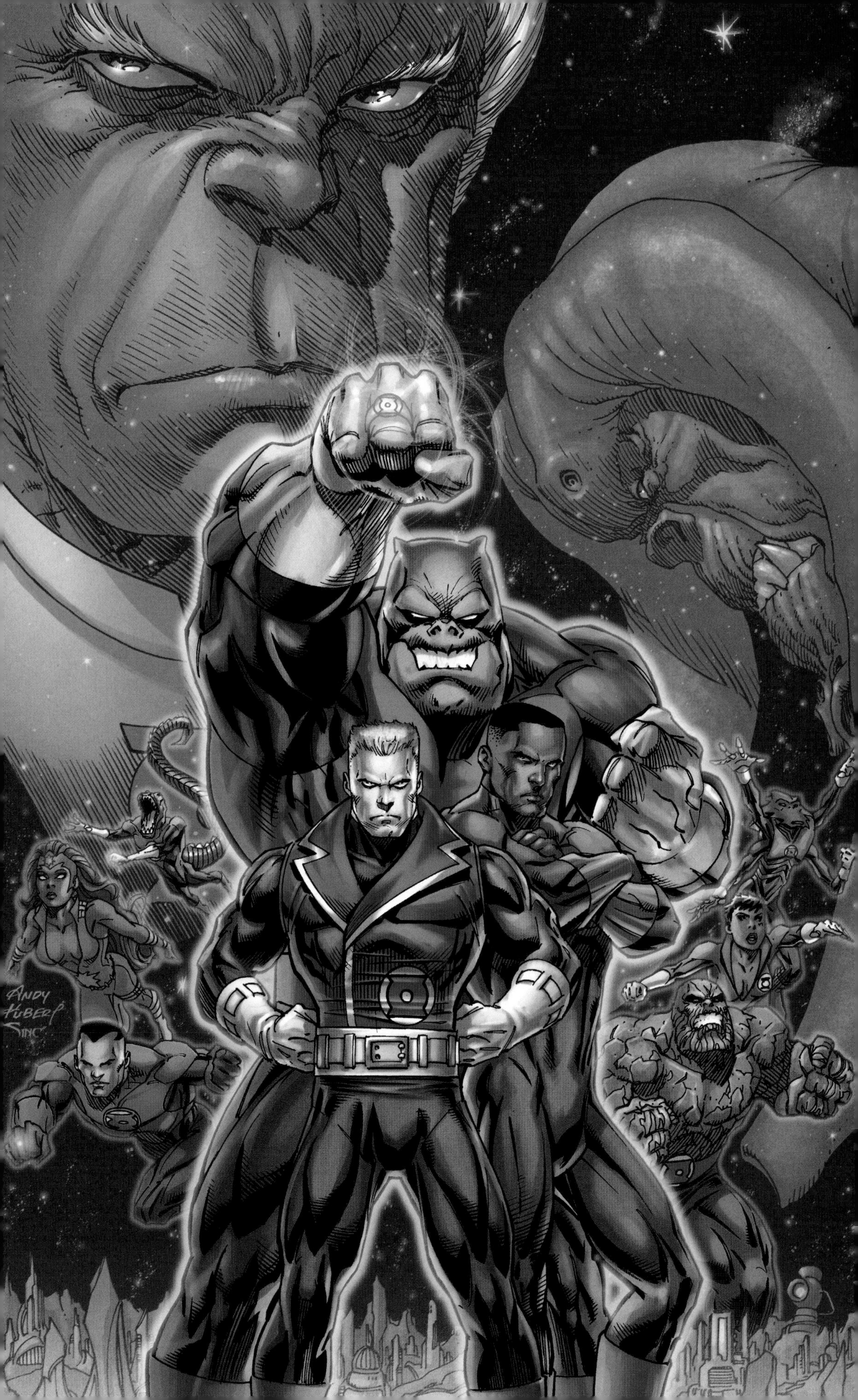
ANDY
KUBERT
SINC

CODA

PETER J. TOMASI writer **FERNANDO PASARIN** penciller **SCOTT HANNA** inker
cover art by **ANDY KUBERT & ALEX SINCLAIR**

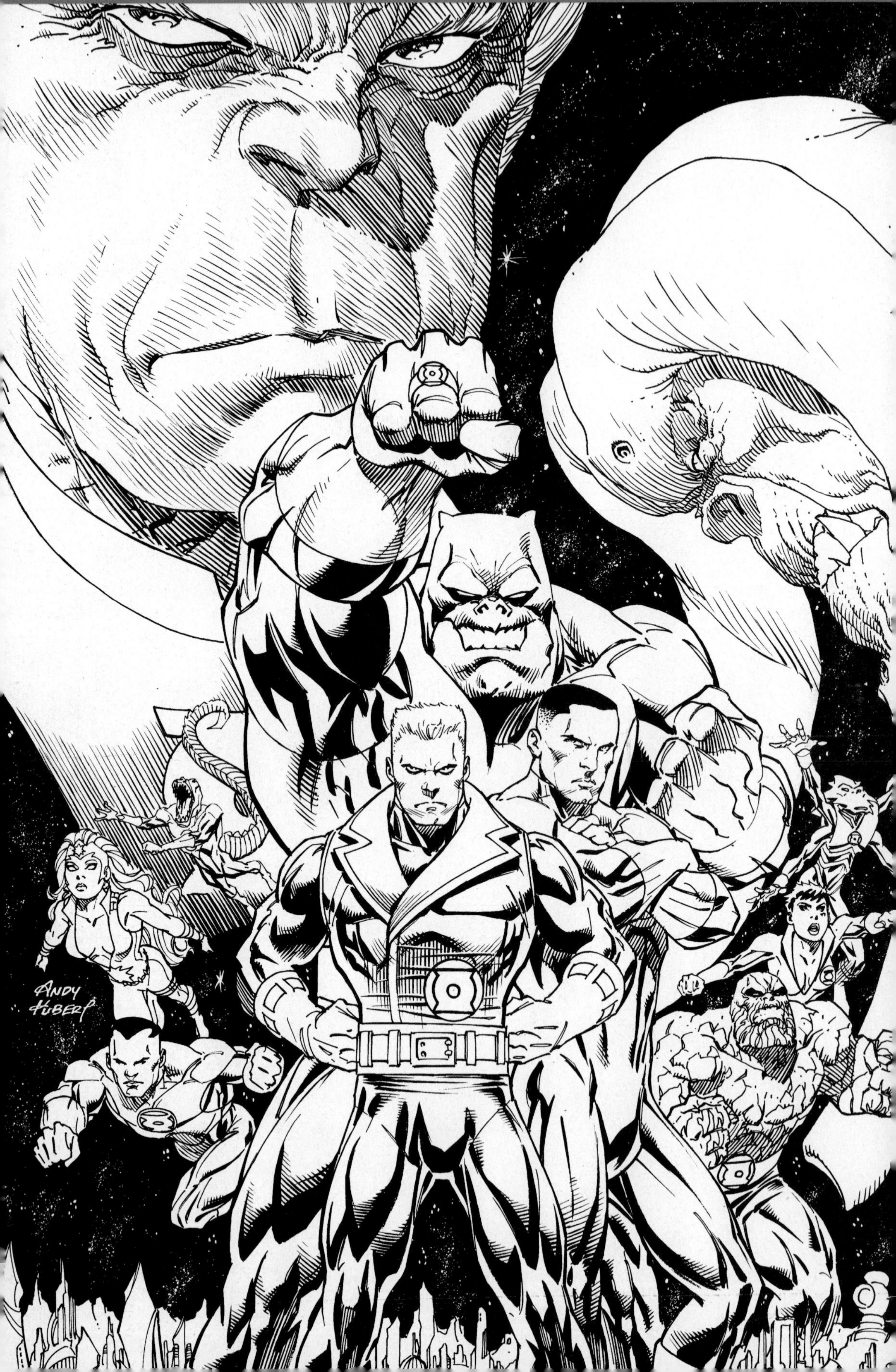
ANDY KUBERT

OA. THE GUARDIANS' PLANETARY CITADEL.
YOU SURE HE'S HERE?
NO I'M NOT SURE, BUT WE'VE CHECKED EVERY-WHERE ELSE.
KKKRRRKKKK
HEY, POOZER, YOU MISS US?

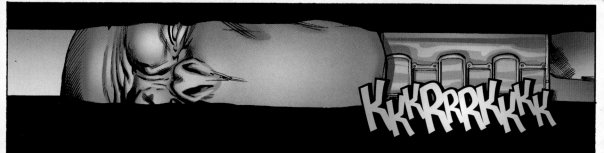

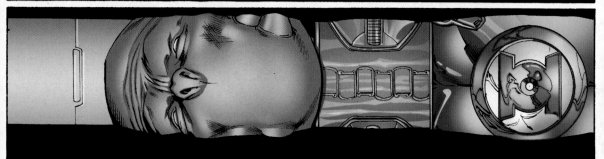

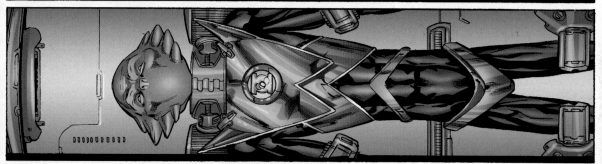

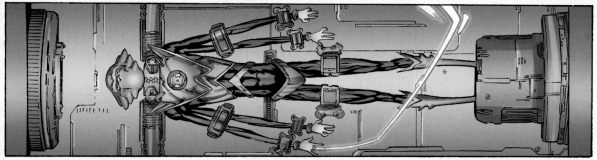

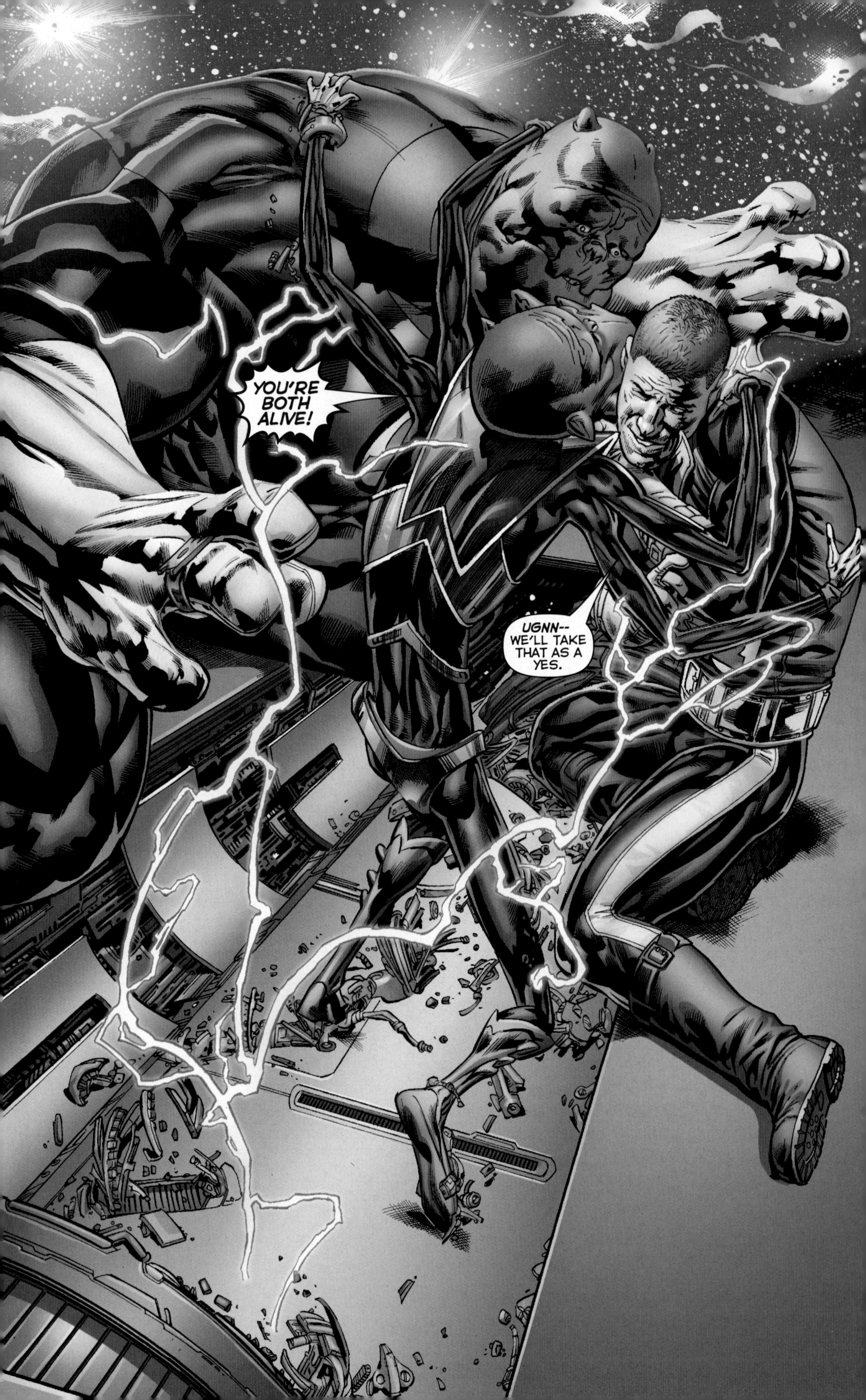
YOU'RE BOTH ALIVE!
UGNN-- WE'LL TAKE THAT AS A YES.

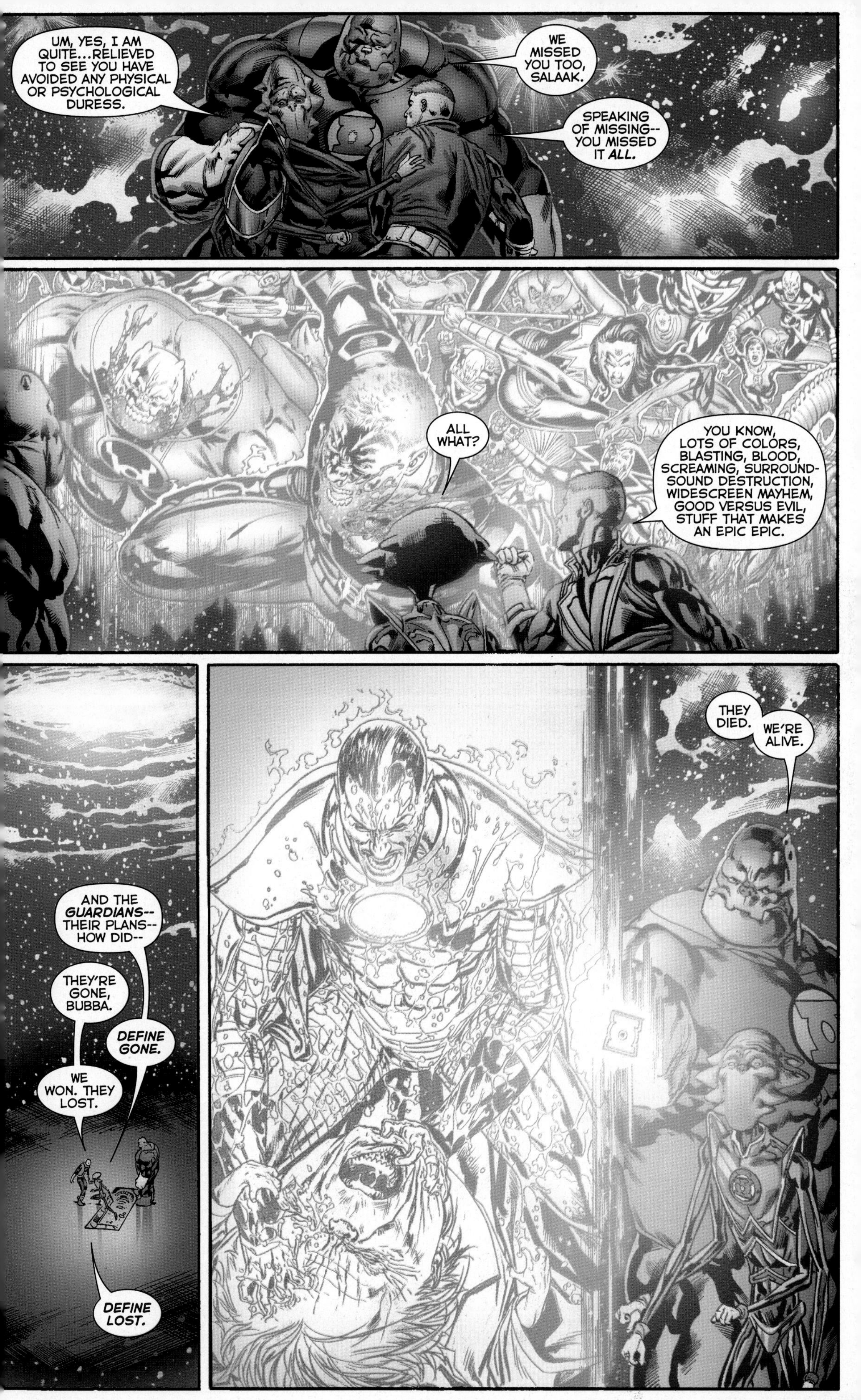
UM, YES, I AM QUITE...RELIEVED TO SEE YOU HAVE AVOIDED ANY PHYSICAL OR PSYCHOLOGICAL DURESS.
WE MISSED YOU TOO, SALAAK.
SPEAKING OF MISSING-- YOU MISSED IT *ALL.*
ALL WHAT?
YOU KNOW, LOTS OF COLORS, BLASTING, BLOOD, SCREAMING, SURROUND-SOUND DESTRUCTION, WIDESCREEN MAYHEM, GOOD VERSUS EVIL, STUFF THAT MAKES AN EPIC EPIC.
AND THE *GUARDIANS*-- THEIR PLANS-- HOW DID--
THEY'RE GONE, BUBBA.
DEFINE GONE.
WE WON. THEY LOST.
DEFINE LOST.
THEY DIED.
WE'RE ALIVE.

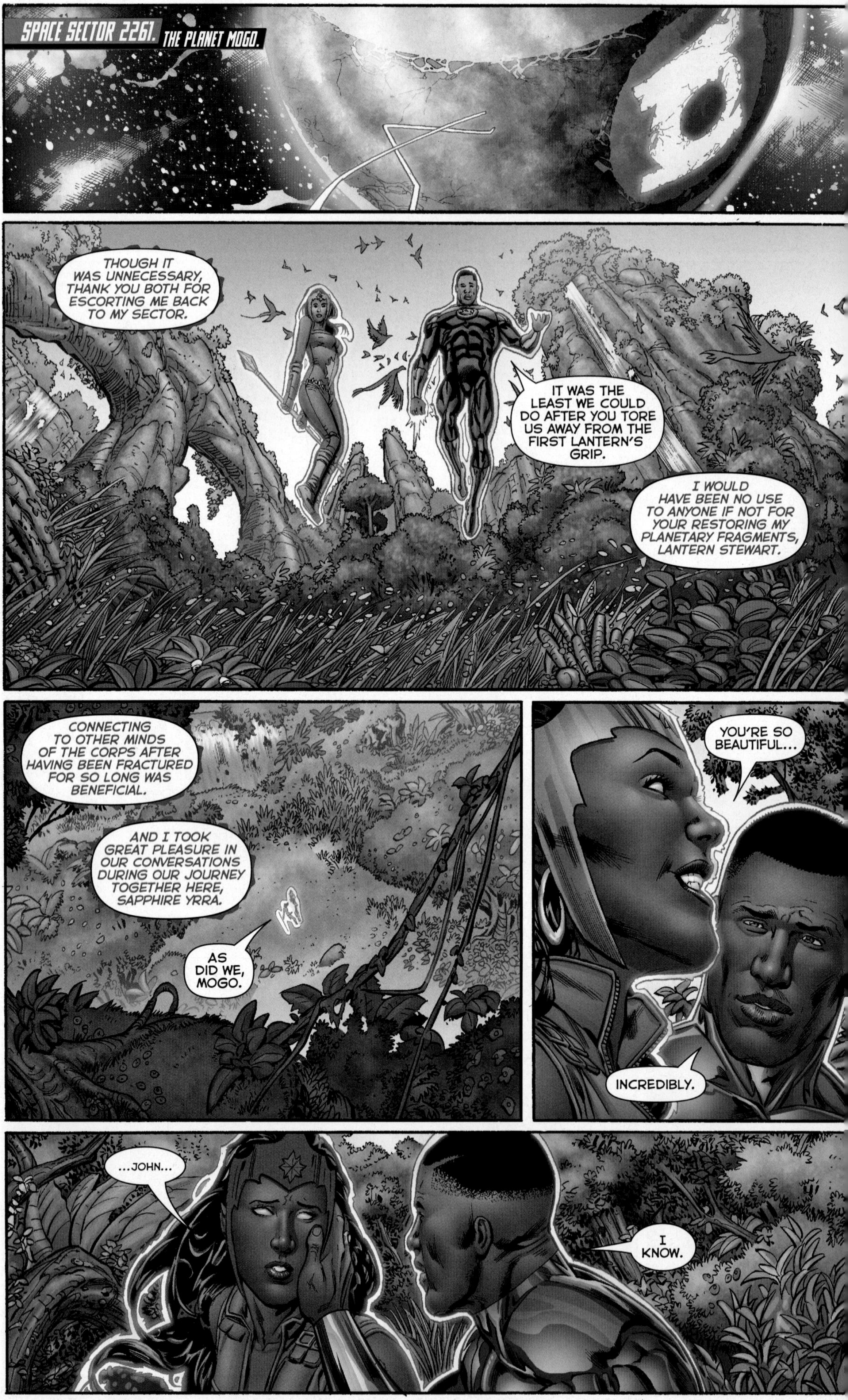
SPACE SECTOR 2261. THE PLANET MOGO.
THOUGH IT WAS UNNECESSARY, THANK YOU BOTH FOR ESCORTING ME BACK TO MY SECTOR.
IT WAS THE LEAST WE COULD DO AFTER YOU TORE US AWAY FROM THE FIRST LANTERN'S GRIP.
I WOULD HAVE BEEN NO USE TO ANYONE IF NOT FOR YOUR RESTORING MY PLANETARY FRAGMENTS, LANTERN STEWART.
CONNECTING TO OTHER MINDS OF THE CORPS AFTER HAVING BEEN FRACTURED FOR SO LONG WAS BENEFICIAL.
AND I TOOK GREAT PLEASURE IN OUR CONVERSATIONS DURING OUR JOURNEY TOGETHER HERE, SAPPHIRE YRRA.
AS DID WE, MOGO.
YOU'RE SO BEAUTIFUL...
INCREDIBLY.
...JOHN...
I KNOW.

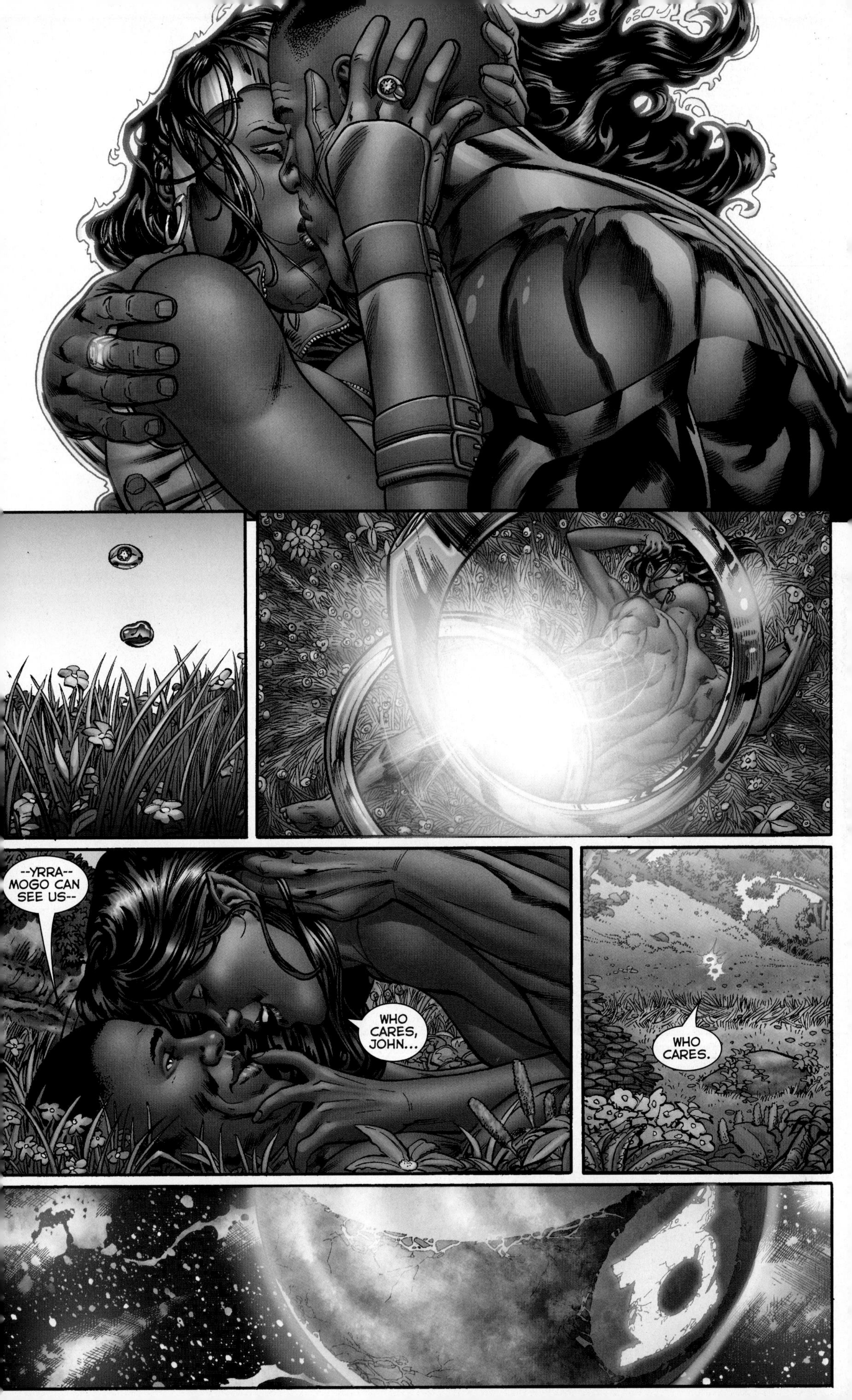
--YRRA--
MOGO CAN
SEE US--
WHO
CARES,
JOHN...
WHO
CARES.

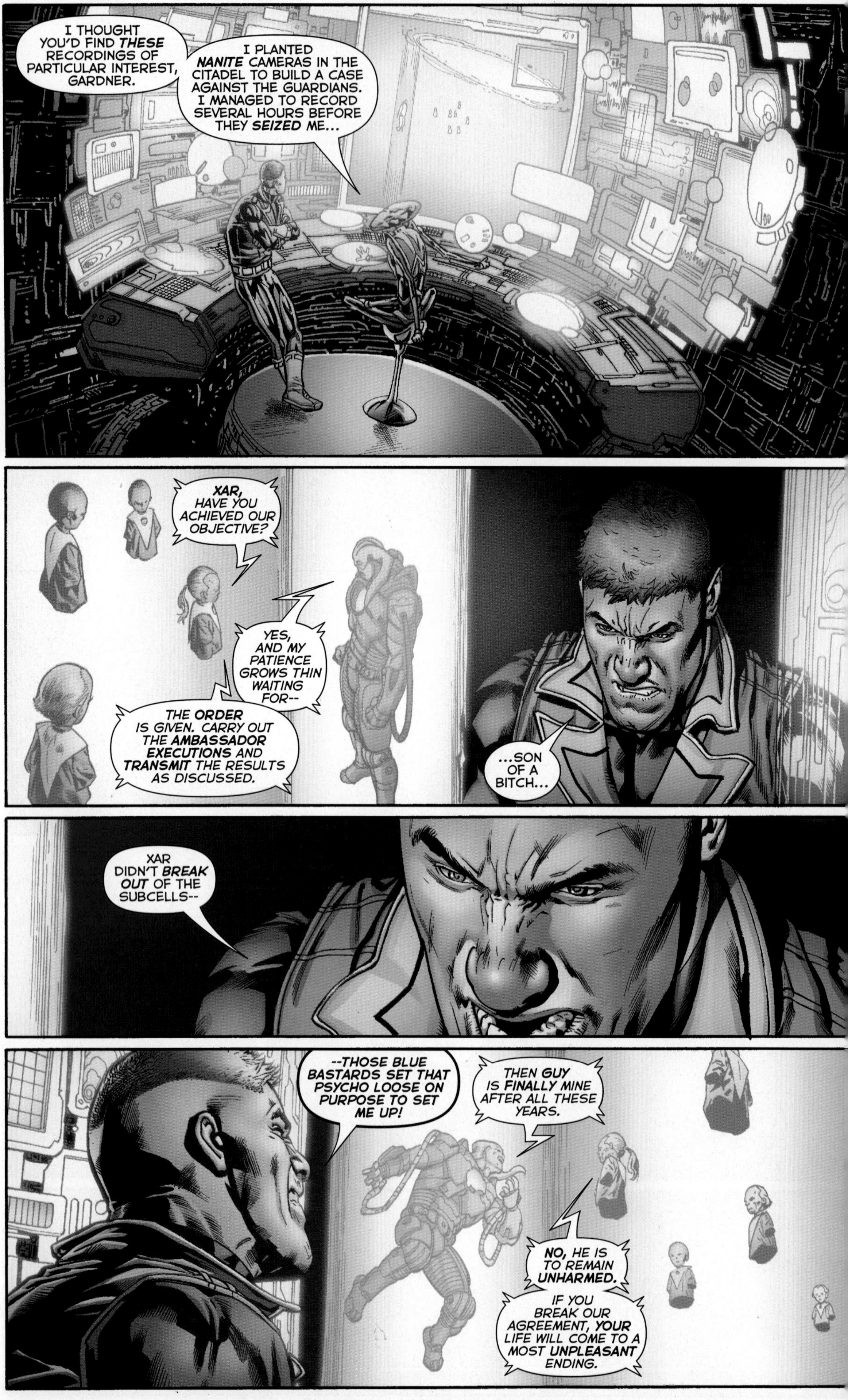
I THOUGHT YOU'D FIND THESE RECORDINGS OF PARTICULAR INTEREST, GARDNER.
I PLANTED NANITE CAMERAS IN THE CITADEL TO BUILD A CASE AGAINST THE GUARDIANS. I MANAGED TO RECORD SEVERAL HOURS BEFORE THEY SEIZED ME...
XAR, HAVE YOU ACHIEVED OUR OBJECTIVE?
YES, AND MY PATIENCE GROWS THIN WAITING FOR--
THE ORDER IS GIVEN. CARRY OUT THE AMBASSADOR EXECUTIONS AND TRANSMIT THE RESULTS AS DISCUSSED.
...SON OF A BITCH...
XAR DIDN'T BREAK OUT OF THE SUBCELLS--
--THOSE BLUE BASTARDS SET THAT PSYCHO LOOSE ON PURPOSE TO SET ME UP!
THEN GUY IS FINALLY MINE AFTER ALL THESE YEARS.
NO, HE IS TO REMAIN UNHARMED.
IF YOU BREAK OUR AGREEMENT, YOUR LIFE WILL COME TO A MOST UNPLEASANT ENDING.

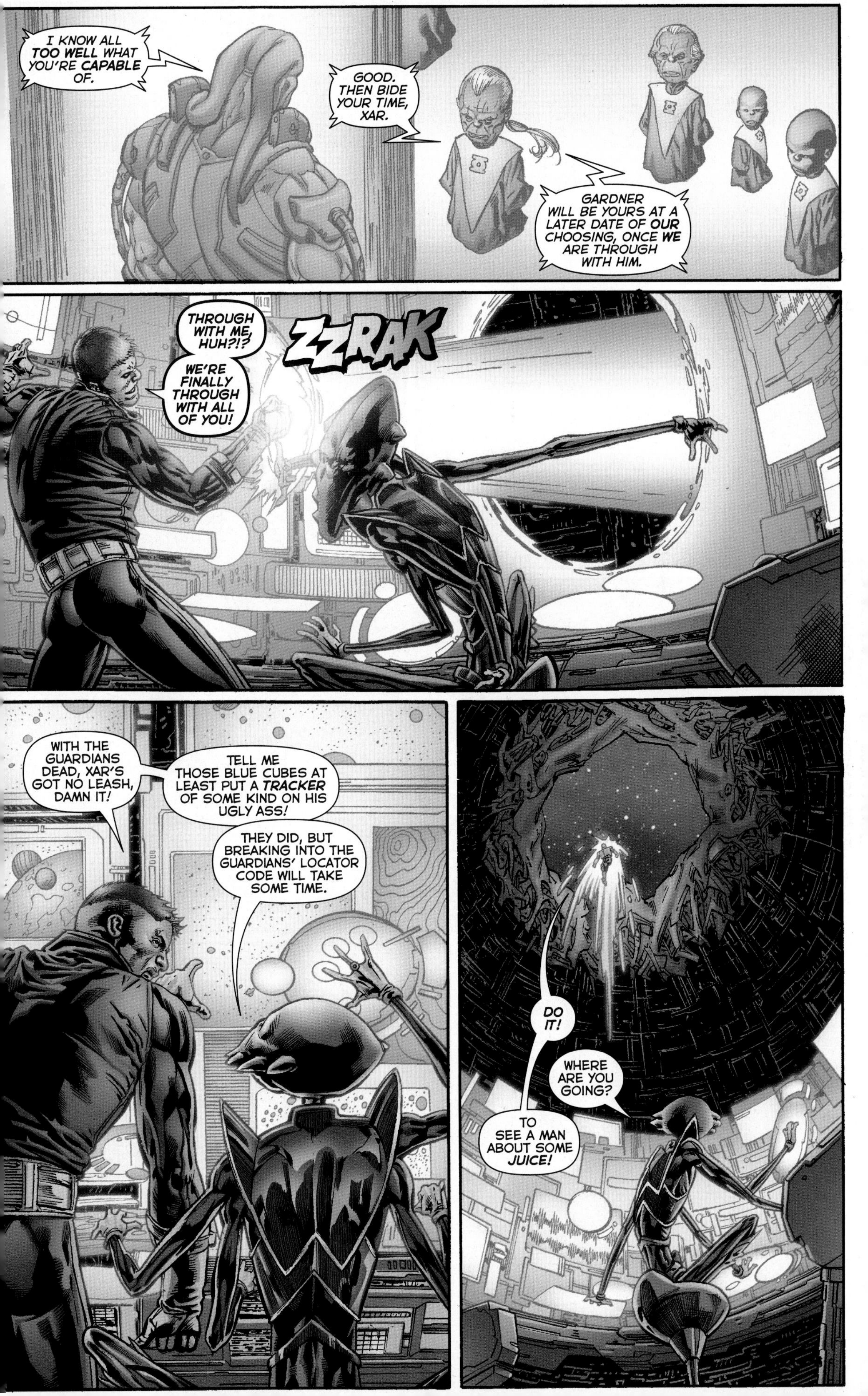
I KNOW ALL TOO WELL WHAT YOU'RE CAPABLE OF.
GOOD. THEN BIDE YOUR TIME, XAR.
GARDNER WILL BE YOURS AT A LATER DATE OF OUR CHOOSING, ONCE WE ARE THROUGH WITH HIM.
THROUGH WITH ME, HUH?!?
WE'RE FINALLY THROUGH WITH ALL OF YOU!
ZZRAK
WITH THE GUARDIANS DEAD, XAR'S GOT NO LEASH, DAMN IT!
TELL ME THOSE BLUE CUBES AT LEAST PUT A TRACKER OF SOME KIND ON HIS UGLY ASS!
THEY DID, BUT BREAKING INTO THE GUARDIANS' LOCATOR CODE WILL TAKE SOME TIME.
DO IT!
WHERE ARE YOU GOING?
TO SEE A MAN ABOUT SOME JUICE!

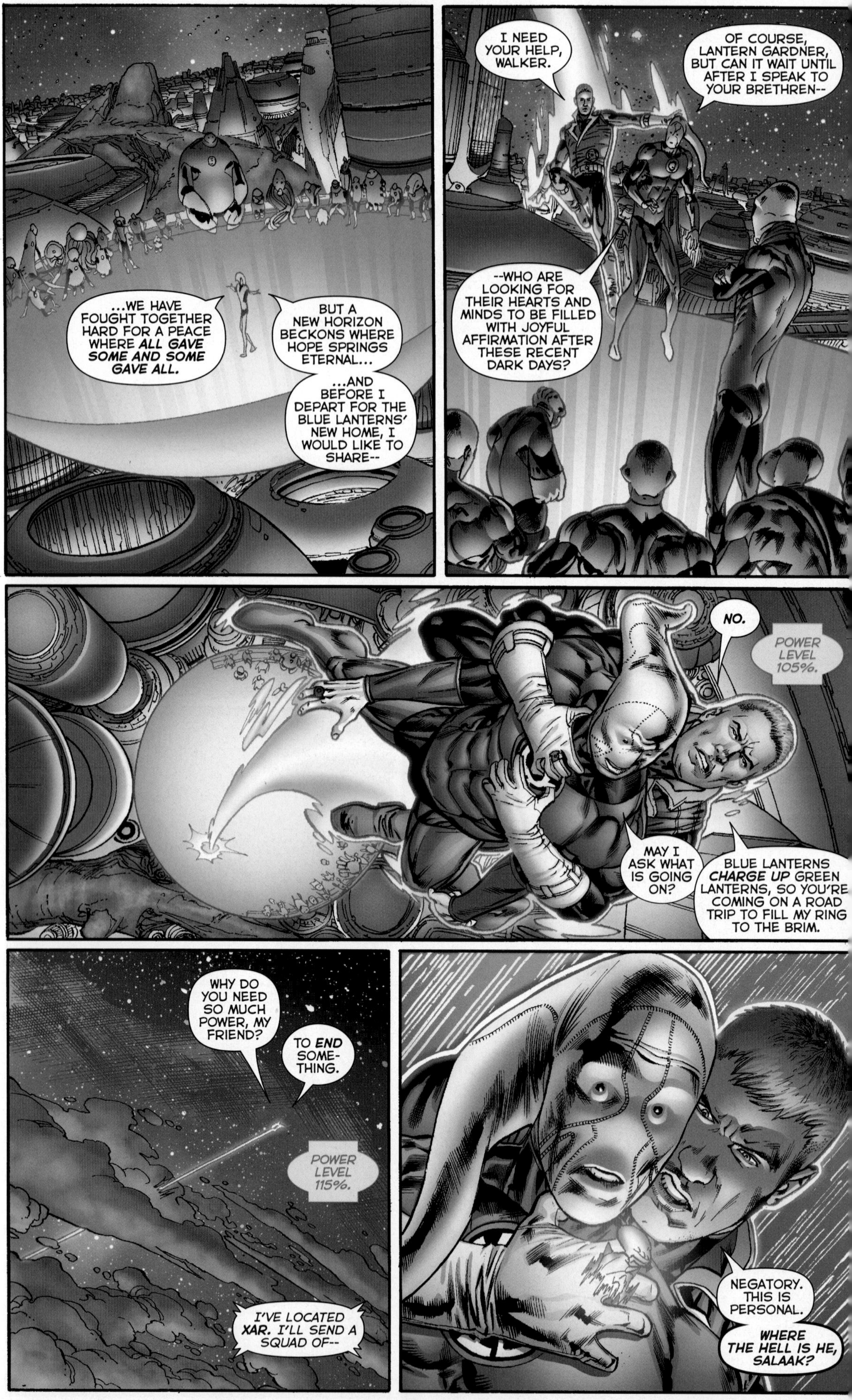
...WE HAVE FOUGHT TOGETHER HARD FOR A PEACE WHERE *ALL GAVE SOME AND SOME GAVE ALL.*
BUT A NEW HORIZON BECKONS WHERE HOPE SPRINGS ETERNAL...
...AND BEFORE I DEPART FOR THE BLUE LANTERNS' NEW HOME, I WOULD LIKE TO SHARE--
I NEED YOUR HELP, WALKER.
OF COURSE, LANTERN GARDNER, BUT CAN IT WAIT UNTIL AFTER I SPEAK TO YOUR BRETHREN--
--WHO ARE LOOKING FOR THEIR HEARTS AND MINDS TO BE FILLED WITH JOYFUL AFFIRMATION AFTER THESE RECENT DARK DAYS?
NO.
POWER LEVEL 105%.
MAY I ASK WHAT IS GOING ON?
BLUE LANTERNS *CHARGE UP* GREEN LANTERNS, SO YOU'RE COMING ON A ROAD TRIP TO FILL MY RING TO THE BRIM.
WHY DO YOU NEED SO MUCH POWER, MY FRIEND?
TO *END* SOME-THING.
POWER LEVEL 115%.
I'VE LOCATED ***XAR.*** *I'LL SEND A SQUAD OF--*
NEGATORY. THIS IS PERSONAL.
WHERE THE HELL IS HE, SALAAK?

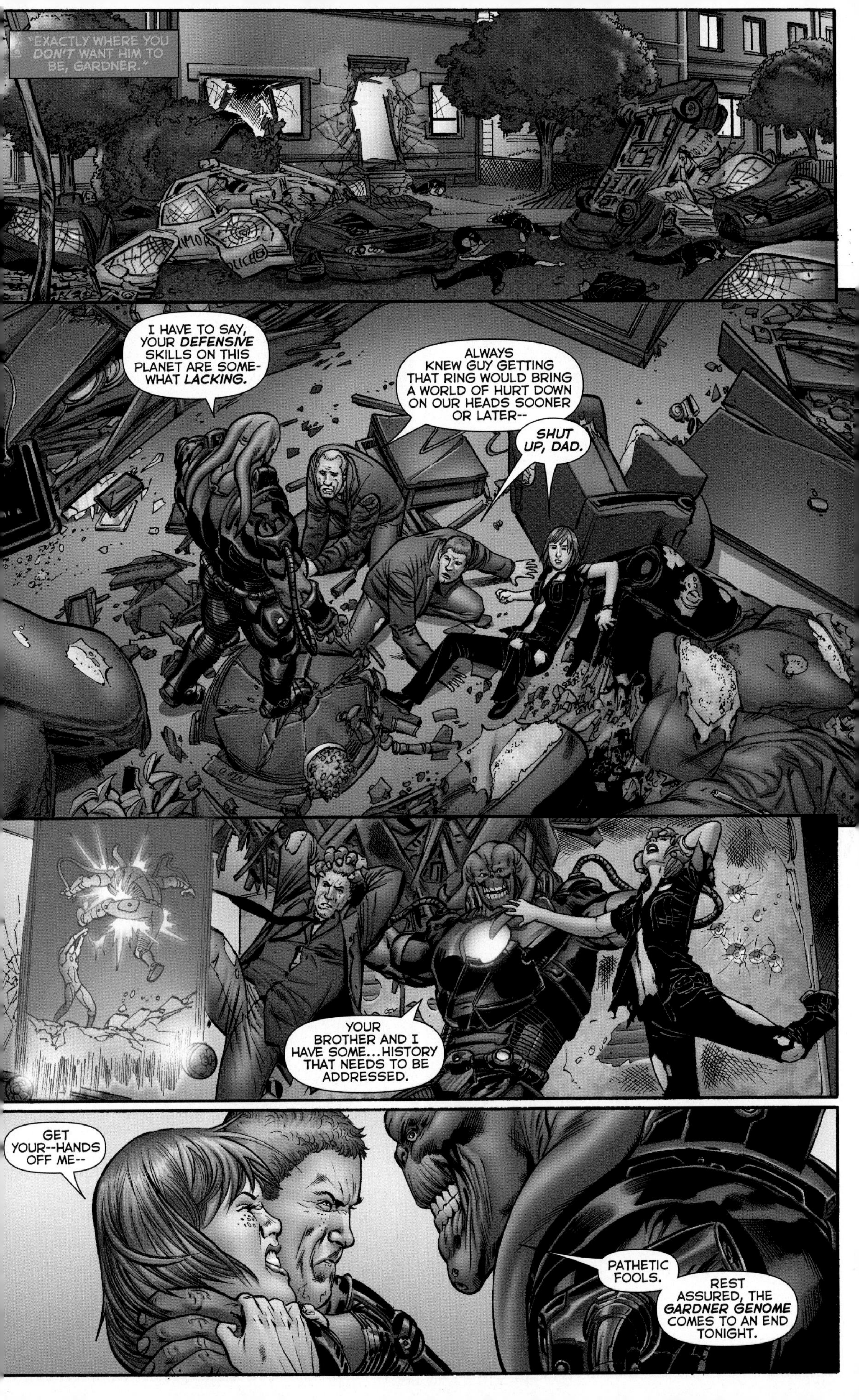

"EXACTLY WHERE YOU DON'T WANT HIM TO BE, GARDNER."
I HAVE TO SAY, YOUR DEFENSIVE SKILLS ON THIS PLANET ARE SOME-WHAT LACKING.
ALWAYS KNEW GUY GETTING THAT RING WOULD BRING A WORLD OF HURT DOWN ON OUR HEADS SOONER OR LATER--
SHUT UP, DAD.
YOUR BROTHER AND I HAVE SOME...HISTORY THAT NEEDS TO BE ADDRESSED.
GET YOUR--HANDS OFF ME--
PATHETIC FOOLS.
REST ASSURED, THE GARDNER GENOME COMES TO AN END TONIGHT.

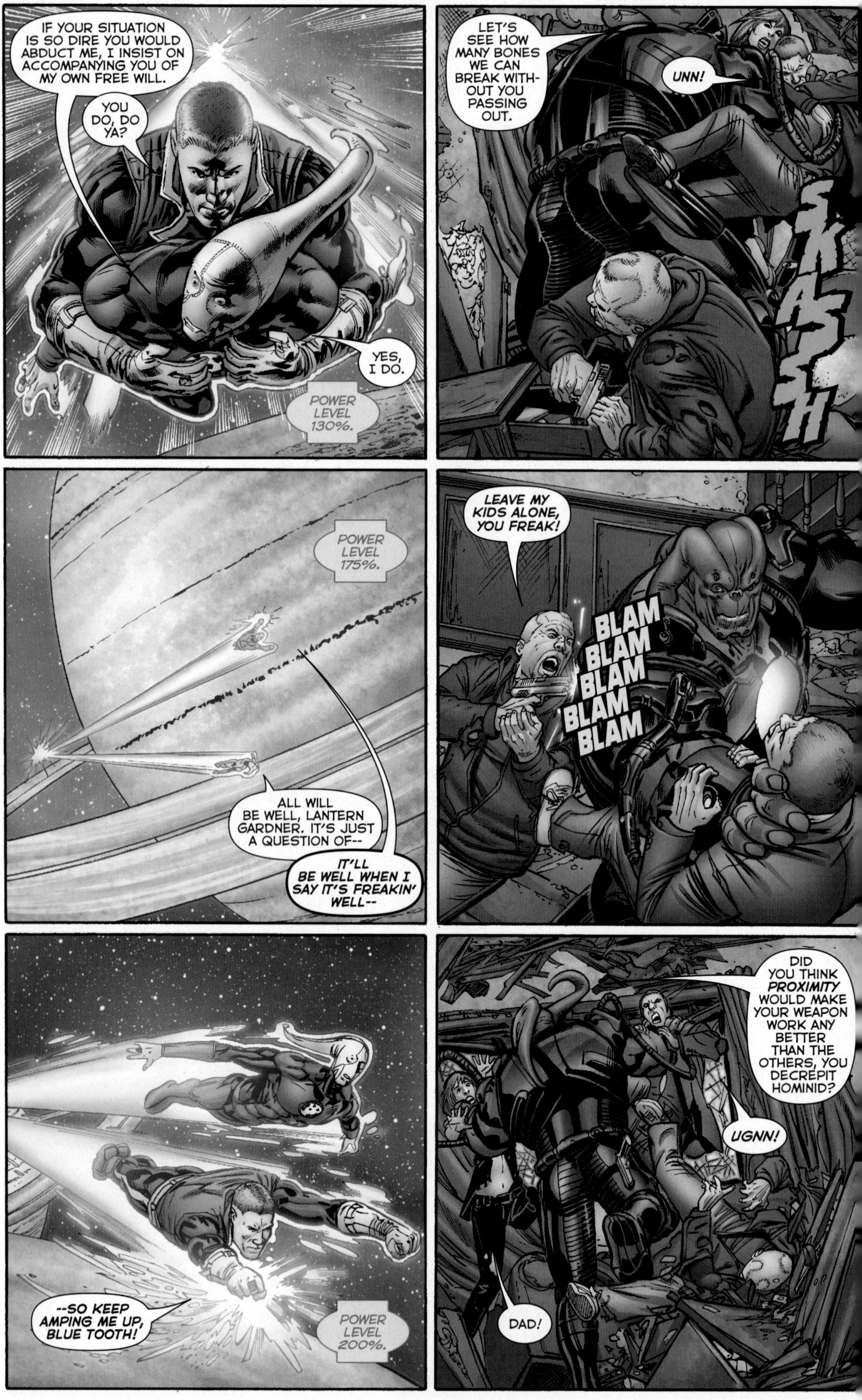
IF YOUR SITUATION IS SO DIRE YOU WOULD ABDUCT ME, I INSIST ON ACCOMPANYING YOU OF MY OWN FREE WILL.
YOU DO, DO YA?
YES, I DO.
POWER LEVEL 130%.
LET'S SEE HOW MANY BONES WE CAN BREAK WITH-OUT YOU PASSING OUT.
UNN!
SKASSH
POWER LEVEL 175%.
ALL WILL BE WELL, LANTERN GARDNER. IT'S JUST A QUESTION OF--
IT'LL BE WELL WHEN I SAY IT'S FREAKIN' WELL--
LEAVE MY KIDS ALONE, YOU FREAK!
BLAM BLAM BLAM BLAM BLAM BLAM
--SO KEEP AMPING ME UP, BLUE TOOTH!
POWER LEVEL 200%.
DID YOU THINK PROXIMITY WOULD MAKE YOUR WEAPON WORK ANY BETTER THAN THE OTHERS, YOU DECREPIT HOMINID?
UGNN!
DAD!

POWER LEVEL 300%

I'M NOT SURE WHAT THE CAPACITY OF YOUR RING IS, BUT YOU NEED TO DISCHARGE THE IMMENSE POWER YOU'VE BUILT UP SOON.

YEAH. *THAT'S THE PLAN.*

IT'S TIME TO DIE.

IT WILL BE INCREDIBLY SLOW AND PAINFUL.

SMASH

YOUR LAST MOMENTS WILL BE RECORDED SO GUY GARDNER CAN WATCH HOW HE FAILED HIS OWN BLOOD-COVERED FAMILY.

THANKS FOR THE *COMPANY,* WALKER.

GOTTA DO THIS ALONE.

POWER LEVEL 325%

SO...

...WHO WANTS TO *SCREAM* FOR THE CAMERA FIRST?

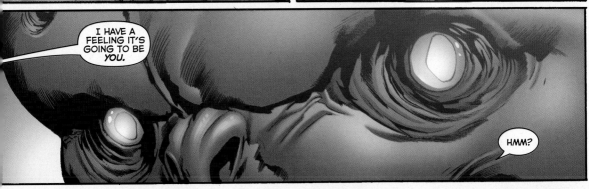
I HAVE A FEELING IT'S GOING TO BE *YOU.*

HMM?

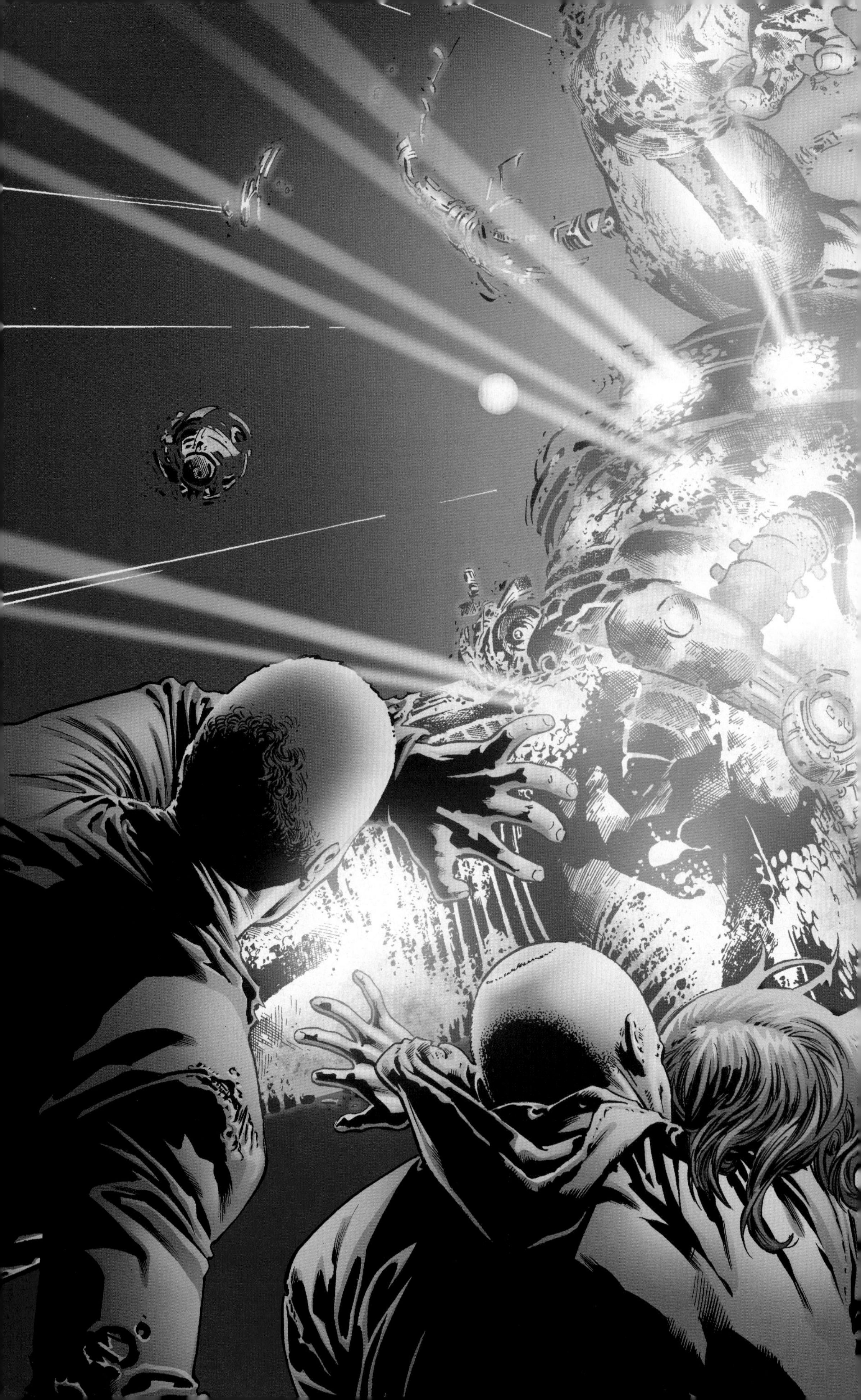

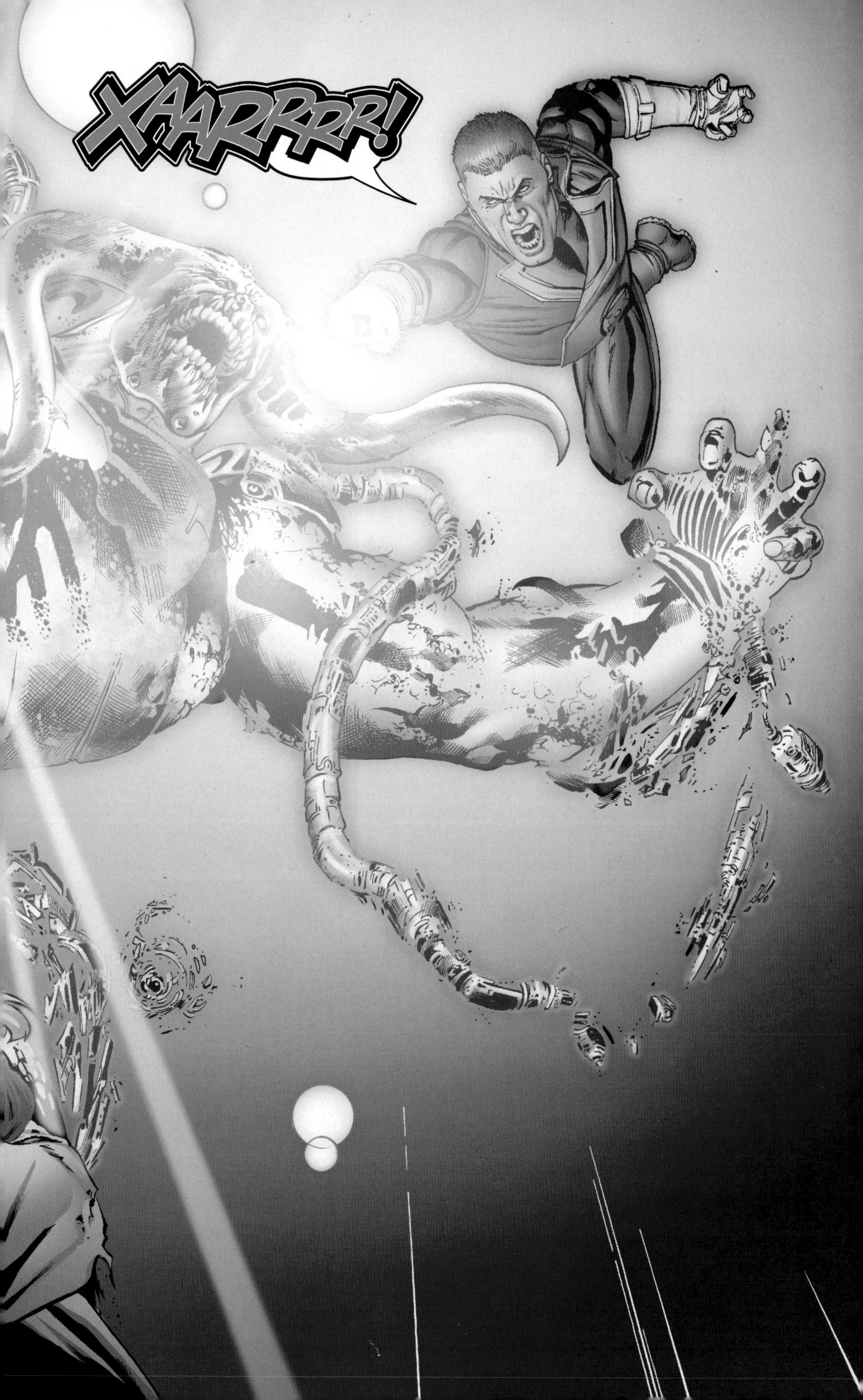
XAARRRR!

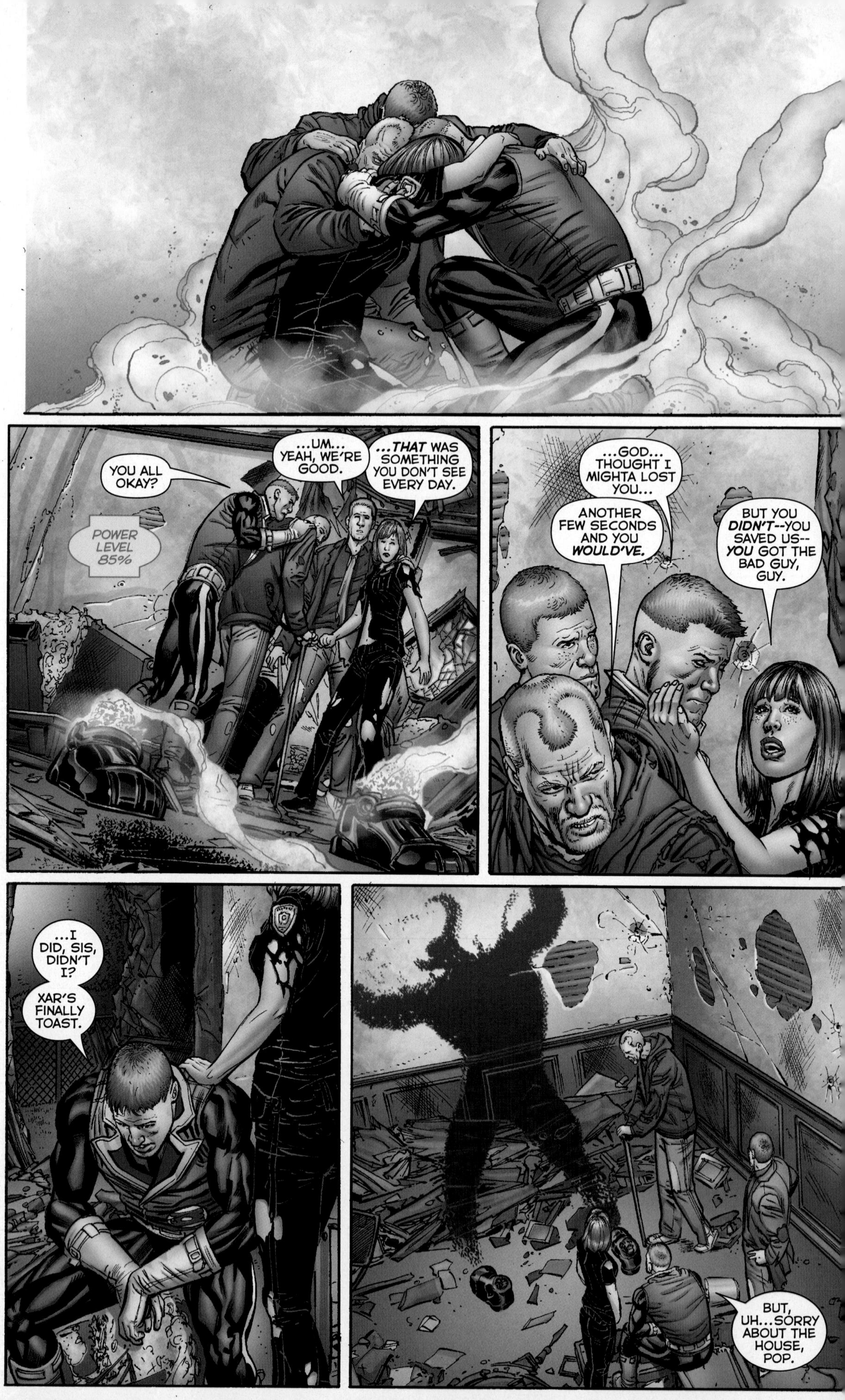

YOU ALL OKAY?
POWER LEVEL 85%
...UM... YEAH, WE'RE GOOD.
...*THAT* WAS SOMETHING YOU DON'T SEE EVERY DAY.
...GOD... THOUGHT I MIGHTA LOST YOU...
ANOTHER FEW SECONDS AND YOU *WOULD'VE.*
BUT YOU *DIDN'T*--YOU SAVED US--*YOU* GOT THE BAD GUY, GUY.
...I DID, SIS, DIDN'T I?
XAR'S FINALLY TOAST.
BUT, UH...SORRY ABOUT THE HOUSE, POP.

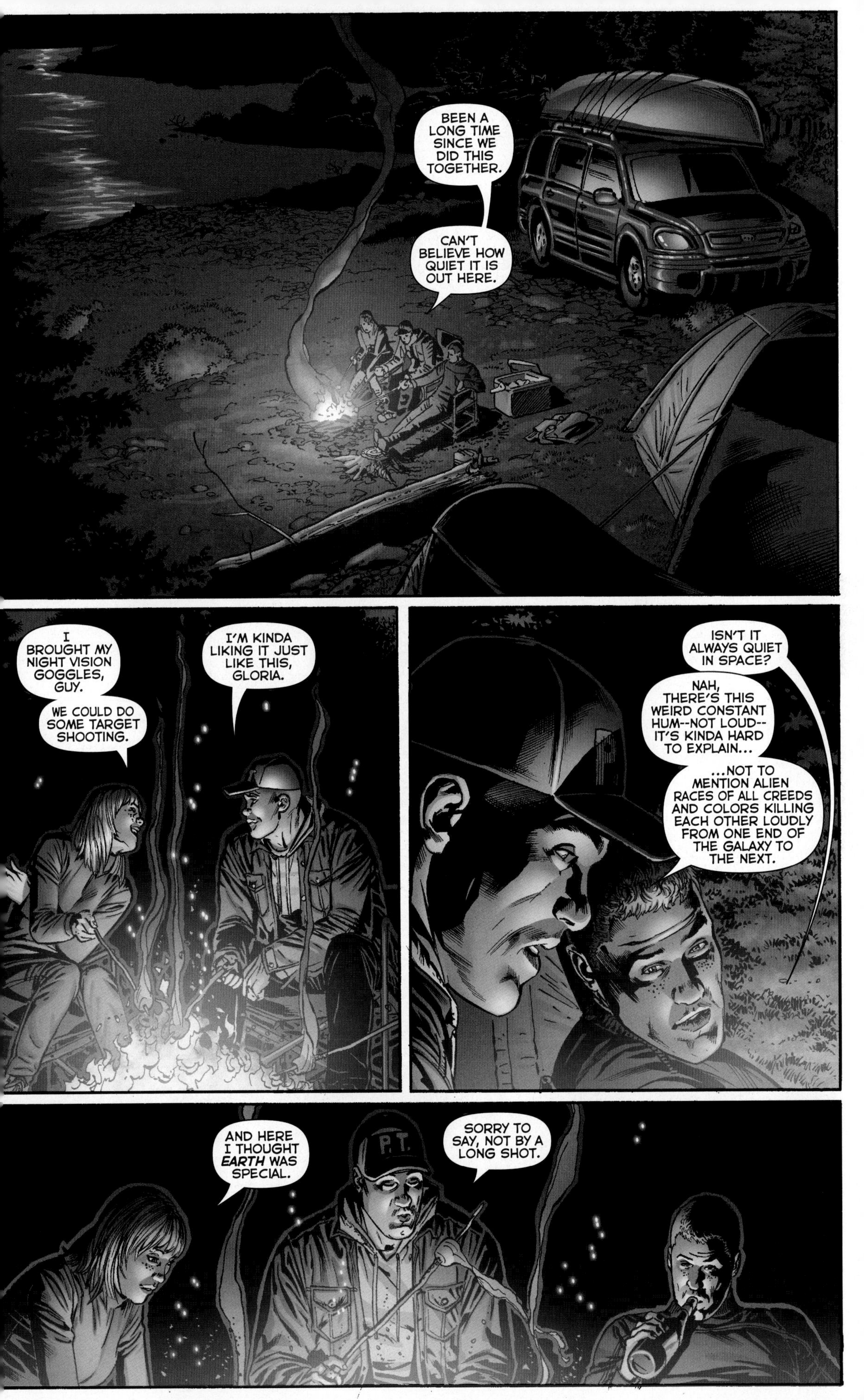
BEEN A LONG TIME SINCE WE DID THIS TOGETHER.
CAN'T BELIEVE HOW QUIET IT IS OUT HERE.
I BROUGHT MY NIGHT VISION GOGGLES, GUY.
WE COULD DO SOME TARGET SHOOTING.
I'M KINDA LIKING IT JUST LIKE THIS, GLORIA.
ISN'T IT ALWAYS QUIET IN SPACE?
NAH, THERE'S THIS WEIRD CONSTANT HUM--NOT LOUD--IT'S KINDA HARD TO EXPLAIN...
...NOT TO MENTION ALIEN RACES OF ALL CREEDS AND COLORS KILLING EACH OTHER LOUDLY FROM ONE END OF THE GALAXY TO THE NEXT.
AND HERE I THOUGHT EARTH WAS SPECIAL.
SORRY TO SAY, NOT BY A LONG SHOT.
P.T.

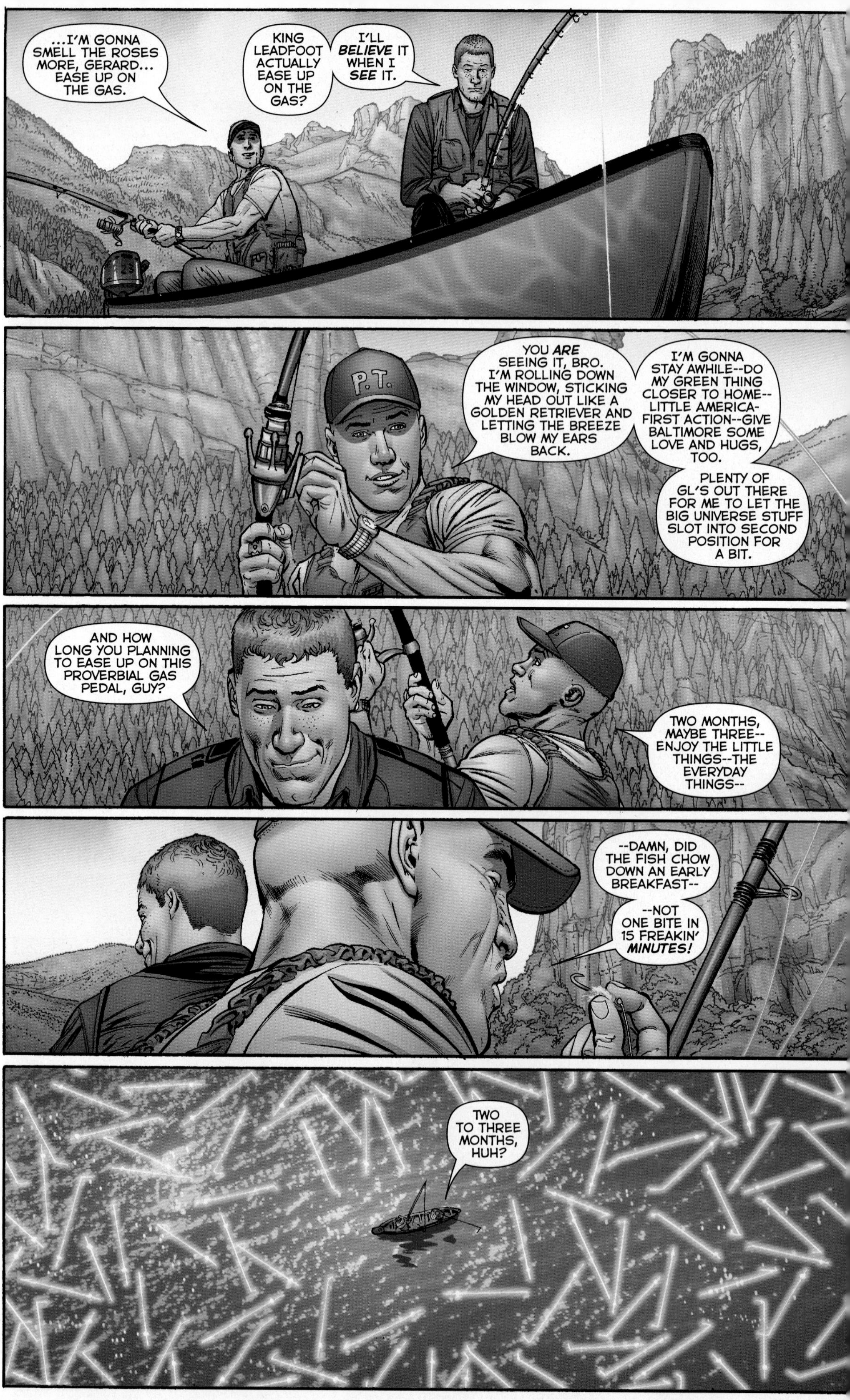
...I'M GONNA SMELL THE ROSES MORE, GERARD... EASE UP ON THE GAS.
KING LEADFOOT ACTUALLY EASE UP ON THE GAS?
I'LL *BELIEVE* IT WHEN I *SEE* IT.
YOU *ARE* SEEING IT, BRO. I'M ROLLING DOWN THE WINDOW, STICKING MY HEAD OUT LIKE A GOLDEN RETRIEVER AND LETTING THE BREEZE BLOW MY EARS BACK.
I'M GONNA STAY AWHILE--DO MY GREEN THING CLOSER TO HOME--LITTLE AMERICA-FIRST ACTION--GIVE BALTIMORE SOME LOVE AND HUGS, TOO.
PLENTY OF GL'S OUT THERE FOR ME TO LET THE BIG UNIVERSE STUFF SLOT INTO SECOND POSITION FOR A BIT.
AND HOW LONG YOU PLANNING TO EASE UP ON THIS PROVERBIAL GAS PEDAL, GUY?
TWO MONTHS, MAYBE THREE--ENJOY THE LITTLE THINGS--THE EVERYDAY THINGS--
--DAMN, DID THE FISH CHOW DOWN AN EARLY BREAKFAST--
--NOT ONE BITE IN 15 FREAKIN' *MINUTES!*
TWO TO THREE MONTHS, HUH?
P.T.

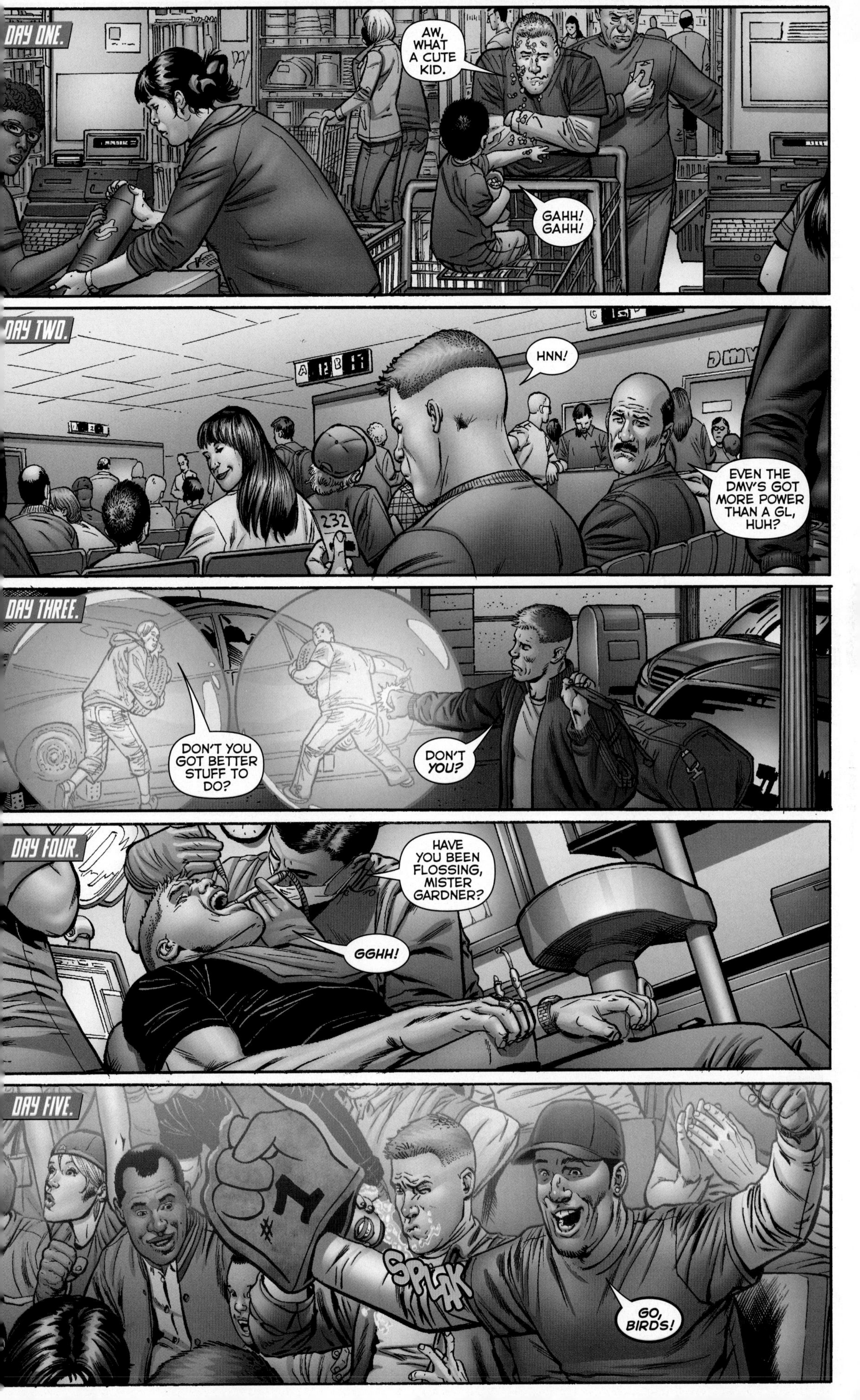

DAY ONE.
AW, WHAT A CUTE KID.
GAHH! GAHH!
DAY TWO.
DMV
HNN!
232
EVEN THE DMV'S GOT MORE POWER THAN A GL, HUH?
DAY THREE.
DON'T YOU GOT BETTER STUFF TO DO?
DON'T *YOU*?
DAY FOUR.
HAVE YOU BEEN FLOSSING, MISTER GARDNER?
GGHH!
DAY FIVE.
SPLAK
GO, BIRDS!

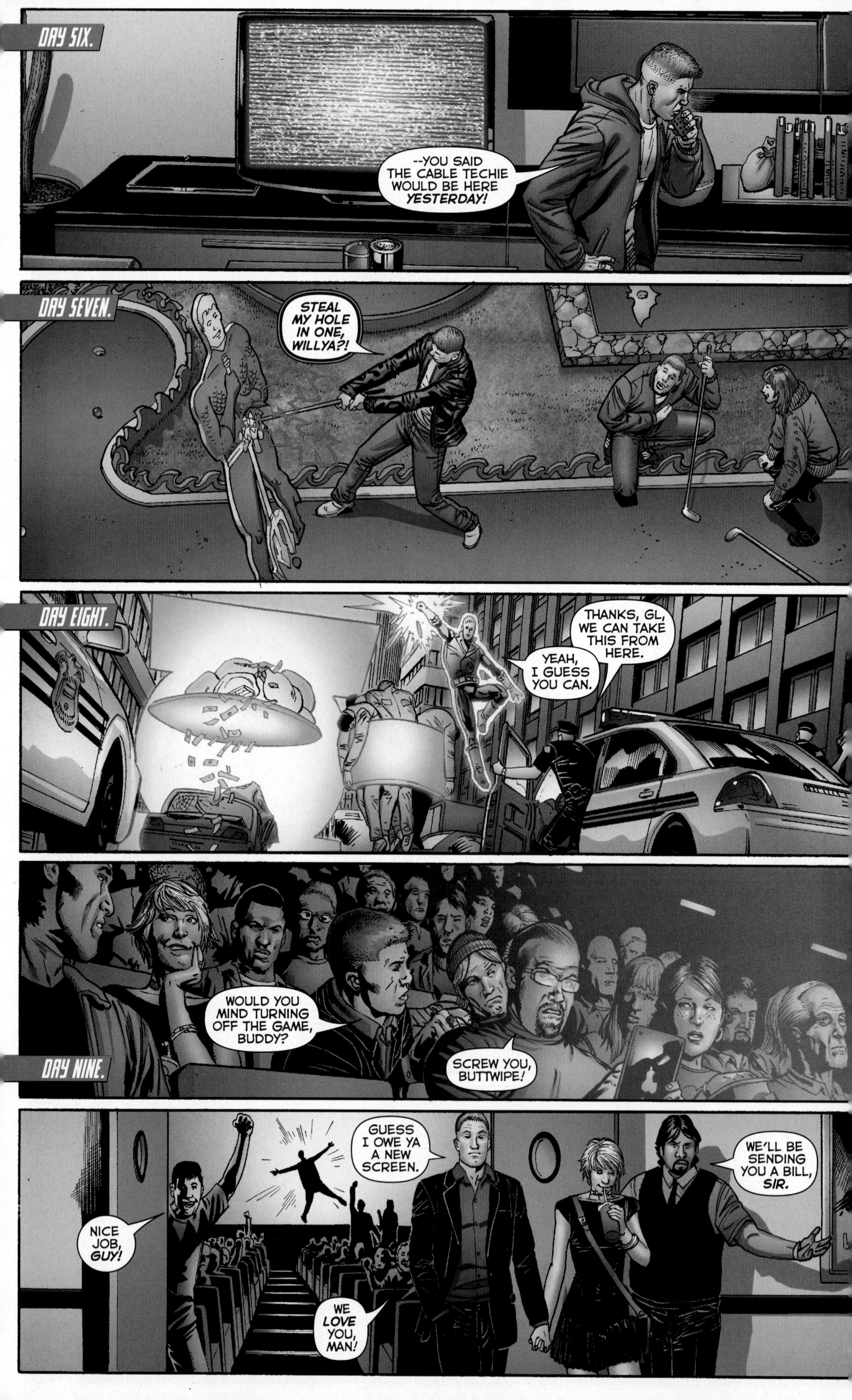
DAY SIX.
--YOU SAID THE CABLE TECHIE WOULD BE HERE *YESTERDAY!*
DAY SEVEN.
STEAL MY HOLE IN ONE, WILLYA?!
DAY EIGHT.
THANKS, GL, WE CAN TAKE THIS FROM HERE.
YEAH, I GUESS YOU CAN.
WOULD YOU MIND TURNING OFF THE GAME, BUDDY?
SCREW YOU, BUTTWIPE!
DAY NINE.
GUESS I OWE YA A NEW SCREEN.
WE'LL BE SENDING YOU A BILL, **SIR.**
NICE JOB, *GUY!*
WE *LOVE* YOU, MAN!

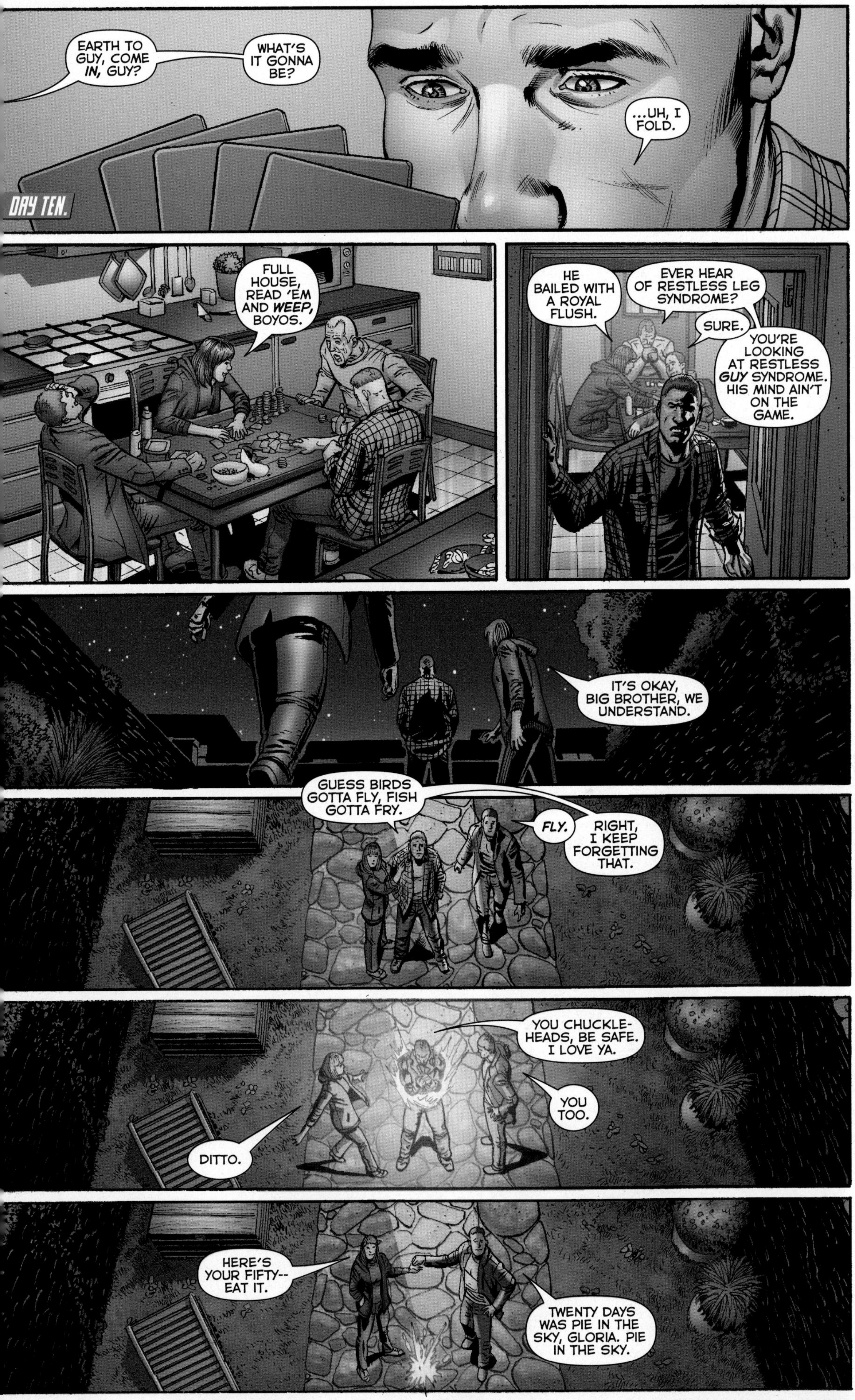
DAY TEN.
EARTH TO GUY, COME IN, GUY?
WHAT'S IT GONNA BE?
...UH, I FOLD.
FULL HOUSE, READ 'EM AND WEEP, BOYOS.
HE BAILED WITH A ROYAL FLUSH.
EVER HEAR OF RESTLESS LEG SYNDROME?
SURE.
YOU'RE LOOKING AT RESTLESS GUY SYNDROME. HIS MIND AIN'T ON THE GAME.
IT'S OKAY, BIG BROTHER, WE UNDERSTAND.
GUESS BIRDS GOTTA FLY, FISH GOTTA FRY.
FLY.
RIGHT, I KEEP FORGETTING THAT.
YOU CHUCKLE-HEADS, BE SAFE. I LOVE YA.
YOU TOO.
DITTO.
HERE'S YOUR FIFTY-- EAT IT.
TWENTY DAYS WAS PIE IN THE SKY, GLORIA. PIE IN THE SKY.

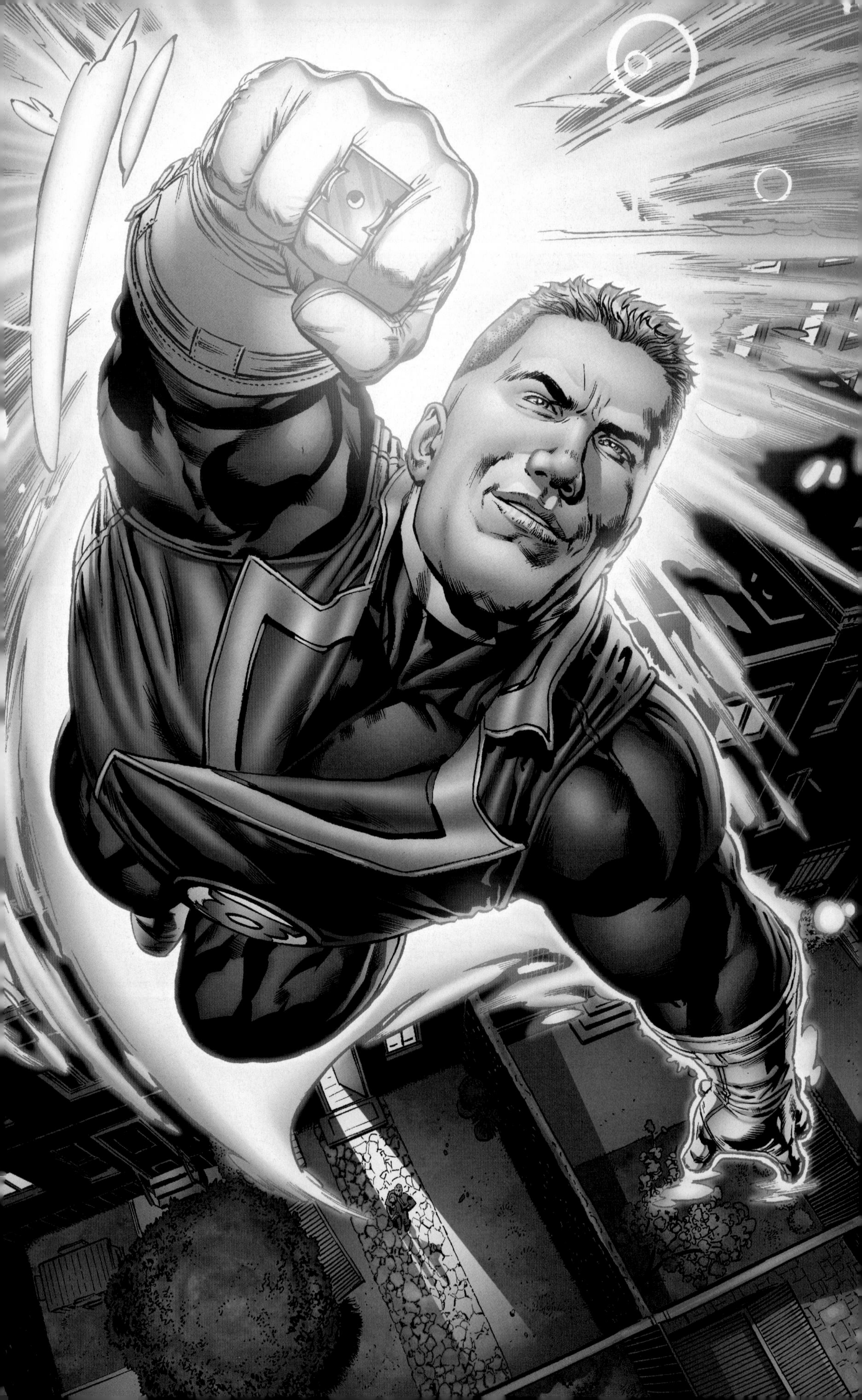

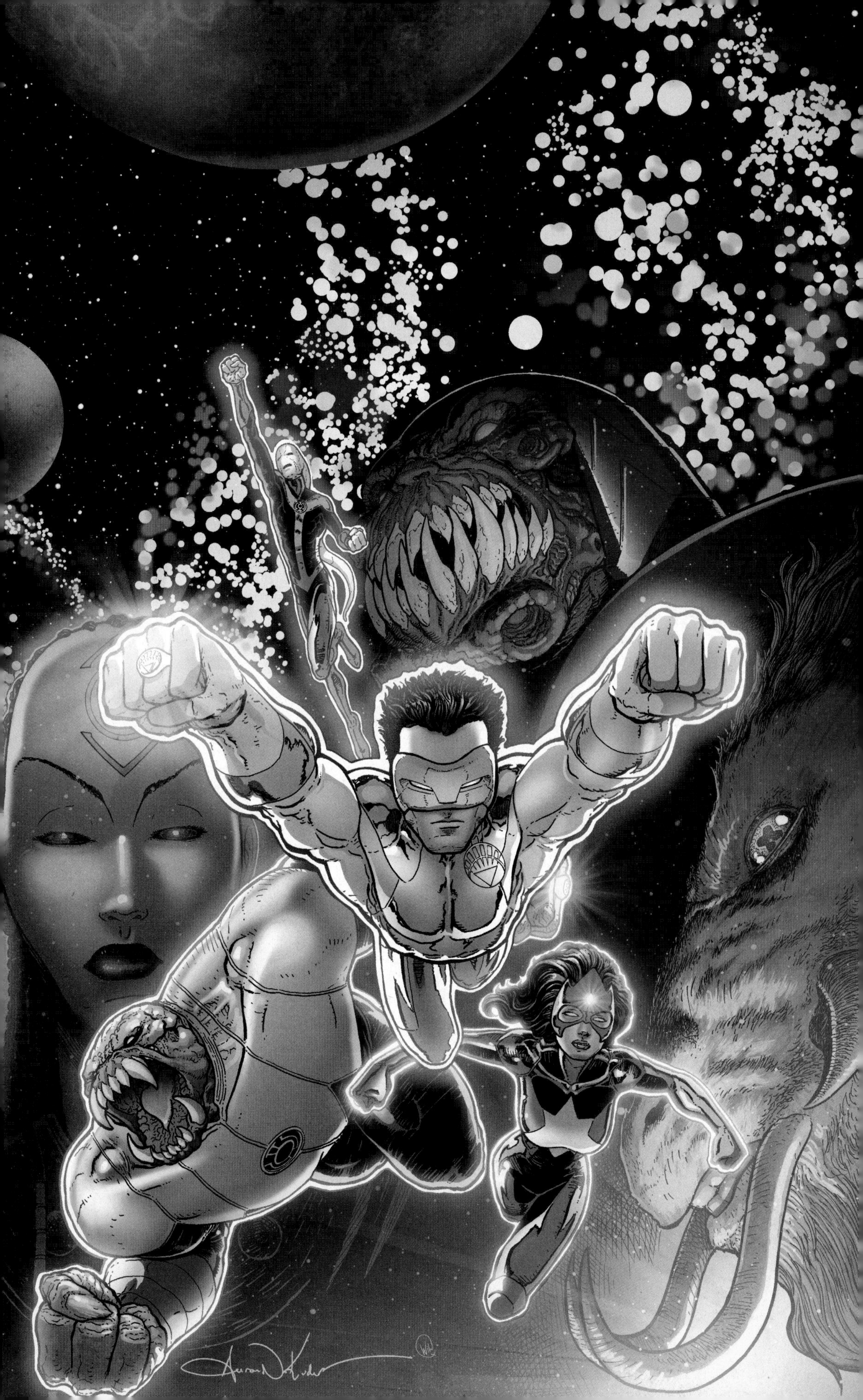

EPILOGUE: REUNION

TONY BEDARD writer **ANDRES GUINALDO** penciller **RAUL FERNANDEZ** inker
cover art by **AARON KUDER & WIL QUINTANA**

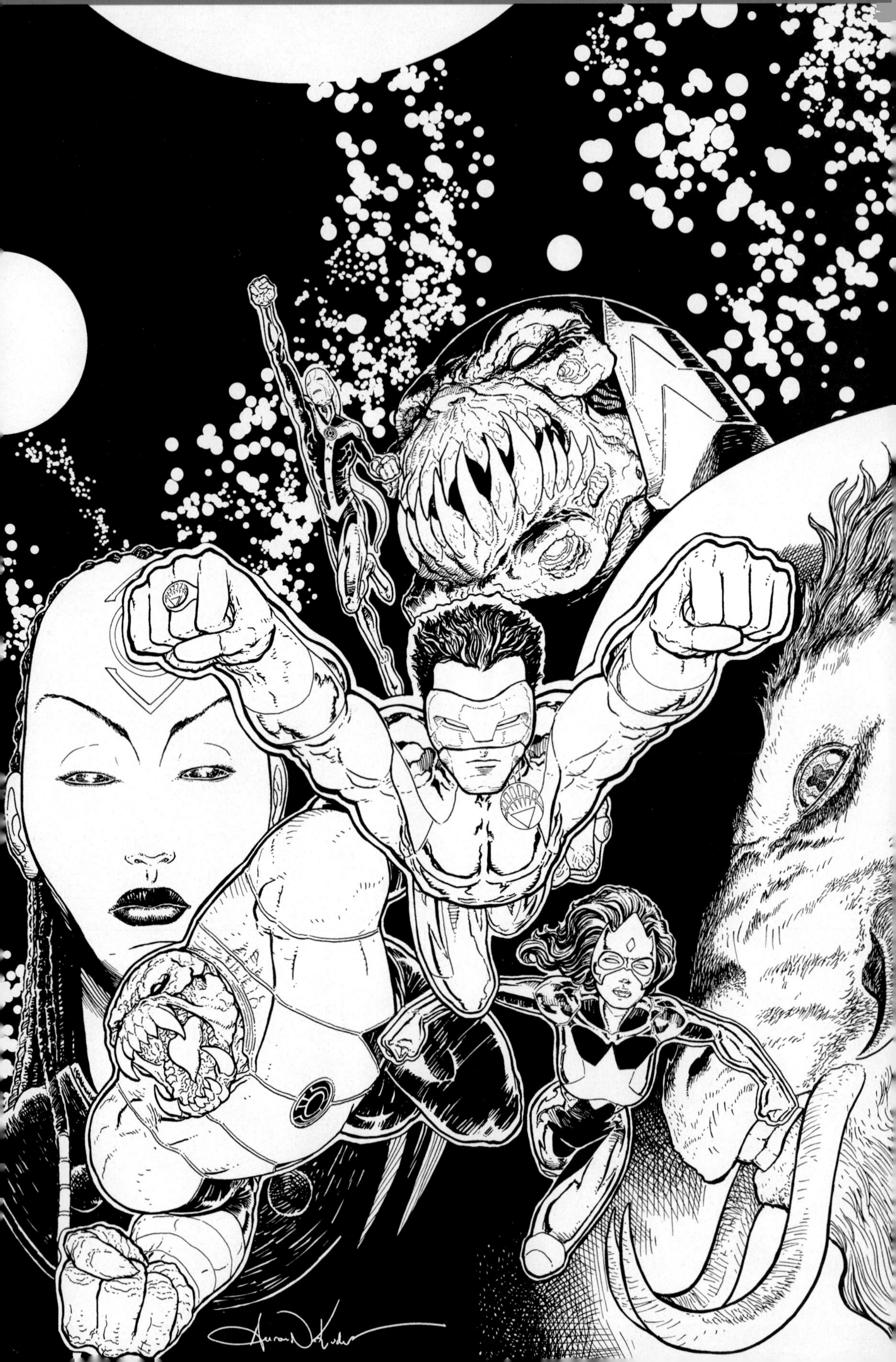

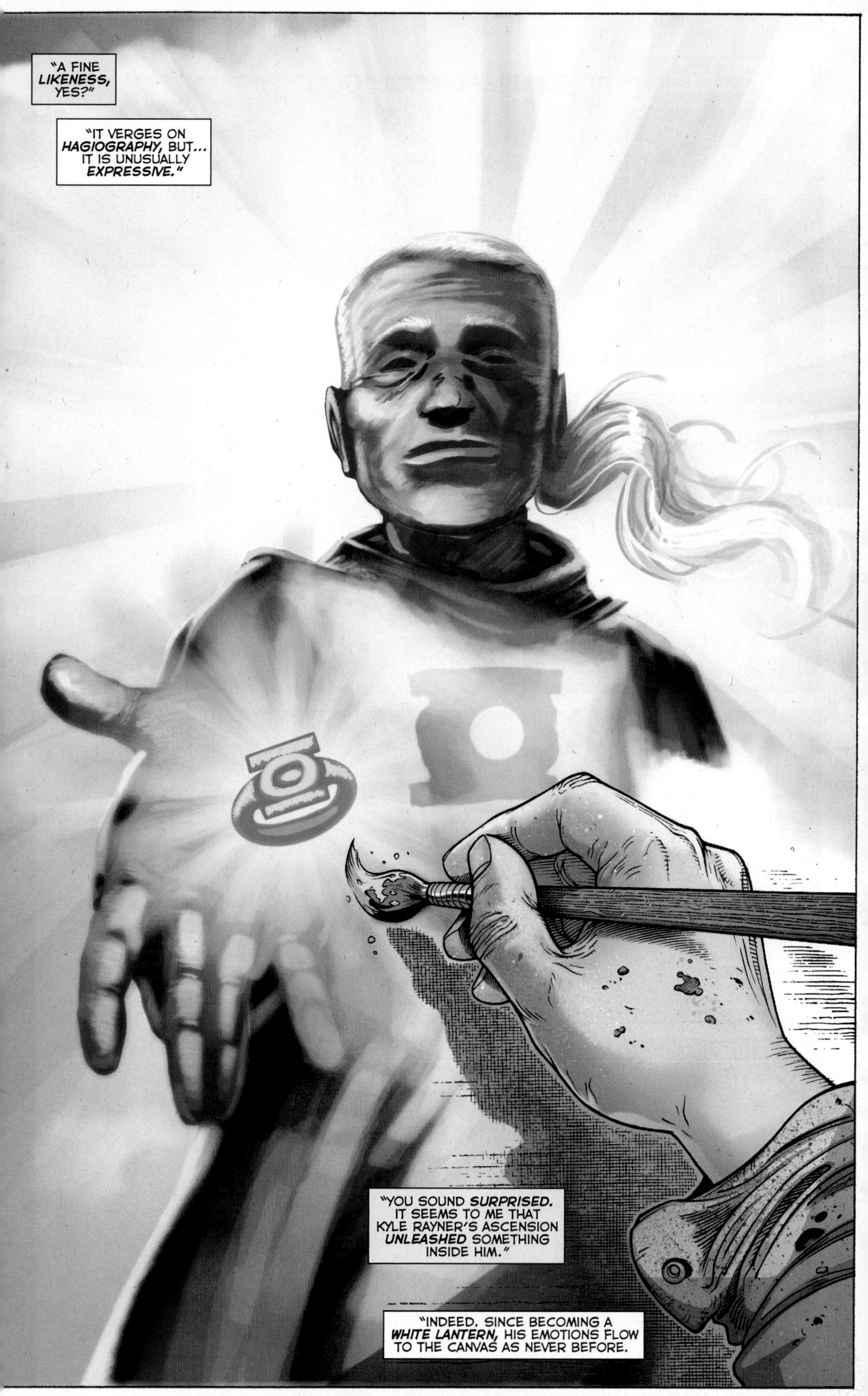
"A FINE *LIKENESS,* YES?"
"IT VERGES ON *HAGIOGRAPHY,* BUT... IT IS UNUSUALLY *EXPRESSIVE.*"
"YOU SOUND *SURPRISED.* IT SEEMS TO ME THAT KYLE RAYNER'S ASCENSION *UNLEASHED* SOMETHING INSIDE HIM."
"INDEED. SINCE BECOMING A *WHITE LANTERN,* HIS EMOTIONS FLOW TO THE CANVAS AS NEVER BEFORE.

"HE MUST COME TO GRIPS WITH THE ENORMITY OF WHAT HAPPENED ON *OA.*

"SMALL WONDER THAT UPON RETURNING HOME HE SEEKS TO POUR IT ALL OUT THROUGH HIS *BRUSH...*

"...TO EXTERNALIZE HIS FEELINGS FOR HIS *ERSTWHILE COMPANIONS.*

"*SAINT WALKER,* CHAMPION OF HOPE.

"FEARSOME *ARKILLO.*

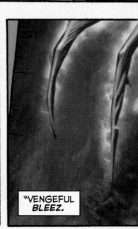

"VENGEFUL *BLEEZ.*

"...AND HIS MISTRESS, *INDIGO-1.*

"RAGING *ATROCITUS.*

"GREEDY *LARFLEEZE,* WHOM WE KNOW ALL TOO WELL...

RING: *TELL ME* SOMETHING.

"GLOMULUS, PUPPET OF AVARICE.

"TACITURN MUNK...

"...AND LOVE'S HUNTRESS, FATALITY.

"CAROL FERRIS, WHO HELPED COMPLETE HIS QUEST...

"...AND SHE WHO GAVE ALL."

IF I'M SUCH A *BIG FAT DEAL* NOW, WHY DO I FEEL LIKE SOMETHING'S STILL *MISSING?*

INSUFFICIENT DATA.

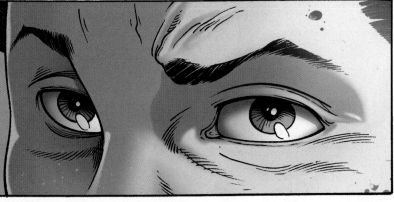

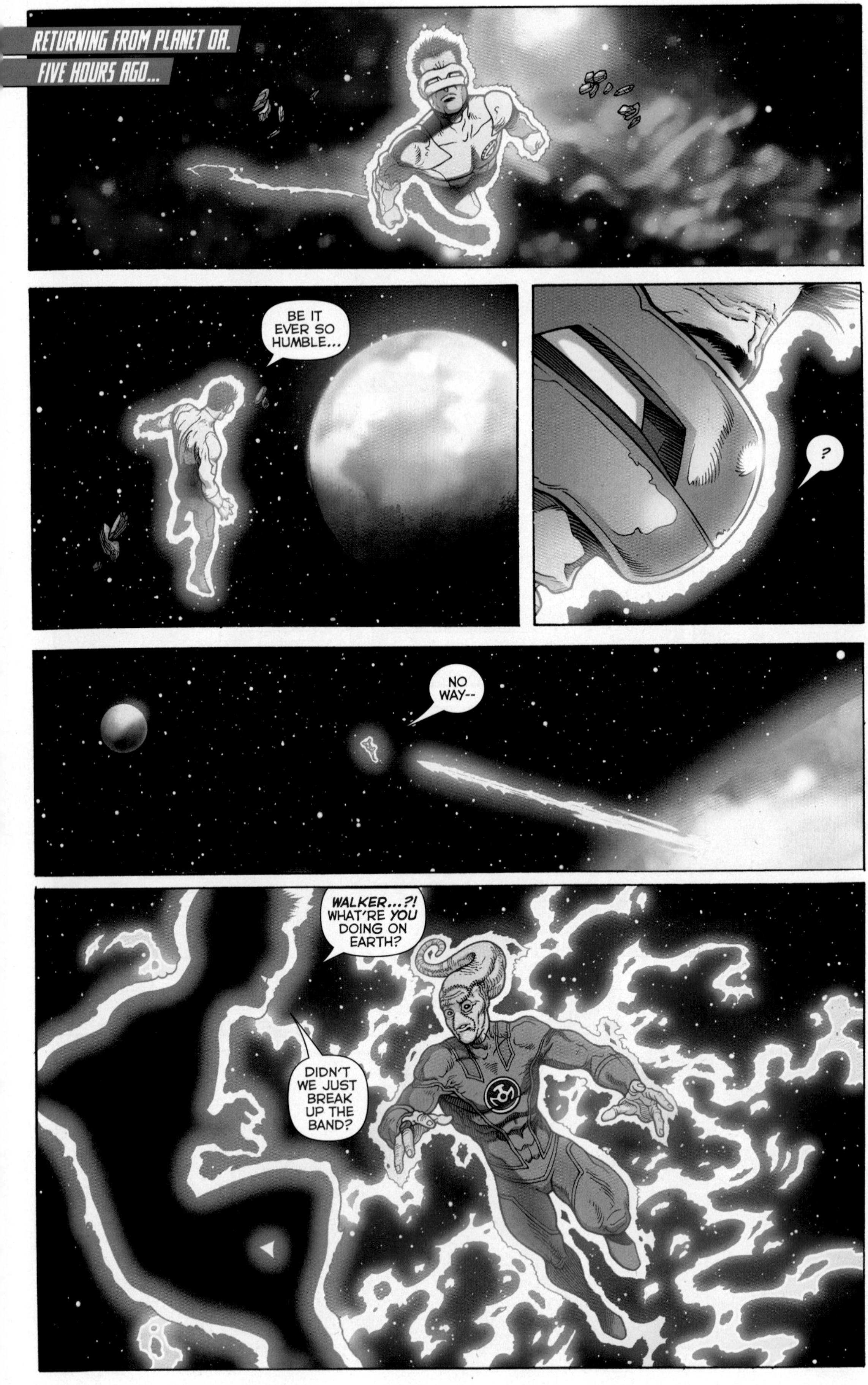
RETURNING FROM PLANET OA.
FIVE HOURS AGO...
BE IT EVER SO HUMBLE...
?
NO WAY--
WALKER...?! WHAT'RE YOU DOING ON EARTH?
DIDN'T WE JUST BREAK UP THE BAND?

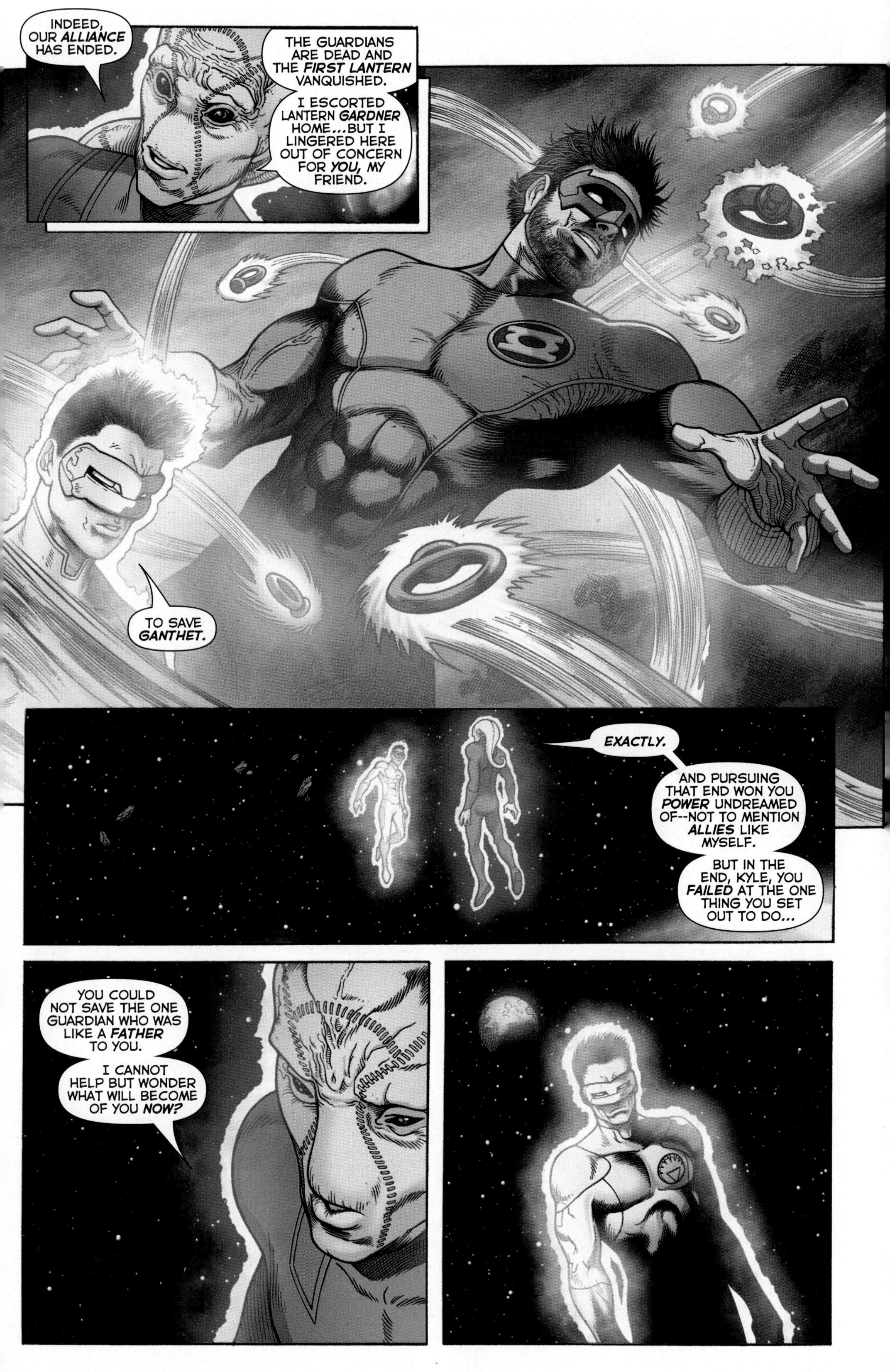
INDEED, OUR ALLIANCE HAS ENDED.
THE GUARDIANS ARE DEAD AND THE FIRST LANTERN VANQUISHED.
I ESCORTED LANTERN GARDNER HOME...BUT I LINGERED HERE OUT OF CONCERN FOR YOU, MY FRIEND.
TO SAVE GANTHET.
EXACTLY.
AND PURSUING THAT END WON YOU POWER UNDREAMED OF--NOT TO MENTION ALLIES LIKE MYSELF.
BUT IN THE END, KYLE, YOU FAILED AT THE ONE THING YOU SET OUT TO DO...
YOU COULD NOT SAVE THE ONE GUARDIAN WHO WAS LIKE A FATHER TO YOU.
I CANNOT HELP BUT WONDER WHAT WILL BECOME OF YOU NOW?

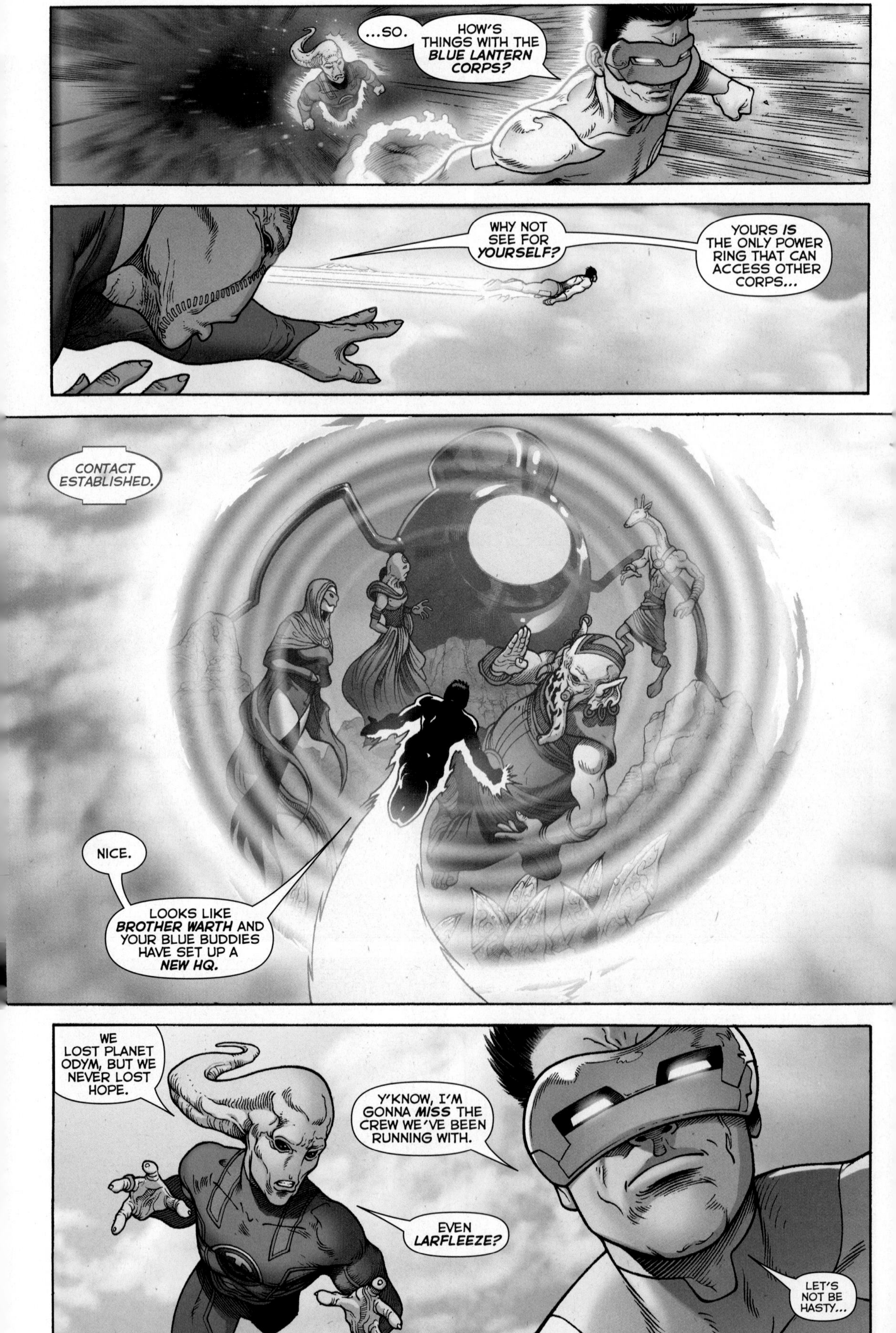
...SO.
HOW'S THINGS WITH THE BLUE LANTERN CORPS?
WHY NOT SEE FOR YOURSELF?
YOURS IS THE ONLY POWER RING THAT CAN ACCESS OTHER CORPS...
CONTACT ESTABLISHED.
NICE.
LOOKS LIKE BROTHER WARTH AND YOUR BLUE BUDDIES HAVE SET UP A NEW HQ.
WE LOST PLANET ODYM, BUT WE NEVER LOST HOPE.
Y'KNOW, I'M GONNA MISS THE CREW WE'VE BEEN RUNNING WITH.
EVEN LARFLEEZE?
LET'S NOT BE HASTY...

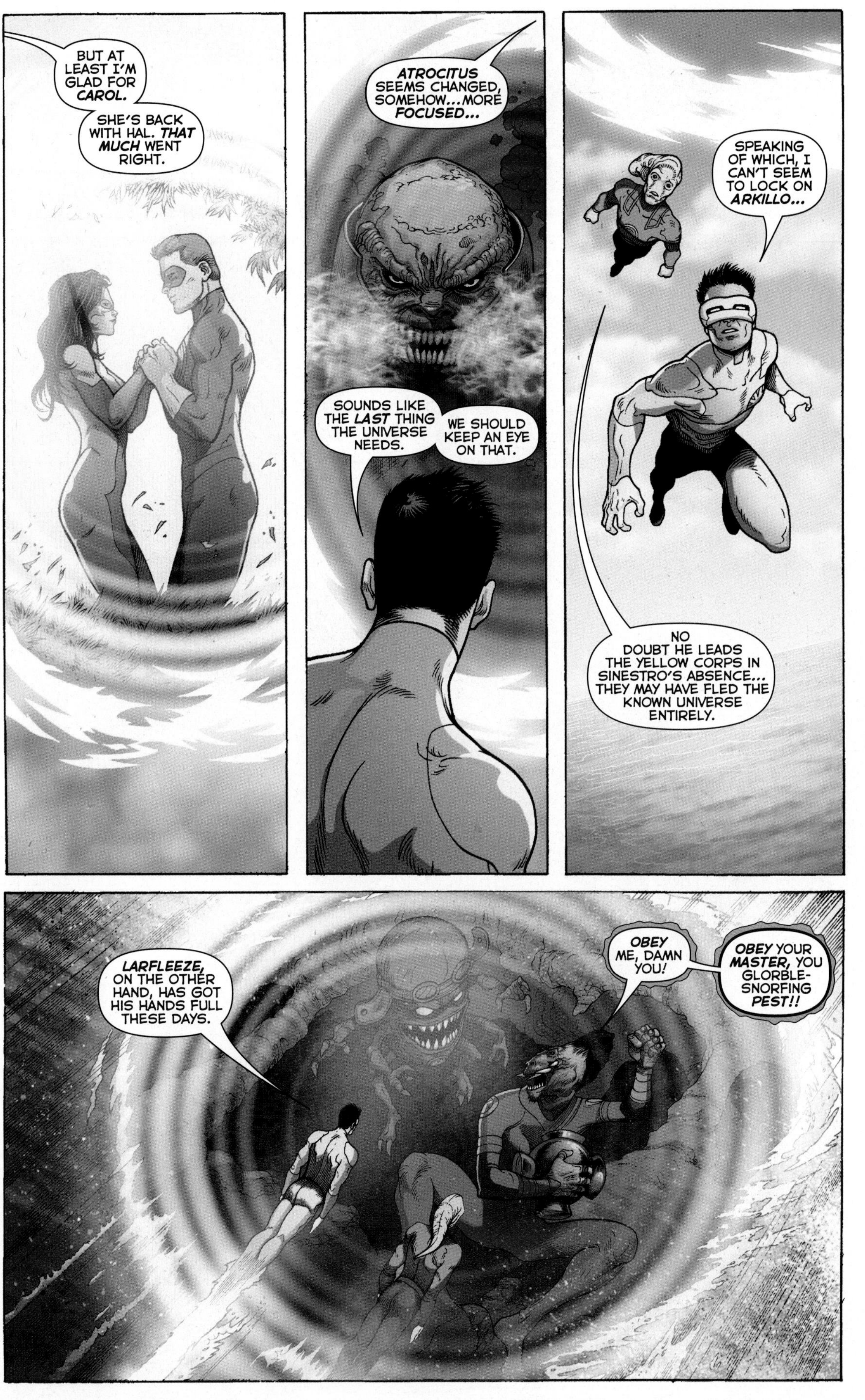
BUT AT LEAST I'M GLAD FOR CAROL.
SHE'S BACK WITH HAL. THAT MUCH WENT RIGHT.
ATROCITUS SEEMS CHANGED, SOMEHOW...MORE FOCUSED...
SOUNDS LIKE THE LAST THING THE UNIVERSE NEEDS.
WE SHOULD KEEP AN EYE ON THAT.
SPEAKING OF WHICH, I CAN'T SEEM TO LOCK ON ARKILLO...
NO DOUBT HE LEADS THE YELLOW CORPS IN SINESTRO'S ABSENCE... THEY MAY HAVE FLED THE KNOWN UNIVERSE ENTIRELY.
LARFLEEZE, ON THE OTHER HAND, HAS GOT HIS HANDS FULL THESE DAYS.
OBEY ME, DAMN YOU!
OBEY YOUR MASTER, YOU GLORBLE-SNORFING PEST!!

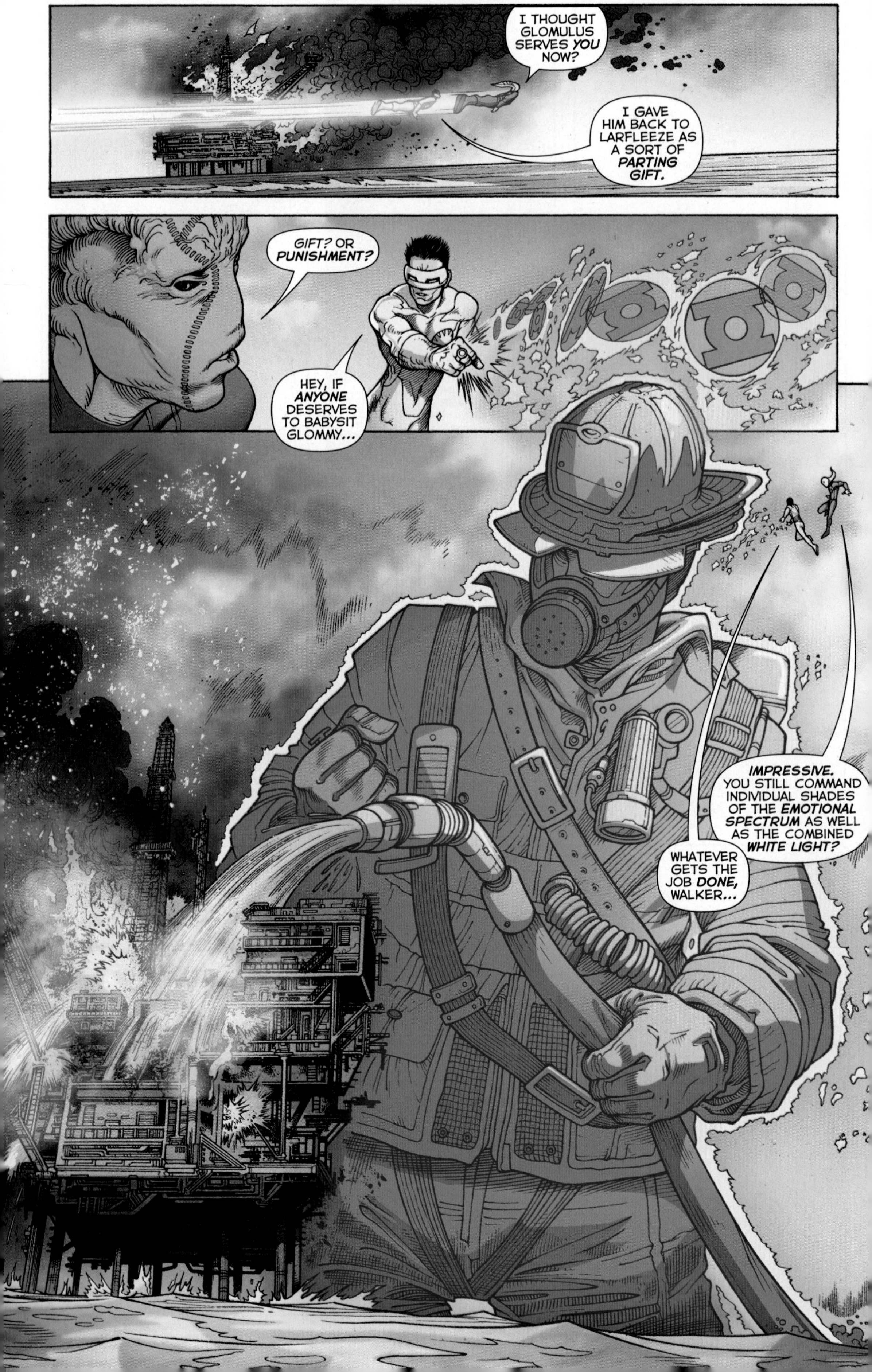
I THOUGHT GLOMULUS SERVES *YOU* NOW?
I GAVE HIM BACK TO LARFLEEZE AS A SORT OF *PARTING GIFT.*
GIFT? OR *PUNISHMENT?*
HEY, IF *ANYONE* DESERVES TO BABYSIT GLOMMY...
IMPRESSIVE. YOU STILL COMMAND INDIVIDUAL SHADES OF THE *EMOTIONAL SPECTRUM* AS WELL AS THE COMBINED *WHITE LIGHT?*
WHATEVER GETS THE JOB *DONE,* WALKER...

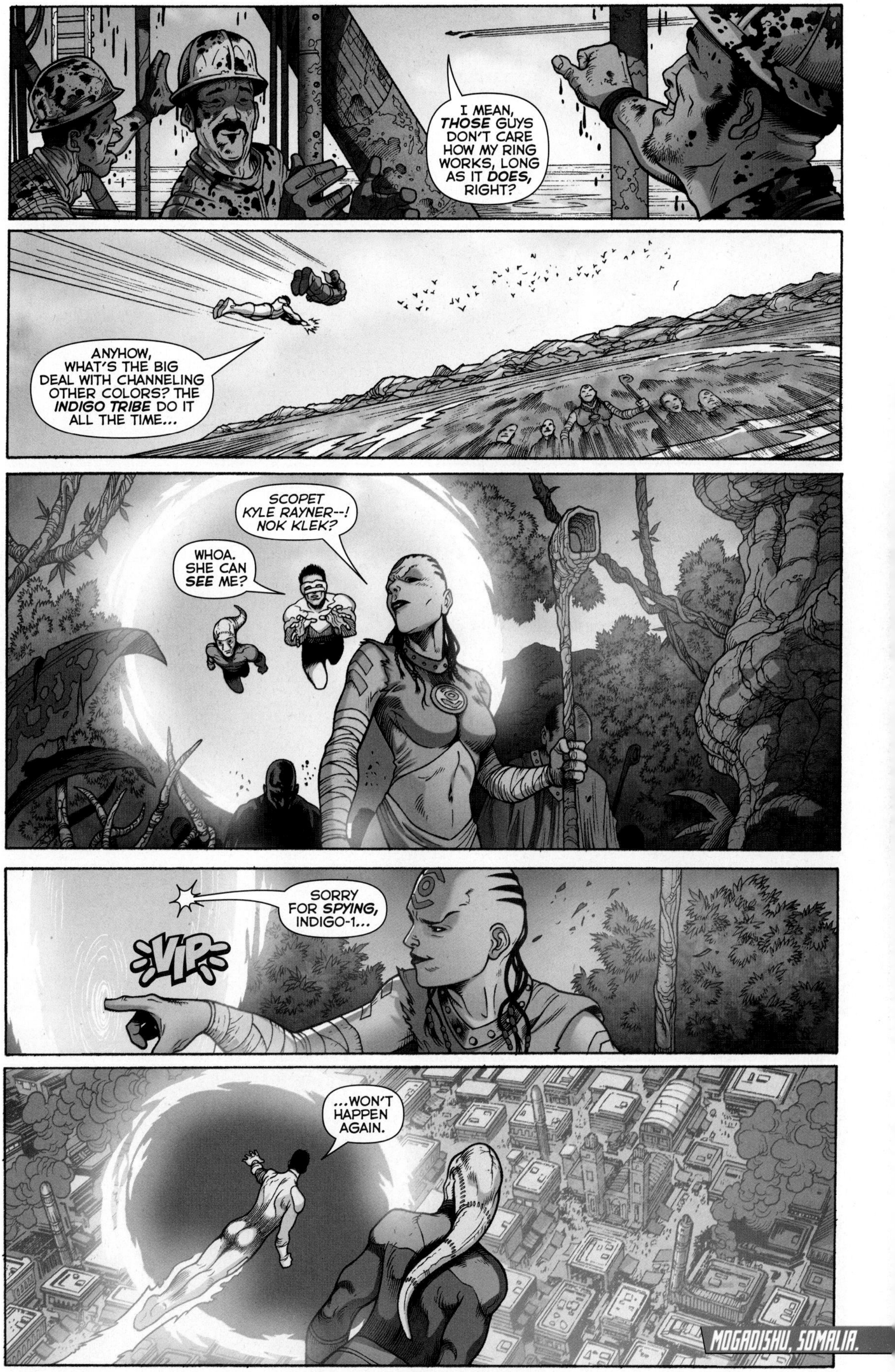
I MEAN, THOSE GUYS DON'T CARE HOW MY RING WORKS, LONG AS IT DOES, RIGHT?
ANYHOW, WHAT'S THE BIG DEAL WITH CHANNELING OTHER COLORS? THE INDIGO TRIBE DO IT ALL THE TIME...
SCOPET KYLE RAYNER--! NOK KLEK?
WHOA. SHE CAN SEE ME?
SORRY FOR SPYING, INDIGO-1...
VIP
...WON'T HAPPEN AGAIN.
MOGADISHU, SOMALIA.

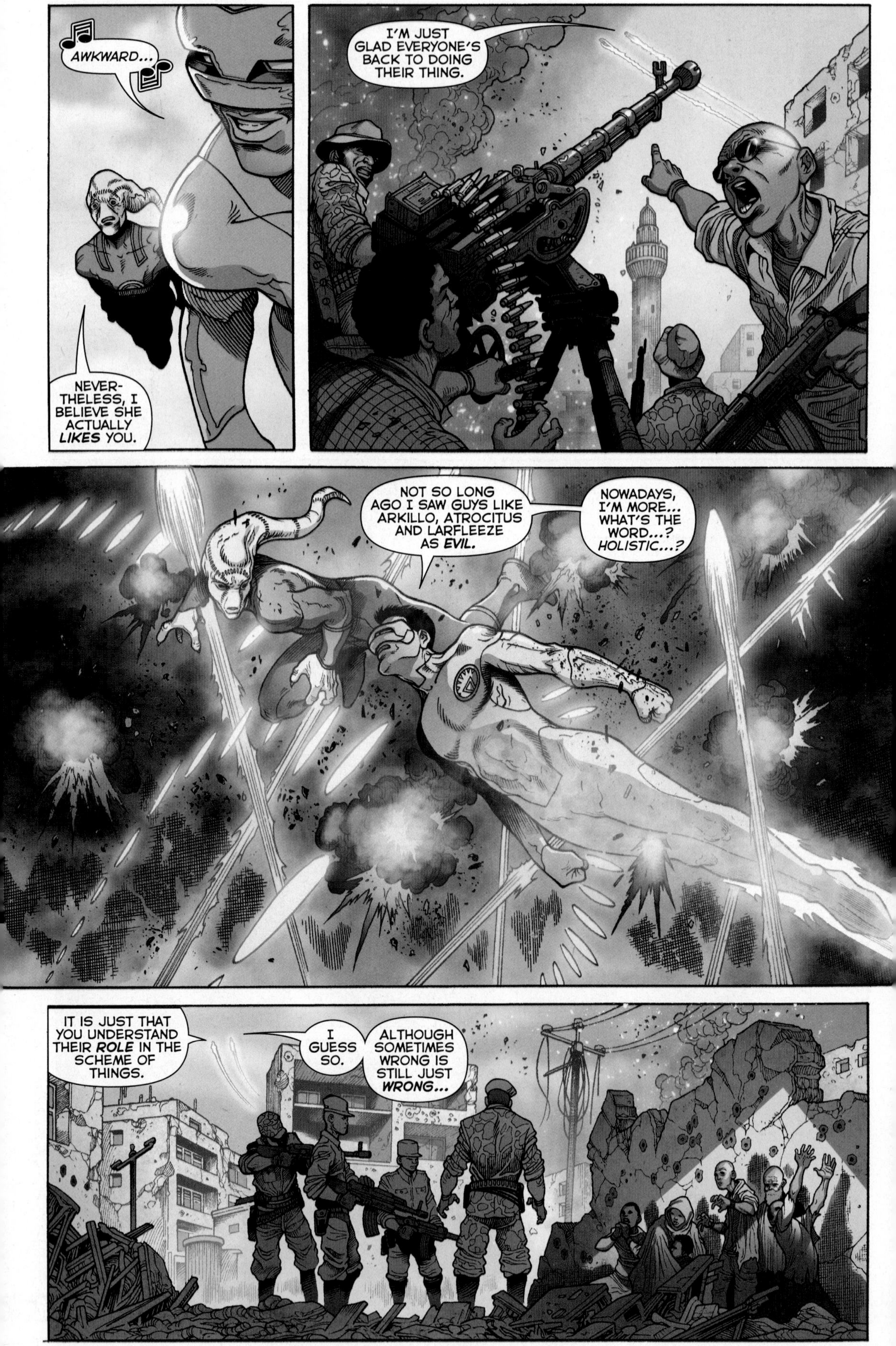

AWKWARD...
NEVER-THELESS, I BELIEVE SHE ACTUALLY *LIKES* YOU.
I'M JUST GLAD EVERYONE'S BACK TO DOING THEIR THING.
NOT SO LONG AGO I SAW GUYS LIKE ARKILLO, ATROCITUS AND LARFLEEZE AS *EVIL.*
NOWADAYS, I'M MORE... WHAT'S THE WORD...? *HOLISTIC...?*
IT IS JUST THAT YOU UNDERSTAND THEIR *ROLE* IN THE SCHEME OF THINGS.
I GUESS SO.
ALTHOUGH SOMETIMES WRONG IS STILL JUST *WRONG...*

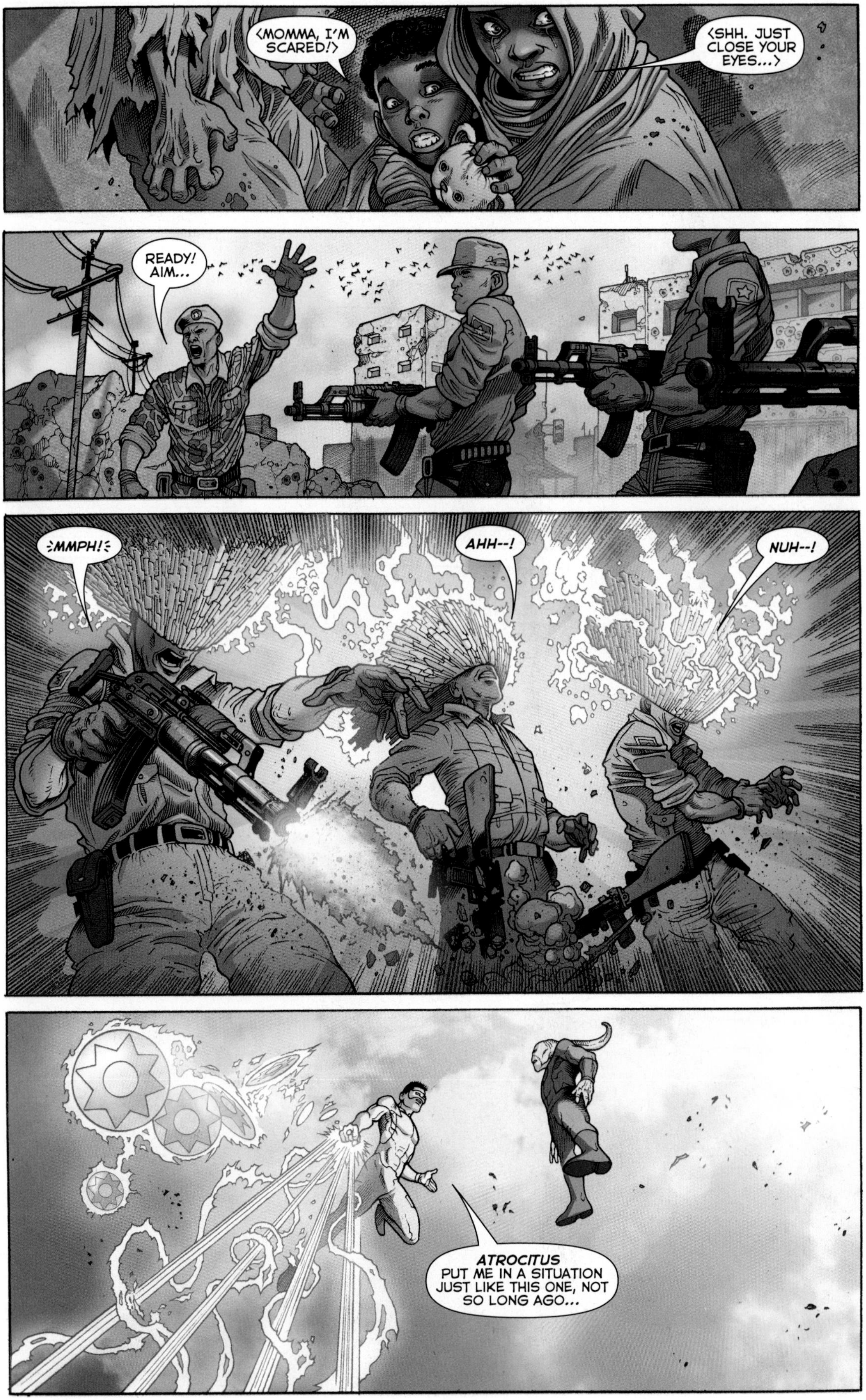
<MOMMA, I'M SCARED!>
<SHH. JUST CLOSE YOUR EYES...>
READY! AIM...
MMPH!
AHH--!
NUH--!
ATROCITUS PUT ME IN A SITUATION JUST LIKE THIS ONE, NOT SO LONG AGO...

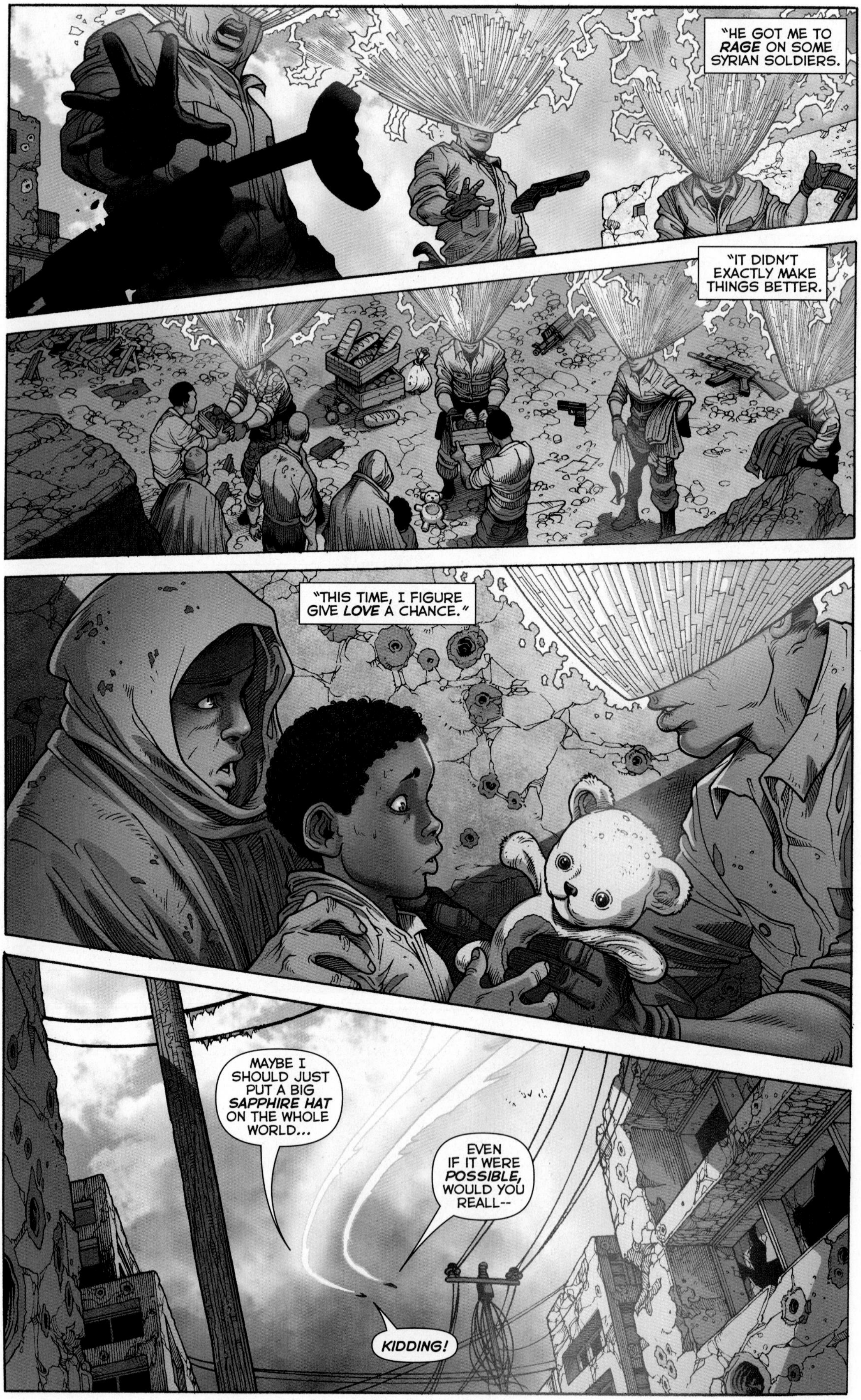
"HE GOT ME TO RAGE ON SOME SYRIAN SOLDIERS.
"IT DIDN'T EXACTLY MAKE THINGS BETTER.
"THIS TIME, I FIGURE GIVE LOVE A CHANCE."
MAYBE I SHOULD JUST PUT A BIG SAPPHIRE HAT ON THE WHOLE WORLD...
EVEN IF IT WERE POSSIBLE, WOULD YOU REALL--
KIDDING!

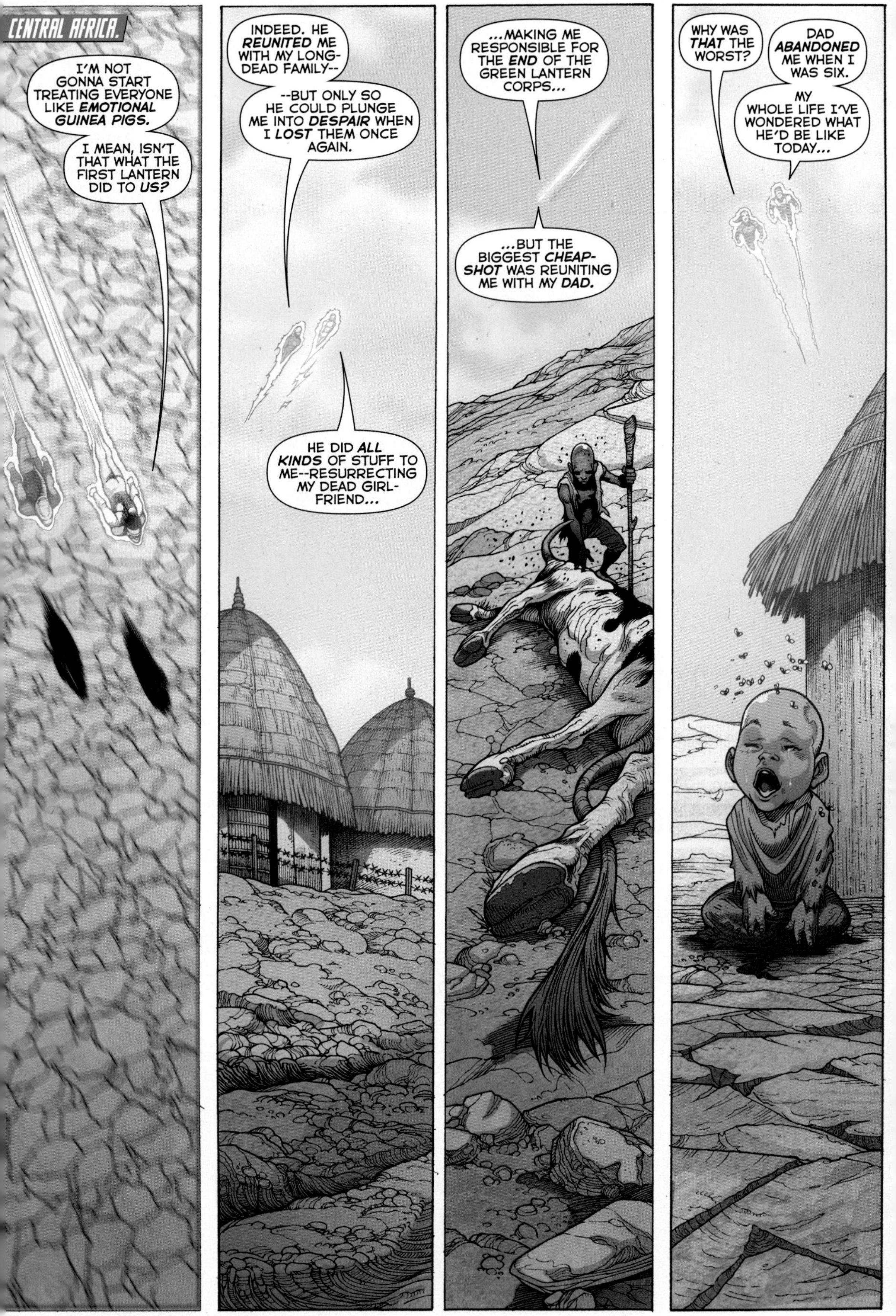
CENTRAL AFRICA.
I'M NOT GONNA START TREATING EVERYONE LIKE EMOTIONAL GUINEA PIGS.
I MEAN, ISN'T THAT WHAT THE FIRST LANTERN DID TO US?
INDEED. HE REUNITED ME WITH MY LONG-DEAD FAMILY--
--BUT ONLY SO HE COULD PLUNGE ME INTO DESPAIR WHEN I LOST THEM ONCE AGAIN.
HE DID ALL KINDS OF STUFF TO ME--RESURRECTING MY DEAD GIRL-FRIEND...
...MAKING ME RESPONSIBLE FOR THE END OF THE GREEN LANTERN CORPS...
...BUT THE BIGGEST CHEAP-SHOT WAS REUNITING ME WITH MY DAD.
WHY WAS THAT THE WORST?
DAD ABANDONED ME WHEN I WAS SIX.
MY WHOLE LIFE I'VE WONDERED WHAT HE'D BE LIKE TODAY...

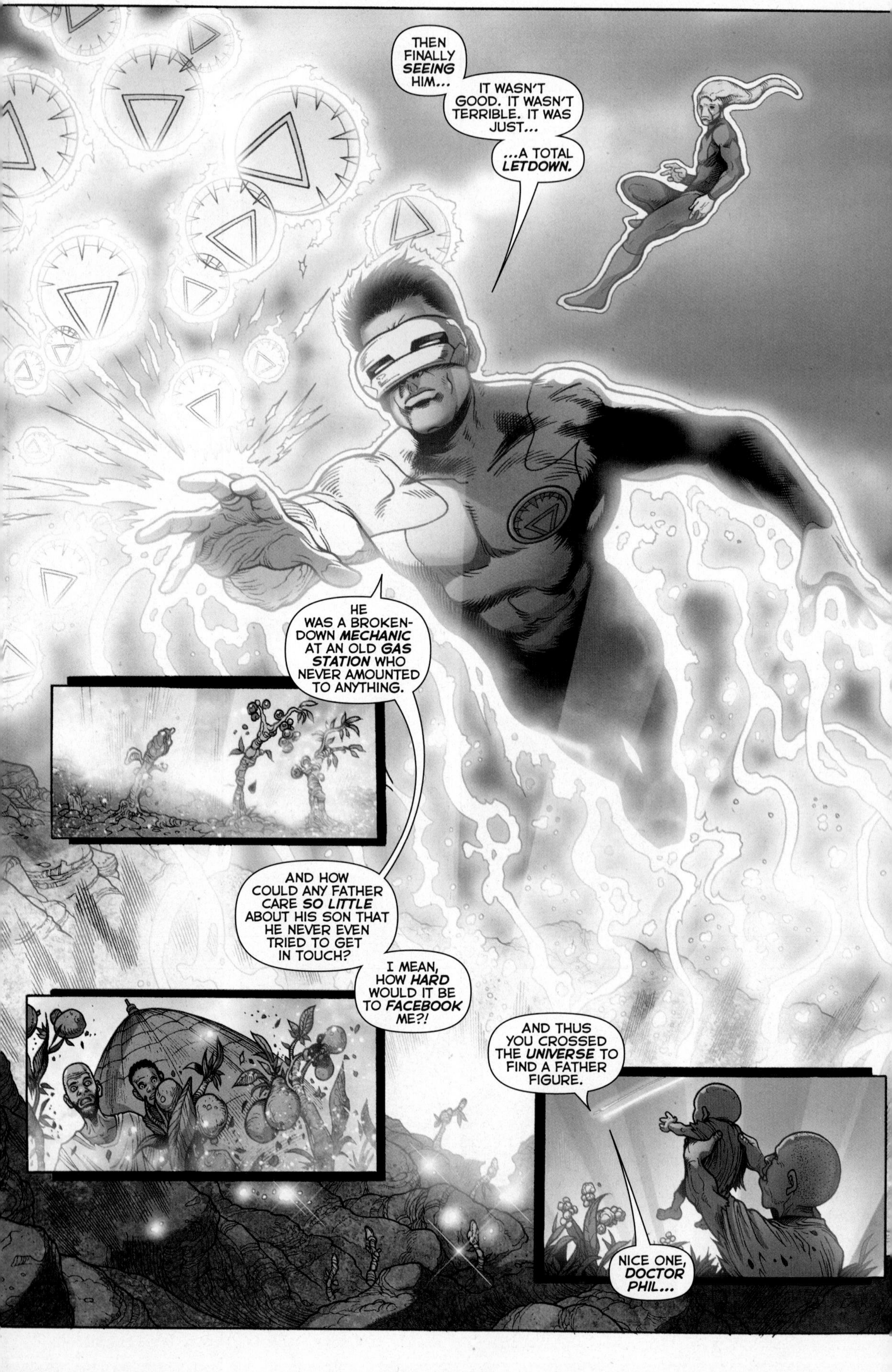
THEN FINALLY SEEING HIM...
IT WASN'T GOOD. IT WASN'T TERRIBLE. IT WAS JUST...
...A TOTAL LETDOWN.
HE WAS A BROKEN-DOWN MECHANIC AT AN OLD GAS STATION WHO NEVER AMOUNTED TO ANYTHING.
AND HOW COULD ANY FATHER CARE SO LITTLE ABOUT HIS SON THAT HE NEVER EVEN TRIED TO GET IN TOUCH?
I MEAN, HOW HARD WOULD IT BE TO FACEBOOK ME?!
AND THUS YOU CROSSED THE UNIVERSE TO FIND A FATHER FIGURE.
NICE ONE, DOCTOR PHIL...

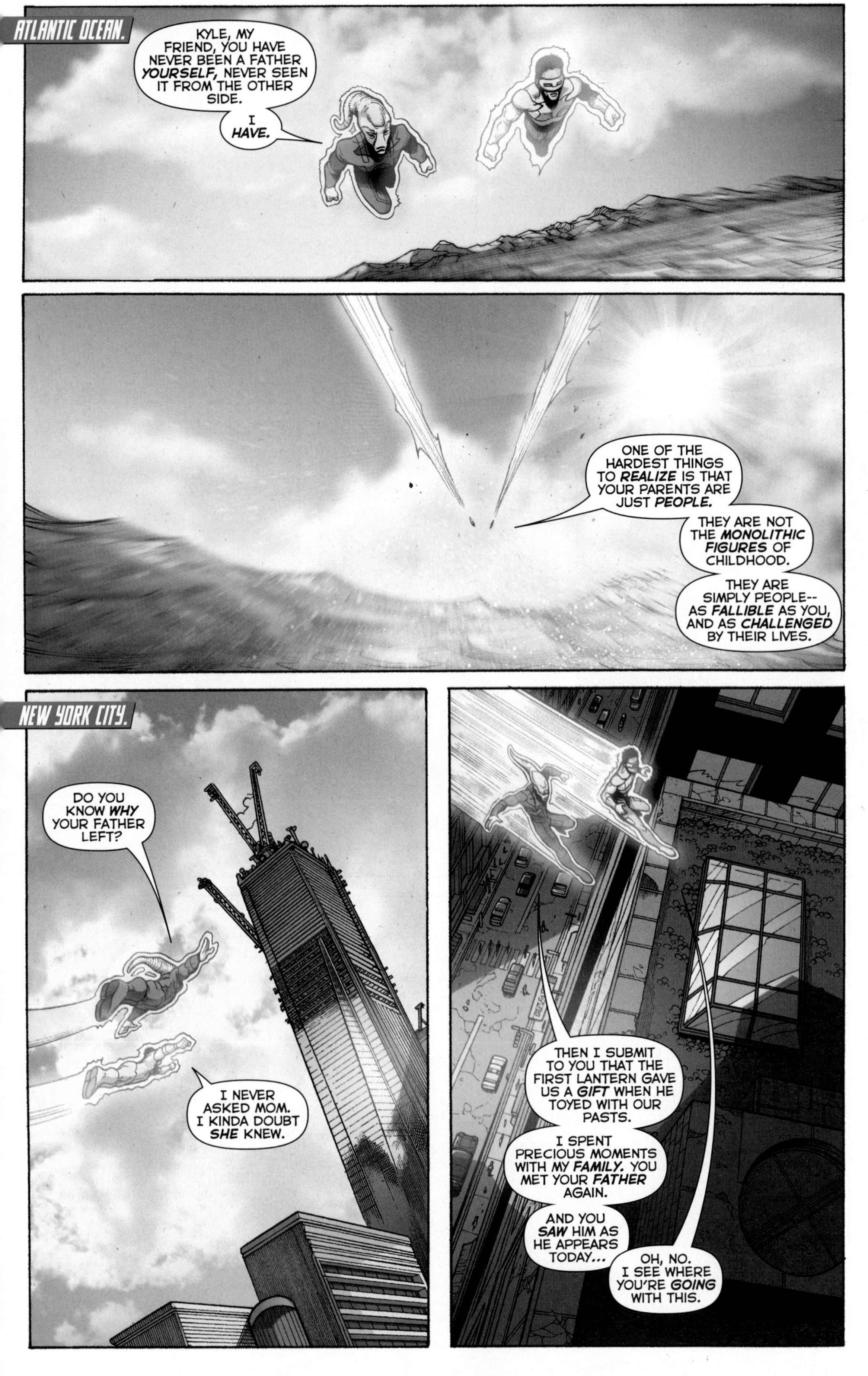
ATLANTIC OCEAN.
KYLE, MY FRIEND, YOU HAVE NEVER BEEN A FATHER YOURSELF, NEVER SEEN IT FROM THE OTHER SIDE.
I HAVE.
ONE OF THE HARDEST THINGS TO REALIZE IS THAT YOUR PARENTS ARE JUST PEOPLE.
THEY ARE NOT THE MONOLITHIC FIGURES OF CHILDHOOD.
THEY ARE SIMPLY PEOPLE-- AS FALLIBLE AS YOU, AND AS CHALLENGED BY THEIR LIVES.
NEW YORK CITY.
DO YOU KNOW WHY YOUR FATHER LEFT?
I NEVER ASKED MOM. I KINDA DOUBT SHE KNEW.
THEN I SUBMIT TO YOU THAT THE FIRST LANTERN GAVE US A GIFT WHEN HE TOYED WITH OUR PASTS.
I SPENT PRECIOUS MOMENTS WITH MY FAMILY. YOU MET YOUR FATHER AGAIN.
AND YOU SAW HIM AS HE APPEARS TODAY...
OH, NO. I SEE WHERE YOU'RE GOING WITH THIS.

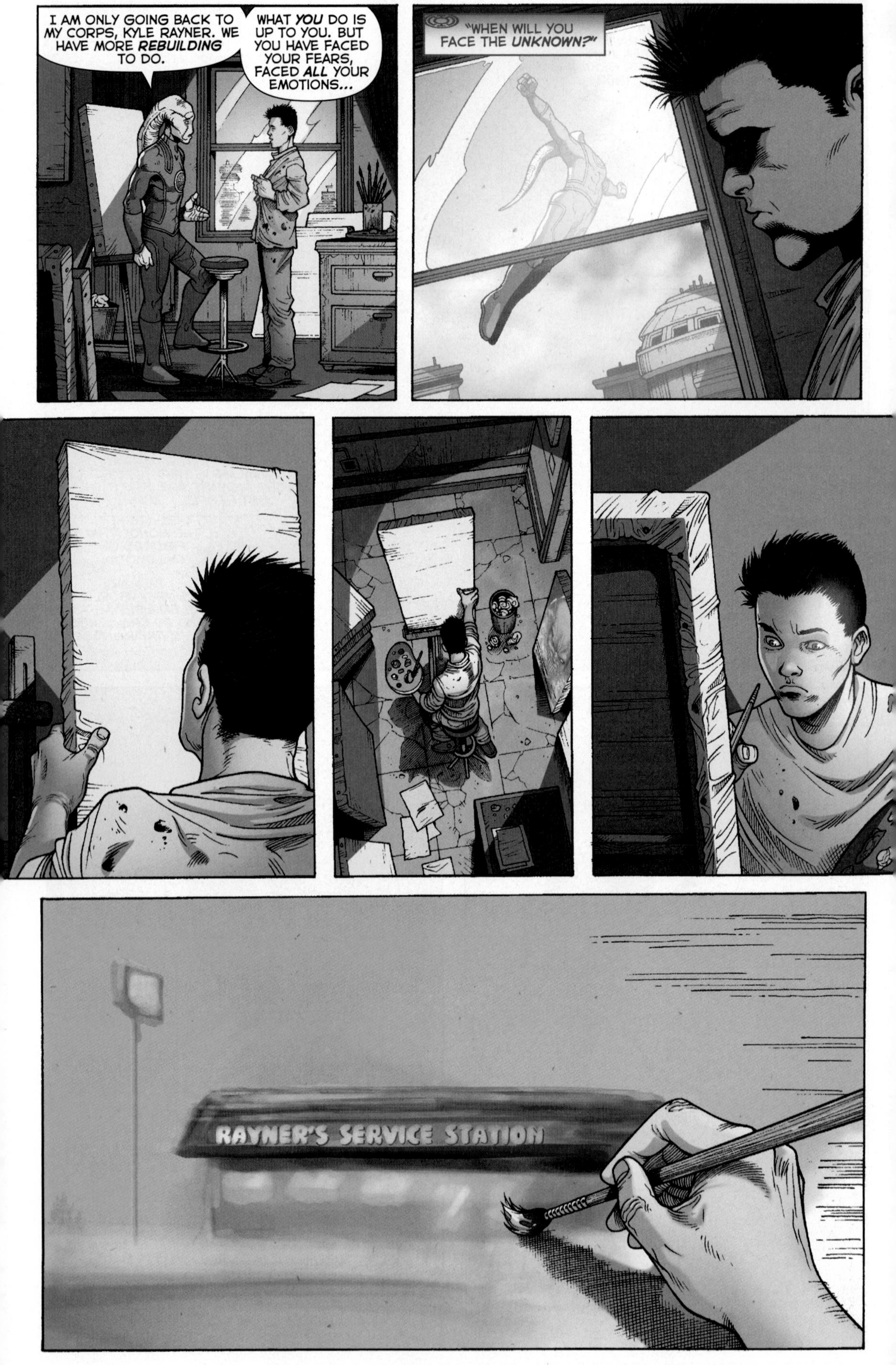
I AM ONLY GOING BACK TO MY CORPS, KYLE RAYNER. WE HAVE MORE *REBUILDING* TO DO.
WHAT *YOU* DO IS UP TO YOU. BUT YOU HAVE FACED YOUR FEARS, FACED *ALL* YOUR EMOTIONS...
"WHEN WILL YOU FACE THE *UNKNOWN?*"
RAYNER'S SERVICE STATION

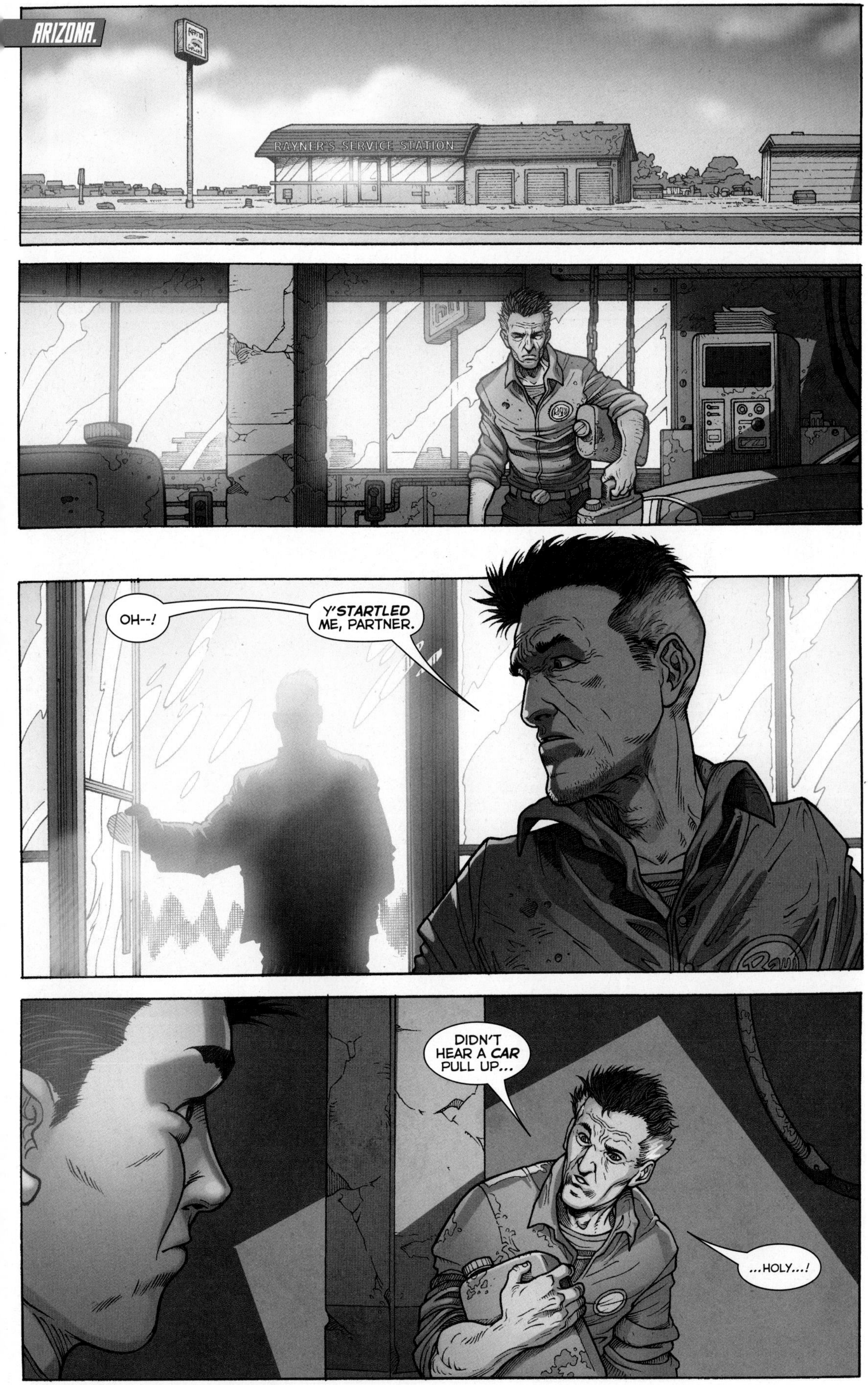
ARIZONA.
RAYNER'S SERVICE STATION
OH--!
Y'STARTLED ME, PARTNER.
DIDN'T HEAR A CAR PULL UP...
...HOLY...!

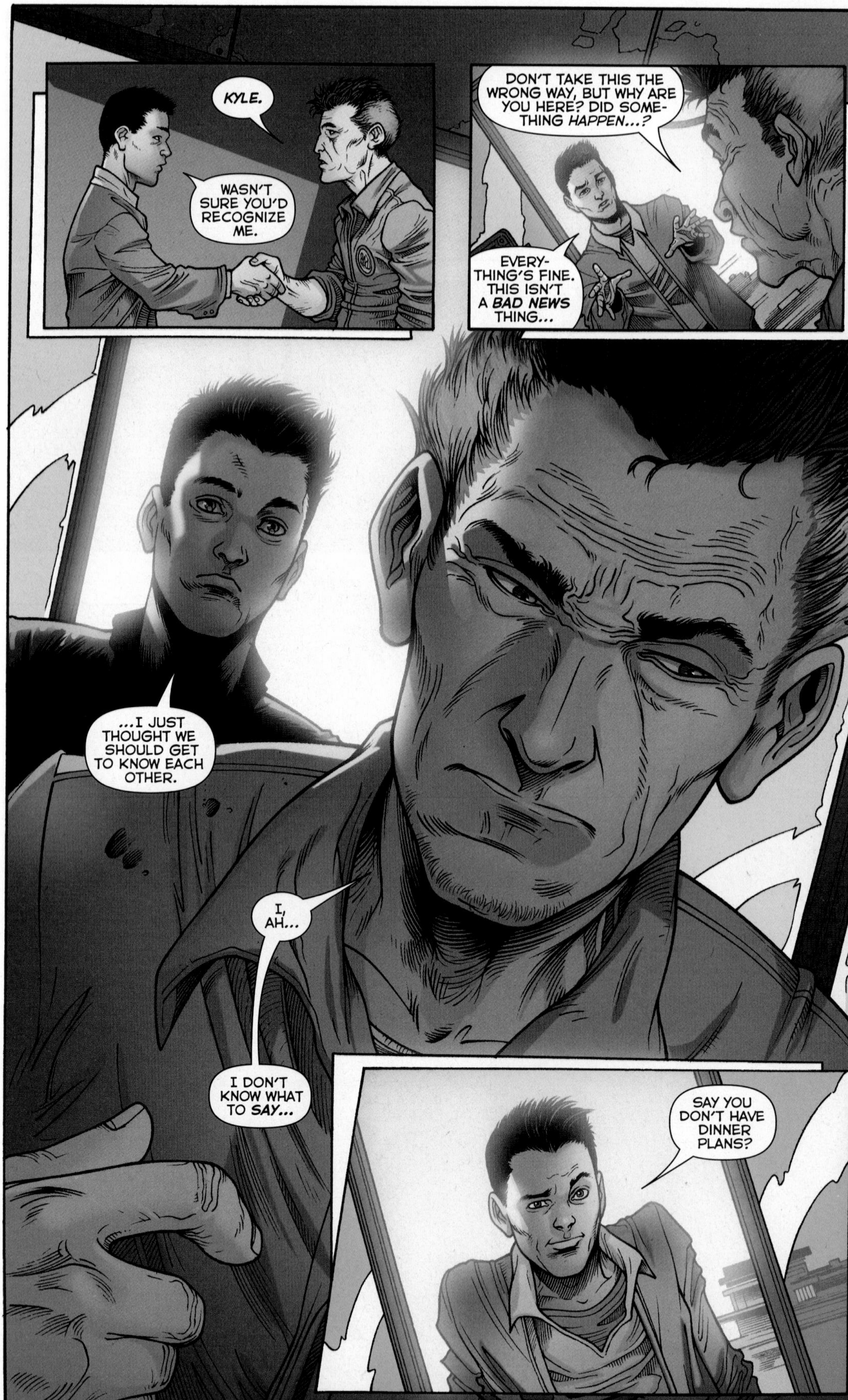
KYLE.
WASN'T SURE YOU'D RECOGNIZE ME.
DON'T TAKE THIS THE WRONG WAY, BUT WHY ARE YOU HERE? DID SOMETHING *HAPPEN...?*
EVERYTHING'S FINE. THIS ISN'T A ***BAD NEWS*** THING...
...I JUST THOUGHT WE SHOULD GET TO KNOW EACH OTHER.
I, AH...
I DON'T KNOW WHAT TO ***SAY...***
SAY YOU DON'T HAVE DINNER PLANS?

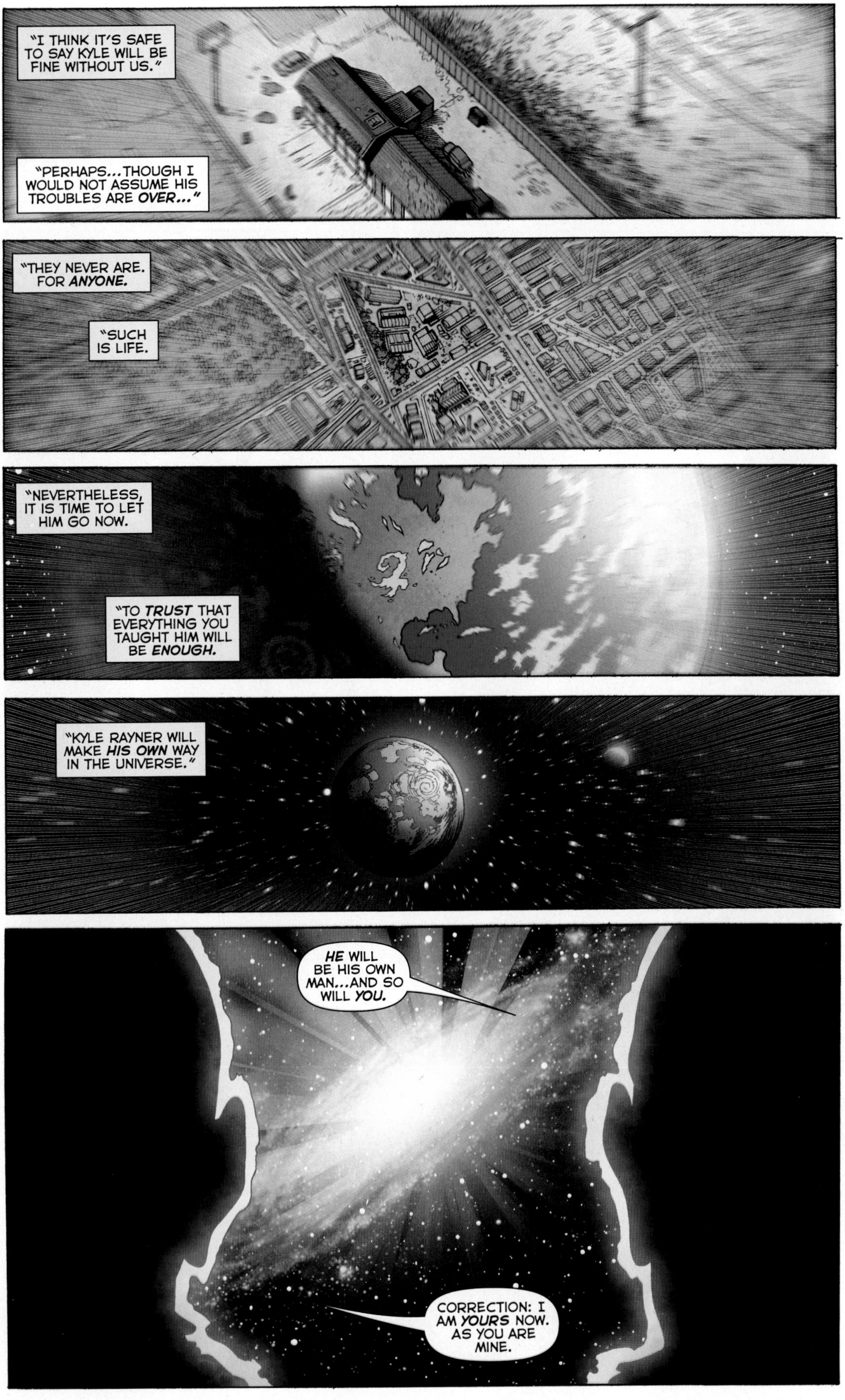
"I THINK IT'S SAFE TO SAY KYLE WILL BE FINE WITHOUT US."
"PERHAPS...THOUGH I WOULD NOT ASSUME HIS TROUBLES ARE *OVER*..."
"THEY NEVER ARE. FOR *ANYONE.*
"SUCH IS LIFE.
"NEVERTHELESS, IT IS TIME TO LET HIM GO NOW.
"TO *TRUST* THAT EVERYTHING YOU TAUGHT HIM WILL BE *ENOUGH.*
"KYLE RAYNER WILL MAKE *HIS OWN* WAY IN THE UNIVERSE."
HE WILL BE HIS OWN MAN...AND SO WILL *YOU.*
CORRECTION: I AM *YOURS* NOW. AS YOU ARE MINE.

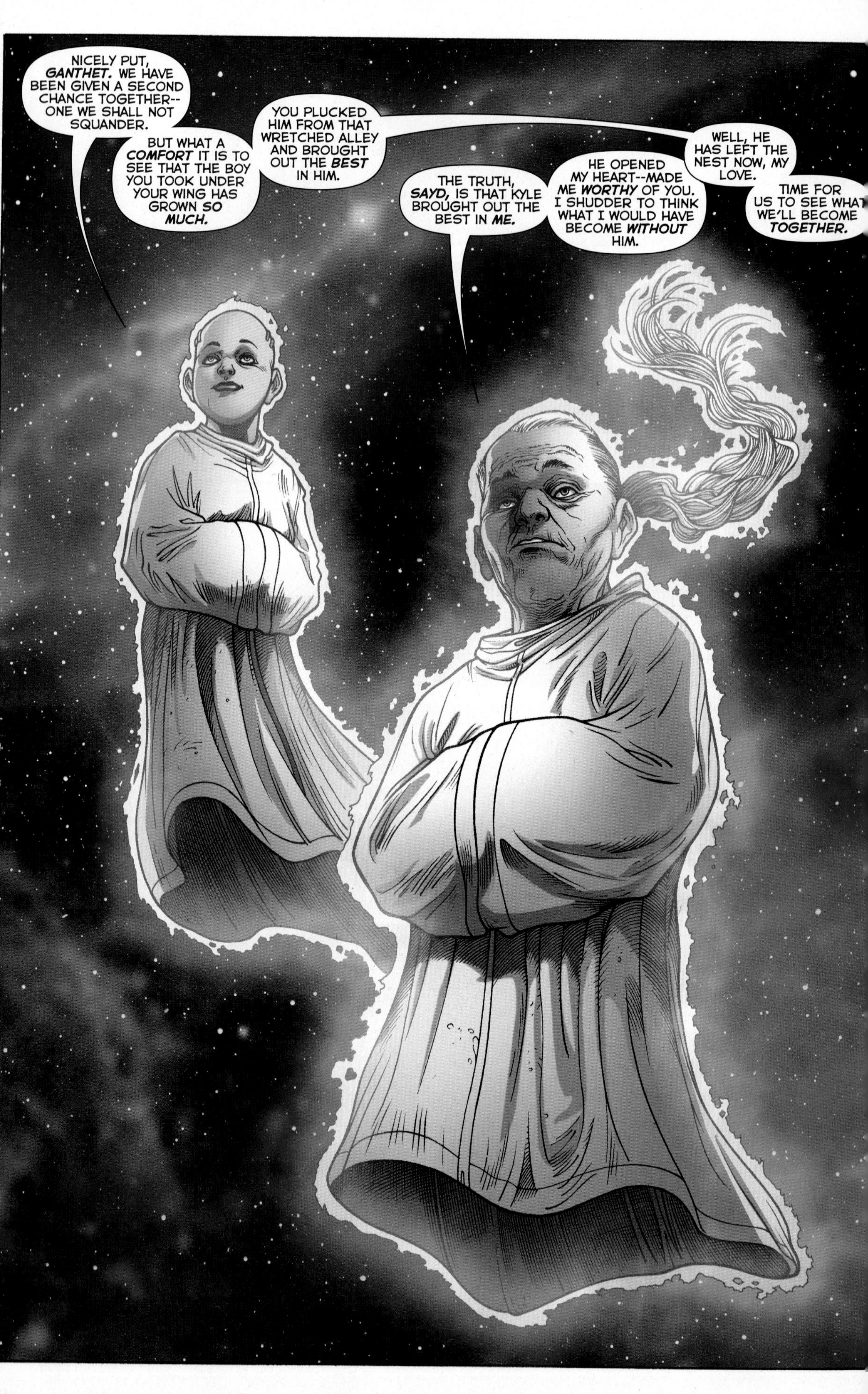
NICELY PUT, GANTHET. WE HAVE BEEN GIVEN A SECOND CHANCE TOGETHER-- ONE WE SHALL NOT SQUANDER.
BUT WHAT A COMFORT IT IS TO SEE THAT THE BOY YOU TOOK UNDER YOUR WING HAS GROWN SO MUCH.
YOU PLUCKED HIM FROM THAT WRETCHED ALLEY AND BROUGHT OUT THE BEST IN HIM.
THE TRUTH, SAYD, IS THAT KYLE BROUGHT OUT THE BEST IN ME.
HE OPENED MY HEART--MADE ME WORTHY OF YOU. I SHUDDER TO THINK WHAT I WOULD HAVE BECOME WITHOUT HIM.
WELL, HE HAS LEFT THE NEST NOW, MY LOVE.
TIME FOR US TO SEE WHAT WE'LL BECOME TOGETHER.

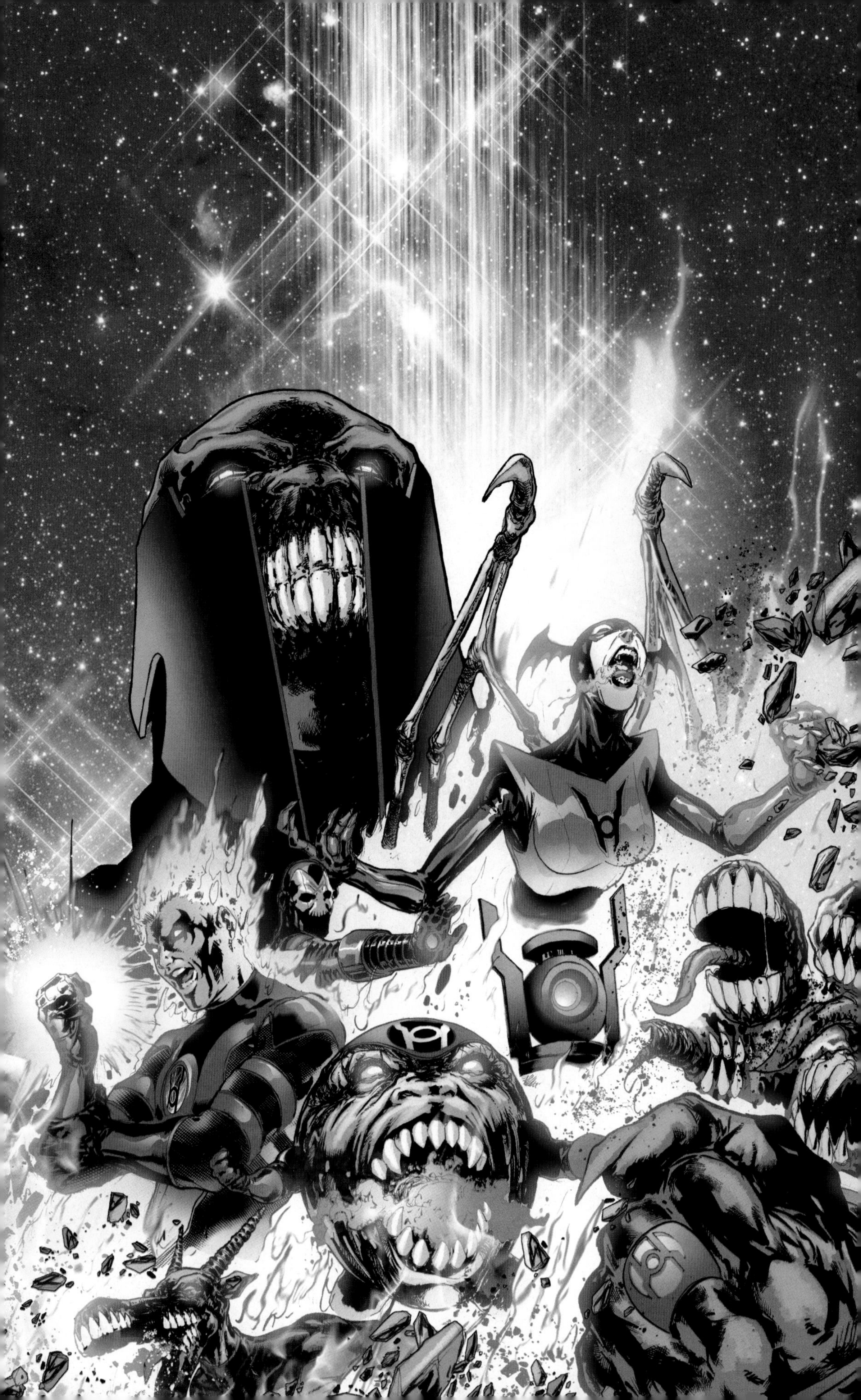

EPILOGUE: A DEATH LONG COMING...

PETER MILLIGAN writer **WILL CONRAD** artist

cover art by **MIGUEL SEPULVEDA** & **RAIN BEREDO**

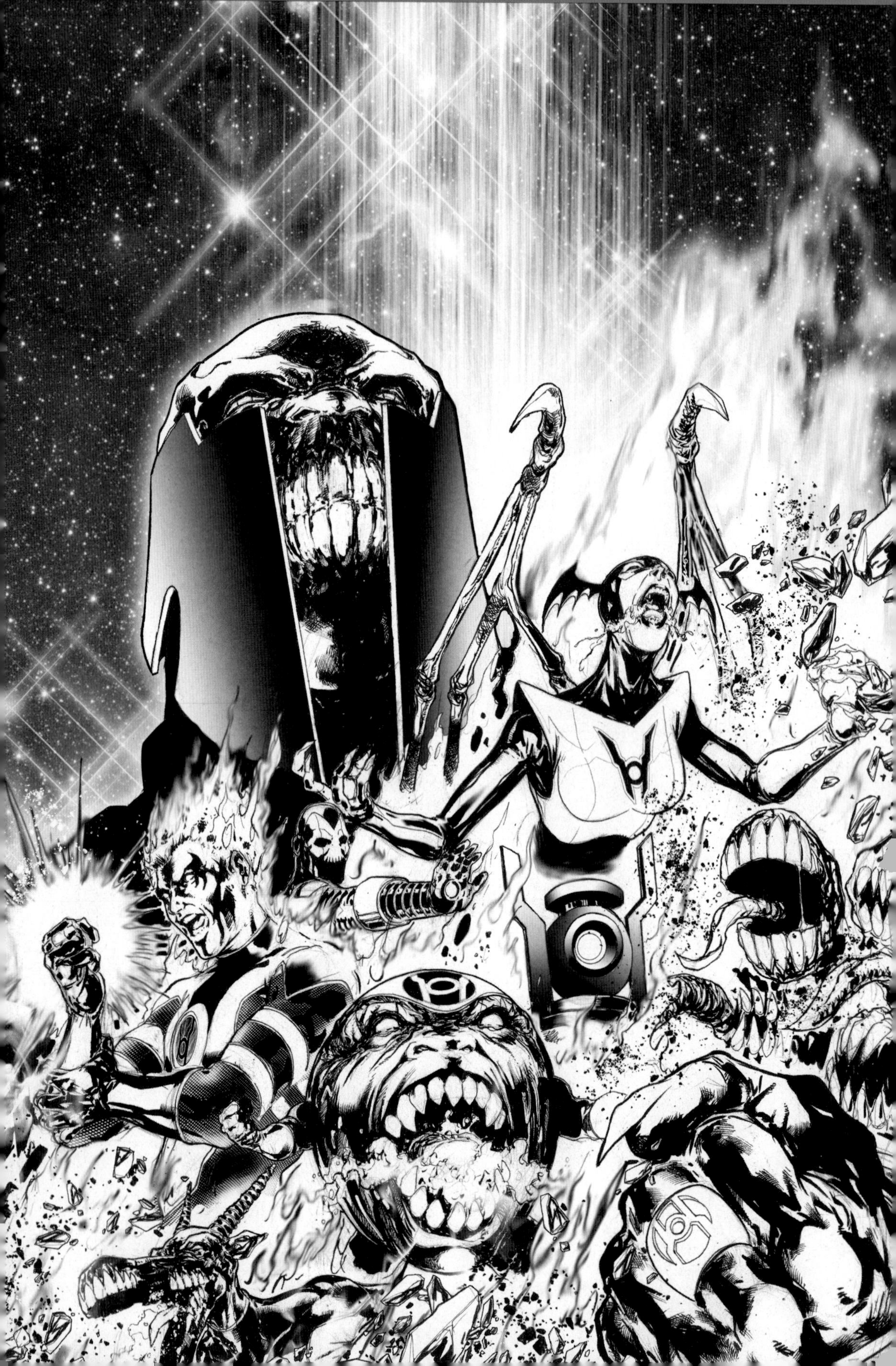

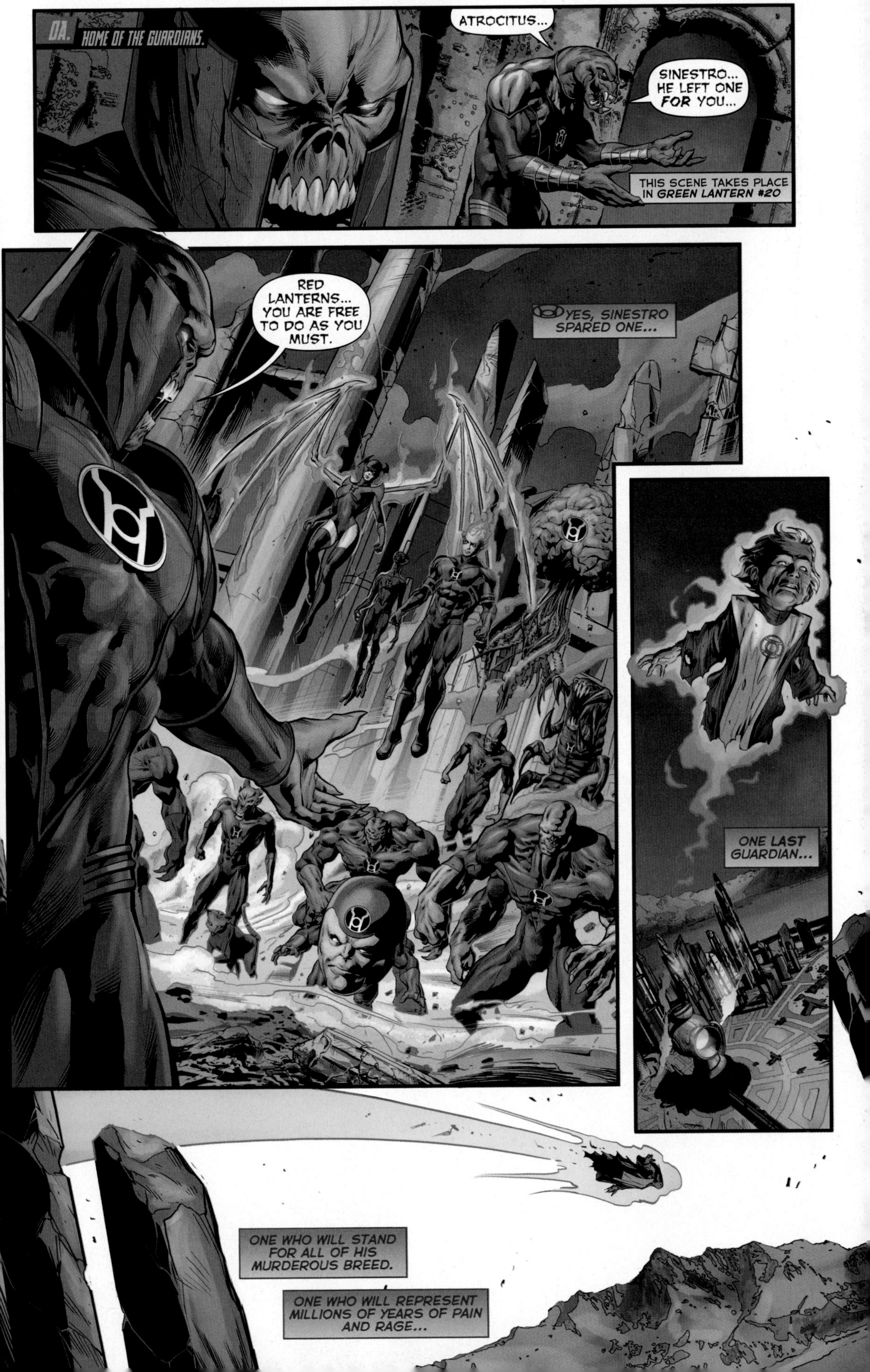
OA. HOME OF THE GUARDIANS.
ATROCITUS...
SINESTRO... HE LEFT ONE FOR YOU...
THIS SCENE TAKES PLACE IN GREEN LANTERN #20
RED LANTERNS... YOU ARE FREE TO DO AS YOU MUST.
YES, SINESTRO SPARED ONE...
ONE LAST GUARDIAN...
ONE WHO WILL STAND FOR ALL OF HIS MURDEROUS BREED.
ONE WHO WILL REPRESENT MILLIONS OF YEARS OF PAIN AND RAGE...

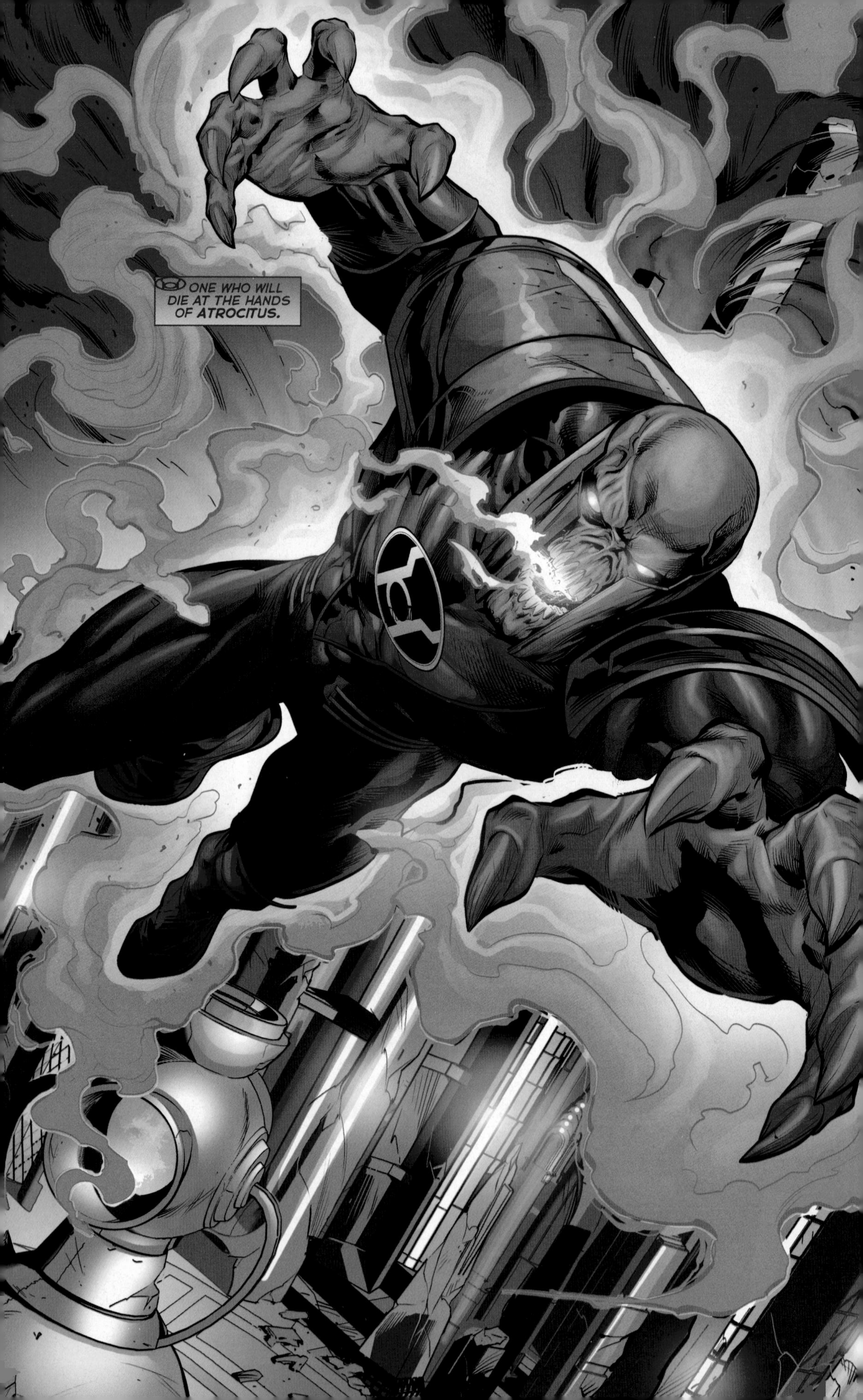
ONE WHO WILL
DIE AT THE HANDS
OF ATROCITUS.

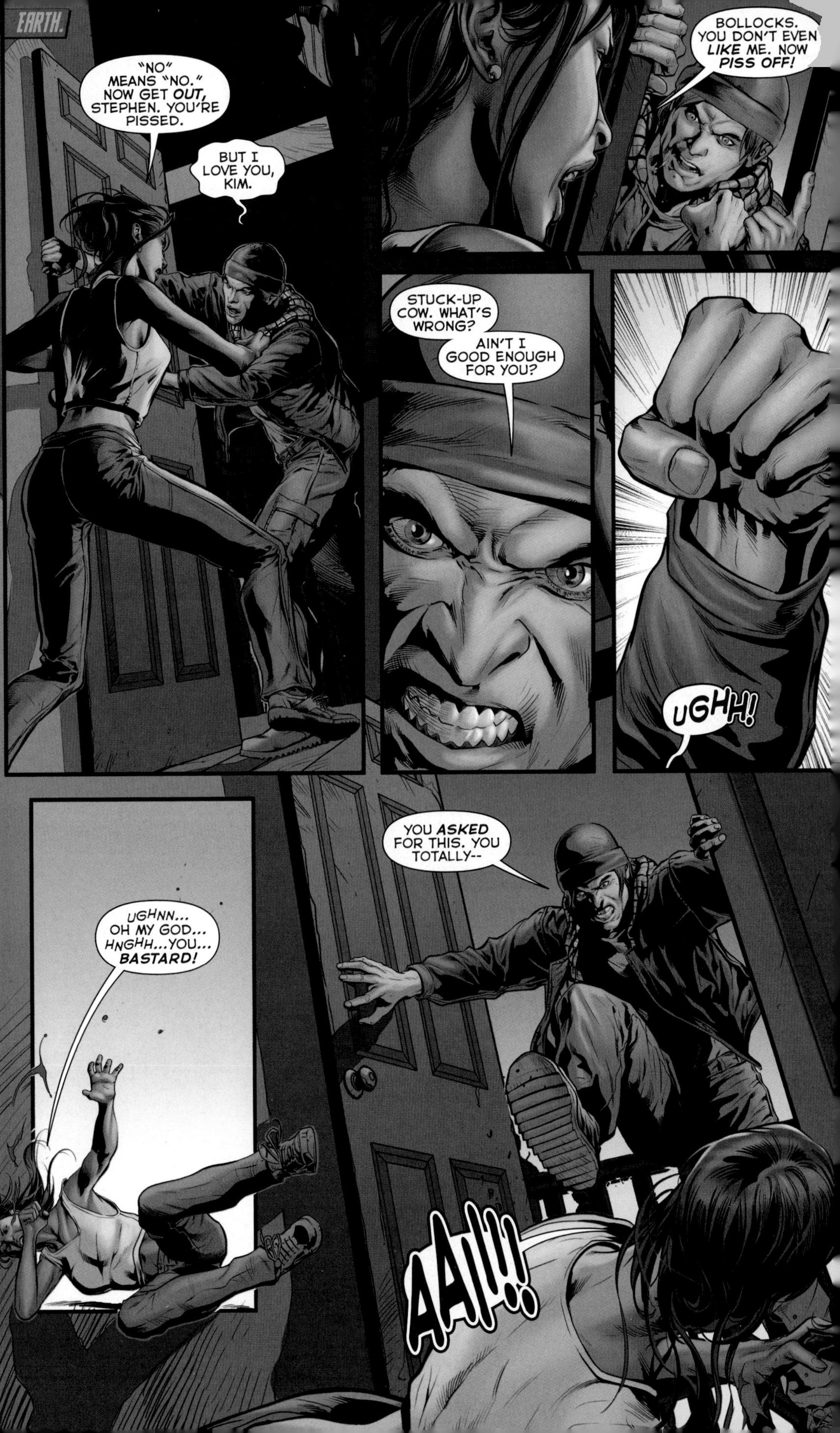
EARTH.
"NO" MEANS "NO." NOW GET OUT, STEPHEN. YOU'RE PISSED.
BUT I LOVE YOU, KIM.
BOLLOCKS. YOU DON'T EVEN LIKE ME. NOW PISS OFF!
STUCK-UP COW. WHAT'S WRONG?
AIN'T I GOOD ENOUGH FOR YOU?
UGHH!
YOU ASKED FOR THIS. YOU TOTALLY--
AAII!!
UGHNN... OH MY GOD... HNGHH...YOU... BASTARD!

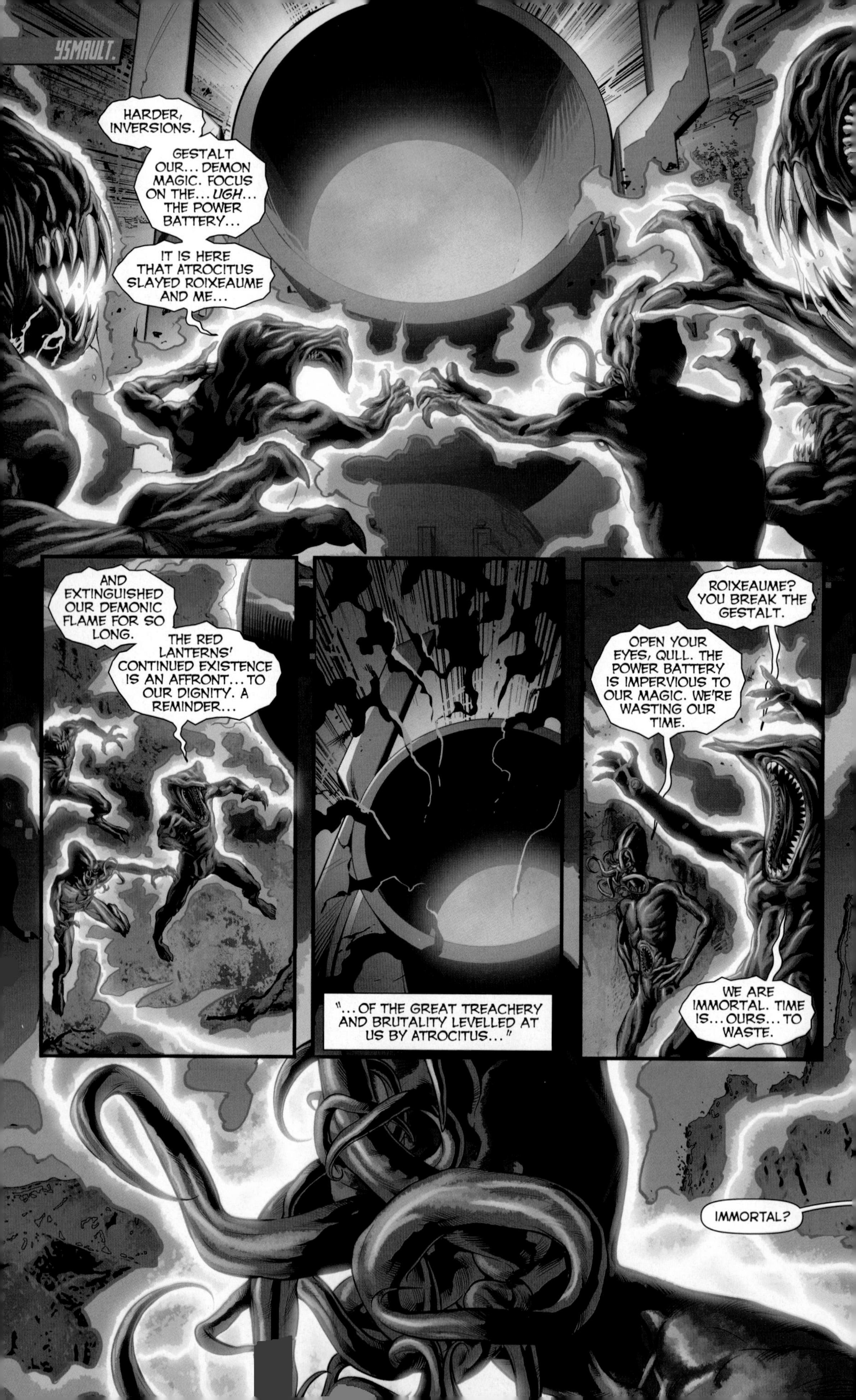
YSMAULT.
HARDER, INVERSIONS.
GESTALT OUR... DEMON MAGIC. FOCUS ON THE... UGH... THE POWER BATTERY...
IT IS HERE THAT ATROCITUS SLAYED ROIXEAUME AND ME...
AND EXTINGUISHED OUR DEMONIC FLAME FOR SO LONG.
THE RED LANTERNS' CONTINUED EXISTENCE IS AN AFFRONT... TO OUR DIGNITY. A REMINDER...
"...OF THE GREAT TREACHERY AND BRUTALITY LEVELLED AT US BY ATROCITUS..."
ROIXEAUME? YOU BREAK THE GESTALT.
OPEN YOUR EYES, QULL. THE POWER BATTERY IS IMPERVIOUS TO OUR MAGIC. WE'RE WASTING OUR TIME.
WE ARE IMMORTAL. TIME IS... OURS... TO WASTE.
IMMORTAL?

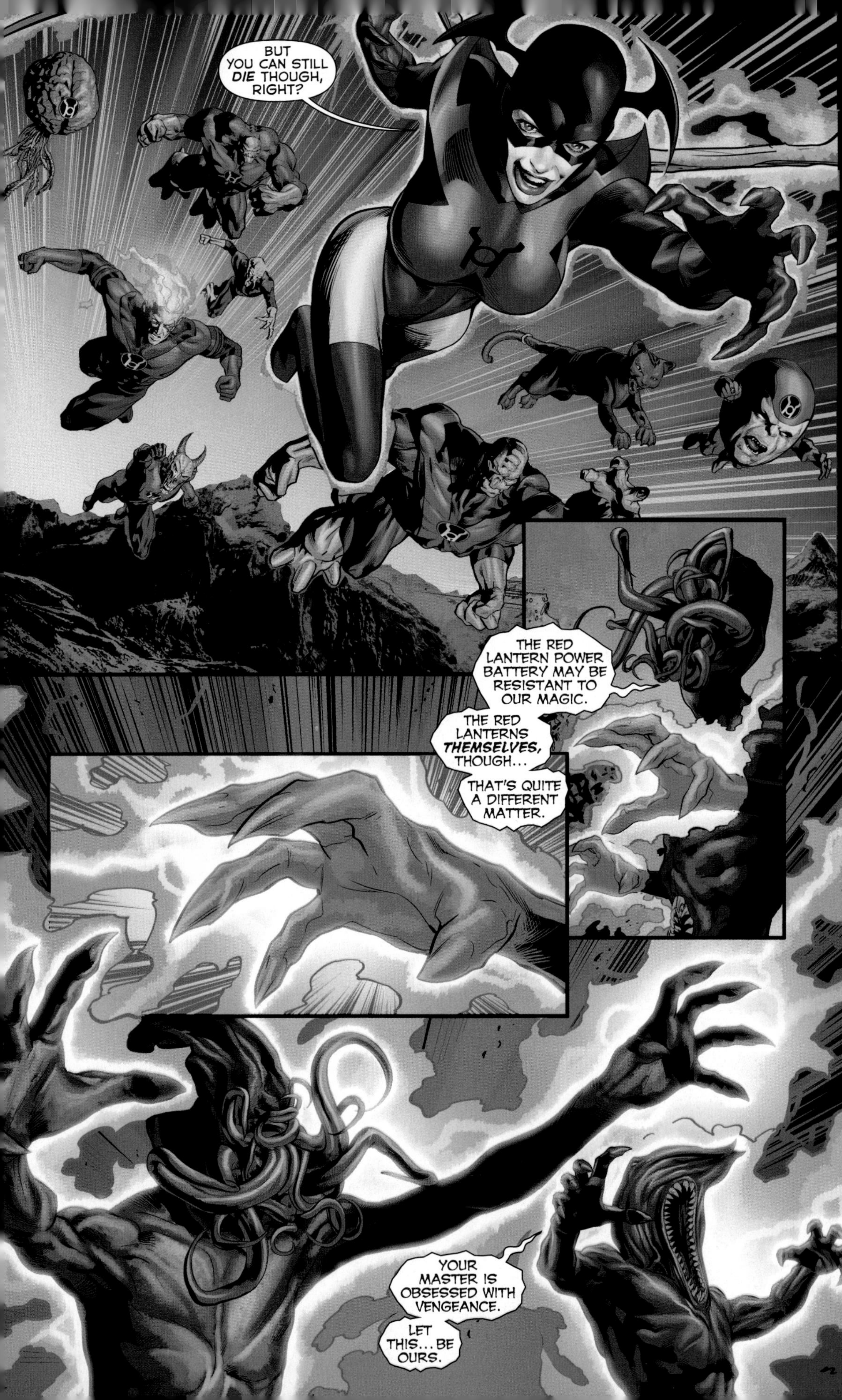
BUT YOU CAN STILL *DIE* THOUGH, RIGHT?
THE RED LANTERN POWER BATTERY MAY BE RESISTANT TO OUR MAGIC.
THE RED LANTERNS *THEMSELVES,* THOUGH...
THAT'S QUITE A DIFFERENT MATTER.
YOUR MASTER IS OBSESSED WITH VENGEANCE.
LET THIS... BE OURS.

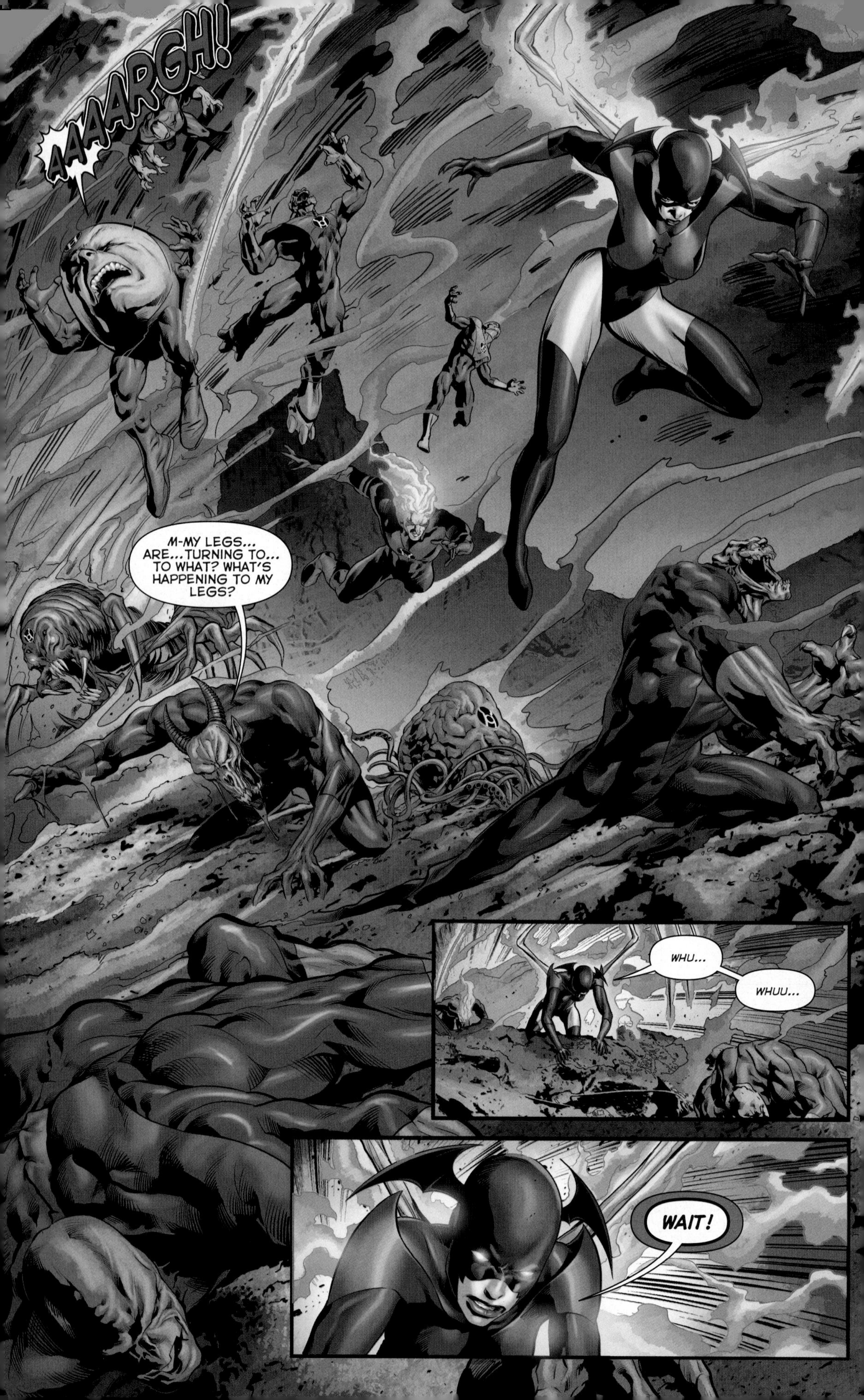
AAAARGH!
M-MY LEGS... ARE...TURNING TO... TO WHAT? WHAT'S HAPPENING TO MY LEGS?
WHU...
WHUU...
WAIT!

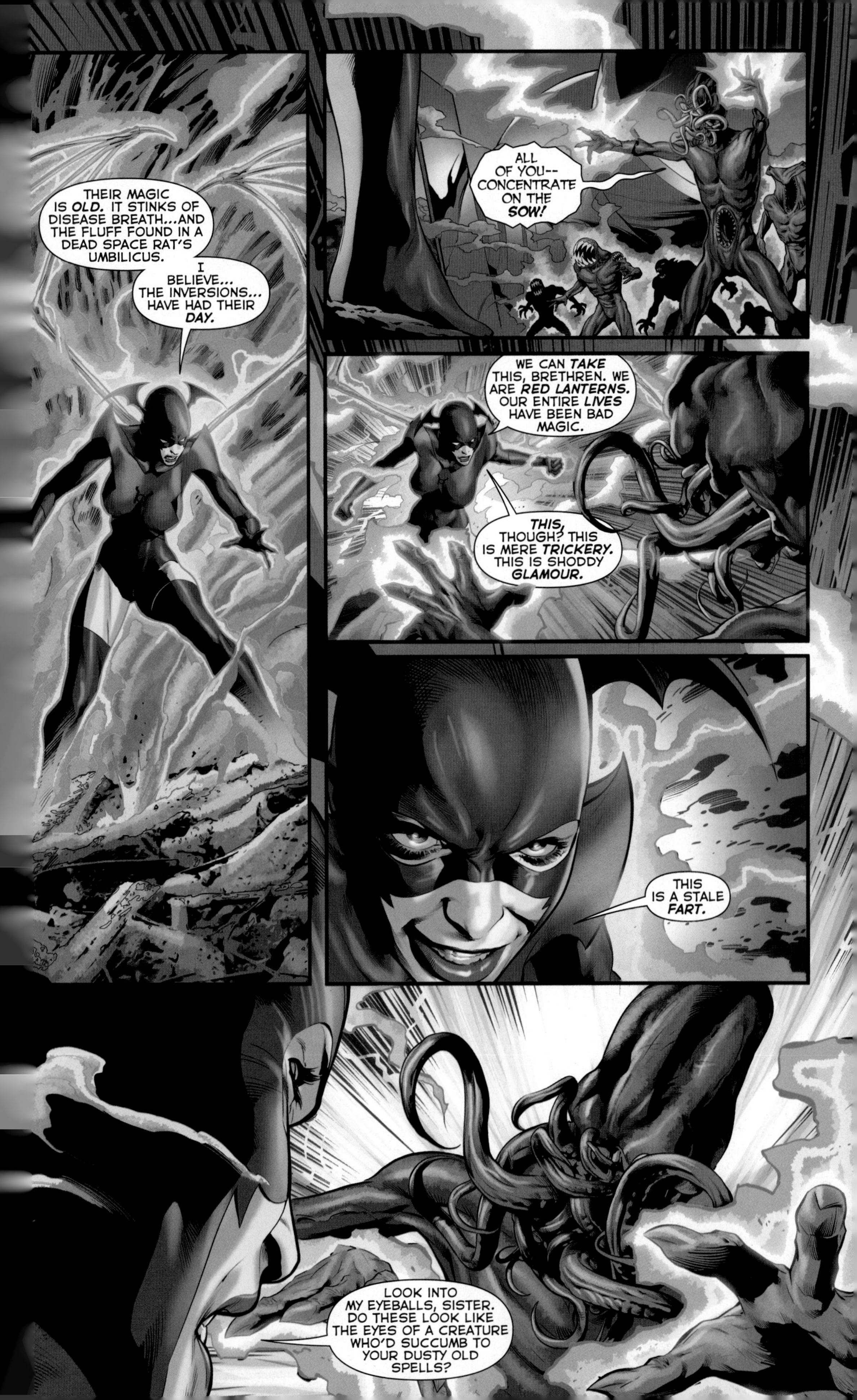
THEIR MAGIC IS OLD. IT STINKS OF DISEASE BREATH...AND THE FLUFF FOUND IN A DEAD SPACE RAT'S UMBILICUS.
I BELIEVE... THE INVERSIONS... HAVE HAD THEIR DAY.
ALL OF YOU-- CONCENTRATE ON THE SOW!
WE CAN TAKE THIS, BRETHREN. WE ARE RED LANTERNS. OUR ENTIRE LIVES HAVE BEEN BAD MAGIC.
THIS, THOUGH? THIS IS MERE TRICKERY. THIS IS SHODDY GLAMOUR.
THIS IS A STALE FART.
LOOK INTO MY EYEBALLS, SISTER. DO THESE LOOK LIKE THE EYES OF A CREATURE WHO'D SUCCUMB TO YOUR DUSTY OLD SPELLS?

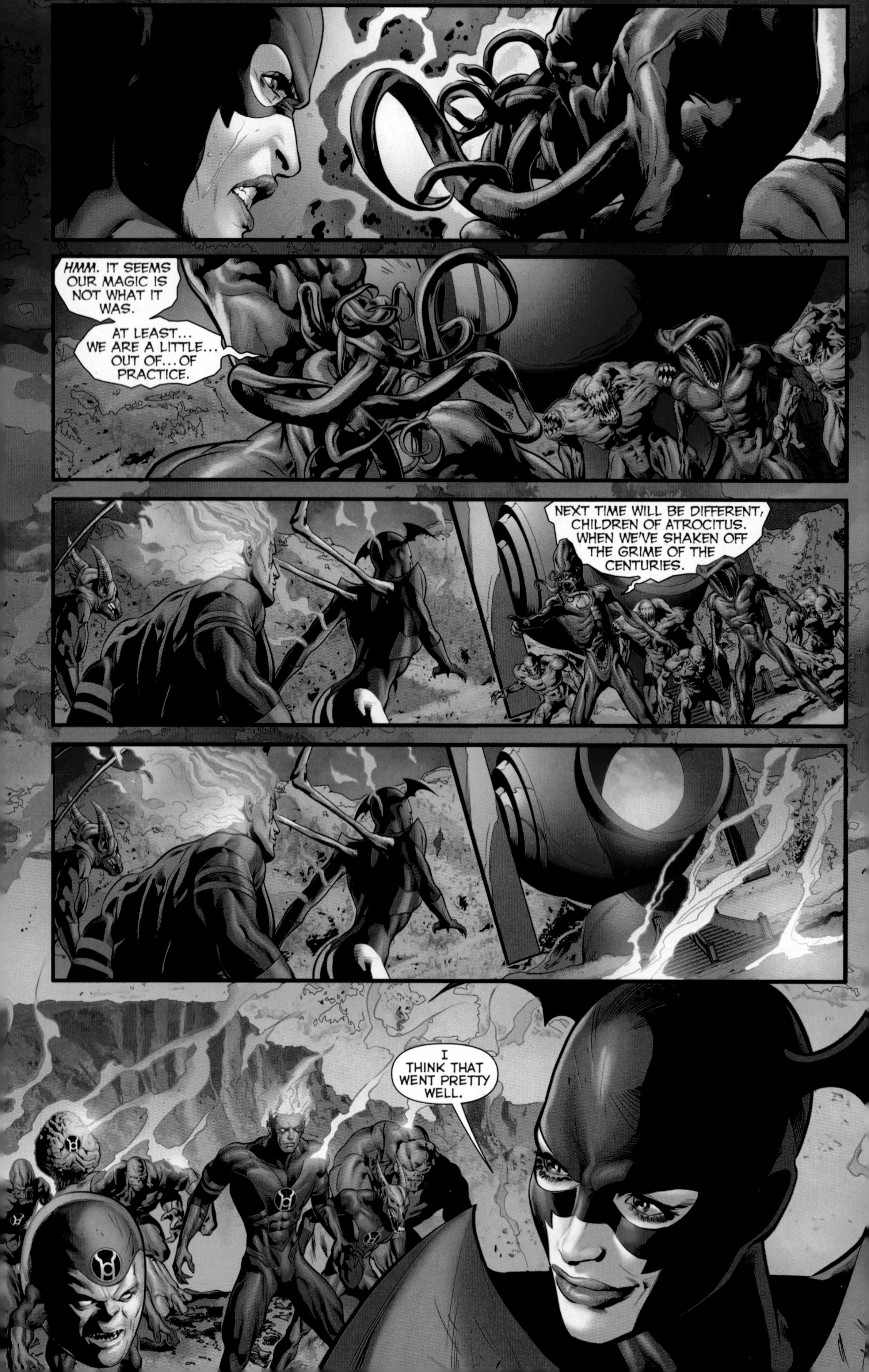
HMM. IT SEEMS OUR MAGIC IS NOT WHAT IT WAS.
AT LEAST... WE ARE A LITTLE... OUT OF... OF PRACTICE.
NEXT TIME WILL BE DIFFERENT, CHILDREN OF ATROCITUS. WHEN WE'VE SHAKEN OFF THE GRIME OF THE CENTURIES.
I THINK THAT WENT PRETTY WELL.

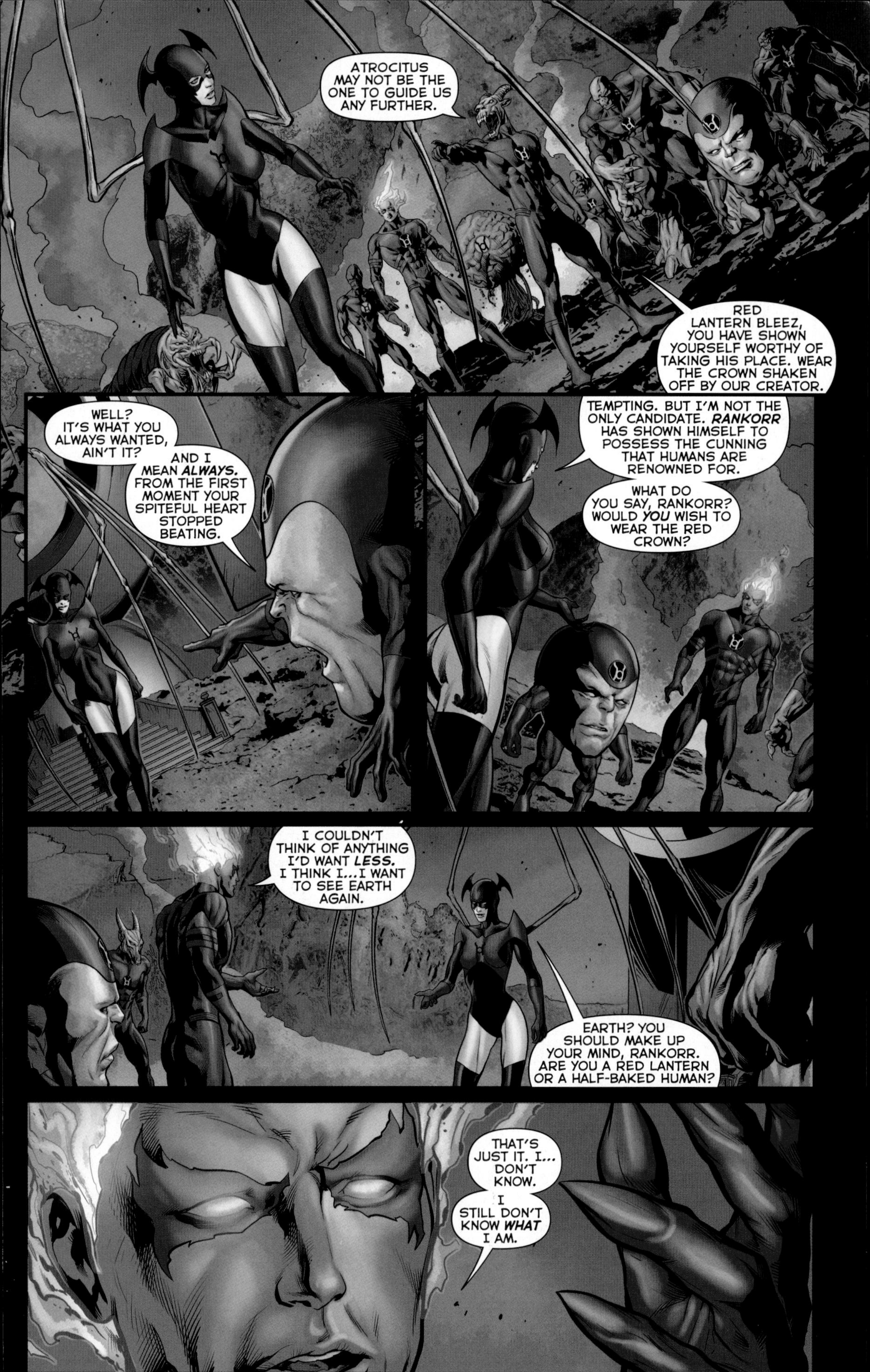
ATROCITUS MAY NOT BE THE ONE TO GUIDE US ANY FURTHER.
RED LANTERN BLEEZ, YOU HAVE SHOWN YOURSELF WORTHY OF TAKING HIS PLACE. WEAR THE CROWN SHAKEN OFF BY OUR CREATOR.
WELL? IT'S WHAT YOU ALWAYS WANTED, AIN'T IT?
AND I MEAN ALWAYS. FROM THE FIRST MOMENT YOUR SPITEFUL HEART STOPPED BEATING.
TEMPTING. BUT I'M NOT THE ONLY CANDIDATE. RANKORR HAS SHOWN HIMSELF TO POSSESS THE CUNNING THAT HUMANS ARE RENOWNED FOR.
WHAT DO YOU SAY, RANKORR? WOULD YOU WISH TO WEAR THE RED CROWN?
I COULDN'T THINK OF ANYTHING I'D WANT LESS. I THINK I...I WANT TO SEE EARTH AGAIN.
EARTH? YOU SHOULD MAKE UP YOUR MIND, RANKORR. ARE YOU A RED LANTERN OR A HALF-BAKED HUMAN?
THAT'S JUST IT. I... DON'T KNOW.
I STILL DON'T KNOW WHAT I AM.

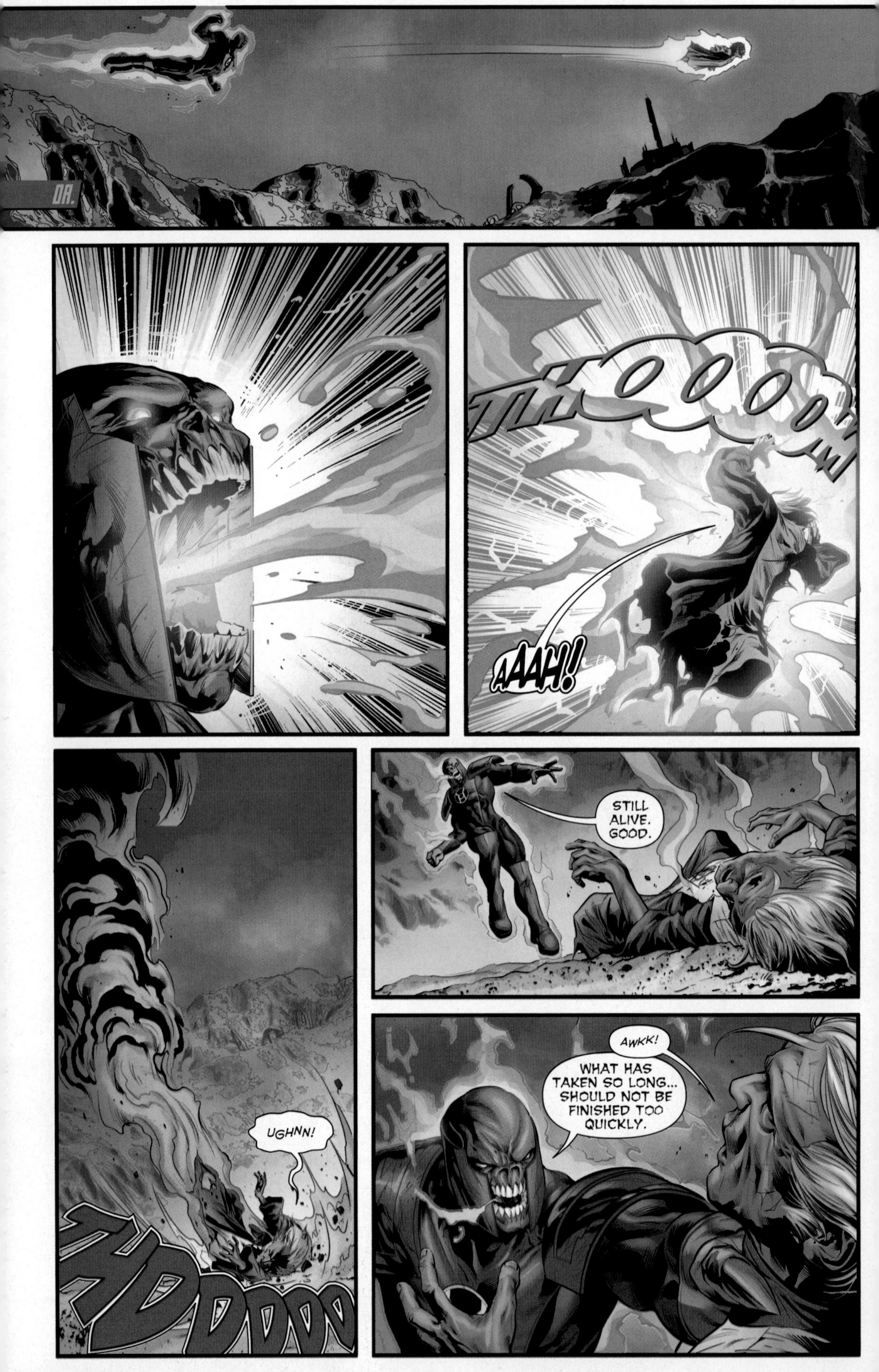
OA.
AAAH!
UGHNN!
STILL ALIVE. GOOD.
AWKK!
WHAT HAS TAKEN SO LONG... SHOULD NOT BE FINISHED TOO QUICKLY.

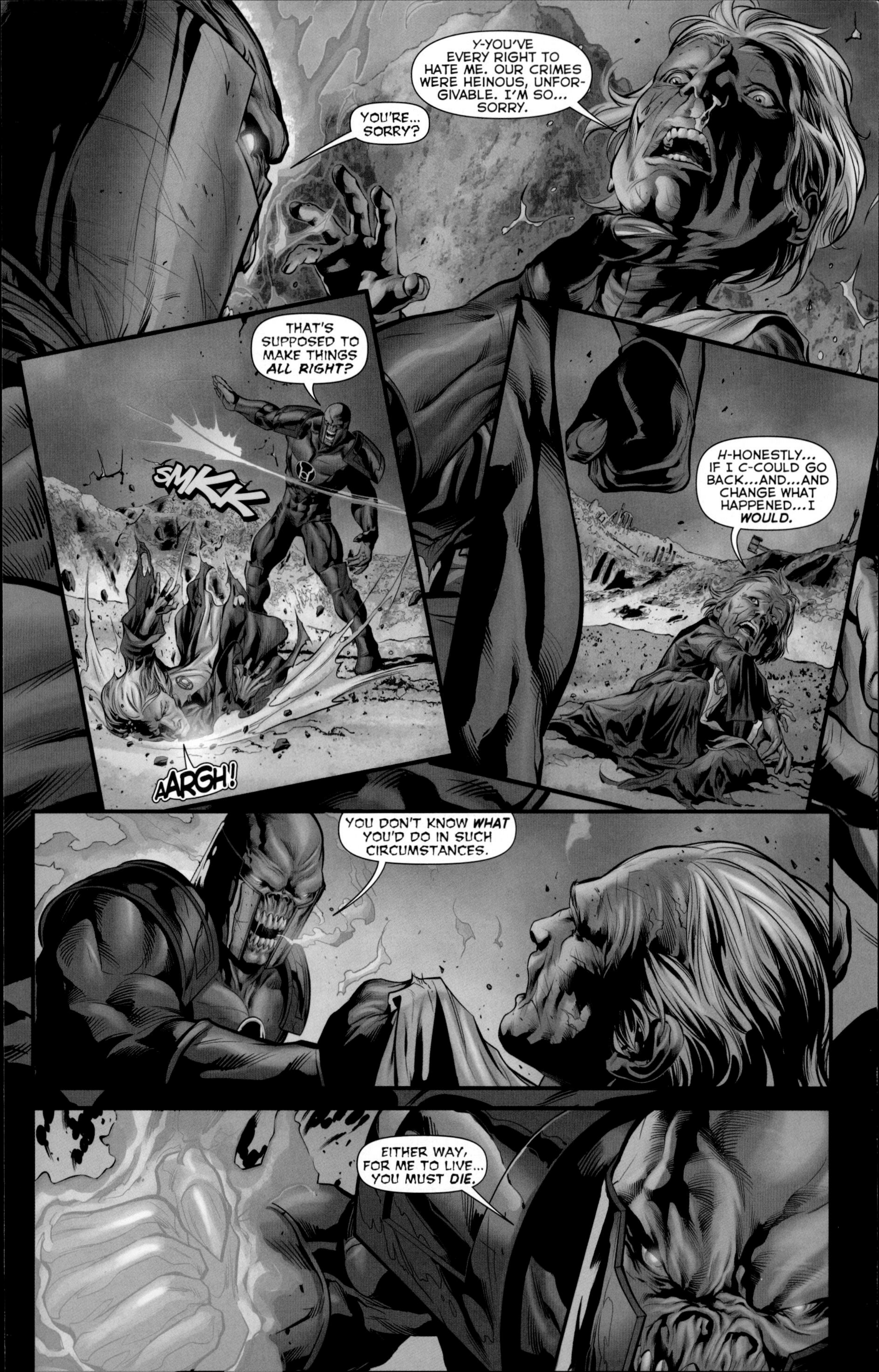
Y-YOU'VE EVERY RIGHT TO HATE ME. OUR CRIMES WERE HEINOUS, UNFORGIVABLE. I'M SO... SORRY.
YOU'RE... SORRY?
THAT'S SUPPOSED TO MAKE THINGS ALL RIGHT?
SMKK
AARGH!
H-HONESTLY... IF I C-COULD GO BACK...AND...AND CHANGE WHAT HAPPENED...I WOULD.
YOU DON'T KNOW WHAT YOU'D DO IN SUCH CIRCUMSTANCES.
EITHER WAY, FOR ME TO LIVE... YOU MUST DIE.

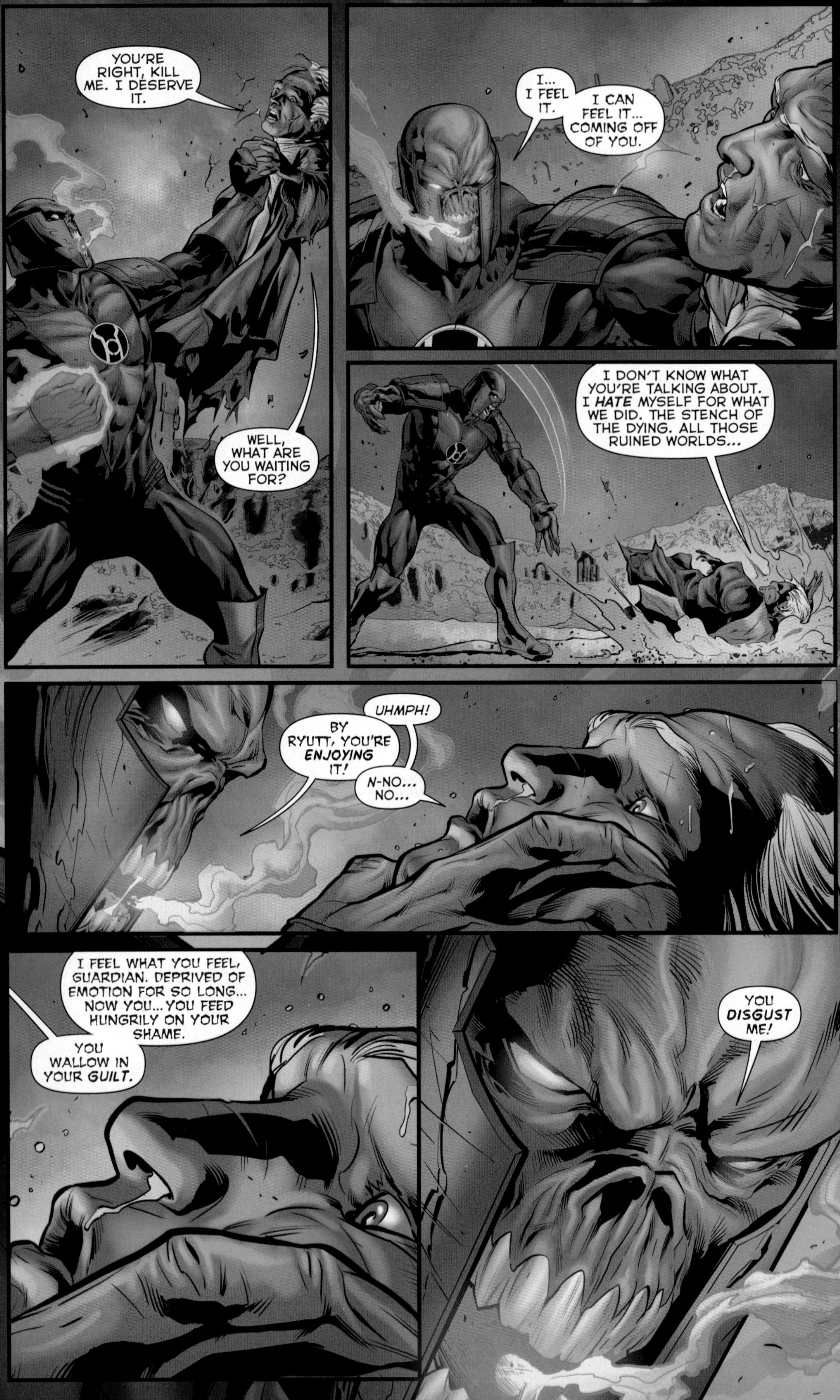
YOU'RE RIGHT, KILL ME. I DESERVE IT.
WELL, WHAT ARE YOU WAITING FOR?
I... I FEEL IT.
I CAN FEEL IT... COMING OFF OF YOU.
I DON'T KNOW WHAT YOU'RE TALKING ABOUT. I HATE MYSELF FOR WHAT WE DID. THE STENCH OF THE DYING. ALL THOSE RUINED WORLDS...
UHMPH!
BY RYUTT, YOU'RE ENJOYING IT!
N-NO... NO...
I FEEL WHAT YOU FEEL, GUARDIAN. DEPRIVED OF EMOTION FOR SO LONG... NOW YOU... YOU FEED HUNGRILY ON YOUR SHAME.
YOU WALLOW IN YOUR GUILT.
YOU DISGUST ME!

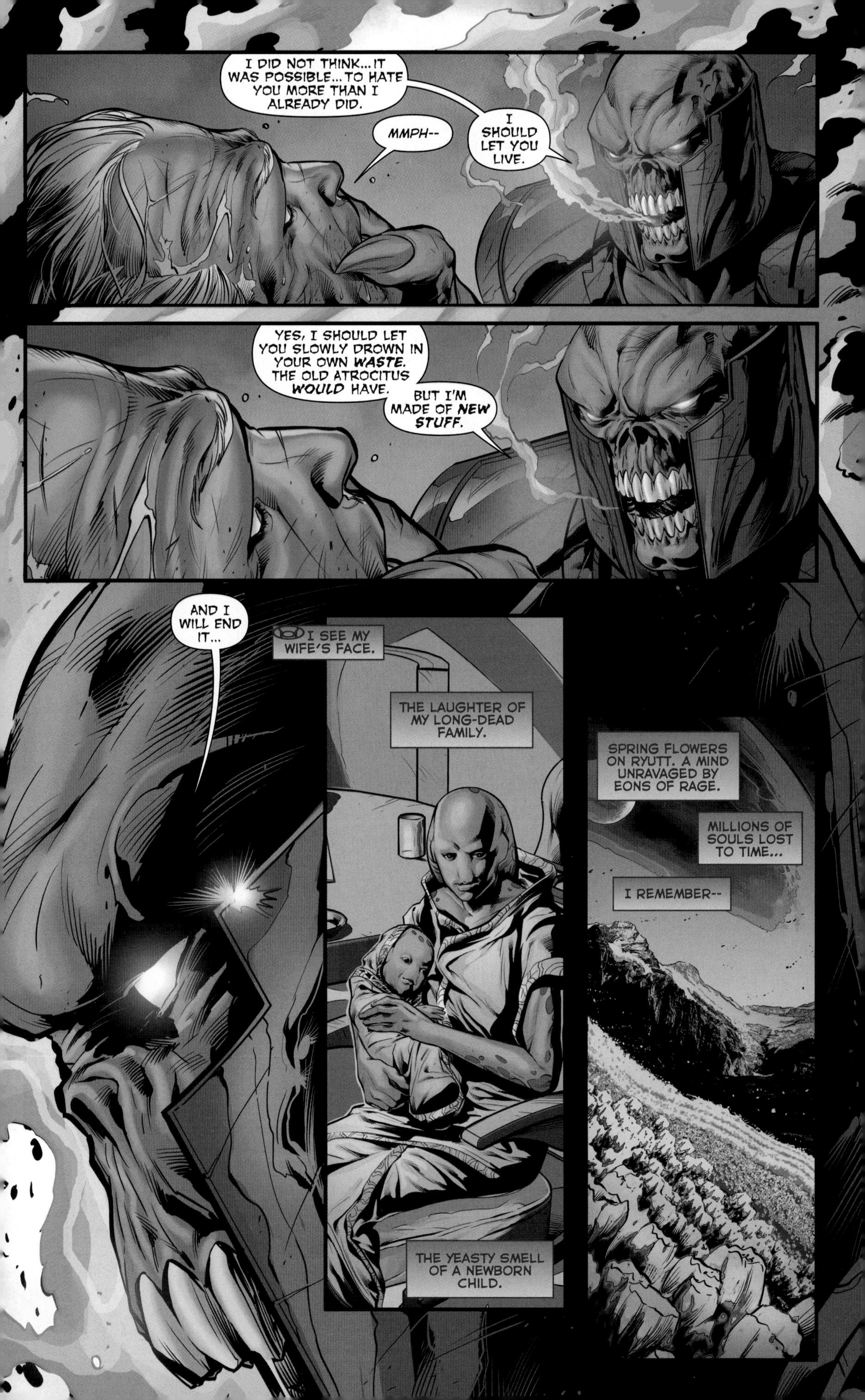
I DID NOT THINK... IT WAS POSSIBLE... TO HATE YOU MORE THAN I ALREADY DID.
MMPH--
I SHOULD LET YOU LIVE.
YES, I SHOULD LET YOU SLOWLY DROWN IN YOUR OWN WASTE. THE OLD ATROCITUS WOULD HAVE.
BUT I'M MADE OF NEW STUFF.
AND I WILL END IT...
I SEE MY WIFE'S FACE.
THE LAUGHTER OF MY LONG-DEAD FAMILY.
THE YEASTY SMELL OF A NEWBORN CHILD.
SPRING FLOWERS ON RYUTT. A MIND UNRAVAGED BY EONS OF RAGE.
MILLIONS OF SOULS LOST TO TIME...
I REMEMBER--

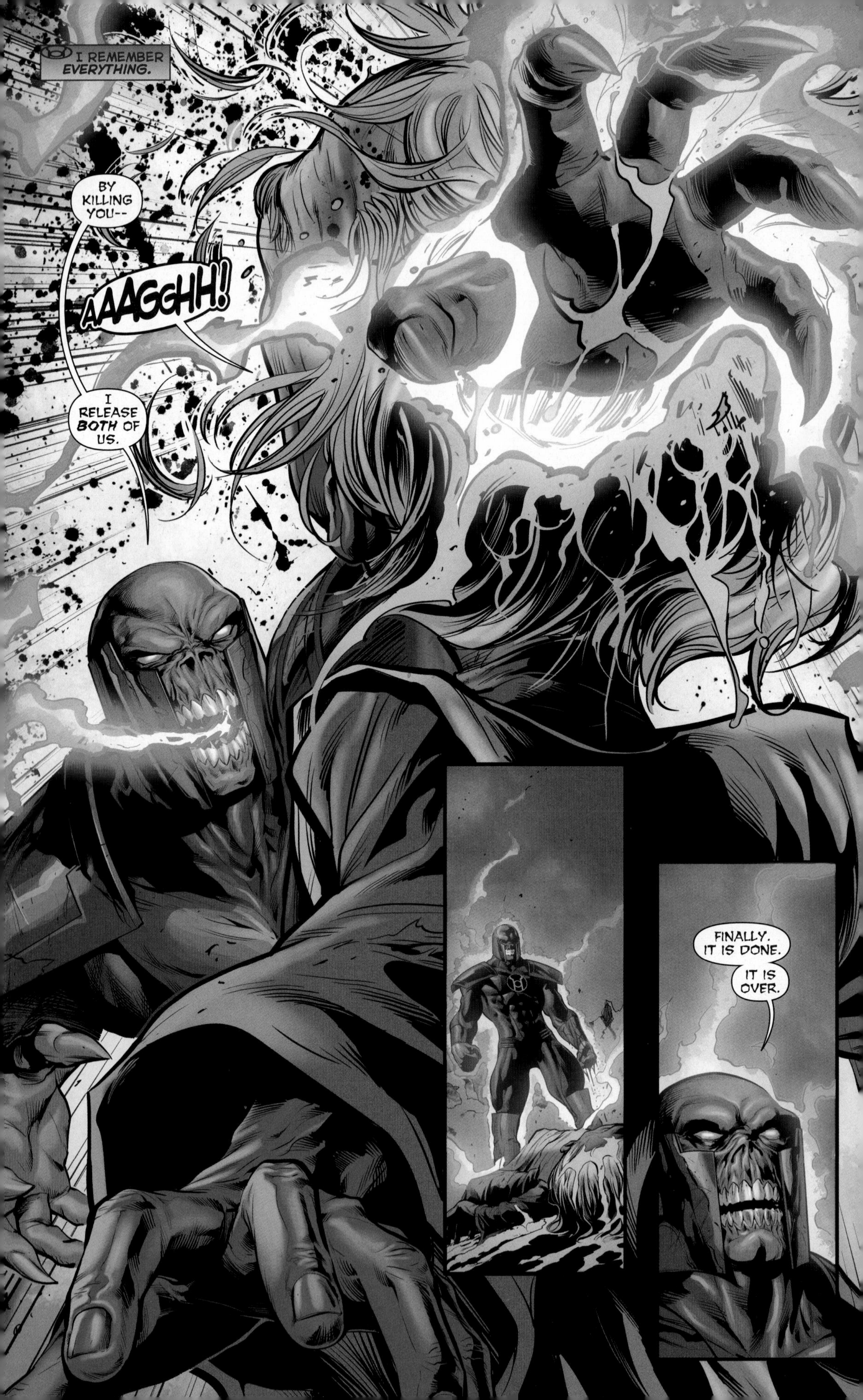
I REMEMBER EVERYTHING.
BY KILLING YOU--
AAAGGHH!
I RELEASE BOTH OF US.
FINALLY. IT IS DONE.
IT IS OVER.

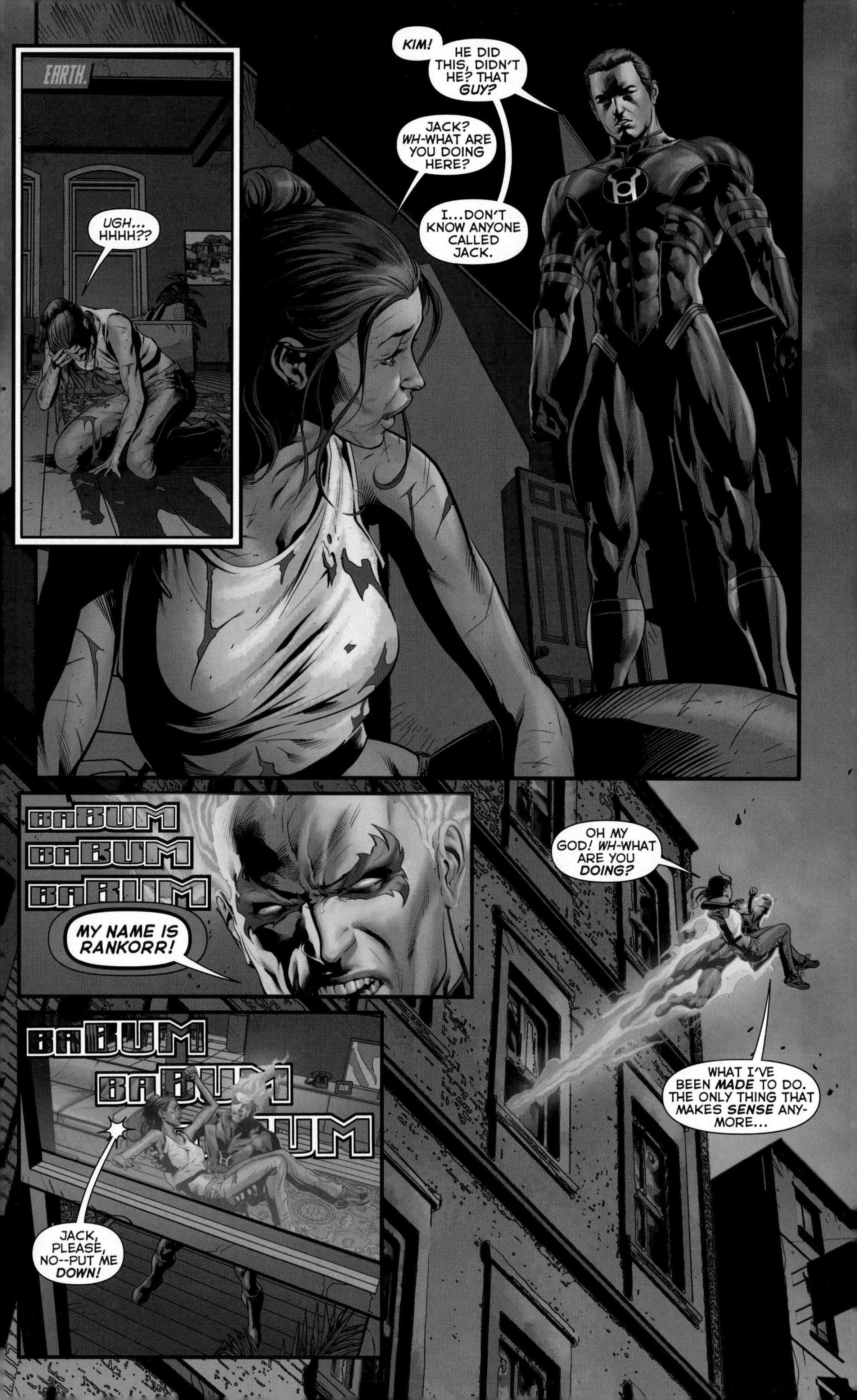
EARTH.
UGH... HHHH??
KIM!
HE DID THIS, DIDN'T HE? THAT GUY?
JACK? WH-WHAT ARE YOU DOING HERE?
I...DON'T KNOW ANYONE CALLED JACK.
BABUM BABUM BABUM
MY NAME IS RANKORR!
BABUM BABUM BABUM
JACK, PLEASE, NO--PUT ME DOWN!
OH MY GOD! WH-WHAT ARE YOU DOING?
WHAT I'VE BEEN MADE TO DO. THE ONLY THING THAT MAKES SENSE ANYMORE...

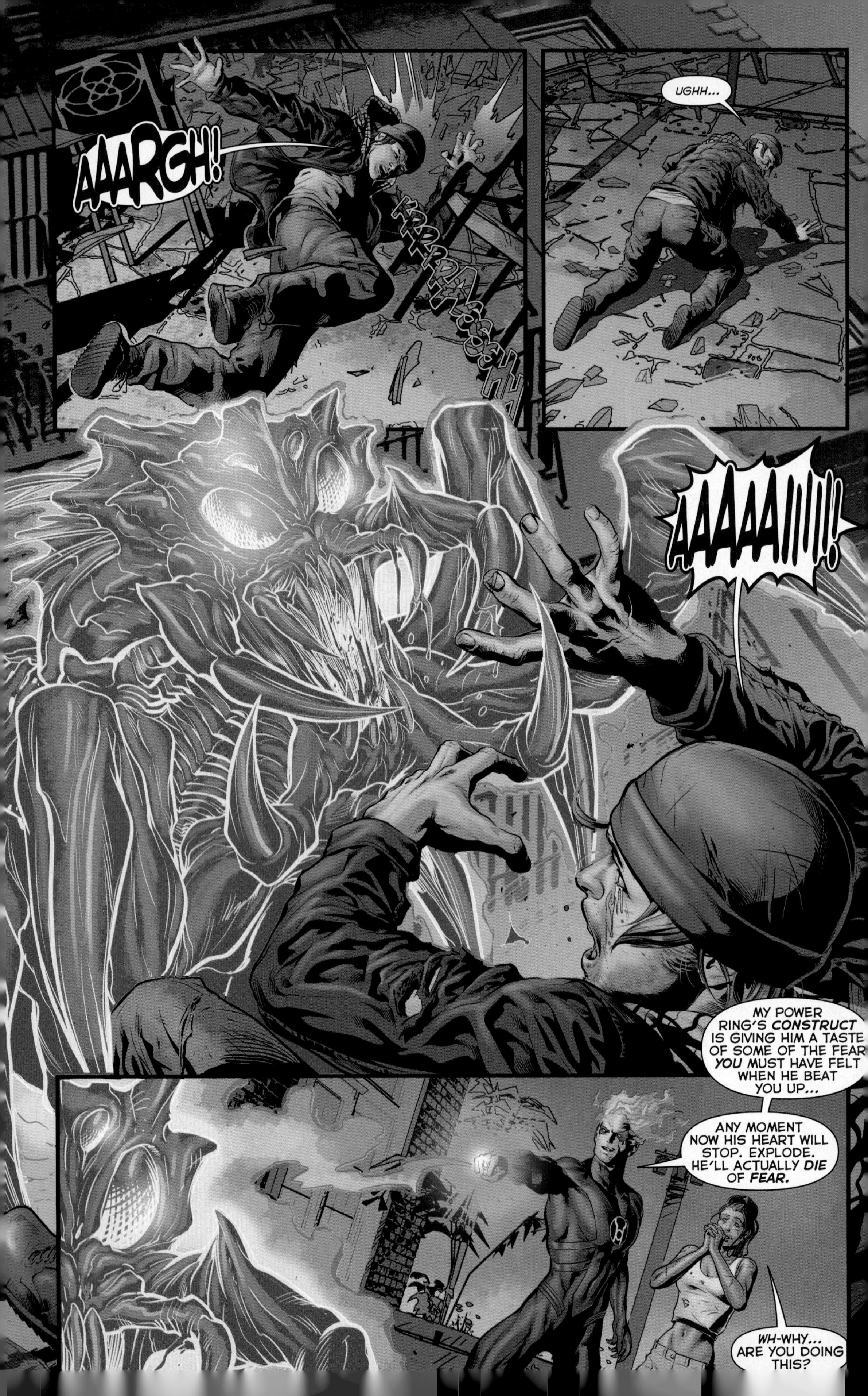
AAARGH!
KRRRASSSHH
UGHH...
AAAAAIIIIIII!
MY POWER RING'S CONSTRUCT IS GIVING HIM A TASTE OF SOME OF THE FEAR YOU MUST HAVE FELT WHEN HE BEAT YOU UP...
ANY MOMENT NOW HIS HEART WILL STOP. EXPLODE. HE'LL ACTUALLY DIE OF FEAR.
WH-WHY... ARE YOU DOING THIS?

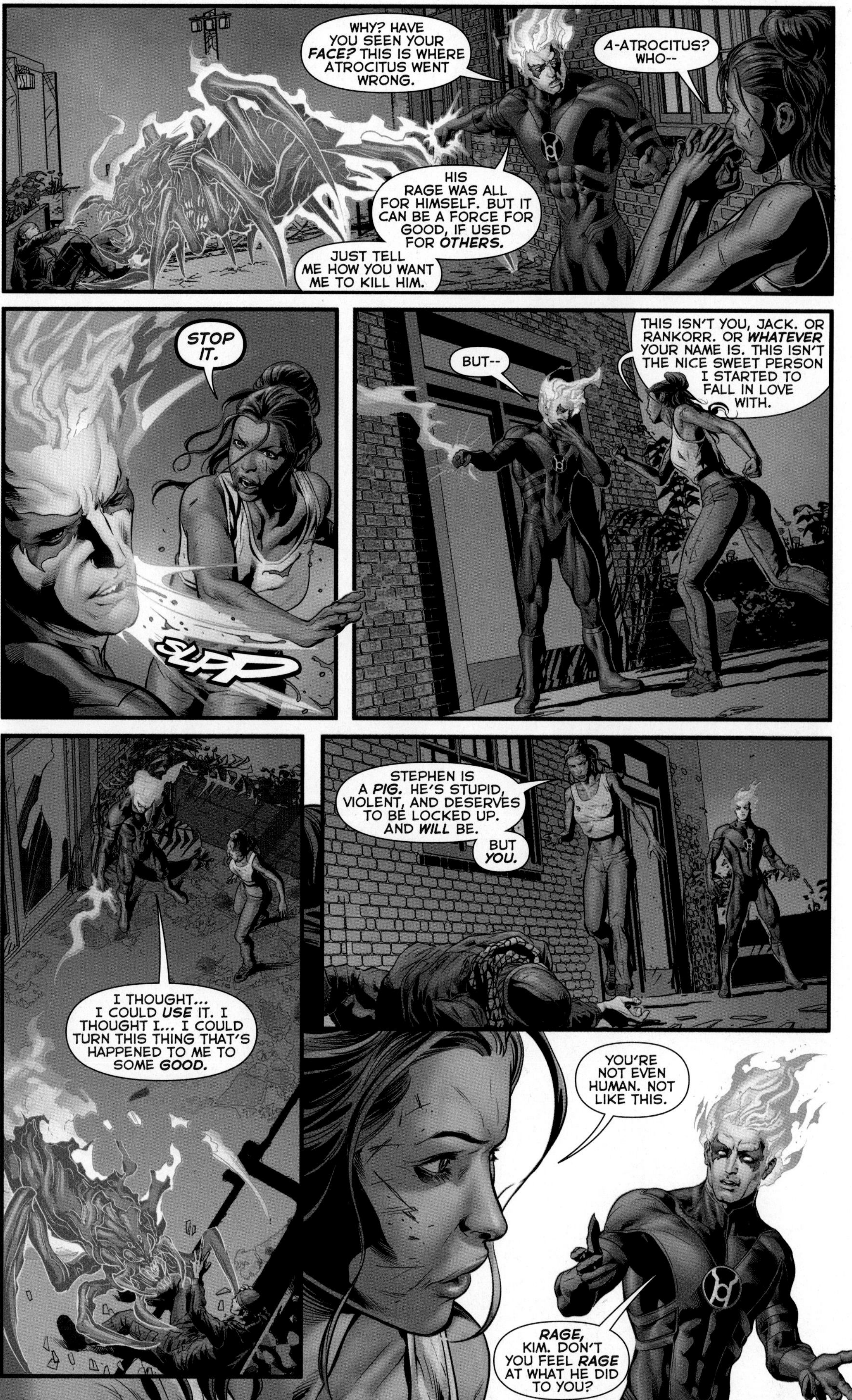
WHY? HAVE YOU SEEN YOUR FACE? THIS IS WHERE ATROCITUS WENT WRONG.
A-ATROCITUS? WHO--
HIS RAGE WAS ALL FOR HIMSELF. BUT IT CAN BE A FORCE FOR GOOD, IF USED FOR OTHERS.
JUST TELL ME HOW YOU WANT ME TO KILL HIM.
STOP IT.
SLAP
BUT--
THIS ISN'T YOU, JACK. OR RANKORR. OR WHATEVER YOUR NAME IS. THIS ISN'T THE NICE SWEET PERSON I STARTED TO FALL IN LOVE WITH.
I THOUGHT... I COULD USE IT. I THOUGHT I... I COULD TURN THIS THING THAT'S HAPPENED TO ME TO SOME GOOD.
STEPHEN IS A PIG. HE'S STUPID, VIOLENT, AND DESERVES TO BE LOCKED UP. AND WILL BE.
BUT YOU.
YOU'RE NOT EVEN HUMAN. NOT LIKE THIS.
RAGE, KIM. DON'T YOU FEEL RAGE AT WHAT HE DID TO YOU?

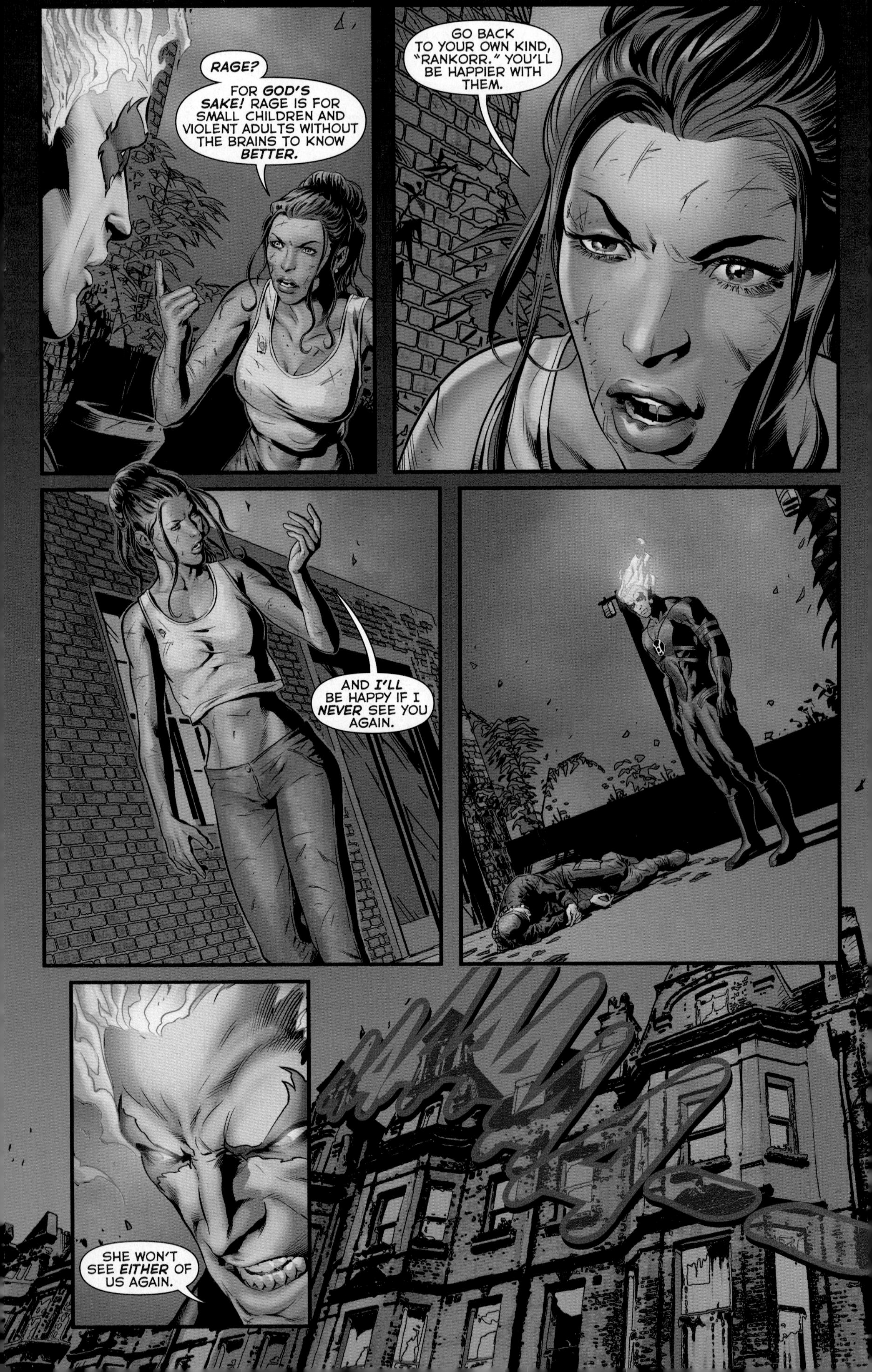
RAGE?
FOR GOD'S SAKE! RAGE IS FOR SMALL CHILDREN AND VIOLENT ADULTS WITHOUT THE BRAINS TO KNOW BETTER.
GO BACK TO YOUR OWN KIND, "RANKORR." YOU'LL BE HAPPIER WITH THEM.
AND I'LL BE HAPPY IF I NEVER SEE YOU AGAIN.
SHE WON'T SEE EITHER OF US AGAIN.

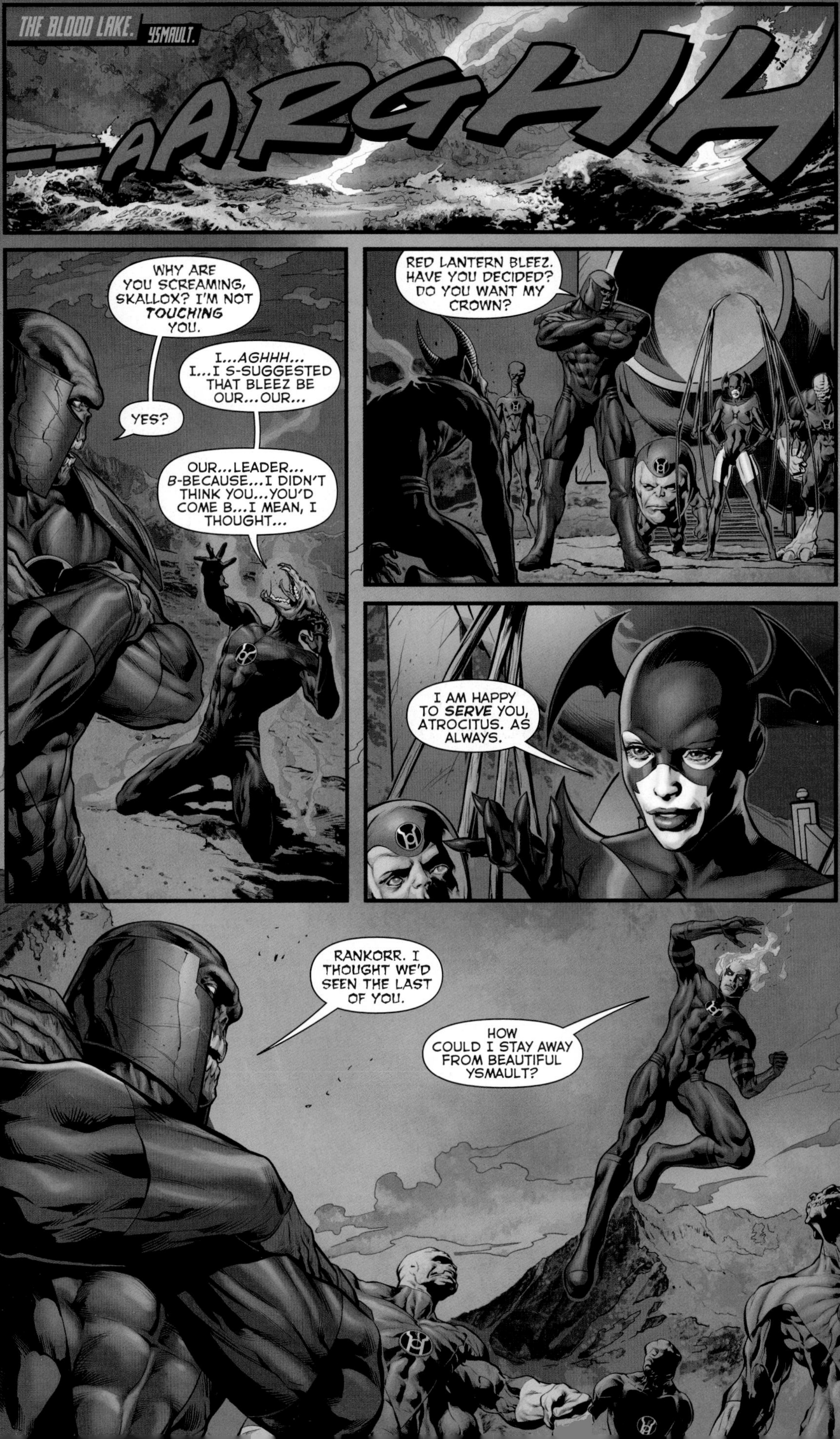
THE BLOOD LAKE.
YSMAULT.
--AARGHK
WHY ARE YOU SCREAMING, SKALLOX? I'M NOT TOUCHING YOU.
I...AGHHH... I...I S-SUGGESTED THAT BLEEZ BE OUR...OUR...
YES?
OUR...LEADER... B-BECAUSE...I DIDN'T THINK YOU...YOU'D COME B...I MEAN, I THOUGHT...
RED LANTERN BLEEZ. HAVE YOU DECIDED? DO YOU WANT MY CROWN?
I AM HAPPY TO SERVE YOU, ATROCITUS. AS ALWAYS.
RANKORR. I THOUGHT WE'D SEEN THE LAST OF YOU.
HOW COULD I STAY AWAY FROM BEAUTIFUL YSMAULT?

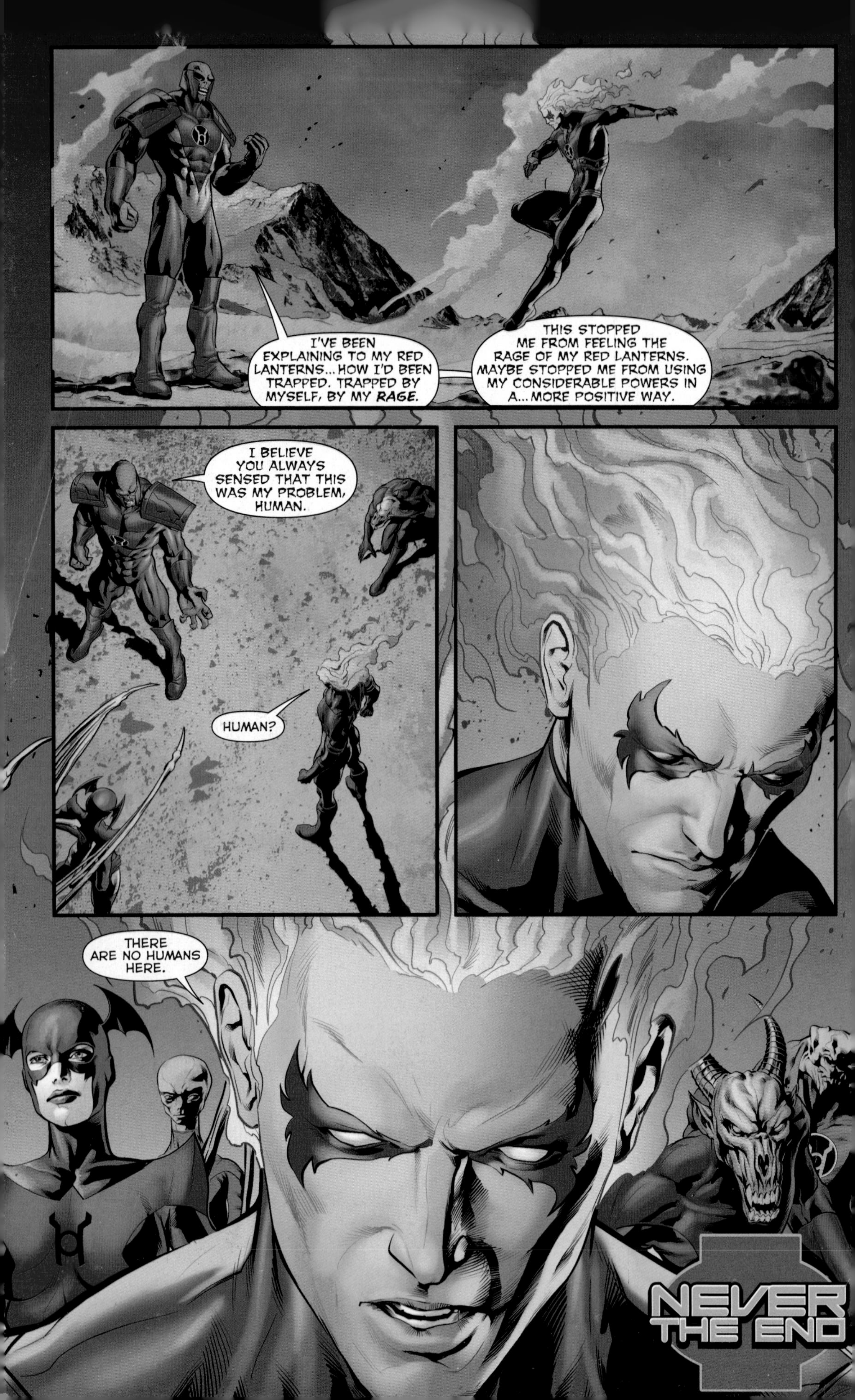
I'VE BEEN EXPLAINING TO MY RED LANTERNS... HOW I'D BEEN TRAPPED. TRAPPED BY MYSELF, BY MY RAGE.
THIS STOPPED ME FROM FEELING THE RAGE OF MY RED LANTERNS. MAYBE STOPPED ME FROM USING MY CONSIDERABLE POWERS IN A... MORE POSITIVE WAY.
I BELIEVE YOU ALWAYS SENSED THAT THIS WAS MY PROBLEM, HUMAN.
HUMAN?
THERE ARE NO HUMANS HERE.
NEVER THE END